THE ARMENIAN PEOPLE
FROM ANCIENT TO
MODERN TIMES

VOLUME II

Also by Richard G. Hovannisian

ARMENIA ON THE ROAD TO INDEPENDENCE
THE REPUBLIC OF ARMENIA *(4 volumes)*
THE ARMENIAN GENOCIDE: History, Politics, Ethics *(editor)*
THE ARMENIAN HOLOCAUST
THE ARMENIAN GENOCIDE IN PERSPECTIVE *(editor)*
THE ARMENIAN IMAGE IN HISTORY AND LITERATURE *(editor)*
ISLAM'S UNDERSTANDING OF ITSELF *(editor)*
ETHICS IN ISLAM *(editor)*
THE PERSIAN PRESENCE IN THE ISLAMIC WORLD *(editor)*
THE THOUSAND AND ONE NIGHTS IN ARABIC LITERATURE AND
    SOCIETY *(editor)*

THE ARMENIAN PEOPLE FROM ANCIENT TO MODERN TIMES

VOLUME II

Foreign Dominion to Statehood:
The Fifteenth Century
to the Twentieth Century

Edited by Richard G. Hovannisian
Professor of Armenian and Near Eastern History
University of California, Los Angeles

St. Martin's Press
New York

Library of Congress Cataloging-in-Publication Data

The Armenian people from ancient to modern times / edited by Richard
   G. Hovannisian.
     p.   cm.
   Includes bibliographical references and index.
   Contents : v. 1. The dynastic periods—from antiquity to the
fourteenth century — v. 2 Foreign dominion to statehood—the
fifteenth century to the twentieth century.
   ISBN 0-312-10169-4 (v. 1). — ISBN 0-312-10168-6 (v. 2)
   1. Armenia—History. 2. Armenians—History. I Hovannisian,
Richard G.
DS175.A715   1997
956.62—dc21   97-5310
                                            CIP

Design by Acme Art, Inc.
First edition: September, 1997
10 9 8 7 6 5 4 3 2 1

CONTENTS

LIST OF MAPS

INTRODUCTION

Richard G. Hovannisian

The history of the Armenian people is long, complex, and in many ways epic and heroic. Emerging as an organized state by the middle of the second millennium B.C., Armenia lay at the ancient crossroads of orient and occident on the highland located between the Mediterranean, Black, and Caspian seas. The Armenian plateau became the buffer and coveted prize of rival empires: Assyrian, Mede, Achaemenian, Parthian, Sasanian, Arab, Seljuk, and Mongol from the south and east, and Seleucid, Roman, Byzantine, and Crusader from the west. Through all the turbulence, however, the Armenians created a rich and colorful culture and defensive mechanisms for survival. Even during long periods of foreign dominion, internal religious and socioeconomic structures allowed them to preserve their distinct way of life.

The dynastic era of Armenian history extended, with interruptions, over a time span of some two thousand years. The pre-Christian period, spanning more than one thousand years, was characterized by strong interchanges with Persian and Hellenistic civilizations. The Ervandian (Orontid), Artashesian (Artaxid), and Arshakuni (Arsacid) dynastic families held sway during this epoch, which for a brief historic moment even gave rise to an Armenian empire in the first century B.C.

The adoption of Christianity as the religion of state at the beginning of the fourth century A.D. introduced a new period that had a profound effect on the spiritual and cultural life and the political orientation of the Armenian realm. Although untold suffering would befall the Armenians in the name of their religion, the fusion of Armenian faith and patriotism provided a powerful defensive weapon in the unceasing struggle for national survival.

The underpinning of Armenian society, before and after the conversion to Christianity, was the military-feudal *nakharar* class—often unruly, divisive, ambitious, and vain, but also valiant and heroic. So long as the *nakharars* remained strong and able to rally against external threats and challenges, the continuum of Armenian life was maintained whether or not an Armenian monarch reigned. Hence, in the long span between the end of the Arshakuni dynasty in the fifth century and the restoration of monarchy under the Bagratunis (Bagratids) in the ninth century, the *nakharars* and the Church provided the structures essential for the continuation of traditional society and a national existence.

The fall of the last major Armenian kingdom on the great plateau in the eleventh century gave rise to an expatriate kingdom in the region of Cilicia, which is bounded by the northeastern corner of the Mediterranean Sea. There, the successive royal families of the Rubenians, Hetumians, and Lusignans came into close contact with the Crusader states and Europe. In face of the threat posed by resurgent Muslim powers, attempts were made to overcome the dogmatic and hierarchical differences separating the Armenian Apostolic, Greek Orthodox, and Roman Catholic churches. Armenian art, architecture, and literature flourished during this period. These and other themes are presented in detail in the first volume of this history.

The fall of the Cilician kingdom late in the fourteenth century left only isolated pockets of semiautonomous Armenian life: Zeitun in Cilicia, Sasun in the heart of the Armenian plateau, and Karabagh (Artsakh) along the eastern perimeter of that highland. Armenia came under the domination of rival Muslim dynasties: the Turkmen Aq Qoyunlu and Kara Qoyunlu, the hordes of Tamerlane, the Safavids and Qajars of Persia, and the Ottoman Turks, who captured Constantinople in the mid-fifteenth century and extended eastward into both Cilicia and Armenia proper during the next century.

Thereafter, the subject Armenians existed as a religious-ethnic minority with the legal status of second-class citizens. Because of the segregated nature of Muslim-dominated societies and the quasi-theocratic foundation of certain Islamic states, the Armenian Church was accorded jurisdiction in internal civil and religious matters. In return, the church hierarchy was held responsible for the conduct of all members of the ethnic community, their payment of taxes and fulfillment of other obligations, and their loyalty and devotion to the reigning sultan or shah. In the Ottoman Empire, this system was undermined by political, economic, and social decay, especially in the eighteenth and nineteenth centuries and by the infiltration of intellectual and political currents inspired by the Enlightenment and the French Revolution. These developments raised serious questions about the relationship between ruler and ruled and about the ability and even desirability of maintaining the status quo in a moribund empire.

The winds of change also affected the Armenian community *(millet)*, first through an intellectual revival and ultimately through plans and pressure for reforms both within and for the community. The articulation of Armenian social and political programs reached the table of international diplomacy at the Congress of Berlin in 1878, but the failure of the powers to resolve the so-called "Armenian Question" was to lead to the eventual elimination of the Ottoman Armenians and their removal from most of their historic lands. The widespread massacres of 1894-1896 were followed by the Cilician pogroms of 1909 and ultimately by the Armenian Genocide beginning in 1915 and culminating in 1922 with the burning of Smyrna and the final Armenian exodus from Cilicia. The "Young Turk" regime, on which reform-minded Armenians had placed so much hope, became in fact the catalyst for the annihilation of the Ottoman Armenians.

The eastern reaches of the Armenian plateau were spared this calamity only because Russian rule had been established there during the nineteenth century. Despite discriminatory practices and the arbitrariness of Romanov governors and bureaucrats, the Russian Armenians made significant organic progress during the century of tsarist rule. Like the Ottoman Armenians, they experienced an intellectual renaissance, which was strongly influenced by European social, political, and economic thought. By the outbreak of World War I in 1914, there were nearly as many Armenians living in the Russian Empire as in the Ottoman Empire. They became the fastest-growing and most affluent element in Transcaucasia, the region extending from the Black Sea to the Caspian Sea south of the Caucasus Mountains.

World War I, the Armenian Genocide, and the Russian revolutions and Civil War shattered the Armenian infrastructures in both the Ottoman and Russian empires. By the end of the world war in 1918, most Armenians either had been killed or displaced. Yet, there was cause for great excitement and anticipation. The European Allied Powers, assisted by the United States of America, had defeated the German Empire and its ally, the Ottoman Empire, and were publicly committed to the restoration and rehabilitation of the Armenian people. But the first modern experiment in Armenian independence lasted less than three years, from 1918 to the end of 1920. The reluctance of the Allied Powers to sustain their pledges with armed force and the collaboration of the Turkish Nationalists led by Mustafa Kemal Pasha and of Soviet Russia led by V.I. Lenin crushed the Republic of Armenia.

That which remained of historic Armenia, an area of less than 12,000 square miles, was transformed into Soviet Armenia and a part of the Union of Soviet Socialist Republics. Seven decades of Soviet rule were characterized by heavy centralization and coercion and the attempted suppression of many traditional ways. Yet, that critical period also gave rise to the contemporary Armenian—literate, highly skilled, adept in the arts, and resourceful individually for self and family and collectively for the preservation of national traits and ideals under creative guises.

The rapid collapse of the Soviet Union in 1991 brought another opportunity for Armenian independence, albeit only on this small, landlocked portion of the ancient and medieval realms. Many of the problems besetting the first Armenian republic quickly resurfaced, including an enervative and disruptive territorial dispute with and economic blockade by the neighboring Azerbaijani republic. Moreover, the aspiration to democracy and the setting up of a framework of democratic institutions have grated roughly against the daily reality of political inexperience and perpetuation of some of the worst abuses of the Soviet system. Critical to the welfare of the new republic is its relationship with the numerous, generally able and affluent, and potentially invaluable communities of the Armenian diaspora. These and related issues are addressed in the second volume of this study.

No comprehensive history of the Armenian people exists in the English language. Many monographs on specific subjects have appeared in recent years, but the ambitious undertaking to present the entire span of Armenian history has awaited this endeavor. Those who teach Armenian history have had little choice but to resort to selected readings from sundry sources in place of a cohesive textbook, and general readers seeking a reliable history of Armenia written in English have often been disappointed with the results. It was to meet this long-standing need that seventeen specialists in various disciplines of Armenian studies were drawn together as contributors to this two-volume work.

Any publication with multiple authors is likely to have chronological and topical gaps, as well as significant differences in organization, style, and attention to detail in the individual chapters. This work is not an exception. It would have been desirable, moreover, to incorporate chapters on art and architecture, music and theater, and other aspects of culture that are important reflectors of the spirit and soul of a people.

Fortunately, a number of excellent monographs and illustrated volumes have been published in English on these subjects. A bibliography of the works cited in the two volumes is included in each of them.

The transliteration of Armenian personal and place names into the Latin alphabet is not consistent in the chapters that follow. As individual authors have strong personal preferences, the editor has in general respected those sentiments. Chapters 3 through 8 in volume I use the modified Hübschmann-Meillet system, which for the uninstructed English reader will not always seem phonetic. The system uses a single character, often with diacritical marks, to represent a single Armenian letter; thus *Mušeł* rather than *Mushegh,* and *Xoranac'i* rather than *Khorenatsi.* And the traditional rendering of "ian" as the suffix of Armenian family names has been altered to "ean"; thus, *Mamikonean* rather than *Mamikonian.* To assist readers unfamiliar with this system, the editor has added the phonetic form after the initial use of the term. A table comparing the Hübschmann-Meillet system with modern Eastern Armenian and modern Western Armenian pronunciations, without diacritical marks, follows this introduction. By and large, the transliteration system used in these volumes is based on the sounds of Classical and modern Eastern Armenian; thus *Trdat* rather than *Drtad,* and *Khachatur Abovian* rather than *Khachadour Apovian.* Exceptions are made in the case of names with a widely accepted alternative form; thus *Boghos Nubar* rather than *Poghos Nupar,* and *Hagop Baronian* rather than *Hakob Paronian.* Moreover, in chapters 5 and 6 of Volume II, a mixed system is used, so that the names of Western Armenian intellectual, political, and clerical figures appear in Western Armenian pronunciation, whereas the names of Eastern Armenian personages are shown in Eastern Armenian pronunciation; thus *Krikor Odian* rather than *Grigor Otian,* but *Grigor Artsruni* rather than *Krikor Ardzruni.*

The preparation of this history has been long and difficult, and the challenges and responsibilities facing the editor have been formidable. A single author may have provided greater consistency in style and content but could not have offered the expertise or most recent findings relating to all periods or topics. The editor wishes to commend the authors for their contribution, cooperation, and forbearance. Robert Hewsen has meticulously produced the useful maps in the two volumes, and Simon Winder, formerly of St. Martin's Press, enthusiastically initiated the long publication process. It is hoped that this collective study will bring the reader the rich historical and cultural heritage, and an appreciation of the continuing saga, of the Armenian people.

Richard G. Hovannisian

TRANSLITERATION SYSTEMS FOR ARMENIAN

Armenian Letter	Hübschmann-Meillet	Eastern Armenian	Western Armenian
Ա ա	a	a	a
Բ բ	b	b	p
Գ գ	g	g	k
Դ դ	d	d	t
Ե ե	e	e	e
Զ զ	z	z	z
Է է	ē	e	e
Ը ը	ě	e	e
Թ թ	t'	t	t
Ժ ժ	ž	zh	zh
Ի ի	i	i	i
Լ լ	l	l	l
Խ խ	x	kh	kh
Ծ ծ	c	ts	dz
Կ կ	k	k	g
Հ հ	h	h	h
Ձ ձ	j	dz	tz
Ղ ղ	ł	gh	gh
Ճ ճ	č	ch	j
Մ մ	m	m	m
Յ յ	y	y *or* h	y *or* h[1]
Ն ն	n	n	n
Շ շ	š	sh	sh
Ո ո	o	o *or* vo	o *or* vo[2]
Չ չ	č'	ch	ch
Պ պ	p	p	b
Ջ ջ	ǰ	dj *or* j	ch
Ռ ռ	ṙ	r	r
Ս ս	s	s	s
Վ վ	v	v	v
Տ տ	t	t	d
Ր ր	r	r	r
Ց ց	c'	ts	ts
Ւ ւ	w	u	u
Փ փ	p'	p	p
Ք ք	k'	k	k
Օ օ	ō	o	o
Ֆ ֆ	f	f	f

1. Pronounced as "h" at beginning of a word; often silent when the final letter of a word.
2. Pronounced as "vo" at beginning of a word.

1

ARMENIA FROM THE FALL OF THE CILICIAN KINGDOM (1375) TO THE FORCED EMIGRATION UNDER SHAH ABBAS (1604)

Dickran Kouymjian

The fifteenth and sixteenth centuries are the dark ages of Armenian history. The poverty of historical sources reflects the disastrous decline of society and culture under Turkic oppression. Thus, this period—from the fall of the Armenian kingdom of Cilicia in 1375 to the forced resettlement of eastern Armenians in Safavid Iran in 1604—is either ignored in standard histories or relegated to a page or two.

To call both these centuries simply the early Ottoman period would be inaccurate. Armenia—a precise geographical entity since antiquity, at times misleadingly referred to as eastern Anatolia or eastern Asia Minor—was conquered by the Ottomans under Sultan Selim the Grim in the second decade of the sixteenth century. To be sure, Armenians in cities such as Kaiseri, Trebizond, and Constantinople had lived under Ottoman rule from the fourteenth and fifteenth centuries and had known the Turks as Seljuks since the eleventh, but it was only in the sixteenth century that the majority of the nation became subject to the sultans.

From shortly after the year 1000 to the second half of the twentieth century, Armenia's fate was inextricably associated with the Turkic invaders from Central Asia, and whether Seljuk, Turkmen, Ottoman, Safavid, or Azeri, all of them belonged to the same Oghuz Turkic linguistic group, one of the four major divisions of the Turkic family of languages. The fifteenth and sixteenth centuries represent the midpoint in the millennium span of Armeno-Turkish relations.

Strangely, during these two hundred years Armenia was never at war, yet it never saw peace. After 1375 Armenia as an autonomous political entity ceased; as a geographical area it remained coveted; as a nation it survived. Rival Islamic dynasties struggled to dominate it and in so doing to exploit its resources. The structure of Armenian life was badly damaged, nearly destroyed, and, finally, changed. Self-rule became a dream to be fulfilled. The core of Armenia's ancient society—the *nakharar* system of hereditary landowning nobility—had collapsed and disappeared. The Armenian Church, deprived of its traditional upper-class support and divided by dissension, accommodated itself to Islamic tutelage in order to endure intact beyond this destructive era. The population steadily fled the wars, pillage, famine, and ruin, augmenting already existing Armenian colonies in the Crimea, Central Europe, Constantinople, and the large urban centers of the Ottoman Empire, Syria, and Iran.

Though the population in Armenia declined, it remained sufficiently Armenian to guarantee national continuation. Yet just as these years witnessed the annihilation of the Armenia of kings, they prepared the way for a cosmopolitan, mercantile nation ready to compete in a modern world dominated by the West.

The fall of the kingdom of Cilicia was a cruel disappointment to all Armenians, even if the jurisdiction of its rulers never reached north of the mountains into Greater Armenia. Colophons or scribal memorials of the thirteenth and especially of the fourteenth centuries from areas as distant as the Crimea, Ilkhanid Iran, Julfa on the Araxes River, Ayrarat, Siunik, Tiflis, Erzerum, Erzinjan, Sebastia, Baiburt, and the Lake Van region acknowledged the successive kings of Cilicia. They are the most important sources from a period graced only by a single historian at its beginning, Tovma Metzopetsi (Thomas of Metzop) (events from 1388 to 1446), and another at its end, Arakel Tavrizhetsi

(Arakel of Tabriz) (d. 1670). Immediately after the destruction of the Cilician kingdom, colophons, in their formular language, stop citing Armenian kings. Only in Siunik and Lori were Armenian rulers, local princes and barons such as the Orbelians, still mentioned. For the rest of Armenia, the church remained the only permanent, widespread national institution. Its catholicoses, patriarchs, and bishops were unfailingly referred to in the colophonic formulae. For a generation or two there were still fragmentary references to remnants of the Cilician nobility in strongholds such as Gaban and Korikos, but by the second quarter of the fifteenth century these too disappeared and the title "King of Armenia" passed into the titulature of the Lusignan house of Cyprus and thence to Venetian and other aristocratic families of Europe.

At the end of the fourteenth century, the Near East had three major powers: the Mamluks of Egypt and Syria, the Ottomans in western Anatolia, and the Timurids in Iran and Central Asia. Armenia and the surrounding areas were ruled by a number of Turkmen dynasties, formed by military adventurers formerly in the employ of Mongol rulers of the late thirteenth and early fourteenth centuries. The Ottomans themselves started out as one of these. The Byzantine Empire had been reduced to its capital Constantinople, and the Crusaders had vanished a century earlier. In Armenia, northern Mesopotamia, and eastern Iran, the most important Turkmen forces were the Kara Koyunlu (Black Sheep) and the Ak Koyunlu (White Sheep) dynasties, named after the emblems on their banners.

As the century was ending, between 1387 and 1402, Timur-Leng marched through Armenia three times on campaigns of terror and destruction as he passed from his base in the distant east to the shores of the Aegean. The History of the Wars of Timur and Shah Rukh by Tovma Metzopetsi and dozens of contemporary colophons chronicle Timur's devastating progress in gruesome and painful detail (Metzopetsi, 1860, 1892; Minorsky, 1953a). Not a kind word is spoken of him. The scribes, following a centuries-old tradition, attribute these calamities to God's punishment for the wickedness and sins of the Armenians. In 1402 Timur crushed the rising Ottoman power through a humiliating defeat of Sultan Bayazid I near Ankara; afterward, he retreated to Central Asia and died. The former Turkmen rulers, like their Armenian subjects, sighed in relief at the simultaneous disappearance of Timur in the east and the Ottomans to the west.

Political and Military History

The Kara Koyunlu (Black Sheep) Dynasty (1410–1467)

Within two years of Timur's last winter in the Near East (1403-1404), spent in Karabagh/Artsakh, the reigning chief of the Kara Koyunlu, Kara Yusuf, came forth from his retreat in Egypt. The clan had remained opposed to Timur and his successors, defending the area during the early raids. In 1406 Kara Yusuf took Tabriz, the principal city of western Iran; in 1409, Mardin; and the following year engaged the rival Ak Koyunlu Turkmens on the plain of Mush, killing their leader, Kara Yuluk Osman. Kara Yusuf's authority now extended over most of Armenia. His rise to power was not without severe consequences for the Christians. In 1407, during a raid into Georgia, he killed King Giorgi VII and took 15,000 prisoners, many of whom were Armenian. In 1411 he seized Baghdad from the Jalayirids and, after establishing his son there, returned to his base at Vagharshakert (Alashkert) in Armenia with his Baharlu tribesmen. Despite Kara Koyunlu incursions during the rest of the decade into areas to the north, there were some years of comparative tranquillity. Tovma Metzopetsi emphasizes that though taxes were high, there was peace, robbers were gone, and reconstruction had begun (Metzopetsi, 1860). This is confirmed by a colophon of 1412 that speaks of the rebuilding of Kars (Khachikian, 1955, no. 136, p. 134; Sanjian, 1969, p. 135).

The Timurids had not renounced claims on the region. From Khorasan, Timur's son, Shah Rukh, led three campaigns in the next fifteen years against the Kara Koyunlu. These are described in detail in Metzopetsi's *History* (Metzopetsi, 1860). In 1420, on the way to meet the first attack, Kara Yusuf died. Once again a leaderless Turkmen army turned to looting. Colophons, especially from Akhlat, which had been taken by Shah Rukh, describe the tragedies and anguish Armenia was subjected to during this fourth Timurid scourge. Iskandar (1420-1437), son of Kara Yusuf, retreated south to Mardin and Mosul only to return when Shah Rukh left the area. According to Armenian witnesses, Iskandar's reign was perceived to be as harsh as any: "He made the Armenian homeland like a desert" (colophon of 1426); "Armenia was subject to devastation and plunder, to slaughter, and captivity" (1425); "Each time, Iskandar plundered and carried off captives from the region of Van and Vostan. He then captured the citadel of Van, and all of us—bishops and *vardapets* [celibate priests], monks, priests, *tanuters* [heads of families], and ladies—took to flight and wandered about in foreign lands and became strangers" (1426) (Khachikian, 1950, pp. 277-88; Sanjian, 1969, pp. 150-63). In 1427 a monk from the Monastery of Metzop complained that Mass had not been performed for six years.

Iskandar also attacked many of the Kurdish chiefs around Lake Van and Lake Urmia. In 1426 he put an end to the fiefdom of Artaz in the Maku area, ruled by Armenian Catholic feudal lords, much to the joy of the Armenians, who, in one colophon, praise the Muslims for allowing them to make repairs on a church that the Catholics had forbidden.

The second raid of Shah Rukh, resulting in Iskandar's defeat, brought more plunder and destruction. Armenians retreated into the mountains, especially in the Vaspurakan area, because prisoners were being rounded up and deported as slaves to Khorasan. This campaign of 1428 was followed by a severe famine; in 1432 witnesses reported the eating of human flesh and the sale of human fat. In between these raids, Iskandar conducted devastating campaigns to restore his authority in the land and prepare for future incursions. The final attack of the Timurids began in 1434. The sources list complaints not only of looting, but also assertions that many Armenians left their mother hearth and emigrated (Khachikian, 1955, no. 448a, p. 419; Sanjian, 1969, p. 180).

Yet Iskandar sought to cultivate the Armenian population, especially the feudal lords and clergy. To reinforce this policy, he took the title "Shah-i Armen," King of the Armenians. He also had as one of his advisors Rustum, the son of Baron Beshken, the head of the Armenian *nakharar* (feudal nobility) house of Siunik. Evidence suggests that from 1425 to 1430, Rustum became the governor of the province of Ayrarat with Erevan as its center. His authority seems to have extended as far as Siunik, where his father still kept the title "prince of princes." During the final Timurid assault, Shah Rukh secured the allegiance of Iskandar's younger brother, Jihanshah, who was appointed governor over Tabriz and Armenia. The latter began persecutions in the Siunik area, forcing the Armenian noble Beshken Orbelian with 6,000 households to emigrate north to Lori, at the time under the control of King Alexander of Georgia, who was married to Beshken's sister. Colophons of the period describe the ravages inflicted on the area, including the sacking of the monastery of Tatev. A northern monastery, Sanahin, became the spiritual center of the displaced Armenians, now subjects of the Georgian king. Iskandar was busy farther west. During a raid against the rival Ak Koyunlu clan, he seized Armenians from Sebastia/Sivas, Kharpert, and Tokat and forced them to resettle in the Ayrarat and Siunik areas. Late in 1437, however, in an attack against his brother Jihanshah, he was defeated and killed; as a consequence, Rustum lost his authority over the Armenians and joined his father in exile. Tovma Metzopetsi comments, nevertheless, that peace was returned to the area (Metzopetsi, 1860).

Jihanshah (1437-1467), faced by various enemies, also looked toward the Armenians for support. Several feudal chiefs were given control of one or more regions and even allowed to use the title "prince" *(ishkhan);* these included the lords of Siunik, Vayots Dzor, Artsakh, and Gugark. Monasteries regained some of their previously sequestered properties. A certain Yakub Bek was appointed in Rustum's place over Ayrarat, with residence at Erevan. More than once during Jihanshah's rule positive actions toward the Armenians were taken. Some Armenian churches were rebuilt; tacit permission was given for the catholicosate to be reestablished in Echmiadzin in 1441; and Catholicos Zakaria of Aghtamar interceded before Jihanshah concerning the payment of taxes from the Bitlis, Mush, and Akhlat areas in the 1450s. But these positive steps were counterbalanced by continued transgressions. In 1440 the population of Georgia was victimized. In Tiflis 8,000 were killed and 9,000 were taken as slaves. Ruthless onslaughts continued into the 1450s targeting Erzinjan, Kemakh, Baiburt, and Terjan. Afterward Jihanshah moved south again toward Bitlis, Mush, and Akhlat, taking 1,500 Armenian prisoners. More ambitious campaigns led him into Mesopotamia, where he conquered Fars and Baghdad in 1455. Two years later he forced his way into Iran, capturing the Timurid cities of Rayy, Gilan, Qazvin, Khorasan, and, in 1458, the capital, Herat.

The final decade of Jihanshah's rule witnessed a continual fight with the Ak Koyunlu, who had begun moving up from their lands around Mosul. Attacks against the Lake Van area resulted in heavy reprisals by Jihanshah, who laid waste Taron and Mush in 1467. The end was near, however, for the Kara Koyunlu dynasty, plagued as it was by internal revolts and confronted by the charismatic leadership of Uzun Hasan, the Ak Koyunlu leader. The decisive battle occurred in November 1467; Jihanshah and his most loyal forces were slaughtered. Shortly after, the Ak Koyunlu became rulers of Armenia. The following four decades of their rule, marked by continual struggles with opposing Turkic dynasties to the east in Iran and the west in

Anatolia, were no more peaceful than the previous forty years of Kara Koyunlu supremacy.

The Ak Koyunlu (White Sheep) Dynasty (1468–1502)

The Ak Koyunlu, an Oghuz Turkmen tribe that may have entered the Middle East as early as the Seljuk invasions, chose Diarbekir as capital. Unlike the Kara Koyunlu, they did not resist Timur, but joined him and therefore were confirmed in their fief of Diarbekir. In the post-Timurid period, the Ak Koyunlu were unable to overcome their rivals, nor were they able to profit much from the weakening of the Ottoman state. They had marital ties with the Greek Comnene rulers and allied themselves with the Karamanid dynasty of central Anatolia against the Ottomans. The most outstanding of their rulers was Uzun Hasan (1453-1478), related by marriage to the Greeks of Trebizond. In consequence, Uzun Hasan tried to intercede with Sultan Mehmed on behalf of the Comnene, but to no avail as the Ottomans took Trebizond in 1461. Subsequently Uzun Hasan, along with the Karamanids, established firm diplomatic contacts with the Venetians in an attempt to trap their common enemy in a pincer action. The policy failed, and at best Uzun Hasan succeeded only in delaying the Ottoman drive eastward.

Still, with the crushing defeat and death of the Kara Koyunlu leader Jihanshah in 1467 and that of his son Ali, the last Black Sheep representative, in the following year, the Ak Koyunlu became undisputed rulers of Armenia, northern Mesopotamia, and Shirvan. Though at first Armenian scribes saw the destruction of Kara Koyunlu power as a deliverance from the oppressive taxation and exactions of the previous half century, and though Uzun Hasan, in an attempt to rationalize levies, issued a *kanunname* (legal decree) that published tax rates and the principles governing their collection, Armenians found out that the Ak Koyunlu were to oppress and tax at least as much as their predecessors. Furthermore, in Uzun Hasan's time restrictions were put on church activities, and Christians were required to wear a blue mark for identification.

Determined to stamp out all semi-independent authority in his lands, Uzun Hasan attacked Bitlis, the decades-old stronghold of Kurdish emirs who controlled that area of Lake Van. Bitlis, Akhlat, and lands to the south and in Jezira were taken. The Ak Koyunlu leader then turned against his old enemies, the Ottomans, who, in addition to absorbing the Pontic state, the last Greek outpost in the east, defeated the Karamanids, the last independent Muslim principality in Anatolia. In 1472, starting from Taron, Uzun Hasan realized a series of successes at Terjan, Erzinjan, and Tokat; he then marched against Karamaniya. But in a series of battles against the Ottomans, he was defeated and nearly lost his life. It was Ottoman military organization, the well-trained Janissary corps, and the use of artillery that beat Uzun Hasan's forces, essentially structured on tribal or at least traditional Turkic nomadic lines and unwilling to accept the use of canons.

In 1476 and 1477 Uzun Hasan launched a cruel assault against his northern neighbor, Bagrat IV of Georgia, during which many Armenians were killed in Tiflis. Throughout these wars, the money to equip the Ak Koyunlu army and manage military affairs came from heavy taxation and levies, the brunt of which was borne by the Armenians. The death of Uzun Hasan in 1478 left the Turkmen realm at the mercy of his young sons' generals. In the end Yakub became the Ak Koyunlu padishah (1478-1490). He soon faced a new threat from the east: the Safyan sheikhs of the city of Ardabil in northwestern Iran. Shi'ites by faith, the sheikhs had already begun to exert a strong moral influence over various Turkmen tribes. In 1488 Yakub attacked Ardabil, defeated the Safyan allies known as the Kizil-Bashi, or redheads—after the color of their headdress—and killed the sheikh, whose young children, it is said, took refuge with Armenian monks in the Aghtamar region (Hakobian, 1932, p. 271). In less than a dozen years, the youngest of these children, Ismail, was to head a Turkmen coalition and to found a new dynasty for Persia—the Safavids. During Yakub's reign, Armenian sources report that Christians could not use saddles or ring bells and had to wear a white belt as a mark of identification (Siurmeian, 1935, p. 68; Armenian Academy of Science, 1972, vol. 4, p. 52).

After two years of internecine struggles, Rustum, the grandson of Uzun Hasan, took control of the family for the next five years, until he was killed near Julfa by Ak Koyunlu rivals. In the following year, 1498, Alwand managed to seize power. But by 1499 the realm was divided in two—Alwand getting Armenia and Shirvan and his brother Muhammad, northern Mesopotamia and Iraq.

The Rise of the Safavids

By 1500 Ismail the Safavid was gathering under his banner Turkmen tribes, especially the seven that made up the Kizil-Bashi confederation. In that same year he attacked southern Georgia and Shirak, then entered

Shirvan and took Shamakhi. The following year Ismail took Tabriz, Alwand's capital. In 1502 he repulsed a counterattack by an Ak Koyunlu coalition of Alwand and Muhammad and thereby all but put an end to the White Sheep dynasty.

In Armenian history, the fifteenth century ends with the heralding of a new Muslim force. The Safavids were also of Turkmen origin, Ismail himself composing poems in the Oghuz dialect. Unlike their predecessors, the Safavids were, as sheikhs of Ardabil, religious as well as secular rulers. And though Muslim and essentially Oghuz Turkic like their western neighbors, the Ottomans, and their eastern ones, the Uzbek Turks (successors to the Timurids in Central Asia), the Safavids were Shi'i. This religious distinction gave Iran (until then predominantly Sunni) an identity apart from its Islamic Turkic neighbors.

During the sixteenth century Armenia and the Armenians suffered terribly; only later in the mid-seventeenth century were they to experience a revival under these same Ottomans and Safavids. The rise to power of a new Iranian dynasty coupled with the eastern push of the Ottomans in the sixteenth century brought into being a different kind of foreign overlordship. In a sense the Ak and Kara Koyunlu acted as intermediate powers in control of Armenia, Shirvan, and the Caspian region and at times Iraq, serving as a buffer zone between the Ottomans in the west, the Timurids in the east, and the Mamluks to the south. That intermediary was now gone. The superpowers—the Ottomans and the Safavids—were to confront each other directly in Armenia. However bad the fifteenth century appeared in terms of the socioeconomic and cultural history of Armenia, the sixteenth century was to be worse.

Armenian-Ottoman Relations

During the absorption of central Asia Minor by Sultan Bayazid I at the end of the fourteenth century, Armenians in larger cities such as Amasia and Kaiseri had come to know the Ottoman Turks only indirectly. The destruction of the Ottoman state in Anatolia in 1402 delayed Armenia's contact with them until the second half of the fifteenth century. The conquest of Constantinople in 1453, the taking of Trebizond in 1461 and the Crimea in 1475, and the final submission of the Karaman state in 1475 brought comparatively large numbers of Armenians in contact with the new empire. Armenians had always been resident in Constantinople and in other cities of the Byzantine Empire, but there is relatively little information on their numbers and activities in such places as

Adrianople, Bursa, Kutahia, Ankara, and Karaman. Armenians lived in these and other cities, some of which already supported bishops. For Constantinople the information is better, though at times confused and contradictory. Several standard histories of Armenia (Chamchian, 1786, vol. 3, p. 500; and Ormanian, 1955, p. 61; for example) assert that after the conquest of the Byzantine capital, Sultan Mehmed established Bishop Gennadius as the Greek patriarch, with jurisdiction over all Orthodox subjects in the empire, and in the following year, 1454, the sultan established the post of chief rabbi over the Jews. Finally, in 1461, according to these and other works, Mehmed brought to Constantinople Bishop Hovakim of Bursa, whom he made patriarch *(patrik)* over all Armenians and non-Orthodox Christians in his territories (Kurkjian, 1958, p. 281). Furthermore, these histories declare that Mehmed, wanting a counterforce against the many Greeks in the capital, brought in from newly conquered areas large numbers of Armenians to help in the repopulation of the war-weakened city (Kiumurjian, 1913, p. 210; Armenian Academy of Science, 1972, vol. 4, p. 301).

The traditional views concerning Mehmed's resettling of Armenians in Constantinople as a counterforce against the Greeks and even the accepted notion of the establishment of the Armenian Patriarchate in the conqueror's time have now been dismissed as "myths" (Berbérian, 1965). A careful examination of the early postconquest history of Constantinople, through sources heretofore not used by Armenian scholars, demonstrates there is no evidence showing that Sultan Mehmed tried to balance Armenians against Greeks. As a matter of fact, a quarter of a century after Mehmed's conquest, the number of Armenians in Constantinople did not exceed more than 1,000 households—some 5,000 to 6,000 souls—in both the city proper and Galata, the former Italian suburb across the Golden Horn. These figures are based on the 1478 census of the shops in Constantinople and Galata conducted by the judge *(qadi)* and police chief *(za'im)* of the city. Five or six thousand Armenians was not a great number among a population estimated at 100,000 to 120,000—just a bit more than 5 percent. It was in fact the smallest among the major groups listed: 9,500 Muslim households, or 57,000 individuals; about 3,750 Greek households, or 22,500 Greeks; and approximately 1,650 Jewish households, or some 9,900 Jews (Berbérian, 1965).

The census figures of 1478 show that the great majority of new settlers, whether forced or voluntary, was in fact Muslim. A quarter of a century later, shortly after 1500, Armenian households represented about one-fourth that of the Greeks, hardly enough to suggest a dramatic increase. The situation remained much the same until the end of the sixteenth century, when there was a wave of Armenian immigrants fleeing the Ottoman-Persian wars and the Jelali upheavals. There was forced resettlement of Armenians in the fifteenth century, but the sources, when specific, refer to very few individuals (Berbérian, 1965, appendix; Khachikian, 1958, no. 260, p. 261; Sanjian, 1969, pp. 283-84).

The question of the Armenian Patriarchate of Constantinople is complex. The Greek Patriarchate was not established by Mehmed, simply because it had always existed. The chief rabbi, who had been encouraged to migrate to the capital, was appointed in 1454, but only as the spiritual leader of the Jews in Constantinople. As for the Armenian "patriarch," Bishop Hovakim was merely the prelate of the capital and held no jurisdiction over the Armenians in the rest of the empire; nor did he possess the title "patriarch." The title was not officially used to designate the head of the Armenians in Constantinople until the reign of Süleyman Kanuni (1520-1566), known in western sources as the Magnificent (Berbérian, 1965, p. 112). Other Armenian sources make it clear that the Patriarch of Constantinople did not get jurisdiction over other Armenian prelates of the empire until the sixteenth and seventeenth centuries, and then only by a gradual process (Berbérian, 1965, pp. 100-11). The question of when exactly the title and authority of "patriarch" was awarded and acquired its full jurisdictional meaning may be understood when the Armenian colophons of the sixteenth century are published.

Still, the numbers of Armenians in the Ottoman capital were steadily increasing, continually augmented by newcomers from both the better-established Armenian middle class of the large urban centers of the empire and lower-class artisans and peasants from the war-torn and famine-stricken, despoiled areas of Armenia. The few accounts of forced immigration of Armenians into Constantinople in the early period make it quite clear that Sultan Mehmed wanted merchants, artisans, and educated persons to contribute to the reanimation of the city. Some colophons even specify that Armenians were at times forced to move on the threat of death. As at other moments when they were unwillingly compelled to leave Armenia, these refugees lamented their exile while vividly describing their hardships and sufferings. By hard work and outward conformity, they made the best of their situation and slowly acquired important positions in trade and finance in Constantinople and elsewhere (Khachikian, 1958, pp. 443 and xxxviii; Sanjian, 1969, p. 326; Hakobian, 1956, p. 46ff.; Armenian Academy of Science, 1972, vol. 4, p. 86).

The Ottoman Empire and the Christians

An examination of state institutions during the centuries of Ottoman ascendancy reveals the astonishing phenomenon of the most powerful Muslim empire being administered and run—except for the sultans themselves—by officials and military men born, almost without exception, as Christians. The elite Janissary corps of the conquering sultans of the fifteenth and sixteenth centuries was originally formed of Christian captives from the Balkans. Later the corps obtained new recruits through the *devshirme* (from the Turkish *devşirmek,* to gather) system. In this system, young Christians, for the most part Orthodox, were periodically collected by force from the European provinces of the empire. They were converted to Islam and taught Turkish while being given an elite education and military training. Most nonreligious posts, including that of the governors of provinces and even the grand vizier, were filled from the corps' ranks. Sons of Janissaries, no matter the rank or distinction of their fathers, were not allowed to join the corps, since they were born Muslims. Thus, the empire was led on the battlefield and in its civil service by individuals who were neither Turks nor Muslims at birth. By the seventeenth century the system had degenerated. The decision to admit Muslims resulted in a tenfold increase in the size of the corps (which consisted of only 10,000 to 12,000 during its glory), leading to a decline in military discipline.

What role did the Armenians play in this system? Simply stated, a very small one. The majority of youths, probably gathered from among the vast Orthodox populations, whether Greek or Slav, of Europe rather than from Anatolia or Armenia. That the Armenians were officially excluded from the *devshirme,* as some have suggested, is inaccurate. A curious reference to the exclusion of the Armenians is found in the 1582 account of Maffei Venieri. It is paraphrased by von Hammer-Purgstall (1827-1835, vol. 5) as follows: "The Armenians are the only ones exempt from the annual recruitment of Christian children destined to be incorporated into the ranks of the Janissaries. They do not become Janissaries until a lapse of twenty-five years." Elsewhere, however, von Hammer-Purgstall affirms that the Janissaries were "recruited by an annual levy of young boys, which after the decree *(kanun)* could take place only in Bosnia, Greece, Bulgaria, and Armenia."

Recruitment commonly took place outside urban centers. Since the major part of Armenia was not conquered until the first quarter of the sixteenth century and areas such as Erzerum, the Ararat Valley, and eastern parts of Vaspurakan were not really secure for the Ottomans until the early seventeenth century or at best at the end of the sixteenth century—prior to which only the main fortresses and cities were in their control—large rural areas of Armenian population were not available for such recruitment. Yet, as will be seen later, a few Armenians did obtain high office through this channel in the sixteenth and early seventeenth centuries.

There were several, presumably large, instances of forced migration *(surgun)* to Constantinople under Mehmed the conqueror from Kaffa in the Crimea and the area of Karaman. But the number of Armenians involved is uncertain and their exact fate unclear except for those from Karaman, who, according to the already cited census of 1478, were designated as "Armenians from Karamaniya" after they had been settled in the capital. Somewhat later Selim ordered the transfer of large numbers of Armenians after his eastern campaigns of 1514 to 1517, but there is no evidence that they entered the Janissary corps or the civil service. The major figures from high Ottoman circles who were of Armenian origin were Sinan, the architect for Sultans Süleyman and Selim II, and Khalil, grand vizier for a year, 1616-1617. That many Armenians did not reach high office in the system does not preclude their service in the lower ranks of the Ottoman administration. There has been, however, very little published on which to base a case in this period. The forced gathering of Armenian youth is mentioned in colophons and other sources for the following years: 1464, 1480, 1519, 1531, 1536, 1543, 1547, 1550, 1590, and 1622 (Berbérian, 1965). Small numbers of individuals were affected; their exact exploitation by the Ottomans is not made clear. Armenian youth taken from Ankara in 1464 were accompanied by their bishop and later joined by their parents, practices forbidden for normal *devshirme* recruiting. Nevertheless, Western and Turkish sources record the forced gathering of youths in areas clearly inhabited by Armenians, for instance: Sis and Sivas, 1456, 1526, 1574; Batum, 1583; Amasia, Malatia, Tokat, Sivas, Marash, Chemishkezek, Erzerum, Baiburt, Kemakh, 1622-1623 (Zulalian, 1959, pp. 247-56). The mere threat of the *devshirme,* arbitrarily and suddenly breaking up a Christian family to serve the Muslim superpower, was one of the important psychological factors that made the late fifteenth and sixteenth centuries such a dreaded period in Armenian history.

Armenia in the Sixteenth Century

The sixteenth century was one of war between the Ottomans and the Safavids over Armenia and the Caucasus. Successive campaigns of three to twelve years were usually followed by famine. The depletion of whatever resources may have been available on the Ottoman side of the shifting border led to general anarchy, further ravaging Anatolia and Armenia at the end of the sixteenth and the first decade of the seventeenth century. This resulted in massive Armenian immigration to the cities of Cappadocia and, farther west, Constantinople, which, together with the forced transfer of Armenians by Shah Abbas in the first years of the seventeenth century, caused a decline in population in larger areas of the historic homeland (Tavrizhetsi, 1896).

The firm establishment of the new Safavid dynasty in Persia was supported primarily in the early period—from 1502 to the offensive of Sultan Selim (1512-1520) in 1514—by the Kizil-Bashi, as both regular and irregular Safavid troops were known. They laid waste great sections of Armenia while consolidating the Persian position in the Caucasus. According to colophons of 1501 from Erzinjan and 1504 from Mush, Armenians subjected to the pillaging of the Turkmen sought refuge in Georgia. By 1509 the Safavids had captured much of Georgia and Shirvan and seized Derbent in Daghestan. Areas all the way to Sivas, formerly controlled by the Ak Koyunlu, were now under direct Safavid rule or subject to their raids. Because of Safavid association with the sheikhs of Ardabil, the Turkmen population with Shi'ite tendencies, especially sufi and dervish elements, provided the Kizil-Bashi with sympathizers in the western areas.

Though the Safavids found support from the same Turkmens who had been loyal to the Kara and Ak Koyunlu dynasties, from the Ottoman viewpoint the new rulers of Persia presented a more complex challenge because of their Shi'ism, a form of Islam that appeared less rigid to many Muslims. Sultan Selim was determined to neutralize this threat while extending the boundaries of the empire. In 1514 he implemented a course of action that was to serve future sultans well as a normal expedient when confronted with any group that was deemed undesirable: elimination by massacre. In a matter of weeks, some 40,000 sufis and dervishes of Shi'i leaning were put to death throughout the eastern regions of the country. In the same year, after assembling a large army, Selim marched from Amasia to Tokat and Sivas, after which the lands of the shah began. He took Erzinjan, Kemakh, and Erzerum, crossed the Araxes above Khoi, and engaged Shah Ismail on the plain of Chaldiran, not far from the spot of the fifth-century battle of the Avarayr. With superior artillery, the Ottomans defeated the Safavids and advanced to Tabriz, which was held for eight days. On Selim's return to Constantinople, he took control of territories ruled by Kurdish emirs and lands of the Dhul-Kadir principality in the Taurus and beyond. The Turks took many Armenians from Tabriz, Erzerum, and surrounding areas to Constantinople. These conquests brought the central and southern areas of the Armenian population into the Ottoman Empire, including the cities of Malatia, Mush, Diarbekir, Birejik, Aintab, and Antioch.

The Safavids struck back almost immediately, establishing a pattern of attack and counterattack for the entire sixteenth century. In 1516 Ismail invaded Georgia and the Caspian coast of Shirvan. In the next decades, under Shah Tahmasp (1524-1576), the Safavids made raids into Armenia as far as Kars, Erzerum, and Terjan. The first of the three Ottoman campaigns into Armenia and Georgia by Sultan Süleyman against Shah Tahmasp began in 1533 when Ibrahim Pasha, the grand vizier, was ordered to seize the fortress of Van. For the next hundred years Van and Erzerum were to be the main staging points for Ottoman thrusts against Persia. In 1534 Süleyman received the obedience of various Georgian princes as well as the Kurdish khan of Bitlis, who ceded his fortresses south of Lake Van. The Kurds, however, were not brought under control completely until the seventeenth century. The outcome of the campaign gave little more to the Ottomans than the area around Van.

The second Ottoman campaign, begun in 1547-1548 with the seizure of the city of Van and attacks against Shirvan, was led this time by Shah Tahmasp's own brother, Alkaf Mirza, who had defected to the enemy side. The next year, 1549, the Georgian army was destroyed, and the western part of the country, along with Armenia, began to be considered as part of the Ottoman Empire. However, the area, which centuries later was to be called Azerbaijan, with its capital Tabriz, still remained in Persian hands. During the three years that followed, Shah Tahmasp made vicious counterraids against Basen, Bardzr Hayk, Vaspurakan, and Turuberan. Süleyman reacted by officially turning Van and Diarbekir into separate provinces among the twenty-one that constituted his empire. During this phase of the bitter rivalry over Armenia and Georgia, the sources concur that, as a group, the Christian inhabitants preferred the Persians to the Ottomans. In Armenia proper, the immediate consequence from the war of 1547 to 1552 was a severe famine in 1552-1553, the result from the peasants' reluctance to go out to distant fields for fear of their lives and of opposing armies and irregular troops requisitioning by force whatever else was available.

In between these eastern wars, Süleyman was waging battle in Europe. The first siege of Vienna was in 1526. Just prior to the third eastern campaign in 1553, Tahmasp seized the fortresses of Akhlat and Arjesh and the country around Basen, Baiburt, Erzinjan, Terjan, Erzerum, Khnus, and Mush. Erzerum, Van, and Artzke were laid waste. Shah Tahmasp, having received word that an Ottoman army had reached Sivas, embarked on a deliberate scorched-earth policy in order to retard an army he could not beat as it progressed through Armenia.

The Turkish attack of 1553 to 1555 was one of the most consciously violent recorded in the annals of the Ottoman Empire. In the winter of 1553-1554, Süleyman stayed at Aleppo to be near the front for an early spring offensive. In 1554 Erevan, "the soul of all Persia," as it was described by Pechevi, the contemporary Ottoman chronicler of these campaigns, was seized and burned (Pechevi, 1961). Nakhichevan was taken, and all provinces between Tabriz and Maragha were totally destroyed. The Karabagh was also seized. Pechevi related in great detail the willful destruction and devastation carried out by the Turks. Under the year A.H. 962/A.D. 1553-1554 he writes:

> . . . The region had become very prosperous, having many rich villages with cultivated lands. The victorious [Ottoman] army destroyed and ruined those prosperous villages and leveled them to the ground. From there the army . . . arrived on the seventeenth day at the city of Erevan, which was the soul of Persia. . . . Everything was burned to the ground. On the twenty-third day it moved on to the Arpa Chai, and in that area too everything was pillaged and destroyed. . . . On the twenty-fifth day it entered the land called Karabagh, which, with its mountains and rich orchards, is a very famous region of the Persian lands. . . . The local population had scattered and disappeared without a trace . . . yet, the army seized enormous riches and spoils. . . . On the twenty-seventh day it reached the plain of Nakhichevan. From dread of the victorious army, the towns and villages, the houses and habitations were so deserted and desolate that the area had become a haven for owls and crows striking terror amongst those who

viewed such a sight. . . . The army, thirsty for booty, again looted and destroyed not leaving one stone upon another. Besides this, for a distance of four to five days' march from the main route, all villages and hamlets, fields and construction were destroyed and ruined to such a degree that not a trace of building or of any life remained. . . . But in addition to this, uncountable quantities of valuable property and stores were looted and destroyed. And the number of handsome young boys and lovely, gentle young girls who were enslaved were of such a large portion that it is impossible for this writer to describe. In no other campaign did such a quantity of wealth come to the [Ottoman] army. There was not a [soldier's] tent in which the number [of slaves] . . . was less than three, and the number of tents with five or more than ten was beyond counting.

On May 29, 1555, at Amasia, this phase of a senseless war was concluded with the first treaty of peace between the Safavids and Ottomans. Süleyman received or kept Mosul, Marash, Van, Alashkert, Bayazed, and western Georgia. The shah kept Shirvan and the area to Tabriz. Thus, at midcentury, the Ottomans dominated the Armenians, the Georgians, and the areas inhabited by the Kurds.

Again during this phase of the war, the Armenians suffered the most. Those who could leave did so, moving toward urban centers farther west in Ottoman lands, or east and south. Most, of course, were unable to escape their lot; contemporary colophons stress over and again the incessant suffering (Armenian Academy of Science, 1972, vol. 4). The Georgians were also victimized, but they still had a kingdom, even if disunited. By real and feigned conversion to Islam and alliances with the Ottomans and Persians, Georgians were sometimes able to play one off against the other. On the other hand, the Kurds, who, though still seminomadic, were orthodox Muslims, encouraged the Ottomans to absorb their territories, which provided a Sunni buffer against the Shi'i Turkmens of the shah. In this period large numbers of Kurds were resettled in Artsakh, Siunik, Shirvan, and the Ararat plain.

During the twenty-three-year hiatus before the next eruption of hostilities, the Ottomans used Armenians and Kurds—according to a colophon of 1566—to construct or reconstruct forts in Van and Arjesh and probably elsewhere (Armenian Academy of Science, 1972, vol. 4, p. 88). Shortly after, in the area from Van to Khoi, the Ottomans encouraged a Kurdish rebellion against the Safavids, who, after the death of Tahmasp (1576), were in the midst of a struggle for succession.

To weaken the Persian state, which was in this period perceived as an important rival for eastern trade, the Ottomans planned to seize all of Armenia and Caucasia at any auspicious moment. Already in the 1560s they had tried to take Astrakhan and the areas north of the Caucasus and the Caspian Sea in order to construct a Don-Volga canal that would have enabled the strong Ottoman fleet to sail from the Black Sea to the Caspian. But the attempt failed even though the Ottomans were helped by the Crimean Tatars who made raids deep into Georgia, Shirvan, and even around Tabriz. The Persian trade with Russia in Shirvan and Derbent was enormous, especially in silk, rice, salt, and petroleum. The annual revenue for the shah was some 25,000,000 aspers (small silver coins, 90 percent pure) from Shirvan alone. Earlier Süleyman had banned the trade of silk from Persian. It was just at this troubled moment that much of the silk trade was taken over by Armenian merchants.

In 1578 Mustafa Pasha, the vizier of Sultan Murad III (1574-1595), at the head of an army of some 200,000, started out from Erzerum on the sixteenth century's fifth campaign in the Perso-Turkish conflict. Though it was to be the longest—1578 to 1590—and the last of the century, it was, unfortunately, not the final campaign of the war. Kars was again fortified, and in August, Mustafa moved to Ardahan and Georgia. Tiflis was taken and destroyed. Ganja was sacked by the Crimean Tatars. Shirvan and Derbent were attacked and pillaged. But little was accomplished against the Persians, and the army—returning to Erzerum—was disbanded. The Persians asked for peace, but the sultan refused and soon started hostilities again with a new commander. Karabagh, Gegharkuni, and Erevan were reoccupied. Murad decided that no major attack on Persia could be undertaken if the Ottoman border areas were not firmly secured. Therefore, in 1582 he ordered the repair of the fortresses of Erevan and Kars. By 1584 the Ottomans had stabilized their control over northern Armenia, Georgia, Shirvan, and Daghestan. In 1585 a major thrust south was made, and Tabriz fell. But the Persians, led by Prince Mirza, retook the town the next year and defeated the Ottoman army in several battles, forcing them to retreat to Van. Then the Persians took Salmast and attacked the Ottoman pasha of Erevan. In 1588-1589, the Persians seized Ganja, Karabagh, and Nakhichevan.

By then the young Shah Abbas (1588-1629) had succeeded to the throne. He was to face a double threat: the traditional Sunni enemy to the west, and the Uzbeks, another Turkic and Sunni power, from the east. In order to gain time to meet the Uzbek menace to Khorasan, Abbas sued for peace, which the Ottomans, who had suffered defeats in Europe, willingly accepted. By the terms of the Treaty of 1590, Persia gave up Tabriz, Mukan, Shirvan, and Georgia, while the Ottomans kept Armenia and Iraq. Because the rivals were preoccupied with a menace at the opposite end of their respective empires, direct hostilities in Armenia and the adjacent areas stopped for more than a decade. Unfortunately, however, there was no peace in Armenia.

The Jelali Movement and Shah Abbas's Deportations

In the second half of the sixteenth century, mostly because of the introduction of cheap silver from the Americas via Europe, the Ottoman state suffered a serious monetary crisis that resulted in the depreciation of its silver standard currency coupled with an increase in prices. Fixed-income groups suffered the most. Among them were the provincial cavalry, the *sipahis,* whose revenue depended on rents (usually fixed) from lands. Those with small holdings were unable to meet the expenses of outfitting the expected number of troops for the unceasing military campaigns and, therefore, had their holdings confiscated. Also affected were irregular soldiers in Anatolia, the *sebkans,* usually landless peasant youths equipped with muskets recruited in time of war as paid soldiers by local governors.

Bands of these individuals were formed; they lived off the people and came to be called *Jelalis.* After the demobilization following the peace of 1590, the Jelalis drew their main strength from the *sebkan* companies but were joined by dissatisfied *sipahis,* local vigilantes, and Kurdish and Turkish nomads. When the regular troops withdrew, the countryside was at the mercy of these bandits. From 1590 to 1610, they set upon Armenian, Cappadocian, and Anatolian towns and villages. Armenian colophons of the first five years of the seventeenth century refer no less than ten times to the exactions of Kara Yazidji, who, with his 20,000 followers, was the best known of these independent leaders. The central government was unable to suppress the Jelalis, who, it seems, had no fixed objective. They were outlaws living off the peasants and lower classes, taking advantage of the Ottoman Empire's inability to organize and rule its eastern provinces properly (Zulalian, 1966; von Hammer-Purgstall, 1827-1835).

After crushing the Uzbek threat in the east, Shah Abbas took advantage of the anarchy prevailing in Armenia and Anatolia as a result of the Jelali movement to launch a major campaign. In 1603 he recaptured Tabriz, then Erevan, and in 1605, Baghdad. To meet the expected Ottoman counteroffensive, Shah Abbas imitated the scorched-earth policy Tahmasp had used in 1553. Starting in the summer of 1604, Eastern Armenia was systematically laid waste. The shah issued a proclamation throughout the areas of Ayrarat and the lower Araxes Valley, ordering all Armenians to gather in designated places for a mass migration. Persian troops then thoroughly burned houses and fields and destroyed everything else that might be used by the advancing Ottoman troops. Armenians from Vayots Dzor, Sevan, Lori, Abaran, Shirakavan, Kars, and Alashkert were assembled on the Ararat plain. To them were added those from Julfa, Nakhichevan, and the surrounding area. Arakel of Tabriz has carefully chronicled the disastrous forced march of hundreds of thousands of Armenians into Persia. Though winter was approaching and though the Armenians as loyal subjects tried to obey to the letter the request of the shah, their petitions to delay the move until the following spring were denied. Almost immediately human caravans extending for miles pushed forward. Thousands died in the crossing of the Araxes River because boats were lacking. Later survivors were split up in groups, and during the winter of 1604-1605, they sought shelter wherever possible in northwestern Persia. In the following year, one group finally got to the shah's capital, Isfahan, where the Armenians were given an area south of the Zangi-Rud River to establish their own town, named by them New Julfa in memory of the city from which most of them originated. Other groups were scattered throughout Persia. (Tavrizhetsi, 1896, pp. 16-92; Alishan, 1893, pp. 414-18; Hakobian, 1951, no. 12, pp. 178-88; "An Armenian Catholic Bishop," 1837). Coincidentally, at almost the same moment, Grigor Daranaghtsi was leading a group of 7,000 Armenians *away* from Constantinople toward the rapidly depopulating eastern provinces as part of the repatriation plan of Sultan Murad the IV.

The Ottomans had little success against Shah Abbas's newly reorganized army, trained in the European manner by the Shirley brothers, English adventurers who also conducted diplomatic missions with the West. Abbas, having neutralized the Kizil-Bashi by relying more strongly on Georgians who had converted to Islam and other Caucasian elements, regained most of the lands lost in the war of 1578 to 1590. He offered peace in 1610, but it was refused by the Ottomans until 1618, when an agreement roughly based on the peace of Amasia of 1555 gave Persia Shirvan, Georgia, and Tabriz. In the 1620s, however, hostilities broke out again. They ended only in 1639, when the Treaty of Zuhab finally stopped a century and a half of war. The treaty gave the Ottomans Iraq, with Baghdad and Mosul, the Van area, and Armenia up to Kars. Erevan, Shirvan, and Tabriz went to the Safavids.

Armenia had been ruined by more than a hundred years of attacks and counterattacks. Foreign travelers testify that Ararat, Alashkert, Bayazit, and the plain of Nakhichevan were deserted. Nomadic Kurds and Turkmens moved into many of the ravished or abandoned areas. The natural economy of the region was destroyed. Artisans and merchants who had managed to escape the forced migrations either joined their countrymen in Persia at a later date or left for more distant lands.

Social and Economic Structure of Armenia

With the fall of the Cilician kingdom in the fourteenth century, how was Armenian life structured? In many respects not much differently from that of previous centuries, at least for the first hundred years. After the disappearance of the Bagratid dynasty and the Artsrunis of Aghtamar in the eleventh century, life in Greater Armenia had continued without kings or autonomous states of large scope. The early fifteenth century showed that the Armenians had learned well how to continue life under non-Armenian and non-Christian rule. They took advantage of any benevolence offered by charitable governors, saved or put aside something for worse times, which they knew were sure to come, and always hoped that conditions in Armenia would become better in the future.

There were still autonomous and semiautonomous Armenian *nakharar* units of varying size, especially in Siunik and Karabagh, but they affected only a small portion of the population. Large numbers of Armenians opted to move. They had learned centuries before that individual salvation might be gained by emigration to more secure lands. The major centers toward which they went were the Crimea, thence to Poland and central Europe, and to the larger urban centers of western Armenia, Cappadocia, and Anatolia. This trend continued in the fifteenth century, with an additional minor movement toward Christian Georgia. In the sixteenth century Georgia became as unsafe as Armenia, and the flow gradually moved east into Persia and farther west toward Constantinople and centers in the Ottoman Empire with already established Armenian communities.

Yet, surprisingly, despite the devastating invasions, accompanied by pillaging and enslavement, despite taxes on a level never before imposed, despite the recurring famines, occasional plagues, locusts, and the relatively large number of earthquakes reported during the period, Armenians also stayed in Armenia. Colophons and other sources testify that they tried to maintain Armenian life as they understood it and, when possible, even to improve or at least contribute culturally to it (Khachikian, 1955-1967; Hakobian and Hovhannisian, 1974; Kouymjian, 1983). At times the struggle must have seemed insurmountable, the nation condemned. The worst moment, when traditional institutions were in danger of total collapse, was the first half of the sixteenth century. This will be discussed later.

The main means of livelihood were agriculture, trade, and craftsmanship. During this period, because of wartime conditions, the areas available for agriculture became further and further circumscribed. In the fifteenth century, the still partially nomadic Turkmen dynasties and their epigones, mostly Turkic and Kurdish nomads, were quick to turn any abandoned or temporarily untended fields into pasturage for their flocks. Through this process many large holdings were permanently removed from tillage. Mountainous areas such as Siunik and Karabagh, where terracing was common and water was abundant without the need for irrigation, continued to provide sustenance to a limited population. This pattern of reduction of the agricultural lands continued even after Ottoman absorption of Armenia in the sixteenth century, as evidenced by the very small number and the relatively smaller size of land grants *(timars)* recorded in Ottoman documents of later centuries for Armenia. In addition, the policy of favoring the Kurds, much less concerned with farming, at least during the sixteenth century—begun by Sultan Selim as an orthodox Sunni Islamic counterforce to the heterodox Shi'i Kizil-Bashis who made up the Safavid ranks—contributed further to the reduction of agricultural lands while increasing the Kurdish population in Armenia. Also underscoring the decline in agricultural production were various plagues vividly recorded by Armenian colophons (Cook, 1972; Faroghi, 1984).

Trade traditionally produced revenue for Armenia in two ways: through the direct selling of goods and by transit fees. Since Armenia was at the juncture of the principal natural highways from east to west and north to south, it benefited by making those segments under its control function efficiently. On the other hand, over the centuries Armenia often suffered by being geographically "in the way." The Mediterranean route from Cilicia through Armenia to Persia, which had in part been responsible for the wealth and prosperity of the thirteenth and early fourteenth centuries in Cilicia and Armenia proper, became virtually inoperative from the Armenian point of view after the fall of the Cilician kingdom. The traditional route through Tabriz and Erzerum to Trebizond on the Black Sea also was destroyed after the fall of Trebizond to the Turks. It was replaced by another route passing from Persia through Shirvan and Derbent into Russia. Persian silk normally traded by Persian, Turkish, and Armenian merchants had become more and more exploited by Armenians in the sixteenth century (both in the Ottoman-controlled areas and in Persia) well before Shah Abbas gave the Armenians a virtual monopoly over the trade in the early seventeenth century. Benefiting by commercial contacts in Europe with the diasporan communities of the Crimea, Poland, and Italy, many Armenians in the western cities of Erzinjan, Sivas, Kaiseri, and cities around Lake Van such as Bitlis, and farther to the east, Julfa and Nakhichevan, took advantage of moments of peace under Black and White Sheep dynasties to engage in trade. By the mid-fifteenth century, sources speak regularly of provincial *khojas* (traders or merchants) who had become sufficiently wealthy, mostly through trade, to endow—at times very modestly—churches and monasteries. They had become the dominant class in Armenian society. By the sixteenth century, these *khojas* and their somewhat later city brothers, often called *chelebis,* had established themselves east in India, south in Aleppo, north in Russia, and west in Constantinople, the Balkans, Italy, the Baltic Sea, and elsewhere (Kouymjian, 1994). This process continued in the seventeenth, eighteenth, and nineteenth centuries, when the *chelebis* gave way to the equivalent of the great financial and industrial magnates of the West, the Armenian *amiras* (Barsoumian, 1982, pp. 171-72).

Artisans and craftsmen were active throughout the land. The crafts most often mentioned in the manuscript sources are naturally enough associated with book production—scores of scribes, miniaturists, illuminators, and binders. There are more than a hundred references to traders or merchants—*khojas.* An extremely large number of crafts and professions are cited. The most common in order of their frequency are goldsmiths, weavers, blacksmiths, coppersmiths, doctors, shoemakers, farriers, millers, and tailors. In addition, over one hundred individuals are known as *varpet,* that is, master craftsman. The eventual publication of the sixteenth-century colophons will allow completion of the picture of the period. For the first decades of the seventeenth century, in addition to scribes, painters, binders, *khojas,* and *chelebis*—the latter almost all from Constantinople or its environs—there are frequent references to goldsmiths, blacksmiths, silversmiths, tailors, farriers, and a variety of other crafts (Khachikian, 1955-1967; Hakobian and Hovhannisian, 1974). Medieval Armenian brotherhoods, which functioned to bring together and protect (when necessary) merchants and craftsmen, were established perhaps as early as the eleventh century in Ani and certainly by the twelfth and thirteenth centuries; among other evidence are the rules and regulations of the Brotherhood of Erzinjan, written in 1280 by Hovhannes of Erzinjan (Kouymjian, 1975, pp. 107-12). These brotherhoods were spread throughout the Armenian world: in the Crimea, Poland, Constantinople, Aleppo, and Vaspurakan. No doubt they were precursors of the Armenian *esnafs* (guilds) of nineteenth-century Constantinople.

Urban Centers, Migrations, and Population in the Fifteenth and Sixteenth Centuries

Just as the Seljuk and Mongol invasions caused a dramatic movement, even a shift of population, that sustained the rise of the kingdom of Cilicia, so too did the Timurid invasions, the Turkmen wars of the fifteenth century, the Ottoman-Persian wars of the sixteenth century, and the forced migrations instigated by the Ottomans and Shah Abbas have their effects on the demography of Armenia. The fall of the Lusignans in Cilicia resulted in a rapid decline in Armenian activity along the coastal cities. In the fifteenth and sixteenth centuries, except for Sis—graced by its catholicosate—little was heard of the many Cilician centers active earlier. In the north, Ani, Kars, and Shirak in general continued to decline in the late fourteenth and early fifteenth centuries, though Ilkhanid coins were still struck in Ani until 1350; and Jalayirid (Mongol) issues from the Ani mint are recorded for the years 1356-1357, 1375-1376, and 1376-1377. A Bishop Hovhannes is mentioned at Ani in 1426; the city was still in existence, probably as a village, in the early seventeenth century, as shown by two colophons (Khachikian, 1955; Hakobian and Hovhannisian, 1974). Kars, however, was virtually dormant in the fifteenth century and presumably in the sixteenth, too, until its fortress was rebuilt by the Ottomans in 1584, after which it again became an important Armenian center. Siunik, Lori, and the area up to and including Tiflis were active during the early fifteenth century, with Tatev in Siunik still the leading monastic institution of the area in the first quarter of the century. Haghbat and Sanahin were also very prosperous, and, unlike Tatev in the south, were able to sustain themselves as dynamic centers into the seventeenth century and beyond. But after mid-century Tiflis and Georgia in general became less important for Armenian life. Echmiadzin was virtually inactive until the re-creation of the catholicosate in 1441, but even then, travelers' accounts of the sixteenth and early seventeenth centuries describe it as nearly abandoned (Hakobian, 1932; Alishan, 1893; Carswell, 1968, pp. 73-87). Vagharshapat maintained itself reasonably well, and Erevan began its steady rise in the sixteenth century. In the fifteenth century Nakhichevan and Julfa on the Araxes were little heard of. Julfa became more important in the second half of the sixteenth century, only to be destroyed at the end of the century by Shah Abbas. The English traveler John Cartwright, in the late sixteenth century, reports 2,000 stone-built houses in Julfa with 10,000 Armenian inhabitants (Cartwright, 1611; Alishan, 1893, p. 419; Carswell, 1968, p. 73). Arakel of Tabriz says, however, that in 1604-1605, 20,000 Armenians from Julfa were deported to Persia—with one-fifth surviving to settle in New Julfa (Tavrizhetsi, 1896, pp. 52ff.). This suggests that the surrounding villages were included. Major urban centers to the east—Tabriz, Maku, Khoi, Maragha, Salmast—had Armenian communities, though that of Tabriz was incontestably the most active. Karabagh/Artsakh, Gandzasar, Artaz, Gegharkuni, and the cities of Shirvan were also animated centers, but it was in Mountainous Karabagh that autonomous Armenian rule seems to have survived best during the dark days of the sixteenth century.

At the end of the sixteenth and the beginning of the seventeenth century, Isfahan (with New Julfa), Tabriz, Amida, and Diarbekir were all important Armenian centers. In Syria, Aleppo, which had a small colony in the fifteenth century, grew in the sixteenth to become one of the major communities in the seventeenth century, benefiting by the settlement of important merchants from cities such as Julfa on the Araxes. Throughout the period the Armenians in Jerusalem, with their own quarter and the monastery of St. James, kept active and visible.

The most thriving center of Armenian culture in the fifteenth century, and perhaps in the sixteenth too, was around Lake Van. The cities and monasteries along and nearby its shores were both individually and as a group the most dynamic of any in Armenia. The region had its own catholicos, established at Aghtamar in 1113. An anonymous Venetian merchant in the first quarter of the sixteenth century reported that the island contained a town of 600 houses called Armenik (Hakobian, 1932, pp. 300-1; Armenian Academy of Science, 1972, vol. 4, pp. 44-45). Cities such as Baghesh (Bitlis), Hizan (Khizan), Van, Arjesh,

Varag, Artzke, Khlat (Akhlat), and Berkri were even more active with large monastic institutions such as Metzop, near Arjesh, and Kadjberuni and Moks in surrounding areas. Mush, with its monasteries, especially St. Karapet and Sasun, was also flourishing. Baghesh was protected in the early sixteenth century by the Kurds, who were praised at least by the local Armenians as being benevolent. Unfortunately, this was not the case everywhere.

In the west, Constantinople slowly became an important center of Armenian life, but a real increase of population started only after the conquest of Greater Armenia by Sultan Selim. At the turn of the sixteenth century, the Polish-Armenian cleric Simeon Lehatsi (Simeon of Poland), resident in Constantinople for several years, reported 80 Armenian houses proper in 1604, but adds there were 40,000 Armenian emigrant hearths (Lehatsi, 1936, p. 26). Authorities interpret this latter count to mean individuals—which puts the Armenian population at the turn of the seventeenth century at about 50,000, including Galata, Uskudar, and the nearby suburbs. There is little doubt that from the seventeenth century on—at least according to population—Constantinople became the most important Armenian city in the world, with some 200,000 Armenians by the late nineteenth century. However, in the fifteenth and sixteenth centuries, the largest and most active diaspora communities were in the Crimea and Poland. The large medieval colony in Egypt had become considerably diminished and impoverished during the fifteenth and sixteenth centuries according to Simeon Lehatsi, who visited Cairo in 1615-1616 (Kapoian-Kouymjian, 1988).

Unfortunately, we have very few population statistics for the period. The only figures close to our period are those of the generally reliable Simeon, who passed through Anatolia in 1612-1613 and 1617 on his way to and from Egypt and Jerusalem. In his travel account, he often gives the population figures for larger cities not only at the moment of his passage, but also for a generation earlier, prior to the devastation and depopulation caused by the Jelali movement. For instance, Sivas had 600 Armenian houses in 1612 but 2,000 before; Tokat 500, but 1,000 before; and of Zeitun's 800 Armenian houses, only 30 remained in his time. From a much earlier period, Ibn Battuta, the Arab traveler, reported that in the 1330s, when he passed through Erzinjan, the majority of the inhabitants were Armenian; but for the fifteenth century, figures for this and other towns remain obscure.

For certain cities of Anatolia and Cappadocia, through the publication of Ottoman *defters* (fiscal and population registers), much raw data with precise population counts on Armenians for the sixteenth century is now available. The fiscal registers of 1520 to 1530 show that Sivas had a large Christian majority: 750 Christian versus 261 Muslim households; and Tokat was about equally divided: 701 Christian and 818 Muslim households (Jennings, 1976, pp. 21-57). Because this information is so new and interesting, an analysis of some of these documents follows.

Ottoman fiscal registers are particularly a phenomenon of the sixteenth century. From those already published, useful and new information is available on the Armenian inhabitants of Baiburt, Trebizond, Amasia, Karaman, Kaiseri, and Erzerum. The registers enumerate the districts of each city, listing the number of adult males *(nefer)* and households *(hane)*, the names of individuals, their marital status, often their trade, and property they owned. Jennings's 1976 study of Ottoman defters of five cities—Karaman, Trebizond, Amasia, Kaiseri, Erzerum—from the period 1500 to 1591, shows a population rise of about 100 percent during this period, in line with the general increase of population throughout the Mediterranean world. But each city had varying increases depending on individual history and demography (p. 51).

From 1523 to 1583 Karaman showed a 195 percent increase, with 2,048 adult males in the latter year. But just 2 percent of the population was Christian and, therefore, useful only as a negative statistic. In part this is explained by the forced deportation from Karaman to Constantinople of Armenian and Greek inhabitants at the end of the fifteenth century. Amasia increased in population by 69 percent from 1523, to reach 3,326 adult males in 1576; of these 77 percent were Muslim and the rest Jews, Greeks, and Armenians. Of all the cities, Amasia was the one longest under Ottoman protection; yet the Jelali troubles of the end of the sixteenth century and the general disorder in the early seventeenth century caused its population to fall by half, to 1,736 adult males, according to a *defter* of 1642. The average household represented by an adult male was composed of four to five members for the period. Thus the Armenian population of Amasia in the sixteenth century was small. Armenian sources bear this statistic out; there was little Armenian activity in Amasia at the time. Its rival in trade, Tokat, was a much more important Armenian (and Ottoman) city. In 1612 Simeon of Poland reports 200 Armenian houses in Amasia and 500 in Tokat.

Trebizond, which had been conquered by the Turks with little destruction in 1461-1463, maintained its predominantly Christian population—85 percent in the *defter* of 1523, with about 15 percent of the population Armenian: 197 adult males out of a total of 1,473. By 1583 the general population had risen by 44 percent, but the Armenian population had dropped by almost 50 percent, because the Armenians moved, willingly and by force, especially to Constantinople.

For Erzerum, the register of 1523 reports that the city was empty and destroyed. Though there were twelve quarters *(mahalle)*, they were empty. This official Ottoman source is a graphic testimony of the havoc caused by the successive wars of the fifteenth and early sixteenth centuries. The *defter* of 1540 reports 21 quarters, but only about 100 adult males, mostly associated with the Ottoman army, for Erzerum was the main staging point for attacks against the Safavids. The scribe records that because Erzerum was on the frontier, the population had been scattered by the Kizil-Bashi and the Georgians: "The city stands empty and in ruins . . . *raya* [Christians] come to settle." After the Ottoman-Persian peace of 1590, a register of 1591 shows a total adult male population of 548, 60 percent of whom are Armenian, the rest Muslim. The three quarters for trades and crafts—tanning, dyeing, and storing of grains—in the city, are composed exclusively of Armenians (Jennings, 1976, pp. 47-49). Armenian sources confirm this rapid rise of Armenians in Erzerum at the end of the sixteenth and especially the early seventeenth century (Kouymjian, 1983, p. 431). When the Ottoman traveler Evliya Chelebi passed through Erzerum in 1645, he commented on the remarkable economic and urban activity of the Armenian city (Chelebi, 1896-1928). Erzerum quickly gained third place, after Constantinople and Izmir, among the most important customs posts in the entire empire.

In many respects the information for Kaiseri (Caesaria, Gesaria) is the most interesting because of the detailed picture it offers of Armenian life in that Cappadocian capital during the sixteenth century. In 1500 there were 2,287 adult males, of whom 86 percent were Muslim, 12 percent Armenian (266 adult males, or about 1,300 souls) and 2 percent Greek. The registers of 1523, 1550, and 1583 show that the city, securely placed far from the Ottoman-Persian front, had a steady and dramatic rise in population of nearly 400 percent, to 8,251 adult males, or about 41,000 people. Of all groups, however, the Armenian population increase of 506 percent was the most rapid, despite the movement of "native" Armenian inhabitants of the city (those of 1500) to the west, especially Constantinople, during the same period. Interestingly, the registers of 1523, 1550, and 1583 divided the Armenian population by communities *(jema'at)* into three distinct quarters: Kaiseriyan (natives

of Kaiseri), Sisiyan (natives from Cilicia and its environs), and
Sharkiyan (those from the east). The Sisiyan may have had allegiance
to the catholicosate in Cilicia and the Sharkiyan to Echmiadzin. The fact
that these Armenians chose to segregate themselves in Kaiseri once
again underlines the enormous cultural diversity within the Armenian
nation, so clear in our own time, with various Armenian immigrants
producing separate enclaves within communities according to geographical origin, dialect, and allegiance to one or the other catholicosate
(Jennings, 1976).

The raw data of these Ottoman fiscal registers can be interpreted
in many ways. Armenian specialists must reexamine them carefully
before too easily accepting the conclusions of those who have already
studied them. The *defters* of Kaiseri provide an important case in point.
In 1500, though the Armenians represented only 12 percent of the entire
population, we know from the register that they had the largest single
quarter, with no close second, and that the Armenian quarter was within
the city walls, whereas the largest Muslim quarters, presumably of new
settlers, were outside the walls. Thus, according to the published figures,
within the inner city—the real metropolitan Caesaria—Armenians represented 24 percent of the population and the Christians as a group, 30
percent. By 1583, though Armenians are still a minority, they are
powerful in the inner walled city, representing 47 percent of the population. Therefore, a more critical interpretation of the data affords a
totally different "impression" about the importance of the Armenian
population in Kaiseri and other Anatolian cities in the sixteenth and
subsequent centuries.

Remnants of Self Rule and the Quest for Liberation

Reference has already been made to the semiautonomous feudal lords,
or *nakharars*, in Siunik and Karabagh, the latter surviving to become
the *meliks* so important in eighteenth- and nineteenth-century movements of liberation. In the mid-fifteenth century, the Orbelian house,
unhindered by the Kara Koyunlu overlords continued to carry on a
feeble existence. Though Baron Beshken Orbelian's son Rustam became governor of Ayrarat for a time, by the sixteenth century Armenian nobility (except in the remote areas of Karabagh) had all but
vanished. There were a few centers of autonomy in the fifteenth
century: at Hamshen west of the Chorokh River between the Black Sea
and the city of Sper—especially in the first twenty-five years of the

century, and at Maku, where the last of the Armenian princes of Artaz held out until the fortress was taken by Iskandar the Kara Koyunlu in 1426. Aghtamar was also the theater of an attempt to reestablish the Artsruni kingdom by Catholicos Zakaria III (1434-1464), who claimed himself to be descendant from the kings and who inspired the movement, actually carried out by his nephew and successor Stepanos IV (1464-1489). In 1465 Stepanos consecrated his brother Smbat "King of Armenia" (Khachikian, 1972, p. 44). Though Smbat had the acquiescence of Jihanshah, his rule was strictly local and lasted only until 1471. There are also the princes of Armenia mentioned by Don Juan of Persia (a late-sixteenth-century court official who renounced Islam while in Europe) and western sources of the same century, when Adal ad-Dawlet, emir of the Dhul-Kadir state, refused passage through the Taurus Mountains to Sultan Selim on his way to fight Shah Ismail in 1514 (Le Strange, 1926, p. 116 and p. 321, note 3). Since there are no other details, the account may be an anachronistic reference to earlier nobles of Cilicia, unless they are to be associated with the later Lentoul Degh, mentioned in 1571 by Vincenzo d'Alesandri, who claimed to have had 10,000 followers in the Taurus, or the Lawand mentioned under 1601 by Arakel of Tabriz, operating in the same area. These were thought by some authorities (A. Alboyadjian, 1941-1961, and H. Hakobian, 1932) to be Muslim converts of Armenian or Georgian origin referred to as Liwon/Levon Oghlu, sons or descendants of Levon, the Cilician king.

The twilight of the Armenian nobility in the fifteenth century produced a transformation in the functioning of the *nakharar* houses, especially in Siunik. The feudal title *tanuter* (head of the house) eventually gave way to the title *paron-ter,* from the secular title *paron* (baron) and *ter* (lord) used principally for upper-ranking clergy. Fearing sequestration of their lands under Muslim regimes, the feudal houses found a way compatible with Islamic usage of protecting their property and domains from heavy taxation and alienation. They deeded them to a monastery as an inalienable pious foundation functioning like the Muslim *waqf* (inalienable, non-taxed charitable trust). Naturally, the *nakharars* first made sure that a member of the family was either a prominent bishop or an abbot of the establishment, in order to keep an eye on family possessions; hence the title *paron-ter.* Through this method, hereditary lands and property were safeguarded for a while longer during the century. Later, little is heard of the old feudal lords and their patrimony, though the title *paron-ter* was in common use at the end of the sixteenth and the beginning of the seventeenth centuries for prelates throughout Armenia and Anatolia.

Already by the mid-fifteenth century, the Armenian Church and its higher clergy were responsible, willy-nilly, for the ordered protection of the nation, its traditions, and its destiny. Indeed, the catholicos took the earliest steps toward freeing Armenia from the malevolent conditions of abusive Islamic rule. This was only natural, for no other individual or group could claim to speak for the entire nation. In 1547 Stepanos Catholicos Salmastetsi (1544-1567) called a secret meeting of clergy and select laymen at Echmiadzin, then under Safavid suzerainty, to discuss steps that might be taken to help the Armenians. It was decided to send the catholicos himself on a mission to Europe. Passing through Venice, Stepanos must have received the advice of the important Armenian trading colony there before he met with Pope Julius III in Rome in 1550. Purportedly on the authority of twenty-seven Armenian bishops, Stepanos accepted union with the Catholic Church as the precondition for the papacy to take action on Armenia's behalf. His petition to the pope, which survives only in an Italian version, is signed by the "Lords of Armenia," presumably prominent personalities wishing to convince the pope that the catholicos was delegated by representatives of the nation. From Rome, Catholicos Stepanos went to Vienna for an interview with the German emperor Charles II and then to Lvov to visit the Polish king Sigismund II. Nothing came of the mission except a clear understanding that church union was a precondition to any western involvement in Armenian affairs.

A second secret meeting was held by Catholicos Mikayel of Sebastia (1566-1577), already co-adjutor at the time of the first meeting of 1547, this time in his native city of Sivas well inside Ottoman territory. During the meeting of 1562, though composed mainly of bishops, Abgar Dpir of Tokat, a layman, was chosen as its representative. Despite the failure of the first mission, it was decided to appeal once again to the pope for help in freeing Armenia from both Ottoman Turkish and Persian yokes. Abgar, accompanied by his son Sultanshah and a priest, again passed by Venice, arriving in Rome in 1564, where he communicated to Pope Pius IV the request of the Armenian catholicos for help. Unfortunately, nothing was forthcoming from this second encounter, except that Abgar, who had claimed to be descended from the Armenian nobility, asserted that the pope was ready to designate him "King of Armenia." Though his son was to stay on in Rome, Abgar returned to Venice, where he devoted himself to the printing of

Armenian books; especially important was the first Armenian Psalter issued under his care in 1565.

Later, when Abgar was forced to stop publishing in Venice, he moved to Constantinople. In the expanding diaspora of the Ottoman capital, he established the first Armenian press in the Middle East, publishing six titles from 1567 to 1569. (The Turks did not start printing until 1717, with the help of the Hungarian renegade Ibrahim Muteferrika.) In 1569 Abgar visited Catholicos Mikayel. But this effort to get help for the nation also failed, and Armenian suffering increased during the depredations of the Turkish-Persian wars.

There are several interesting facets to these endeavors for liberation. In the first place, they were led by successive catholicoses of Echmiadzin, with the cooperation of the higher and lower clergy and upper-class or "establishment" laymen. Furthermore, they were supported by Armenians both in Eastern (Persian) and Western (Turkish) Armenia. Contrary to the great resistance offered by the northern bishops against union with the Catholic Church negotiated by Armenian kings and catholicoses of Cilicia, the bishops in the north had no problem two hundred years later with exchanging church union for western help. The final chapter of this sixteenth-century struggle for liberation was the relationship between Catholicos Azaria (1584-1601) of Cilicia and Pope Gregory XIII (1572-1585). In a letter sent to the pope and preserved in Rome, the catholicos, after the visit of a papal delegation to Sis, expressed his and several of his bishops' willingness to enter into union. At the same time he beseeched the pope's protection for the Armenian "sheep" menaced by foreign "wolves."

The Church and the Nation

The most important result of the Turkish Islamic conquest and continued occupation of Armenia was the elimination of Armenian self-government. By the fifteenth century, there was no Armenian secular authority for writers of colophons to invoke, only foreign rulers, catholicoses, and local bishops. The Armenian Church was left weakened by the loss of royal and princely patronage, yet alive, sheltered usually behind the walls of remote monasteries. With the removal of the political forces that shaped and nurtured Armenian society, the continuity and direction of the nation henceforth resided almost exclusively in the Armenian Church. How did it act in serving as a unifying and guiding institution?

In part, the question has already been answered by showing that at the end of the sixteenth century, the catholicoses, especially of Echmiadzin, made the only initiatives toward the liberation of Armenia, speaking, they claimed, for the entire nation. In later centuries the power of the church increased dramatically. Though ultimately controlled by the rising Armenian bourgeoisie, the church was the unrivaled instrument of leadership until the development of the Armenian revolutionary movement in the latter part of the nineteenth century.

The Background

The catholicos had been settled in the Taurus Mountains and Cilicia since the time of Grigor II Vkayaser (1065-1105) in the late eleventh century. In 1147 the patriarchal seat was moved from Dzovk to Hromkla, and from there to the royal capital of the Rubenid dynasty, Sis, in 1293 after the brutal sack of Hromkla by the Mamluks of Egypt. Once again, if only for less than a century, the spiritual head of the nation had his seat in the royal capital, as in the time of the Bagratid dynasty and much earlier the Arsacids of the fourth and fifth centuries. The Armenian Church, however, was far from unified. Though the kings of Cilician Armenia styled themselves and, indeed, thought of themselves as leaders of the entire nation, their political authority did not extend beyond Cilicia. In fact, besides the unusual visit (1253-1256) of King Hetum II to Greater Armenia on his way to the Mongol capital of Kara Korum in deepest Central Asia and King Oshin's journey to Bitlis in the early fourteenth century to convince the northern bishops of his unionist policies, the kings seldom came into contact with the population of Armenia proper. So too from the twelfth to the fourteenth centuries, the catholicoses and major bishops stayed in Cilician territory. Many of the prominent clergy—as in centuries past—were of the nobility and associated closely with the court.

The Armenian Church already was decentralized with an independent catholicos established on the island of Aghtamar since 1113, a patriarchate at Jerusalem after 1311, and powerful clergy led by the abbots of the principal monasteries in Greater Armenia, sometimes called as a group the northern bishops, who doctrinally opposed attempts at church union. In the north, there were also the United Brethren (Frater Unitores), Catholics under the Dominican order, who settled in the Nakhichevan area in the early fourteenth century and at one time had 700 clergy and more than thirty establishments. Both the fifteenth and sixteenth centuries were to see dramatic changes in the structure and administration of the church. By the end of the period, the main lines of Armenian Church authority were set in place, not to change until the present.

The history of the Armenian Church in Cilicia has been characterized by attempts at reconciliation with the universal Christian church: at times with the Byzantine Church, at times the Catholic Church. Spearheaded by catholicoses and kings, often for ulterior motives, union was actually consummated several times, even though it had little effect on the beliefs and practices of the Armenian Church, which remained autocephalous. In the mid-fourteenth century a western or westernized royalty, fearing the gradual encroachment of the Mamluk sultans, hoped—as the Byzantine emperors were to hope a century later—to acquire European military aid through union with Rome.

Clearly the kings were right in believing that without military support from the West, the kingdom of Armenia would be destroyed, but they were wrong, as the Byzantine emperors were wrong, in believing that union actually would produce any concrete assistance from the pope or European kings. The westernizing inclination of Kings Levon IV and V only alienated the Cilician clergy who were not then any more willing than the northern bishops to support a foreign policy of reconciliation based on doctrinal changes. Thus, while King Levon V was desperately fighting a losing battle in his citadel in Sis, the catholicos and Armenians loyal to the church, in the city below, had already sworn allegiance to the emir of Aleppo, commander of the Mamluk army. The subsequent capture and captivity of Levon V in Cairo, his ultimate ransom by the king of Castille, his decade of activity in Paris and London trying to create enthusiasm for a crusade against the Mamluks for Armenia's sake, and his death and burial with the kings of France in 1393 are well known (de Lusignan, 1906).

Though the Armenian kingdom had ceased to exist by the end of the fourteenth century, the title "King of Armenia" was passed on through the court of Cyprus to European nobility for the next two centuries. Nevertheless, the disappearance of the kings was not coterminous with the disappearance of their subjects. A large Armenian population existed in Cilicia until the "Final Solution" of the Turks from 1915 to 1922. The catholicos also survived, maintaining his residence at Sis until 1915. Lacking the financial and sovereign support of Armenian rulers, however, the prestige of the Cilician catholicosate declined and the caliber of the leading clergy ostensibly was diminished.

The Catholicosate of Aghtamar

During this period, the catholicos of Aghtamar (reconciled earlier with the catholicos of All Armenians at Echmiadzin) benefited by his geographical position in the center of Armenia. Closer than Sis to the Armenian population and the remaining semiautonomous centers in the north of the country, he took advantage of the sporadic protection of Kurdish emirs and the Kara Koyunlu rulers by asserting an authority on the Armenian Church and nation beyond the immediate confines of the Van region. From the 1420s to 1464 Catholicos Zakaria, through his ceaseless activity, was to exert a major force in national affairs. As a leader in the events surrounding the reestablishment of the catholicosate in the north in 1441, he was later, with the support of Jihanshah, able to assume the office of catholicos of All Armenians and was even resident in Vagharshapat for a time, as was his successor Ter Stepanos. But these were for short periods and against the wishes of most of the northern clergy. By the late sixteenth and early seventeenth centuries, Aghtamar's authority began to shrink, becoming once again a strictly regional patriarchate with the title catholicos.

The Assembly of 1441 and the Establishment of the Catholicosate at Echmiadzin

The Armenian catholicosate had moved to Sis in 1292 seeking the security and protection of Armenian rulers. Now, though there was no kingdom left in the north, Greater Armenia could claim a higher population density and a larger number of surviving *nakharar* houses. However, in the late 1430s or early 1440s Sis was not in any better position than Vagharshapat and the suburban Echmiadzin, for there was just as much or as little benevolence on the part of the Mamluk rulers of Egypt as that of Kara Koyunlu rulers in the north. The major factor in the desire to have the catholicosate back in the Ararat Valley was the clergy itself, the leading bishops of the northern monasteries. In the fourteenth century these monasteries were Gladzor, Tatev, Hermoni, as well as Haghbat, Sanahin, and Ayrivank/Geghart, which eclipsed by far Sis and the once-great but now fading Cilician centers such as Hromkla,

Skevra, Drazark, and Akner. The only monastic rivals to the northern establishments were those of the Van region, which were to become powerful in the fifteenth century, and Upper Armenia (Bardzr Hayk), especially the Avaz and Kapos Vank in the Erzinjan area. Indeed, the leaders of the move back to Echmiadzin were Tovma Metzopetsi, the abbot of the declining Tatev Vank, and Hovhannes Kolotik, abbot of St. Hermoni Vank. Prior to the reestablishment of a catholicosate in the north, Tovma had actually moved from Tatev, which had become unsafe during the long period of wars between the Timurids and the Black Sheep dynasty, to Metzop Vank near Bitlis. He was in close contact with Catholicos Zakaria of Aghtamar and no doubt convinced the latter to acquiesce in reinstalling a catholicosate in the north. It is reasonable to assume that Aghtamar itself might have become the original location contemplated by Tovma. In 1431 Rustam, the son of Prince Beshken Orbelian, and for a time probably governor of Ayrarat province, gave seven villages to Echmiadzin in order, it is thought, to supply the ancient center with the resources to support a pontiff. Rustam and Beshken were close associates of Tovma Metzopetsi and the hereditary Orbelian-Berthlian feudal lords of Siunik.

Contemporaries called forth other reasons for the move (Ormanian, 1914; Tournebize, 1910a; Kiuleserian, 1939). Since the fall of the Armenian kingdom of Cilicia, many of the catholicoses had obtained their offices by bribes and even assassination. Not only had learning declined at Sis, but the Cilician bishops were on close terms with the Franciscans, who had become powerful under the last Armenian kings. Furthermore, Catholicos Constantine VI (1430-1439) seems to have supported the movement toward union initiated at the Council of Florence-Ferrara in 1438-1439, where the Armenian representatives from Aleppo and the Crimea, though arriving after the council had adjourned, nevertheless accepted a union with the Catholic Church and signed an agreement with the pope. They returned, however, to Kaffa perhaps because Constantine VI had died, and the agreement was never ratified. The northern clergy felt that moving the catholicosate deep into Armenia would take it away from Roman influence, especially after the Armenian lords of Artaz, themselves converts to Catholicism, had been destroyed by Iskandar at Maku in 1426. It also seems that Armenian desires coincided with a policy of Jihanshah to cultivate the Muslim and Christian clergy. That the Kara Koyunlu were conscious of the need for the cooperation of the Armenian feudal lords and church leaders, while at the same time exploiting and periodically plundering the country, seems clear from the occasional good relations between Armenians and both Jihanshah and his brother Iskander, as witnessed by the title of Shah-i Armen that the latter took. In any case, when it was finally decided to call a national assembly or a meeting of Armenian clergy and grandees, Jihanshah seems to have given his approval. His emir at Erevan, Yakub, not only agreed that the meeting take place in his domain at Vagharshapat and the adjoining Echmiadzin, but also threw a grand reception for those participating in the two-day affair—all of which is elaborately described by Tovma Metzopetsi.

Tovma was not only one of the major organizers of the move to choose a catholicos for Echmiadzin but also is the principal source for the proceedings. Most of the facts about the assembly of 1441 comes from the often-cryptic remarks found in the colophon he attached to his *History*. He reports that 300 bishops, clerics, and dignitaries from various parts of Armenia came to Vagharshapat (Metzopetsi, 1892; Khachikian, 1955, no. 587, pp. 522ff.). (Another colophon reports 700, but Tovma's number seems more reasonable.) The major candidates were Grigor Jalaliants, who already held a major office in Vagharshapat and was formerly bishop of Artaz; Zakaria, abbot of Havuts Tar monastery; and Catholicos Zakaria of Aghtamar. The catholicos, and probably Tovma himself, thought that the election of Grigor, already a proven leader, would place a respected and qualified person in the position and at the same time put an end to the existence of two catholicosates. Grigor IX Musabekiants, the reigning catholicos at Sis, did not attend the meeting, and his role in the entire proceedings is unclear.

Internal power struggles among the candidates and their supporters produced a deadlock. A compromise was chosen in the figure of an ascetic vardapet, Kirakos Virapetsi, who had little previous administrative experience. His pontificate lasted only two years (though colophons continue to mention him as catholicos until 1447), when he either resigned—in disgust, some say—or was removed by more powerful forces. Grigor Jalaliants was elected catholicos in 1443. Zakaria of Aghtamar, who was of course against Grigor and the northern clique, continued his independent catholicosate and even succeeded with the help of Jihanshah in having himself declared catholicos of All Armenians, sojourning in Echmiadzin for some time in 1461. He is cited as catholicos in colophons as late as 1464 (Khachikian, 1958, no. 2646, p. 218, and no. 270, p. 223; Sanjian, 1969, pp. 285-86, 376).

The sources of the period, almost exclusively colophons, present an unclear picture of the position of the catholicos in Vagharshapat.

Most references to either catholicos (Sis or Echmiadzin) are as *hayrapet* (patriarch) rather than the less frequently used *katoghikos* (catholicos); furthermore, the catholicos was resident in Vagharshapat, and most colophons refer to that city, rather than Echmiadzin on its outskirts. Echmiadzin had become an antiquity, a museum—frequented only occasionally by pilgrims and travelers—without regular services and with no great monastic complex around it. It was to remain so until the early seventeenth century, when a revival and expansion of the site took place. According to travelers, it was often closed during this period, with the keys in the hands of lay doorkeepers, at times even Persians. The colophons make it clear, however, that for most Armenians, certainly those in the north, there had been a restoration of the catholicosate to the Ararat valley in 1441.

Nonetheless, the sources do not speak of a "transfer" of the catholicosate from Sis. After his election and consecration, Kirakos sent his respects to the catholicos in Cilicia, the elderly Grigor IX. It is unclear how Grigor reacted. That he did not himself move his residence is a historical fact; yet there seems to be no firm evidence that he protested the elections carried out at Vagharshapat either. Seemingly, he continued to live as catholicos until 1445, as attested by two colophons of 1444 and one of 1445 (Khachikian, 1955, no. 648, p. 576; Sanjian, 1969, p. 202). Starting in the following year, Karapet (1446-1477) is regularly mentioned as catholicos at Sis in colophons not only from Cilicia proper but also from Bitlis and Arabkir (Khachikian, 1955, no. 679a, p. 603, and 1958, no. 277, p. 229, and no. 368, p. 285; Sanjian, 1969, pp. 208, 287, 297).

The Catholicosate of the Great House of Cilicia, as it came to be called in time, continues to this day. On occasion it has claimed that since there was no transfer, formal or informal, of the office to Vagharshapat, the legal succession of the head of the Armenian Church continued and continues through the Cilician catholicoses. The position of the Catholicosate of Echmiadzin is that the assembly and election of 1441 was clearly recognized by most bishops and the people as a return and, in fact, a transfer, to the original Holy Echmiadzin. The sources support both positions, even though a colophon of 1446 from Arabkir suggested that a purely "Cilician Catholicosate" came into being with the consecration of Karapet, which coincided with the finding of the previously lost relic of the right hand of St. Gregory (Khachikian, 1955, no. 679a, p. 603).

No matter how the legalistic interpretations are argued, the de facto relationship of the two catholicosates remains quite clear for the coming centuries. There was a reconciliation between them, including also the Catholicos of Aghtamar, marred only twice when violent disputes reappeared between Sis and Echmiadzin in the mid-seventeenth century and at the end of the nineteenth century. In the mid-twentieth century, the two centers fell into disagreement after the election of Zareh Catholicos in Antelias, Lebanon, in February 1956. But these quarrels are not to be seen as a division in the Armenian Church, since none of them involved doctrinal questions, but rather disagreements over diocesan jurisdiction. Today the Catholicosate of Echmiadzin is recognized by everyone, even by the Catholicos of Cilicia, as the Mother See, although in terms of ecclesiastic rank and absolute and unique control over their respective orders, they are equal.

The Catholicosate of Aghtamar continued into the twentieth century (though with a locum tenens from 1895 to 1915) until it too became a victim of the Armenian genocide. Throughout the fifteenth and sixteenth centuries and until 1815, there was also a catholicos of Caucasian Albania, resident at Gandzasar in Karabagh; it became and remained a hereditary pontificate in the Armenian Hasan-Jalaliants feudal family maintaining the ancient title "catholicos," but administering to local needs only.

From the fourteenth century, there was an Armenian patriarchate in Jerusalem, which had its origins when Bishop Sargis, refusing to accept the union concluded with the Roman Church by the Council of Sis in 1307, declared independence from Cilicia. In 1311 he prevailed on Sultan Malik Nasr of Egypt to confirm him as *patrik*, or patriarch. In the fifteenth and sixteenth centuries, however, the patriarchate maintained very close ties with the catholicos in Sis and did not come under the jurisdiction of Echmiadzin until the nineteenth century, and then only with the agreement of the Cilician catholicos. Its major administrative function was to attend to the Holy Places under Armenian control, the local community in Palestine, and the continual flow of Armenian pilgrims.

As Ottoman power increased and the Armenian prelate of Constantinople gradually became the patriarch of all Armenians in the empire, when Cilicia with its catholicosal see was incorporated by Sultan Selim in 1517, and later when Erevan and Vagharshapat came under Ottoman rule for long periods, the jurisdictional question in the Armenian Church became confused and disputed. During the second half of the fifteenth and much of the sixteenth century, the catholicos at Sis had the strongest say in the succession of prelates/patriarchs and the affairs of the church in Constantinople. Toward the end of the sixteenth century, however, as large numbers of Armenian refugees emigrated to the Ottoman capital, the shift toward Echmiadzin became clear, since most newcomers originated, as already discussed, from areas directly under Echmiadzin's jurisdiction. Nevertheless, only in the eighteenth and nineteenth centuries would the patriarch of Constantinople enjoy an overwhelming dominance in church affairs.

Corruption and laxity were evident among some clergy in all the ecclesiastical centers of the Armenian Church during the fifteenth and sixteenth centuries. Considering the terror and destruction of the period, church leaders found it necessary once and for all to adjust themselves to dependency on non-Christian rulers. Furthermore, despite the immense disruption in authority and revenue, and the decreasing numbers of faithful caused by constant emigration and assimilation to Islam, the church and its leaders reached a modus vivendi on jurisdictional questions and somehow survived along with the nation. As already mentioned, the upper clergy even were able to initiate attempts toward the liberation of Armenia. As a national institution, the church, at least as it was represented by some of its more able catholicoses and bishops, recognized its responsibility to assume secular as well as spiritual leadership when Armenian authority had disappeared.

Art and Culture

Constant warfare, destruction, and the loss of royal patrons had their predictable effect on all intellectual and cultural activities in Armenia. The result was general and felt systematically during the fifteenth and sixteenth centuries. The first three-quarters of the sixteenth century especially was far worse than the fifteenth. Surviving artifacts were produced almost exclusively by the clergy, mostly monks, working in Armenian monasteries. Among exceptions are ceramics of the sixteenth century (and later) from Kutahia.

The influence of the Armenian Church on intellectual and artistic life cannot be overstated. Surviving secular works from these centuries are nearly as rare as they were in the previous ones. Virtually all surviving architecture up to 1600 is religious, except for fortresses. Nearly all painting is devoted to themes from Christian iconography. Only in literature were secular themes more actively employed in the form of ballads and poems, histories, scientific and medical treatises, and a few philosophical works.

The Monasteries and Their Schools

The sponsors or the continuators of Armenian art were the large monastic complexes, the only institutions that had the means to sponsor even the relatively few remains of material culture that have survived from these centuries. Colophons and inscriptions of donations record numerous examples of how churches and monasteries began to be enriched. Already in the fifteenth century it became common for surviving noble families, especially in Siunik and the northern regions, to give property—villages, orchards, fields—to monasteries to avoid having them pass to Muslim civil authorities. In the Van area at the Theotokos Monastery at Bitlis and at Aghtamar itself, the practice is also regularly recorded.

The church sometimes was able to buy outright large properties and entire villages, as attested by colophons of Aghtamar during the life of Catholicos Zakaria III in the mid-fifteenth century (Khachikian, 1955, 1958). For a time the church replaced the feudal lords as the largest landowner, and like the feudal lords, it collected various taxes from its lands for the operation of its establishments, including monasteries and the schools or universities attached to them.

The famous monastic universities of the late fourteenth century associated with Hovhannes Orotnetsi, Grigor Tatevatsi (Gregory of Tatev), and others continued a precarious existence in the north in the first decades of the fifteenth century, falling into eclipse in the latter part of the fifteenth and the entire sixteenth century. Those that played the most active role in the fourteenth century were Tatev and Hermoni in Siunik, and Metzop in the Van area. The focus of activity had by the fifteenth century shifted to the more stable Van area. The monasteries of Kadjberuni, Khizan, Bitlis, Aghtamar, and Arjesh flourished during the early part of the century, while later, those in the Erzinjan area—the Avag and Kapos Vanks on Mt. Sebuh—showed a moment of comparative splendor, especially under Bishop Hovhannes, when students from the Crimea, Greater Armenia, and Cappadocia studied there. Throughout the sixteenth century, however, these institutions struggled simply to survive. In the first-half of the seventeenth century, a perceptible resurgence of monastic institutions, concomitant with the general flourishing of Armenian life, took place.

Architecture

The great building activity in northern Armenia of the twelfth and thirteenth centuries came to a rude stop in the latter part of the fourteenth century. During the fifteenth and sixteenth centuries, churches and monasteries in Siunik, Karabagh/Artsakh, and Ayrarat struggled to preserve existing structures in the face of continued pillaging and intentional destruction during the Timurid and Turkmen periods. During two and a quarter centuries, from 1375 to 1604, only three or four churches were constructed in the north, mostly in Siunik, during the better moments of the first half of the fifteenth century. The collected inscriptions from Tatev, Haghpat, and Sanahin lack references to construction or reconstruction. Most are either short memorials on small *khachkars* (literally cross-stones—monolithic, intricately carved with a cross) or inscriptions on tombstones. The situation had so deteriorated that when a new church was built at the monastery of Metzop in the fifteenth century, a Greek architect was brought in to do the work.

In the central areas around Lake Van and the city of Diarbekir/Amida, the situation was somewhat better, thanks especially to the efforts of a certain Stepanos of Pir, a *vardapet* (archimandrite) from the Rshtunik area, who, in that area of Lake Van, "constructed more than ten domed and lime-plastered churches" and repaired many others, according to a colophon written at Aghtamar in 1445 (Khachikian, 1955, no. 653, pp. 579-81; Sanjian, 1969, p. 203). Also active in this early and mid-fifteenth century was the architect Nekamat who, under the prelacy of Mkrtich Naghash, poet and painter, built the wondrous domed church of St. Theodorus in Amida. Because it was more splendid and higher than the mosques and minarets of the city, it was torn down, to be rebuilt after the intercession of the Islamic officials in 1447, as recorded in a detailed colophon of 1449 (Khachikian, 1955, no. 704, pp. 622-29; Sanjian, 1969, pp. 209-14). As for the sixteenth century, no construction is recorded except for a domed chapel in 1555 and a few minor restorations made at the end of the century at St. Karapet in Mush. In no other century had the art of construction in Armenia been so severely affected by the conditions of the time as in the sixteenth. On the other hand, throughout this period Armenian architects were active in diasporan colonies, building churches in Constantinople, Lvov, the Crimea, Moldavia, and Russia.

Manuscript Production and Miniature Painting

Just as the lack of construction reinforces the notion of the decline in the arts, so too does the scarcity of manuscripts. For the first time since the ninth century, there was a decline in the number of manuscripts produced from one century to the next, perceptibly fewer sixteenth-century manuscripts exist than fifteenth-century ones. A survey using catalogs of some 18,000 of the estimated 30,000 surviving Armenian manuscripts and using only dated examples revealed the following results (Kouymjian, 1983, pp. 433-34). Manuscript production clearly begins to decline after 1350, and continues to fall until the Timurid campaigns end at the turn of the century, when there is a rapid rise in production up to 1420. This is followed by a sharp drop, coinciding with the death of Kara Yusuf, and until about 1440, when another steady rise in production peaks out at 1460, followed by another steep decline up to 1500. The most dramatic plunge in production occurs during the years of Sultan Selim's eastern campaigns up to the early 1520s and again during the wars of Süleyman in the late 1530s and early 1540s. In both of these periods almost no manuscripts were copied. The half century from 1500 to 1550 was definitely the lowest point in the activities of Armenian scriptoria from the ninth century until printing definitively replaced manuscript copying in the nineteenth century. Afterward, from about 1545 and continuing to the seventeenth century, there was a steady rise in the copying of manuscripts, surpassing, by the turn of the eighteenth century, every previous period of production, even though graphically vivid declines marked the beginning years of the last Ottoman Turkish campaign of the century, around 1575 to 1580, and again just after the forced immigration of Shah Abbas of 1604-1605.

This statistical analysis, thus far only partially published, confirms what was already apparent from research based on historical sources. If one were to remove from the statistical base manuscripts executed in the Crimea and cities of western and central Anatolia in the second half of the fifteenth and sixteenth centuries, the picture would appear even darker. The most active centers of manuscript production were almost entirely in the Lake Van area and, in the later period, Jerusalem and Aleppo. The second half of the sixteenth century, however, also shows the Van region in decline, giving way to Constantinople and eventually to New Julfa.

Miniature painting, which had undergone a period of continuous activity in the fourteenth century, both in the north at the schools of

Glatzor and Tatev and in the newly flourishing centers in Vaspurakan, also showed a decline. A few manuscripts of the first half of the fifteenth century from the north monasteries, especially Tatev, are illuminated. But the major workshops are in the central areas, both at Khizan to the southwest of the lake and at Van and Aghtamar to the southeast. The Khizan artists showed a certain innovation and excitement in their iconography and in the agitated style they employed. The outstanding artist of that school in the fifteenth century was Khachatur of Khizan, flourishing in the 1450s. Miniatures executed at Van, Aghtamar, Artzke, and other monasteries in the mid and latter part of the century present a much more conservative, static approach, somewhat dull in their attitude toward the subjects. Outside these areas, Kapos Monastery near Erzinjan produced a few illustrated manuscripts, as did the scriptoria of Crimea and Jerusalem. The end of the century and the first half of the sixteenth century are characterized by a dearth of illuminations paralleling the sharp drop in manuscript production. By the final quarter of the sixteenth century, however, the Khizan school is once again active through such artists as Sargis, Martiros, and Khachatur. They skillfully decorated a series of interesting manuscripts dating from the 1570s to the early seventeenth century, spreading the influence of the Khizan style to other centers where they worked, especially Constantinople and New Julfa. The most outstanding artist of this period is Hakob Jughayetsi (Hakob of Julfa), who executed a series of richly decorated and colorful works from the 1580s to the 1620s. During this revival, artists such as Khachatur of Khizan consciously turned to older Cilician Gospels of the thirteenth century and copied both their style and iconography. The abundance of European-printed Bibles, replete with engravings of Old and New Testament scenes, provided Armenian artists with convenient model books.

Only a few examples of art in other media from these centuries have survived. They include the famous carved doors of 1486 from the monastery of Lake Sevan showing a monumental Pentecost. The embroidered processional banner of 1448, among the treasures of the Echmiadzin, shows St. Gregory, Trdat, and St. Hripsime on one side, and Christ in glory with the symbols of the Evangelists on the other. Some silver bindings of the late sixteenth century are known, two of which are similar enough to each other to suggest that a workshop in the Lake Van area produced prefabricated plaques. Tooled and stamped leather bindings and woven and printed doublures of manuscripts and altar curtains also affirm that leather crafting and the textile industry were operative in the period. After a long decline, *khachkar* production also resumed, especially in old Julfa, where the masters Hayrapet and Grigor were active from 1550 to 1605, and in Noraduz near Lake Sevan. The distinguished sixteenth-century ceramics produced by Armenians in the western Anatolian town of Kutahia are also to be noted.

It is perhaps not coincidental that the Armenian venture into printing in 1511 to 1513 coincided with the absolute low point of manuscript production. Hakob Meghapart was able to publish, with the help of Venetian printers, five titles in those years, just six decades after printing was invented. Armenian was the tenth language in which books were printed, only sixty years after Gutenburg's invention. That in itself demonstrates the wide familiarity Armenians had with new discoveries and their desire, individually and collectively, to exploit innovation. In the later sixteenth century, Abgar Dpir produced books in Venice and Constantinople; afterward his son, Sultanshah, along with Hovhannes Terjantsi (Derjantsi), issued Armenian books in Rome (1584) and Venice (1587). This modest beginning did little to assuage the clergy's need for liturgical works, as is clear by the letter of 1585 addressed to Pope Gregory XIII by Catholicos Zakaria of Sis. Zakaria asks the pope to use the resources at his disposal to print the Bible in Armenian, because the cost of copying locally was so high the Bible had become rare.

Printing was to spread rapidly to nearly every center of Armenian life in the next two centuries. The tradition established by Hakob and Abgar in the sixteenth century is carried forward today wherever Armenians have settled.

Literature

Though several important church leaders were also poets, literature of the time, written almost exclusively in the monasteries, was philosophical, scientific, or historical.

Belles lettres was confined exclusively to poetry, ballads, or troubadour songs. A popular genre was the elegy or lamentation. Two of the most famous, by Arakel of Bitlis and Abraham of Ankara, were on the fall of Constantinople to the Turks in 1453. Another elegy by Tadeos of Sebastia described the *devshirme* (forced conscription of Christian boys) of 1531 (Anasian, 1957). The famous poets of the period were Arakel of Siunik (ca. 1350-1425); Grigor of Akhlat (Tzerents, 1350-1426); Arakel of Bitlis (ca. 1380-1450); Mkrtich Naghash, the poet, painter, and catholicos of Sis of the fifteenth century; Hovhannes

Tlkurantsi (John of Tlkuran, 1489-1529); Nahapet Kuchak and Hovasap of Sebastia (1510s-1560s); and a group of centagenarian poets from Tokat—Minas, Khachatur, Stepan, and Hakob—of the sixteenth century. Philosophical and scientific writers tended to be the heads of the great monasteries or their universities as in the fourteenth century.

Grigor Tatevatsi (d. 1410) and Tovma Metzopetsi (1378-1446) were the leading teachers of the late fourteenth and first decades of the fifteenth century. Though they had to move their schools from monastery to monastery, they still attracted more than a hundred students at a time. Tatevatsi was a scientist and philosopher who left a large legacy of written works, as did his students Matteos Jughayetsi (Matthew of Julfa) and Arakel Siunetsi (mid-fourteenth to the first quarter of the fifteenth century). Active in both science and medical writing was the famous doctor Amirdovlat of Amasia (d. 1496) working in Constantinople, and the already-mentioned poet Hovasap (Armenian Academy of Science, 1972, vol. 4, pp. 515-20).

Armenian historiography suffered seriously during the period, producing only a single important work, the *History* of Tovma Metzopetsi, to which is added the famous colophon about the assembly of 1441. It covers in great detail the devastating raids of Timur, starting in 1386, and those of the Kara Koyunlu rulers Kara Yusuf, Iskandar, and Jihanshah. There is also a long colophon of Grigor Tzerents (d. 1426) on the years 1386 to 1422 (Khachikian, 1955, nos. 300-300b, pp. 272-88; Sanjian, 1969, pp. 150-63), but nothing else for two centuries except terse, minor chronicles and the abundant but often cryptic colophons. Only with late sixteenth-early seventeenth century works of Grigor Daranaghtsi (Kamakhetsi, 1576-1643) and especially the valuable *History* of Arakel of Tabriz (end of the sixteenth century to 1670) does the long and consistent Armenian historical tradition revive.

Conclusion

The sixteenth century ends in Armenia with one of the severest famines of a century of famines. Two hundred years earlier a kingless, geographically divided Armenia, under foreign Islamic domination for the greater part of three centuries, suffered the third, the Timurid, wave of central Asiatic Turkic hordes in as many centuries. Between the dread and terror of these terminal points, there was mostly war, hunger, and oppression. Many Armenians chose to escape through migration. Some assimilated to the religion of the conqueror. Colophons of 1366 and 1422 and other sources allude to Islamic conversion by Armenians, though there does not seem to have been the kind of massive conversion that went on among Greek communities of western Anatolia during the thirteenth to fifteenth centuries (Khachikian, 1950, no. 577, p. 473; Vryonis, 1971). In order to maintain their power and influence under the changed regime, Armenian nobles in the north—though not to the degree of their Georgian cousins—converted to Islam. But on the whole Armenian Christians seemed to have been as fiercely against conversion to Islam as they were to accepting Catholicism. It is certain that especially in the sixteenth century, some Armenian youth became Muslim through the process of the *devshirme*. It is no coincidence that Armenian figures such as the architect Sinan was of the mid-sixteenth century and the Grand Vizier Khalil of Kaiseri was of the very early seventeenth century. After 1593 the majority of Janissaries were Muslim-born. In the subsequent century the problem was not a lack of manpower for the corps but a burdensome surplus.

Arakel of Tabriz, in discussing the depredations and suffering caused to the Armenians by Shah Abbas, was so affected that he could not continue. The Mekhitarist father Ghevond Alishan, in the middle of the nineteenth century, while discussing the work of Abgar Dpir, laments that the sixteenth century was surely culturally worse than the fifteenth, for he can barely find any material in the vast manuscript collection at his disposal about activities in Armenia proper. Alishan also complains that the language has been debased and that few scribes can write the *grabar* (classical literary language) properly. The early twentieth century historian Leo, in recalling Alishan's words, points out that the brighter side of this process is the firm strides made toward a more facile and popular language, the *ashkharhabar*. He says, perhaps ironically, that never had there been so much singing in Armenia as in the sixteenth century, referring to the extraordinary number of bards and minstrels who were actively composing poetry and songs. But here Leo exaggerates a bit, not considering what he knew too well: namely, that many of the poems and ballads were lamentations, nostalgic yearnings for the homeland, for a secure haven, for the arrival of a new spring in Armenia, songs for the exiled refugee or sedentary sufferers.

And yet the nation survived. Armenian continued as the language of the Armenians. Manuscripts were produced and beautifully decorated, even in the homeland, which foreign travelers described as having become a desert through the destruction and pillaging of successive wars. In the next century, the seventeenth, with the help of diasporan communities in

Constantinople, western Asia Minor, New Julfa, and Europe, more Armenian manuscripts were produced than at any other time. And the language flourished. In the second hundred years of the history of Armenian printing, some 150 entirely Armenian titles were published almost exclusively outside Armenia proper, compared to the dozen or so of the sixteenth century.

The fifteenth and sixteenth centuries saw, in addition to the far-reaching geographical shift of Armenian population, a major change in social and political institutions. Not only had government by Armenians disappeared with the destruction of the Cilician kingdom, but regional Armenian sovereignty also dissolved as the *nakharar* families gradually lost their lands, the traditional source of their power and regional hegemony. Only in the most remote areas were these chieftains able to hold onto their titles and estates; a group of them would even reemerge actively a century later in Karabagh. The Armenian feudal class had been destroyed or had faded away. From the point of view of class structure, the nation had entered the modern period, one dominated by a bourgeoisie of urban merchants, financiers, and clergy. Privilege by noble birth had been essentially eliminated.

By in the fifteenth century in northern and central Armenia, reinforced and strengthened in Constantinople in the sixteenth century, new power was given to the Armenian Church. Within traditional Islamic legal practice, Christians and Jews constituted protected, though clearly inferior, communities with separate status on the basis of their religion. The Ottoman state machinery exaggerated this process through its *millet* (independent non-Muslim religious communities) system. Already in fifteenth-century Armenia, the heads of leading monasteries, often scions of still-powerful feudal families, decided matters relating to marriage and divorce, inheritance, and criminal disputes between Armenians. As the decades passed and the church continued to remain the spokesman of the nation before Islamic rulers, its authority increased. This power was strengthened in Constantinople especially in later centuries, when the Armenian patriarch was to accumulate near absolute authority over his countrymen and also to become the person directly responsible for the nation before the sultan and the Ottoman administration.

Though the drama of the fifteenth and sixteenth centuries brought Armenia and the Armenians into the modern era, the future did not provide peace or privilege for all of them. The church, which continued to accumulate power and wealth, did not receive its authority or mandate from the people, but rather acquired it from the sultan or the shah, as the case might be. It was from foreign Islamic rulers that the heads of the Armenian Church were to derive so much of their power. Unfortunately, peasants and villagers continued to live an insecure life, slaves of the taxes imposed by local governors and the state. Armenian city dwellers, even the minority who enjoyed considerable privilege in the system, were always conscious of their legalized second-class status. Yet travelers alluded to the industriousness and seriousness of purpose of Armenians, elaborating further that these traits have distinguished them from other peoples of the area and have been the major cause of their material success. Perhaps through this work ethic and the Christian belief in a more hopeful future, Armenians, individually and collectively, were able to compensate for the psychological trauma the nation had suffered and, unknowingly, had already prepared for continued and even more intense future suffering.

FOR FURTHER INFORMATION

For the sources of, or more information on, the material in this chapter, please consult the following (full citations can be found in the Bibliography at the end of this volume).

Ajarian, 1942-1962.

"Ak-Koyunlu," in *İslam*
    Ansiklopedisi, 1st ed.

Alishan, 1888.

Anasian, 1961.

Andreasyan, 1964.

Arakel Tavrizhetsi, 1896.

Arakelian, 1964.

Baltrusaitis, and
    Kouymjian, 1986.

Barkan, 1958.

Brosset, 1874.

Dédéyan, 1982.

Der Nersessian, 1978.

Grigor Daranaghtsi, 1915.

Hammer-Purgstall, 1834-1846.

*Haykakan Sovetakan
    Hanragitaran,* 1974-1986.

"Kara-Koyunlu," *Encyclopaedia
    of Islam,* 1960.

"Kara-Koyunlu," in *Islam
    Ansiklopedisi,* 1st ed.

Kapoïan-Kouymjian, 1988.

Kouymjian, 1982, 1988.

Mutafian, 1993.

Nève, 1861.

Safrastian, 1961, 1964, 1967, 1972.

Vryonis, 1971.

Woods, 1976.

For further information on physical, historical, and economic geography and anthropology, please consult the following (full citations can be found in the Bibliography at the end of this volume).

Gregory, 1968.   Le Strange, 1939.

Hewsen, 1978-1979.   *Soviet Armenia,* 1972.

Hughes, 1939.   Toumanoff, 1963.

2

ARMENIAN COMMUNITIES IN EASTERN EUROPE

Krikor Maksoudian

The history of the Armenian communities in Eastern Europe is of interest to Armenian as well as Western scholars. To this day, however, there is no comprehensive work about that segment of the Armenian experience. There are only monographs and articles on certain communities, individuals, monuments, works of art, and events. One will also find chapters about Armenian history and the Armenian dispersion.

Until after World War I, the study of the Eastern European Armenian communities was an esoteric field of Armenian scholarship. The descendants of Armenian immigrants living in Eastern European countries were looked upon as the "lost tribes" of the Armenian nation, which was still concentrated in its historic homeland and in neighboring countries. The dispersion of the Armenian people throughout the world after the genocide of 1915 and the emergence of large communities even in such distant regions of the world as North and South America, Australia, Western Europe, and elsewhere, and the concern of Armenian intellectual, religious, and political leaders about maintaining the Armenian identity have brought to the forefront the case of the old communities—particularly the assimilation of the Armenians—in

Eastern Europe. The rhetoric of modern writers and orators focuses Armenian attention on drawing lessons from the extinct "colonies" in Eastern Europe so that the communities existing today will survive and instill a strong sense of identity in the younger generations.

Setting aside modern rhetoric and present-day concerns about the future of the Armenian dispersion, scholars have studied certain aspects of life in the Armenian communities of Eastern Europe—namely, the art, architecture, literature, printing, language, and law. Modern studies reveal the vitality and longevity of some of these Armenian colonies even after the seventeenth century, when large numbers of Armenians were allegedly assimilated.

Crimea

The Armenian communities in the Crimean peninsula were established long before those in Poland, Ukraine, Transylvania, Wallachia, Moldavia, and Bukovina. In fact, most of the immigrants in these countries came from the Crimea.

Armenian contacts with the Crimea date back to the eighth century. From the sixth to the twelfth century, the southern coastline of the Crimea was under Byzantine control. Armenian contingents fighting in the Byzantine armies were stationed there frequently. During the course of the eleventh and twelfth centuries, large numbers of Armenian immigrants arrived from Constantinople, Armenia Minor, and Greater Armenia. Those from Constantinople and Armenia Minor came via the Balkans or the Black Sea, whereas those from Greater Armenia crossed the Caucasus.

In the eleventh century, immigrants from Armenia Minor and Greater Armenia fled their ancestral homelands because of the Seljuk raids. The penetration of nomadic elements into Armenia and eastern Anatolia disrupted the way of life of the local sedentary population and forced them to migrate elsewhere. Armenian immigrants from Constantinople and its environs probably migrated because of the religious intolerance of the Byzantine authorities toward the Monophysites. This element probably reached Crimea several decades earlier than that fleeing the Seljuks. Though it is not clear why the early Armenian immigrants chose Crimea as their destination, the mild climate of the southern part of the peninsula, the fertility of its soil, and the commercial opportunities were probably major attractions. One of the earliest vestiges of Armenian presence in Kaffa (the modern town of Feodosiia) is an inscription in Armenian bearing the date 1027.

The political situation of Eastern Europe in the thirteenth century and new conditions favorable for commercial enterprises made Crimea even more appealing to Armenian settlers. In 1239 the Mongols, under Batu Khan, invaded Crimea, which thereafter became a part of the Golden Horde. Under Mongol domination the Armenians fared relatively well, as long as they paid their tributes. During the middle decades of the thirteenth century their numbers increased considerably, and they began to settle in various cities and towns throughout the peninsula. As he passed through the town of Sudak in 1253, the Flemish diplomat William of Rubruck came across Armenians.

Toward the end of the thirteenth century, the Armenian communities in the Crimean peninsula and their ecclesiastical traditions and customs had already attracted the attention of the local Greek element. The author of a colophon in a Greek synaxarion noted that the Armenians celebrated the Easter of 1292 a week after the Greeks; thus the Armenians had already established churches and religious institutions in their new land.

In 1267 the Genoese came to terms with the Mongols of the Golden Horde and monopolized the trading privileges in the southern and eastern regions of the Crimea. The Genoese consulate, which was located in the city of Kaffa, extended its jurisdiction over all the Genoese colonies in the peninsula. Thus the Genoese virtually controlled the entire region, despite the presence of Mongol authorities and officials. The Armenians, with their extensive commercial ties, were useful to the Genoese. Favorable conditions created by the Genoese attracted more Armenians. Genoese sources report that in 1316 there were three Armenian churches in Kaffa: two were under the jurisdiction of the Armenian catholicos and one was subject to Rome.

The Armenian merchants of the Crimea were in close contact with the Armenian communities in the lower course of the Volga River. These communities had been established by the Mongols, who had transported large numbers of Armenians there from Ani in 1235 and 1262. Well aware of the commercial possibilities and the better way of life in the Crimea, the leaders of these communities negotiated with the Genoese and made a treaty with their consul to migrate. The Genoese were as anxious as the Armenians to populate the Crimean peninsula with Armenians. Not only were the Armenians commercially useful, they also could provide warriors to secure the protection of Genoese interests. According to the information in the colophon of an Armenian manuscript, in 1330 "the princes, nobility, and the common people left Akhsarai and, taking up arms, fought against the Tatars to break through their lines. They came to Crimea, where they settled in Feodosiia, Kazarat, Surkhat, and the environs of these towns."

In Armenian texts written in the Crimea, scholars have noticed words that are characteristic of the dialect of the Shirak district, where the city of Ani is located. This substantiates the claim of the Crimean Armenians that they are the progeny of immigrants from Russia who were themselves descendants of the people of Ani.

The Armenian communities in the Crimea extended from Belogorsk to Feodosiia and to the foothills of the Crimean or Yalta Mountains in the north. Nineteenth-century Armenian travelers describe several Armenian monuments in this region, some of which were still extant at that time. Despite the very heavy toll reaped by the Black Death in 1346-1347, the Armenian communities survived and continued to flourish throughout the fourteenth and fifteenth centuries.

The author of a colophon gives us specific information about the numbers of Armenian who migrated to Crimea in 1330.

> At that time we became strong and increased in number, and built villages and districts. The princes and the nobility filled the mountains and plains from Gharapazar to Surkhat and Feodosiya with monasteries and churches. . . . We built one hundred thousand houses and one thousand churches. Out of fear of the Huns fortifications were built around the city of Feodosiya.

On the basis of this colophon, scholars have suggested that at least half a million Armenians lived in the region during the fourteenth and fifteenth centuries. This is a very large number for the Middle Ages and may be somewhat inflated. Yet we know from Genoese sources that the Armenian population of Kaffa alone was 46,000. Furthermore, there were very large communities in Sudak, Surkhat, Eupateria, Kazarat, Belogorsk (Karasubazar), Simferopol (Akmechit), Bakhchisarai, Balaklava (Chembale), Armiansk (Orabazar), Inkerman, and elsewhere. The Armenians also lived in villages in the vicinities of these cities. The communities grew larger as more Armenians arrived from Cilicia after the fall of the Armenian kingdom in 1375. Life for the Armenians in Armenia in the fourteenth and fifteenth centuries had become unbearable under nomadic Turkic dynasties. Continuous wars between the

Ottomans and the Safavids throughout the sixteenth and the early decades of the seventeenth centuries laid waste the country. The Armenian population of the cities and villages of Greater Armenia abandoned their homes and sought the safety of the Crimean peninsula. Our sources refer particularly to immigrants from villages in the modern Nakhichevan and Baiburt regions who were engaged in commercial enterprises and cultural work in the Crimean towns.

In the early decades of the fifteenth century, the Armenian presence in the Crimea was very impressive. In his letter of 1432, Pope Eugenius IV refers to the city of Sudak as being *in partibus Armeniae maioris*. Western sources occasionally called the Crimean peninsula *Armenia maritima* and the Sea of Azov as *Lacus armeniacus*.

In southern Crimea the Armenians lived in traditional communities whose ethnic integrity was both politically and economically expedient for the Genoese. Armenian contingents under the command of Armenian commanders protected the Genoese colonies of Surkhat, Katta, and others. The seaport city of Kazarat was the seat of an Armenian official who had under his command an Armenian detachment and kept a close eye on the activities of the local Tatars. The Armenians built the fortifications of the city of Kaffa and were in charge of its safety. In 1475 they defended the city against the onslaught of the Ottoman navy, yielding to the superior Ottoman forces only after the escape of the Genoese consul. Acknowledging the fact that the Crimea was for the most part inhabited by Armenians *populatum esse in maiori parte Armenus*—one of the Genoese consuls describes them as *boni mercatores, nobis fidelissimi* who are of great service to the state—*civitati magnum beneficium*.

Information on the early history of the Armenian communities of the Crimea reveals that the Armenian immigrants represented a segment of thirteenth-century Zakarid Armenian society. Under Genoese control, the communities maintained their internal autonomy. The sources distinguish three major classes among the immigrants of 1330: princes *(ishkhank)*, nobility *(aznvakank)*, and common people *(zhoghovurd)*. The feudal order was ultimately replaced by the merchant class, which continued to play an active role in the life of the communities until the eighteenth century.

The region of Crimea was organized as a prelacy of the Armenian Church in the middle of the fourteenth century. The new episcopal jurisdiction was known as *Hayots hiusisayin koghmank* (The Northern Regions of the Armenians [or Armenia]). The town of Surkhat, where the seat of the bishop was located, was the ecclesiastical metropolis of the Armenians. The church occupied a central place in the life of the community. In Kaffa alone, the number of churches rose to forty-four after the great migration of 1330, and many were built in the traditional Armenian architectural style. The common people had a voice in the election of their prelates. In 1474 they refused to accept the candidate of the merchant class and proposed the name of another bishop acceptable to them. This tradition, which seems to have its antecedents in Ani, was later transferred to Constantinople by thousands of Crimean Armenians who flocked there at the end of the fifteenth and throughout the sixteenth centuries. The practice of expressing popular dissent ultimately led to the secularization and modernization of Armenian society in the Ottoman Empire.

The Armenians of Crimea specialized in agriculture and the crafts. In cities they lived in their own quarters and spoke their native tongue but conducted business transactions with non-Armenians in local languages, such as Italian, Greek, and particularly Kipchak Turkish.

The favorable conditions under which the Armenian communities flourished during the course of the fourteenth and fifteenth centuries came to an abrupt end in 1475, when the Ottoman navy attacked and laid siege to Kaffa. The city fell, and the rest of the Genoese colonies in the Crimean peninsula were seized and placed under the control of a Tatar khanate, which officially accepted the suzerainty of the Ottoman sultan in 1478. The Armenian communities did survive under the Tatar khans but lost their former luster and importance.

The Ottoman conquest of the Crimean peninsula and the ouster of the Genoese from the region were catastrophic for the Armenian merchants and for the economy. Right after the conquest and during the early period of the Tatar domination, the local Tatars and the Turks were hostile toward the Armenians, since the latter had defended the Genoese colonies. Several Armenians were executed, and many were forced to convert to Islam. As many as sixteen Armenian churches in Kaffa alone were converted to mosques. Thousands of Armenian families fled to other Eastern European countries or to the Gallipoli peninsula. The Ottomans took captive several thousand people and transported them to Constantinople, where they joined their kinsmen, established new quarters, and formed the nucleus of a small community.

The conquest of the Crimea by the Turks, however, did not completely drain the Armenian communities of their population. Economic revival in the peninsula at the end of the sixteenth century and relative political stability under Tatar rule attracted new immigrants from several beleaguered Armenian communities in eastern Anatolia.

The Crimean towns served as havens not only for Armenian refugees fleeing the cruel valley lords of Anatolia but also for Armenian culture. Already in the thirteenth century the Armenians had a monastery called St. Sargis and a scriptorium in Kaffa. The most important cultural center was the monastic complex of *Surb Khach* (Holy Cross) in Surkhat. According to one theory, the name "Surkhat" is the corrupt form of *Surb Khach*. In the scriptoria of the monasteries of Kaffa, Surkhat, and Sudak, Armenian scribes copied numerous codices, most of which were illuminated by local Armenian artists. Some of these centers—for example, Surb Khach Monastery, the Church of the Archangels Gabriel and Michael, and the Church of St. John the Baptist—are still extant and have been studied by modern historians of architecture.

According to paleographer Ashot Abrahamian, more than 500 manuscripts copied in the Crimean peninsula survive today in various libraries of the world. In a work devoted to the Armenian miniature art of the Crimea and published in 1978, Emma Korkhmazian has examined 111 manuscripts with illuminations of artistic merit, dating from the thirteenth century to 1727. The chronological distribution of these manuscripts is informative. Eight manuscripts were illuminated before 1330 (i.e., the date of the mass migration of the Armenians from the lower Volga basin); sixty codices illuminated between 1330 and 1475 (i.e., the Ottoman conquest of Kaffa); no manuscripts exist from 1474 to 1575; and the remaining forty manuscripts were copied and illuminated after 1536. These statistics indirectly reflect the economic and cultural state of the Crimean Armenian communities.

During the fourteenth century, the sponsors of miniature artists included not only the rich merchants but also common craftsmen. Codex No. 3797 of the Matenadaran (Repository of Manuscripts) of Erevan, a collection of homilies copied in 1347, was sponsored by painters, goldsmiths, shoemakers, blacksmiths, tailors, viniculturists, and the like. At a time when an unstable political situation left the cultural life of Greater Armenia in a precarious state and the kingdom of Cilician Armenia was waning, Crimea became a major center of Armenian art.

The artistic traditions of the Crimean scriptoria were later transported to other parts of Eastern Europe and to Constantinople. These traditions were influenced predominantly by the style of miniature art produced in Western Armenia, particularly in the Baiburt-Erzerum region. In their new environment, the Armenian artists also were influenced by contemporary Western art.

In the fourteenth and fifteenth centuries, when the political situation was more permissive, Armenian students from the Crimea were sent to study in various monastic centers and medieval "universities" in Greater Armenia. Hakob of Crimea, who died in 1416, was one such student sent to the renowned University of Gladzor. After completing the course of his studies, he spent the rest of his life in the monasteries of Western Armenia and became an authority on the Armenian calendar and related fields. Armenian literature flourished in the Crimean communities only after the arrival of immigrants from the town of Tokat in the sixteenth and seventeenth centuries. Among the foremost writers were several distinguished chroniclers who kept the historiographical tradition alive and several talented poets whose works have survived and are now published. Two of them are interesting, since they are probably among the earliest modern Armenian satirists. The first is the priest Stepanos of Tokat, who migrated to Crimea in 1604-1605 after escaping the horrors of the Jelali uprisings in his homeland. He spent all of his life in exile at the Monastery of Surb Khach, where he had as a pupil a young boy named Martiros. Martiros, a native of Kaffa, also became a satirist. To further his education Martiros went to Tokat and then to Jerusalem, where he was ordained a priest in 1651. From 1659 to 1660 he became patriarch of Constantinople, and in 1661 he received episcopal ordination at Echmiadzin and was appointed prelate of the region of Crimea. Martiros died in 1683 on the patriarchal throne of Jerusalem. His literary works include several letters and invectives in verse about various contemporary priests. From the biographies of Hakob, Stepanos, and Martiros we can see that the Armenian communities in the Crimea were not deprived of culture and that they maintained a considerable amount of cultural relations with centers in Greater Armenia and Armenia Minor. The major Armenian centers in the Crimean peninsula also disseminated Armenian culture to the Armenian communities in various Eastern European countries.

In 1778 the Armenians of Crimea migrated to Russia under peculiar circumstances. In 1774 the Russians had succeeded in forcing the Ottomans to accept the independence of the Khanate of Crimea, an act that put the khanate under immediate Russian influence. In order to speed up the annexation of Crimea to the empire, the Russians decided to strike at the economy of the peninsula by persuading the Armenian and Greek population, who were the most active in conducting commercial enterprises, to migrate to Russia. The Armenians of Russia and especially their prelate, Archbishop Hovsep Arghutian, were very much in favor of this move, since the Russian court had promised the Armenian immigrants important privileges and an entire area in which to settle. The Armenians parted from their second homeland with great reluctance and settled in the region of Rostov-on-Don. They named their new habitat Nor (New) Nakhichevan and built villages, cities, and a monastic complex called Surb Khach in memory of the institution in Surkhat. The Armenians of Nakhichevan have survived and maintained their identity until the present day, and several nineteenth- and early twentieth-century Armenian intellectuals and political leaders were born and raised there. The Monastery of Surb Khach, which was in Armenian hands until the Soviet government took it away several decades ago, was recently restored and reconsecrated as a church.

Soon after the migration of the Armenians and Greeks, the Russians succeeded in annexing Crimea to the empire in 1783. At the end of the eighteenth and beginning of the nineteenth century, several Armenians from various areas migrated to Crimea and formed new communities, particularly in the larger cities. The latter were still active until World War II.

Armenians had lived on the Crimean peninsula for over six hundred years by the time they left in 1778. Since the great migration of 1330, eighteen generations maintained their Armenian identity on Crimean soil. Various factors contributing to the longevity of these communities are of great interest to the student of Armenian history. One such factor is the large number of Armenians living in close quarters in a relatively small area. The communities of the Crimea were tightly knit around traditional Armenian institutions such as the family and the church. In this environment even the Armenians in union with Rome, whose history goes back to Genoese times, were never Latinized; they retained their identity and in 1778 joined the rest of their brothers and sisters in migrating to Russia. New waves of immigrants from Armenia Minor and Greater Armenia occasionally replenished the Armenian population of the communities, particularly after 1475. The constant inflow was instrumental in preserving the Armenian language and traditions. We must note that immigrant scribes, miniature artists, writers, poets, and chroniclers were responsible for the revival of the arts and literature in the seventeenth-century Crimean communities.

The demographical distribution of various ethnic groups in medieval Crimea probably was another major factor in the preservation of the Armenian identity. The region was for the most part inhabited by Tatars who were Muslims. There also was a small concentration of Greeks and a very small number of Italians. The Armenians were the largest "minority" in the Crimea. As Christians, they refrained from intermarrying and mingling with the Muslim element. The sources speak of periodic atrocities, forced conversions, and executions perpetrated on the Armenians by the Muslim overlords of Crimea. The Armenians also were distant from the Greeks and Italians on theological grounds. They lived in their communities, aloof from others.

The stable economy of the Crimean peninsula and the prosperity of the Armenians, save for certain intervals shortly after the Ottoman conquest in 1475 and during the sixteenth century, was another factor why the Armenian communities continued to survive and thrive. Yet in 1778 the number of Armenians was nowhere near half a million. In that year only 12,000 Armenians migrated to the region of Rostov. The large numbers had dwindled as a result of the Ottoman conquest in 1475, when the majority of the population migrated to the north.

Because of their geographical position, the Armenian communities in the Crimea were not isolated from their homeland or the other communities in Asia Minor and Eastern Europe. Commercial transactions took Armenian merchants to these regions, and merchants from the Crimea traveled far and wide. The early seventeenth-century Armenian chronicler Grigor Kamakhetsi speaks about Crimean merchants who frequently visited the quarters of Crimean Armenians in Constantinople and were very active in the affairs of the Armenian community in the Ottoman capital.

During the seventeenth and eighteenth centuries, merchants from New Julfa and the towns of the Nakhichevan region frequented the seaports of the Black Sea, and some had established headquarters in Feodosiia. This element probably carried certain ideas about a national awareness, which inspired a few hundred young Armenians from the Crimea at the beginning of the eighteenth century to volunteer to join the forces of Davit Bek to liberate Eastern Armenia.

The hierarchy of the church provided another form of contact with other Armenian communities. Catholicoi, patriarchs, prelates, and bishops as well as learned *vardapets* (doctors of theology) frequently visited the Armenian communities of Eastern Europe, keeping the Armenians of these regions informed about the situation of their brothers and sisters in the homeland and elsewhere. After the Ottoman conquest of the Crimea, the Armenian prelacy of the region became subject to the Armenian patriarchate of Constantinople. Exactly when this happened is not clear, but the spiritual and administrative tie with the capital was instrumental in maintaining close relations with Armenian centers.

The life and travels of Martiros of Crimea, mentioned earlier, can give us some insight into the movements of men of the cloth in a world where there was almost no system of communication comparable to that of our own. Throughout the late Middle Ages and modern times, until the mid-nineteenth century, the major hierarchical sees of the Armenian church and some of the major monasteries sent bishops or priests especially to affluent communities to raise funds and promote interest among the people for pilgrimage. This institution, which has been studied only superficially, was called *nvirakutiun* and the holder of the office a *nvirak*. The functions and duties of the *nviraks* included bearing the blessings of the particular holy institution he represented, carrying encyclicals and letters, distributing holy chrism among the different churches, raising money for various purposes, and performing a series of other errands that focused the attention of people living in distant communities on the monasteries of the homeland. The *nviraks* usually were learned monks who spent several years in important communities such as Kaffa and busied themselves with intellectuals pursuits, preaching in local churches, writing, copying codices, and teaching in schools. These men kept the cultural and religious traditions of the Armenian people alive in distant lands.

Grigor Kamakhetsi mentions several *nviraks* who taught and preached in Crimea. One of them was a certain Ghazar Vardapet from the town of Baberd (modern Baiburt) who had first migrated to Poland and mastered the art of miniature painting and theology. He subsequently went to Aleppo in Syria, where the rank of *vardapetutiun* was bestowed upon him by the catholicos of Cilicia. Returning to Europe, Ghazar spent some time working in Kaffa until he was deported by the order of the Tatar khan.

Of all the factors just cited, demography is perhaps the most important in concluding that the Armenian experience in the Crimea was very similar to that in the Armenian homeland and Asia Minor. The existence of a predominantly Muslim population in its immediate environment prevented the Armenians from assimilating.

Poland/Ukraine

The important Armenian communities of medieval Poland were concentrated in the eastern part of the country and especially in the regions seized from Ukraine during the fourteenth century, namely, Galicia, Volhynia, and Podolia. The Armenian sources refer to these territories, as well as to Poland, as *Lehastan* or *Erkirn Ilakhats* (land of the Ilakhs). There were large concentrations of Armenians in Kamenets-Podolskii (Podolsk) from the eleventh to the nineteenth century; in Kuty from the eighteenth to the twentieth; in Lvov from the thirteenth to the twentieth; in Luck from the fourteenth to the eighteenth; in Stanislav (Ivano-Franiivsk) from the seventeenth to the eighteenth; in Jazlowiec (Yabluvinka) from the thirteenth to the eighteenth; in Zamostya from the sixteenth to the eighteenth; and in Zolotsiv from the seventeenth to the eighteenth.

The Armenian presence in these regions dates back to the tenth century. Ana, the wife of Prince Vladimir (978-1015), was an Armenian, and, according to Slavic legends and early sources, the princes of Galicia and Kiev employed Armenians living in Kiev as mercenaries. After the Seljuk penetration into Greater Armenia and the fall of Ani in 1064, waves of Armenian immigrants found their way north to the western Ukraine. New immigrants arrived in the twelfth century. The Mongol conquest of Kiev in 1240 and the unstable political situation there forced many Armenians to migrate to Galicia and Volhynia, where settlements of Armenians already existed in Kamenets-Podolskii and the surrounding villages. By 1250 the Armenians had built a church in Kamanets.

The communities in the western part of Ukraine increased in size during the fourteenth and fifteenth centuries, when three major waves of immigrants arrived. The first wave came from the lower Volga region via the Crimea and was responsible for turning the Crimean settlements into major communities in 1330. The second wave came from Cilicia after the fall of the Armenian kingdom in 1375, arriving via Wallachia or the Crimean peninsula; the third came from the Crimea after the Ottoman conquest of that region in 1475. During the course of the sixteenth through eighteenth centuries, a constant flow of smaller waves of immigrants followed from Greater Armenia and Armenia Minor—particularly from the region of Tokat and the Crimea.

Unlike the immigrants who concentrated in large numbers in the southern regions of the Crimean peninsula, the Armenians of Poland and Ukraine were scattered in small numbers over a very vast region.

Recent studies have shown that there were over fifty Armenian communities in Ukrainian, Polish, and Romanian towns and villages. One of the largest of these was in the city of Lvov. First settled by Armenians in the thirteenth century, Lvov became the center of an Armenian prelacy in 1364. At that time there were already two Armenian churches there and a monastery. The renowned cathedral, which still stands, was built in 1363 with the support of two Armenian merchants, Hakob, son of Shahnshah of Kaffa, and Panos of Vaysur. Records indicate that at its peak in 1633, the Armenian community of Lvov and its suburbs consisted of 2,500 individuals. The other communities were also relatively small. In 1672, when the Ottomans conquered Kamenets-Podolskii, there were only 1,200 Armenian families there, and Luck had only 800 in the seventeenth century. The Armenian population in the other cities was far less numerous.

In 1340 the Polish king Casimir III occupied Galicia and Volhynia. Considering the contribution Armenians, Jews, and Ukrainians could make to the advancement of commerce, the king granted them the right to practice their laws and maintain their traditions. The Armenians established their courts not only in Lvov but also in Kamenets-Podolskii and a number of other towns. In 1519 the royal court approved the use of an adaptation of Mkhitar Gosh's Armenian codification of laws, which thereafter was used in the Armenian law courts and tribunals.

The Armenians in the major towns were free to conduct their own community affairs. In Lvov they lived in their own quarter and elected elders (forty-two of them, called *avags*) and judges *(voyt)*. In certain towns such as Kamenets-Podolskii and Zamostia, there were Armenian magistracies in the seventeenth century. The documents and papers of the Armenian courts in these towns are still extant and are in Kipchak Turkish, the official language for business transactions. Modern scholars depend on these documents to reconstruct the Kipchak language.

The Armenian communities were composed of various classes of people. The least known are the farmers, peasants, and all those elements living in the country. Because this class, the lowest and the poorest, lived in very small numbers in isolated communities, its members were probably more prone to assimilation. Many were in fact serfs on lands owned by Polish feudal lords. The craftsmen and the merchants, on the other hand, lived in the Armenian quarters of cities and were allowed to organize themselves into guilds. The Armenians excelled as goldsmiths, silversmiths, painters, weavers, and the like.

As in the Crimean peninsula, so also in Poland did the Armenian merchants play a major role in eastern trade, traveling all over Russia, the Crimea, the Ottoman Empire, Persia, and other lands. In the fifteenth and sixteenth centuries, the Armenian merchants were given the right to participate in commercial enterprises in Poland, and in 1505 they were exempt from paying customs duties on imported goods. In the sixteenth century, most of the stores in Lvov belonged to Armenians; by the seventeenth century, the Armenian merchants of Lvov had branches in Constantinople, Ankara, Isfahan, Moscow, Gdansk, and other cities. Some of these merchants managed to advance themselves into the ranks of the Polish nobility and gradually were assimilated.

Like everywhere else, in Poland the Armenian Church played an important role in the life of the community. However, in the communities of Poland, unlike the other Armenian communities inside and outside of Armenia, church-related matters were decided upon by elected representatives of the community, namely the elders. Since the churches and church property belonged to the community, changes in the status of the church had a strong bearing on the life of the community.

Despite the rhetorical references of modern writers and orators to the assimilation of half a million Armenians in Poland, the separate communities survived there for several centuries. According to seventeenth-century Polish historian Sebastian Petricz, the Armenians of Lvov refused to integrate with the natives and married only within their community. We know from other historical sources that the Armenians continued to maintain their identity even after the seventeenth century—that is, after their forced conversion to Catholicism. The longevity of these communities in an environment so different from that of the Crimea and the Ottoman Empire deserves comment.

With the exception of the Armenian community of Kamenets-Podolskii, the major centers in Poland and the Ukraine were spared from the destruction, devastation, and carnage of other parts of the world where Armenians dwelled. The major communities prospered and even increased in number. The mass migration of Armenians to Poland occurred at a most opportune time, when Casimir III was organizing the defense of his realm and giving privileges to minorities to advance trade. Armenians played an important role as soldiers as well as merchants. In the seventeenth century, Armenian detachments protected the caravans of merchants as well as the border against the advancing Ottoman armies. The "Knights of the Virgin Mary," an Armenian military organization founded in the 1630s, was active until the end of the seventeenth century. In 1683 a 5,000-man Armenian army participated in the defense of Vienna, fighting against the Ottomans. This military involvement, as well as the autonomy Armenians enjoyed in their internal affairs and the disintegration of communities in general, kept the Armenian identity strong.

At the beginning of the sixteenth century, the jurisdiction of the tribunal of Lvov was extended to deal with cases involving Armenians and non-Armenians. Over the course of time the tribunal of Lvov acquired the prestigious rank of a higher court in relation to the Armenian tribunals in other cities. For as long as the Armenians enjoyed their legal privileges and the tribunals functioned, the Armenian identity remained intact.

As in the Crimea, so also in the Armenian communities of Poland and the Ukraine was there a constant flow of immigrants from the homeland, various parts of the Ottoman Empire, and certain older colonies. This migration had adverse effects on the situation in Greater Armenia and Armenia Minor, but it replenished and revitalized the communities in Eastern Europe. Recently published statistics about the Armenian population of the city of Lvov give us some idea about the flow of immigrants. In 1407 there were 301 Armenians living in the city; in 1417 the number increased to 337; throughout the rest of the fifteenth and sixteenth centuries, the number remained constant; and in 1575 there were only 60 families. A sharp increase is detected in 1600, when the number of families rose to 100. In 1620 there were 70 older families and 60 newcomers. By 1633 the number of Armenians living in and around Lvov was estimated to be 2,500. Some of the newcomers apparently moved elsewhere, and the number of families dropped to 82 in 1640. The records from 1678 show only 14 families, indicating a sharp decline. Between 1655 and 1675, 52 families arrived from Van, Constantinople, and Isfahan who did not settle down in the region of Lvov. In the early part of the eighteenth century, the number of families had increased to 73. Thus a sedentary element formed the core of the community in Lvov, which occasionally was inflated by newcomers who lived there for a while and then moved elsewhere. The sedentary element maintained the local traditions and rights acquired through the centuries, providing a base for the immigrants to adapt to their new habitat and in turn being revitalized by them.

The communities of Poland and the Ukraine were geographically remote from the homeland, a factor that could contribute to the isolation of the Armenians in these areas from the mainstream of

Armenian life. Yet there was constant contact not only with the
nearby communities but also with the homeland. Besides merchants,
prelates, and intellectuals, catholicoi of All Armenians visited Lvov
and the other towns. At the beginning of the seventeenth century, it
became fashionable for Armenian intellectuals, particularly *vardapets,* to go to Poland to become acquainted with the Western
intellectual tradition. The communities of Eastern Europe were not
always at the receiving end; they contributed a great deal to the
movement of intellectual revival among the Armenians. According
to the seventeenth-century historian Arakel of Tabriz, the contacts
of Armenian *vardapets* in Poland with learned Latin clergy prompted
a revival of interest in Eastern Armenia concerning grammar, rhetoric, and philosophy. Lvov, Lazlovitz, Kamenets-Podolskii, and
Zamostia were important cultural centers with schools and scriptoria,
and over two hundred codices copied in Poland and the Ukraine are
now extant in various libraries throughout the world. Most of these
manuscripts were copied by scribes born in Eastern Europe, including a small number from various towns in the homeland. In the
sixteenth and seventeenth centuries, the scriptoria in Poland were so
well known that students of calligraphy went there to master the art.
The demand for manuscripts was so great that the seventeenth-century traveler Simeon of Zamostia, the son of an immigrant from
Kaffa, supported himself as a scribe.

In the seventeenth century the Jesuits founded a seminary in Lvov,
promoting Armenian studies and literature. In 1616 Hovhannes
Farmatanents of Baghesh (Bitlis) established a printing press and began
publishing religious books. The first known play is Armenian, a tragedy
about the martyrdom of St. Hripsime that was written and presented in
Lvov in 1668.

Because of the intellectual give-and-take between the homeland
and the colonies in Poland and the Ukraine, certain traditional literary
genres flourished. Among the Polish-Armenian intellectuals one may
mention the names of several chroniclers, historians, and writers who
made substantial contributions to Armenian literature. Historiographical
tradition in the Armenian communities in this part of the world was
established in the course of the fifteenth and sixteenth centuries and was
continued until the nineteenth century. Among the towering intellectual
figures were Stepanos Lehatsi (Stephen of Poland, seventeenth century),
well known for his translations from Latin, and Stepanos Roshka (1670-
1739). The latter was a Uniate priest born in Kamenets who became the

vicar of the archbishop of Lvov. He was educated in Poland, Rome, and at the Mekhitarist Monastery in Venice. Roshka is the author of several historical, grammatical, and theological works in Armenian, including a lexicon of Classical Armenian that remains unpublished. This work is still of exceptional value, since several hitherto unknown Armenian authorities are cited in it. Another major work by him is the *Ecclesiastical Annals,* a chronicle of church history wherein he has recorded important events, particularly those concerning the Polish-Armenian communities. Historiography and other intellectual pursuits played a definite role in maintaining and fostering the Armenian identity in Eastern Europe.

Various nonacademic institutions also played a major role in extending the life of Armenian communities in Eastern Europe. Among these were the guilds, hospitals, and churches. Until the seventeenth century, the Armenian Church was instrumental in fostering an Armenian Christian identity separate from that of Roman Catholics and the Orthodox. Several patriarchal encyclicals issued by fourteenth- through seventeenth-century catholicoi and addressed to the Armenian communities in Poland and the Ukraine bear testimony to the close contacts between the center of the Armenian Church and these colonies. The church strengthened the ties between the communities and the homeland. The fact that the architect of the cathedral of Lvov emulated traditional Armenian architectural patterns is symbolic of the attachment of the dispersed Armenians to their cultural tradition.

During the course of the seventeenth century, the Armenians of Poland resisted for forty years the pressure of local authorities to convert to Catholicism. The seventeenth-century Armenian historian Arakel of Tabriz claims Nikol Torosovich, the Armenian bishop of Lvov, was the person responsible for their ultimate conversion. This is a simple explanation for a complex issue. From Arakel himself and other sources we learn that the Polish government favored the forced conversion of the Armenians to Catholicism. Bishop Nikol was apparently a controversial figure disliked by the people, but he was not the cause of the problem. Ever since the sixteenth century a general reaction against the Protestant movement had triggered a change in the hitherto tolerant policy of the Polish government toward the Jews, the Orthodox, and the Armenians. During the seventeenth century, when the Armenians were pressured to convert, the Jews as well as the Orthodox were persecuted. Under the circumstances, Bishop Nikol probably was left with no other choice than to accept the supremacy of Rome.

Catholicos Movses of All Armenians excommunicated Bishop Nikol in 1629, but in 1654 Nikol went to Constantinople to meet Catholicos Philippos, Movses's successor, and swear his allegiance to the see of Holy Echmiadzin. Rome was well aware of Nikol's dual policy and did not trust him. In the 1660s a special seminary was established in Lvov where Latin Armenists prepared clergymen for Armenia to replace the old priests. Their efforts bore fruit. The prelacy of Poland, with its center at Lvov, officially severed its relations with Echmiadzin and accepted the supremacy of the pope in about 1689, during the tenure of Bishop Vardan Hunanian.

Conversion to Catholicism did not break the ties between the Armenians of Poland and their native land. Bishop Vardan Hunanian himself had traveled extensively throughout Greater Armenia and engaged in scholarly pursuits. In 1699 when Israel Ori visited the pope to offer him the letter of the Armenian *meliks* (hereditary landowners of feudal lineage in southeastern Armenia and Karabagh), who requested Western help for the liberation of Armenia, he had beside him as a translator Stepanos Roshka. In 1701, Ori passed through Poland, visiting the Armenian communities. Two decades later a number of Armenians from Poland applied to join the forces of Davit Bek and fight for their fatherland.

The traditional view that thousands of Armenians living in Poland and the Ukraine were assimilated as an immediate result of forced conversion to Catholicism is not warranted. No single event cannot explain the waning and gradual disappearance of some of the communities in Eastern Europe. As already shown, the Armenian communities in Poland and the Ukraine were not very populous. The rise of feudal lords and of a feudal socioeconomic structure in Poland at the end of the fifteenth century limited the growth of cities. Despite attempts in the seventeenth century to build new cities, the economy of the country declined because of continuous wars and major shifts in world trade. After the 1660s better markets than those in Poland attracted the Armenian merchants to Russia, Persia, and the Ottoman Empire. Economic problems and the religious persecutions of the seventeenth century forced many Armenians to migrate to Wallachia and elsewhere. The numbers of Armenians decreased sharply when Podolia fell to the Ottomans in 1672, and many Armenians migrated to the Balkans, particularly to the region of Plovdiv. All of these factors make the general picture much more complex. It is interesting to note that after their conversion to Catholicism, the Armenians of Poland and the

Ukraine maintained their national identity for as long as their institutions could function. Conversion to Catholicism did not mean attending non-Armenian churches. The Armenians still maintained their churches and their ancient rite.

The major blow to the status quo of the Armenian communities in Poland probably came in 1784 following the first partition of Poland, when the Armenian tribunals were shut down. After the Russian take-over of Podolia in 1793, the Armenians of that region were completely cut off, and the Armenian Catholic bishops of Lvov could no longer tend to the spiritual needs of the Armenians in that region of their prelacy. For a while the Russians allowed the Armenian Catholics to maintain the Armenian rite, but in the 1820s they were deprived even of that.

Lvov was under Austrian control throughout the nineteenth century. The Armenian community in and around the city remained under the jurisdiction of their bishops, and the Armenian rite was maintained until the beginning of the twentieth century. In the 1880s the bishopric of Lvov had about 3,000 Armenians. In 1902 Vahan Kurkjian, an Armenian intellectual from the United States, visited Lvov, known as Lemberg at that time. He gives the following information: 500 Armenians lived in Lvov and another 500 in Stanislav. They had lost their native tongue, but the 3,000 villagers living in Kuty were still Armenian speakers. There were twenty priests of the Armenian rite who tended to the spiritual needs of the faithful. Next to the cathedral of Lvov was a convent where some of the nuns were of Armenian origin. After World War I, when Galicia became a part of Poland, the Armenian community of Lvov was still active. The Armenian archbishop Joseph Theodorovich undertook the task of renovating the fourteenth-century cathedral. In the 1930s the Armenians of Lvov had a cultural organization and published journals and pamphlets, some of which were about the cathedral. After World War II, Galicia was united with Ukraine. According to the *Armenian Soviet Encyclopedia*, there were in the 1970s as many as 1,500 Armenians living in Lvov. Recent reports indicate that thousands of Armenians live in various Polish cities. Many Poles also trace their family trees from Armenian ancestors.

Bulgaria

The origins of Armenian communities on the territory of present-day Bulgaria go back to the Byzantine period (sixth through tenth centuries).

The Danube frontier of the empire was very vulnerable, as nomadic elements living on the northern borders of the "inhabited world" made frequent inroads deep into Byzantine territory and terrorized the sedentary population. The logical solution to the problem was to settle warrior frontiersmen in the Balkans. The Byzantine emperors, who since the time of Justinian I were trying to pacify Armenia and destroy its feudal social order, transported Armenian feudal and warrior elements to the Balkans, thus resolving two problems at once: pacification of Western Armenia and protection of the Danube frontier. The imperial policy is clearly reflected in an apocryphal letter addressed to Khusro II, King of Kings of Persia, by the emperor Maurice (582-602). In this document, which is preserved in the *History* of the seventh-century Armenian historian Sebeos, the Byzantine emperor makes the following proposal:

> There is an unruly and disobedient race in our midst, creating confusion. Come now, let me gather those on my side and deport them to Thrace and you gather those on your side and order them to be taken to the East. If they die, our enemies will die, and if they kill, they will kill our enemies, and we shall live in peace. For if they remain in their land, we shall have no rest.

Beginning with the early ninth century, Paulician heretics of Armenian origin replaced the earlier political exiles in the Balkans. New exiles were sent to this region in the ninth and tenth centuries. Besides heretics, Monophysite Armenians as well as Duophysites penetrated the area. According to the testimony of the tenth-century Armenian historian Stepanos Asoghik, one of them by the name of Samvel Anetsi (Samuel of Ani) who was originally from the district of Terjan in Western Armenia became king of Bulgaria in 976 and ruled until 1014. Ironically, his great archenemy, the Byzantine emperor Basil II, known as "the slayers of the Bulgars," was also of Armenian origin and had Armenian detachments in his armies fighting in his campaigns against Samvel Anetsi.

In the eleventh century, after the annexation of Bulgaria to the Byzantine Empire, large Armenian communities were established at Burgas and especially at Philippopolis (modern Plovdiv). The latter was the center of what appears to have been a newly organized prelacy of the Armenian Church and was also the site of a Chalcedonian Armenian monastery. Smaller Armenian communities existed in other Bulgarian towns and villages.

In the fourteenth and fifteenth centuries, new waves of Armenian immigrants arrived from Cilicia and particularly from the Crimea. Ottoman conquests in Bulgaria during the last two decades of the fifteenth century were responsible for the refuge of some Armenians to Wallachia, Transylvania, and Galicia. Yet whenever political and social stability prevailed in the Balkan peninsula, Armenians fleeing their homeland considered it a haven. This trend continued until the twentieth century.

The Armenian immigrants in Bulgaria and the other Balkan countries, like their brothers and sisters in Poland and the Ukraine, were scattered in relatively small numbers over large areas. For example, in the seventeenth century there were only 100 Armenian families living in Plovdiv. The community grew as refugees arrived from Kamenets-Podolskii in 1675. The situation was similar in Sofia, where an older community existed prior to the seventeenth century. During the course of the seventeenth and eighteenth centuries, refugees arrived from Nakhichevan and southwestern Armenia, so inflating the Armenian population that by the end of the eighteenth century there were as many as 1,600 Armenians living there. During the seventeenth and eighteenth centuries, the Armenian community of Trnovo was very active because of its commercial significance. When Trnovo ceased being a commercial center, the Armenian population moved away. In the city of Varna there also was an Armenian quarter in the seventeenth century. The Armenian population increased in the second half of the nineteenth and the early decades of the twentieth century. The Armenian community of Ruschuk (Ruse) traced its history back to the sixteenth century. The majority of the smaller communities that flourished in the seventeenth and eighteenth centuries were merchant colonies from southeastern Armenia, particularly from the region of Nakhichevan. Most of them disappeared as Bulgaria lost its commercial ties. After the merchants had left, the Armenian population of the larger communities in Plovdiv, Sofia, Ruschuk, and Varna labored to maintain a livelihood as expert craftsmen.

In the late eighteenth and nineteenth centuries, Armenian refugees from Greater Armenia, Persia, the different regions of the Ottoman Empire, and Europe continued to go to Bulgaria, even though the economic situation was not very inviting. There were several reasons for this. The political and economic situation in the Balkans was comparatively better than that in the hinterlands of Anatolia and Greater Armenia. Armenian Monophysites living under Polish rule escaped religious persecution by taking refuge in Bulgarian towns under the Ottomans, since the Ottoman segregated administrative system allowed them to worship according to their faith. For Armenians in both Eastern Europe and the Ottoman Empire, Bulgaria was an easily accessible land. Armenians had no racial, religious, or national conflicts with the local Bulgarians.

Despite the nineteenth-century Ottoman oppression in the Balkans that forced many Armenian families to leave, the larger communities survived. After the establishment of the Bulgarian principality in 1878, Bulgaria became the principal refuge of Armenians escaping the brutality of the Turks. The massacre of the 1800s, those of 1909 in Cilicia, and the holocaust of 1915 brought numerous Armenians to the major cities of Bulgaria.

The 1,400-year Armenian presence in Bulgaria is well attested in historical sources, architectural monuments, manuscripts, and art. Scholars think that prior to the Ottoman occupation of the Balkans, many Armenians living in the peninsula were assimilated. Lack of channels of communication with the homeland and the religious persecutions of the Byzantines may have contributed to the loss of several thousand Armenians. During the Byzantine period, Armenian Chalcedonians founded in 1084 one of the oldest cultural centers of Bulgaria, namely, the Monastery of Bachkova. The Chalcedonian element was, however, the first to assimilate. These as well as the adherents of the national church made substantial contributions to Bulgarian art and architecture. Armenian calligraphers and miniature artists were active in the Balkans from as early as 1007.

The survival of several communities in Bulgaria since the Middle Ages and the early years of the Ottoman period of occupation is, however, evident. Several factors may have contributed to this longevity. Bulgaria was geographically very close to the Crimea and the Ottoman capital, where there were large concentrations of Armenians. Because of this there was an ongoing relationship among the communities, particularly in religious matters, since the Armenian church authorities in Bulgaria were at first in contact with those in Crimea and later were placed under the direct control of the Armenian patriarchate of Constantinople. Under Ottoman rule the communities of Bulgaria pulled closer to those in the Crimea and Anatolia. The older communities were more readily replenished with new blood coming from the east. Here as well as elsewhere the church, art, architecture, and letters played a major role in maintaining the Armenian identity of the communities. There was no mass conversion of Armenians either to the Orthodox faith or to Catholicism, and the Armenians of Bulgaria remained much closer to the mainstream of Armenian life. Toward the end of the nineteenth century, especially after the massacres of the 1890s, many Armenian intellectuals escaped to Bulgaria. Armenian life was bustling there in the early decades of the twentieth century and during the two decades between the two world wars. In 1933 many Armenians repatriated to Soviet Armenia, and a second group, consisting of 6,000 people, left for Armenia in 1946. In the 1950s and 1960s many Armenian families migrated to the Middle East, the United States, and Canada. But Armenian communities still remain in the major towns of Bulgaria. According to the statistics of 1976, there were about 25,000 Armenians in the country.

Romania

The history of the Armenian communities in the historic districts of Bukovina, Moldavia, and Wallachia dates back to the fourteenth century and perhaps even earlier. A major Armenian migration headed toward these regions probably originated in the lower Volga basin, accompanying the wave of immigrants that went to the southern Crimea in the 1330s. In 1350 the Armenian immigrants built a church in Botoshan and another one in 1395 in Iąsh. In 1401, Prince Alexander of Moldavia permitted the Armenians to establish a prelacy at Suchava.

The Armenian communities in Bukovina and Moldavia grew during the course of the fifteenth century particularly— that is, after the Ottoman conquest of Constantinople and the fall of Kaffa in 1475. In 1484, however, the Ottomans transported the Armenians of Kilian and Akkerman to Constantinople. Soon thereafter, in 1497, seven hundred Armenian families left Suchava for Hungary, Poland, and Galicia because of Polish aggression.

The middle of the sixteenth century was a particularly bad period for the Armenians of Moldavia, since religious persecutions drove them away to Transylvania. In the last quarter of the sixteenth century, however, the Serpeka dynasty of Armenian origin ruled. Armenian participation in the popular movements protesting the heavy taxation under Prince Duca in the seventeenth century was catastrophic for the communities. Several Armenian families were forced to flee to the Carpathian Mountains, but at the end of the seventeenth century the old

Armenian communities were replenished with new waves of immigrants. These communities were still active until the end of the
eighteenth century, though they suffered setbacks during the Russo-
Turkish wars. In the 1790s Archbishop Hovsep Arghutian, the prelate
of the Armenians of Russia, helped 4,000 Armenians from Moldavia
migrate to Russia. Nonetheless, the communities outlasted the Austrian
occupation of Moldavia and were later actively involved in Romanian
politics and cultural movements.

Individual Armenians probably first appeared in Wallachia in the
thirteenth century. Communities were established in the second half of
the fourteenth century, with the earliest immigrants arriving from the
Crimea. After the fall of Kaffa in 1475, larger numbers arrived to
replenish the older communities. More refugees came from Ottoman
territories in the sixteenth and seventeenth centuries, some settling in
Dobruja. In 1620 the Armenians built their first church in Bucharest,
and as a result of the continuous influx of population from the Ottoman
Empire throughout the eighteenth, nineteenth, and early decades of the
twentieth century, the Bucharest community grew in size. The Armenians of Wallachia did not suffer as many setbacks as their kinsmen in
Moldavia, and the communities were relatively more stable. Save for
the tightening of Ottoman control during the period of the Phanariot
Greeks in the eighteenth and early nineteenth centuries, the Armenians
enjoyed relative peace and prosperity. They were engaged mostly in
commercial enterprises both in Wallachia and Moldavia and monopolized much of the transit traffic between the Ottoman Empire and
Poland. These communities were more affluent than those in Bulgaria.

Since late medieval times, the Armenians participated in the
political and cultural as well as social life of Wallachia. It is interesting
to note that this participation did not lead to assimilation and collapse
of Armenian community life. The Armenians brought their art, architecture, literature, and crafts and made contributions in a number of
areas such as publication of newspapers and books, erection of buildings, and politics. Certain individuals of Armenian ancestry achieved
great success in political and cultural areas and are considered today
very much a part of Romanian history. According to the testimony of
the seventeenth-century Turkish traveler Evliya Chelebi, the Armenians lived in harmony with the local Romanians. This kind of coex-
istence continues until the present time.

The contributions of the Armenians to Romanian culture are so
substantial that several Romanian scholars have studied the history of

the Armenian communities in Romania. One of them, N. B. Iorga, a renowned historian and national figure in Romania, wrote on various aspects of Armenian history and was a relentless champion of the Armenian cause.

The Armenian communities in Romania have survived until the present. Besides the large community in Bucharest, there were and still are Armenians in Constanta, Tolbuhin (now in Bulgaria), Silistra, Tulca, and several other towns. In most of these places there are Armenian churches and monuments.

During the late Middle Ages the communities in Moldavia and Wallachia were well organized. In Moldavia the Armenians also had tribunals, which continued to function until the beginning of the Austrian occupation. Near Suchava there are at least two Armenian monasteries that are still open; the Monastery of Hachkatar Surb Astvatsatsin is still a place of pilgrimage for the Armenians of Romania.

In most of the Armenian communities there were Armenian schools that were still functioning in the 1950s and 1960s. The Romanian Armenians had local presses where newspapers, journals, and books were published in the Armenian language. Most of these had been founded in the second half of the nineteenth century and later. The Armenians in Romania had a very active cultural life and kept in very close touch with intellectual movements in other Armenian communities. Though the repatriation of thousands of Armenians to Soviet Armenia in 1946 and 1948 and the immigration of thousands of others to the Middle East and the West in the 1950s and 1960s have devitalized the communities, they are still in existence.

At the beginning of the nineteenth century, the situation of the Armenian communities in Moldavia and Bukovina was little different from those in Poland and Ukraine and contributed greatly to the preservation of the Armenian identity. The first half of the nineteenth century was a most critical period for the Armenians in general. The times required a decision to be made and steps to be taken for a transition from a medieval to a modern society. The transition led to a revival of national culture and greater self-awareness. In cities such as Tiflis, Moscow, Smyrna, and Constantinople, a mainstream of Armenian life and new definitions of national identity and nationhood were forged by the intelligentsia. Certain communities on the periphery of the Armenian dispersion plunged into the mainstream, maintained their identity, and flourished. Others could not do so; some of these communities survived as fossils whereas others ultimately died out. The

Armenian communities in Romania belong to the first category. The constant influx of new immigrants from the Ottoman Empire; the national church; institutions such as schools, libraries, newspapers, hospitals, social, cultural, and political groups; and continuous contact with the religious, cultural, social, and political life of the homeland and the major Armenian communities outside pulled the Romanian Armenians into the mainstream of Armenian life. In addition, the period of Armenian national revival coincided in Romania with that of an economic boom, as Romanian grain was in great demand. The old Armenian communities in Romania—although geographically not much closer to the homeland and the Ottoman capital than the cities of Poland and the Ukraine—also flourished and were economically in a position to respond to the changes in Armenian life.

In modern times, the closing down of several institutions and the flux of immigrants since the 1950s have weakened the vitality of the Romanian communities, and assimilation is taking its toll despite very close cultural contacts with Soviet Armenia.

Hungary

Armenian presence in Hungary and Transylvania, which was a part of Hungary until 1920, is attested from as early as the tenth century. In the fourteenth century the Armenian community of Hungary must have been quite large, since we know that they had a bishop by the name of Martin who presided in Transylvania. The major wave of immigrants, however, came in 1497 from Suchava in Bukovina and settled in Transylvania. Others followed, fleeing religious persecutions in Moldavia in 1551. During the seventeenth century there were new waves of immigrants from the same region. The historical sources do not speak of other migrations of Armenians to Hungary or Transylvania after the seventeenth century.

In their new habitat, the Armenian immigrants from Moldavia gradually acquired rights. In 1680 they were given the privilege to conduct their own internal affairs and engage in commerce. In the 1680s they played a major role in unifying Hungary and in the war against the Ottomans. In 1696 they were allowed to elect their own judges and hold tribunals.

Like their kinsmen in Poland and the Ukraine, the Armenians of Hungary and Transylvania were forced to convert to Catholicism at the end of the seventeenth and the beginning of the eighteenth century. This was brought about when the Hapsburgs extended their control over Transylvania and the Armenian Catholic prelates of Lvov were given a free hand to impose their will on the Transylvanian communities. As a result, ties between the Armenians of Transylvania and the communities in the Balkans were severed. Yet the Armenian communities survived until the early decades of the twentieth century.

The Armenians of Transylvania founded two major cities—Gherla and Elizabethspol (Dumbraveni)—and several towns and villages. These cities and towns, referred to as Armenopolis (Armenian city), were autonomous, self-contained, and distinguished for their Armenian courts. The majority of the Armenian population, probably no more than 20,000 people, resided in these towns, which were renowned for their tanneries and candle factories. The Armenians of Transylvania were for the most part engaged in foreign trade and contributed a great deal to the economy of Hungary.

One of the great aspirations of the Armenians of Transylvania was to establish an Armenian Catholic bishopric in their district. After several years of negotiation they achieved this goal, which made it possible for them to be semiautonomous in religious matters, establish their own schools, and maintain the Armenian language. In the eighteenth and nineteenth centuries the Mekhitarists of Venice regularly sent *vardapets* to educate them and even founded a monastery and a school. For several generations the Armenians maintained their identity and were very creative in literature and especially historiography.

Like their kinsmen in Romania, the Armenians of Transylvania and Hungary became actively involved in the sociopolitical life of Hungary. In 1848 the several Armenian cities and towns participated in the Hungarian revolution against Hapsburg domination. Three generals of Armenian descent were among the military leaders of the revolution. When the Hapsburgs crushed the rebellion in 1849, two of the three Armenian generals were executed and the Armenians suffered great financial losses. The Armenian cities and towns were forced to pay war indemnities and lost their privileges. The Armenian population, which hitherto had been in an economically stable state, was impoverished. The economic stress forced many to move away to seek work elsewhere. The Armenians also lost their right to have a bishop.

Despite the difficulties, the Armenians of Transylvania made a final attempt to revive their towns in the 1870s and 1880s, but to no avail. The communities dwindled, and non-Armenians moved into the

Armenian towns. There are no Armenians now in the city of Gherla, the last stronghold. The last Armenian in the city, a Roman Catholic priest and scholar, died in the 1960s.

At the beginning of the nineteenth century, the Armenian communities in Transylvania were in a fossilized state, severed from the mainstream of Armenian life politically, ecclesiastically, culturally, and also linguistically. As already noted, unlike the communities in Bulgaria and Romania, the ones in Hungary were not replenished by new blood. The great changes in Armenian life throughout the nineteenth century in no way affected the social, political, and cultural life of the Transylvanian communities.

Unlike the Armenian community of Lvov, which had converted to Catholicism but was under an Armenian archbishop, the Transylvanian Armenians could not even maintain their identity as Armenian Catholics. After losing their right to have their own jurisdiction, they were put under that of a local non-Armenian bishop. In the second half of the nineteenth century, the priests who served in the churches no longer understood the language of the liturgy, and most of them officiated in Latin. The only Armenian ecclesiastical presence was that of the Mekhitarists of Venice, who were forced to close down their school after the rebellion of 1848.

The Armenians of Transylvania initially spoke the dialect of immigrants from Bukovina. By the nineteenth century they were already linguistically isolated, since modern literary Armenian, with its eastern and western branches, became the standard idiom of communication. The Hapsburgs denied the Armenians of Transylvania the opportunity to learn modern literary Armenian in their schools. The Transylvanian dialect was used only in funerary orations and formal speeches. At the end of the nineteenth century, only a few old people could still communicate in their dialect.

During the nineteenth century the Armenians of Transylvania culturally and emotionally related less to their fellow Armenians in the homeland than to their own past and communities and towns. The most patriotic among them found satisfaction in writing local histories. Armenians of Transylvania were assimilated. There were still small pockets of Catholic Armenians in Transylvania in the 1950s; unfortunately, there is no recent information about them. The communities disappeared because the affluent as well as the middle class and the poor moved away from the old towns and cities. The young went to school in various

Hungarian cities and never returned, and the political upheavals of the twentieth century scattered the few who were left.

Certain facts regarding Armenian communities are noteworthy. The larger communities in Eastern Europe and the Crimea first appeared in the fourteenth century, with the arrival of large migrations from Russia and Anatolia. The large numbers mentioned in early modern historical works must be seriously questioned because, from all appearances, the number of Armenians in Eastern Europe was not very large. Most communities were revived by the arrival of new immigrants from the homeland, from other parts of the Ottoman Empire, or from neighboring communities. Most of the major communities survived until the nineteenth century, and some are still extant today. The Armenians reached Eastern Europe at a time when new cities were being founded and older ones encouraged to flourish. The Armenians succeeded in acquiring privileges and some autonomy in conducting their community affairs. The medieval way of life and confinement to ethnic quarters in cities and ethnically homogeneous villages with commercial, legal, religious, and social privileges automatically segregated the Armenians from other ethnic groups. Under such circumstances the Armenians did not find maintaining their identity too difficult.

The communities that kept pace with the mainstream of Armenian life survived, and some even thrived; those that were hindered from doing so because of religious, political, or cultural barriers were fossilized and gradually disappeared. Immigrants from thriving communities within the mainstream of Armenian life founded new colonies and communities, whereas those from fossilized communities disappeared completely. This point can be substantiated by comparing immigrants from the Crimea with those from Transylvania. The former founded or replenished several communities, while the latter were assimilated. While local Armenian institutions played an important role in the life of an Armenian community, a sense of belonging to a nation was generated only through participation in the mainstream of Armenian life.

FOR FURTHER INFORMATION

Alboyadjian, 1941-1961.   Simeon Lehatsi, 1936
Kurkjian, 1958.

3

EASTERN ARMENIA FROM THE SEVENTEENTH CENTURY TO THE RUSSIAN ANNEXATION

George Bournoutian

The Formation of Eastern Armenia

At the start of the sixteenth century, Armenia became the center of conflict between the Ottoman sultans and the Safavid shahs of Persia. After continuous warfare between the two empires, a compromise was finally reached by the Treaty of Zuhab in 1639. Under this agreement, the Ottomans recognized almost all of Transcaucasia as being part of Persia. The plain of Shuragial and the Arpachai River became a sort of boundary; Armenian lands east of that zone were considered part of Persia, and all lands west of it fell into the Ottoman sphere. The terms "Eastern" or "Persian" Armenia and "Turkish" or "Western" Armenia were soon coined by contemporary travelers, geographers, and historians.

For the next eight decades Eastern Armenia remained under the control of the Safavids, who divided it into two administrative units:

Chukhur-i Sa'ad, or the territory of Erevan and Nakhichevan; and Karabagh, formed from the combined regions of Karabagh, Zangezur (Siunik) and Ganja. Chukhur-i Sa'ad was composed of sections from the historic Armenian provinces of Ayrarat, Gugark, and Vaspurakan. Karabagh contained the ancient provinces of Artsakh and Siunik, while Ganja or Gandzak represented the historic Armenian province of Utik. The Safavids appointed two governors *(beglerbegi)* bearing the title of khan to rule the two units that fell under the general administrative supervision of the province of Azerbaijan.

Although the devastating wars that had ruined towns, destroyed monasteries, and decimated the population had ceased, the Armenians in Eastern Armenia periodically suffered under the misrule of their Muslim overlords, particularly during periods of weakness of the central government in Isfahan. A number of khans behaved like despots, leaving the Armenian and Muslim population little recourse save for prayers, bribes, and petitions. By the end of the seventeenth century, internal conditions in Persia encouraged the rise of Shi'i fundamentalism, which in turn made life for the Christian subjects more difficult. In the meantime, the economic influence of the Armenian merchants in Persia, Russia, and India had gradually begun a revival of a national consciousness among the higher clergy and the remnants of the landed aristocracy—the only leadership the Armenians still possessed. Realizing their military limitations, a number of Armenian emancipatory pioneers sought aid from Catholic Europe. Failing to receive concrete help from the West, at the start of the eighteenth century the Armenians turned to the rising star in the north. Religious, geographical, and political considerations made the Russian Empire the natural choice for the Armenians.

Russo-Armenian Relations
Prior to the Eighteenth Century

Russo-Armenian relations can be traced as far back as the tenth century, when Armenian merchants came into contact with Kievan Russia both via the Balkans and Byzantium, the Black and Caspian seas, as well as the Caucasus. Turkish and Mongol invasions of Armenia brought an exodus of refugees northward, and by the mid-thirteenth century Armenians had established colonies in the Crimea, Ukraine, and as far west as Poland. Armenians became so well known as traders that items in which they dealt became collectively known as "Armenian goods." In

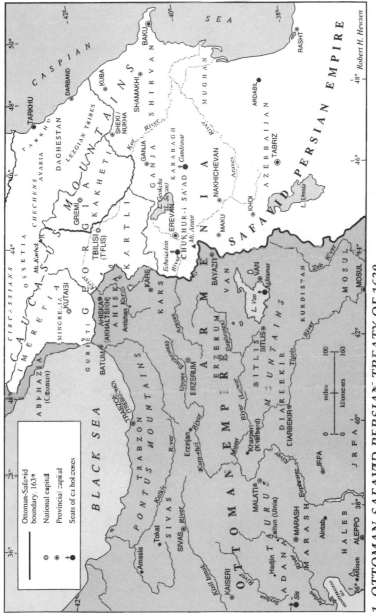

1. OTTOMAN-SAFAVID PERSIAN TREATY OF 1639

Robert H. Hewsen

SAFAVID PERSIAN EMPIRE

OTTOMAN EMPIRE

CASPIAN SEA

BLACK SEA

CAUCASUS MOUNTAINS

Legend:
Ottoman-Safavid boundary, 1639
National capital
Provincial capital
Seats of cat holicoses

RASHT
BAKU
TARKHU
DARBAND
KUBA
SHAMAKHI
SHIRVAN
SHEKI/NUKHA
ARDABIL
DAGHESTAN
LEZGIAN TRIBES
AVARIA
CHECHENS
KAKHETI
GREMI
TBILISI (TFLIS)
KARTLI
GANJA
KARABAGH
Gandzasar
MUGHAN
TABRIZ
AZERBAIJAN
KHOI
MAKU
NAKHICHEVAN
EREVAN
CHUKHUR-i SA'AD
L. Sevan
Gokcha
Mt. Ararat
L. Urmia
ARMENIA
Echmiadzin
BAYAZIT
VAN
L. Van
Aghtamar
KURDISTAN
Zab River
MOSUL
CIRCASSIANS
OSSETIA
Mt. Kazbek
IMERETIA
MINGRELIA
KUTAISI
GURIETI
ABKHAZIA (Tsoman)
BATUM
AHISKA (AKHALTSIKHE)
Ardahan
KARS
ERZERUM
Upper Euphrates River
Euphrates
ARARAT
BITLIS
MOUNTAINS
DIARBEKIR
Tigris River
PONTUS MOUNTAINS
TRABZON (TREBIZOND)
Kelkit River
Erzinjan
Kara-chai
Murat River (Lesser Euphrates)
Kharpert (Kharberd)
URFA
SIVAS
Tokat
Amasia
KAISERI
Kizil Irmak River
TAURUS
MALATIA
MARASH
Hadjin
Zeitun (Ulnia)
ADANA
Sis
Antioch
Seyhun River
Jeyhun
Aintab
ALEPPO
HALEB
JEZIRA
MEDITERRANEAN SEA

miles 0 100
kilometers 0 160

the fourteenth century a small Armenian trading colony settled in Moscow. A century later Armenian merchants were firmly established in that city, where they imported silk, horses, and precious stones and exported pelts and metals. Armenians were especially favored by the Mongol rulers and were permitted to trade throughout their domains in Russia, Persia, Central Asia, and China.

The sixteenth century witnessed a great expansion of Armenian trade activity in Russia and Poland. This was as a result of the Russian conquest of Kazan (1552) and Astrakhan (1556) from the Tatars, which allowed Russia control of the Volga River and access to the Caspian Sea. By the end of the sixteenth century, the Russians had reached the Caucasus and had established colonies along the Terek River. Stable trade routes were finally available between Europe and Asia, via Russia, which encouraged additional Armenian trading activity in the expanding Russian Empire. Responding to early overtures from a number of Georgian and Armenian leaders who wished an end to Perso-Turkish rivalry and its resulting devastation, Russian forces attempted to penetrate Transcaucasia. Their plans were abandoned, however, after several of their divisions were routed by the Muslim mountain tribes of Daghestan. The Russians retired beyond the Terek River.

In the second half of the seventeenth century, the Persian Armenian merchant community, which after its forced migration from Eastern Armenia at the beginning of the century had established a major international trade center in New Julfa, sought to take advantage of the favorable conditions in Persia and Russia and negotiated various trade agreements with the Russian state in the hope of increasing their trade. Astrakhan continued to be the starting point of this trade. Armenians who had built a church there in 1639 opened additional warehouses in that city. A few decades later the enormous profits from this commerce enabled the Armenian merchants to present Tsar Alexei Mikhailovich (1645-1676) with the Almazi (diamond) Throne in 1660. Such gifts resulted in the conclusion of a trade treaty (1667) between the Armenian merchants of New Julfa and the Russian throne, which granted them the monopoly of selling certain Persian goods, mainly silk, in Russia. By the third decade of the century, the Armenians had not only built a church in Moscow but had opened a tanning factory as well. At the same time a number of Armenians entered the Russian diplomatic service, and some Armenian artisans found employment at the Russian court. By the end of the seventeenth century, thanks to the safety and ease of travel and the benevolence of the Russian throne, Armenian colonies sprang up in the various commercial centers of Russia. The Russian Armenians not only prospered, but, like their Persian counterparts, they received privileges from the state. The right to construct and maintain their own churches and practice their religion freely, exemption from military service, citizenship, the right to build schools and establish printing presses, the right to join the diplomatic service, and even some degree of self-rule were lavished on the Armenians by the grateful tsars. Thus the Armenian trading colonies in Persia, Russia, India, and Western Europe were not only in close commercial contact with each other but, after centuries of isolation and foreign domination, their leadership was in a position to reflect on the political future for their people. Liberation from foreign, particularly Muslim, rule, autonomy, and even independence were their next goals.

Early Emancipatory Movements

Favorable political and economic conditions in Persia began to shift with the decline of the Safavid state in the late seventeenth century. The religious persecution and the ensuing economic deterioration once again reminded the Armenians of the precarious position of living under foreign domination. More Armenians emigrated to Russia and India with a newly stimulated quest for emancipation.

One of the motivating forces behind the emancipatory movement was the Armenian Church. The Armenian Holy See, which in the mid-fifteenth century had returned to Echmiadzin in Eastern Armenia, had periodically been a center of Armenian liberation activities. In the sixteenth century the first moves were made in the hope of receiving the support of the papacy and the cooperation of a European power to liberate Armenia. For a short time, the church even was ready to accept some form of papal authority and unite with Rome. Various missions and projects led by Catholicos Stepan Salmastetsi (Stephen of Salmast) in 1547, Catholicos Mikayel in 1562, and Catholicos Azaria Jughayetsi (Azaria of Julfa) in 1585 ended in empty promises and failure.

Such efforts were not limited to the clergy; laymen who may also be termed emancipatory pioneers participated as well and at times came closer to a successful outcome. The most notable efforts came from within the region of Karabagh and Zangezur. When the Safavids took control of Eastern Armenia, they came in contact with a number of small principalities in Karabagh which were ruled by local Armenian mountain chieftains called *meliks*. Realizing the impregnability of these mountain fortresses, the Safavids, like the Turkic and Mongol rulers before them, granted the *meliks* an autonomous status under Persian suzerainty. The five major principalities of Karabagh were Gulistan, Jraberd, Varanda, Khachen, and Dizak, which were ruled by the Beglarian, Israelian, Shahnazarian, Hasan-Jalalian, and Avanian families respectively. Several prominent *meliks* existed in Zangezur as well. The remoteness of that region had fostered a separate religious center in Gandzasar, with a number of prominent and active catholicoses and patriarchs. Rivalries among the *meliks* prevented them from becoming a formidable force against the Muslims, but unstable conditions in Persia eventually forced them to forgo their internal squabbles and join others in seeking aid from Europe.

In 1678 Catholicos Hakob Jughayetsi (Hakob of Julfa) (1655-1680) called for a secret meeting at Echmiadzin and invited several leading *meliks* and clergymen of Armenia. There he proposed to head a delegation to Europe in order to find a protecting power for the Armenians. After conferring with the ruler of Georgia, Erekle I (1688-1703), a seven-man mission proceeded to Constantinople. The catholicos died on the way and the group abandoned its plan. One of the delegates, a young man named Israel Ori, continued on, however. Ori, the son of Melik Haikazian of Zangezur proceeded to Venice and then France where he spent a number of years in the army of Louis XIV, rising to the rank of major. He fought the English, was captured and released, and later settled in Prussia as a merchant. He married and eventually entered the service of Prince Johann Wilhelm of the Palatinate before whom he laid his plan for an independent Armenia and to whom he offered the crown of a restored Armenian throne. The prince seems to have responded favorably, for he gave Ori letters addressed to the king of Georgia and the *meliks* of Armenia. Ori returned to his homeland in 1699.

A meeting of leading *meliks* and churchmen was called, but enthusiasm soon gave way to dissent when a number of leaders, led by Catholicos Nahapet of Edessa (Kuchak) (1691-1705), questioned the wisdom of possibly having to accept papal suzerainty. Nevertheless, a number of prominent *meliks* lent Ori their support and sent him back to Prussia. Johann Wilhelm, encouraged by Ori's return, suggested that he go to the court in Vienna and ask his overlord, Emperor Leopold, for aid. The emperor also showed interest in the Armenian project but pointed out how little could be accomplished without the cooperation of Russia, whose territory lay between Europe and Armenia.

Resolute, Ori continued on to Russia and in 1701 managed to receive an audience with Peter the Great (1689-1725). Peter, who had his own plans for the southern regions, immediately dispatched a delegation of his own to Armenia with letters to the catholicos regarding a proposed expedition against the Ottoman and Persian empires. The Russo-Swedish War, however, delayed the project and forced Ori to return to Europe. In 1704 he again returned to Russia and entered the service of Peter. After serving the tsar for a few years, he was given a military title and made special envoy to Persia in 1708. Ori was to assess the internal conditions of Persia and to solicit the aid of the Armenians in Isfahan for the Russian plan. When he finally arrived in Isfahan (1709), however, Persian suspicions as well as the intrigues on the part of the French envoy rendered his mission a failure. Ori left Persia and was on his way to St. Petersburg when he died at Astrakhan in 1711.

Eastern Armenia in the Early Eighteenth Century

Although nothing concrete came out of Ori's efforts, they were significant in that Armenian lay and religious leaders came in closer contact with the Russian state and began to see it as the natural ally of the Armenians. The further decline of the Safavids encouraged more Armenians to settle in Russia. By 1716 the Armenians enjoyed the protection of Peter the Great, and the Armenian Church was granted formal recognition when Archbishop Minas Tigranian was named Prelate of All Armenians in Russia, with his see in Astrakhan.

By the second decade of the eighteenth century, the Safavid Empire was in its last stages of collapse. The Georgians, the most effective military force in Persia, and Armenians, the major contributors to the economy, were both alienated by the actions of Shah Soltan Hosein, which had allowed the resurgence of Shi'i fundamentalism. In 1721 the Sunni subjects of the empire rebelled in the Caucasus and Afghanistan. When a number of Russian merchants were killed in Shirvan, the Russian governor of Astrakhan urged Peter to invade Persia. Peter, who had just concluded the Treaty of Nystad with Sweden and had ended his northern campaign, found the timing ideal and reactivated his armies. The fall of Isfahan to the Afghans (1722) and the promises of Armeno-Georgian cooperation assured the Russians' success. The Russian troops crossed the Terek and occupied Derbent, a major city on the Caspian Sea. Peter continued his drive south and gained control of the Caspian littoral. Meanwhile the Ottomans sent messages of protest to Peter, who, assuring them of his peaceful intentions, concentrated his forces along the Caspian and himself left the region returning to Astrakhan.

In order to assume control of Eastern Armenia and Georgia, as well as to safeguard these strategic neighboring provinces from Russia, the Turks violated the 1639 agreement and entered Transcaucasia in 1723. The Georgians sent urgent messages to Peter but Russia, fearing to antagonize the Ottomans, concentrated its effort on the Caspian coast. Russian assurances of support, however, had encouraged the Armenians to armed resistance, and, together with the Persians, they fiercely defended Erevan and Ganja. Although the Turks were successful in capturing those fortresses, as well as most of northeastern Persia in 1724, the Armenian region of Karabagh-Zangezur fought on. The Armenians there were armed and had found a formidable leader in the person of Davit Bek.

Not much is known about the early life of Davit, except that he had been in the service of Vakhtang VI, king of Georgia, and in 1722, together with a number of Armenian warriors in the service of Georgia, was sent to Zangezur at the request of the Armenian *meliks* who were being harassed by their Muslim neighbors. After defeating the Turkic tribal lords, Davit had to face the arrival of the Ottoman army in 1724. Gathering the Armenian forces, Davit Bek and another commander, Avan Yuzbashi, managed to wreak havoc on the Turks from their various mountain hideouts and fortresses, hoping all the time for the arrival of Russian troops. Russian forces, however, never reached Armenia, for Peter, not wanting to face another Russo-Turkish war, made peace with the Ottomans in 1724. Transcaucasia was divided between the Russians and the Turks, with Eastern Armenia and Georgia falling into the Turkish sector. The Armenians were abandoned. When Peter died a year later, Russia lost interest in Transcaucasia altogether. By 1725, with the exception of the armed resistance in Karabagh and Zangezur, the Turks were in full control of Eastern Armenia, where for the next decade they installed their own garrisons and governors in the major population centers. The fortress of Erevan served as the administrative headquarters of the Turkish pasha in charge of the region. Surrounded by hostile forces, Davit Bek, Mkhitar Sparapet, and the relatively small force of Armenian volunteers fought on despite heavy odds and loss of life. The *meliks* resumed their rivalries, and Davit Bek spent much of his efforts in keeping them united and loyal. Sources disagree on the date of Davit's death, which was sometime between 1726 and 1728, but he and his successors managed to keep much of the highlands in Armenian hands until the revival of Persia once again changed the political setup in Eastern Armenia.

The Reorganization of Eastern Armenia

Persia found a new champion in the person of Nader Khan Afshar, who aligned himself with the last Safavid prince and who managed to defeat the Turks, forcing their withdrawal to the 1639 boundaries in 1735. At the same time he also convinced the Russians, who had lost thousands of troops to disease in their bases along the Caspian, to withdraw from the region. By 1736 he was crowned Nader Shah, founding the Afshar dynasty. In response to the heroic defense by the Armenians, Nader recognized the autonomy of the *meliks* of Karabagh and rewarded them by recognizing Karabagh and Zangezur as semiautonomous enclaves. Catholicos Abraham Kretatsi (Abraham of Crete) had managed to befriend the shah, and Echmiadzin received various tax exemptions as well as other privileges. Soon after the region of Chukhur-i Sa'ad also was divided into the administrative units of Erevan and Nakhichevan. Hence by the second half of the eighteenth century, Eastern Armenia was composed of four khanates: Erevan, Nakhichevan (which included a number of settlements south of the Araxes River), Karabagh (which included Zangezur), and Ganja. To ensure the loyalty and obedience of the various Turkic tribes in Eastern Armenia, Nader took a number of hostages to Persia proper. The decade of wars and Turkish occupation, however, had resulted in additional Armenian migrations to Russia where the Empresses Anna and Elizabeth, in 1734 and 1744 respectively, extended Russian hospitality and once again encouraged the Armenians to settle in their realm, practice their religion, and enjoy the protection of the crown.

Eastern Armenia in the
Second Half of the Eighteenth Century

Nader's assassination (1747) once again caused the collapse of central authority and ushered in a struggle for succession among the various tribes of Persia. Nader's death also allowed some of the Turkic tribes to

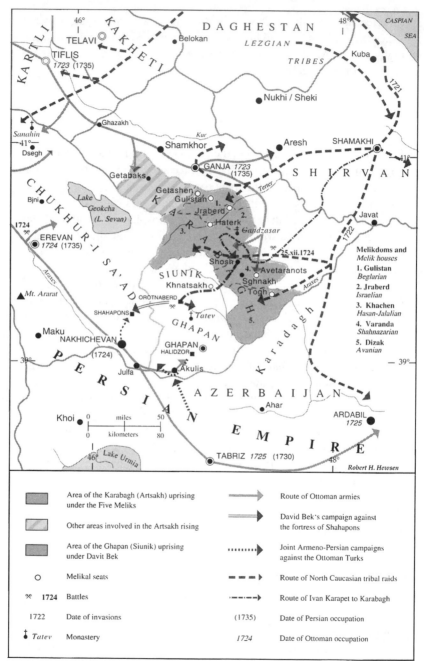

2. THE MELIKS OF KARABAGH DURING THE PERSIAN WAR OF PETER THE GREAT

Map labels:

KARTLI · KAKHETI · DAGHESTAN · CASPIAN SEA
TELAVI · Belokan · LEZGIAN · TRIBES
TIFLIS 1723 (1735) · Kuba
Sanahin 41° · Dsegh · Ghazakh · Kur · Nukhi / Sheki
Shamkhor · Aresh · SHAMAKHI
CHUKHUR-I-SA'AD · GANJA 1723 (1735) · SHIRVAN
Getabaks · Getashen · Gulistan
Bjni · Lake Geokcha (L. Sevan) · Jraberd · Haterk · Gandzasar · Javat
1724 · EREVAN 1724 (1735) · Terter · 25.xii.1724
Araxes · Shosh · Avetaranots
Mt. Ararat · SIUNIK · Khnatsakh · Sghnakh · Togh
SHAHAPONS · OROTNABERD · Tatev · GHAPAN · Araxes · Karadagh
Maku · NAKHICHEVAN (1724) · GHAPAN · HALIDZOR
Julfa · Akulis · AZERBAIJAN
Khoi · Ahar
ARDABIL 1725
P E R S I A N   E M P I R E
Lake Urmia · TABRIZ 1725 (1730)
Robert H. Hewsen

Melikdoms and Melik houses
1. Gulistan *Beglarian*
2. Jraberd *Israelian*
3. Khachen *Hasan-Jalalian*
4. Varanda *Shahnazarian*
5. Dizak *Avanian*

Legend:

- Area of the Karabagh (Artsakh) uprising under the Five Meliks
- Other areas involved in the Artsakh rising
- Area of the Ghapan (Siunik) uprising under Davit Bek
- ○ Melikal seats
- ✳ 1724 Battles
- 1722 Date of invasions
- ‡ *Tatev* Monastery
- Route of Ottoman armies
- David Bek's campaign against the fortress of Shahapons
- Joint Armeno-Persian campaigns against the Ottoman Turks
- Route of North Caucasian tribal raids
- Route of Ivan Karapet to Karabagh
- (1735) Date of Persian occupation
- 1724 Date of Ottoman occupation

reassert themselves in Eastern Armenia. The Qajars took control of their fiefs in Ganja, Erevan, and Nakhichevan, while the Javanshir tribe emerged once more in Karabagh. By allying himself with Melik Shahnazarian of Varanda, who at that time was warring with the other *meliks,* Panah Khan Javanshir and his son Ibrahim Khan managed to gain a foothold in the exclusively Armenian stronghold of Mountainous Karabagh. The Javanshirs soon allied themselves with Erekle II (1762-1798), the ruler of Eastern Georgia, and together they divided Eastern Armenia into their respective protectorates. More Armenians emigrated from the region and settled in Tiflis (present-day Tbilisi), the capital of Erekle, where they found royal favor in exchange for their trading abilities. Eventually a new leader in the person of Karim Khan Zand emerged in southwestern Persia. By 1762 he managed to subdue all of Persia and take a number of hostages from the khans of Erevan, Nakhichevan, Ganja, and Karabagh. Thus, until his death in 1779, Eastern Armenia and the rest of Transcaucasia tentatively remained under Persian suzerainty.

The reign of Catherine the Great (1762-1796) witnessed a major revival in Armenia-Russian ties. By the third quarter of the eighteenth century, Russia, which since the death of Peter the Great had generally ignored the Armenian struggle, renewed its interest in the Christians of Transcaucasia. Thus after her war with the Ottomans (1768-1774), Catherine, in 1778, in order to undermine the economy of the Turkish-controlled Crimea, relocated the Armenian community of that region to a new settlement along the Don River, which was named Nor (New) Nakhichevan (now incorporated into Rostov-on-Don). Her benevolent policy toward the Armenians in Russia during her reign enabled a number of Russian Armenian merchant families, some of whom had left New Julfa, to attain a substantial degree of economic as well as political power, particularly in Moscow and St. Petersburg. The most important of these was the Lazarev (Lazarian) family, who became active in Armenian emancipatory efforts and who later founded the Lazarev Institute of Oriental Languages in Moscow. Catherine's victories against the Turks and her interest in Transcaucasia reawakened the Armenian leadership there and once again encouraged clerics and laymen to seek Russian support in their struggle for autonomy.

Individuals such as Hakob Shemakhetsi, the merchants Agha Shahamir and Movses Baghramian of India, Movses Sarafov of Astrakhan, and the Lazarevs were among those who envisioned an autonomous Armenia under the protection of Russia. To this end they continuously petitioned Catherine and her advisors for support, promising financial and military aid in the event of a Russian invasion of Transcaucasia. Armenians continued to emigrate to Georgia, and especially Russia, where they distinguished themselves in the diplomatic and military service as well as in the mercantile and artisan communities. Armenian notables were regularly received at court, and new Armenian churches were constructed in Nor Nakhichevan and St. Petersburg.

A figure who exemplifies Armenian liberation aspirations in this period is Joseph Emin (1726-1809). An Indian Armenian whose family had immigrated from Persia, Emin, who had witnessed Britain's successful domination of India, became convinced that it was superior weapons and European strategy that had conquered Asia and that Armenians should learn Western techniques of warfare. He went to England, joined the British army, and rose to a position of some prominence where he found powerful friends in the persons of the Duke of Cumberland and Edmund Burke. Realizing, however, that little could be expected from the British, who generally favored the Muslims, Emin in 1761 went to Russia and began his campaign for the liberation of Armenia. He met Erekle II of Georgia and presented him with a plan for a joint Armeno-Georgian force trained by Emin in the latest Western methods. He also advocated the opening of modern schools and the reorganization of the feudal Georgian kingdoms into a new state under Russian protection. Although Erekle had solicited the protection of Russia, neither he nor the Armenian catholicos Simeon would risk an open rebellion against the Persians without concrete assurances from St. Petersburg. Catherine, who was at war with the Ottomans and who also was occupied with conflicts in Europe, did not venture to commit her troops against a war with Persia. Peter the Great's probe into the Caucasus had ended in disaster, and neither the Armenians nor the Georgians had substantial armed forces. Emin traveled all over Transcaucasia in the hope of gaining support for his plan but failed to stir the *meliks* or the leaders of the Church, who were not only divided and fighting the Javanshirs but who feared a repetition of the Russian betrayal during the time of Davit Bek. Disappointed, Emin left the region in 1768. The dream of an Armenian province under Russian protection had to await a later date.

The death of Karim Khan Zand in 1779 once again left Persia adrift among rival tribal chiefs. New Armeno-Georgian petitions and the prompting of the Potemkin family convinced Catherine to commit

Russia to a long-term presence in Transcaucasia. In 1783 she annexed the Crimea and by the Treaty of Georgievsk placed Eastern Georgia under the protection of Russia. The treaty, however, frightened the khans of Eastern Armenia and the Ottomans. With no stable government in Persia, the khans had begun to act as independent rulers vis-à-vis Georgia and their Armenian subjects. The arrival of a strong Christian force would rearrange the balance of power in the region. The Ottomans feared that the Russian presence in the region would encourage their own Armenian subjects to seek redress from centuries of injustice at the hands of corrupt administrators and would place the Russian forces close to their rear flank. The treaty angered Agha Mohammad Khan, the leader of the Qajar tribe, who was in the process of establishing a new dynasty in Persia. Agha Mohammad envisioned the revival of the Safavid Empire and sent angry messages to his "vassal" Erekle. For the moment the Qajar chief was occupied with defeating his enemies in Persia, but by 1794 he was ready to reclaim Persian possessions north of the Araxes. The khans of Eastern Armenia, save the khan of Karabagh, submitted without delay. Erekle's urgent messages of the impending attack on Georgia were not taken seriously by the Russians, however, and in 1795, after receiving a token submission from Ibrahim Khan of Karabagh, Agha Mohammad Khan entered Tiflis and ordered the infamous massacre, during which the Armenian minstrel Sayat Nova and many other Christians lost their lives. After taking thousands of slaves, the khan retreated south. Having reestablished the boundaries of the Safavid Empire, Agha Mohammad was crowned shah in 1796. Shocked by the sack of a Russian protectorate, Catherine declared war on Persia and ordered her troops to annex Eastern Armenia and the rest of Transcaucasia. Russian troops had well advanced into Transcaucasia and had taken the Khanate of Ganja when Catherine's death in 1796 ended the Russian campaign. Her son Paul, unhappy with his mother's policy and favorite generals, recalled the Russian force. The Christians now awaited the renewed wrath of the Qajar shah, but, as fate would have it, after the conquest of Karabagh, he was assassinated in Shushi in the same year. Persia was once again the thrown into the conflict of succession, the khans of Eastern Armenia and the rest of Transcaucasia renewed their autonomous activities, and the Armenians, who had come so close to liberation, were once more abandoned and left with shattered hopes.

Socioeconomic Conditions
in Eastern Armenia, 1639 to 1800

Eastern Armenia, located on a major international trade route, functioned as an important economic center under Safavid rule. Caravans
from China, Central Asia, India, and Persia crossed Eastern Armenia
on their way to the Ottoman and Russian empires. Erevan and
Nakhichevan served mainly as depots for goods transiting to the west
(Ottoman Empire and Western Europe), while Ganja became one of
the stopovers—via Georgia—for the trade with Russia. Good, safe
roads, uniformed tariffs, and comfortable caravansaries enriched the
region and the predominantly Armenian merchants. In addition to
goods from other regions, Eastern Armenia produced and exported
sizable quantities of wheat and silk (Karabagh and Ganja), dried fruit,
salt, hides, and copper (Erevan). Its large nomadic tribes were major
producers of wool and carpets.

The fall of the Safavids and the Turkish occupation of the region
halted most of the trade. Local warfare, unstable conditions, and the
departure of a significant number of Armenian merchants throughout
the remaining decades of the eighteenth century did little to revitalize
the once-prosperous region. It was only in the first decade of the
nineteenth century that Eastern Armenia was to regain some of its
economic importance, and that, as will be seen, came as a result of new
political developments.

The population of Eastern Armenia consisted of Muslims and
Armenians. The Muslims were themselves divided into Persians, Turks,
and Kurds, each element playing a distinct role in the region. The
Persians, the elite of the land, formed much of the administration and
part of the army; the Turkic groups were divided into settled and
semi-settled branches, with members from both groups forming the
balance of the army; while the Kurds led a traditional nomadic existence.
Thus a good part of the Muslim population of Eastern Armenia was
engaged in some sort of nomadism and utilized close to half of its
territory for that purpose. The settled Turkic groups and the majority of
the Armenians lived as peasants. Villages were divided into farming and
communal grazing areas in an open field and common pasture system.
The elders divided the agricultural plots according to the number of
animals and laborers in a family. The lands of large villages were farmed
communally, while in small settlements each plot was farmed by a single
family. Agricultural lands followed the two-field rotation system; half

the plot was planted, half left fallow. Oxen and wooden plows were used by farmers. Animal manure was not only necessary for replenishing the soil but, when dried, was used as fuel.

Irrigation was an important factor from the earliest of times. Scarcity of rain would normally have made for poor agriculture and scanty population; that the region was populous and an important food-producing area can be explained by the inhabitants' skill in irrigation, which had begun in the Urartu era nine centuries B.C. From the various rivers water was conducted to the fields by canals, which sometimes extended twenty or more miles. The water not only irrigated the fields and gardens, but turned the village mills.

The major crops grown in Eastern Armenia were wheat, barley, rice, cotton, millet, flax, beans, and various oil seeds. Other crops of importance were cochineal, which was the source of the highly prized red dye of Armenia, honey, beeswax, nuts, fruit, and silk. Numerous gardens and orchards in the region annually produced thousands of tons of fruit, various greens, and vegetables. A large variety of grapes assured the production of wines and raisins. The peasants consumed some of the produce and after taxes generally had a small surplus left to sell in the urban centers of Eastern Armenia. Life was on the frugal side, and although the peasants in Eastern Armenia lived better than most of their counterparts in Persia proper, few could afford luxury items. Bread, butter, yoghurt, and cheese, accompanied by various greens, was the usual diet. Rice and meat were reserved for holidays or special occasions. Few had beds; most slept on mats, and most utensils were made of wood. A large number of taxes and a complicated land tenure system collected the revenues and compensated the administrative officials.

In most villages large individual farms belonged to a single clan, the members of which lived together in one household. Usually the land of these clans could not be sold unless the family became too large or quarreled among themselves. The family organization was patriarchal. The sons all inherited equal shares; the daughters were sometimes allotted half of a son's share. If a daughter married during her parents' lifetime, as commonly happened, she forfeited any inheritance and received only a dowry. The eldest male headed the clan. He was called *aqa* or *arbab* in Persian, *tanmets* or *tanuter* in Armenian, and his word was final in any argument. Armenian as well as Muslim women did not speak in the presence of men or strangers (even at home) and were usually secluded or veiled. They did not venture outside the house or farm, except to visit the baths. Apart from religion and customs concerning marriage and divorce, there were few differences between Muslim and Armenian family life. Age-old habits, prejudices, and superstitions were equally shared by both groups.

By the end of the eighteenth century, the Armenian population of the territory had shrunk considerably. Centuries of warfare and invasions combined with the tyranny of local khans had forced the emigration of the Armenians. It is probable that until the seventeenth century, the Armenians still maintained a majority in Eastern Armenia, but the forced relocation of some 250,000 Armenians by Shah Abbas and the numerous exoduses described in this chapter had reduced the Armenian population considerably. The census conducted by the Russians in 1830-1831 indicates that by the nineteenth century Armenians of Erevan and Nakhichevan formed 20 percent of the population. The Armenians of Ganja had also been reduced to a minority. Only in the mountain regions of Karabagh and Zangezur did the Armenians manage to maintain a solid majority. The Armenian population was generally concentrated in the fortress cities of Erevan, Nakhichevan, Ganja (later Elisavetpol, Kirovabad, now Ganja), Shushi (Shusha), Sardarabad, and in the villages surrounding the town of Vagharshapat, which contained the Holy See of Echmiadzin.

The four khanates which formed Eastern Armenia were all divided into districts *(mahals)* and had a sizable bureaucracy. Although a small fortress town, Erevan was the main city of Eastern Armenia. Located on the plain of Ararat, the city was composed of three sections, which themselves were subdivided into ten subsections, or *mahalles.* The plan of the city was much like that of other urban centers of Eastern Armenia and Persia, with distinct commercial and residential sections. The numerous shops in the traditionally covered bazaar were surrounded a mosque, bath, and caravansary. This complex formed the nucleus of the city, where all important events occurred and all business was transacted. The various city officials, tradesmen, and artisans gathered there daily to pray, work, wash, collect dues, sell or buy wares, drink coffee or tea, and smoke their water pipes. Muslim and Christian religious functionaries, supported by donations and taxes, served their respective communities and were concentrated in the urban centers. Education and many of the social services were handled by the religious hierarchy and institutions of both groups.

Numerous Muslim and Armenian artisans lived in the fortress cities of Eastern Armenia. Since the Christians were considered "unclean," the Muslims generally controlled the preparation of food and personal services. Although some professions had an equal number of Muslims and Armenians, the highly skilled professions were dominated by Armenians. In the rural areas almost all the crafts were controlled by Armenians. Excepting the smallest trades, all urban tradesmen and artisans were organized into guilds, or as they were called in Transcaucasia, *hamkar*. Most guilds were divided along religious as well as professional lines. These guilds functioned to maintain a monopoly over a product or service. They also managed to control the market, so that each member could be assured a livelihood, to insure quality and to establish minimum prices, to serve as a welfare organization, and to act as a pressure group in protecting the interests of their members. A complex system of cooperation as well as of apprentices, journeymen, and masters governed the entire system.

With the advent of the nineteenth century, Persia once again achieved relative stability when the Qajars consolidated their power and aspired to re-create the Safavid Empire. Russian interests in Transcaucasia forced the attention of the Qajars to stabilize Eastern Armenia and to assure the cooperation of its Christian inhabitants. Qajar commanders were sent to Erevan, Nakhichevan, and Ganja, while the heir-presumptive, Abbas Mirza, controlled the adjacent province of Azerbaijan. Eastern Armenia thus once again assumed an important defensive and offensive position, while the Armenian Church inadvertently became involved in the upcoming conflict in Transcaucasia.

The Role of the Armenian
Church in the Russo-Persian Conflict

The Safavid state from its inception had sought the cooperation of the Armenian leadership and the Armenian Church. By the end of the seventeenth century, the Russians also began to consider an alliance with the Armenians crucial for their future expansion. Russo-Armenian relations and the pleas for Russian aid in the eighteenth century gave Russia high hopes of recruiting Armenian support. Since the Armenians lacked a national government or leader, the Russians regarded the church leadership to be spokesmen of the people.

The Armenian Church had assumed political leadership of the Armenian people as early as the fall of the last Armenian kingdom in Cilicia (1375). This was especially true after the fifteenth century, when the Muslims emerged as the only power in the Middle East, for Islam recognized the representatives of certain religious groups as the leaders of their people. Within the Armenian Church, the catholicos, or supreme patriarch, who, as elected by religious and lay members of the community, came to be regarded by the Muslims as the spiritual and political head—and inaccurately referred to as the "caliph"—of the Armenian people. As previously mentioned, Echmiadzin had lain in Persian-controlled territory since 1639, and Persia, in exchange for the commercial success of the Armenian merchants, had granted the Armenian Church numerous privileges. The Church was not only free from taxation but could own endowed property, and its members could travel without restrictions, permits, or road tolls. The shahs in various decrees always addressed the catholicos as the leader of the Armenians. The church thus became the tax collector of the community for the Persian throne, petitioned for Armenian interests before their rulers, and represented these interests in the Islamic courts of law. By the eighteenth century the church had gained considerable wealth and power and had invested most of its capital in land, the basic source of income in a preindustrial society. The church bought, rented, and received as bequests large plots of land in Eastern Armenia and received a percentage of the produce of these lands from the peasants who lived there.

The fall of the Safavids weakened the church and threatened their various monasteries and possessions, which were spread all over the four khanates. Without the protection of the throne, the church was on its own and suffered economic losses during the Turkish occupation of Eastern Armenia. Catholicos Abraham Kretatsi, as noted, managed to obtain major concessions from Nader Shah, but it was not until the second half of the eighteenth century that the See of Echmiadzin began to regain some of its earlier stature, thanks mainly to the efforts of Catholicos Simeon Erevantsi (1763-1780), one of the most energetic patriarchs of the modern era. Erevantsi conducted a precise cadastral survey of church property, founded a seminary, established a printing press at Echmiadzin, constructed a paper mill, began the church archives (now incorporated into the Matenadaran archives in Erevan), and revised the liturgical calendar. He petitioned the Muslim courts to regain usurped church property and, thanks to the benevolent rule of Karim Khan Zand, generally obtained favorable rulings. His successor, Ghukas Karnetsi (1780-1799), formed a permanent council of bishops to assist the patriarch, thus distributing some of his power and indirectly contributing to the rise of future factionalism. Ghukas's death at the end of the century coincided with the renewed Persian and Russian interest in

Transcaucasia and of their active solicitation for the support of the Armenians and their church.

The election of the catholicos on the eve of the nineteenth century was one of the most hotly contested. The main candidates were archbishops Eprem Dzorageghtsi (Ephrem of Dzoragegh), Davit Enegetsi, Daniel Surmaretsi, and Iosif Argutinskii (Hovsep Arghutian). Eprem was supported by the conservative faction of the council, who favored a church free from political consideration. Davit was favored by the Persians. Daniel, who was the patriarch of Constantinople, was a popular choice of the Armenians in Erevan—although few believed he would leave the glamor of the city on the Bosporus for the dusty village of Vagharshapat. Iosif, whose family had been pro-Russian and who was the prelate of the Armenians in Russia, was naturally supported by the Russians.

The Russians and their supporters in Echmiadzin, led by Bishop Nerses Ashtaraketsi, hoped that Iosif would be conferred. Long an advocate of the Russian annexation of Armenia, Iosif was related to Russian nobility and had powerful friends in St. Petersburg. With Persia involved in the turmoil of succession, Russia and its supporters had a good opportunity to maneuver their candidate into position. Davit was immediately bypassed and Daniel was asked to decline his candidacy. As an added measure, the Russian envoy to Constantinople pressured the Sublime Porte to convince Daniel to stay in the Ottoman Empire. Eprem was offered Iosif's position as prelate and also declined to be nominated. Thus, after a year of political machinations, Iosif Argutinskii was elected Catholicos and Russia felt sufficiently sure of its dominant role in Transcaucasia to annex Eastern Georgia. In early 1801 Iosif left Nor Nakhichevan for Echmiadzin, where he was officially to take his position as Catholicos of All Armenians. The history of Eastern Armenia and the Holy See of Echmiadzin might have been different had Iosif not fallen ill and died in Tiflis. Since he had not been consecrated there was no need to observe the customary period of mourning, and the election process resumed immediately. Although Daniel remained a strong candidate, the Persians, who by now had resolved their dynastic dispute in favor of Fath Ali Shah, the nephew of Agha Mohammad Khan, favored Davit, the pro-Persian candidate. Thus when Daniel was elected catholicos in 1801, Davit, supported by the Persian khan, usurped his seat. For the next six years there were technically two catholicoses (with Davit at Echmiadzin and Daniel at Diadin), which caused bitter feelings among many Armenians, who, unhappy with the despotic rule of the khans in the region, now had no avenue of petition.

Russian Annexation of Eastern Armenia

At the start of the nineteenth century, Russia, for the third and last time since the reign of Peter the Great, began to move beyond the Caucasus. As discussed earlier, Russia not only involved itself in the affairs of the Armenian Church but in 1801 annexed Georgia outright, a territory that technically was under the suzerainty of Persia. The Russian advance, however, was met with an unexpected response; Persia after a decade of internal chaos had firmly consolidated under the Qajar dynasty and, led by a few capable commanders, initiated a variety of defensive and offensive measures.

Following the Russian annexation of Georgia, its royal family of Georgia was exiled (Alexander, one of the Georgian princes, escaped to Persia and joined the war against Russia) and was replaced by a Russian administration. In 1804 Russia, under the pretext that Ganja belonged to the Georgians, invaded that territory and sparked the first Russo-Persian War (1804-1813). General Pavel Tsitsianov, Russian commander of the Caucasus, received important help from the Armenians of Ganja and Karabagh, who had waited so long for the arrival of the Russians and who had been maltreated by the local khans. Early in 1804 Tsitsianov managed to penetrate half of Eastern Armenia and marched on to Erevan. The local population, especially the Armenians, dissatisfied with the incompetent and corrupt governors, was ready to aid the Russians. A large Persian army arrived in time and stymied Russian efforts. Tsitsianov withdrew from Erevan, annexed two northern districts of the khanate, and until his death in 1806 concentrated his efforts on other fronts. A number of Armenian families, tired of Persian tyranny, left with the Russians and settled in Tiflis. Although the Russians had taken Karabagh and Ganja by 1806, the death of Tsitsianov, the war with Napoleon in Europe, and the conflict with the Ottomans left a lull in the Russo-Persian War and caused the Russians to slow their advances and maintain the status quo. Moreover, Tsitsianov's replacement, General Ivan Gudovich, lacked his predecessor's nerve and bided his time in Tiflis. It is important to note, however, that from 1806 onward the periphery of Eastern Armenia, or the khanates of Ganja and Karabagh, had thus become part of Russian-occupied lands. Part of the Armenian population of these khanates, especially some of the *meliks,* had fled the region during the rise of the Javanshirs and their penetration into the mountains. Others had left the area during the campaigns of Agha Mohammad Khan and had settled in

Tiflis and the Georgian-controlled districts of Kazakh and Shamshadin. The division in the church and lack of leadership and arms also hampered the Armenians from taking advantage of the occupation and regaining political control of these historic Armenian lands. Karabagh and Ganja tentatively remained Russian-occupied territories, and since the fate of the war was not clear, no political decision was made. This partition of Eastern Armenian was to have major consequences in the future, problems that continue to this day in Karabagh.

Russian inactivity allowed the Persians time to reorganize. In 1807, in the Polish city of Finkenstein, Persia signed a treaty with France by which Napoleon became an ally, sending Persia military hardware and technical advisors. Under the guidance of the energetic and capable heir-apparent, Abbas Mirza, the Persians began to modernize their forces and build new fortresses. In the meantime, Persian leaders tried to end Armenian and local sympathies toward Russia or at least to neutralize them. A new capable governor, Hosein Quli Khan Qajar (whose title was *sardar*, or military commander) and other responsible administrators were appointed in Erevan and Nakhichevan (1807), which became the centers of the Persian counteroffensives in the region. The first act of the new governor was to welcome Daniel as the catholicos-elect. When Daniel died in 1808, the Persians did not hesitate to confirm Eprem, even though he was the prelate of the Armenians in Russia.

Hosein Quli Khan realized that Armenian support was very important to the well-being of the two khanates in Armenia left under Persian control. Armenian merchants and craftsmen were important for the economy of the region, and a satisfied Armenian and Muslim population would give the lie to the Russian claim of liberating them from tyranny. A number of social and economic reforms were carried through hastily, especially after the Treaty of Tilsit (1807) between Napoleon and Tsar Alexander I of Russia invalidated the Finkenstein agreement. The benevolent policy of the new Persian administration bore some fruit, as there was little enthusiasm for the Russians during General Gudovich's march on Erevan in 1808. The Russians did not succeed in penetrating the fortress of Erevan and suffered a humiliating retreat. A number of Armenian families, fearing a return of the Muslim repression, left with Gudovich for Georgia. Thus the Armenian population of Eastern Armenia was shrinking while that of Georgia was increasing. The next ten years were extremely beneficial for the Armenians of Erevan, however. The church and the Armenian leadership were given numerous privileges, and Safavid land grants that had lapsed or had been usurped during the long period of chaos were reaffirmed by the Persian administration. The relatively competent administration tried, and succeeded to some degree, to rejuvenate the socioeconomic life of this part of Eastern Armenia. By the second decade of the nineteenth century, these efforts resulted in one-fourth of all Persian exports, valued at more than a quarter of a million pounds sterling, to pass through Erevan. It is important to remember, however, that although living conditions did improve, these reforms came too late, were mainly as a result of the Russian threat, and solely affected the region of Erevan.

The Russian treaty with the French forced the British to reexamine Persia's strategic location, and an envoy was dispatched to Tehran to negotiate with the Persians. Since France had essentially abandoned Persia, the shah accepted British aid, which brought funds, arms, and British military advisors to Persia. British officers completed the fortifications begun by the French and continued to train Persia's new army in Persian Azerbaijan and Eastern Armenia. The Russo-Ottoman War of 1806-1812, the Russian conflict with Sweden and England, and the raids by the Daghestani tribes on the Russian garrisons in the Caucasus gave the Persians ample time to reorganize their forces. Napoleon's invasion of Russia left the army in Transcaucasia without reinforcement and vulnerable to Persian attack. The sardar of Erevan contemplated an alliance with the Ottomans, but when a Persian Kurd killed a Turk during the negotiations, talks broke off. The Russians were nevertheless pinned down by Persian raiding parties, and once again the Armenians were instrumental in defending Ganja and especially Karabagh and saving the Russian garrisons from total destruction. A Russo-British rapprochement and eventual alliance (1812) brought about most British advisors and greatly reduced British support for Persia at this crucial time. Soon thereafter the Treaty of Bucharest (1812) ended the Russo-Ottoman conflict and Persia was left to face the Russians alone. The newly formed Persian troops fought well, and although they lost a number of crucial battles, they were not ready to concede the war. The British, now an ally of Russia, had no need to continue their large subsidies and strongly advised the shah to sue for peace or lose all support. They offered to act as intermediaries and to aid Persia in negotiating a fair settlement. Left with no other alternative, the Persians signed the Treaty of Gulistan (1813) by which they ceded all the territory north of the Araxes and the Kura rivers except for Erevan and Nakhichevan. In addition, they renounced their claims to Georgia and Daghestan.

The Russians became the masters of half the territory of Eastern Armenia, but neither they nor the Armenian leadership did anything to combine Karabagh and Ganja and make it an Armenian enclave. The divided Armenian leadership was concentrated in Tiflis, Erevan, and Echmiadzin. Everyone's immediate concern was the liberation of the khanates of Erevan and Nakhichevan. Having no crystal ball, none realized the terrible future consequences of their laxity. Thus the fate of Karabagh and Ganja was left to the Russian administrators, who incorporated Ganja into the Georgian province, while Karabagh was combined with the khanates of Baku, Sheki, Kuba, and Shirvan to form the Muslim provinces of Transcaucasia. A son of Ibrahim Khan Javanshir and a Russian military governor were put in charge of Karabagh and ruled in Shushi.

The Persian defeat slowly renewed their mistrust of the Armenian population. A number of Persian leaders blamed the Armenians for their losses in Karabagh and Ganja. Abbas Mirza, a major supporter of the Armenians, had to struggle to maintain his popularity in the face of defeat, especially since he had pushed Westernization against the advice of the Muslim religious hierarchy. The situation worsened when, in 1814, Nerses Ashtaraketsi, Catholicos Eprem's assistant, left for Tiflis as the new Armenian archbishop. There he openly began to organize anti-Persian activities and petition the Russians to complete the liberation of Eastern Armenia. The next ten years can be viewed as the nadir in Armeno-Persian relations. Erevan's administration ceased its protection of the Church, and Armenian property was usurped and taxes increased. The situation became so intolerable that the catholicos left Echmiadzin and sought refuge in an Armenian monastery under Russian control on the Armeno-Georgian border. Since he had not resigned, no other catholicos could be elected, and the affairs of the Church were left in limbo. This action hindered the Persians from taking away certain disputed endowments (although some were seized anyway), but it left the Armenians with virtually no leadership and even more at the mercy of their enemies. Hasan Khan, the brother of Hosein Quli Khan of Erevan, was especially wary of the Christians and lost little opportunity to harass them with his cavalry and to extort tribute whenever possible. Some Muslim officials followed his example and tried to usurp Armenian property. Others hoped to amass their fortunes, by milking both their Armenian and Muslim subjects, and to depart to safer provinces in the interior. More Armenians abandoned Erevan and Nakhichevan and settled in Georgia or in Persian Azerbaijan.

By 1825 the Persian leadership was ready to resume war with Russia. The Armenian secular chief of Erevan, Sahak Melik Aghamalian, whose daughter was married to Prince Alexander of Georgia, an ardent enemy of Russia, was asked to solicit Armenian cooperation. Taxes were reduced and some usurped property was returned in the hope of enticing Eprem to return to his see. Eprem refused and the Armenian population, tired of years of war and promises, remained generally aloof.

Since neither side was pleased with the Gulistan agreement, it was just a matter of time before new hostilities erupted. The Russians viewed the Persian presence near their main administrative base at Tiflis as a major threat, and the Persians felt their prestige in Central Asia and other regions would suffer if they let their Muslim population remain under Russian rule. Abbas Mirza wished to convince his detractors of his prowess as a commander and assure himself the future throne of Persia. Taking advantage of the death of Alexander I and the Decembrist uprising in Russia (1825), the Persians invaded Karabagh and Shuragol early in 1826 and began the second Russo-Persian War (1826-1828). The Persians, who had caught the Russians off guard, scored initial victories. The local Muslim population heeded the call of *jihad* (holy war) and rose in rebellion in Ganja and Karabagh, but the Armenians once again stood fast by the Russian garrisons. General Alexei Ermolov vacillated for fear of leaving Tiflis undefended. The new Russian tsar, Nicholas I, who mistrusted Ermolov, soon replaced him with General Ivan Paskevich, who arrived with large reinforcements and artillery. In a few months the superior Russian forces bombarded and captured the Persian fortresses in Abbasabad, Ordubad, Sardarabad, Nakhichevan, and eventually Erevan. When the Russians crossed the Araxes and threatened Tabriz, capital of the Persian Azerbaijan province, the Persians sued for peace and signed the Treaty of Turkmenchai (1828). The khanates of Erevan and Nakhichevan, or the rest of Eastern Armenia, now became part of Russia, and the Araxes River became, and remains, the border between the two countries (today the border with the Republic of Armenia). The treaty, in addition, awarded Russia an indemnity of 20 million rubles, exclusive naval rights in the Caspian Sea, and other economic and political prerogatives in Persia, which exposed the Qajars to Russian manipulation.

The outbreak of the war fulfilled the dreams of Nerses Ashtaraketsi, who hoped that Eastern Armenia, with Russian aid, would finally gain autonomy. A major emancipatory figure, Nerses was born in 1771 in the village of Ashtarak in the Erevan province. He became involved in the internal politics of Echmiadzin and was convinced that Armenian hopes lay with the Russians. He was raised to the rank of bishop by Catholicos Ghukas and played an important role in the election of Iosif Argutinskii. He was made archbishop and had disagreements with Eprem who advocated a more conservative course. Angered by the passivity of the catholicos, Nerses left for Tiflis, where he hoped to convince the Russians to complete their annexation of Eastern Armenia. A decade later he founded the Nersisian Academy in Tiflis, a school where later a number of nineteenth-century Armenian intellectuals and nationalists were to receive their Armenian reawakening and education.

During the second Russo-Persian War, Nerses designed an Armenian national banner and gathered some 1,000 Armenian volunteers under such leaders as Harutiun Alamdarian and Grigor Manucharian. Although the Armenian units were not a major force and did not change the course of the war, they were nonetheless instrumental in a number of pitched battles, especially in Oshakan, Ashtarak, and Echmiadzin, where a small number of local Armenians joined them. Nerses followed the Russian army to Echmiadzin and, citing the Armenian contributions to the Russian victory, began an immediate campaign for the restoration of an Armenian homeland under the supervision of the church and the protection of Russia. He realized, however, that a large part of the Armenian population had gradually left Eastern Armenia and that the Armenians had become a minority in much of the land. He therefore set out to convince the Russian commanders and diplomats to include the Armenian repatriation in their talks with the Persians. Largely because of his efforts and the support of the pro-Armenian groups in Russian military and diplomatic circles, that idea was formally incorporated into article 15 of the Treaty of Turkmenchai, which allowed population transfers across the Araxes River for a specific period. Some 30,000 Armenians were encouraged to repatriate from northern Persia. Soon after, at the conclusion of the Russo-Turkish War (1828-1829), this same policy was instrumental in bringing another 25,000 Armenians from Western Armenia into Erevan and Nakhichevan. An equal number of Persians, Kurds, and Turkmen left Eastern Armenia for Persia and the Ottoman Empire. Thus, after more than a hundred years, the Armenian population in parts of Eastern Armenia slightly surpassed that of the Muslims. These migrations began a trend that continued after the Crimean War (1853-1856) and the Russo-Turkish War of 1877-1878, and finally created a solid Armenian majority in a part of the Armenian homeland—a development that was later to have great political significance.

Those Armenian leaders, both secular and ecclesiastic, who had envisioned an autonomous Armenia under the benevolent Russian guidance were somewhat disappointed, for both Nicholas I and Paskevich were conservatives who advocated russifying all the non-Russian areas of the empire and bringing them under the control of the central administration. Although Nerses was decorated for his efforts, he was immediately "promoted" to the position of Armenian prelate of Novorossisk and Bessarabia and removed from the Caucasus. Eprem found Russian policies too burdensome and resigned (1830) and the new catholicos, Hovhannes, supported the Russian policy. A few years later the Russians enacted a set of rules and regulations known as the *Polozhenie,* which regulated the power of the church far more than the Persians had ever attempted. As a concession to the Armenians and their supporters, the territory of Erevan and Nakhichevan was for a short time (1828-1840) renamed the *Armianskaia Oblast'* (Armenian Province), creating an illusion of semiautonomy. Karabagh and Ganja, however, still remained outside this province and were placed in the Georgian-Imeretian and Caspian provinces respectively. By 1840 even the simple title of "Armenian Province" was too much for the centralists at St. Petersburg, and was removed. The numerous administrative reorganizations that followed did little to fashion Eastern Armenia into what its leaders had envisioned and the region became simply known as Russian Armenia.

Initially, following the Russian conquest, socioeconomic conditions in Eastern Armenia deteriorated. The new administration was unfamiliar with the region and relied heavily on the Muslim officials and landlords. Trade declined and taxes were increased, but in time Russian administrative reforms slowly brought Eastern Armenia into the fold of the empire and the Armenians began to benefit from their greater contact with Russia. New political and social ideas from Russia exposed some Armenians to the intellectual life of the West. At the same time, however, Eastern Armenia lost its strategic and commercial significance and became a backwater of the Russian Empire. Its most influential and talented citizens immigrated to Tiflis, Baku, Moscow, St. Petersburg, and other urban centers of the empire. Nonetheless, Eastern Armenia, mainly as the result of the new concentration of Armenians and to the continued presence of the Holy See had emerged as a distinct geoplotical entity. It was in this little corner that ultimately the survivors of massacres and deportations would find the determination to begin a new chapter in the history of the Armenian people.

FOR FURTHER INFORMATION

For the sources of, or more information on, the material in this chapter, please consult the following (full citations can be found in the Bibliography at the end of this volume).

Bournoutian, 1983, 1992, 1994.

Busse, 1972.

*The Cambridge History of
Iran,* vol VII.

Emin, 1918.

Gregorian, 1972.

Hovannisian, 1967.

Kazemzadeh, 1974.

Lockhart, 1938, 1958.

4

EASTERN ARMENIANS UNDER TSARIST RULE

Ronald Grigor Suny

Russian Annexations and the Armenians

For nearly a century, from the 1730s until 1828, Eastern Armenia was once again dominated by the Persians. When the empire of the shahs was prosperous and ruled by men of ability, the Armenians and Muslims who lived around Erevan, in Karabagh or Nakhichevan, were ruled directly by Persian officials, but at other times, when the Persian Empire was weak or under attack, the local Caucasian peoples enjoyed a modicum of autonomy or recognized the authority of the Georgian king, Erekle II (1744-1798). Many Armenians, among them wealthy businessmen and merchants, lived in Georgia itself, most of them in its capital, Tiflis (Tbilisi), and enjoyed the protection of the king. Because the Georgians were primarily a rural people, peasants and nobles living in the countryside, the overwhelming majority in the city of Tiflis was Armenian. This Armenian middle class was involved in small handicraft production, local trade, and the lucrative transit trade from Persia to Russia. The silks and other goods that flowed northward through the hands of Armenian middlemen were known to the Russians as *armianskie tovary* (Armenian goods), and the first prevalent image of Armenians in the Christian empire north of the Caucasus was that of the wily merchant.

Besides the important Armenian colony in Georgia, there were influential communities in Astrakhan at the mouth of the Volga, Armavir in the North Caucasus, Nor Nakhichevan near the Russian town of Rostov-on-Don, and in the Crimean towns of Karasubazar, Staryi Krym, and Theodosia (Feodosiia). Still farther away from the Armenian heartland were clusters of Armenians in Bessarabia, Lvov and other parts of Poland, and in the Russian capitals, Moscow and St. Petersburg. Though these communities were only loosely connected with one another, most of them felt some allegiance to the Armenian Apostolic Church, headed by the catholicos in Echmiadzin, then still in Persian territory. Beginning in the eighteenth century, many Armenians in Georgia and in the peripheries of the Russian Empire looked northward to the Orthodox tsars for political protection. In 1763 the Armenians of Astrakhan received a special charter and were permitted to form the first Armenian Apostolic diocese in Russia. The empress Catherine II (1762-1796), eager to use the purported entrepreneurial talents of the Armenians, in 1779 invited Crimean Armenians to settle within her empire. The migrants founded Nor Nakhichevan and were given special tax privileges. When the Crimea was annexed to Russia in 1783 after one of the series of Russo-Turkish wars, those privileges were extended to Armenians on the peninsula. Long in contact with Italian and Greek traders, the Armenians of the Black Sea coast were among the most Westernized and cosmopolitan of their countrymen. In their enthusiasm for things European, many Crimean Armenians had abandoned the Armenian Church and embraced Catholicism.

In 1801 Russia annexed the eastern Georgian kingdom (Kartli-Kakheti) and began a three-decade campaign to bring the rest of Transcaucasia under its rule. From 1804 to 1813 Russia fought with Persia over Azerbaijan, and in 1806 the Caspian port of Baku was captured. Determined to hold on to his Caucasian provinces, the shah appointed the loyal and able Hosein Quli Khan to become khan of Erevan (1807-1827). Hosein's efforts to improve relations with the Armenian Church, fortify Erevan, and develop the economy of the region won him support among the local population, the majority of which was Muslim. A Russian attempt to seize Erevan in 1808 failed, but in the Treaty of Gulistan, which ended the first Russo-Persian War (1804-1813), the Persians gave up territory in Karabagh, Shirvan, Daghestan, Talysh, Lori, Kuba, Sheki, Baku, and Ganja, as well as their claims to Eastern Georgia. Large Armenian populations came under Russian rule, but Erevan and Nakhichevan remained khanates within the Persian Empire.

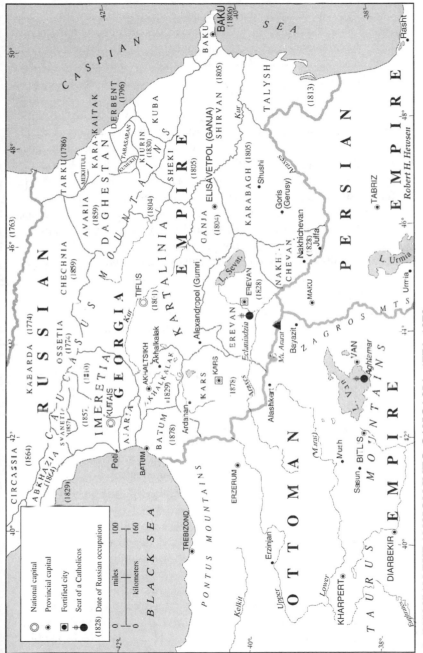

3. RUSSIAN EXPANSION INTO CAUCASIA, 1774–1878

Robert H. Hewsen

CASPIAN SEA

BLACK SEA

RUSSIAN EMPIRE

PERSIAN EMPIRE

OTTOMAN EMPIRE

CIRCASSIA (1864)

ABKHAZIA (1829)

KABARDA (1774)

OSSETIA (1774)

CHECHNIA (1859)

AVARIA (1859)

DAGHESTAN

TARKU (1786)

DERBENT (1796)

KARA-KAITAK

TABASARAN

MEKHTULI

KUBA

KIURIN (1830)

KAZIKUMUKH

SHEKI

SHIRVAN (1805)

BAKU (1806)

TALYSH (1813)

GEORGIA

IMERETIA

SVANETIA (1857)

AJARIA

SAMTZKHE (1810)

KARTALINIA

KUTAIS

TIFLIS (1811)

ELISAVETPOL (GANJA)

GANJA (1804)

KARABAGH (1805)

Shushi

Goris (Gerusy)

Nakhichevan (1828)

Julfa

NAKH-CHEVAN

MAKU

L. Urmia

Urmia

TABRIZ

Alexandropol (Gumri)

Akhalkalak

AKHALTSIKH

Akhalkalak (1829)

KARS (1878)

Ardanan

Ardanan

BATUM (1828)

Poti

BATUM

L. Sevan

EREVAN (1828)

Etchmiadzin

M. Ararat

Bayazit

Alashkar

Kars

Erzerum

VAN

Aghtamar

L. Van

SASUN

BITLIS MOUNTAINS

Mush

ZAGROS MTS

PONTUS MOUNTAINS

TREBIZOND

Erzinjan

Kelkit

TAURUS MOUNTAINS

KHARPERT

DIARBEKIR

Upper

Lower Euphrates

Murat

Kur

Araxes

Araxes

Kur

Rasht

0   100   160 miles
0   kilometers

50° 48° 46° 44° 42° 40° 38°

Relations between Armenians and Persians in the Erevan khanate soured after the Treaty of Gulistan, and several important Armenian leaders promoted a pro-Russian orientation. In 1814 the influential clergyman Nerses Ashtaraketsi left Echmiadzin to become archbishop of Tiflis, and there he engaged in agitation against the Persians. In 1822, Catholicos Eprem moved to Karabagh, already under Russian suzerainty. When a second Russo-Persian War (1826-1828) broke out, Nerses urged young Armenians to join the Russian military campaign against Persia and free their countrymen and homeland. Armenian volunteer brigades were formed. On October 1, 1827, Russian and Armenian forces under the overall command of General Ivan Paskevich took the fortress of Erevan, and on February 10, 1828, the Treaty of Turkmenchai ceded Erevan and Nakhichevan to the Russians. The border between Russia and Persia was established on the Araxes River, approximately where it has remained to the present time.

When the Treaty of Adrianople ended the Russo-Turkish War of 1828-1829, Russian conquests were supplemented by the Black Sea port of Poti and the towns of Akhalkalak and Akhaltsikh, but several regions in which Armenians lived (Kars, Ardahan, Bayazit, and Erzerum) were given up to the Turks. With the fighting over and the Russian hold over Transcaucasia secure, tens of thousands of Armenians living on the Turkish and Persian sides of the new border migrated into Russian territory, while Muslims left for Turkey and Persia. Before 1828 there had been approximately 87,000 Muslims and 20,000 Armenians in Erevan khanate. After the migrations the number of Armenians reached 65,000 and the number of Muslims fell to just over 50,000, including about 10,000 Kurds. The city of Erevan still had a Muslim majority. Of its 11,400 citizens, more than 7,000 were Muslims and less than 4,000 were Armenians. Only later in the century, after population transfers following the Russo-Turkish War of 1877-1878, would the Armenians form a dominant majority in Erevan province, and not until the early twentieth century would Armenians constitute a majority in the provincial capital. Nevertheless, the most important result of the Russian conquest of Transcaucasia and the subsequent migrations was the formation of a compact Armenian majority on a small part of their historic homeland. It was to be here, in Eastern Armenia, that the future republics of Armenia—the independent Republic of Armenia (1918-1920), the Armenian Soviet Socialist Republic (1920-1991), and the "restored" Republic of Armenia (1991 to the present)—would be established.

Immediately after the conquest of Erevan, Armenians in Russia began generating ideas for an autonomous Armenian region, complete with its own flag and Armenian administrators. In St. Petersburg wealthy men, such as Khristofor Ekimovich Lazarev, and influential Russophiles, such as Alexandr Khudabashev and K. Argutinskii-Dolgorukii, worked out a plan for an autonomous Armenian principality under Russian protection. But the emperor Nicholas I (1825-1855) rejected such a notion and approved instead the formation of an Armenian district (*Armianskaia Oblast'* in Russian, *Haikakan Marz* in Armenian) which would be run by Russian administrators. The Russian diplomat and writer Alexandr Griboedov complained to Paskevich about the bureaucratic and insensitive manner in which Russian governance was imposed.

> We have taken the power from the beks and khans and in exchange we have given the people the confusion of alien laws. Our urban and city [officials] made no effort to adapt to local customs. . . . They judge by drawing things out and signing directives and decisions which the inhabitants obey, not by conviction, but as if by force. (Griboedov, 1953, pp. 614-38)

Only in February 1830 was a Russified Armenian, Major-General Vasilii Bebutov, named commander *(nachalnik)* of the Armenian district. Ten years later the district was abolished altogether, and the Armenian areas became part of the Georgian-Imeretian province. Another reorganization in 1849 resulted in the formation of Erevan province. Henceforth Armenia was to be governed just like any other part of the Russian Empire.

Russian policy was aimed at integrating the ethnic borderlands into the bureaucratic absolutist system of Russian administration as fully as possible. Caucasia was generally treated as an area of military concern. Persia and Turkey were regarded as hostile powers through most of the nineteenth century, and the mountain tribes of the North Caucasian mountains were not finally subdued until the 1860s. Most of the governors of the Caucasus, understandably, were military men, and Russian rule was subordinated to overall strategic and foreign policy considerations. The principal advisors to the emperor were divided about whether Transcaucasia should simply be exploited as an economic colony or developed to enhance the welfare of the local peoples. Foreign Minister Count Karl Nesselrode favored developing trade through the region, a process that he believed would have a "civilizing" effect on the Armenians and Georgians. But Minister of Finance Egor Kankrin argued that the territory could be left as an "Asian province, although better governed" and treated as "our colony, which should bring the state rather significant profits from the products of southern climes" (Kazemzadeh, 1974, p. 254). The colonialist view meant that the local development of industry and the near monopoly of trade in Armenian hands would be discouraged by the state. The imposition of tariffs hurt trade through the area in the 1830s, and little Russian investment occurred.

The officials sent by the tsar to govern the peoples of Transcaucasia were of two types—those who totally disregarded local traditions and customs, such as Paskevich and Baron Hahn, and tried to impose Russian laws on the non-Russian peoples; and those, such as Tsitsianov, Ermolov, and Baron Rozen, who believed in a gradual integration of the Caucasians into the centralized Russian system. In 1844 Nicholas I appointed Count Mikhail Semenovich Vorontsov (1782-1856) to be the first viceroy *(namestnik)* of the Caucasus. During his stay in Transcaucasia (1845-1854), Vorontsov transformed the attitudes of Armenians and Georgians toward the Russian state, dispelled the resistance of Georgian nobles and Armenian businessmen to Russian officialdom, and provided new security with Russian arms. He encouraged economic development and tried to help Armenian merchants by having tariffs lowered and a free transit of European goods permitted through Transcaucasia. He declared the Armenian middle class of Tiflis to be "hereditary eminent citizens of the Russian Empire" *(pochetnye grazhdane)* and freed them from military recruitment, certain taxes, and corporal punishment. This class of propertied Armenians, known to Georgians as the *mokalakebi* (city folk), emerged as the most influential social group in Transcaucasian towns, as a new capitalist-industrial environment began to take shape in Caucasia. Wealth, enterprise, and talent were the means to advancement, rather than noble birth, and these Armenian merchants and industrialists fared far better economically than the declining Georgian nobility who relied on their pedigree and peasant serfs for their welfare. Thanks to the innovations of Vorontsov and the developing economy of Transcaucasia, the Armenian middle class dominated Tiflis and grew influential in other cities. By the middle of the nineteenth century, the prospering Armenian bourgeoisie had become loyal supporters of Russian rule. Many russified their names, sent their children to Russian schools, and tried to adopt the cultural patterns of the master nationality.

The most important imperial decision concerning the Armenians in the first half of the nineteenth century was the decree issued by Nicholas I in 1836 that governed relations of the tsarist government and the Armenian Church. The *Polozhenie* (Statute) excluded the church from political affairs and subordinated it to the ultimate power of the tsar, but at the same time the Armenian Apostolic Church was given considerable autonomy, in contrast to the Georgian Orthodox Church, which had lost its independence after the Russian annexation. The *Polozhenie* guaranteed the Armenian Church the security of its considerable properties, granted freedom of worship to Armenians, freed the clergy from taxation, and gave the power over Armenian religious schools to the church (though their curriculum had to be approved by the Holy Synod of the Russian Orthodox Church and communicated to the Ministry of the Interior). Echmiadzin was given primacy over the six dioceses of the Armenian Apostolic Church in Russia—Erevan, Georgia, Karabagh, Shirvan, Nakhichevan-Bessarubia, and Astrakhan—while preserving some autonomy for each locality. The catholicos was to be chosen by a national assembly of clergy and laymen, which would submit two names to the tsar, who would make the final choice. The new catholicos was then to swear an oath of allegiance to the Russian crown. To make sure of the church's obedience, a Russian procurator was to attend the Armenian Church's Synod as representative of the tsarist government. Rather than creating antagonism between church and state, the *Polozhenie* established a working relationship and cooperation. For nearly fifty years the state interfered minimally in Armenian affairs, perceiving little threat to its interests, and the church often used the policing powers of the state to enforce its decisions among the Armenian people.

The Formation of National Awareness

The consolidation of Russian rule over Eastern Armenians had a revolutionary impact on Armenian society. From isolated, discrete communities with a loose allegiance to the national church as their spiritual authority, the Armenians of the Russian Empire now had a single state authority over them and closer association with the head of the national church, now living within the empire. The new social and political developments in Russia and Europe created a receptive environment for the work of a small number of Armenian intellectuals determined to create a shared sense of nationality among their people. What is most often described as the national cultural awakening or the modern Armenian renaissance was, in fact, not a spontaneous release of a deep-seated Armenian spirit but the product of hard political and intellectual work by Armenian scholars, teachers, and political activists.

Several characteristics of the Armenians in Russia worked against the development of a national communality: the territorial dispersion of the Armenians from Erevan to Tiflis, Moscow to Bessarabia, Astrakhan to the Crimea; the deep social differences between the more prosperous and better-educated urban middle class and the poor and benighted peasantry of the Transcaucasian villages; and the conflicting cultural and political aspirations of the young Armenian intelligentsia increasingly at odds with the traditional clerical authorities.

The Russian conquests of Caucasia brought the peasantry of Eastern Armenia under the same state authority as the more westernized Armenians of Crimea and Nor Nakhichevan. Contacts were now possible between the urban centers of Russia and the villages of Erevan province. In a real sense the coming of the Russians represented a "liberation" from centuries of Muslim dominance and the opening of channels to European enlightenment. But the positive aspects of Russia's entry into Caucasian affairs were tempered by the kind of "civilization" that Russians brought with them—a mixture of militarism, autocracy, bureaucratic insensitivity to cultural specificity, and obscurantism that tried to limit the influence of European ideas. Russian rule, thus, had a contradictory effect on the Armenians. For many it opened roads to the West, taught new ways of thinking, and expanded the expectations of what the future could hold. But at the same time, the full power of the Russian state was directed to creating a conservative mentality, support for the status quo, and acceptance of Armenian subordination to Russian authority.

Given the dispersion of the Armenians throughout Caucasia and Russia and the deep social divisions between peasants and city dwellers, unifying Russian Armenians on the basis of shared social interests or common territory was impossible. Either they would remain, as in centuries past, a loose religious community held together by their church, or they would come together on a new basis—common awareness of nationality and a belief that they shared interests. Building on the work of the scholar monks of the Catholic Armenian Mekhitarist order of Venice and Vienna, Armenian intellectuals, both in Russian cities and in Istanbul and Izmir, began to work out the notion of an

Armenian nation. Their concept of Armenia, one based on a secular sense of nationality rather than the traditional understanding of a religious people, was an affront to the clerical leaders of the Armenians, and a bitter struggle was waged for several decades between those who were creating a new "imagined community" for the Armenians and those who defended the hallowed concept of a Christian society.

Before the nineteenth century almost all education for Armenians was in the hands of the church. The aim of such teaching was to train clerics for service and to preserve the literary monuments of classical Armenian culture. Caucasian Armenians, however, had no schools before the Russian annexations, and the first schools established by the government—a noble *uchilishche* (school) in 1802 and an Orthodox seminary in 1816, both in Tiflis—were alien to most Armenians. Armenians had founded schools in Astrakhan (the Agababov school in 1810), in Nor Nakhichevan (1811), and in Moscow (the famous Lazarev Institute in 1815), but not until 1813 did the energetic Nerses Ashtaraketsi open the *Zharangavorats* (seminary) in Echmiadzin. Ten years later he established the premier school for Armenians in Transcaucasia, the Nersisian Jemaran (academy), in Tiflis. These schools were the nuclei of a small network of places of learning in churches and homes, usually involving a single dedicated teacher. By the end of 1836 Caucasian Armenians had twenty-one Armenian church schools (and 824 churches).

As education expanded, the church hierarchy attempted to keep learning within a strictly prescribed religious framework, but young priests and university-educated lay instructors, such as the writer Khachatur Abovian (1805-1848), worked to stretch the peripheries of education and introduce western literature, the latest science, and a demythologized history. Students were pulled in one direction by the rigid traditional instruction of most of the higher clergy and in another by the younger *kahananer* (married priests) and lay teachers. Typical of this first generation of "enlighteners" was Gabriel Kahana Patkanian (1802-1889), the father of the patriotic poet Rafayel Patkanian (Kamar-Katipa) (1830-1892) and the teacher of the radical journalist and political activist Mikayel Nalbandian (1829-1866). Gabriel Patkanian had studied with his father, Serovbe, who in turn had been educated by the Mekhitarist fathers in Venice. Gabriel attempted to bring secular and Western subject matter into his teaching but came up against powerful political and religious opposition. By order of the Catholicos Nerses V (1843-1857), he was dismissed from his school in Nor Nakhichevan and exiled to Georgia (1845). Even as Echmiadzin

imposed a uniform religious curriculum in its church schools throughout Russia, the number of schools continued to grow. In 1850 the first
three-year elementary schools with instruction in Armenian were
opened by the church in Transcaucasia. By 1860 there were twenty-
nine such schools; by 1885, there were 270. But at the same time
powerful bishops and the catholicos himself used their influence and
even the Russian police to censor books and newspapers printed in
Armenian and purge the schools of suspect teachers.

The young men coming out of Armenian church schools and
Russian state schools went on to university in Moscow, St. Petersburg,
and Dorpat (now Tartu, Estonia), as well as in Europe (Heidelberg,
Berlin, and Jena). Unlike their Armenian compatriots from Ottoman
Turkey, who were much more likely to be trained in France and Italy
and imbibe Mekhitarist influences, the Armenian intellectuals of Russia
came under Russian and German teachings. Idealist philosophy and the
accompanying idea of nationality as the soul of a people made a
considerable impact on the thinking of these students. But like their
contemporaries in Turkey, these intellectuals were vitally interested in
the burning cultural issue of the day—the creation of a living Armenian
literary language. Eastern Armenians spoke a dialect peppered with
Georgian and Russian words, while Erevantsis, Karabaghtsis, and Crimean Armenians often had trouble understanding one another. Almost
all books, as well as the first Armenian newspaper in Russia—*Kovkas*
(Caucasus) (Tiflis, 1846-1847)—were printed in the classical Armenian
language, *grabar,* used by the church. The Westernizing intellectuals
with their commitment to spreading education and culture wanted to
base the new standard literary language on one or another of the spoken
dialects *(ashkharhabar).* The most powerful advocate of *ashkharhabar*
was the teacher-writer Abovian, who in the early 1840s wrote the first
novel in modern Eastern Armenian, using the Erevan dialect. This work,
Verk Hayastani (Wounds of Armenia), was a patriotic attack on the
effects of Russian rule on Armenia and did not spare the conservative
clergy. The Russian censors removed a telling passage from the first
edition in 1858 where Abovian warned his reader:

> If you are Russian, speak Russian: if you are Turkish, speak Turkish.
> . . . The Armenian language has its own words. . . . And if you know
> your language, if you speak your language, the Russians will snatch
> the very bread from your hands. They will send you to Siberia.

Prophetically Abovian had foreseen his own end. In 1848, the year of revolutions in Europe, the young writer disappeared. Some say he was killed by the tsarist authorities; others, also with little hard information, claim he was exiled to Siberia.

An equally tragic fate befell another radical nationalist, Mikayel Nalbandian. After antagonizing church officials in Nor Nakhichevan, Nalbandian moved to Moscow where together with the scholar Stepanos Nazariants (1812-1879) he started a newspaper in *ashkharhabar*—*Hiusisapail* (Northern Lights) (1858-1864). Their aim was to provide a secular alterative to the largely clerical literature available to Armenians. Nalbandian's credo was summed up in the foreword to his translation of Eugène Sue's popular French novel, *The Wandering Jew:*

> We Armenians have lacked secular learning up to the present time; for better or worse, we have had and continue to have only religious learning. . . . The times have passed when the priests could reinforce whatever direction they chose by apportioning and weighing and measuring out the light of wisdom to the nation. The transformation of the world has been amazing, yet what is even more amazing is that there are still so many people who do not believe that this transformation has taken place. (Nalbandian, 1940-1948, vol. 2, p. 65)

Hiusisapail represented an anticlerical tendency among Armenian intellectuals, and the pro-church party struck back in the pages of *Meghu Hayastani* (The Bee of Armenia) and *Masiats Aghavni* (The Dove of Ararat). Nalbandian argued for a new conception of the Armenian nation, one based on the common people. For him Armenians were no longer to be thought of solely as a religious community but one based on the principle of nationality. Nationality could be created only by implanting consciousness in the common people. Such enlightenment would take place in the national schools, where the principal task would be to teach Armenians to speak their own language. He wrote: "The heart and soul of the nation can keep their quality and distinctiveness pure only by being fashioned under the influence of the national language. Whoever denies this truth denies his nationality" (Nalbandian, 1940-1948, vol. 1, p. 455). Women were to play an important role in the formation of national consciousness, not by leaving the home but by returning to traditional nurturing activities:

Armenian women! Today I am addressing you. National regeneration
and salvation are only dreams if the domestic life of the nation has
withered away. Mothers are to teach their children the national
language. Mothers are to implant the seeds of nationality in their
young hearts so carefully and intently that neither the freezing storm
of the north nor the torrid climate of the south can wither the budding
shoots. (Nalbandian, 1940-1948, vol. 1, pp. 456-57)

By the early 1860s, Nalbandian had become a notorious figure, hated
by the leadership of the church and under suspicion for subversive
activities by the Russian police. After visiting the Russian radical
thinkers Alexander Herzen and Nikolai Ogarev in London, Nalbandian
was arrested on his return to Russia. His apartment was searched, and
his "subversive" pamphlet on land reform—*Erkragortsutiune vorpes
ughigh janabarh* (Agriculture as the True Way)—was discovered. He
died in exile in 1866.

The imposition of Russian administration on Armenians scattered
from Erevan to Moscow brought a divided and diverse people together
under the same laws, taxes, and political authority. Economic development and the establishment of a network of schools made possible the
emergence of a lay intelligentsia that was able to generate a new sense of
Armenian nationality. This mid-century national awareness was at one
and the same time the product of the intellectual revival that the Mekhitarist and Armenian Church fathers had begun, as well as a Westernized
reaction to the traditional view of Armenians as a primarily religious
community dominated by the church. Beginning with the *kahanas* of
Gabriel Patkanian's generation and proceeding with the university-trained
scholars and writers such as Abovian and Nazariants, a secular intelligentsia was formed. It found its most outspoken representative in the bold,
somewhat reckless, and ultimately victimized Nalbandian. By 1858 a
secular and secularizing generation of Armenian intellectuals had arrived
in Russia. That was the year of *Hiusisapail* and *Verk Hayastani*. Two
hundred subscribers signed up in advance to receive the Moscow-based
newspaper. Clearly there was a growing interest in western ideas, for a
concerted challenge to the traditional leadership of church and community, and for a clearer identification of Armenians as a nationality. In the
absence of a fixed territory where most Armenians lived or an Armenian
state with the usual political institutions, the making of the modern
Armenian nationality became the obligation and the major cultural
achievement of the small but determined Armenian intelligentsia.

Economic and Social Developments

The great social transformations of the nineteenth and early twentieth centuries that changed European life—the development of capitalist markets, the spread of industrial production, the move from villages to cities, and the increased activity of the lower and middle classes—had an enormous effect on the Armenian communities in Russia. In Tiflis, Moscow, and Baku especially, urban middle-class Armenians were among the pioneers in developing machine production of textiles, tobacco processing, the oil industry, and long-distance trade. The great majority of Russian Armenians, however, remained on the land, and their customary way of life changed quite slowly. Commercial agricultural production, particularly in cotton and wine grapes, came to the Ararat Valley late in the century, but most Armenian peasants in Erevan province continued to grow just enough to feed their families and pay off their obligations to their landlords and the state. Some of the poorest left the villages to enter the new working class in Baku, Batum, or Tiflis. Social differences between Armenians remained acute—they may even have grown greater in the century after the Russian conquests—but the new prosperity of the middle class gave Armenians increased power, influence, and visibility. It was not long before their very success created a bitter envy and hostility from competitors of other nationalities.

By mid-century there were about 565,000 Armenians in Caucasia. This number rose three-fold by 1917, to 1,783,000, in part because of natural growth, in part because of additional conquests (1877-1878) by Russia of Kars and other Ottoman districts inhabited by Armenians. Erevan province had a bare majority of Armenians by the second half of the century, and it remained economically backward. With only 11.2 percent of its people living in towns in 1863, Erevan province had the lowest percentage of urban population of any province in European Russia. Less than 20 percent of the town dwellers were artisans or workers. More Muslims than Armenians lived in the towns of Erevan (6,900 to 5,800 in 1865), Ordubad, and Nakhichevan, but the garrison town of Alexandropol, the largest in the province, was overwhelmingly Armenian (14,733 Armenians to 461 Muslims), as was Novo-Bayazit. In general, Armenians tended to live in larger settlements than Muslims and dominated the urban population overall (27,000 to 15,000).

At the time of the conquest of Eastern Armenia, the former Persian khanate was in desperate economic straits. Much of the region was depopulated, and even with the mass migrations of Muslims and

Armenians, hundreds of villages remained empty. Peasants made up almost 90 percent of the population of the *Armianskaia Oblast'*. Merchants and artisans accounted for about 6 percent. The upper class of landholders and the Muslim and Armenians clergy were freed from taxes and supported in their influential positions by the Russian state. In Persian times all land in the khanate had been held by the khan, with the nobles operating the estates and collecting the taxes from the peasants. But with the coming of the Russians the Muslim *beks* and khans and the Armenian *meliks* pressured the government to recognize them as fully empowered owners of private land. As part of his effort to secure the loyalty of the Caucasian elites, Viceroy Vorontsov convinced the government to issue a new law (December 6, 1846) that gave the landlords hereditary tenure over the lands they had held at the time of annexation. The more informal and often arbitrary system of taxation and control over the peasants, which had been characteristic of the Persian Empire, was replaced by a more regulated system, not unlike that found in serf-owning Russia.

To work the difficult terrain, peasants in Russian Armenia used the heavy *gutan* and the *aror* or *jut* (wooden plows with metal plowshares), pulled by teams of six to ten animals with three or four people pushing and prodding. Households worked together in what was called *haragashutiun* (association). There was almost no fertilizing, and when land became exhausted it was left fallow or used as pasture for a few years. Productivity was low, and the rents to the landlords were paid not in money but in kind through the whole nineteenth century. Peasants worked for larger landowners, and those who lived in the mountainous regions, where the growing seasons started later and were shorter, spent many months in the valleys to earn more money. To further supplement their income, poor peasants either sent their women to work as domestic servants or sold handicraft products on local markets. The peasant household was a large economic unit, made up of several generations of relatives *(gerdastan)*. At the head of a household, which might have as many as fifty members living under one roof, was the eldest male, father and grandfather to many of the younger members. Such large family units were necessary for survival, for the work and income of all its members were pooled to insure enough for all to eat. As conditions improved through the nineteenth century, the size of such households decreased, until as a rule a typical household consisted of parents with their married sons and small children; sons with grown children would soon form their own households.

Armenian peasants clearly divided the roles and the work of men and women. Field work was strictly masculine. Women did not plow, plant, or harvest; they were responsible, however, for the threshing of the grain. Men raised the sheep and goats and sheared them, but the women cleaned the wool and spun it into the thread that made up most of their clothing, carpets, and fabrics. All housework was organized by the *tantikin,* the oldest woman in the household, who ran a disciplined matriarchy inside the walls of her home. She had the power to choose brides for her sons, who in turn would enter the household as the lowly *hars* (bride) who was not even permitted to speak to the older men in the family. She was obligated to wash the feet of the men and of honored guests. While some women had great power and influence in family life, Armenian peasant society was dominated by men. All important decisions in the villages were made by the men, and even the terms used for relatives suggested the importance of the male line. Those related on the male line were called *azgukun* (literally, of the same kinship group, *azg*); those related on the female line were called *barekam* (literally, well-wisher, now the word used exclusively in Eastern Armenian for "relative" and in western Armenian for "friend").

More than two-thirds of peasants in Erevan province lived on land owned by the state; the rest lived on the lands of the *beks,* khans, and clergymen. The largest landowner among Armenians was the monastery of Echmiadzin. In the first half of the century Armenian and Muslim peasants increasingly came under the authority and control of their noble landlords, and their legal status approximated that of Russian serfs. But beginning in 1861 the Russian government began a long process of emancipating the landlord serfs, and on May 14, 1870, the peasant reform was extended to the Armenian and the Muslim provinces of Transcaucasia (Erevan, Baku, and Elisavetpol). As in 1846, all land was recognized as belonging legally to the nobles, but now the peasants were given the use of their plots in perpetuity, for which they were obligated to pay the landlord dues and had the right to buy their plots over time. Nobles kept one-third of their estates as their own, and the rest was distributed in small allotments to the peasants. Pastures, orchards, and vineyards remained with the lords, and peasants received such small holdings (some received nothing at all) that they were forced either to sell their petty properties or to rent additional lands at high prices. Very few peasants in Armenia were able to save enough money to buy their land from the nobles. Thus the Armenian and Muslim peasants of Eastern Armenia remained in a legal limbo called "temporary obligation," a kind of semiserfdom, which lasted until 1912. Personally free but economically dependent on the nobles, the 15 to 20 percent of the Armenian peasantry affected by the reform could neither buy their land nor leave it without great difficulty. Their fellow peasants on state lands also remained obligated, to the state, until 1901.

Though it is difficult to generalize about the complex results of the tsarist attempts to "emancipate" the peasants, two conclusions are possible. First, the degree of freedom granted to the peasants in the prerevolutionary period was not particularly significant. Economic and social dependence undercut the legal rights granted by state decree. Second, the government failed in its attempts to improve the life of the peasantry because it was never willing to undermine or reduce significantly the power of the Muslim and Armenian elites.

Agricultural output did increase in the second half of the nineteenth century in Erevan province, though unevenly. In the early 1890s, Armenia suffered from the grain crisis that hit the rest of the Russian Empire, and grain had to be imported from central Russia into Transcaucasia. From 1900 to 1913 grain production actually fell somewhat in Armenia. But at the same time new crops with commercial potential were being developed, most importantly cotton (which increased ninefold between 1870 and 1900) and wine grapes. The success of viniculture led to the creation of a successful wine and cognac industry. In 1887 the entrepreneur Nerses Tairov built a large winery in Erevan, and three years later he added a cognac factory. The Georgian D. S. Sarajev and the Russian Shustov, who had plants throughout Russia and outlets in Europe, also entered the Armenian wine business. Shustov took over and improved Tairov's plant and increased production twelve times. By 1913 Armenia was producing 82 percent of all the cognac in Transcaucasia and more than the rest of Russia together.

There were few industrial enterprises in Erevan province. Armenians worked in copper mines and smelteries, in Alaverdi (Tiflis province) and Zangezur. The father and brother of Anastas Mikoyan, later president of the Soviet Union, worked in Alaverdi, and the young Mikoyan witnessed the brutal conditions in which the miners worked. Copper production grew in the late nineteenth century but suffered from the world industrial crisis of 1901 to 1903 when copper prices fell 19.7 percent in three years. There was much improvement during the years of the Russo-Japanese War (1904-1905) when demand for copper was high, but the boom was soon followed by a depression. Only in 1913 did the industry recover. By that year Armenia provided 12.5 percent of the empire's copper. The company that dominated Armenia's copper industry, the Caucasian Industrial Metallurgical Society, was French-owned, and as in the cognac business Armenians played a minor role in the capitalist development of Russian Armenia.

The Armenian bourgeoisie was far more important in the larger cities of Transcaucasia-Baku, and Tiflis. In the decades when capitalist industry spread south of the Caucasus mountains, Transcaucasia was marked by severely uneven development. The oil capital, Baku, was responsible for 90 percent of the wealth produced in the region. Tiflis accounted for only 4 percent, and Erevan for even less. Not surprisingly, then, the Armenian merchants who had dominated trade in Transcaucasia for centuries turned their attention in the nineteenth century to the new forms of industry that promised great profits—to textile manufacturing, tobacco processing, and oil. Among the earliest men to exploit the "black gold" of Baku were Armenians, including M. I. Mirzoev, who drilled the first successful well in 1871. By 1900 Armenians owned almost a third of the oil companies in the region, though foreign capitalists such as the Rothschilds and the Nobel brothers were challenging their dominance of the industry. As monopolies began taking over smaller companies in the early twentieth century, the Armenian-owned Mantashev company merged with several Russian companies to form one of the giants of the industry, the Russian General Oil Company. Until 1901 Baku was the leading oil center in the entire world, outproducing all the fields in the United States combined. In a few short decades oil had turned Baku into a capitalist city in a feudal land, a proletarian oasis surrounded by a peasant population. Armenians gravitated to the city, along with Russians, Azerbaijanis, and Persians, and formed a multinational workforce. The Muslims generally were given the least skilled and least well-paid jobs, while the Armenians and Russians tended to join the skilled workers and white-collar employees. At the bottom of society the workers gradually turned toward radical politics and made contact with the embryonic socialist movement. At the top the men of great property dominated the municipal government and allied with the tsarist authorities to maintain the order that permitted them to enjoy a life of extraordinary wealth and privilege. The social cleavages between the lower classes and the upper in Baku grew deeper, while at the same time ethnic differences kept the different religious communities apart. Ethnicity and religion reinforced some social distinctions. Christians usually fared better than Muslims, but on occasion, during strikes or political demonstrations, temporary alliances were formed by workers of different nationalities.

The most important Armenian community in the Russian Empire was in Tiflis, the seat of Caucasian government. Armenians made up the largest ethnic group in the town until the 1917 revolutions. In 1865 approximately 31,000 of its 71,000 inhabitants were Armenian, while only 15,000 were Georgian and 12,000 Russian. Increasingly Georgians from the countryside migrated into town. By 1897 the number of Georgians in Tiflis had risen by 158 percent, to over 38,000; Russians by 190 percent, to 36,000; while the number of Armenians had risen by only 88 percent, to 55,500. No longer a majority, merely a plurality, the Armenians of Tiflis were faced by a growing Georgian working class and an increasingly hostile Russian officialdom. Yet even as their demographic dominance in Tiflis declined, the Armenians continued to hold on to political and economic power in the city. The mayors of Tiflis were almost always Armenians, and the city council *(duma),* first elected by men of property in the 1870s, was dominated by rich Armenian merchants and industrialists. The wealthiest families—the Arzumanov, Avetisian, and Mantashev in the oil industry; the Adelkhanov in leather goods; the Tumaniants, Kevorkov, Avetisov, and Pitoev in commerce; the Egiazarov, Ter-Asaturov, Bozarjiants, and Enfiajiants in tobacco—made up a fraternity of entrepreneurs who worked together in a variety of joint-stock companies to maintain the position of the local bourgeoisie in the face of Russian and foreign competition.

From Consensus to Conflict

Up to the 1880s Armenian aspirations and Russian state interests seemed to coincide. Although Armenian peasants had to endure landlords and state officials who perpetuated their inferior status and economic backwardness, the Armenian middle class and many intellectuals believed that their welfare was best served by working within the tsarist system. Russian protection made commerce possible; security for property provided an incentive for industry. Russian education and access to Europe seemed to promise a future of greater enlightenment and culture. During the Crimean War (1853-1856), when Russia stood alone against the Ottoman Empire and most of the European powers, Armenians in Russia supported the tsar against the Turks. Though Caucasian Armenians were not placed under any military obligation until 1887, during both the Crimean War and the Russo-Turkish War of 1877-1878 they formed volunteer units to fight against the enemy of the Russian state.

A Russian Armenian general, B. O. Bebutov, emerged as a hero of the Crimean War, as did the young officer, Mikhail Loris-Melikov (1826-1888). While Russian forces did poorly in the main theater of battle, Crimea, they fared much better on the Caucasus front. On November 15/27 (Gregorian/Julian calendar), 1855, the Turks surrendered Kars, the major fortified town in eastern Anatolia and a town that centuries before had been the center of an Armenian kingdom. It was apparent to many Armenians that Russian arms were their best hope for bringing their compatriots in Turkey under a more modern, less repressive regime. Russia, however, was forced to cede Kars back to Turkey in the humiliating Treaty of Paris (1856).

Two decades later when Russia and Turkey again went to war, Armenian generals once more participated in the fighting. General A. A. Gukasov led the Russian armies that occupied old Bayazit and Alashkert, where local Armenians joyfully greeted the Russian troops. Kars was taken once again, this time by General Hovhannes Lazarev, and Armenian volunteers fought alongside Russians in the battles for Ardahan and Erzerum. The Russian Armenian press praised Russia's efforts to "liberate" the Armenians of Turkey, and a general consensus developed among educated Armenians that Armenia's most effective ally was tsarist Russia. But for a second time Russia was humiliated diplomatically. After imposing conditions on Turkey in the Treaty of San Stefano that would have left Russian troops in Turkish Armenia until political reforms were implemented, Russia was compelled to pull its armies back. At the Congress of Berlin (1878) the European Powers, led by Great Britain, demanded that Russian troops be withdrawn from Turkish Armenia immediately. The Russo-Turkish border was redrawn, however, and Kars and Ardahan were annexed to the Russian Empire. By this act over 100,000 Armenians were added to the empire's population.

The Russo Turkish War of 1877-1878 stimulated interest in the "Armenian Question" throughout Europe. Russia put itself forward as the true champion of the oppressed Turkish Armenians, but Britain was unwilling to see its ally Turkey fall under the influence of Russia or be progressively carved up by its imperialist rivals. Within Russia pro-Russian feelings ran high among Armenians, and in the last years of the reign of Alexander II (1855-1881) a zenith of Armeno-Russian collaboration was reached. When revolutionaries threatened the stability of his empire, the emperor turned to the hero of the Russo-Turkish War, Count Loris-Melikov, to head the Russian government and establish order. Generally perceived as a liberal, at least in the

Russian context, Loris-Melikov was able to carry out a number of political reforms while simultaneously tracking down the radicals who opposed autocracy. But on the very day of his greatest triumph (March 1, 1881), hours after the tsar signed a draft for a consultative assembly to advise the autocrat, Loris-Melikov suffered his greatest defeat. Populist terrorists threw a bomb at the emperor's carriage and mortally wounded Alexander. Within a few weeks Loris-Melikov was dismissed by the new tsar, Alexander III (1881-1894). The era of reform was over. An age of reaction began.

In the last two decades of the nineteenth century, the Russian government turned against the Armenians, as state officials began to see them as a potential danger to the empire. The conflict between the tsar and his Armenian subjects had its origins in the long developmental process that Armenians had undergone since 1801. The very success of middle-class Armenians in establishing themselves as the dominant class in urban Transcaucasia made them visible targets for the social and ethnic resentments of other nationalities and the Russian government. The powerful and ambitious merchants and industrialists who came to head the Russian-Armenian communities rivaled businessmen from other nationalities, pushed aside the traditional Georgian nobility, and became an almost unchallengeable political and economic force in the major cities of Caucasia. At the same time, both in Russia and Turkey, a well-educated Westernized intelligentsia, often the children of the bourgeoisie, had formulated a sense of nationality and promoted the teaching of the Armenian language and the national cultural heritage. These developments had occurred earlier and more rapidly among Armenians than among Georgians, Azerbaijanis, or Ottoman Turks. Social and cultural differences between Armenians and their neighbors became more apparent during the nineteenth century, as each national intelligentsia emphasized the distinctiveness of its people. Once Armenians became a subject of international concern, they appeared to the conservative governments of the Russian and Ottoman empires to be a subversive force, a disruptive element aiming to set up a separate state of its own.

The Russian government had long been interested in increasing the strength, unity, and uniformity of its vast realm. Laws and regulations had been issued to improve the central administration's control over the peripheries of the empire. To the national minorities this process was seen negatively as Russification *(obrusenie),* and the leaders of ethnic communities resisted to the best of their ability the whittling away of their privileges and local powers. The government, on the other hand, believed that the elimination of different legal systems and enclaves of local autonomy was essential for Russia's ability to govern itself effectively and defend itself from foreign threats. Three separate processes can be understood (and are often confused) within the concept of Russification. First, there was the phenomenon of spontaneous Russification, the more or less evolutionary acculturation or assimilation of non-Russians into the Russian-speaking cultural community. Many Armenians in the tolerant years of Alexander II had adopted Russian endings for their names, sent their children to Russian schools, and taken on mannerisms of their Russian overlords. Second, there was administrative Russification, the introduction of Russian institutions, laws, and bureaucratic practices in the ethnic areas. The entire first two-thirds of the nineteenth century had witnessed the steady replacement of Georgian and Armenian laws and customs by the norms of Russian bureaucratic absolutism. Third, there was cultural and linguistic Russification, the imposition of Russian language, culture, even religion, on non-Russians. Though spontaneous and administrative Russification had been part of Armenian life in Russia since 1800, forced cultural and linguistic Russification was not attempted until the reign of Alexander III.

The tsar was personally very nationalistic. A fervent anti-Semite, he also loathed the Poles, whom he considered disloyal, and listened attentively to those of his advisors who preached a chauvinistic vision of "Russian principles, Russian strength, Russian people." Russian was to be the state language, and the teaching of other languages was to be curtailed. Although this policy of cultural and linguistic Russification was applied neither consistently by the central government nor with conviction by local authorities, the periodic, fitful implementation of laws aimed against the ethnic minorities created in their wake a powerful opposition to autocracy. Ironically, the very policy of forced cultural Russification resulted in a stronger identification with one's own nationality.

Russification efforts began in earnest in 1885, first in the Baltic region and in Poland, and then in Transcaucasia. The zealous governor of the Caucasus, Prince A. M. Dondukov-Korsakov (1820-1893), ordered all Armenian parish schools closed and their replacement by Russian schools. The Caucasian authorities believed that nationalism and a revolutionary spirit, "patriotism and populism," were rampant among Armenian students and had to be eradicated. Five hundred schools, attended by 20,000 pupils and employing 900 teachers, were shut down. Almost immediately the Armenians organized secret schools. A year later the government decided to reopen the Armenian schools, but their staffs were purged and stricter state surveillance over teachers was established. This unilateral abrogation of the *Polozhenie* of 1836 and the callous treatment of the educational system run by the church had a galvanizing effect on the Russian Armenian communities. The Russophilia prevalent among Armenians rapidly eroded. Elements within the church grew more hostile to the Russian state, and the young Armenian intellectuals emerged from the school crisis more nationalist and more radical. Within a few years many of the veterans of this struggle would become involved in the formation of the first Armenian revolutionary organizations within Russia.

Although Armenians did not turn to revolutionary activity in any significant numbers until the very end of the nineteenth century, the intellectual influences of the first generation of Armenian "enlighteners," with their emphasis on Western learning and the idea of the nation, had led many young Armenians to question the principles of the traditional order. Reason and science were considered preferable to faith and obedience to custom. Nationality seemed a more compelling principle on which to build a state than loyalty to a foreign dynasty. Though there were grave risks in questioning the religious and political authorities in Russia, some committed individuals were prepared to follow the examples of Russian radicals, such as Alexander Herzen or Nikolai Chernyshevkii, or Armenian martyrs to the cause of liberation, such as Mikayel Nalbandian. In April 1869 a group of enthusiasts in Alexandropol formed the first circle dedicated to Armenian liberation in the Russian Empire, the so-called Barenpatak Enkerutiun (Society of the Noble Aim). Nothing came of this short-lived society, nor of the efforts of the unfortunate Tigran Navasardiants, who in 1879 was arrested for distributing portraits of Nalbandian.

In the 1870s and 1880s the most influential tendency among educated Armenians was not revolutionary politics but the liberalism represented by the newspaper *Mshak* (Tiller). Edited for twenty years (1872-1892) by the popular and influential Grigor Artsruni (1845-1892), *Mshak* promoted a pro-Russian attitude among Armenians, advocated economic development along capitalist lines, and polemicized against the newly fashionable doctrines of socialism. Reform rather than revolution was the preferred way to improve Armenian life in Russia. While Russian radical youth turned to peasant socialism (populism, or *narodnichestvo*), their Armenian contemporaries for the most part remained liberal and nationalist. But some young Armenians, inspired by the romantic nationalism found in the novels of Raffi (Hakob Melik-Hakobian) (1832-1888), began to search for new ways to serve their people.

When the initial European interest in the plight of Turkish Armenians began to die down, a small number of young Armenians in the Caucasus decided to adopt the Russian populists' notion of "going to the people." They called for "going to the homeland" *(depi erkir)*. For Russian Armenians the turn to revolutionary struggle was actually a commitment to the liberation of Armenians in Turkey, not of those in Russia. This led in the 1880s and 1890s to an organizational separation of radical Armenians from Russian and Georgian revolutionaries. Whereas the Armenians were nationalists and were willing to fight alone against their Turkish enemies, the Russians and Georgians were more often socialists and revolved to join in a multinational effort against Russian autocracy.

The closing of the Armenian schools in 1885 mobilized large numbers of students into the nationalist movement. Stirred by the government's provocative act, the young Armenian populist, Kristapor Mikayelian, issued a leaflet addressed to his "Brother and Sister Armenians":

> Our schools are for us as sacred as the holy temple; from our glorious past we have been left two holy things—the national church and the national schools. These two holy things, having preserved our language, have preserved us as a nation.... Our schools are being closed with the help of bayonets. Let each Armenian family become its own separate Armenian school. Victory will be ours. (Arkomed, 1929, pp. 51-66)

A number of Caucasian radicals traveled in 1886 to Geneva and there drew up a program for a new party. The following year the six revolutionaries formally established the party, and in November 1887 the first issue of its newspaper, *Hnchak* (Bell), appeared. Socialist but not specifically Marxist, the Hnchak party was led by the charismatic Avetis Nazarbekian and his wife, Maro Vardanian. Their goal was an independent, socialist Armenia; their means was armed struggle.

Meanwhile in Transcaucasia other Armenian young people were forming their own revolutionary organization. Mikayelian and his friends founded Eritasard Hayastan (Young Armenia) and began organizing other revolutionary circles in Turkey and Persia. The Hnchaks and the Caucasian radicals tried to create a common organization, but the Tiflis circle was not socialist enough for the Hnchaks. In 1890 the Hai Heghapokhakanneri Dashnaktsutiun (Armenian Revolutionaries' Federation) was founded in Tiflis. At first the more strictly socialist Hnchaks were the more active of the two parties. But by the mid-1890s the Hnchaks were split between radicals and moderates, and the Dashnaks became the more influential Armenian political party, a position they never relinquished.

From its inception, the Dashnaktsutiun subordinated the social question to the national. Concerned that Armenian survival was at stake if some action was not taken soon, their first declaration rang with such phrases as "this is not the time to wait." The Dashnak manifesto called on the whole nation, young and old, rich and poor, even the clergy, to unite in the fight for national liberation ("Manifest H. H. Dashnaktsutian," 1958, p. 1). The Dashnaks did not see themselves as the representatives of any single group or class but as the revolutionary vanguard of the entire nation. As a coalition of socialists and nonsocialist nationalists, the Dashnaks were prepared to subordinate the struggle against Russian autocracy to the most immediate task—the defense and eventual liberation of the Armenians of Turkey.

For the Russian government, the appearance of an Armenian revolutionary movement was the fulfillment of its expectations about Armenian subversion and separatism. The Russian police believed that "the idea of revolution has penetrated all the classes of Armenian society, those that have much wealth and those that have nothing" (Ter Minassian, 1973). Even the Catholicos of All Armenians was suspect. No longer was the tsarist regime interested in supporting the Armenians against the Ottoman Empire. When in 1890 an ill-equipped army of Armenians, led by Sargis Gugunian, crossed the frontier into Turkey, the tsarist forces pursued and arrested them. The Russian police intercepted collections of money in support of the liberation movement in Turkey. The Armenophobe governor of the Caucasus, Prince Grigorii Golitsyn (1838-1907), launched a campaign against Armenian educational and charitable institutions. Censors prohibited the use of the words "Armenian people" or "Armenian nation." The government encouraged anti-Armenian journalists, such as the notorious chauvinist Vasilii Velichko. Leading Georgian poets took up their pens to draw vicious portraits of Armenians. Fears of revolutionaries were combined with fears of foreigners and hatred of the bourgeoisie into a single murky image of the Armenians as a pariah nation isolated within the Russian Empire.

Armenian Society and the Crisis of Tsarism

At the turn of the century there were more than 1,243,000 Armenians living in the Caucasus. Almost half of them, 506,000, lived in the backward, nonindustrial province of Erevan. These Armenians, the least transformed by the profound social and economic developments of the nineteenth century, were still largely peasants, still largely unconcerned about the great political issues of the time. Their compatriots in other parts of Transcaucasia and Russia had been far more affected by the capitalist industrialization that had begun intensively in Russia in the 1880s. By 1897 there were approximately 30,000 Armenian wage workers in Transcaucasia, most of them employed in the oil industry of Baku and the factories and workshops of Tiflis and Batum. Almost completely unprotected by the law or by trade unions (which were illegal until 1906), these workers occasionally joined their comrades from other nationalities in strikes or demonstrations, but until the late 1890s one could not speak of any kind of organized labor movement in Transcaucasia. Within a few years, however, labor discontent combined with nationalist anger to create a massive Armenian opposition to the Russian autocracy, a movement that included not only the urban workers and intellectuals but the peasants of Erevan province as well.

The years 1901 to 1903 were a time of a worldwide industrial depression, and the effects of economic slowdown were felt in Transcaucasia. The ill-organized workers of southern Russia, Baku, Tiflis, and Batum engaged in a rising number of strikes in those years, responding to the agitation by Marxist revolutionaries. Georgian and Russian workers joined the young Social Democratic propaganda circles and unions, but Armenians were more reluctant to give themselves to the multinational class struggle against capitalism and autocracy. The leading Armenian radicals, the Dashnaks, discouraged Armenian workers from participating in strikes and directed all efforts toward the struggle in Turkey. The Hnchaks spent more time organizing workers, but their primary goal also was liberation of Ottoman Armenia. Some young intellectuals, among them Stepan Shahumian, Arshak Zurabian, and Bogdan Knuniants, threw in their lot with the Georgian and Russian

Marxists and joined the newly formed Russian Social Democratic
Workers' Party (RSDRP). But they constantly met frustration as they
tried to interest Armenian workers in the all-nation struggle against
autocracy.

Suddenly the tsarist government itself provoked the great majority of the Russian Armenian community to abandon its passivity and
support the revolutionary movement. On June 12, 1903, Tsar Nicholas
II (1894-1917) ordered the confiscation of Armenian Church properties by the state. This violation of the *Polozhenie* of 1836 was motivated by the government's belief that the Armenian Church was
instigating separatism and Russophobia among Armenians. But the
effect of the tsar's decree was to create precisely the kind of revolutionary sympathies that the government sought to prevent. Armenians
of all classes marched in solemn processions to protest the confiscation. Demonstrations turned violent. Rocks were thrown. Shots fired.
People were wounded and killed. Catholicos Mkrtich I (1892-1906,
known as Khrimian Hairik), refused to accept the new law. Insurrection broke out in Baku, coinciding with economic strikes by workers
throughout Caucasia. In October Hnchaks wounded the governor-gen-
eral of the Caucasus, Prince Golitsyn. Tsarist officials reported to their
superiors that a revolutionary situation had been created in Transcaucasia. As Armenians of all political persuasions turned against the
Russian government, the Dashnaktsutiun decided to take upon itself
the self-defense of Caucasian Armenians. For the first time the major
Armenian political party devoted a significant portion of its manpower
to the fight in Russia. Workers were now prompted to join in strikes
and demonstrations. Terror was directed at tsarist officials who were
considered anti-Armenian.

At the same time that Armenian revolutionary activity increased,
a general revolutionary crisis shook the tsarist empire. On January 9,
1905, the soldiers of the tsar fired on a peaceful demonstration of
workers in St. Petersburg, killing dozens. "Bloody Sunday," as that
event was thereafter known, precipitated a year of violence—mutinies,
general strikes, and peasant uprisings. In Baku, Armenians and
Azerbaijanis fought each other in the streets, both sides massacring the
innocent and helpless. With the tsarist order in Caucasia in danger of
collapse, Nicholas II responded to the urgings of his more liberal
advisors and decided to make concessions to the opposition. He appointed a new viceroy of the Caucasus, Count Illarion I. Vorontsov-
Dashkov (1837-1916), a man considered a friend of the Armenians. On

August 1, 1905, the Council of Ministers repealed the act confiscating Armenian Church properties. And on October 17 Nicholas issued a manifesto promising all the people of the empire civil rights and the establishment of a representative legislature, the Duma.

The last twelve years of the tsarist regime (1905-1917) may be viewed as a constitutional experiment that ultimately failed. The tsar had been forced to limit his absolute powers, but he remained unwilling to make the deep political and social reforms demanded by the liberal and radical elements in Russia. The First State Duma was elected in 1906. Four Armenians—Khristafor Bagaturov, Artem Aivazov, Kegham Ter-Petrosiants, and Levon Tumaniants—were among the deputies elected from Transcaucasia. Since the Dashnaks, Hnchaks, and many Marxists had boycotted the elections, those selected were close to the liberal Constitutional Democratic (Kadet) Party. Confrontation rather than cooperation marked the Duma's brief existence. The tsar soon dismissed the legislature and called for new elections. But the Second State Duma, which met in 1907, was even more radical than the first. This time Dashnaks and Social Democrats fully participated in the elections. Five Armenians—Stepan Ter-Avetikiants, Hovhannes Saghatelian, Sirakan Tigranian, Hovsep Atabekian, and Arshak Zurabian—were in the Caucasian delegation. On June 3, 1907, the tsar dismissed the Duma and in a political coup d'etat changed the electoral law to favor the rich and the noble who tended to support the monarchy.

The new law allowed only one representative from the Armenian community in Transcaucasia. Hovhannes Saghatelian, a Dashnak, was elected both to the Third State Duma (1907) and the Fourth (1912). Despite persecution by the government, the Dashnaktsutiun remained the most influential party among Russian Armenians. Their organizations lost members after 1907, and their newspapers were subjected to interference from the authorities. Hundreds of Dashnaks were put on trial in 1912, but the skillful defense by renowned lawyers such as Alexandr Kerenskii (later prime minister of Russia in 1917) and Pavel Miliukov (foreign minister in 1917) resulted in light sentences and acquittals for many. Forced into a semilegal existence, the Dashnaks nevertheless maintained much of their authority in the eyes of the peasants and workers.

The Armenian middle class, on the other hand, gradually abandoned its support for the revolutionaries and made its peace with tsarism. Enough avenues for political participation on the local level (the city dumas) and self-expression (in the press) were open to encourage acquiescence with the Russian political system. Vorontsov-Dashkov worked to convince the government that the Armenians were a loyal people who deserved to be supported, particularly when Russia was concerned about its traditional enemy, the Ottoman Empire. Fearing German influence in Turkey, Nicholas and his foreign minister, Sergei Sazonov, responded positively to a petition from Catholicos Gevorg V (1911-1930) for reforms in Turkish Armenia. Negotiations among the Great Powers resulted in a reform act signed by the Russians and the Turks on February 8, 1914. Eastern Anatolia was to be divided into two large provinces over each of which would be appointed a foreign inspector-general. Just as the mechanisms for supervised reform were being put into place, war broke out in Europe. Within months Turkey and Russia were in the final struggle that would bring down both the Ottoman and the Romanov empires.

Shortly after the outbreak of hostilities between Germany and Russia in August 1914, Vorontsov-Dashkov met with leading Armenians in Tiflis to urge the creation of volunteer units to fight with the Russian army. The catholicos, the mayor of Tiflis, Alexandre Khatisian, and many other Russian Armenian leaders enthusiastically embraced the Russian offer. Eventually 150,000 Armenians would serve with the regular Russian troops. The catholicos met with the emperor and declared that the salvation of Armenia was dependent on Russia. The tsar assured the holy father that "a most brilliant future awaits the Armenians" (Khatissian, 1950, p. 87).

Nicholas, however, was soon in no position to fulfill his promises to the Armenians. After initial victories in the war with Turkey, most of Ottoman Armenia was liberated by the Russian army. But the Russian advances and the evident Armenian enthusiasm for the tsar's armies were the final incentives for the Young Turk government in Istanbul to begin massive deportations and massacres of its own Armenian subjects. The death marches of 1915 emptied Turkish Armenia of its Christian population. A second major advance by the Russian army, in 1916, found few Armenians to greet the victorious troops. The dream of an "Armenia without Armenians" proposed by some Russian nationalists was now a real possibility.

The Russian war effort, for all its successes in the Caucasus and Anatolia, was disastrous on the Western Front. The losses to the Germans created severe economic dislocations in the rear and great discontent in the population. In the winter of 1916-1917 food shortages increased the hostility that many workers and soldiers held toward the royal government. In late February 1917 women in Petrograd marched into the streets demanding bread. They were joined by factory workers, and from these modest beginnings a movement swelled that soon brought down the 300-year-old Romanov dynasty. Transcaucasia greeted the February Revolution with joy, and Armenians anticipated that the new Russian regime would make good on the promises left unfulfilled by the deposed tsar.

The history of Armenians in Russia was the story of both progress and persecution, of profound social and political transformation and of cultural and linguistic rejuvenation. Russification had been attempted but had failed. After more than a century under the Russian Empire, the Armenians emerged more nationally aware, more self-conscious, and more able to defend themselves. From a dispersed and divided community they had created national institutions alongside their ancient church to promote their interests as a people. Political parties, schools, newspapers, as well as a considerable amount of economic power, made the Armenians of Russia a force to be reckoned with by the Russian government. Although only one of the crucibles in which the Armenian revival had taken shape, the Russian Armenian community would become the major Armenian community to survive intact the Great War, the genocide of Turkish Armenians, and the Russian revolutions. Eastern Armenia, not the central districts of the Armenian plateau, would provide that part of the homeland on which an independent, a Soviet, and then again an independent republic of Armenia would be built.

FOR FURTHER INFORMATION

Allen and Maratoff, 1953.   Kazemzadeh, 1974.

Gregorian, 1972.   Lynch, 1901.

Hovannisian, 1967.   Suny, 1993.

5

MODERN ARMENIAN LITERATURE AND INTELLECTUAL HISTORY FROM 1700 TO 1915

Vahé Oshagan

T he Armenian intellectual revival in modern times was a complex
process extending over 150 years, from 1700 to 1850. It entailed
not only the enlightenment of a nation plunged into ignorance during
three centuries of servitude, but also its political liberation from Turkish
and Persian rule.

Beginnings of the Revival in the Ottoman Empire

The first phase of the Armenian revival covers the period from 1700 to
1800 and is characterized by the slow emergence of a native intelligentsia and by the establishment of certain social and cultural infrastructures. The second phase of fifty years is marked by numerous foreign
contacts, increased social conflicts, and the speeding up of the cultural
life in the major urban centers. Already in the seventeenth century seeds
of impending change and conflict appeared in the form of bridgeheads
of Catholic penetration into the Ottoman Empire. Jesuit missionaries

landed in the Ottoman Empire in 1609 and 1668. The Capuchins arrived
in 1626. The College of Propaganda Fidei was founded in Rome by Pope
Gregory XIV in 1640, and the Jesuit preacher Clemens Galanus landed
in Constantinople shortly thereafter. The first Armenian historians of
the seventeenth century, Krikor Taranaghtsi (Grigor Daranaghtsi) and
Arakel Tavrizhetsi (Arakel of Tabriz), began to write around 1640, and
the first Armenian printing presses were established in Constantinople
in 1587 and 1677. But the most remarkable event of the seventeenth
century was doubtless the appearance of the towering figure of Eremia
Chelebi Kiumurjian (1637-1695). Historian, poet, pedagogue, musician,
miniaturist, editor, and translator versed in nine languages, his scores of
books in Armenian and Turkish on historical, historiographic, and
literary subjects make him the most important man of letters during the
entire pre-1800 period. The historian Leo (Arakel Babakhanian), concerned more with Kiumurjian's social impact, says that "he was the first
lay intellectual to influence the course of events, a man who created and
directed public opinion, the first Armenian writer in the European sense
of the word, and whose work contains the seeds of the future growth of
Armenian journalism." Fanatically anti-Catholic, Kiumurjian established a printing press in Constantinople in 1677 that "pioneered the
printing activity of the following century," says Mekhitarist scholar
Father Nerses Akinian. This outstanding man appears to us today as the
prototype of the Western Armenian man of letters we meet along the
centuries—self-made, versed in many languages and in the sciences,
hailing from no definite literary tradition and contributing to none but
working on his own and dying either too young or too old, without
having accomplished his destiny.

Another sign of the revival in the seventeenth century was the
emergence of a lay intelligentsia made up of various dignitaries whose
claim to prominence was primarily in their moral and economic power.
The most eminent of these were the *amiras,* wealthy and astute bankers
and money-changers who managed the finances of Turkish *pashas* and
whose piety and philanthropic spirit gave them immense authority in
the Armenian community. Another class of dignitaries who enjoyed
considerable prestige were the *chelebis* (meaning "godly" in Turkish).
Like the *amiras,* they were wealthy merchants with close ties to
government circles and high civil servants whose affairs they managed. The *chelebis* patronized social and cultural activities in the
community, building churches, schools, orphanages, hospitals, found-

ing printing presses, publishing books, and funding students. Then there were the *mahdesis* (meaning "pilgrims" in Arabic), who were highly respected by the Armenians for their saintly lifestyle and devotion to religion. So were the more worldly *aghas* (Turkish for "landlords" or "lords"), who were respected because of their wealth, age, and wisdom. Another class that wielded authority was made up of the *badvelis* (Armenian for "teachers" or "preachers"), mostly church-trained lay teachers whose vast erudition, especially in religious matters, gave them a venerable position in society. Finally there were the *khodjas* (meaning in Persian "masters"), the rivals of the *amiras* and *chelebis*. They formed an entrepreneurial class of wealthy, enterprising merchants on a global scale but who were especially active in Persia and India as well as in the internal and external commerce of the Ottoman Empire during the seventeenth and part of the eighteenth century.

The clergy was the last element of the cultural elite of the period. Traditionally, the clergy had been the most educated element of the Armenian population. It allied itself with the lay intelligentsia and formed the ruling class, with the patriarch at its head. This array of men of letters, of wealth, and of fanatical fervor was formed slowly in the two centuries of the revival, and it counteracted the threat posed by the advent of first the Catholic then the Protestant missionaries into the Ottoman Empire.

Parallel to the awakening of cultural interest, in the seventeenth century there was a sudden surge of national liberation activity thanks to the vigorous initiatives of Israel Ori, a native of Armenia born in 1659 into an aristocratic family. As a young man, Ori was driven by the obsession of enlisting European powers in a concerted military adventure to liberate Eastern Armenia from Persian domination and to create an independent state. He failed, but his indomitable will and his constant travels helped create a psychological climate in the Armenian ruling classes that favored more openness to the West.

Except for the works of Eremia Chelebi Kiumurjian, there was very little literary activity in the Armenian world during the seventeenth century. Backwardness and the humiliating status of *raya* (chattel) had almost stifled the Armenians' creative energies. Only a score of books, all of a religious nature, saw the light of day. However, a certain tradition of popular lyrical poetry as well as troubadour poetry did survive, kept alive by its sheer momentum.

The Age of Enlightenment

The eighteenth century may be labeled the "Age of Enlightenment" in the Armenian world. It was characterized by the slow but steady emergence of a middle class in the major cities, bringing in its wake the need for better public education, for mass media, and eventually for power. The traditional ruling classes—the *amiras,* the *khodjas,* and the *chelebis,* in concert with the Armenian patriarch of Constantinople, whom they controlled, consolidated their hold over the community through greater and more frequent acts of public benevolence. No less important were the cultural initiatives of the Armenian Apostolic Church and of the Armenian Catholic Mekhitarist Congregation in Venice, founded by Mekhitar of Sebastia in 1717.

What makes this elite remarkable is the fact that it was committed to the preservation of the traditional culture, to the faith and the language of its forefathers, and to the survival of the Armenian nation. Although the *amiras, khodjas,* and *chelebis* retained their dominance for generations, they had no concerted impact on the revival. Their activities were erratic and discontinuous, and they often neutralized one another. Thus, in spite of their altruism and patriotism, these groups constituted a powerful force of conservatism and restraint in the path of ambitious and daring intellectuals, especially in the nineteenth century. Allied to the Armenian Church, they exercised a fly wheel action, propelling and restraining the revival at the same time.

Modern Armenian culture is an essentially urban phenomenon and has flowered in large cities at the periphery of the Armenian world, at the points of contact with foreign cultures—with English culture in Madras and Calcutta; with French culture, in Smyrna, Constantinople, and Paris; with Italian culture, in Venice; with German culture in Dorpat (now Tartu, Estonia), and Vienna; with Russian culture, in St. Petersburg, Moscow, and Tiflis. This fact gives modern Armenian culture a somewhat cosmopolitan character, provoking inner tensions that other cultures, developing within their own and stable national structures, do not experience.

The absence of national political life for over 400 years has developed strong centrifugal and individualistic tendencies among Armenians and has given rise to an incipient xenophilia that has been the major cause of a permanent desire to emulate Western cultural models, resulting in certain "alienation" of the ethnic literature. All this has fostered a permanent state of tension within Armenian life, giving rise to class conflicts and religious and denominational dissensions. The gradual separation of the nation, beginning in 1800, into two divergent eastern and western parts and the much larger context of racial antagonism between Turks and Armenians have kept the Armenians, especially the elites, in a constant state of alertness and anxiety. These anxieties have created a centripetal reflex and craving for a closed social life, for unity and isolation. The final constant of Armenian cultural life has been the ideology of absolute priority of the group's interests over those of the individual, an imperative to which all else—artistic demands and experimentation, individual rights, freedom of expression, and dissent—have been subordinated.

For the Western Armenians, the eighteenth century opened with the founding the Benedictine Order of Mekhitarists in 1717 on the island of San Lazzaro in Venice, dedicated to piety, literary scholarship, and service to the nation. The founder was a young priest, Mekhitar (1676-1749), born in Sebastia. After taking the orders as a member of the Armenian Apostolic Church in Constantinople, Mekhitar was converted to Catholicism and organized a small group of disciples. Predictably, this action drew the ire of the Apostolic Church. Unable to withstand the church's harassment, Mekhitar took refuge in Venice, to pursue in freedom his religious devotion and his mission of enlightenment. To this end, he decided that the first priority was the forging of an effective instrument by which the Armenian masses could be enlightened. Because the *ashkharhabar,* or the language of the people, was a hopelessly inefficient and unreliable tool for that purpose, Mekhitar felt that he had to write a complete and definitive grammar of the Armenian language. Thus, in 1727 he published the first volume of the *Grammar in Armeno-Turkish* (the manuscript of the second volume is still in Venice), followed three years later by a grammar of *grabar* (krapar), or classical Armenian. But the major contribution of the indefatigable monk to Armenian scholarship is his celebrated *Bargirk Haikazian Lezvi* (Dictionary of the Armenian Language). Published in 1749, three weeks after his death, it contained 100,000 items and took twenty-five years to complete. For a long time both works were the basic tools used by scholarly researchers who published classical Armenian texts, popularized of Armenian history, restored the linguistic structure of the Armenian language, and translated Greek, Latin, and European masterpieces. Perhaps more important was the example of total dedication Mekhitar inspired in his disciples and the spiritual vigor with which he imbued them for generations to come. It was through the dedication of his followers that Mekhitar achieved his triple goal of preparing Catholic priests of deep religious devotion, accomplished scholars, and highly motivated patriots.

At the same time, the clergy of the Apostolic Church in Constantinople also set itself the task of modernizing the infrastructure of the national culture. Between 1700 and 1710 four new printing presses were founded in Constantinople and forty volumes of books were published, almost all of a religious nature. The driving force of this sudden surge of activity was Hovhannes of Baghesh, otherwise known as Archbishop Golod. Elected patriarch of Constantinople in 1705, he threw himself body and soul into the task of easing the vicious denominational conflicts that had been ravaging the Armenian *millet* for over fifty years. But he made little headway. He also commissioned the translation of some twenty volumes of Latin and Italian books on religious topics. During his tenure of thirty-six years, Golod published more than ninety volumes, founded two seminaries, and trained and ordained forty priests. The boost he gave to learning was continued by his student and successor, Patriarch Hagop Nalian, an even more passionate apostle of modernization. He authored ten volumes of religious instruction and interpretation of religious texts. As a theologian, linguist, and author, Nalian ranks with the most illustrious patriarchs, and although his work bears no comparison with the lasting and worldwide effects of Mekhitar's, he nonetheless played a key role in consolidating the authority of the Apostolic Church at a crucial time in its history.

On the strictly literary plane, the first half of the eighteenth century produced no less than thirty poet-versifiers writing in classical or vernacular Armenian or even in Turkish. Many of these were patriarchs. The annals of the period are rich in men of letters of all sorts, such as Baghdasar Tbir (1683-1768) of Constantinople, poet, musician, historian, scientist, educator, Enlightenment activist, author of three books on Armenian grammar (which were used in Armenian schools for over 100 years) a book of lyrics, and a treatise on logic, and editor of more than ten manuscripts of major medieval Armenian authors. There were also historiographers, translators of Italian and Latin texts, interpreters (polyglot Armenians who worked in foreign consulates as translators), linguists, and versifiers. It was, all in all, a dynamic period for the newly forming middle class in the cities, the future *esnafs,* or guildsmen, who controlled much of the inner commercial market in Constantinople. Around this time, in 1750, the Great Khan of Constantinople was built, a vast three-storied commercial complex with 166 rooms from where the *amiras* and the Armenian merchants conducted their affairs.

This was a time of construction of churches and monasteries, financed largely by the *amiras,* who consolidated their power over the church and the community. By the middle of the eighteenth century, ten printing presses functioned in the capital, but only religious books were published; it would be another ninety years before the periodic press appeared. Two kinds of schools for public instruction existed—one had the classes in the Great Khan for the training of trade apprentices, and the other took place in the small rooms adjacent to the churches where priests taught religion to neighborhood children as well as reading and writing. Only in 1789 were minorities in the Ottoman Empire given the right to open their own schools. But this short period of cultural activity was followed by many years of lethargy until the first quarter of the nineteenth century.

The Revival in the Communities in India

In the East, the hopes and struggles for national liberation had always been more active. Prominent among the eighteenth-century intelligentsia was Joseph Emin. He deployed immense energy in trying in vain to interest the British government, the Armenian catholicos, and then the Georgian king in his plans to create a sovereign Armenia. In 1792 he published in London his autobiography, *The Life and Adventures of Joseph Emin, an Armenian,* in which he expounded his ideas about the liberation of the Armenian nation from Oriental tyranny through education and armed struggle. It was with him that the Enlightenment theories that man is born free and obeys only the natural laws of reason penetrated into Armenian political consciousness and influenced the ideology of the period.

The centers of this consciousness were the Armenian communities in India, of Madras and Calcutta, established at the beginning of the eighteenth century as a result of massive emigration from the region of New Julfa (Nor Chougha; Isfahan) in Persia. Close commercial relations with the British through the East India company had brought prosperity to the Armenians and had awakened them culturally. In 1772 a printing press began to function in Madras, another one in Calcutta in 1796, as an elite group of intellectuals calling themselves "the Madras Group" came into being in the early 1770s. Soon the ideology of the national liberation movement that had been developing for two centuries took shape in the works of the leading intellectuals. Movses Baghramian's *Nor Tetrak vor Kochi Hortorak* (New Booklet of Exhortations) in 1772 (which Leo considers the foundation of Armenian political literature) advocated armed struggle against the oppressors and exhorted the Armenians to open up to the ideas of Western Enlightenment and to work toward national self-consciousness so that the ideology of the national liberation struggle could strike root. Shahamir Shahamirian (1723-1797) is the author of two important books—*Girk Anvanial Vorokait Parats* (Snare of Glory) in 1773 and *Tetrak vor Kochi Nshavak* (Booklet of Aim) published in 1783. The first laid down the social and economic structures of the future free Armenia, which Shahamirian imagined to be a republic with a parliament freely chosen by the people and endowed by a constitution that would guarantee the rights and duties of the various governing bodies and citizens and institute the separation of church and state. In *Aim,* Shahamirian writes about the ideal communal constitution for the Armenians in Madras. Both books are animated by the vision of a double liberation of the Armenians—first from ignorance through education and enlightenment that prepares the ground for the second liberation, this time from political slavery through armed struggle. They further envision the general form of the future free and sovereign Armenia, its legal system and constitutional structures, the separation of church and state, and the republican framework chosen through universal suffrage. The small Madras community of only 1,000 Armenians also boasted a highly enlightened and wealthy upper middle class that financed the publication of these and other books and their diffusion in the Armenian world, the founding of schools, and the work of the Mekhitarists in faraway Venice and Trieste. Finally, these same wealthy merchants decided to enrich the colony with a newspaper. So in 1794 an educated priest, Father Harutiun Shmavonian, was brought to Madras from Persia to edit and publish the first periodical publication in the Armenian world, *Aztarar* (The Monitor). The journal published commercial news and general information about the Armenian colonies in the world but was forced to cease publication after eighteen issues.

By the turn of the century, the Armenian community in Madras had lived out its brief existence. It was the turn of the Calcutta community to carry the torch. A printing press was founded in 1797, the following year a school was opened, and ten years later a second press was founded. Books began to be published, and in 1818 the first journal, the weekly *Hayeli Kalkatian* (Mirror of Calcutta) appeared, almost exclusively in classical Armenian, to please the highly conservative community.

Gradually the revival gathered speed. Other journals were published and European authors, such as William Shakespeare, René de Chateaubriand, Samuel Johnson, and others were translated. In 1821 an important step was taken when the first Armenian college, the Philanthropic College (Mardasirakan Jemaran) was opened in Calcutta. The following year a printing press was added, and four years later a library was opened. The college became a hub of cultural activity around the imposing figure of its principal for forty years, Hovhannes Avdalian (1793-1860). Originally from Persia, Avdalian had acquired an impeccable English education and specialized in education and philology. He became the leading intellectual of the entire epoch, training a whole generation of teachers and men of letters who played an important role in the growth of the spirit of the revival.

But with prosperity and culture, a certain decadence had set in. Mixed marriages, neglect and disuse of the Armenian language, weakening of traditions, and assimilation within English society had contributed to the decline of the Armenian community in Calcutta. It was at this moment, in 1839, that an intellectual from Persia, Mesrob Taghiatiants, entered the scene. A heady young man with an English education, he saw his literary function as that of a popularizer of other cultures and an educator of the masses. He first translated English historical works; then edited the journal *Azgaser* (The Patriot) of the Ararat Association, which he helped found; wrote poetry and essays; and worked as a teacher. Then in 1846 he published the first of his three historical novels inspired by ancient Armenian literature, *Vep Vardgesi* (The Epic Novel of Vardges), the first work of fiction in modern Armenian literature. Partly historical and partly psychological, its style and tone were heavily influenced by European preromanticism and many English authors. (Taghiatiants had translated works by Shakespeare, John Milton, Daniel Defoe, and Sir Water Scott.) Artistically speaking, Taghiatiants's novels were rather crude, but their didactic and pseudorealist style seems to have set the tone for most of the novels that were to follow in the coming century.

After 1850, the Armenian community of Calcutta, like the other communities in India, declined and, by the year 1900, ceased to count in the Armenian world. Yet these communities played an important role in the nineteenth-century revival in both the Eastern and Western Armenian world through their close contacts with the Mekhitarist congregations in Venice and Trieste, which they supported financially out of love for the national culture.

The Revival of the Eastern Armenians

The revival of the Eastern Armenians was much slower than that of the Western Armenians. It started in the mid-eighteenth century with the appearance of an exceptionally gifted poet minstrel, Sayat Nova (1712-1795), who was born in Aleppo but lived and produced in Tiflis. Artistically, Sayat Nova was certainly the most accomplished minstrel of the some 400 others in the region in his time, and he gave an important impetus to the popular lyrical poetry. But his was an oral tradition, and its impact was not very great in the urban centers.

In the eighteenth century, Eastern Armenian society was made up of a largely rural population in Armenia itself and an urban mass in cities outside Armenia proper, such as Tiflis, Baku, and Batum, whose prosperity increased with the growth of commerce and industrialization of the Caucasus. Armenian businessmen and educated people with European connections were also instrumental in transmitting new social ideas and commercial know-how to the population. At the same time, an intelligentsia radicalized through contacts with Russian culture emerged from the middle and lower-middle classes, drawing the cities and countryside closer. Thus, during the nineteenth century, traditional rural society was gradually enlightened and transformed, and a sense of nationality of secular nature developed among the Armenians. Many Armenians had settled in Moscow or St. Petersburg either as businessmen or as students and lived in small, closed communities. Tiflis was another important cultural center for Armenians. The remoteness and the sorry plight of the homeland moved the hearts of these expatriates and turned some, especially the students, into cultural activists. Out of this ferment the first signs of a renaissance appeared.

The first stirring occurred in communities far away from the homeland, as was the case with the Western Armenians. In 1780 a printing press was opened in St. Petersburg, and some classical Armenian texts were published. The opening of a school in Astrakhan in 1810 marked the start of an educational activity that would increase as the renaissance developed. Soon the fame of the school and that of its principal, Serovbe Patkanian, spread far and wide, setting an example to others. In 1815 an event of major consequence took place in Moscow: the opening of the prestigious Lazarian College, or Academy (Jemaran), founded by the Lazarian family, a veritable dynasty of wealthy, enlightened Armenian businessmen from New Julfa. The family also had distinguished itself in the Russian armies during the Armenian liberation struggles and was a great patron of education. Very soon the Lazarian Academy became an important center of learning (it existed until it was seized by the Bolsheviks in 1918) with the full program of a Russian gymnasium, under the able leadership of Harutiun Alamdarian. By 1850 the academic syllabus of the college had a markedly Orientalist and Armenological direction with an elite majority of Armenian teachers and students from all over Russia. Many of them, poets, intellectuals, and leaders, would soon spearhead the cultural renaissance in Russian, or Eastern, Armenia. In 1836 its library holdings numbered 8,000 volumes, its press published books in thirteen different languages, and it became the first point of contact of Armenian intelligentsia with the modern world.

In 1824, fifteen years after the founding of the Lazarian College, another important center of learning, the Nersisian College, began in Tiflis, at the other end of the Russian Empire. Lasting one hundred years, it was the work of Nerses Ashtaraketsi (1770-1857), prelate of the Armenians of Tiflis (he became catholicos in 1843), a leading figure in the national liberation struggle of the Armenians. Like the Lazarian College, Nersisian College counted among its students and faculty some of the most liberal-minded political activists, poets, and writers of the time, such as Khachatur Abovian, Stepan Nazarian, and Harutiun Alamdarian. These two institutions taught the Armenians what Western education meant and gave birth to a class of true intellectuals.

Printing presses and publications continued apace with education. In 1821 a press started to function in Moscow, then in Tiflis in 1826, where Father Mikayel Chamchian's *Grammar of the Armenian Language* was published. In 1827 a press was set up in Shushi. In 1828 a book of archives was published in St. Petersburg. That same year students of the Nersisian College published, under the guidance of Alamdarian, a book of poetry. The following year a press was founded in the Lazarian College, which published a collection of student poetry called *Musaik Araratian* (Muses of Ararat). In 1829 the Treaty of Adrianople between Russia and Turkey inaugurated a period of peace for the Armenians during which the cultural progress gathered momentum. During the next decade the Armenian theater took its first steps in Nor Nakhichevan, Tiflis, and Shamakhi. And when in 1834

Sargis Tigranian published in Moscow a grabar translation of Racine's *Athalie,* he gave the first sign of the coming of classicism into Russian Armenian letters.

Fifty years later, in 1874, a third college, Gevorgian Jemaran, was founded by Catholicos Gevorg IV of Echmiadzin. At first it was dedicated to the training of teachers and the preparation of students for the priesthood, but gradually its religious character weakened and it became almost equivalent to a lay college with a strong accent on Armenian scholarship. Later in the century the college became a hotbed for political activism.

One last center of learning that played an important role in the renaissance was the German University of Dorpat. In the 1830s a group of Armenian students from Russian Armenia had gone there to pursue humanistic studies. In this academic environment these students—writers, poets, musicians—felt the powerful impact of the romantic poetry of Johann Goethe and Johann Schiller as well as the shock waves of the 1830 Revolution in Paris. They were fired up with nationalist fervor, with the ideals of the Enlightenment, and the revolutionary spirit of the times. They wrote passionate poetry about the woes and hopes of Armenia, set it to music, and sang it.

The period between 1830 and 1850 was a time of great excitement and challenge. Scores of schools were opened under the influence of the Mekhitarists from the West and of the newspapers and ideas that reached from Madras and Calcutta from the East. The enlightened class soon realized the urgency of educating and upgrading the masses. Liberation of the homeland would come later. And to do all this, they needed effective means of communication—a language and a forum. Thus the first steps in forging a new literary *ashkharhabar* were taken in the Lazarian and Nersisian colleges, where teachers actively studied the dialects of the students from various regions of Armenia, then purified them of foreign borrowings and gradually developed a common language understandable by all. By 1846 Stepan Nazarian had written a book in defense of the new literary *ashkharhabar,* declaring that the dialect of the Ararat district should serve as the basis for the future language. This started a polemic that continued until 1855 with the publication of Rafayel Patkanian's (he used the pseudonym Kamar-Katipa) poetry in *ashkharhabar,* which assured that form's final victory. By 1850 students in Dorpat were singing their patriotic songs in *ashkharhabar.*

Other men of letters also were aiming at the enlightenment of the Armenian people from the 1830s to 1850s. Several travelogues were published in Venice, Calcutta, and Tiflis, as were some novels and tales of mainly moralistic nature. Memorialist and autobiographical literature, too, developed rapidly. Other important figures were Harutiun Araratian, Father Manvel Gumushkhanetsi and Khachatur Abovian. There was a revival in other genres, too. Books of parables, moralistic tales, and novels were published in Smyrna, Constantinople, and Moscow, and popular ballads dedicated to Armenian heroes of Russo-Turkish wars.

The Western Armenian Revival

Among the Western Armenians, things began to fall into place in the 1840s. Politically, the hopes aroused by the tanzimat proclamation of Sultan Abdul-Mejid in 1839, promising reforms for the non-Muslim subjects of the Ottoman Empire, were still very much alive. Culturally, the revival seemed to be gathering pace. Some thirty-seven schools, including two colleges, with 4,620 students, were operating in Constantinople; several museums, printing presses, hospitals, and public libraries were functioning; and eight different journals were published. Between 1843 and 1848 some thirty promising students were sent to European, mainly French, universities for higher education paid for by the *amiras* and some wealthy middle-classers. Also, in 1843 the Mekhitarists of Venice began publishing the first scholarly periodical, *Pazmavep* (Polyhistory), while in 1847, their counterparts in Vienna began to publish *Evropa* (Europe), a literary and scholarly journal in almost faultless literary Armenian. At the same time, the patriarch of Constantinople founded its own journal called *Hayastan,* a symbol of its intellectual and social authority. In 1847, the Protestant community was officially recognized by the Ottoman government.

By 1850 an intelligentsia had gradually taken shape, made up first by a group of Westernized, highly motivated and professional young people. They represented the best minds of the time—Nahabed Rusinian, the daring innovator in the field of linguistics; Krikor Odian, jurist, writer, humanist, and the driving force behind the Ottoman Constitution of 1878 and the Armenian National Constitution of 1863; Stepan Vosganian, already mentioned; Khachadur Misakian, the erudite linguist and writer, and Hovhannes Hisarian, the editor, writer, and archaeologist-ethnographer. Then there were the brothers Mgrdich and Krikor Aghaton, the first an editor, jurist, and political figure in the Ottoman administration, and the second an internationally noted agronomist, economist, editor, and high civil servant in the Ottoman administration; Nigoghos Zorayan, the economist, political scientist, and free thinker; Garabed Utudjian, the agronomist and editor; and others, almost all university graduates from Paris.

The second group of the intelligentsia was the previously mentioned *amiras*. Many of the *amira* families (in the eighteenth century their number had reached 150) held hereditary positions of great responsibility in the royal palace which they often used for the benefit of their community. Of these families (such as the Dadian, Duzian, and Bezdjian), none was so famous as the Balians, the prestigious architects to the sultan for more than a century and a veritable dynasty. Two of the Balians, the brothers Nigoghos and Hagop, both graduates of the University of Paris, took an active part in community affairs by supporting and financing theaters, schools, and other cultural projects in the capital, especially Hagop, whose house became the meeting place for the cultural elite.

Thus, by the middle of the nineteenth century, the preparatory phase of modern Armenian literature appeared to be complete. Several important developments had occurred. A start had been made in structuring a tolerably well-made and polished literary language; and frequent contacts with advanced cultures (English in India, Russian and German in Eastern Armenia, French in the Ottoman Empire and in Europe, Italian and classical in Venice) had brought a sense of progress and activated critical thinking. Also, an intelligentsia of sorts and an elite had asserted themselves; some elements of a literary tradition in prose, verse, and journalism were in place; and a middle class had begun to take shape in the big urban centers. Finally, Eastern Armenia had passed under Russian rule, but the liberation of Western Armenia from the Ottomans was no more than an idea in some minds.

The first literary texts in the West were in grabar as the authors were men of religion. After the books of Taghiatiants, the most important event was the publication in Constantinople, in 1850, of the poetry of Father Mgrdich (Mkrtich) Khrimian (1820-1907) entitled *Hravirak Ayraratian* (Invitation to Ararat), which was fashioned after the classical model of Virgil's *Pastoral Poems*. But Khrimian was also a spontaneous, elementary writer whose words sprang from deep, hidden sources of Armenianness; from love and understanding of the land, its traditions, and the peasants' feelings. His book, an exhortation to love the land and to liberate it from oppression, had a tremendous impact on the minds of the enlightened people. The following year a volume of poems by Father Edvard Hurmuzian (1799-1876), entitled *Purastank* (Flower Gardens) and inspired by Virgil's poetry, appeared from the Mekhitarist Congregation press in Venice. The poems lacked solid poetic qualities but they established the presence of classicism in Armenian letters. By the 1830s the classical taste also had penetrated into the Mekhitarist sensibility, thanks to massive translations of the ancients as well as through poems by eminent scholars and poets of the congregation. The dominant figure in Armenian classicism was Father Arsen Pakraduni (Bagratuni) (1790-1866) whose *Haik Diutsazn* (Haik the Hero) is the masterpiece of the epic genre in Armenian letters. It is also one of the longest epics in world literature (22,332 lines), glorifying the patriotic spirit within the context of Christian ethics and the Old Testament, in the purest classical tradition of Tasso, Virgil, and Homer. But the real theoretician of Armenian classicism was Father Edvard Hurmuzian, whose *Ardzern Banasteghtsutiun* (Handbook of Poetry), published in Venice in 1839 is the first attempt to make a theoretical study in aesthetics, that of classicism, in Armenian. Armenian classicism, almost exclusively confined to the Mekhitarists and their students, was concerned with two main themes. One was the national ethos—the unending struggle for national liberation, the heroic and glorious past of Armenia, the beauty of the motherland, the mythic figure of Haik (Haig) the ancestor, and the virtues of Haikanush, his wife. The other was the general aesthetic issues of classicism, such as the sense of order and harmony, the respect for rationality, the edifying nature of poetry, the choice of noble sentiments and heroes, the epic breath, and the role of the supernatural in the destiny of the Armenian people. But the scope and duration of the school was severely restricted by writers' use of the grabar as the only dignified language worthy of classical texts and also the mythic nature of the content. In any case, hardly anyone of importance outside the Mekhitarist sphere of influence ever tried to write in the classical vein.

First Signs of Revival—The Mekhitarists and Smyrna

While the rise and fall of the Indian communities was taking place, the Mekhitarist world had moved forward. In the second half of the eighteenth century, a new and more prepared generation of scholars trained in the spirit and discipline of Mekhitar of Sebastia entered the scene. First on the list of priorities was the perfecting of grabar by translating classical texts into Armenian and then by arduously purifying and renewing the grammar. The *Nor Haikazian Pararan* (The New Haikazian Dictionary) prepared by the "Three Vartabeds," Fathers Gabriel Avedikian, Khachadur Surmelian, and Mgrdich Avkerian, begun in 1784 and completed in 1834, remains unsurpassed in its scholarship and scope. The Mekhitarist fathers also launched research in historical and archaeological fields. The leader was Father Mikayel Chamchian, whose epoch-making three-volume *Hayots Batmutiun* (History of the Armenians) was published in 1786, covering the entire history of the Armenian nation. The project used all available historical published and unpublished material from Greek and Roman sources, and it became the cornerstone of all historiography for a hundred years, influencing writers as well as historians. Another scholar of great merit was Father Ghugas Injijian, whose work on the archaeology, ethnography, and geography of ancient Armenia, published after his death, was of much help to later scholars. Other areas of interest have been theology, literature, and philology. The work of Father Gabriel Avedikian on Grigor Narekatsi (Gregory of Narek) was the starting point of much subsequent research on the medieval mystic. Avedikian also distinguished himself as a grammarian and patristic scholar.

By the mid-1800s the Armenians of the Ottoman Empire had been much weakened by constant struggle against Catholic penetration and by internal dissensions among different groups of the ruling elites. The urban masses, separated from the rest of the world and especially from the Turkish population, lived huddled around their church and their *amiras*. But the peasantry was worse off and barely survived the unbridled exploitation by Kurdish chieftains and Turkish overlords. All cultural life was thus the work of isolated and haphazard initiatives by *tbirs, badvelis,* priests, and *amiras,* who very slowly and painfully set up the infrastructure of the revival a century later. And when, in 1789, Sultan Selim allowed the *millets* to have their own parochial schools next to the churches, the *amiras* were quick to respond. Within five years, in Constantinople they had opened six schools, one hospital, and had founded a printing press.

Smyrna, with its compact, very conservative, prosperous Armenian community of around 10,000, was active too. Like Constantinople, it was a cosmopolitan city and an international port, open to all sorts of influences from the outside world. Armenian businessmen profited most from this reality. They also controlled the chamber of commerce as well as much of the local and international silk market. In 1759 a printing press was active in the city, and a community hospital was built in 1802. Smyrna had the most imposing cathedral in the empire. The real glory of the community, the Mesrobian College, built in 1825 by the Abroyan family, was the first lay college in the entire empire. The school was free of charge, many foreign languages were taught, and European plays were staged—all for the first time in the Ottoman Empire. The principal, Father Hovnan Vanantetsi, a nationally renowned figure, was also one of the first to write poetry. It seems natural that the revival of the Western Armenians should start from such a cultured environment.

But the humiliating conditions of life of the Armenians, their inferior status in society, their isolation and insecurity, all resulted in an excessive reliance on the church, which, as the custodian of the culture, fostered their conservatism. During the reign of Sultan Mahmud (1808-1839), the situation of the minorities became somewhat more tolerable with the suppression of the frightful Janissaries and the tanzimat proclamation.

The Question of Western Armenian *Ashkharhabar*

By the nineteenth century Constantinople had become the spiritual and social center of the Armenians. It had a population of around 125,000, many of whom had come from the provinces, bringing their various dialects that carried strong Turkish influences. Thus the need for a common, efficient, and purified language became more pressing. To meet the challenge, the intellectual elite, made up of graduates from European universities, set to work. Garabed Utudjian, editor of *Masis*, the organ of the patriarchate; Nahabed Rusinian; Nigoghos Zorayan; Nigoghos Balian; and men of letters such as Krikor Odian and Minas Cheraz as well as Mekhitarist linguist Father Arsen Aydenian started the difficult task of forging a literary *ashkharhabar* from the popular vernacular. This effort was countered by pro-grabar intellectuals such as Father Madatia Karakash, Hagop Kurken, Reteos Berberian, and others who favored an *ashkharhabar* derived from grabar only. The "quarrel" lasted some 20 years, from 1860 to around 1880, and the *ashkharhabar* formed from the living language of the people was victorious. In the end, the founding of the journal *Hairenik* in 1891 by young writers Arpiar Arpiarian, Levon Pashalian, and Arshag Choban-ian finally established the hegemony of the Western *ashkharhabar*.

A major breakthrough came with the publication in Smyrna in 1840 of the first periodical in literary *ashkharhabar, Arshaluis Araratian*

(Dawn of Ararat), edited by Ghugas Baltasarian. The periodical was a significant step toward modernization because of its high quality and its *ashkharhabar* language. The next important development was the activity of Stepan Vosganian (1825-1901), one of the great figures of the century. The first literary critic and all-around intellectual of the Western Armenians, Vosganian represents the prototype of a long line of Armenian intellectuals nurtured in and identified with European, and particularly French, culture. Educated in Paris, he became the champion of liberalism, of the positivist philosophy of Auguste Comte, and took part in the French Revolution of 1848. Thus, Mesrobian College, under the leadership of Vosganian and others such as Krikor badveli Peshdimaldjian, Andreas Papazian, and Kevork badveli Chaprasdian, became a real powerhouse of erudite, dedicated, and Francophile teachers, translators, and journalists who influenced almost all aspects of literature.

Armenians have always had a passion for translation. In modern times, translating European literature into Armenian has served the triple purpose of enlightening the uneducated public, perfecting a literary language, and catching up with the civilized world. The Mekhitarists indulged in this passion fully, liking particularly the moral and didactic nature of much of the classical texts. Thus, between 1825 and 1850 Mekhitarist scholars translated some 130 volumes of European literature, including major works of Greek and Latin antiquity as well as scores of Italian and French classics and romances. Although almost all these translations were done in grabar, they nevertheless influenced the taste of the lay intelligentsia. Also, between 1816 and the 1850s some of the most widely read authors of European preromanticism were translated all over the Armenian world. The works of Edward Young, François Fénelon, Bernardin de Saint Pierre, and others satisfied a popular taste for melodramatic and exotic literature with religious and pastoral undertones. This taste persisted up to the end of the nineteenth century, influencing all the literary genres and even the lifestyles of the upper middle class in the big cities. When in 1852 the Dedayan brothers of Smyrna opened a press and a printing house and set up a team of expert translators, they found a ready market, especially in Constantinople, which they proceeded to flood not only with best-sellers of such authors as Alexandre Dumas *(fils)*, Eugène Sue, and Jules Verne but also with the works of major romantics including Victor Hugo, Alphonse de Lamartine, Sir Walter Scott, and others. In the following forty years the Dedayan Press produced over 200 volumes of translations, an output second only to the achievement of the Mekhitarists. While this powerful flow of preromantic and romantic translations was an important factor in shaping the nascent Armenian literature, to a certain extent it inhibited the natural growth of authentically national genres, especially in prose, a phenomenon generally associated with modernization efforts of emerging literatures in the nineteenth century. It also consolidated the hold of French cultural values on the Western Armenians. The massive translations by the Protestant missionaries of religious literature in an insipid, bland *ashkharhabar* also helped slightly to purify the language.

In the field of classical scholarship, further important work was done by the Mekhitarists of Vienna. This congregation had come into being in 1810 after a schismatic group of monks, breaking away from the mother congregation in Venice in 1773, had settled in Vienna. The congregation had become culturally active only after 1838. Influenced largely by the German academic atmosphere, it devoted its considerable energies to critical analyses of classical historians, to linguistics, and to archaeological research. Its main concern was the study and revival of the fifth-century grabar, the "Language of the Golden Age." The first important figure in this field was Father Ghevond Hovnanian (1817-1897), who conducted intense research into medieval Armenian and wrote a four-volume "Grammar of the Armenian Language," still unpublished. Another linguist was Father Hovsep Katerdjian (1820-1882), translator of Cicero, Xenophon, and Bossuet, and considered the founder of the literary school of the Vienna Mekhitarists. Author of a *Universal History* in four volumes (of which only two have been published [Katerdjian, 1849, 1852]), he is celebrated for the exquisite quality of his grabar. Another scholar of note was Father Madatia Karakashian (1818-1903), author of an important *Critical History of the Armenians* (1895). No less imposing was the figure of Father Hagovpos Dashian (1866-1933), an important contributor in the field of classical Armenian language and manuscript study, a translator and a co-author with Father Kerope Sbenian of a two-volume *Study of the Classical Armenian*. Perhaps the best-known scholar was Father Arsen Aydenian (1824-1902), whose *Critical Grammar of Ashkharhabar Modern Armenian Language* (1866) is considered an epoch-making achievement in the study of the Armenian language, its dialects, and its periods. His work has contributed perhaps more than that of any other Mekhitarist work to the establishment of the *ashkharhabar* as the literary language of modern times. The Mekhitarists of Vienna supplemented their books and research by starting the publication in 1887 of a scholarly journal called *Handes Amsorya* (Monthly Review), which continues to publish valuable work in scholarship. The combined contribution of the two Mekhitarist congregations—the Venice branch specializing in scholarship and literature, the Vienna branch specializing in linguistic scholarship—has been enormous, especially in the nineteenth century, in studying and consolidating the Armenian language and medieval culture. The Mekhitarists also have been very important forces in disseminating nineteenth-century European ideological and cultural currents into Western Armenia. Additionally, they have been active in the field of education, opening schools, twenty-eight in all until World War I, all over the Armenian world, from Hungary in 1746 to France and Italy in 1918. In a word, they have been an indispensable factor in the revival of Armenian culture in modern times.

Western Armenian Romanticism

Western Armenian romanticism arrived and developed in two different centers almost at the same time—in the Mekhitarist Congregation in Venice and in Constantinople. Its first signs appeared in Venice in the poetry of Father Ghevond Alishan (1820-1901), who published in 1857 and 1858 five small volumes of verse, two of which, *Bnuni* (About Nature) and *Hairuni* (About Fatherland), throb with feverish love for nature and Armenia. His was a poetry of strong but restrained emotion, expressed in grabar and cast in the classical garb, rather bookish at times, but also, at others, breaking out in flights of liberated imagination. It was this love of nature, of fatherland, of religion and life that characterized Western Armenian romanticism for thirty years. An important component of Mekhitarist romanticism came from the European environment as the aftershocks of the 1848 February republican revolution in Paris and of French romanticism reached the shores of the Adriatic. The Mekhitarists were quick to act, as they thought of themselves as a relay station for transmitting the spirit of the political and literary revolutions of Europe to the Armenians in the Ottoman Empire.

In Constantinople, the situation had changed after 1858. The generation of university graduates of the 1840s had returned from France and had taken over many of the important posts in the community. In 1852 the journal *Hayastan,* organ of the patriarchate, had been changed to *Masis* and had become the most influential daily of the community under the editorship of Garabed Utudjian. In 1856 Harutiun Sevadjian (1831-1874), the rebel intellectual, began publishing

"Meghu," a voice of dissent new in Armenian life. The same year, Mgrdich Beshigtashlian (1828-1868) helped found the first permanent theater in Constantinople and started staging classical tragedies in *ashkharhabar* and dramas inspired from ancient Armenian history.

Beshigtashlian, a graduate of Muradian College in Padua, was the first major romantic poet of the West Armenians. Muradian was founded in 1834 by an Iranian-Armenian merchant and placed under Mekhitarist administration. Beshigtashlian formed part of the large group of West Armenian intellectuals educated in the Mekhitarist schools and in the spirit of European romanticism. He was very active socially and culturally in Constantinople, notably in the founding of the Western Armenian theater and of the Hamazkiats Association, the first serious organization for the advancement of learning through schools. In 1862, when the Zeitun rebellion erupted, his patriotic and passionate poems electrified the public, popularizing the romantic mood, and he became the first man to assert the moral authority of the writer in Armenian society. His tragic love affair with Srpouhi Vahanian, his early death from tuberculosis, and his melancholic and tender lyricism represent the first image of the romantic poet in Armenian popular imagination.

We find the same themes and style in the works of Beshigtashlian's contemporary, Bedros Turian (1852-1872). His historical plays, full of pathos and heroics, were mainly inspired from ancient Armenian history but had less impact than those of Beshigtashlian. The main themes of the few poems he wrote in his short life—love, solitude, nature, death— were all in the pure romantic Lamartinian tradition. Turian is unequaled in Armenian literature for the utter sincerity and purity of his talent, and his death from tuberculosis has endeared him to all Armenians, especially the young, who share best his desperate love of life. Today he has come to symbolize the prototype of the Armenian romantic poet— highly talented, very patriotic, poor and ungainly, unloved and unappreciated, fervently religious, and doomed to an untimely death.

The romantic period ended with Turian's death in 1872. It had lasted only fifteen years, leaving the stage to second-rate poets, journalists, sundry prose writers, and polemicists, until around 1885. This was a period of conflicts between, on the one hand, a rising middle class, Catholic clergy, and Protestant missionaries, and, on the other hand, the Apostolic Patriarchate allied to the *amiras* who ended up losing some of their prerogatives. The National Constitution (1860-1863) also helped curb *amira* power considerably, guaranteeing a democratic, lay participation in communal matters. At the same time, the non-Apostolic churches strengthened their positions and weakened the power of the patriarchate. With the *amiras* split on many issues, especially school matters, the age-old racial hostility between Turks and Armenians heightened with the ascension to the throne in 1878 of the "Red Sultan," Abdul-Hamid II. One outstanding man of letters was Kevork badveli Peshdimaldjian, renowned teacher, apologist of the faith, lexicographer, and poet. The other was Garabed badveli Deroyents-Chamurdjian, equally famous theologian and erudite ideologue of the true doctrine, editor, linguist, and author of 150 volumes of books, of which only five or six are known. Thus, despite the aggressiveness of the rising middle class, the mood of the mass of Armenians was conservative, attached to its institutions, and resigned to its fate.

During the 1870s and 1880s the creative imagination appeared exhausted, even though a certain momentum was kept alive thanks to the constant appeals by the press for unity, enlightenment, tolerance, and love among Armenians. During those arid decades, the dominant figure in the press and public eye was Madteos Mamurian (1830-1901) of Smyrna, editor of the literary and political weekly *Arevelian Mamul* (Oriental Press), which he founded in 1871. He was the most accomplished and informed intellectual of the times, European educated and a symbol of wisdom and stability. Mamurian cut the figure of a "master," and his periodical was the voice of moderation, although in one of his novels, *Sev Lerin Marde* (The Man of the Black Mountain), the hero, Zora, a freedom fighter, advocates armed resistance to the Russian oppressors. He was a serious social critic and an advocate of Westernization.

The year 1875 was an important one in Armenian intellectual history. By this time major elements of the cultural infrastructure (schools, cultural associations, printing presses, periodic press, churches, clubs, etc.) were in place, and the middle class was pretty well established in authority and imposed its utilitarian ideology. Also, some contacts had been made with the Eastern Armenians, and the provinces were showing the first signs of resistance to the oppressive regime. In literature, the literary Armenian was almost complete, there was a poetic tradition of sorts, and the prose had developed into different genres—the novel, the short story, the theater, and the satire.

Khachatur Abovian and His Generation

Eastern Armenian poetry was born with the work of Abovian, of the University of Dorpat. Of all the students at the university who wrote, sang, or recited patriotic and nostalgic verses inspired by the homeland, its souvenirs, its suffering, and its beautiful nature, none had a greater impact on the times than Abovian. Before going to Dorpat, he had studied at the Nersisian Academy. A versatile talent, he tried his hand at almost all the genres—poetry, stories, essays, novels, plays, folk-lore—and was an innovator in many of them. His short career started in early youth with love lyrics inspired partly from popular poetry. During his Dorpat years, he fell under the influence of German romanticism, writing most of his inflamed and romantic poetry. He soon realized, however, that his public, the common people, needed to be educated and that the Armenian writer had to use the people's language in order to be understood. From then on, Abovian dedicated his life and work to enlightening the public. But his reformist activities soon brought him into sharp conflict with conservative elements and the clergy, causing him endless suffering. Armenian literature thereafter took on a social vocation, that is, it tried to appeal to the people, move their feelings, and direct their will. His masterpiece—*Verk Hayastani* (Wounds of Arme-nia), written in 1840 but published only in 1858—opened the new age. The novel was conceived and written more like a poem, so intense was its emotionality. It gave a graphic and tearful description of the tragic condition of Armenians in the countryside and in Erevan under Persian oppression; the hero, Aghasi, at the head of a band of partisans, fights against the overlords and for the liberation of Erevan, but dies in the end. He is thus the first rebel hero, the first *"fedai"* in Armenian literature, the prototype of the freedom fighter in Raffi's and Madteos Mamurian's novels. Abovian's novel and his patriotic poetry succeeded in placing the tragedy of Armenia and of the Armenians at the center of the enlightenment effort.

Contemporary to Abovian, Rafayel Patkanian (1830-1892) joined his voice to those trying to create a new literary Armenian that could be understood by the masses. He too was a liberal-minded reformist, and his short-lived journal *Ararat,* published in Tiflis from 1850 to 1852, gave full expression to this new spirit.

In the decade between 1850 and 1860, political themes started to appear in the journals, largely inspired by the Russian intellectual scene and by the ideologies of the radicals such as Mikhail Bakunin and Alexander Herzen. But the Armenians were most influenced by Visarion Belinsky's realist aesthetics, his social and political pragmatism, and, above all, his idealization of the "people," glorified by the Populists. The center of this new literary activity was the small group of Armenian students studying at the medical faculty of Moscow University. It was the continuation of the spirit of Dorpat students, and very soon some of the members of the group stood out as the most prominent playwrights, political activists, and journalists of the revival.

Another major literary event of those years was the publication of Stepan Nazarian's journal *Hiusisapail* (Aurora Borealis) in Moscow, in 1858, in close cooperation with Mikayel Nalbandian. Their common aim was the enlightenment and modernization of Armenian society, but whereas Nazarian favored a moderate approach to social change, Nalbandian was the prototype of the intellectual committed to radical and revolutionary change, to the democratization of Armenian society, and to the triumph of liberal ideals and the new *ashkharhabar*. Nazarian, an accomplished linguist, also championed the cause of *ashkharhabar,* advocating that it should be based on the dialect of the district of Ararat. Soon other young writers joined the team of *Hiusisapail,* which became the spearhead of the generation of reformers and revolutionaries. For six years Nazarian fought desperately to promote liberal education in Armenian schools, to open schools to train an enlightened clergy and a modern, lay intelligentsia, and to do away with intolerance and superstitions. He also translated scores of edifying, preromantic novels. He was the true personification of the spirit of Westernization and renewal.

Nalbandian led an agitated existence, harassed by both the tsarist authorities for his contacts with exiled Russian revolutionaries and by the Armenian establishment for his extreme liberal and reformist ideas. His literary production was scant but intense—his patriotic poems set to music were immensely popular, and he also wrote the first ethnographic novel in Armenian literature, *Minin Khoske, Miusin Harsn* (A Promise to One, A Bride to the Other), in 1857. A staunch champion of *ashkharhabar,* he believed that the function of the Armenian writer was to enlighten the Armenian people through a proper education in literary *ashkharhabar.* He was the first literary critic to formulate, in around 1865, the notion of a "national literature."

Nalbandian's contribution to literary ideas included the theory of "realism" or "art as a mirror of reality," a notion that covered, besides Abovian's *Verk Hayastani,* such works as Perj Proshian's *Sos ev Vartiter* (Sos and Vartiter), which he valued highly; Vartan Pasha's *Akabi* (published in Constantinople in 1851 in Armeno-Turkish, that is, Turkish words in Armenian characters); and others.

Another important enlightenment figure was Rafael Patkanian, a graduate of Lazarian College and Dorpat University. Like many of his contemporaries, he was a linguist and a poet whose revolutionary lyrics, turned into music, inflamed the youth of his time from St. Petersburg to Tiflis. He too aimed at perfecting the vernacular. So, to pass from words to acts, he founded in 1854 the literary society known as "Kamar Katipa," whose purpose was to promote the use of the popular language for the expression of ethnic culture. Both he and Abovian shared the view that only through the creative literary work could *ashkharhabar* develop into an effective and elegant language. That was how Abovian's novel, coming after Patkanian nationalistic poetry and essays inspired by the daily life of the ordinary people, consecrated the triumph of the vernacular, which was the first condition for the success of the revival.

Smbat Shahaziz (1841-1901), the poet, was also caught up in the patriotic enthusiasm of his classmates in Lazarian College. His literary career was intimately tied to *Hiusisapail,* where he published most of his poetry. In 1865 appeared his most important work, *Levoni Vishte* (Leon's Lament). This long poem described the emotional experiences of an Armenian university student traveling from Moscow to Armenia. In it, the main character, Levon, laments the backwardness, servility, and moral degradation of his compatriots whom he meets in the cities en route. Levon vows to struggle and liberate his country from its chains and his people from its ills. Although the long poem owed much to Alexander Pushkin's *Evgenii Onegin* and Lord Byron's *Childe Harold,* it was the first long poem in Armenian literature to have been inspired by the life of the people.

From 1860 to 1890 Eastern Armenian literature developed further the romantic, patriotic, and populist strains of its founders. New novelists gradually brought into focus the dominant literary style of descriptive, didactic, and socially oriented prose that has characterized the novels, the short stories, the plays, and even to some extent the poetry of the Eastern Armenians. It has been a literature of commitment to the welfare of the "people," to the land and traditions of the race, a mixture of romanticism and popular realism. Underlying it was a naive belief in progress and in the moral role of the writer that has lasted well into the Soviet era. Russian writers such as Nikolai Gogol, Mikhail Lermontov, Nikolai Chernyshevskii, and Pushkin above all were a constant source of liberal and populist inspiration for them.

The 1870s opened with the founding in 1872 in Tiflis of the periodical *Mshak* (Tiller) by Grigor Artsruni (1845-1892), a "Westernizer," one of the most accomplished and well-traveled intellectuals of his time. *Mshak* was the first major journal to appear in an important Armenian urban community, and it became the outspoken champion of Westernization, European enlightenment, and liberalism. With these and other advanced ideas—on education, religious tolerance, and national liberation—Artsruni set his journal the task of continuing the momentum that Nazarian had generated with *Hiusisapail*. *Mshak* was published until the 1920s, remaining always in the forefront of the revival effort, of the intellectual struggle for a democratic and egalitarian society.

The Triumph of Romanticism

Artsruni also opened wide the pages of his journal to promising writers of his time, foremost among whom was Raffi, born as Hakob Melik-Hakobian (1835-1888), the most prolific and talented novelist of the nineteenth century. He authored a score of historical and ethnographic novels, stories, and sketches of city life whose main purpose was to depict the sorry plight of the Armenian rural population in the Ottoman Empire. He also aimed at inspiring in his compatriots a pride in their past and their historical heritage and at awakening in them the revolutionary spirit. Raffi's novels, written with fiery imagination, intense emotion, and fine observation of detail, constituted the centerpiece of the romantic fiction in Eastern Armenian literature. He is rightly considered the ideological father of the Armenian revolutionary movements that started in the middle of the 1880s. One of his heroes in particular, Vardan, in the novel *Khente* (The Madman), symbolized for generations to come the figure of the Armenian freedom fighter.

Raffi's work was the most successful application of the ideas of enlightenment and political awakening. Other novelists concentrated mainly on criticism of society's ills, all the while remaining within the realm of mild realism and sentimentalism so dear to the public. One such novelist was Perj Proshian (1837-1907), whose *Sos ev Vartiter* followed closely the model of *Verk Hayastani*. He also published several ethnographical novels, reinforcing the general trend set by Abovian's slogan "Literature for the people and about the people." But when literature draws very close to life, especially country life, whose picturesque appealed so much to city people, the need for imagination and the attention to style seem to lessen. Both *Mshak* and another conservative journal, *Meghu Hayastani* (Bee of Armenia) (1858-1886), supported this pragmatic aesthetic, which was a major cause in the gradual decline of poetry after 1885. Another secondary writer of those years was

Ghazaros Aghayants (1840-1911), whose novels of rustic inspiration were very popular.

Eastern Armenian literature had by now a history of some thirty-five years. During this time a literary Armenian had been formed, based on the dialect of the plain of Ararat, and a semblance of tradition had come to life in prose and in journalism, both heavily influenced by foreign cultures. But poetry had lagged behind, and there were still no major literary historians, no literary critics, no linguists, and no great translators. The theater had matured. Early patriotic and sentimental plays by students at Moscow University in the late 1850s and in Tiflis during the 1860s and comedies in the local dialect were crude beginnings of a genre whose first major representative was Gabriel Sundukian (1825-1912). His work heralded the coming of the realist theater in Eastern Armenian literature around the years 1870-1880. A student of Abovian's, Sundukian also studied at St. Petersburg and was influenced by Belinskii's theories about the moral function of the theater. Sundukian's plays exposed the evils and ills of emergent capitalism in the Caucasus. In his comedies and melodramas, especially *Bebo* (1871), written in the dialect of Tiflis, he derided the corruption in the Armenian middle class, the superstitions of the lower classes, and their exploitation by the bureaucracy of Tiflis. His influence on future generations of playwrights has been great, and his plays still attract a large public. By the middle of the 1880s, Eastern Armenian literature had established contacts, through *Mshak,* with Western Armenian literary circles (mainly in the journal *Arevelk* of Arpiar Arpiarian, appearing in Constantinople), thus broadening its field of interest and action. In 1882 the new liberal newspaper *Ardzagang* (Echo) of Abgar Hovhannisian came to join *Mshak* in its crusade of modernization, followed in 1888 by Mkrtich Barkhudarian's *Handes Grakanakan ev Patmakan* (Review of Literature and History) from Moscow. Then in 1889 it was the *Murj* (Hammer) of Avetik Aratskhaniants followed by Father Giut Aghanian's *Luma* in 1896. The 1880s was the scene of a bitter polemic between two groups of intellectuals polarized around the journals *Mshak* and *Meghu Hayastani,* followed later by *Nor Dar* (New Century). *Mshak,* progressive and liberal, was the champion of Westernization, which was fiercely opposed by the latter two conservative and regressive journals. In the 1890s this feud turned sour, and bitter invectives were often exchanged. In any case, it was in these journals that the main characteristics of Eastern Armenian literature—its sense of the rural culture and of the common man, its utilitarian, didactic, and prose-oriented nature—found their best expression.

All major novelists and prose writers so far had worked within the romantic tradition established by Abovian and Raffi, but by the 1890s a more realistic aesthetic had begun to tempt one of the more talented writers, Alexandr Shirvanzade (1858-1935). He had started his career in *Mshak* and soon asserted his talent as the novelist of the disinherited classes of society. More than any other writer of his time, he had a firsthand knowledge of the ugly side of life, from tsarist jail to the oil fields of Baku. He continued the realist tradition of Sundukian, and his novels, especially his best-known one, *Kaos* (Chaos, 1896), depicted the drama of a dying rural society, the birth of an industrial proletariat, and the iniquities of a rising bourgeoisie. His twenty-six novels and novellas constitute an ambitious project of capturing the spirit and reality of an entire epoch, from 1879 to the coming of the revolutionary times, in 1900. After 1900 Shirvanzade turned to the theater, pursuing the same themes of social criticism.

Avetis Aharonian (1866-1948), called the "Bard of Armenian Grief," was another prolific novelist and story writer who drew his inspiration from the immense tragedy and heroism of recent Armenian historical experience as well as from Armenian village life, native traditions, and domestic dramas. He was a master of style and his colorful, romantic imagination, together with his powerful sense of reality, made him unique in Eastern Armenian letters. "The true novelist," he says, "is first of all a poet, a visionary and a prophet, and the seat of divine inspiration."

In the last decades of the nineteenth century, Eastern Armenian literature entered a new phase with the coming of the poet Hovhannes Hovhannisian (1864-1929). His passionate love of nature and of suffering mankind, his tender lyricism and limpid verse were new in Armenian poetry and thus prepared ground for the emergence of three major poets who changed and vitalized the entire poetic scene—Hovhannes Tumanian (1869-1923), Avetik Isahakian (1875-1957), and Vahan Terian (1885-1920). With these new and talented poets there appeared also, at the turn of the century, a group of literary critics who helped initiate a serious discourse on the nature and purpose of literature. With Tumanian, a breath of poetry swept into the popular legends, epic tales, and ballads, an inimitable style that raised the ordinary folktale into the realm of art. Above and beyond realism or romanticism, Tumanian's art created a genre of its own, where popular wisdom, sense of beauty, and love of simple country life are combined. For the first time in Armenian culture, a poet became the voice of the national conscience and the symbol of national unity. Tumanian was one of the few intellectuals in Eastern Armenia who organized urgent help for the Western Armenians fleeing from the Turkish genocide of 1915. Isahakian also touched a very sensitive popular vein in his folk poetry as well as the more universal theme of love. In 1897 his first volume of poetry, *Erger ou Verker* (Songs and Wounds), appeared. His work captures the simple yet powerful emotions and deep humanity of the Armenian peasant folk through legends, lyrical and epic poems, short stories, and his own epic novel *Usta Karo* (1925). His poetic versatility, his travels, and his extensive connections outside Armenia earned him the title "master." But perhaps the most gifted and private poet of all Eastern Armenian literature was Terian, who embraced communism in 1917 and was active in various advisory functions. In his collection of poems *Mtnshaghi Andurdje* (Twilight Daydreams) in 1908, Terian exhibited a talent that excelled in capturing the fleeting sensations, the feelings of sadness, loneliness, and profound despair at the hopelessness and void of human existence. Later on his poetry developed the themes of an ideal patriotism and a craving to escape from life into dreamland and an utopian world. The "Poet of Melancholy," he is the most "Western" of all Eastern Armenian poets and is almost an anomaly in a culture where public and private domains are not clearly differentiated.

By the time the Russian revolution exploded in 1917, Eastern Armenians could claim, after a century of evolution and struggles, to have a well-formed literary language, a sense of professionalism and of national traditions in prose, and, in particular, the novel In poetry, too, Tumanian and Terian were certainly nationally known and held great promise for the future.

Western Armenian Prose

The earliest forms of the novel were almost copies of the French and English preromantic fiction that had been translated in the early 1850s. These novels of Hovhannes Hisarian (1827-1906) and Armenag Haiguni (1835-1866), published in the 1850s and 1860s, were mainly exotic and sentimental works so popular in Europe in the early part of the century. So were the score of pseudonovels and novels written until the end of the 1870s. Only in 1878 did a novelist, Hovsep Shishmanian, or Dzerents

(1822-1888), appear on the scene with three historical novels, intending to mobilize Armenian political power for the struggle to liberate Western Armenia or at least Cilicia. These novels, largely inspired by Sir Walter Scott, were a great success with the public for their colorful details and heroic scenes, but do not rank as historical novels in the true sense of the word. Another novelist of the 1880s was Srpouhi Dussap (1842-1901), whose novels were constructed around feminist themes of emancipation of the woman and her rights and again inspired by European and French romantic literatures. Dussap did not lack talent and an understanding of human nature, but the violent controversy aroused by the themes in a still-conservative and traditionalist society such as Armenia distracted attention from the merits of her work.

The short story was the genre best suited to a society newly awakened to modern literatures and where the vehicle best fitted for literary expression was the newspaper. Here again, the model was taken from French literature, but the hundreds of stories published in the press were closer to life's reality than was the case with the novels. But the genre had to wait until the 1890s for the coming of a real master.

Satirical literature has always been popular with Armenians, perhaps because it is the only way a victim can retaliate in an oppressed society. Started in 1856 by Harutiun Sevadjian (1831-1874) in his journal *Meghu,* the genre was perfected in the 1870s and 1880s by Hagop Baronian (1841-1892), a writer combining a generous soul with a scathing satirical verve and a refined sense of humor. Baronian remains to this day the uncontested master of the genre, and his hilarious plays, especially *Baghdasar Aghbar* (Brother Baghdasar) and *Metsapativ Muratskanner* (Honorable Beggars) are still very popular with Armenian audiences. His social satire, in his prose texts, is also very much alive today and is a mine of information about life a century ago in the Ottoman Empire. Although influenced by Molière's art, Baronian's plays, sketches, and descriptions of urban life with its picturesque throng of characters carried an ethnic stamp that was missing elsewhere. Sevadjian, Baronian, and many other satirists laid the basis of the "realist" school that was to flourish from the late 1880s to the end of the century.

The periodic press has always been a vital component of Western Armenian literature, and perhaps three-quarters of all published texts have first appeared in its pages. It has proved to be the easiest if not the best way of enlightenment, of communication and bonding between the far-flung communities. Almost every writer has either edited or published a newspaper or formed part of an editorial body. During the nineteenth century and while in the throes of awakening, the Armenians managed to publish some 300 periodicals.

The 1880s were remarkable from many points. The Treaty of Berlin in 1878 had internationalized the Armenian question but had also cast fears in the sultan's heart of foreign intervention and Armenian secession from the empire. As a result, in the early 1880s repression in the provinces had increased, obliging Armenians to form secret political societies and parties in order to defend themselves and to fight back. This only escalated the repression, resulting in increased misery and bloodshed. Soon the newspapers in Constantinople were flooded with horror stories from the Armenian provinces. The reports suddenly awakened the Armenians to the brutal reality at their doorsteps.

Western Armenian Realist School

Thus, a breath of reality had blown across the minds and had swept away some of the latent romanticism and the habit of escape from the painful reality into a dream world or into prayer. One last romantic however lingered on, Eghia Dermirdjibashian (1851-1908), a poet with mystical leanings, an eclectic mind nourished by Goethe, Hugo, Auguste Comte, and positivist philosophy. He called out for a renewal of Armenian culture through Eastern sources of inspiration. But times were changing; men with nerves of steel and a sense of action were needed. One such man was Arpiar Arpiarian (1852-1908)—writer, intellectual, journalist, political and cultural activist. In 1884 he founded the journal *Arevelk* (The Orient) to nurture a new generation of realist writers and intellectuals and also established cultural contacts through Artsruni's *Mshak* with the Eastern Armenians. He engaged in political activity to awaken his compatriots to the need to unite and face the Turkish menace of extermination, which he felt coming, sooner or later. Arpiarian was a passionate and prolific writer but only a few of his longer stories are known to the public at large, especially one novella, *Karmir Zhamuts* (The Red Offering), which is a powerful story of class conflict that ends with a plea for national reconciliation. He traveled a great deal, writing, publishing, lecturing, organizing. Soon his efforts bore fruit and a new generation of "realists" entered the literary scene.

Many of the new wave of writers were destined to perish in the 1915 catastrophe. Among them were some of the most brilliant minds of Armenian literature, the fruit of 150 years of unrelenting effort. The first name to appear in print in 1887 was that of Krikor Zohrab (1861-1915), the quintessential product of Western Armenian social evolution. After the failure of his novel *Anhetatsats Serund Me* (A Vanished Generation), he turned to the short story, whose format suited him admirably. Lawyer and celebrated orator, political figure, engineer, writer, man of the world, he produced the most accomplished short stories of domestic dramas and character studies in Armenian, which capture many dramatic aspects of the life of the affluent Armenian society in Constantinople. His themes range from the war of the sexes and class exploitation to moral and social alienation in big cities, to love and its aberrations. Zohrab stands well above his contemporaries in the depth and breadth of his understanding of life and human nature, especially that of women. This "Prince of the Short Story," as he was known, died in the 1915 genocide. In 1888 appeared one of the important novels of the nineteenth century, Dikran Gamsaragan's (1866-1940) *Varzhapetin Aghchike* (The Teacher's Daughter), a tale of sin and love that tried to lay bare the bigotry of the Constantinople middle class private and social life, the immorality hidden behind the respectability as well as the conflict of social classes. It was the first work of a totally unknown young man of twenty, a novel written as a document about the manners of his day. The novel marked the triumph of the new spirit of realism that the journal *Arevelk* had begun.

The period 1885 to 1915 was filled with a number of popular novelists whose rather coarse works catered mainly to the crowd. In fact, these popular novels have had the longest and most stable tradition, beginning in the early years of the 1850s, at the start of Western Armenian novel, and continuing right up the present. However, they have had no impact on the evolution of the genre. The last realist novel of the nineteenth century was Erukhan's (Ervant Sermakeshkhanlian) (1870-1915) *Amirain Aghchige* (The Amira's Daughter), published in 1905 under the title *Merzhvats Ser* (Rejected Love). Like Gamsaragan's quasi-realistic novel, this work details certain aspects of the private life of the upper and lower classes in Constantinople at the turn of the century, centered on the emotional and economic abuse of the poor by the rich but leaving more disturbing facts unsaid. It is a "class novel" in that the author and the heroes are constantly conscious of their position in society and can never liberate themselves from their value systems. It suffers from, among other things, the author's inability to be objective and to avoid taking sides in the conflicts in the novel, a shortcoming typical of the vast majority of writers. The realist trend in Western

Armenian literature continues mainly in the short story, gradually giving shape to a certain Armenian variant of the realist aesthetic. Armenian realism presents a reality cleaned of its sharply immoral and shocking aspects, has didactic aims, and never questions the social hierarchies.

An important figure of the epoch was Arshag Chobanian (1872-1954), publicist, translator, and literary critic of great versatility who was very active in acquainting the French public with the treasures of Armenian medieval poetry. He was also a poet, an essayist, a scholar, and the founder-editor of one of the most serious Armenian literary journals, *Anahid*. A writer of considerable renown was the satirical novelist Ervant Odian (1869-1926), a prolific writer and publicist who is remembered today mainly through his epistolary novel *Unker Panchuni* (Comrade Panchuni) (1910), which satirizes the activities and ideology of Eastern Armenian socialist revolutionaries come to politicize the Western Armenian country folk. Finally, in 1910, Rupen Zartarian (1874-1915), a gifted prose writer from the provinces, published a collection of brilliant short stories and popular legends *Tsaigaluis* (Nocturnal Light), highlighting the beauty of the countryside and the wisdom of the simple peasants.

Around the turn of the century, these new genres coincided with an upsurge of literary activity in the provinces that continued the momentum of Mgrdich Khrimian and of Father Karekin Srvantsdiants's ethnographic work on Armenian traditions and his transcription of the popular epic "David of Sassun" in 1874. Two writers, Melkon Gurdjian, or Hrant (1859-1915), and Tlgadintsi (Hovhannes Harutiunian) (1860-1915), now turned their attention to the life of the country folk. Gurdjian focused interest on the suffering of the migrant workers from the countryside living in utter misery in the slums around Constantinople, describing in the dialect of the victims their hopes and pains. Tlgadintsi gave an emotional picture of everyday life in the provinces, the simply healthy ethic of the villager as well as his defects and foibles. This was truly the literature of the Armenian heartland.

All this contrasted sharply with the cosmopolitan and refined lifestyle of the Armenians living in big cities. Writers from the countryside moved to reject city literature as a reflection of a "corrupt" life and pitted themselves against the "Bolsetsi," or Constantinople intelligentsia. This "return to the racial sources" had hardly taken shape when a new movement, this time from the city, sprang up. The work of a group of very talented young poets and prose writers who had entered the literary scene between 1900 and 1910, with a totally fresh source of inspiration, a generation with a new vision of life and art, was probably an expression of the spiritual energies that the intense repression of the Turkish regime had sublimated in them. It was destined to be the last phase of Western Armenian literature, labeled "the literature of artists" by critics.

Renewal in Western Armenian Poetry

This renewal started in 1901 with a poet of great talent, Vahan Tekeyan (1878-1945). He introduced a poetry of a rather cerebral nature with a very refined sense of style that was new in Armenian poetry. The serene, measured verses of a twenty-three-year-old youth held great promise for the future. Tekeyan was to reveal the full measure of his talent after the massacres. In 1901 the first play by the most accomplished Armenian playwright, Levon Shant (1869-1951), appeared. Shant brought into Armenian theater some of the concerns of European thought: the themes of the conflict between idealism and sensualism, between the individual's destiny and the interests of society, and the emancipation of the self from the shackles of the body. Very often Shant took his subjects from Armenian history. One of the distinctive features of his theater was the use of poetry, mythology, metaphysics, allegory, symbolism, music, and elaborate stage scenery to mask the brutal sides of human nature and convey the often-complex metaphysical message. But this is a theater of essentially moral issues, of passions unleashed between strong personalities, in *Hin Astvatsner* (Antique Gods) (1909), *Kaisre* (The Emperor) (1916), and *Shghtaivatse* (The Enchained) (1918). Shant began his career as a poet and novelist concerned mainly with social issues such as superstitions, women's freedom, and the rights of the elite. Adom Yardjanian (Siamanto) (1878-1915) was remarkable for the violence and power of his verse and the freedom of his imagination. The epic breath blowing through his lines gave enormous power to the language and helped to revitalize the morale of the Armenians and enable them to resist the Turkish moral aggression, after the bloody massacres of 1894 to 1896. His books *Diutsaznoren* (In the Epic Manner) (1901), *Hogevarki ev Huisi Jaher* (Torches of Agony and Hope) (1907), and *Karmir Lurer Barekames* (Red News from My Friend) (1909) are all testaments of revolt and heroism. In his poetry the Armenian language attained its most powerful expression. Although his output was meager, his writing voices the Armenian nation's outrage against man's inhumanity to man.

In 1906 Misak Medsarents (1886-1908) asserted his intense yet refined experience of beauty through poetry as the way to truth and survival. Medsarents had a totally individual and lyrical temperament intoxicated with sounds, smells, and pure sensations, a creature of nature destined to die very young, the equivalent of John Keats in Armenian poetry. His two collections of poems, *Dziadzan* (The Rainbow) and *Nor Tagher* (New Lyrics), both published in 1907, inspired by the Armenian countryside and the popular culture, have immortalized the most exquisite qualities of Western Armenian lyrical sensibility. In the same year appeared *Sarsurner* (Shudders), the first volume of the most talented Armenian poet, Taniel Varoujan (1884-1915). A man of great vitality of spirit, his poetry was a synthesis of controlled, sensual classical beauty and of romantic emotion and imagination. His art revived the virile powers of the language and exalted the hidden energies of the race. He was the driving force behind the revival of pagan Armenian culture in 1914 and of a movement to revitalize the creative force of the nation by an appeal to instinctual, racial virtues, a movement that gave birth to the avant-garde journal *Mehian* in 1914. His important books were *Tseghin Sirte* (The Heart of the Race) (1909), wherein he exalted the virtues of the Armenian nation, and the *Hetanos Erger* (Pagan Songs) (1912), which sang the glory of pagan energy, beauty, and love. In the last collection of his verse, entitled *Hatsin Erge* (The Song of Bread) and salvaged by friends and published posthumously in 1921, Varoujan glorified the virtues of the peasant's life and spirit. In 1906 Diran Chrakian, or Indra (1875-1921), entered the literary scene with his highly original, mystifying introspective prose book *Nerashkhar* (Inner World), a kind of metaphysical exploration into the world of subtle meanings and intuitive truths, a surreal statement about the essence of language and reality that at times went into the realms of Far Eastern esoterical wisdom. Chrakian's world of mystical flights has not yet been fully explored. He also published a collection of poems called *Nojastan* (The Cypress Grove) (1908), where his brooding imagination fixed itself on God and death. The year 1907 saw the arrival of a prose writer, Zabel Yesayan (1878-1943), an accomplished stylist formed in the European artistic milieu and gifted with a broad understanding of human nature and who, later in life, was to become one of the best novelists of modern Armenian literature.

The impact of such a concentration of gifted artists was slow to develop because of the severe censorship that had been instituted in 1898 and also because as a result of the widespread massacres of 1894 to 1896 in the provinces, a large segment of the political and literary intelligentsia had fled to Europe, in particular Paris. From there they continued to wage ideological war against the sultan's government. Part of this émigré community returned to Turkey upon the downfall of the sultan in 1908. From then until 1915 the talents of the new generation blossomed and developed their aesthetic ideals. Other budding writers included Hagop Oshagan (1883-1948), the critic and short story writer who later was to become the greatest and most prolific novelist and critic in Western Armenian letters, and Gosdan Zarian (1885-1969), the cosmopolitan writer and novelist. These men and others supported the new movement and the journal *Mehian* (1914), which served as a forum for the formulation of their ideas. Most of these talented and promising men were caught in the genocide seven years later and perished, with around 200 other intellectuals.

The final chapter of the Western Armenian literature covers the four years following the World War I Armistice of 1918, when the remnants of the once-glorious Armenian literati flocked to Constantinople from exile to restart their cultural life. In a short, dramatic effort, the Armenians tried to get back on their feet with a sudden burst of creativity and feverish cultural activity in the city full of horror stories and morbid memories of butchered friends and relatives. But that revival came to an abrupt end with the triumphant return of Mustafa Kemal (Ataturk) to the capital in 1922.

The 1920s ushered in a new era in the long and tragic history of Armenian culture, with the onset of communism in Armenia in the east and the birth of the diaspora in the Western Armenian world.

FOR FURTHER INFORMATION

For the sources of, or more information on, the material in this chapter, please consult the following (full citations can be found in the Bibliography at the end of this volume).

Basmadjian, 1971.
Bedrosian, 1991.
Etmekjian, 1964.

Oshagan, 1982, 1984, 1986.
Shirinian, 1990.

6

THE EASTERN QUESTION
AND THE TANZIMAT ERA

Hagop Barsoumian

The Eastern Question

By the end of the seventeenth century, the Ottoman Empire had entered a period of military, economic, and administrative decline. As a consequence, the Turks were gradually forced out of the Balkans and the Near East. The recession of Turkish power created a political vacuum that European diplomacy tried to fill in an orderly fashion. However, in general, the European major powers rivaled each other and even entered into open conflict in their attempts to take advantage of or to fill the political gap created by the weakness of the Ottoman state. The Eastern Question, which essentially was this intricate European diplomatic problem, kept the powers preoccupied until the end of World War I.

The Russian Advance

Both Austria and Russia exploited Ottoman military debility. While Russia unremittingly pursued an aggressive policy vis-à-vis the Ottoman Empire, with a clearly perceived goal in mind, Austria, after an initial spurt of successful military campaigns at the end of the seventeenth century, slackened and eventually ceased to confront its erstwhile enemy. Beginning with Peter the Great, tsarist foreign policy was directed toward reaching first the shores of the Black Sea and then the "warm waters" of the Mediterranean. The turning point in Russian-Turkish relations was the Treaty of Kuchuk Kainarji, signed on July 10, 1774. Not only did the treaty signal the beginning of Russia's advance in the Black Sea region and the Balkans, but it established the right of Russia to intervene in Ottoman internal affairs on behalf of its coreligionist Orthodox Christians. This treaty set the tone for relations between the two neighboring states until their dissolution by the end of World War I.

Until the 1790s Russian advances in the Balkans, as well as in the Caucasus, were made in cooperation with the Habsburg Empire, the other great power in the region, and the support of Great Britain, while France and Prussia simply acquiesced. This unusual harmony in international diplomacy ended when Prime Minister William Pitt the Younger publicly stated that Russian expansion at the expense of the Ottoman Empire was contrary to British interests. Despite internal opposition deploring British support for the autocratic and despotic rule of the sultan over his Christian subjects, British policy in the Balkans and the Near East henceforth was to maintain the territorial integrity of the Ottoman Empire. Tsarist territorial expansion in the Balkans and in Asia was perceived as a threat to the safety of imperial trade routes to British possessions in the Far East.

In spite of this British opposition, at the turn of the nineteenth century Russia had come to dominate the Black Sea and had advanced to the banks of the Dniester River, at the entrance to the Balkan peninsula. The geographical proximity of mighty Russia, on the one hand, and its propaganda presenting itself as the liberator of all the Orthodox Christians, on the other, raised the hopes of all the Balkan peoples who looked for Russian assistance to cast off the heavy yoke of Turkish domination.

Nationalism in the Balkans

Russian penetration into the Balkans coincided with the spread of nationalism there. Cultural nationalism, developed at the end of the eighteenth century in the works of some German writers (such as Herder, Novalis, Schleiermacher, and Fichte) reached the Balkan peoples through the writings of native intellectuals. At first, the spoken vernaculars were raised to the level of literary languages, replacing the dead classical languages—Classical Greek for the Greeks and Church Slavonic for the Slavic peoples. In addition, secular works written in the modern languages disseminated the ideas of the Age of Enlightenment and the French Revolution, while historical writings glorified the past of each people, rekindling its national consciousness.

The existence of large expatriate communities abroad also contributed to the national revival of these peoples. These communities—in Austria, Italy, France, Germany, and especially Russia—continued to maintain close relations with their compatriots in the homeland. Enjoying more freedom and security, as well as higher educational and living standards, they flourished economically and culturally. They harbored nationalist intellectuals, provided a fertile ground for the dissemination of progressive ideologies, and offered a safe haven for the organization of secret revolutionary groups.

Simultaneously, the Balkan merchants had established commercial relations with West European countries that they visited on business trips. They were thus exposed to the liberal and enlightened rule of European governments and to the life-style of European society, and naturally compared what was seen in Europe with conditions in the homelands. They saw Ottoman rule as arbitrary and oppressive, with its burdensome and discriminatory taxation system and insecurity of life and property. The Balkan merchants were struck by the supportive policy of European governments, which encouraged competitors through various means, while they lived under the constant threat of confiscation of capital, sometimes ending even in imprisonment and death. The rule of the sultan was perceived as an impediment to merchants' economic progress and a menace to their personal well-being and safety. As a consequence, the usually conservative-minded traders began to entertain hopes for the overthrow of the sultan. Thus the intellectual and the merchant, fostering desires for complete change, one for ideological motives and the other for economic considerations, developed into agents of revolutionary propaganda and activity.

Emancipatory Movements

The Serbian Rebellion (1804–1830)

In the beginning, the Serbs did not rise in rebellion against the authority of the sultan but against the lawless Janissaries, who, after ransacking and plundering Serbian villages, hanged seventy-two leaders. Under the leadership of a local rebel, Kara George or George Petrovich, in February 1804, the Serbs started to attack Janissary outposts as a preventive measure. The mediation of Austria failed, for the sultan refused to give any guarantees against mistreatment by the Janissaries and did not allow the rebels to retain their weapons. The warfare resumed, but the rebellion had taken a more ominous turn; the Serbs were now fighting the sultan's government. In the following three years several Turkish armies were defeated. In the meantime, Kara George tried in vain to win the support of Austria, Russia, and France successively. In the aftermath of the alliance of Sultan Selim III with Napoleon in 1806, Tsar Alexander I offered the Serbs his full support, while the sultan proffered virtual autonomy to Serbia.

During the second phase of the Serbian revolt, the new leader, Milosh Obrenovich, skillfully exploited the international political situation as well as the sultan's weakness. The Turks preferred to come to terms with Obrenovich, who was successfully leading the new revolt that had started in 1814. The agreement with the Ottoman government provided the Serbs with a national assembly and permission to retain their arms. Eventually, after the Treaty of Adrianople (September 14, 1829), Serbia became an autonomous principality, with Obrenovich as the hereditary prince but under the suzerainty of the sultan (decree of August 28, 1830). Serbia would be made independent in the Treaty of Berlin (July 13, 1878).

The Greek Revolution

Unlike the Serbian revolt, the Greek Revolution, with its ideological foundation and international diplomatic complexities, had a deep impact on the subject peoples of the Ottoman Empire. The Greek communities abroad, well advanced culturally and economically, also were hotbeds of revolutionary propaganda. The first serious secret revolutionary organization, disguised under an innocuous name, Philike Hetairia (Society of Friends), was founded in Odessa, Russia, in 1814 by Greek merchants. Its leader, Alexander Ypsilantis, a high officer in the Russian army, unfurled the flag of revolt on March 18, 1921, in Moldavia (Romania), hoping to win the support of the coreligionist Romanians. But the Romanians were not interested in an essentially alien cause; soon the "Sacred Battalion" of young patriotic Greeks was crushed and Ypsilantis fled to Austria.

The torch of the revolt was taken up by the Greeks in the homeland proper, when, on April 6, 1821, a group of Greek notables proclaimed their insurrection against the sultan. In the beginning, the rebels successfully attacked Turkish garrisons and drove the Turkish forces out of the Morea. Within a year the Greeks controlled all of Morea and captured Athens, Thebes, and the fortress of Missolonghi in the north. Several attempts by the Turks to defeat the rebels failed. Sultan Mahmud II, in despair, called on his vassal Muhammad Ali, governor of Egypt, who dispatched his able son Ibrahim at the head of an expeditionary force. After capturing Crete, Ibrahim Pasha reached the Morea in the winter of 1825 without opposition. By then the Greeks were deeply divided and were on the verge of a civil war. Ibrahim's army advanced, ruthlessly slaughtering the Greeks on its way. In a coordinated attack Turkish and Egyptian forces seized Missolonghi in April 1826, where with the valiant defenders of the fortress the renowned English poet, Lord Byron, lost his life. It seemed that the revolution was doomed, but then the European powers intervened.

News of the atrocities committed by the invading forces aroused European public opinion in defense of the Greeks. Philhellenic organizations in France and Britain actively supported the Greek cause and sought the intervention of the major powers. In August 1827 Great Britain, France, and Russia offered to intervene. The Greeks accepted the offer, whereas the Turks refused. The Allied fleets in the eastern Mediterranean received instructions to intercept supplies destined for the Egyptian army and help bring about a cessation of hostilities. At the Battle of Navarino Bay (October 20, 1827), the Egyptian and Turkish fleets were completely destroyed.

At this juncture, under Allied pressure, Muhammad Ali evacuated his forces, while Russia declared war against the Ottoman Empire in April 1828, as a response to the sultan's abrogation of an earlier convention. This war too ended with the defeat of the Ottoman armies and the signing of the Treaty of Adrianople in 1829. In an adjunct agreement, the Treaty of London (February 3, 1830), the sultan recognized the independence of Greece.

Latent Balkan Nationalism

The successful struggles of the Serbs and the Greeks were not lost upon the other Balkan peoples. Nationalism was now well rooted in the region. Soon the entire peninsula was to be marked by the continuing growth of secret societies. Despite difficulties of communication, nationalism was to spread from the Balkans to the Asiatic parts of the empire. The misrule and tyranny of the Turkish state was equally unbearable to all. Mistreatment and exploitation were common, especially in the economic sphere, with the heavy taxation of the subjects of the sultan, Christian and Muslim alike.

Pan-Slavism, with its emphasis on the racial affinity and political solidarity of the Slavic peoples in Europe, fanned nationalistic feelings in the Balkans on the one hand and served as a vehicle of Russian expansionist policy on the other. Russia was perceived as the champion and liberator of all the Slavs. In spite of the open rebellion of Serbs and Greeks and the concealed uneasiness of the other national groups, the Ottoman state was as torpid and lethargic as ever, oblivious to its internal difficulties and problems. There were voices, however, both within and without the empire that signaled the need for change and reform. External events and pressures were to force the sultan to initiate some reforms.

The Tanzimat

In the history of the Ottoman Empire, the forty-year period between 1839 and 1878 is characterized by the series of reforms that are collectively called Tanzimat (Reorganization or Reform). Unlike the previous reforms, which were simply attempts to revive old Ottoman institutions, these were endeavors to modernize and Westernize both the regime and the society of the Ottoman state. The reforms culminated in the creation of an Ottoman constitution in 1876; one year later the reformist trend came to an abrupt end as Sultan Abdul-Hamid II suspended the constitution and began his autocratic rule. Two reform edicts form the cornerstones of the tanzimat period: the Noble Rescript of 1839 and the Imperial Rescript of 1856.

The Noble Rescript of 1839

It was in the aftermath of the disastrous defeat of the Ottoman armies by the Egyptian forces of Muhammad Ali and the armed intervention of Great Britain, Russia, and Austria saving the Ottoman realm from the Egyptian threat that the young sultan, Abdul-Mejid, issued the imperial decree called the Noble Rescript of the Rose Chamber—Hatt-i Sherif of Gulhane—on November 3, 1839. This decree inaugurated the tanzimat period.

By the mid-1830s the maintenance of the territorial integrity of the Ottoman Empire and the strengthening of it formed the primary goal of British foreign policy in the Near East. The Foreign Office viewed the realm of the sultans as a vital link for British imperial trade with India and its Far Eastern colonies. In order to invigorate the Ottoman state, to prevent rebellions by any disgruntled peoples, especially in the Balkans, and to avoid giving any pretext for Russian intervention on behalf of its coreligionists, the British advised and exerted pressure on the sultan's government to introduce new reforms.

Many Ottoman statesmen and public servants had warned various sultans of the need for reform to revitalize the empire, but the emphasis invariably was on the military field. Even the reforms of Mahmud II (1807 1839) were intended to strengthen the army first, then the central government. Now, for the first time, the reforms concerned the subjects of the sultan.

The decree provided guarantees for the "perfect security of life, honor, and fortune" of all the subjects. It enunciated the abolition of tax farming and abuses associated with it, the establishment of a regular system of taxation, and the setting up of an orderly recruitment for the army. It also provided for public and fair trial for all crimes, as well as equality before the law for all subjects "of whatever religion or sect they may be." More than any other stipulation, it was the last principle that was the most sweeping novelty, for it was breaking with Islamic law and tradition. These high-sounding principles did not constitute a bill of rights or an act of legislation; the sultan, as a manifestation of his munificence and care for his subjects, had granted the decree; he could rescind it anytime he wished. Moreover, for its application he was accountable to no authority, spiritual or civil.

The Noble Rescript was followed by a number of other reform measures in the legal, financial, educational, administrative, and military fields. Seemingly, the Ottoman state had entered into a period of innovation, modernization, and regeneration. But soon the discrepancy between the ideal of the reforms and the ignominious reality of Ottoman life were exposed to all, both within and without the empire. The sincerity and efforts of Turkish reformers were not sufficient to dissuade the European powers from insisting on the need for new reforms.

The Imperial Rescript of 1856

Under the strong pressure of the French, Austrian, and especially British governments, the sultan promulgated a new reform edict, the Imperial Rescript—Hatt-i Humayun—on February 18, 1856. The new decree reconfirmed the principles of the 1839 Noble Rescript, such as the abolition of the much-abused tax farming and the full equality of all Ottoman subjects before the law, regardless of religion. The edict dealt also with the status of non-Muslims, individually and collectively. In the previous year, the degrading poll tax was abolished and conscription in the army for non-Muslims recognized, with the option of payment of an exemption tax equal to the abolished poll tax. The new rescript clearly stated that no class of subjects should be "inferior to another class on account of religion, language, or race." In addition, it enjoined the non-Muslim *millets* to reform their organizational structure, allotting laymen greater representation and control in *millet* affairs. One of the fundamental changes brought about by this decree was, then, the reorganization of the *millets*.

The Armenian *Millet*

The Millet *System*

Originally the Arabic term *"millet"* was used to denote the community of Muslims in contradistinction to the non-Muslims, who were called *dhimmi* (in Arabic) or *zimmi* (in Turkish). The *dhimmis* were "the protected and tolerated people" who accepted a subordinate status and who paid a poll tax as a price for their protection. In a Muslim state, the individual's place in society was determined first and foremost by his religion.

In the Ottoman context, *millet* gradually came to designate the non-Muslim communities. Each *millet* was a self-contained religious entity, enjoying autonomy in its internal affairs. For its governance, it was allowed to maintain traditional customs, laws, and institutions dealing basically with personal status, such as marriage, divorce, and inheritance. The *millet* was permitted freedom of worship within certain bounds: During Muslim religious ceremonies noise and display were to be avoided; often no bells could be built on churches; and so forth.

Discrimination against the *zimmis* had two dimensions: on the *millet*-wide community basis and on the individual level. It was in the latter situation that the non-Muslims felt their legal, social, and financial disabilities most strongly. Such practices as the wearing of a large sign of the cross on the chest for Christians or the star of David on the back for Jews had been discarded; but as late as the mid-nineteenth century distinctive clothing, the show of deference to Muslims, the interdiction against a *zimmi* to bear arms or to ride on a horse, the nonacceptance of the testimony of a non-Muslim against a Muslim in a court of law, and other such discriminatory measures were still in use. The most concrete and burdensome aspect of this inequality was the payment of higher taxes, which affected the daily life of the *zimmi*.

What mattered for the Ottomans was the orderly administration of their multireligious and multiethnic empire and most of all the systematic taxation of all subjects. Since the middle of the seventeenth century, the empire had been losing territory and sources of income, its expenditures continued to grow rapidly, and yet the sultans did not cease to spend lavishly. The *millet* system provided an expedient vehicle for administrative purposes. As a method of administration for an empire with diverse races, languages, cultures, and religions, the *millet* system was an offensive scheme, which functioned well so long as the non-Muslims accepted their status of inferiority and subservience. Once they refused to accept the restrictions and bonds imposed on them, then the whole system gradually collapsed. Ideas of liberalism and nationalism created yearnings for independent nationhood, which replaced the notions of social order represented by the system of religious communities.

At the turn of the nineteenth century, there were three major *millets* in the Ottoman state: the Greek Orthodox, the Armenian, and the Jewish. The Greek Orthodox *millet* was the largest; it included, in addition to Greeks, Serbs, Bulgarians, Romanians, Macedonians, Vlachs, some Albanians and Arabs, and others. The head of the *millet* was the universal patriarch at Constantinople. The Jewish *millet* incorporated the various Jewish congregations: the indigenous Rabbinite (followers of Talmudic Judaism) and Karaite communities and the Iberian immigrants who came to Constantinople from Spain after 1492, fleeing persecution, who soon formed the majority of Ottoman Jewry.

The Armenian Millet

All the Armenians living within the borders of the Ottoman Empire were members of the Ermeni (Armenian) *millet,* which was the second largest. The central government recognized only the authority and responsibility of the Armenian Patriarch of Constantinople for the management of *millet* affairs. Some of the unclassified Christians of the empire were assumed to belong to the Armenian *millet*. The Assyrians, for example, voluntarily joined the Armenian *millet* in 1783.

From the second quarter of the nineteenth century, the Armenian *millet* was to acquire greater importance and influence, politically and economically, especially after the secession and independence of Greece. The Armenians were then considered the most reliable elements in the empire, and the *millet* was called Millet-i-Sakika (the loyal *millet*). However, during the last quarter of the nineteenth century, this state of affairs would change, because of the mistreatment and persecution of Armenians by the Turkish government.

The Armenian Patriarchate of Constantinople (Istanbul)

As an institution, the Armenian Patriarchate was the creation of the Ottoman state. Recent research has refuted the presumed date of its establishment in 1461. The patriarchate is thought to have been set up during the second quarter of the sixteenth century (between 1526 and 1543). Through a long period of evolution, it grew from a mere vicariate to a universal center of religious and civil authority. By the middle of the eighteenth century, this process of transformation and growth reached its completion when the patriarchate acquired jurisdiction over all the Armenians of the empire, except for the few localities under the authority of the catholicosate of Sis (whose territory comprised essentially Cilicia), the catholicosate of Aghtamar (whose control was limited to a number of towns and villages in the south of Lake Van), and the patriarchate of Jerusalem (which exercised authority over communities in Palestine, southern Syria, Lebanon, Cyprus, and Egypt). The catholicoi, including the catholicos of Echmiadzin, needed the assistance of the patriarch of Constantinople for their dealings with the Ottoman central government. In ecclesiastical hierarchy the patriarchate was inferior to the three catholicosates, but in real life it carried more prestige and weight than its spiritual superiors until the middle of the nineteenth century. While the three catholicosates were located in geographically isolated places, the patriarchate was situated in a sprawling and cosmopolitan imperial metropolis.

The patriarch was both the spiritual and civic leader of the entire Armenian population of the empire. As *milletbashi* (head of the *millet*), the patriarch ranked equal to a pasha. His investiture came directly from the sultan through the issuance of an imperial decree. The patriarch was personally responsible for the administration of his *millet* and for the collection of state taxes. As a corollary to this responsibility, he enjoyed complete jurisdiction over the Armenian *millet*, that is, over its religious, charitable, and educational institutions. Within the patriarchal premises he had his own court and prison, where he could try all cases except those involving "public security and crime." His mere word was sufficient for the authorities to send any individual—cleric or layman—into exile. People dreaded this almost absolute power of the patriarch over their lives.

The patriarch enjoyed many other privileges, such as the right to own property, to be exempt from taxation, and to appoint tax collectors for the gathering of state taxes from members of his *millet*. Among his jurisdictional protocols, the patriarch was vested with the authority to grant permission for the construction and repair of churches, monasteries, schools, and printing establishments. In fact, he had total control over religious and secular education in his *millet,* as well as over publications.

The patriarch was both the symbol and the real head of the Armenian Church, and as such it was incumbent upon him to defend the national church against the encroachments of Catholic priests and Protestant missionaries, who began to gain converts in the eighteenth and nineteenth centuries.

The Emergence of the Catholic Armenian Millet

Since the days of the Cilician kingdom, Armenians had been in contact with the Catholic Church. The latter had tried to bring the Armenian Church under its sway, but all the attempts had failed. Catholic propaganda was resumed with new vigor and militancy thanks to the diplomatic and financial support of such Catholic Western powers as France and Austria. As early as the seventeenth century, the Jesuit and Capuchin congregations penetrated the Ottoman Empire; the latter funded its own school in Constantinople in 1679 and soon won over some converts, including priests from the Armenian Church. At first, the Armenian Church resisted the Catholic missionaries with some success, the Ottoman government lending its own support to the Armenian Church, which it considered endogenous. In this period Patriarch Avedik Evdokiatsi, who had vigorously opposed the Catholics, was even abducted by the French in 1703, when he was on his way to Jerusalem, and reportedly was imprisoned in Paris.

Despite the efforts of the patriarchs, Catholicism spread among Armenians, thanks to the lure of education, culture, and political support. The number of Armenian Catholics grew, but they had neither a separate church nor legal status of their own. To the authorities they were still members of the Armenian *millet*. Since the efforts to eradicate Catholic influence among Armenians failed, the church attempted to win back its "schismatic" members.

At this time the Catholics were divided into two major camps, the Collegians and the Abbotians. The Collegians (named after the College for the Propaganda of the Faith, whose headquarters were located in Rome) insisted on the supremacy of the pope and denied the validity of the sacraments of the Armenian Church, while the Abbotians (named after Abbot Mekhitar), comprising mainly the Mekhitarists of Venice and their followers, faithfully kept many of the traditions of the Mother Church and were favorably disposed toward union. The first two attempts at unity, in 1810 and 1817, were initiated by the patriarchs; both failed. The third attempt was ordered by the Ottoman government in 1820. After three months of discussion, a declaration of faith called *Hraver siro* (Call to Love) was formulated as a compromise between the Armenian Apostolic and the Catholic doctrines (April 2, 1820). Within a short time, the Collegians, hostile to the unity, thwarted and disrupted the reconciliation. Considering the riots instigated by the Collegians as rebellion against the state, the government used force to restore order and peace in the community. Scores were thrown into prison and many sent into exile, while a few were hanged, from among both the Catholics and members of the national church.

Heeding the advice of lay leaders, the patriarch appointed a Catholic priest as vicar in the patriarchate for Catholic Armenians. During the Greek Revolution, Sultan Mahmud II, as a defiant gesture against the Allied powers, issued an edict, in December 1827, for the banishment of Catholic Armenians from the capital to the interior. As a consequence, thousands suffered, many dying from the cold and rigors of the journey. The Treaty of Adrianople provided not only for the return of these Catholics but also their right to have their own church and separate administration. The election of the Catholic cleric Hagopos as head of the Armenian Catholic Church was ratified by an imperial decree on May 24, 1831, which, in effect, signified recognition of the separate status of that community as a distinct *millet*.

Eventually the bishopric was raised to the status of patriarchate by the decree of April 17, 1834.

The Emergence of the Evangelical Armenian Millet

Unlike Catholicism, Armenians came into contact with Protestantism only in the beginning of the nineteenth century. The formation of the American Board of Commissioners for Foreign Missions in 1810, at Bradford, Connecticut, was the turning point in the spread of Protestantism in the Near East and other parts of the world. Before their arrival American and British missionaries had the Bible printed in Classical Armenian, in the vernacular, and in Armeno-Turkish (meaning Turkish written with Armenian characters), and had it distributed among Armenians as early as 1811. At first the Armenian Church leaders welcomed this dissemination of the Holy Scriptures, but soon they discovered the dogmatic differences in the Bible printed by the missionaries and the real intent of the latter, whose purported motive was the conversion of Muslims and Jews.

In 1824 three celibate priests from the Armenian Congregation of St. James of Jerusalem embraced the new dogma. Encouraged by this success, the board dispatched three of its ablest missionaries (Eli Smith, H.G.O. Dwight, and William Goddell) during 1830-1831 to the Ottoman Empire to work among the Armenians. Missionary effort now went forward with vigor and dynamism. The American missionaries were well received by the patriarch and the people. In 1834 the missionaries opened their first school in Constantinople, to be followed soon in Smyrna (Izmir) and in most cities and towns of Western Armenia and Cilicia. The methodical work of the missionaries was rewarded: Many were won over. The national church responded by electing a tough-minded and resolutely anti-Protestant bishop, Hagopos Seropian, to the patriarchal throne. The new patriarch, supported by the lay leadership, was so indiscriminate in his persecution of individuals suspected of Protestant sympathies that his severity backfired. He was forced to be more moderate.

In the meantime, new missionaries had arrived; new schools, especially Bible-study Sunday schools, were opened; and the number of Evangelical Armenians increased. Free education was the most effective lure in the hands of the missionaries, who, in addition to the study and interpretation of the Gospel, imparted to their students such modern concepts as liberty, equality, and nationality. The Mother

Church fought back by opening many schools, including the Jemaran in 1839, and offering quasi-free education to Armenian youth. Moreover, some of the new converts were publicly excommunicated, among them a cleric, as individuals who had forsaken the national church.

By 1845 the number of Evangelical Armenians had risen to 8,000, alarming the leadership of the Mother Church. New and effective measures were undertaken that succeeded in reducing the number of Protestant Armenians. The Evangelicals now demanded separation from the national church and the creation of a Protestant Church. The ambassadors of Prussia, of the United States, and especially of Great Britain, Sir Stratford Canning, had shown great interest in the spread of Protestantism. The British ambassador seemingly approved the conciliatory overtures of Patriarch Madteos Chukhadjian but covertly lent support to the Protestants.

In the midst of reciprocal accusations, Evangelical Armenians announced, on July 1, 1846, the formation of the First Evangelical Armenian Church of Constantinople, at the residence of American missionary Dwight, along with the election of the first pastor of that church, the Reverend Apisoghom Utudjian. In the same year, three other Evangelical churches were organized, followed by many others in the Armenian-inhabited provinces. At the intercession of the British ambassador, an imperial edict was issued in November 1847, establishing a separate *millet* for the Evangelical Armenians.

The Armenian Community of Constantinople

Constantinople, or Istanbul, was the site of the powerful patriarchate. In addition, the most important Armenian community of the Ottoman Empire lived in the sultan's capital, as it was the largest as well as the most advanced culturally and economically.

Constantinople, the original Greek name of the famous city that Christians continued to use, had an Armenian colony long before the Ottoman conquest of the Byzantine capital in 1453. Under Ottoman rule, the number of the Armenian inhabitants of the city increased steadily. By voluntary or forced migration, Armenians moved to the new Ottoman capital from all corners of Armenia, Anatolia, Iran, and even the Crimea. By the end of the eighteenth century, the number of Armenians living in the capital was estimated at 150,000; around the mid-nineteenth century this number had risen to 225,000; and by the 1880s to over 250,000 or, according to some sources, as many as 300,000.

Armenians lived clustered in certain quarters of the city, such as Kum Kapu, Galatia, Uskudar, and in some outlying villages that were completely Armenian-inhabited: Khas Kiugh, Kadi Kiugh, Makri Kiugh, Micha Kiugh, and so forth. Armenian society was divided and stratified. There was perennial competition between "insiders" and "outsiders." The "insiders" *(nersetsi)* were those who had been settled in the capital for a long time, considered themselves "natives," and were extremely proud of it. The "outsiders" *(drsetsi)* were the newcomers from the provinces, known also as *gavaratsi* (i.e., provincial); the urban "natives" looked down on them. The "natives" were stratified into various social groups: from the very wealthy *amiras* (derived from the Arabic word *amir,* meaning "chief" or "commander") and middle-class guild members to the poor and impoverished masses.

The *amiras,* who numbered less than two hundred, formed the most powerful and dominant segment of the whole *millet.* Great wealth and the holding of a high government office were the prerequisites for the honorific title *amira.* The majority of the *amiras* were bankers *(saraf)* of either the *viziers* or the provincial governors, while others held such positions as Director of the Imperial Mint (the Duzian family), Chief Imperial Architect (the Balian family), and Superintendent of Gunpowder Mills and manager of industrial factories (the Dadian family) The above mentioned high positions were kept in these families as a monopoly almost on a hereditary basis.

The *amiras* formed a well-defined social elite, whose members could be easily distinguished from the rest of the population by the clothes they wore and the beasts they rode. They enjoyed unequaled prestige in Armenian society. They were viewed by their contemporaries as aristocrats and were gratuitously perceived even as descendants of noble *nakharar* families. They carefully cultivated self-images as great benefactors and philanthropists through charitable donations and generous support for churches, schools, hospitals, and publications. Thus, *amiras* were largely responsible for the higher education of those young men who were eventually to initiate and lead the cultural revival of Western Armenians.

The political power of the *amiras* in the Armenian *millet* and their social status were based as much upon their economic power as on the influence they acquired within the Ottoman administration. To exercise their power on the *millet,* they brought the patriarchate under their sway. Their almost absolute control over the *millet* continued to the mid-1840s.

The Armenian merchants of the capital formed another high stratum in Armenian society. Commerce in the Ottoman Empire was disproportionately in the hands of the Armenians and the Greeks, and, to a lesser extent, the Jews, the Bulgarians, and others. The Armenian merchants had established commercial relations with important European trade centers. They imported eastern wares, such as Indian spices, jewelry, shawls, Persian and Damascene fabrics, and Western articles, such as mirrors and glassware from Venice, amber from Germany, and expensive fabrics from France. They sold the European merchandise throughout the empire, Iran, and South Russia, while certain Eastern and locally produced goods were sold in the European markets.

Some of these merchants were familiar with Western business practices. During the first half of the nineteenth century, many among them acted as agents and middlemen for European trading firms. In the second half of the century, some established either their own branches in major European centers or simply moved their businesses abroad. For example, in 1861 there were thirty Armenian business firms in Manchester, many of them quite large.

The middle class of Armenian society consisted of the members of the guilds. The guild, similar to the *millet,* was an administrative device. Until the 1850s the guilds (*esnaf* in Turkish) were the backbone of the Ottoman economy. At the end of the eighteenth century, the Armenian craftsmen and merchants of the capital were organized into sixty-five guilds, and in the middle of the next century, their number rose to ninety-eight; according to the official Turkish records, the number of Armenians enrolled in these guilds approached 40,000 in the second half of the nineteenth century. Some of these guilds had built up a considerable reputation. The Armenian goldsmiths, for example, had their separate marketplace, and their creations were known all over Europe. These guilds supported most of the institutions of the *millet* without having any say in their administration.

The great majority of the Armenian working population of Constantinople belonged to the guilds. But there were also the poor and unskilled laborers who could hardly eke out a living, as the Turkish Census Office indicated in its statistical information published in the second half of the nineteenth century: There were 35,979 craftsmen, merchants, and grocers; 32,399 pupils and students; and 14,998 "people with no occupation." These latter lived a precarious existence.

The ranks of the poor were continuously swelled by new arrivals from the provinces. Mostly illiterate and unskilled peasants, these *pandukhts (bantukht)* (migrant workers) came to the capital, in greater and greater numbers, in search of a seasonal job, with the intention of sending back savings from their meager earnings. The general misery and poverty in the provinces had forced these Armenian peasants— sometimes the town dwellers, too—to the capital as well as to Smyrna (Izmir). In 1860 there were 15,000 *pandukhts* in Constantinople and 4,000 in Smyrna; in the 1870s their number had risen to 45,000 and 5,000 respectively. The *pandukhts* lived crowded together in a few *khans,* or inns, dwelling in extremely unhealthy and appalling conditions, many falling sick (often to tuberculosis) and dying. They worked in heavy menial jobs as porters, water carriers, street sweepers, domestic servants, and similar low-paying and backbreaking labors.

As they continued to live year after year in those unbearable conditions, and as more of them arrived, the *pandukht* phenomenon turned into a permanent aspect of Armenian society in the capital. At first the intellectuals, then the leadership, and gradually the ordinary people took great interest in their plight. The *pandukhts* maintained strong ties with their *erkir* (an Armenian word denoting homeland), graphically reminding their better-off compatriots in Constantinople of the wretched and miserable conditions in which the Armenians in the provinces lived. They awakened in the hearts and the minds of the bourgeois and cosmopolitan Armenians in the capital an awareness, and even a concern, for the *gavar* (province, in the sense of homeland) that for a long time had been neglected, if not actually ignored. Some Armenian writers depicted in a vivid manner the grim and desolate life of the *pandukhts* and their *karot* (i.e., yearning or homesickness) for their families and homeland.

The Armenians in the Provinces

The Urban Population

Armenians lived scattered all over the Ottoman Empire, from the Balkans to Egypt, but they lived mostly concentrated in Western Armenia and Cilicia. In the 1850s there were about forty towns and cities in which Armenians formed a relative or absolute majority or a sizable minority.

According to the last official Ottoman census of 1844, published in the Ottoman yearbook of the same year, there were 2,400,000

Armenians living in the empire. Of these about 350,000 lived in such urban centers in Asia Minor as Van, Karin (Garin; Erzerum), Erznka (Erzinjan), Sebastia (Sivas), Tigranakert (Diarbekir), Kharpert (Kharput; Harput), Mush, Baghesh (Bitlis), Evdokia (Tokat), Kesaria (Kaiseri, Caesaria), Palu, Dersim, Adana, Marash, Hadjin, Zeitun, Aintab, Edesia (Urfa, Edessa), and so on. To this 350,000 should be added another 300,000, who lived in Constantinople, Smyrna, and the Balkans. Thus, the total of urban Armenians would amount to about 650,000, or 27 percent of the total Armenian population.

Whether they formed the majority or were a minority, Armenians kept commerce and most of the handicrafts in the urban centers of Western Armenia and Cilicia under their control. They practiced the same trades as those in Constantinople. The craftsmen were organized into guilds. The goldsmiths of Van were not alone in enjoying a great reputation; so did the blacksmiths and, especially, the armorers of Karin, the coppersmiths of Evdokia, the rug-makers of Kesaria, Sebastia, and Kharpert, as well as the manufacturers of various types of cotton, wool, and silk cloth of these towns and cities.

These handicrafts had been in slow decline since the eighteenth century, if not earlier. After the 1830s the rate of decline accelerated. The craftsmen used primitive tools and methods and were ill-equipped to compete with better-quality and cheaper European goods. While some of these handicrafts simply disappeared, others continued to survive. This economic deterioration strongly affected Armenian society in the provinces. Reports sent to the patriarchate constantly referred to economic dislocation and urged the patriarch to intercede in order to protect native crafts from ruinous foreign competition.

Some enterprising Armenians started to employ modern machines and production methods. Such were the factories of the Barikian brothers and Krikor Kurkjian in Kharpert, the Kassardjian brothers in Kesaria, and many others who imported steam-powered machines from Europe and even from the United States. The government provided no assistance or subsidy; on the contrary, it exploited these productive businesses by taxing them more.

The Rural Population

The majority of Armenians—over 70 percent—lived in rural areas and toiled on the soil. As the Ottoman state was a military-feudal regime, the peasantry in general and the Armenian peasantry in particular bore the burdens of the system.

The Armenian rural population, as well as those in towns who were involved in agriculture, were exploited in various ways: onerous taxation, corvée, misuse of their lands by others, illegal appropriation of their products, expropriation, forced loans, and cheap labor. Rural people were subjected to a great variety of taxes. The tithe *(ushr)* was supposed to amount to a tenth of the annual produce. Invariably it was collected at a higher rate, from 12.5 to as much as 50 percent. For example, in 1864, according to official records, the tithe was collected at 15 percent in Erzerum. There were property taxes *(emlak)* on houses, landholdings, and pasture-land, another tax on all animals *(aghnam),* as well as one on fruit-bearing trees. Taxes were paid also for the use of roads and on such occasions as birth, marriage, death, transfer of goods, and so forth. The percentage of the amount of any tax varied from place to place and from year to year. This arbitrariness was the worst aspect of Ottoman taxation. Armenians always paid more than their Muslim neighbors. Moreover, they paid the degrading poll tax.

Periodically, the central government would enjoin all its subjects to pay exceptional war taxes *(avariz)* to help defray war expenditures. These "occasional" taxes would be collected year after year, becoming in effect another regular tax. All these state taxes were collected through tax-farming, a system of tax collection in which the highest bidder acquired the right to collect taxes in a specific province. The tax-farming system allowed the tax collector *(multezim)* to exploit fully the temporary right he had purchased, by taxing people to the maximum possible. As a result tax-farming led to extraordinary abuses and excesses.

In addition to these official taxes, the Armenian peasant also paid several taxes to the Turkish or Kurdish *agha* (feudal lord), who "owned" or "protected" the village or the district. He was expected to work without pay on the land of the *agha,* even supplying his own tools. There were always a variety of corvées, owed to different masters. In many regions, the cultivated land and the orchard of the Armenian villager or town dweller were trampled on and used as pasture by the herds of sheep and cattle of Kurdish nomads. Every summer some twenty-four Kurdish tribes from Mosul would move north to Vaspurakan (Van) and graze their sheep there, ruining many villages. Moreover, these armed nomads would appropriate, covertly or overtly, the products of the Armenian villagers.

During the long centuries of Turkish rule, most Armenian peasants lost their land. Frequently their fertile and well-maintained pieces of land were simply taken over by Turks or Kurds. For example, in the region of Palu and Charsanjak Armenian peasants were dispossessed of their lands by some twenty-five Turkish and Kurdish *aghas;* in Kharpert three-fourths of the arable land belonged to the Turks, while Armenians, who were more numerous, owned only one-fourth. Using a more subtle method, the Turkish or Kurdish *agha* saw to it that the Armenian villager paid taxes at such high rates that he would be unable to pay some of them; then the *agha* would "kindly" lend him money at the extraordinary rates of 50 percent interest or more. Within a few years, the peasant would be forced to sell his land to pay back his "banker."

Most landless Armenian peasants worked as sharecroppers for their landowners, paying rent as much as half, and sometimes more, of the crop. Many of these sharecroppers turned into *maraba* (landless peasant), connoting a condition of serfdom. The Armenian peasant paid dues and gave gifts to his church and clerics. Donations were made at the birth and baptism of a child, at the marriage and death of an individual. Donations were also made on numerous religious feast days. In addition, the peasant worked without pay, for a certain number of days, on land owned by the church or the nearby monastery.

Concurrent to this economic exploitation, the Armenian peasant was subjected to political oppression. In general, landless and poor, but sometimes landowning and well off, he was denied any political rights. He suffered all the legal handicaps of a *zimmi,* and even more. Actually he was called *raya,* a term that originally meant "subject" (flock), but that had gradually taken on the derogatory meaning of "cattle." The peasant, in other words, had only obligations and duties to fulfill: He was to work hard and pay taxes, as "human cattle."

He was also labeled *giavur (giaour),* meaning "infidel," with the connotation of impiety. The Armenians, in general, and the Armenian peasant, in particular, were periodically harassed and even persecuted on religious grounds. For the judgment of a dispute with a Muslim, the Armenian had to rely on the fairness and justice of the Muslim court, where his testimony was not admissible. Naturally, he suffered all the economic and legal consequences of this unequal treatment.

But the constant fear and dread of the Armenian—man and woman—was forced conversion. The usual victims of this mistreatment were young girls, who would be kidnapped and forcibly married and converted to Islam. This happened so frequently that it had become part of the "normal" life of the Armenian village. Among thousands of recorded cases, the citing of one example should be enough. In 1810 a pretty young girl engaged to a young Armenian peasant in the province of Karin was kidnapped by the Turkish *agha* of the village. The young girl refused to renounce her faith, despite beatings and torture; she was finally killed. For having refused conversion, her three brothers were also killed. Sometimes young boys also suffered the same fate. According to the precepts of Islam, kidnapping and forced conversion in times of peace were unlawful and immoral; but in the prevailing conditions of the Ottoman Empire it was a brutal reality.

Apart from cases of individuals, forced Islamization occurred on a massive scale. Sometimes entire villages were compelled to renounce their ancestral faith. In the beginning of the nineteenth century, in the Hamshen district alone, the inhabitants of about one hundred Armenian villages, approximately 10,000 people, were forced to forsake their faith and convert to Islam. As the nineteenth century progressed, involuntary conversion turned into a deliberate state policy to undermine the very physical existence of the Armenian nation.

The Armenian Constitutional Movement

While such were the deplorable conditions in the provinces, in the capital the leadership of the *millet* was engrossed in an internal struggle, albeit a reforming one. The *amiras* were in full control of the Armenian *millet*. The *esnafs*, guild representatives, participated in *millet* activities, but to a very limited extent. Their participation was more symbolic than real. In general, they rubber-stamped the decisions made and the policies charted by the *amiras*.

The Amira-Esnaf *Conflict*

It was the combination of internal dissension and external pressures that brought changes in the political structure of the *millet*'s administration. The apparent cause for the discord among the *amiras* was the question of the Armenian College, founded in 1838 at Uskudar, a suburb of the capital. This institution of higher learning, called Jemaran, was the brainchild of two imperial architects. At its opening, many *amiras* pledged to support the school, which was called to combat the lure of Catholic and Protestant high schools. But once the college was opened, old rivalries and conflicts emerged. The *amiras* were divided along professional lines into two camps: the bankers and the technocrats. The bankers simply withheld their financial contributions. Moreover, they refused to help the patriarch in the collection of state taxes in the *millet.* The patriarch then appointed a committee of twenty-four, with two technocrat-*amiras* and twenty-two *esnaf* representatives to administer the financial affairs of the *millet* and to manage all the national institutions. For the first time the *esnaf* representatives were members of an executive body with decision-making power. Despite its goodwill and exemplary sacrifices, the committee found itself unable to raise the necessary funds and reluctantly resigned. The patriarch followed suit. Both resignations aroused popular resentment. The government closed the college (October 3, 1841). Upon government intervention a committee of twenty-seven *esnafs* was formed; it too failed in its task and resigned (November 18, 1842). The *amiras,* who came back to power, proved unable to manage the affairs of the *millet* any longer without *esnaf* support. The new patriarch, Madteos Chukhadjian, a very popular figure whom the *amiras* elected, organized a mixed council with sixteen *amiras* and fourteen *esnafs* (1844). The *amiras* had made a major concession by sharing power with the *esnafs.* Consequent to this compromise, peace returned to the community, and the college was reopened (October 1, 1846).

While a relatively harmonious relationship prevailed between the *amiras* and the *esnafs,* the former now clashed with the patriarch on the appointment of prelates to the various sees. The *amiras* complained to Grand Vizier Mustafa Reshid Pasha, who, heeding the advice of his assistant Hagop Grdjigian, ordered the patriarch (May 7, 1847) to proceed with the election of two separate and independent councils: one for the administration of the secular affairs of the *millet,* the Supreme Civil Council, and the other for spiritual and religious matters, the Spiritual Council. To the Supreme Civil Council were elected nine *amiras* and ten *esnafs,* with Hagop Grdjigian as the logothete, a kind of executive director of the council, while the Spiritual Council consisted of fourteen elected clerics. This system of the two councils continued until the adoption of a constitution in 1860.

The Young Intellectuals

Despite the haughty behavior of the *amiras,* it was obvious that they were losing their grip on the *millet* in general and their influence in particular in the Supreme Civil Council. Their membership had declined to only two by 1855, while *esnaf* representation was getting stronger, rising to fourteen in the same year. However, the real challenge to *amira* leadership came from a new quarter—the young intellectuals. These young men, most of whom were related to the *amiras,* had returned to their birthplace during the decade of 1840 to 1850 after receiving their higher education in Western Europe. In Europe they had not only familiarized themselves with Western liberal and progressive ideologies but had observed with keen interest the workings of the democratic political system. Concerned with the conditions at home, they could not fail to take note of the irregularities and flaws prevalent in the *millet* administration. They resented the arbitrary and capricious ways of *amiras* and joined forces with the *esnafs.*

To put an end to *amira* hegemony, the young intellectuals articulated the need for written regulations, defining the functions, duties, jurisdictions, and method of election of the patriarch and of the two councils and the three committees—educational, economic, and judicial. But *amira* opposition to such regulations frustrated their efforts within the council. In 1855 the issue of a written set of regulations was presented by the young intellectuals before the National Assembly, with the support of the *esnafs.* The assembly elected a constitutional committee with the task of formulating a National Code of Regulations *(Azgayin Kanonagrutiun).* Garabed Amira Balian, the Chief Imperial Architect of the sultan and a dominant figure, led the opposition to the code. He wielded such great power that almost single-handedly he was able to thwart the committee's work.

At this juncture two new developments affected the course of events: the promulgation of the Imperial Rescript of 1856 and the resignation of the popular patriarch, Hagopos Seropian. These two events accelerated the resolution of the conflict by intensifying it. The National Assembly, meeting on November 18, 1856, reelected the patriarch and elected a new constitutional committee. This committee, after arduous work, presented its draft to the National Assembly on March 22, 1857. This draft was approved unanimously and submitted to the Sublime Porte for its ratification. After some delay, the government rejected it. For the constitutionalists it was clear that the *amiras* had used their influence to prevent the ratification of the Code of Regulations. Thus, the first serious attempt at adopting a constitution had proved abortive.

But this setback was temporary. Soon the constitutionalists, among whose leaders were Dr. Nahabed Rusinian, Dr. Servichen, Nigoghos

Balian, Krikor Odian, and Krikor Margosian, drafted a new code acceptable to the conservative camp. By then most members of this intelligentsia
were in the employ of viziers and other high Ottoman officials as family
physicians, advisors, or assistants. Like the *amiras,* they used their influence within the Ottoman governing circle in promoting the ideas and plans
for the reorganization of the *millet.* In the meantime, the latest draft of the
code was unanimously accepted by the National Assembly on May 24,
1860. After some delay and a couple of popular demonstrations, imperial
ratification was finally granted on March 17, 1863.

This Code of Regulations incorporated a long preamble and 150
articles. The powers of the patriarch were curtailed, but he continued to
serve as the symbol and the representative of the Armenian *millet.* The
laity formed six-sevenths of the National Assembly, the clerics making
up the rest. The organization and the hierarchy of the *millet* administration were clearly stipulated. One of the notable features of this constitution was the predominance of the Armenians of Constantinople in all
the bodies of the *millet.* This constitution, with some modifications, is
still in use in the administration of the Armenian Church in the diaspora.

The document of 1860 was named the Armenian National Constitution, for the word constitution *(sahmanadrutiun)* had a more European
ring and connotation than "code of regulations," and this pleased its
liberal framers. This was, however, only an illusion, even a delusion.
The term "code of regulations" was more appropriate, for the document
simply regulated the internal affairs of the *millet.* Neither in individual
nor in collective spheres did the Armenians acquire any new rights. The
existing system was merely rearranged and reorganized. The constitution provided no safeguards or guarantees for the Armenians against
mistreatment, abuses, and exploitation by the state officials as well as
by Turkish and Kurdish feudal lords. Perhaps one of the most striking
aspects of the constitutional movement was the nonparticipation of
"provincial" Armenians in it. Armenians from the provinces were
neither asked to take part in the deliberations, nor did they demonstrate
any interest in getting involved.

In spite of its many shortcomings, the Armenian National Constitution was a major achievement within the nineteenth-century Ottoman context. It clearly signified the triumph of liberalism and
democratic principles in the *millet* over arbitrariness and absolutism,
characteristics more of the Ottoman regime than the *millet.* Moreover,
it was a moderate but unmistakable step toward the political regeneration of the people.

The Tanzimat and the Armenians

The tanzimat reforms changed the structure of the Ottoman government, at least outwardly, but did very little to reshape the society and improve the political and economic conditions of the subjects. They affected life in the capital and one or two major cities, while in the provinces they produced no positive developments or change; on the contrary, in religiously mixed regions they created unwarranted tensions and even conflicts. Most scholars now must agree that in order for these reforms to have effectively permeated Ottoman society, it would have been necessary to have had either a strong-willed and firmly committed sultan or a social revolution to change radically the theocratic character of the state and society. Neither condition existed. For the Armenians the tanzimat gave rise to the constitutional movement, yet the Armenian constitution had little effect on the economic and political status of the provincial population.

The Tanzimat Reforms and the Provinces

The reforms did not improve the lot of the Armenian people in the empire. If anything, they affected their destiny in a negative way. By establishing new administrative organs, such as provincial and district assemblies with Armenian representation, the reforms introduced the principle of equality to resentful Muslims, on the one hand, and, on the other, revealed the impossibility of their application, a fact that simply disrupted the existing way of life. In other words, they worsened the conditions of Armenians.

This deterioration was evidenced in the decline of the status of Armenian peasants. In the 1860s the *maraba* (landless peasant) phenomenon spread rapidly in some Western Armenian provinces, especially in mixed areas of Armenians and Kurds. The *maraba*, in fact, depended completely for their very existence on the Turkish *agha* or the Kurdish *beg* (chieftain), in general, and, in rare cases, on their Armenian landlord. The Armenian peasants in Taron (Mush) and Vaspurakan lived as quasi-serfs, an ambiguous and illegal serfdom, but real all the same.

In the 1870s another system of quasi-serfdom, the *khafir*, emerged. In the regions of Mush, Sasun, Shadakh, and the neighboring districts, the Kurdish *khafirs* (chieftains) started to sell the villages they "owned" with their Armenian inhabitants and their possessions. The Armenian peasant and his family "belonged" to the Kurdish *khafir;* the latter milked the peasant, while the womenfolk worked in his household. In certain places, at the marriage of an Armenian peasant the *khafir* reserved the right of "visit" to the bride on the first night. In the reports sent to the patriarchate by special envoys, the condition of these peasants was described simply as slavery.

The central authorities were well informed, but they simply did nothing; this inaction was interpreted by contemporary observers as acquiescence, if not encouragement, of such mistreatment. This reading of the situation was accurate: The Turkish government was not averse to the weakening of the Armenian peasantry. It was no longer interested even in the appearance of implementing the reforms. It was pursuing a policy of total subjection of the peoples in the empire, especially the non-Muslims. The Zeitun Rebellion was a direct result of this policy.

The Zeitun Rebellion of 1862

Zeitun was one of the few mountainous regions where Armenians had maintained their autonomy. The town and its villages were Armenian-inhabited and ruled by local *ishkhans* (princes). At various times Zeitun had been attacked, but the Zeituntsis had either successfully defended themselves or come to terms with their aggressors.

The Turkish government did not view the autonomy of Zeitun benignly; it tried to undermine the strong position of Zeitun by settling Circassians in the vicinity and inciting them against the Zeituntsis. As this strategy did not pay off, in the summer of 1862 a 12,000-strong regular Turkish army, supported by 6,000 irregulars, attacked Zeitun, on the pretext of alleged nonpayment of taxes. The outlying villages were looted and destroyed; the town, however, was not only saved but its 5,000 defenders defeated the Turkish invading forces on August 2, 1862, inflicting heavy casualties and capturing two field cannons and a large amount of ammunition. The blockade instituted by the Turkish commander threatened the Zeituntsis with starvation. The latter eventually requested the intercession of the French king Napoleon III. Under French pressure the blockade was lifted, but, in exchange, the government was allowed to build a garrison and to station some troops there. Zeitun, thus, lost part of its autonomy.

The Zeitun rebellion, essentially a local affair, had deep and far-reaching repercussions among all the Armenians, both in the Ottoman Empire and tsarist Russia. On the one hand, it inspired pride and self-confidence because of the heroic struggle of the Zeituntsis, and, on the other, it awakened nationalist feelings and desires. If the adoption of the constitution was the culmination of Armenian liberalism, the Zeitun rebellion was the fledgling beginning of Armenian nationalism. The decaying Ottoman Empire would have collapsed had it not been for the European powers whose conflicting interests led them to support the decrepit empire. The Serbian and Greek revolts served as a warning that the empire needed fundamental changes. It was mainly under foreign pressure that several successive reforms were introduced.

The tanzimat measures, however, failed in their pompously proclaimed goals. The conditions of the Armenians in the empire did not improve. Mistreatment and oppression continued unabated, and even increased in intensity. The Ottoman government professed reform but pursued a policy of complete subjugation, subservience, and exploitation.

Popular discontent and eventually rebellion would gradually spread among the Armenians, whose demands for better treatment, politically and economically, would give rise to the international issue known as "the Armenian Question," which became an important part of the Eastern Question.

FOR FURTHER INFORMATION

Anasian, 1961.

Barsoumian, 1982.

Krikorian, 1978.

Nalbandian, 1963.

Ormanian, 1955.

Sarkiassian, 1938.

Walker, 1980.

7

THE ARMENIAN QUESTION IN THE OTTOMAN EMPIRE, 1876–1914

Richard G. Hovannisian

The plight of the Armenian population and its struggle for civil rights and administrative reforms became known as the Armenian Question in the Ottoman Empire. That question first found entry into the chambers of international diplomacy in 1878 as the result of the empire's military reverses and internal decay. The tanzimat reforms of the preceding decades proved to be an inadequate response to the breakdown of traditional social, economic, and political relations. They introduced the principle of equality, but in fact remained largely unimplemented and only aroused the suspicions and resentment of Muslim elements whose customary superiority was threatened by the reforms. The confusing and uneven application of the tanzimat measures actually aggravated the situation by weakening the quasi-protection afforded subject groups in semifeudal societies without instituting a new system for safeguarding life and property.

Most Armenians in the Ottoman Empire were peasants, notwithstanding Western stereotypes of shrewd and crafty Armenian merchants with whom Europeans were most in contact. During the nineteenth century, shifting political and economic relationships contributed to a sharp rise in dispossessed, landless Armenian peasants and the condemnation of many to a marginal existence in squalid urban slums. During the patriarchal reign of Archbishop Mkrtich Khrimian (1869-1873), details of the affliction of the provincial Armenians were gathered and publicized. A picture of unjust and exorbitant taxation, corrupt and oppressive administration, inadmissibility of Christian testimony in Muslim courts of law, and depredations by nomadic Kurdish and other tribal elements was clearly etched in these reports.

At the same time that conditions for most Armenians were deteriorating, national self-awareness was on the rise. Hundreds of Ottoman Armenian youth, sons of the privileged classes, were returning from study in the West, imbued with the social and political philosophies of the age of romanticism and revolt. This enthusiastic elite engaged in journalism, education, and literary criticism, breaking the restrictive bonds of the Armenian classical language to write in the vernacular—the utilitarian language. The authors and poets exhorted their people to recover their national collective memory and honor, so long tarnished and forgotten. Stimulated by American and other foreign missionary institutions in the Near East, a network of Armenian schools and newspapers gradually spread from Constantinople and Smyrna to Cilicia and eventually to the towns and villages of the eastern provinces—Turkish (Western) Armenia.

It was this dual development, the conscious Armenian demand for individual and collective security of life and property on the one hand and the burgeoning insecurity of both life and property on the other, that gave rise to the Armenian question as a part of the larger Eastern question. There were certain peculiarities to the Armenian Question. Most other Christian subject peoples lived in the Balkans and were in the process of separation from the Ottoman Empire. The Arab Muslim provinces had never been colonized significantly by Turkic tribes, and by and large they maintained an autonomous existence. But the two to three million Armenians of the Ottoman Empire lived in every province. There were far more Armenians in Constantinople than in any city on the Armenian plateau. Armenians also made up a large proportion of the population of Cilicia and played a vital role in the crafts and trades of western Anatolia. It was true that most Armenians of the Ottoman Empire continued to live on the lands of their historic ancient and medieval kingdoms on the great highland plateau in the east. Yet even there they were no longer predominant. Over the centuries Turkic and

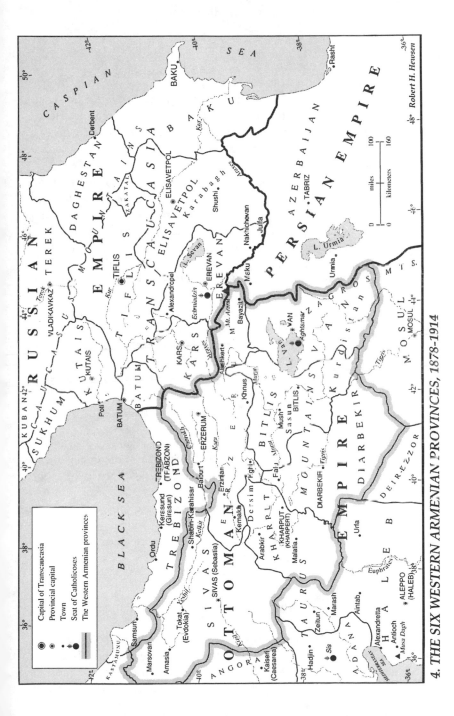

4. THE SIX WESTERN ARMENIAN PROVINCES, 1878-1914

Kurdish peoples had migrated into the area and when combined out-numbered the Armenians. The Muslim elements were disparate from racial, sectarian, social, and economic points of view, yet the Ottoman administration lumped them together into the Muslim *millet* and even-tually counterposed them to the Armenians for political reasons. Hence, Armenians were in some places a plurality, but only in a few districts were they an absolute majority in the provinces known as Turkish or Western Armenia.

The demographic distribution of the Armenian population had a significant effect on the formulation of Armenian political thought. Armenian petitions to the Sublime Porte repeatedly requested action against corrupt officials and predatory tribes and the chronic instances of abduction, pillage, and extortion. They sought a system of direct taxation, civil justice, and local representation. Thus, at the time that Greeks, Serbians, Romanians, Bulgarians, and others were gaining autonomy and even independence, Armenian supplications modestly asked for security and good government. Except for the mountaineers of Zeitun and a few other isolated enclaves, the Armenians of the Ottoman Empire were not willing or able to take up arms to defend themselves. Consequently they received little attention from the Euro-pean states when those powers pressured the Ottoman government to make major concessions to the rebellious Balkan peoples.

By the time the Western Armenians began to articulate their own programs for political, social, and economic reforms, the Ottoman Empire was entrenched in a period of reaction. Sultan Abdul-Hamid II (1878-1909) was driven to paranoia by the specter of the final partition and dissolution of his realm and viewed Armenian agitation as treachery. Each Armenian appeal aroused more antagonism and suspicion. And each halfhearted European attempt at intercession only deepened the paranoia. If the Armenians were to follow the example of the Balkan Christians, there might be nothing left of the empire except a truncated Turkish state in western Anatolia.

Internationalization of the Armenian Question

Revolts by Balkan Christians in 1875 and severe acts of Turkish retri-bution, including the massacre of the men, women, and children of several Bulgarian villages, created an uproar in the liberal press of Europe. Even the British Conservatives, headed by Benjamin Disraeli

(Lord Beaconsfield), could not remain immune to public pressure. When the first reports of massacre reached London, Prime Minister Disraeli tried to forestall action, upholding the Conservative traditional policy of containing the Russian Empire and furthering British political and economic interests by limiting the partition and slowing the collapse of the Ottoman Empire. The Suez Canal had only recently been opened, redoubling British interest in the eastern Mediterranean as a lifeline to India. Yet Disraeli could not withstand the rising tide of criticism and tried to deal with the crisis by proposing a conference in Constantinople of the ambassadors of the European powers—Great Britain, France, Russia, Germany, Austria-Hungary, and Italy—to mediate and find a way to resolve the most serious grievances of the Balkan Christians.

The conference finally convened in December 1876, but Sultan Abdul-Hamid maneuvered to undercut the Europeans by promulgating a constitution that had been drafted by Midhat Pasha, Grigor Otian (Krikor Odian), and other sincere advocates of reform. The constitution provided for the separation of legislative, executive, and judicial powers and guaranteed civil rights, equality of all citizens before the law, religious freedom, and security of life and property. Had the sultan been as sincere in implementing the constitution, he could have eliminated the major grievances of the subject nationalities, Armenians included. But proclamation of the constitution forced adjournment of the conference of ambassadors and, in fact, left matters even worse in the Balkans. Sultan Abdul-Hamid, having warded off European intervention, soon prorogued the constitution and the parliament for which it had provided.

The Balkan crisis heightened Russo-Turkish tensions until April 1877, when the Russians, invoking a clause of a previous treaty, crossed the frontier into the Romanian principality of Moldavia, evoking a declaration of war from Abdul-Hamid. The Russo-Turkish war of 1877-1878 was fought in the Balkans and on the Armenian plateau. The dominant circles of the Armenian *millet* traditionally had shared Turkish suspicions of Russia and feared the implications of a regime committed to "Autocracy, Orthodoxy, and [Russian] Nationality." Patriarch Nerses Varzhapetian issued a pastoral letter calling on his people to work and pray for the victory of Ottoman arms. Yet for the Armenian population in the border regions of Alashkert, Bayazit (Bayazed), Mush, and Van, Russia seemed to offer the only hope of deliverance from the terrible anarchic conditions. This view was strengthened when, after the Russian armies began to advance on the great fortress city of Kars, Kurdish tribal levies and irregulars *(bashibazouk)* looted and burned Armenian villages in that district as well as in Alashkert and Bayazit. Hence, when the Russian armies, led by Russian Armenian generals M. T. Loris-Melikov, A. A. Gusakov, and I. I. Lazarev, captured Kars in November 1877 and then the fortress of Erzerum three months later, they were welcomed by many Armenians as liberators.

At the end of 1877, the Russian armies in the Balkans, commanded by the tsar's brother, Grand Duke Nicholas, overcame stiff Turkish resistance at Plevna and advanced to Adrianople (Edirne), the gateway to Constantinople. There, in January 1878, the Turkish command sued for an armistice and preliminary negotiations for peace began. By then even Patriarch Nerses and the Armenian National Assembly had put aside their Russophobia to instruct the Armenian primate of Adrianople to petition the grand duke to include in the peace treaty specific provisions for the self-administration of the Armenian provinces. The massacre and plunder of scores of Armenian villages in the east by Kurdish and Circassian bands, financed by the regular Turkish army, influenced the patriarchal circles to seek Russian intercession through the good offices of the pan-Slavist prewar Russian ambassador to Constantinople, Count I. I. Ignatev. The Armenians were encouraged by the grand duke's sympathy and a draft clause relating to self-government of the Armenian provinces, but soon the armistice collapsed and the Russians marched to San Stefano on the outskirts of the Ottoman capital.

The Russian offensive set off international war jitters, as Disraeli's government sent a naval squadron to the Dardanelles to prevent Russian occupation of Constantinople. Conflict was averted by the Russo-Turkish peace treaty of San Stefano, signed on March 3, 1878. The treaty virtually ended Ottoman hegemony over the Balkans, as Serbia, Montenegro, and Romania, following the previous example of Greece, were granted independence, and a large Bulgarian state with an outlet on the Aegean Sea was made autonomous. On the Caucasus front, Russia was awarded the districts of Batum, Ardahan, Kars, Alashkert, and Bayazit, whereas the rest of the occupied territories of Western Armenia were to be returned to the sultan. Armenian leaders were disappointed that there was no provision for Armenian self-administration. Their only compensation was article 16, which made Russian withdrawal conditional:

> As the evacuation of the Russian troops of the territory which they
> occupy in Armenia, and which is to be restored to Turkey, might give
> rise to conflicts and complications detrimental to the maintenance of

good relations between the two countries, the Sublime Porte engages to carry into effect, without further delay, the improvements and reforms demanded by local requirements in the provinces inhabited by Armenians, and to guarantee their security from Kurds and Circassians. (Great Britain, 1878; Hertslet, 1891, p. 2686)

General Loris-Melikov would stand firm in Erzerum until Tsar Alexander II was satisfied that there were adequate guarantees for the security of the Christian population.

Receipt of the treaty terms in London immediately put Prime Minister Disraeli and Foreign Secretary Robert Salisbury into action. Salisbury denounced the treaty as a surrender of the Turkish Armenian strongholds to Russia and with them the lucrative overland trade route from Trebizond over Alashkert and Bayazit to Persia and beyond. Enlisting the support of Austria-Hungary, which was also deeply concerned about the spread of Russian influence in the Balkans, the British now demanded a European congress to conclude an equitable Eastern settlement. Tsar Alexander II, already beset by grievous internal crises, could not risk hostilities with a major European power and acquiesced in the British demand. With German chancellor Otto von Bismarck issuing the invitations as the "honest broker," plenipotentiaries of the European powers gathered for the Berlin Congress in June 1878.

When Patriarch Nerses and the Armenian National Assembly learned of these developments, they were not discouraged. On the contrary, it was the reluctant Russian orientation that had brought them disappointment, and they now hoped that a British orientation would lead to a measure of self-government. As the British knew that the Armenians did not seek separation from the Ottoman Empire, they might sponsor a program of good government and of Armenian self-administration to steady the empire. With this objective, a delegation led by former patriarch Mkrtich Khrimian set out for the European capitals to explain the Armenian case to the diplomats who would proceed to Berlin. Using the administrative statute of Lebanon as a model, the Armenians asked that the eastern provinces be granted a Christian governor, civil courts, local self-administration, mixed Christian-Muslim militias, suffrage for all male taxpayers, and the use of most tax revenues for local needs. Lord Salisbury received the delegation politely but without making any commitments, and the Armenians received similar receptions in Paris and Berlin.

To the bitter disappointment of Khrimian "Hairik" (the endearing word for "father") and his associates, no one took note of the Armenian delegation outside the conference hall. Within, Salisbury aggressively pushed the British policy of eliminating the most threatening aspects of the San Stefano treaty. Serbia, Montenegro, and Bulgaria were cut back in size, Bosnia and Herzegovina as well as most of the land set aside for Bulgaria were returned to the sultan. On the Caucasus front, the districts of Alashkert and Bayazit were also restored to Abdul-Hamid, thus keeping the main overland trade route out of Russian control. There was no discussion of Armenian self-administration, and the question of reforms, instead of falling to Russian supervision, was to become the responsibility of the European powers collectively. In place of San Stefano's article 16, Berlin's article 61 read:

> The Sublime Porte undertakes to carry out, without further delay, the improvements and reforms demanded by local requirements in the provinces inhabited by Armenians, and to guarantee their security against the Circassians and Kurds.
>
> It will periodically make known the steps taken to this effect to the powers, who will superintend their application. (Great Britain, 1878; Hertslet, 1891, p. 2796)

In the long run, the conversion of article 16 to 61 was succinctly stated by the Duke of Argyll: "What was everybody's business was nobody's business" (Campbell, 1896, p. 74). On July 13, 1878, the day that the treaty was signed, Archbishop Khrimian wrote the plenipotentiaries that his delegation regretted that its legitimate and moderate demands had been ignored. The Armenian nation had never been the instrument of a foreign power and, although more oppressed than any other Christian people, had caused no trouble to the Ottoman government. It had hoped to find the same protection afforded to other Christian nations, especially as it was "devoid of all political ambition." The protest concluded:

> The Armenians have just realised that they have been deceived, that their rights have not been recognised, because they have been pacific. . . .
>
> The Armenian delegation is going to return to the east, taking this lesson with it. It declares nevertheless that the Armenian people will never cease from crying out until Europe gives its legitimate demands satisfaction. (Walker, 1980, p. 170)

Khrimian Hairik repeated the message shortly after returning to Constantinople. There in the Armenian cathedral in the Kum Kapu quarter, he preached a memorable sermon filled with metaphors. All the big and little powers had gathered in Europe, he said, to partake of the "dish of liberty." The Balkan peoples had come to Berlin with their metal spoons and ate of the tasty *herisa* stew. But the Armenians had only paper petitions, and when they timidly placed their paper spoon into the *herisa,* the paper dissolved and the Armenians received nothing. Despite Khrimian's generally conservative disposition, his message came to be regarded by many as a revolutionary call to forge an "iron spoon" through self-reliance and self-defense (Nalbandian, 1963, pp. 28-29).

Both Austria-Hungary and Great Britain profited from their diplomatic support of the Ottoman Empire. Austria was given the right to administer in the name of the sultan the districts of Bosnia and Herzegovina. This was a major affront to Serbian nationalists and, after Austria simply annexed both districts in 1908, led to the assassination of the Austrian heir-apparent and the outbreak of World War I. Before the Berlin Congress opened, Great Britain already had its reward. In a secret agreement with the Sublime Porte, the British were given a long-term "lease" over the island of Cyprus, with its strategic coaling stations due north of the Suez Canal. In return, Great Britain pledged itself to prevent any further Russian encroachments in the Asiatic provinces of the Ottoman Empire and "to join his imperial majesty the sultan in defending them by force of arms." The sultan, for his part, pledged to introduce "necessary reforms" to improve the administration and protect the Christian and other subjects in those provinces (Walker, 1980, p. 114; Hertslet, 1891, pp. 2722-33). The British thus required reforms unilaterally through the Cyprus convention and collectively through the Congress of Berlin. In the eastern provinces, meanwhile, horrified Armenians witnessed the evacuation of General Loris-Melikov's divisions. As had been the case during the Russian withdrawal from Erzerum in 1829, thousands of native Armenians departed with the tsarist armies in 1878 to settle in Transcaucasia.

Despite the setback caused by the Treaty of Berlin, Armenian leaders had not lost hope. Great Britain was regarded as the most advanced and most civilized country in the world and could be trusted to supervise Armenian reforms in a far more enlightened manner than Russia, whose attitude toward the Armenians, their church and aspirations, was suspect. In addressing the Armenian National Assembly, Patriarch Nerses Varzhapetian declared that he had faith that the needed reforms would evolve from article 61. As the chief spokesman of the Ottoman Armenians, the patriarch swore fidelity to the sultan and emphasized that efforts to surmount Armenian misfortunes would be made within the framework of the beloved Ottoman homeland. At a time when several of the Balkan nationalities had already won complete independence, the Armenians still shunned any hint of separatism.

The Armenian Question was internationalized by the Treaty of Berlin, but the Armenians gained no advantage from that new status. On the contrary, Kurdish and Circassian tribesmen spread havoc over the eastern provinces, harshly striking those districts from which the Russian armies had just withdrawn. Neither the petitions of the patriarch nor the posting of additional British consuls in Western Armenia helped to alleviate the situation. The consular reports detailed the daily occurrences of bribery, extortion, abduction, and murder and described the courts of justice as a farce and the police and gendarmeries as a scourge.

For three years, until 1881, the European powers, outwardly cooperating under the joint responsibility of article 61, issued collective and identic notes reminding the Sublime Porte of its obligations. But in 1881 Germany, seconded by Austria-Hungary, refused to act in concert. In the same year Tsar Alexander II was assassinated; his son, Alexander III, quickly initiated a period of reaction during which the Russian Armenians, along with other minorities, suffered severe discrimination and the St. Petersburg government dropped any pretense of concern for the Turkish Armenians. In Great Britain, William Gladstone had returned to office, dislodging Disraeli, but the British Liberals were no more successful in moving the sultan to effective reforms than the Conservatives had been. Thus the European powers, already deeply engaged in the scramble for empire in Africa and the Far East, shelved the Armenian Question for fifteen years.

The Armenian Revolutionary Movement

Feeling abandoned and betrayed, a growing number of Armenians began to espouse extralegal means to achieve what they now regarded as the natural rights of man. They came to believe that, like the Balkan Christians, the Armenian people would have to organize, even take arms, to achieve their goals. Small, locally based groups emerged at Van, Erzerum, and other localities, with the members reading clandestine literature and engaging in target practice. The rudimentary programs of these groups called for defending the honor of the nation against those who violated the people, their religion and culture. The Pashtpan Haireniats (Defense of the Fatherland) society, formed in Erzerum in 1881, adopted the slogan "Liberty or Death," and advocated Armenian self-defense. The arrest of most of its members the next year suppressed the movement, but the fact that so many young people had participated in the society was a source of inspiration to like-minded Armenians everywhere, memorialized in the patriotic song "A Sound Reverberated from the Armenian Mountains of Erzerum." The appearance of societies such as the Pashtpan Haireniats reflected the growing chasm between fathers and sons, as the youth were no longer willing to accept their parents' patience, endurance, and even fatalism in the face of gross violations of fundamental human rights. It was the generation of the sons that took to heart the metaphor of Khrimian Hairik's "iron spoon."

The Armenakan society, organized in 1885 at Van, is generally considered the first Armenian political party, although its program and area of activity was limited. The inspiration of Mkrtich Portukalian, an erudite educator, organizer, and proponent of self-defense who had propagated his views as teacher and head master in Van, the party took its name from *Armenia,* the newspaper that Portugalian founded in Marseilles after his expulsion from the Ottoman Empire that same year. The Armenakan platform called for Armenian self-determination, to be achieved through revolutionary means but coming after a long period of preparation through enlightenment, propaganda, organization, and military training. The party did not favor open agitation or demonstrations and did not include Armenian independence even as a long-range objective. Their revolutionary rhetoric notwithstanding, the Armenakans continued to seek reforms through peaceful means and European intervention, emphasizing that the general Armenian movement should become manifest at a time of renewed international interest in the Armenian question. Education and enlightenment were essential prerequisites to Armenian self-government. What made the party revolutionary, therefore, was its advocacy of self-reliance and armed resistance against state terror.

The Armenakan society gained some adherents in Constantinople, Trebizond, Salmast in northern Persia, and elsewhere, but by and large it drew its membership and concentrated its activities at Van. Armenakan youth defended Armenian villages from raids and organized acts of retribution. In 1896, when massacre and plunder had enveloped the Armenian plateau, Armenakan detachments, together with those of the Hnchakists and Dashnakists, took arms to defend their city. Subsequently, most Armenakans integrated into the larger revolutionary organizations or else, through stages, moved toward liberal, evolutionary programs, such as that adopted by the Constitutional Democrat (Sahmanadir Ramkavar) party, which was organized in Cairo in 1908.

The Hnchakian Revolutionary Party, subsequently renamed the Social Democrat Hnchakian Party, became the first Armenian party with a national and international structure and detailed political program. Organized in Geneva in 1887 by Maro Vardanian, her fiancé Avetis Nazarbekian, and several other Russian Armenian intellectuals who had been influenced both by Russian populism and by Marxism, the party took its name from its newspaper, *Hnchak* (Bell), clearly reminiscent of Alexander Herzen's Russian-language *Kolokol* (Bell). The short-range goal of the Hnchakists was the emancipation of Turkish (Western) Armenia; the long-range objective was creation of an independent socialist state within the framework of a socialist world order.

Concentrating on the short-range platform, the Hnchakist press detailed the impoverishment and repression in the Ottoman Armenian provinces. The only real solution, therefore, was the liberation of Western Armenia through revolution. In preparation for the uprising, the Hnchakian Party would emphasize education, self-defense, and the revolutionary tactics of agitation and terror against external oppressors and internal informers and collaborators. In view of the fact that the land of historic Armenia was now shared by non-Armenian elements, efforts should be made to draw them into a common struggle against state terror. Following the emancipation of Western Armenia, a popularly elected legislative body would guarantee complete freedom of press, speech, assembly, and conscience and the right to hold office regardless of wealth or position. The government would be based on broad provincial and communal initiative.

In stressing self-sufficiency, the Hnchakists still regarded European intervention as an important element in winning independence, but they also cautioned against the danger of exchanging Turkish misrule for that of the imperialist powers. The only sure way to prevent such an eventuality was realization of the long-range goal of also emancipating Russian Armenia and Persian Armenia and bringing a united socialist state into a world socialist order. While adhering to Marxist tenets, the Hnchakists saw no serious contradiction between patriotism and socialism or between nationalism and internationalism. Like most other Marxist societies, the Hnchakists adopted a tight-knit, centralized structure. The party's central committee and organ remained in Geneva, its clandestine literature finding fertile soil among the discontented Armenian youth of the Ottoman and Russian empires. Field workers soon established branches in Constantinople, Cilicia, Anatolia, Western Armenia, Transcaucasia, and in the Armenian communities of the Balkans, the United States, and elsewhere.

As the Hnchakian Revolutionary Party began to infiltrate the Ottoman Empire, Armenian intellectuals in the Russian Empire were active both in antigovernmental Russian movements and in separate Armenian societies. It was a time of great ferment, especially since the Eastern Armenians had been subjected to the discriminatory measures of Tsar Alexander III. The closure of Armenian schools and other acts of repression by the tsarist regime caused some Armenian internationalists to focus attention on the particular woes of their own people. In that process, they came to the realization that their own tribulations were dwarfed by those of the Western Armenians. Implementation of the reforms foreseen in the Treaty of Berlin and training for self-defense became a part of the credo of the Eastern Armenian intellectuals who had passed through the Russian Zemlia i Volia (Land and Will) and Narodnaia Volia (People's Will) movements. Tiflis, the cultural, economic, and political center of the Russian Armenians, abounded with legal, semilegal, and illegal societies, the more militant of which planned to organize guerrilla bands and have them slip across the frontier into Western Armenia. There was an insatiable thirst for firsthand accounts of what was transpiring in the *erkir* (homeland), as the Western Armenian provinces came to be known.

The proliferation of many small groups of both socialist and non-socialist orientations detracted from effective, coordinated action and created the need for a unifying umbrella organization. It was out of that need that the Federation of Armenian Revolutionaries (Hai Heghapokhakanneri Dashnaktsutiun) took form at Tiflis in the summer of 1890. The primary organizers, Kristapor Mikayelian, Simon Zavarian, and Stepan Zorian (Rostom), were imbued with socialist ideologies, yet in order to form the broadest possible coalition they avoided explicit use of the term and managed to persuade many socialists that the goal of Armenian "economic and political freedom" was founded on socialist precepts. Hnchakist representatives also agreed to enter the federation, but their party soon went its separate way because of insufficient emphasis on socialism by the Dashnaktsutiun and, as was common in the revolutionary movement, because of strong clashes of personality.

By the time of the first party congress and adoption of a platform in 1892, the organization had been recast and consolidated as the Armenian Revolutionary Federation or Hai Heghapokhakan Dashnaktsutiun. Its program resembled that of the Hnchakists to the degree that it focused on the emancipation of Western Armenia and included planks on security of life and labor; freedom of speech, press, and assembly; redistribution of land to those who worked it; equality of all nationalities before the law; establishment of universal military service in place of the military exemption fee; compulsory education; and a progressive system of taxation. Unlike the Hnchakists, however, the Dashnaktsutiun adhered to the Russian populist and Social Revolutionary view of peasant communes containing the seeds of the new society. Rejecting the Marxist scheme of historical development that necessitated capitalistic exploitation and dehumanization as a precursor to revolution and the triumph of socialism, the Armenian Dashnakists and Russian Social Revolutionaries believed that it was possible to avoid the worst abuses of advanced capitalism, and through the existing peasant communes, to pass directly from a semifeudal to an egalitarian society.

The immediate objective of the Dashnaktsutiun was the economic and political freedom of Western Armenia. Measures would be taken to raise the revolutionary morale of the people, to organize armed units to bond with the peasant masses, and to train the Armenians in self-defense. During the period of time needed to spread these ideas and prepare for the armed struggle, the Dashnaktsutiun would battle all exploiters, including corrupt officials, traitors, and usurers. Like the Hnchakian party, the Dashnaktsutiun accepted the Narodnaia Volia's reliance on terroristic measures against the enemies of the people. Yet the Dashnaktsutiun remained aloof from the Hnchakist tactic of mass demonstrations. The most fundamental difference between the two parties, however, was that the Hnchakists alone called for the complete separation and independence of Western Armenia; the Dashnakist program was limited to freedom and autonomy within the framework of the Ottoman Empire. The Dashnakist organ, *Droshak* (Banner), was emphatic in pointing out that the terms "freedom" and "independence" were not synonymous. Under the prevailing circumstances, independence was not a realistic objective. Taking into consideration the dispersal of the Armenian people, the party adopted a decentralized structure, vesting in the regional committees flexible latitude according to local conditions and needs. It was not until renewed anti-Armenian measures in the Russian Empire beginning in 1903 that the Dashnaktsutiun was radicalized sufficiently to adopt an explicitly socialist platform and become a member of the Second Socialist International in 1907. And it was not until 1919 that the party revised its program to bring it into conformity with the entirely unplanned but nonetheless de facto existence of an independent Armenian republic.

The Armenian revolutionary societies faced enormous obstacles. They opposed an imperial regime with extensive military and bureaucratic means of repression. Matters were made even worse in 1891 when Sultan Abdul-Hamid brought frequently rebellious Kurdish elements under official auspices by providing them money, uniforms, and officers and organizing them into irregular cavalry units, ostensibly to patrol the frontiers much like Russian Cossacks, but in reality to keep the Armenians in check. Armenian resistance to the so-called Hamidiye cavalry units could now be regarded as insubordination and insurrection against the state and the sultan.

No less weighty than the instruments of repression was the centuries-long conditioning of the Armenian people to second-class, inferior status under foreign domination. Hence, although the vast majority of Armenians groaned under the breakdown of law and order and the arbitrariness of the sultan's official and unofficial representatives, most were afraid that resistance and acts of defiance would lead to massive retaliation and even greater suffering. Internally, revolutionary ideologies alarmed not only those who feared retribution but also and especially those of the Armenian privileged classes who saw in the militant, socialist-oriented revolutionary platforms frightful threats to their own position and well-being. The anticlericalism of many revolutionary intellectuals posed an ominous challenge to the traditional role of the Armenian Apostolic Church and the governance of the Armenian *millet* in the Ottoman Empire.

Adherents of the new revolutionary societies realized that the campaign to free the Armenian people from a servile mentality would be a lengthy process. Their programs all emphasized education, enlightenment, propaganda, and preparation. To join a revolutionary society required unusual commitment in view of the possibility of punishment by death. Even at the height of their popularity, the secret societies and their armed bands could attract only a relatively small following of active members and even fewer who were willing to abandon home and family in exchange for the abnegation and commitment required of the freedom fighter, the *fedayi*. Still, a significant number of young people gave up all hope in legal, peaceful methods of change and instead moved toward the idealistic image of a free, autonomous, even independent, Armenia. The endurance of the fathers was now matched by the impatience of the sons.

Demonstration and Revolt

Demonstration, confrontation, revolt, and massacre characterized the decade of the 1890s (Walker, 1980, pp. 131-36; Nalbandian, 1963, pp. 118-28). The newly formed Armenian revolutionary societies began to agitate for reforms and renewed European attention to the Armenian question. The Hnchakist Party in particular utilized the tactic of mass demonstration to hasten the process. The first encounter occurred in Erzerum in June 1890, when Turkish authorities combed the Armenian cathedral and the Sanasarian secondary academy in search of weapons. Even though no arms were discovered, an aroused Turkish mob attacked Armenian shops and homes a few days later. Then, when two hundred angry Armenian youths gathered in the churchyard to draw up a petition of protest, they refused to disperse upon order of the authorities. Shots were fired, a melee ensued, and a number of protesters were killed or wounded. It was presumed that the Hnchakists were responsible for this first significant confrontation and open act of Armenian defiance.

A month later blood was again shed, this time outside the Armenian Patriarchate in the Kum Kapu quarter of Constantinople. Several Hnchakists, led by Harutiun Djangulian, Mihran Damadian, and Hambartsum Boyajian (Murad), interrupted the saying of mass to read a manifesto of demands and to denounce the indifference of Patriarch Khoren Ashegian and the Armenian National Assembly. They forced the terrified patriarch to join in a procession to the Yildiz palace to deliver the manifesto of grievances to Sultan Abdul-Hamid and to demand implementation of article 61 of the Treaty of Berlin. Even as the procession was organizing, police and soldiers surrounded the demonstrators. Again a skirmish ensued. Shots were fired, several persons, including at least one Turkish policeman, were killed, and many lay bloodied. The Kum Kapu encounter, an intentional act of agitation, alarmed both the Turkish sultan and the Armenian patriarch. On the other hand, the confrontation had shown that in repressive societies even peaceful demonstrations would end in violence. That conclusion was tested and proved true time and again. And although no tangible improvements resulted from the Kum Kapu affair, the Hnchakist press extolled the courage shown and the awakening in progress.

The Hnchakists continued to organize demonstrations in 1891 and 1892, none of them so dramatic as Kum Kapu, and growing numbers of intellectuals and youthful nationalists joined or secretly supported the clandestine organization. Then, in 1893, the Hnchakists were apparently behind the posting of Turkish-language placards *(yaftas)* in Yozgat, Amasia, Tokat, Marsovan, and other places in Anatolia, calling upon the Muslim population to rise up against the sultan and his oppressive regime. Again, with no tangible effect upon the intended audience, the act of provocation led to the arrest, imprisonment, torture, and hanging of many actual or suspected members of the Hnchakian Revolutionary Party.

The first real test of revolutionary armed resistance came in the remote mountains of Sasun, due south of the plain of Mush in the province of Bitlis. The Armenians complained of the exactions made by Kurdish notables *(aghas),* who demanded tribute in kind *(hafir)* in return for protection or, perhaps more accurately, for refraining from raids. But even the *hafir* often did not spare the Armenians from the havoc caused by nomadic Kurdish tribes from the Diarbekir region moving to summer pasture. Moreover, as the semifeudal system broke down, government tax collectors arrived to take their share. The impoverishment and plunder made the rugged mountaineers of Sasun receptive to the gospel of resistance preached by Hnchakist intellectual Damadian and intellectual-warrior Murad. Armenians of the Talvorig village cluster took arms to defend themselves against Kurdish raids in the summer of 1893. Damadian was arrested and sent to Constantinople that year, but Murad and his partisans continued to exhort the Sasunites to break the stranglehold of their Kurdish overlords.

In the summer of 1894 both nomadic Kurdish tribes and government tax collectors appeared for their exactions. The Armenians, emboldened by Murad's band, resisted. The surprised Kurdish chieftains and Turkish officials leveled the charge of sedition against Sasun and complained to the governor of Bitlis, Hasan Tahsin, who sent a military expedition to assist the Kurds. For more than a month the Armenians withstood the regulars and irregulars, but with supplies nearly exhausted they agreed to lay down their arms in return for an amnesty and having their grievances heard by the government. The Turkish commander gave his word to honor the conditions, but instead the disarmed population was brutalized. The villages of Shenik and Semal were looted and burned; priests were tortured, murdered, and mutilated; men were bayoneted; women were raped and disemboweled; and children were slashed and smashed. People who had fled to the caves and crevasses of

Mount Andok were hunted down by regulars and irregulars who showed no mercy regardless of age or gender. As many as 3,000 Sasunites perished in the carnage (Walker, 1980, pp. 136-42).

Word of the Sasun massacre spread quickly. The British consuls at Erzerum and Van relayed the available details to Ambassador Philip Currie in Constantinople. Their attempts to inspect the site of the massacre were blocked by officials who claimed the region was unsafe because of a cholera epidemic. The British, who by their insistence on the revision of the Treaty of San Stefano in 1878 were most responsible for the absence of adequate guarantees for the protection of the Armenians, now sharply protested to the Sublime Porte. As missionaries and correspondents broadcast the details of the brutality, the outcry in Europe prompted the British, French, and Russian ambassadors to propose a joint commission of inquiry. Rejecting the suggestion as interference in the internal affairs of the Ottoman state, the Sublime Porte ultimately consented to a compromise that allowed European observers to accompany a governmental commission of inquiry. The hearings were held in Mush in early 1895 in an atmosphere of intimidation. Nonetheless, several Armenian eyewitnesses were courageous enough to testify about the causes and character of the massacres. Not surprisingly, the Turkish commission found that the Armenians had engaged in seditious action that had necessitated pacification by the armed forces. The European observers disagreed:

> The absolute ruin of the district can never be regarded a measure proportionate to the punishment even of a revolt; *a fortiori,* in the present case, the only crimes of the Armenians, namely, those of having sheltered or perhaps concealed Murad and his band, of having committed some isolated acts of brigandage against Kurds, or disregarded the authorities, and possibly of having offered some slight resistance to the Imperial troops under circumstances which have not been cleared up, cannot possibly justify the state of misery to which the people and the country have been reduced. An equal responsibility rests on the local authorities, civil and military, for the absence of all measures to prevent a pseudo-revolt . . . or to put a stop later to the strife between the Armenians and the Kurds, and the losses of all kinds which were the consequences. (Great Britain, 1895, 1896)

The Sasun crisis drew the European powers reluctantly back to the Armenian problem after a break of some fifteen years. But the Concert of

Europe no longer acted in unison, as Germany, Austria, and Italy—the future Triple Alliance—showed no interest in pressuring the Sublime Porte, while Russia, outwardly cooperating with Great Britain, was not enthusiastic about supporting Armenian reforms or taking any action that would cause political ferment to spread into Transcaucasia. Nonetheless, in May 1895, after lengthy diplomatic exchanges, the British, French, and Russian ambassadors sent a memorandum to Sultan Abdul-Hamid to remind him once more of his obligations under article 61 of the Treaty of Berlin and to propose a new program of reforms. The project provided that the Armenian provinces of the empire would be consolidated, nomination of governors confirmed by the European powers, Armenian political prisoners granted amnesty, émigrés allowed to return, reparations accorded to victims of Sasun and other affected districts, forced converts to Islam restored to their original faith, a permanent control commission established in Constantinople, and a high commissioner appointed to execute the reform provisions. Moreover, nomadic Kurds were to move only under governmental surveillance and were to be encouraged to adopt a sedentary way of life. The Hamidiye corps, to be disarmed and without uniforms in peacetime, would be attached to regular army units if activated (Great Britain, 1896).

Throughout the summer months, diplomatic exchanges continued, as the Sublime Porte tried to stonewall the program and then to dilute the provisions as much as possible. In London, Lord Salisbury assured the Turkish ambassador that Queen Victoria's government did not seek autonomy or special privileges for the Armenians, only simple justice and equitable treatment. As the negotiations dragged on, the Hnchakists launched another major demonstration. Prior to the Bab Ali (Great Door or Sublime Porte) demonstration in September 1895, the Hnchakists informed the foreign embassies that a peaceful march would be organized to protest the Sasun massacre, political arrests, and terrorization of the Armenian people, which were clearly intended to eliminate the Armenian presence on their historic lands. On September 30 some 2,000 demonstrators set out from the Kum Kapu quarter in the direction of the Sublime Porte with petitions for civil liberties, the right to bear arms, the rehabilitation of Sasun and end to Kurdish migration, the recruitment of Armenians into the police and gendarmerie, and the territorial reorganization of the six Turkish Armenian provinces in conformity with historic, geographic, and ethnographic considerations.

En route to the Bab Ali, the demonstrators were intercepted by the police. Words were exchanged before the police commander slapped a demonstrator, who swiftly pulled out a revolver and shot the officer. In the fracas that followed, a score of Armenians were killed and a hundred wounded. Then throughout Constantinople Muslim theological students *(softas)* appeared with clubs, reportedly supplied by police agents, and beat to death all Armenians they could find. The massacre continued until October 3, striking especially porters, dockers, and other migrants from the provinces. Thousands of Armenians fled to the protection of their churches and did not venture out for a week. Once again the European ambassadors protested the senseless killings, including the murder of wounded persons in the courtyards of police stations.

It was ironic that while blood was flowing in the streets of the Ottoman capital, Sultan Abdul-Hamid finally accepted a compromise Armenian reform measure, much less comprehensive than the original May plan but nonetheless sufficient to give some hope and to elicit expressions of satisfaction from the European ambassadors. But if the promulgation of reforms was Abdul-Hamid's ostensible response to European pressure, his actual response was to teach both the Armenians and the Europeans a lesson that they would not forget for a long time. The 1895-1896 massacres were at hand.

The Massacres of 1895–1896

Approximately 100,000 Armenians were killed, hundreds of town quarters and villages were looted and gutted, many villages were forcibly converted to Islam, and a new Armenian exodus resulted from the bloody pogroms that started in October 1895 and did not abate until clubs, axes, and bayonets had again been put to use in Constantinople eleven months later. The twenty-five-year process of eliminating the Armenians of the Ottoman Empire had begun.

No sooner had the Sublime Porte informed the European embassies that the compromise reform measure was being promulgated than the first violent outbreak occurred at Trebizond. A skirmish in the Armenian quarter was followed on October 8 with a bugle call as the signal for a mob that reportedly included uniformed soldiers to go on a rampage of death and destruction. Armenian shops were looted, merchants killed on the spot, homes ransacked. In one day nearly a thousand Armenians lay dead in the city and surrounding villages; survivors were left to face economic ruin. But this was just the beginning. That same month massacres took place at Erzinjan, Erzerum, Gumushkhane,

Baiburt, Urfa, and Bitlis. At Erzerum, the British consul reported that a thousand Armenian businesses had been plundered and several hundred Armenians killed with the direct participation of army regulars. Near Bitlis, the inhabitants of entire villages were compelled to abjure their Christianity and convert to Islam under threat of death. In all these locations, the massacres were preceded by false rumors of an imminent Armenian attack. Muslims were agitated and armed and often during Friday prayers exhorted to take punitive action against the insolent infidels. First the marketplaces were attacked, then the residential quarters. And in nearly every instance, the passivity or complicity of Ottoman officials was established. The pogroms usually lasted from two days to a week before the authorities finally intervened.

The massacres in the very regions where the reform program was supposed to be implemented prompted renewed protests and threats from the British, French, and Russian ambassadors on November 5, but all such diplomatic notes, unsustained by a show of force, elicited declarations of innocence and hurt from the Sublime Porte, which cast the blame for the disorders first and foremost upon the Armenians themselves. The massacres continued in November, at Diarbekir, Sasun, Kharput, Malatia, Arabkir, Sivas, Amasia, Marsovan, Gurun, Kaiseri, and Aintab. Thousands perished in the violence and even larger numbers faced starvation and ruin during the winter of 1895–1896. The next month Urfa was struck a second time with greater ferocity. On December 28 soldiers joined the mob to break through Armenian barricades and kill all in sight. Kerosene was poured over buildings and the quarter put to flames. Some 3,000 men, women, and children crowded into the cathedral, but the troops set fire to the church and shot anyone who tried to escape. The Armenians were learning the price for looking to the West and daring to challenge the theocracy of Sultan Abdul-Hamid. And once again the European powers stood by passively, limiting themselves to joint and identic notes of protest to the Sublime Porte.

The Armenians resisted at a few places. Zeitun took arms in October, capturing the Turkish garrison and officials. A large Turkish expeditionary force surrounded the town and tried to starve it into submission, but the rugged mountaineers endured. The crisis eased only in January 1896, when through European mediation the Zeitunites agreed to lay down their arms and to permit the exile abroad of several Hnchakist agitators in return for a general amnesty, remission of past taxes, and the appointment of a Christian subgovernor. In June the

Armenians of Van also showed that they were prepared to defend themselves as armed detachments of Armenakans, Hnchakists, and Dashnakists joined forces to spare the city the now-established pattern of massacre, plunder, and fire.

The exact number of victims of the pogroms of 1895-1896 will never be known. Before the last acts of violence had passed, Johannes Lepsius, using German and other sources, compiled the following statistics:

People killed	88,243
Towns and villages plundered	2,493
Villages forcibly converted to Islam	456
Churches and monasteries desecrated	649
Churches turned into mosques	328
Victims left destitute	546,000

(Lepsius, 1897, pp. 330-31)

The massacres again aroused world opinion against the "terrible Turk" and led to one of the most audacious and celebrated acts of the Armenian revolutionaries. Although the Armenian Revolutionary Federation had generally refrained from the Hnchakist tactic of public agitation and demonstration, the Dashnaktsutiun now authorized a plot to shock the Europeans into action. The scheme involved the capture of the Ottoman Bank, which since the declaration of financial insolvency by the sultan's government in 1882 had been placed under the joint administration of the European creditor states. Located in the Galata quarter of Constantinople, the Ottoman Bank controlled the financial pulse of the empire. On August 26, 1896, twenty-six heavily armed Dashnakists, led by the youth Babgen Siuni, stormed the bank, took hostage the European personnel, and threatened to blow up the money vaults, hostages, and themselves if their terms were not met within forty-eight hours. In notes relayed to Turkish and European officials, the conspirators denounced the state-sponsored massacre of 100,000 Armenians and demanded the immediate implementation of a European-supervised reform measure for the six Western Armenian provinces of Van, Diarbekir, Bitlis, Erzerum, Sivas, and Kharput. The demands of the Dashnakist revolutionaries differed very little from previous reform plans, including civil rights; financial, economic, and judicial improvements; restoration of Armenian goods and properties; return of Armenians dislocated or forced to flee abroad; and amnesty for Armenian political prisoners. Still unwilling to turn away from the West, the Dashnakists insisted on a European high commissioner to oversee the reforms and a European-officered mixed Muslim-Christian gendarmerie.

On behalf of the powers and with the consent of the Sublime Porte, an official of the Russian embassy negotiated with the revolutionaries through the night of August 26. Tired, hungry, and discouraged by the death of Babgen Siuni in the initial assault, they agreed to end the siege and to be transferred with their personal weapons to an English yacht and from there to a French vessel and exile. In return, Armenian grievances would receive due consideration. Hence, without any guarantees except for another European vague assurance, the conspirators, having lost their charismatic leader and nine others killed or wounded, sailed away. Their mission had been successful only to the degree that it had alarmed the European powers. It brought no salutary step toward resolution of the Armenian question.

The most immediate outcome of the daring raid, memorialized in the popular revolutionary song "Bank Ottoman Gravads Eh Dashnaktsutian Komiten" (The Ottoman Bank Is Occupied by the Dashnakist Committee), was more bloodshed. As in the Hnchakist demonstrations at Kum Kapu, Bab Ali, and elsewhere, the Armenian stirrings in a repressive system led to increased victimization. Some observers accused the revolutionaries of intentionally provoking a Turkish overreaction. The contention was that the revolutionaries were willing to sacrifice a large number of Armenians in one stroke in order to save the rest by forcing the European powers to intervene. The difficulties associated with the Armenian question made such reasoning logical, but there is little hard evidence that the revolutionaries willingly set up their own people for slaughter. Nonetheless, massacre was the Turkish response to the Armenian seizure of the Ottoman Bank.

Even while Siuni's comrades still held the bank, police agents, some dressed as theological students, were organizing a mob, passing out clubs and iron bars. There were even reports that Abdul-Hamid's extensive espionage network had previously uncovered the plot but that the authorities allowed the bank to be taken in order to impress the Europeans with the murderous recklessness of Armenian terrorists and to rationalize the preceding pogroms. By nightfall on August 26, the armed mobs were attacking Armenian shops and any hapless Armenian in their way. A new orgy of clubbings, knifings, and mutilations was unleashed. Armenians indiscriminately were bludgeoned and hacked to death in the quarters of Pera, Galata, Pangaldi, Tophane, Beshiktash, and Kassim Pasha and in the villages of the Bosporus, including Bebek, Rumelihisar, Kandili, and Khaskoy. The massacre lasted for two days, claiming 6,000 lives and prompting thousands of panic-stricken Armenians to flee from the capital of the Ottoman Empire. The European protest notes deplored the abhorrent killings and pointed to evidence of the coordinated, organized nature of the massacre and the complicity of the authorities. As before, the response of the Sublime Porte was denial and subterfuge. And, as before, the massacres produced another half-hearted European reform scheme. The Europeans soon turned from the Armenian Question to other affairs (Nalbandian, 1963, pp. 176-78; Walker, 1980, pp. 164-68).

The European powers, for their own selfish reasons, needed the Ottoman Empire to survive, and this required reforms to eliminate the worst abuses. Yet mutual rivalries, jealousies, and suspicions, along with the unwillingness to use force, precluded the enactment of real changes. Meanwhile, Sultan Abdul-Hamid, desperate in his attempts to preserve the insufferable status quo, allowed his regime to degenerate into pogroms. While the period from 1894 to 1922 can be seen as a continuum of violent acts to eliminate the Armenian presence in the Ottoman Empire, the objectives of Abdul-Hamid in the 1890s were quite different from those of the Young Turks in 1915. The beleaguered sultan resorted to massacres in his futile efforts to maintain the old order, whereas the Young Turks perpetrated genocide to overturn the status quo and create a new order and a new frame of reference in which there was no place at all for Armenians.

New Directions

Disappointment and disillusion weighed heavily upon the Armenians after 1896. The bloody retribution of Abdul-Hamid split the Hnchakian Party. Many members believed that Europe had turned its back on the Armenians because of the party's socialist ideology. They blamed Avetis Nazarbekian and the organs abroad for their provocative calls for insurrection, and they insisted on radical changes in strategy and structure. Socialist rhetoric should be dropped and instead the party should concentrate entirely on the nationalistic objective of emancipating Western Armenia. Attempts to reunify the party were unsuccessful, as the nationalist dissidents organized the Reformed Hnchakian Party. The international socialist intellectuals continued to dominate the Hnchakian central organs and managed to retain the loyalty of many members in Cilicia, Sivas, Kaiseri, the Balkans, and elsewhere. The Reformed Hnchakists, on the other hand, gradually moved toward the right and eventually merged in 1921 with the Armenakans, Sahmandir Ramkavars, and other groups in the formation of the nonsocialist, liberal Ramkavar Azatakan (Democratic Liberal) Party. The internecine feuds weakened the Hnchakian movement and left the field open for the expansion of the Armenian Revolutionary Federation.

In the decade following the great pogroms, Armenian revolutionary activities were carried on by small guerrilla bands that roamed the Armenian mountains at Sasun, Mush, and Bitlis, continuing to strike officials, informers, and hostile tribal elements. The *fedayis* clustered around a charismatic leader, often known only by a first name and an honorific title, such as Hrair Dzhoghk, Serob Aghbiur, and Andranik Pasha. The daring feats of these bands won the sympathy and support of many inhabitants yet could not reverse the economic impoverishment of the peasantry and the continued exodus from the lands of historic Armenia.

In 1904, while Sasun was again in ferment and the Hamidiye Kurdish cavalry and Turkish regulars were engaged in punitive action, the third general congress of the Dashnaktsutiun, meeting in Sofia, shifted attention from the evils of the system to the personal culpability of the sultan. Subscribing to the view that individuals do affect the course of history and that therefore the removal of despots could lead to a freer society, the Dashnaktsutiun resolved to eliminate Sultan Abdul-Hamid II. Kristapor Mikayelian, a party founder and the chief conspirator, organized the plot in 1905. The scheme was ironically foiled by quirks of fate. Mikayelian was killed accidentally by the explosives intended for the sultan, and when his revolutionary companions subsequently proceeded with the plan, Abdul-Hamid survived unscathed. He had altered his normal Friday routine only slightly, yet the diversion was long enough to shield him from the massive explosion that demolished his waiting carriage and members of his retinue.

It was significant that men and women of different ethnic and religious origins had participated in the Yildiz palace assassination plot. The Dashnaktsutiun had now associated with other societies struggling against the common oppressor. Antipathy to Abdul-Hamid was not an Armenian monopoly. In Geneva, Paris, and other émigré centers, reformists and revolutionaries of all the Ottoman nationalities conceived programs of change. The Turkish groups, in discord on many details, shared the belief that the reigning sultan was the major source of affliction. Both Ahmed Riza and Murad Bey, leaders of rival elements of the so-called Young Turks, held that only efficient, just government could obviate the total disintegration of the Ottoman Empire. The Young Turks generally were modernists, but they were also patriots, rejecting regional autonomy as a solution to the empire's woes. The rightful demands of the Armenians, they insisted, could be satisfied not through self-rule or European intervention but by establishment of a properly functioning central government.

Opposition to Abdul-Hamid developed within the official structure of the empire itself, especially among the students and faculties of the technical institutes and the army officer class. These men, too, felt scandalized by the ruinous policies of the sultan and, like the Young Turks abroad, were motivated by nationalistic concepts. Toward the end of the nineteenth century, however, both internal and external foes of Abdul-Hamid were badly undermined by suppression within Turkey and effective espionage and propaganda abroad. Hamidian agents urged the Young Turks to return home, stressing that the desired reforms would never become reality as long as the attacks on the person and character of the monarch persisted. Cooperation, not defiance, was the avenue to change. Murad Bey and other Young Turks were swayed by the logic and returned to Constantinople, only to become bitterly disillusioned.

The faltering opposition movement received a strong boost in 1899, when Abdul-Hamid's brother-in-law and two nephews fled abroad. Prince Sabaheddin, one of the nephews, assumed a major role in the anti-Hamidian struggle. Before Sabaheddin's active involvement, the Armenian societies had been reluctant to collaborate with the Young Turk movement, particularly because of its negative stand regarding regional-national autonomy. But in February 1902 the Dashnaktsutiun and Hnchakian parties, heartened by the conciliatory statements of Sabaheddin and desperate in their battle against Abdul-Hamid, did participate in the first Congress of Ottoman Liberals. Meeting in Sabaheddin's residence in Paris, the forty-seven delegates representing Turkish, Arab, Greek, Kurdish, Armenian, Albanian, Circassian, and Jewish groups entered into an entente against the sultan. The resolutions of the congress demanded equal rights for all Ottoman citizens, local self-administration, measures to defend the territorial integrity of the empire, and restoration of the constitution that had been suspended since 1877. Yet even during this initial gathering, fundamental differences pulled the delegates into opposing factions. The adoption of an Armenian-sponsored resolution inviting the European powers to honor their obligations to the oppressed Ottoman peoples was roundly denounced by Ahmed Riza and other Turkish nationalists. Ahmed Riza berated Sabaheddin's support for the majority resolution and reasserted the contention that the Armenians needed neither European protectors nor a special status but could prosper, together with all other ethnic and religious elements, in the constitutional Turkey of the future. His view was crystallized in the exclamation "Autonomy is treason; it means separation!"

In the months after the Congress of Ottoman Liberals, Prince Sabaheddin organized the League of Administrative Decentralization and Private Initiative, cosmopolitan in principles and with the immediate objective of rousing individual citizens from apathy and instilling the will to resist tyranny. Having allowed the Ottoman homeland to slip into the grasp of despots, the "good people" were in fact responsible for the sad state of affairs. Administrative decentralization and the enhancement of interracial and interreligious harmony formed the bases of Sabaheddin's program. It was this idealistic goal of federation to which many Armenian leaders were attracted and in which they discerned the most promising solution to the Armenian question. But Sabaheddin's principles were not those that were to win out in Turkey.

Within the Ottoman Empire, meanwhile, army officers revived the anti-Hamidian current. Their secret circles, the most notable of which were in the corps headquartered at Salonika, combined with Ahmed Riza's faction abroad in 1907 to become a formal society, the Ittihad ve Terakki Teshkilati (Committee of Union and Progress). It was as the spokesman of this new group that Ahmed Riza attended the second Congress of Ottoman Liberals, held in Paris at the end of 1907. The meeting, which had been organized primarily on the initiative of the Dashnaktsutiun, pledged its constituent societies to a united campaign to overthrow Abdul-Hamid's regime by the swiftest means possible, not excluding revolution, and to ensure the introduction of representative government.

Quite apart from the deliberations in Paris, events in the empire were already moving toward confrontation. When Ittihadist officers in Macedonia found themselves about to be exposed, they led their regiments toward Constantinople as a defensive measure and, as the mutiny spread, demanded implementation of the Ottoman constitution. Lacking sufficient loyal troops to quell the insubordinate officers, Abdul-Hamid bowed to the ultimatum on July 24, 1908. The Armenians hailed the victory of the army and its Ittihadist commanders, and manifestations of Ottoman Christian and Muslim brotherhood abounded in the streets of the capital. A gust of optimism rustled into the remotest districts of the empire.

The Young Turk Regime

Unfortunately for the Armenians, the new parliamentary regime was beset forthwith by deep domestic and international crises, for these contributed to the ultimate assertion of Turkish chauvinism over Ottoman liberalism. Capitalizing upon the upheavals of 1908, Austria-Hungary annexed Bosnia and Herzegovina outright, Bulgaria asserted full independence, and the Cretans declared union with Greece. The initial impact of these troubles emboldened the Turkish traditionalist elements to stage a countercoup in April 1909. But the military again saved the situation, as the so-called Army of Deliverance marched swiftly into Constantinople and dispersed the forces of the reaction. Sultan Abdul-Hamid, who had become the rallying standard of the old vested interests, was deposed and exiled to Salonika. The turmoil did not abate, however, without renewed tragedy for the Armenians of Cilicia.

The historic region of Cilicia was divided in one of the later Ottoman administrative reorganizations into the province *(vilayet)* of Adana and the counties *(sanjaks)* of Marash, Aintab, and Alexandretta in the *vilayet* of Aleppo. The city of Adana lay at the center of a great alluvial plain that reached to the Gulf of Alexandretta on the Mediterranean Sea and to the feet of the Taurus and Amanus mountains, which protected such Armenian strongholds as Hadjin, Zeitun, and Musa Dagh. Armenians had lived in Cilicia since antiquity, and it was here that the last Armenian principality and kingdom had existed between the eleventh and fourteenth centuries. The region was mixed ethnographically and confessionally, with several distinct Christian and Muslim peoples. The Armenians played a major role in the crafts, commerce, and newly developing industry, availing themselves more than any other group of the educational opportunities provided by American and European schools at Adana, Tarsus, Aintab, Marash, and elsewhere.

After the Young Turk revolution, many Armenians were emboldened to believe that they could now enjoy freedom of speech and assembly. The audacious prelate of Adana, Bishop Mushegh, expounded in nationalistic rhetoric, proclaiming that the centuries of Armenian servitude had passed and that it was now the right and duty of his people to learn to defend themselves, their families, and their communities. For Muslims, however, the new era of constitutional government undermined their traditional relationship with Armenians and threatened their legal and customary superiority. At the same time that Abdul-Hamid's partisans in Constantinople initiated the countercoup to restore the authority of the sultan, conservatives of similar sentiments lashed out at the Armenians of Adana. A skirmish between Armenians and Turks on April 13 set off a riot that resulted in the pillaging of the bazaars and attacks upon the Armenian quarters. The violence also spread to nearby villages. When the authorities finally intervened two days later, more than 2,000 Armenians lay dead. An uneasy ten-day lull was broken on April 25 with an inferno. Army regulars who had just arrived in the city and who encountered Armenian resistance now joined the mobs. Fires set in the Armenian quarters spread rapidly in all directions. Armenian Protestants and Catholics, who had remained generally aloof from nationalistic movements, were not spared as the massacre and plunder fanned out over the width and breadth of Cilicia, extending all the way to Marash in the northeast and Kessab in the south. Hakob Papikian (Hagop Babigian), member of a parliamentary commission of investigation, reported that there had been 21,000 victims, of whom 19,479 were Armenian, 850 Syrian, 422 Chaldean, and 250 Greek (Papikian, 1909, p. 48). Thousands of widows and orphans now stood as a grim reminder of the first massacre of the Young Turk era. Several Turks and Armenians were hanged in Adana for provoking the violence, but the most responsible persons, including the governor and commandant, got off with no real punishment.

After the Young Turks regained control in Constantinople and sent Abdul-Hamid into exile, they ascribed the massacres to reactionaries and conducted a public memorial service for both Turkish and Armenian citizens who had sacrificed their lives "in defense of the revolution." They passed over in silence the fact that a number of Ittihadist supporters had participated in the carnage. Despite the Cilician massacres, the Dashnaktsutiun remained loyal to its entente with the Young Turks. The party's fifth general congress in 1909 pledged continued support of the government and rejected any move toward separation. In September the Ittihadists and Dashnakists entered into a protocol of agreement to implement the constitution fully and to extend its guarantees to the provinces in order to avoid a repetition of the tragedy at Adana, to unite against reactionary elements, and to counteract harmful rumors that the Armenians aspired to independence.

The agreement came at a time when the Ittihadist government had declared a state of siege and limited constitutional rights because of the attempted coup against it. The state of siege was not lifted in Constantinople for four years. During that period the minister of interior, Talaat Bey, enunciated his thesis that equality could be achieved only when the entire citizenry had become "Ottomanized." To Talaat, Ottomanization came to mean Turkification. By 1911, however, the undemocratic methods of the Ittihadist leaders had given rise to splinter groups. The Liberal Union (Ahrar firkasi), supported by Prince Sabaheddin, many non-Turkish groups, and most disgruntled Young Turk intellectuals, called for an end to the extraconstitutional regime and state of siege. The Ittihadists responded in the spring of 1912 by dissolving parliament and conducting a rigged, controlled election that gave them an overwhelming legislative majority. The maneuver did not pass unchallenged, as the military again moved in the name of the revolution. The so-called Savior Officers coerced the cabinet to resign and raised the prolonged state of siege. Moderate liberals, pledged to upholding the principles of the Young Turk revolution, dominated the cabinet for the rest of the year.

During the many crises from 1908 through 1912, the Dashnaktsutiun stayed loyal to the constitutional regime. The party ordered its guerrilla forces to cease all oppositional activities and to disarm, and it campaigned actively in the parliamentary elections. After the 1909 massacres, the Dashnaktsutiun was roundly criticized by the Hnchakists and others for continuing to collaborate with the Ittihadists. The Dashnaktsutiun, at its sixth general congress in 1911, also chastised the Ittihadist leadership for retreating from the principles of constitutionalism and interracial collaboration and resolved to join the opposition groups unless the Young Turks mended their ways. Nonetheless, when the combined armies of Greece, Bulgaria, Serbia, and Montenegro invaded the last remaining Ottoman possessions in Europe in 1912, the Dashnaktsutiun and Armenian leaders, such as Patriarch Hovhannes Arsharuni, exhorted the Armenian citizenry to patriotic endeavors and the Armenian units in the Ottoman army to valorous deeds. Andranik (Ozanian) and other *fedayis* broke with their party and organized volunteer detachments in the Bulgarian army.

The victory of the Balkan states, their occupation of Macedonia and much of Thrace, and their demand for extensive territorial concessions, including Adrianople, weakened the moderate Turkish cabinet and culminated in an Ittihadist restoration. In a coup directed by Enver Bey in January 1913, one cabinet minister was assassinated and the grand vizier was compelled to tender his resignation. The Ittihadist ultranationalists had gained ascendancy. From that juncture until the end of World War I, the policies of the Ottoman Empire were to be formulated by a clique headed by Minister of War Enver, Minister of Interior Talaat, and Military Governor of Constantinople, subsequently Minister of the Marine, Jemal.

The Final Reform Plan

Armenian political societies enjoyed a semilegal status between 1908 and 1915. They maintained party clubs and newspapers and vied for the parliamentary seats allotted to the Armenians. Yet these privileges in the post-Hamidian period did little to diminish the hardships of the rural population. Predatory bands in the eastern provinces could not be controlled by legislative decree. The threats to life and property became greater still when several thousand Armenian youth, subject under the constitutional regime to conscription, were sent off to the Balkan front. The European consuls filled their dispatches with descriptions of the widespread anarchy. In Constantinople the petitions of the patriarch were answered with promises of action, but improvements did not follow. Armenophiles the world over again urged European intervention. By 1912 those cries no longer fell on deaf ears. The tsar of Russia, after a calculated silence of fifteen years, now proclaimed his profound concern for the wretched Armenians of the Turkish empire.

Although the ruling classes of Imperial Russia regarded the Armenian political societies with no less anxiety and loathing than had Sultan Abdul-Hamid, both domestic and external considerations motivated Tsar Nicholas II to speak out. Most of his 2 million Armenian subjects had been alienated by the ill-advised attempts to russify the minorities of the empire and by specific Armenophobe measures of tsarist functionaries in Transcaucasia. The upheavals in the Caucasus between 1903 and 1907 had clearly demonstrated that the disaffection had permeated every level of Armenian society. But Tsar Nicholas, who had managed to stay on the throne during the empire-wide Russian revolution of 1905, could regain Armenian loyalties by centering attention on the Turkish Armenian cause, a cause dear to many Russian Armenians. The imperial counselors believed, moreover, that the aggravations in Western Armenia could easily lead to a rebellion, which might then sweep into Transcaucasia. Influenced by these factors, the Russian government eased Armenian press censorship and actually encouraged the Eastern Armenians to engross themselves in the Western Armenian problem and to organize committees to enlist the support of official European opinion.

Russia's interests in the Middle East also figured in the decision to resuscitate the Armenian question on the international level. In 1907 Russia and Great Britain had arrived at a limited agreement that divided Persia into zones of influence, with most northern districts included in the Russian sphere. For Russia to consolidate its Persian gains and perhaps even to extend its zones, peace in the Caucasus and in adjoining Western Armenia was essential. Furthermore, the increasing sway of Germany in Ottoman economic and military affairs alarmed the Russian strategists. The possibility that the very provinces facing the Caucasus might become Kaiser Wilhelm II's outposts was in itself sufficient cause for Russia to advocate a reform measure that could serve to block German expansionism into Western Armenia.

Uplifted to unprecedented optimism by the most recent expressions of international concern and taking into consideration the fact that the European powers had already placed controls on several departments of the Ottoman government, Armenian patriarchal circles in Constantinople prepared statistical data and memoranda for use by the proponents of reform. A commission of the Armenian National Assembly examined the patriarchal archives, tax ledgers, and parish reports to demonstrate that, despite decades of massacre and persecution, the Armenians still formed a plurality in their historic homelands.

European travelers and scholars in the mid-nineteenth century had given the number of Armenians in the Ottoman Empire as 2,500,000, and the Armenian Patriarchate in 1882 showed 2,660,000. According to the statistics of 1912, however, there were only 2,100,000, the 500,000 decrease presumably being the result of the massacres of 1894 to 1896 and 1909 as well as the continued Armenian exodus to the Caucasus, Europe, and the United States. The 2,100,000 Armenians in 1912 were distributed as follows:

The six provinces of Turkish Armenia	1,018,000
Peripheral areas of the six provinces	145,000
Cilicia	407,000
Western Anatolia and European Turkey	530,000
(Armenian Delegation, 1919, pp. 44-46)	

The peripheral areas that the Armenians excluded from the core region of Western Armenia were largely Muslim populated and had become a part of the six provinces through nineteenth-century provincial reforms. Armenian political leaders regarded the changes as gerrymandering for the purpose of decreasing the overall proportion of Armenians in the six provinces commonly referred to as Turkish Armenia. The patriarchal statistics showed that in the core region, Armenians formed 38.9 percent of the population, with Turks 25.4 percent, and Kurds 16.3 percent. In a provincial breakdown, the Armenians numbered as follows: Erzerum, 215,000; Van, 185,000; Bitlis, 180,000; Kharput, 168,000; Sivas, 165,000; Diarbekir, 105,000. The Christian element, which also included Nestorians and Greeks, formed a plurality of 45.2 percent. In advancing these figures, the Armenians themselves could be charged with manipulation, since they excluded part of the Kurdish-populated southern *sanjaks* and the Turkish-populated western *sanjaks* and established a Christian plurality only by placing heterodox Muslims such as the Kizilbash in the category of "other religions." In sharp contrast to the patriarchate's statistics, the Ottoman government claimed that there were only 1,295,000 Armenians (7 percent) of the total population in the empire and that in the six eastern provinces their number was 660,000 (17 percent) compared with 3 million Muslims (Turkey, 1919, p. 7).

After the Ittihadist coup of January 1913, members of the party's central committee, usually Talaat and Midhat Shukri, met several times with Dashnakist spokesmen Armen Garo (Garegin Pasdermadjian), Vartkes (Hovhannes Serenkiulian), and Aknuni (Khachatur Malumian) to urge the most influential Armenian society to steer the patriarchate as well as all national aspirations away from dependence on foreign governments. Talaat warned his close Armenian acquaintances, two of whom were deputies in the Ottoman parliament, that their people had fallen under the sinister spell of the Europeans, the true enemies of Turks and Armenians alike. But the rift between the Ittihad ve Terakki and the Dashnaktsutiun had become so deep by 1913 that the Armenian leaders were convinced that without external intercession, the collective future of the Western Armenians would remain bleak.

Acting under this premise, the Armenian National Assembly prepared what it regarded to be a workable reform program and presented the draft to André Mandelstam, the Armenophile chief dragoman of the Russian embassy. The main provisions of the plan were later incorporated into a Russian scheme, which was relayed in mid-1913 to the embassies of Great Britain, France, Germany, Austria-Hungary, and Italy. Russia's action drew sharp German protests, and soon the six major powers of Europe were again entangled. Though German ambassador Hans von Wangenheim, bolstered by his colleagues of the Triple Alliance, strongly objected to Russian intervention, he was compelled to accept the proposal that the six ambassadors at Constantinople discuss the question. The summer residence of the Austrian ambassador became the usual site for the meetings. There, in June and July, the six ambassadors and their appointed commission haggled over the Russian plan, which included:

1. Unification of the six Armenian *vilayets,* with the exclusion of certain peripheral districts, into a single province.
2. Selection of an Ottoman Christian or European governor for the province.
3. Creation of an administrative council and a provincial assembly consisting of both Muslim and Christian elements.
4. Formation of a mixed Muslim-Christian gendarmerie commanded by European officers in Turkish service.
5. Dissolution of the Hamidiye Kurdish cavalry units.
6. Publication of official decrees in Turkish, Kurdish, and Armenian, with the right to use those languages in legal proceedings.
7. Extension of the franchise only to sedentary elements.
8. Permission for each nationality to establish and administer private schools for which special taxes might be levied on members of that community.
9. Selection of a special commission to investigate the extent of Armenian losses caused by usurpation and to supervise restitution in the form of currency or land.
10. Exclusion from the province of Muslim refugee-immigrants *(muhajirs).*
11. Institution of similar improvements outside the province for areas inhabited by Armenians, particularly Cilicia.
12. Obligation of the European powers to ensure the enactment of the program. (Mandelstam, 1917, pp. 218-22; Hovannisian, 1967, pp. 30-33)

The Ottoman government, excluded from the preliminary negotiations, attempted to counter the Russian project by declaring general reform measures for the entire empire. The Turkish maneuver was rejected by the representatives of the Franco-Russo-British Entente, who were, however, unable to convince the ambassadors of the Triple Alliance to accede to the Russian proposals. Because of the stalemate, Russian ambassador M. N. de Giers for the Entente and von Wangenheim for the Triple Alliance agreed to continue talks, which lasted throughout the remainder of 1913. At last, after numerous impasses and the exchange of voluminous correspondence between the Constantinople embassies and their respective foreign ministries, a Russo-German compromise was attained, which, with several modifications, was accepted under duress by the Turkish government as the Reform Act of February 8, 1914.

The final accord, though sanctioned by all six European nations, was signed only by Ottoman Grand Vizier and Foreign Minister Said Halim and Russian chargé d'affaires K. N. Gulkevich, acting in the absence of Ambassador de Giers. Among the numerous modifications of the original Russian plan was the creation of two Armenian provinces, one incorporating the Trebizond, Sivas, and Erzerum *vilayets* and the other the Van, Bitlis, Kharput, and Diarbekir *vilayets*. A foreign inspector-general, the supreme civil authority, was to be selected for each province. The division of Western Armenia into two separate areas and the reduction of the Armenian proportional strength by the inclusion of all peripheral areas as well as the Trebizond *vilayet* were obvious concessions to the Ottoman government. Moreover, no mention was made of restitution for Armenian losses, the exclusion of *muhajirs,* the extension of the reform measure to Armenians living beyond the two inspectorates, or the obligation of the European powers to guarantee the execution of the program. While the terms "Armenian" and "Christian" were used repeatedly in the original Russian project, neither was employed in the compromise settlement. Instead, "ethnic elements" and "non-Muslims" were substituted as an additional concession to the Ittihadist rulers. The agreement did not formally pertain to "Turkish Armenia" but rather to "Eastern Anatolia." Although the act of February 1914 did not fulfill all Armenian expectations, it did represent the most viable reform proposed since the internationalization of the Armenian Question in 1878.

Once the compromise settlement had been adopted, the governments of the Triple Alliance and the Triple Entente initiated a new round of negotiations to determine of what nationality and personality the two inspectors-general should be. The men who ultimately gained the approval of all parties concerned were Major Nicolai Hoff, secretary-general in the ministry of war of Norway, and Louis Westenenk of the Netherlands, formerly assistant resident in the Dutch East Indies. By the summer of 1914 Hoff (promoted to lieutenant colonel) was in Van, the administrative center of one of the Armenian inspectorates, and Westenenk was in Constantinople preparing to depart for his post at Erzerum.

It was a moment of great optimism for the Armenians. Their long and extremely costly struggle for civil rights and regional autonomy verged on fruition. In due course, the Armenian question might be consigned to history. Ironically, however, it was the Ittihadist dictators of the Ottoman Empire who planned to consign the matter to history just a few months later by sweeping the Western Armenians, through deportation and massacre, from their homelands of three millennia. The most tragic and traumatic event in the long and turbulent history of the Armenian people was to unfold during the Great War.

FOR FURTHER INFORMATION

Ahmed, 1969.	Nalbandian, 1963.
Campbell, 1896.	Sarkissian, 1885.
Lepsius, 1897.	Ter-Minessian, 1973.
Lynch, 1901.	Walker, 1980.

8

WORLD WAR I AND THE
ARMENIAN GENOCIDE

Christopher J. Walker

From the late 1820s until the Hamidian massacres of the mid-1890s, and even in a lingering way thereafter, Ottoman Turkey was to some extent an ally of Great Britain. There was a serious quality to the friendship between the two empires, which survived Britain's nonparticipation in the Russo-Turkish war of 1877-1878 and the annexation of Egypt in 1882. Anglo-Turkish friendship often had a symbolic, almost sacred quality about it. The British public saw its own empire as a splendid, almost numinous civilizing force, an effortless and supreme "dominion over palm and pine," whose main characteristics were peace and the rule of law; and one of the great strategic guarantees of its continued prosperity was the unwritten alliance with Ottoman Turkey, a state that was perceived to block the advance of imperial Russia toward the Mediterranean and the Persian Gulf, an advance that would have had incalculable results for British possessions. Ottoman Turkey was therefore vital for the preservation of Britain's empire; or so the conventional wisdom went, until Lord Salisbury relocated the center of Britain's Near Eastern power from Constantinople to Cairo, in about 1897. A decade later, the Triple Entente of 1907 brought the historic enemies of Britain and Russia into alliance. The perception dimmed of Turkey as a sustaining force of the British Empire, though it persisted in part until 1914. A further feature that changed the perception was the threat posed to

Britain's global enterprise by the Ottoman Empire's growing alliance with (as it was seen in London) a sinister, ambitious power: the kaiser's Germany.

Germany had been making military and economic inroads into Ottoman Turkey since 1882. In that year General (later Field Marshal) von der Goltz had arrived in Constantinople with a number of German officers, in order to train and develop the Turkish army. Their mission bore fruit in the Ottoman victory over Greece in 1897. In the economic field, a loan negotiated by the Deutsche Bank financed the Anatolia Railway Company, and two sections of the projected Berlin-Baghdad railroad were completed. Politically, there was a strange compliment between the empires of Germany and Turkey. Germany had not sought to put pressure on Abdul-Hamid in regard to a sensitive matter: the reform of the administration of Turkish Armenia. Berlin was uninterested in the subject, and in 1883 Otto von Bismarck had indicated that he was unwilling to press the sultan on the introduction of reforms, as stipulated under article 61 of the Treaty of Berlin.

Moreover the temperament of Kaiser Wilhelm II was vain, unbalanced, and dictatorial, and he found himself drawn to Ottoman Turkey. The main aim of his eastern policy was to win the monopoly of the Berlin-Baghdad railroad, and at the same time he believed in a nebulous manner that he had some sort of mission to the east: part of destiny lay there. He visited Ottoman Turkey twice: once in 1889, the year after his accession, and again in 1898, shortly after the massacres of the Armenians organized by the sultan. This latter visit evoked distaste from the powers of Europe. Nevertheless in 1899 the concession for the Ismid-Konia section of the railroad was granted, so in practical terms the visit could be counted a success. In the first decade of the twentieth century, German trade with Ottoman Turkey expanded rapidly, while the rate of increase of that with Britain slowed down.

Despite the diplomatic cooling that occurred between London and Constantinople after 1896, when, in 1908, the Ottoman constitutional revolution took place, Britain was cheered from all sides, on the grounds that it had created the spirit of democracy and respect for the rule of law that Turkey now adhered to. Yet Britain at that time was absent, with no ambassador in the capital. Within a month too it had shown that it was less than enthusiastic about the constitution; the British foreign secretary, Sir Edward Grey, feared that a demand would follow for constitutions in Egypt and India, where Britain's power was based not on constitutional authority but force. Sir Edward wrote a chillingly cynical memorandum along those lines to the new British ambassador; and Britain's lack of interest in the constitution is noticeable, even in the early months after 1908. The way was left open for Germany to complete the task that it had begun in the 1880s. Enver Pasha, hero of the revolution, went to Germany, not Britain, to study strategy after 1908.

But the German military advisors were not successful in boosting the fortunes of their Ottoman ally. Turkey was badly beaten in the Balkan War of 1912. A new and larger German military mission arrived in Constantinople in 1913, headed by General Liman von Sanders, accompanied by 42 German officers. The Entente Powers protested, but to no effect. The lure of Germany for Turkey (and for Enver Pasha in particular) seemed to override all other considerations.

In the run-up to the outbreak of war, the Entente Powers for their part brushed aside approaches made to them by those leading Ottoman ministers who held some reservations about complete adherence to the pro-German policy favored by Enver. Thus, Interior Minister Talaat Pasha visited Tsar Nicholas II at his summer resort in May 1914, but the visit achieved nothing. (The Ottoman minister's sincerity in seeking a Russian alliance is at the same time somewhat questionable.) Similarly, Ottoman naval minister Jemal's visit to France in July ended in failure. Britain had so downgraded its relations with the Ottoman Empire that its inability to take any sort of diplomatic initiative came as no real surprise. Shortly before the outbreak of the war, it had come into conflict with Turkey over the Persian Gulf and the Aegean Islands. Diplomatic lethargy and failure in London, together with the Young Turks' conviction that an alliance with one power was a necessity and that neutrality was impossible, led to the success of Enver's pro-German plans.

Immediately after the Young Turk (or Ittihadist) revolution of July 1908, the attitude of the Turks toward the other nationalities of the empire had been one of welcoming them as equals. However, this attitude did not last. The position of the Turks was compromised by the constitution; their automatic imperial superiority was at once undermined. Moreover, they had no idea where their future lay. The options had emerged as Ottomanism, Islam, or Turkism. Ottomanism meant strengthening the institutions of the existing empire and making them available for all its citizens, irrespective of ethnic origin. It gained a brief vogue, but never had much chance when compared with the other more exciting ideologies. Islam meant deepening relations between all Muslim peoples and nations within the empire and throughout the world, and perhaps creating a political unit out of the faith. There was a problem here too. It raised the possibility of a confrontation with the Christian powers, unknown since the Crusades. Moreover, the empire to the east of the Ottoman Empire, that of Iran, although Muslim was Shi'i, would never accept the authority of the Sunni Ottomans. And anyway many of the Young Turks, and certainly those who organized the revolution of 1908, were atheists and positivists. Islam to them was little more than a vehicle through which they might mobilize the masses.

There remained Turkism: Turkish nationalism based on the Turkish race. This was an idea that developed and gained popularity among Turkish thinkers from the 1890s. It grew from ideas expounded by Europeans who were friendly to the Turks and who perhaps also sought to weaken imperial Russia. The idea that the Turks were not just the ruling elite in a declining empire, but had a vast kinship, based on race and the Turkic languages, stretching from the Balkans to Siberia, was attractive, something to revive them after the hangover of democracy. Turkism soon became the central ideology of the Young Turks. It gave them a clear new vision of their position, following the ending of the old hierarchies that had occurred with the 1908 revolution. Within a few years it had been accepted by most leaders of the Committee of Union and Progress as a central ideology.

The Armenians failed to grasp the nature of Turkism. They continued to see themselves principally as Christians. If the Young Turks had adopted Islam as the guiding ideology, they would have understood the nature of the situation. Religion was an integral part of being an Ottoman Armenian, so a nonreligious ideology was hard to comprehend. They found it almost impossible to see what it meant to be up against a nonreligious, race-based ideology.

The chief Turkish ideologist was Ziya Gökalp, who was born in Diarbekir, a Kurdish city, in 1875; the Kurdish locality may have encouraged him to stress Turkishness more forcefully as an identity. The subtext to his ideas makes it clear just what a threat Turkism was to Armenians. (His published prose writings, despite their cloudy metaphysics and unsubstantiated assertions, are moderate to the point of banality. His true beliefs were revealed in his verse and conversation.) He held that the country of the Turks was not Turkey, or even Turkestan; it was a broad and everlasting country, Turan. One of his slogans was *Bütün Türkler bir ordu*—"All the Turks are one army." This was a fearful threat to any nation in the way of such a grand union of Turkic peoples, but it was a threat that found little resonance with the Armenians, even though their homeland was most at risk from the "one army." They continued to believe that their woes came from Islam, from the Muslim nature of the Ottoman Empire, and from local tyrannical Muslims.

It should be pointed out that Islam has in fact a definite (though often obscured) place for Christian peoples ("people of the book"), which race-based Turkism does not. Perhaps reflecting this matter, in the course of the events of 1915, the occasional expressions of horror by individual non-Armenians at the fate of Armenians were apt to come from Muslim leaders. Religion has a place for a conscience, which racist ideologies do not.

In April 1909, at the time of the counterrevolution, there had been a serious attack on Armenians at Adana. Some Armenians consider this to be the first assault on the Armenians, constituting a prelude to the events of 1915. But the evidence is inconclusive, especially since the events took place during the counterrevolution when the committee was without power, and the local Armenians were behaving in a somewhat provocative manner, without regard to Turkish sentiments. After April 1909 Armenian activists took pains to repair the inter-communal damage. However, antiminority sentiments were evident at the Young Turks' secret conclave of 1910, held in Salonika, where there was talk of crushing the non-Muslim communities "by force of arms." (The terminology of Muslim and non-Muslim was used, not because the Young Turks were believers, but because it was the only legal and communal language that existed in the polity of the Ottoman Empire.) In 1911 the minorities were described as a *"quantité négligeable"* at a similar forum. Throughout 1912 and 1913 conditions for Armenians in the countryside in Turkish Armenia reverted to the instability, discrimination, and even violence of the days of Sultan Abdul-Hamid. At the official level, no steps were taken to solve the all-important problem of the land taken from Armenians at the time of the 1894 to 1896 massacres. Reports from Constantinople and the provinces in 1913 and early 1914 indicated that the attitude toward Armenians and other Christian peoples was threatening.

Nevertheless, at this time, in the years before the outbreak of World War I, the Armenians were prepared to give considerable support to the empire. Significantly, but overlooked by both Turkish and Armenian historiographers, they fought bravely in the Ottoman armies during the 1912 Balkan War. Eight thousand Armenian troops enlisted in Ottoman ranks. (This was the first time that members of Muslim and Christian nationalities had fought side by side for the defense of the sultan's realm.) The British ambassador wrote that "the several thousands of Armenian troops have fought better than any of the other non-Turkish elements, and numbers of them have been killed and wounded, while many have shown exceptional bravery" (Great Britain, Public Record Office, F0424/235, p. 349, November 23, 1912). In other words, Armenians loyally believed in Ottomanism at this time.

But disillusion set in. Within a year the Dashnakists, who always tried hardest for a modus vivendi with the Young Turks, realized that the efforts were bound to fail, and they turned to supporting the attempts of the European powers to bring reform to the Ottoman Empire. The leader of a more conservative Armenian faction, Boghos Nubar, son of a distinguished Egyptian statesman of Armenian descent and founder of the Armenian General Benevolent Union, called for reforms as stipulated by the Treaty of Berlin (1878). Leaders of neither of these two major Armenian factions sought the breakup of the empire or Armenian independence.

Similarly when the Dashnaktsutiun held its Eighth General Congress in Erzerum in July 1914, on the very outbreak of war, the pattern, was thus of the party disengaging itself from activist Ittihadist (Young Turk) schemes for overrunning the Caucasus, while affirming loyalty to the empire.

Just before the outbreak of war in Europe, on August 2, 1914, Turkey signed a secret pact with Germany, undertaking to go to war if Russia attacked Austria or Germany. At the time of signing, the Young Turks put six proposals to the German ambassador, on general strategic matters, the Capitulations, the Aegean Islands, and so forth. For the Armenians the fifth proposal was of special significance. It was that "Germany would assume the responsibility of rectifying the eastern frontiers of the Ottoman Empire in a manner suitable for the establishment of a link with the Muslim peoples of Russia" (Kurat, 1967, p. 300). Such a link could hardly be established without the neutralization or destruction of a large part, and perhaps all, of the Armenian presence there. This is an important motive for the anti-Armenian measures that followed. The theme was repeated in the proclamation of war aims issued by the Ottoman government after the empire's entry into the war on October 30, 1914. Its tone was almost of gratitude for the opportunity of the war, and it spoke of seeking a natural frontier, including and uniting "all branches of our race." In this context the Young Turks clearly saw the empire as a Turkish rather than an Ottoman entity (Toynbee, 1917, pp. 28-29).

By contrast, most Armenians showed an old-fashioned loyalty to Ottomanism. Many enlisted in the Ottoman army; services were held in churches for an Ottoman victory. However, the pattern was not one of universal loyalty. The Hnchak Party, at this time still quite influential, pledged defiance of the empire at their party conference in Constanta Romania. And before Turkey entered the war, Ottoman deputy and leading Dashnak Garegin Pasdermadjian (Armen Garo) fled to Tiflis to assist in the formation of Armenian volunteer partisan units for operation against Turkey. (On the other side, the Turkish government organized Georgian partisan units and recruited numbers of Caucasian Muslims for sabotage operations in Russian Transcaucasia.) This was an act of disloyalty, but seen in the context of the time, when most parties to the conflict were acting for sectional interests, it was not quite as treacherous as it has sometimes been painted. In Zeitun, in Cilicia, some Armenians who were probably Hnchaks made contact with the Russian headquarters in the Caucasus, offering military help; nothing came of their very risky offer.

Soon after the Ottoman declaration of war, the empire was in action on several fronts. In the east, Enver Pasha attempted to destroy the Russian army in Transcaucasia and after initial success met with disaster at Sarikamish (January 1915). In the same month Halil (Khalil) Pasha seized, but was rapidly ejected from, Tabriz in Persian Azerbaijan; and Jevdet Bey, brother-in-law of Enver, was similarly unsuccessful in Khoi in February. In the west, British warships threatened the Dardanelles and mounted an unsuccessful assault on March 18. At this time, at least until the middle of February, there was no outward display of hostility toward Ottoman Armenians. Indeed, in February Enver had publicly thanked the Armenians for their conduct during the Sarikamish campaign. His letter, addressed to the Armenian bishop of Konia, testified to their loyalty (Lepsius, 1919).

But in the last ten days of February 1915, violent and extreme measures were initiated against Ottoman Armenians. Those who had enlisted in the Ottoman armies were disarmed and brutally compelled to perform manual labor, often until they dropped from exhaustion. Those who had not enlisted were ruthlessly searched for arms. (Armenians had been permitted legally to hold arms since the revolution of 1908, either for self-protection against the Kurds or to protect the revolution from reactionaries.) They were directed to give them up, and in order to make the point, the authorities jailed, in a number of towns, as many as 400 to 500 men until the arms were delivered. The authorities also threatened mass reprisals if they did not get the numbers of weapons they demanded. These figures were in most cases quite unreasonable, so Armenians were driven to purchasing weapons from their Turkish neighbors. When the arms were gathered, the authorities would, on some occasions, photograph them and send the pictures to Constantinople as "evidence of treachery," adding a touch of farce to somber proceedings. All this was accompanied by cruel tortures during the interrogations; of this, the chief of police in the capital made no secret. The arms searches became a pretext for a general persecution of Armenians.

The situation of those Armenians, estimated at 100,000, who were serving in the Ottoman armies was described thus by Sister Alma Johannson, a Swedish nurse working with the Deutscher Hilfsbund (German League of Assistance) in Mush:

> When the war began, all Armenians liable for military service were conscripted as soldiers. Only those who had enough money to buy their way out, who had Turkish friends, or who bribed the Turks, escaped. The men left behind were used to carry supplies to the Turkish army at the Russian border. There were no pack animals left, so they had to carry the loads on their backs. (There are, of course, no railways anywhere in this region.) The winters are always very long and harsh in this region of Mush and Erzerum, and it often took the men two or three weeks to reach their destinations. They were provided with neither the money nor the clothing necessary for such a trek. If they had any money, it was soon taken from them by the military gendarmes. Those who were too exhausted to continue were beaten until they tried to struggle on or until they fell down dead. The survivors took their dead companions' clothes to protect themselves a little better against the cold. . . . At that time vagrants who could not find any other employment were being recruited as gendarmes and then had the right to do whatever they wanted. The outcome is one long sequence of cruelty and inhumanity. (Sommer, 1919, p. 6)

With the Armenians disarmed and with many of their fit men dead or dying, the way was open for the next, more terrible stage in the process. From the documented observations, it is clear that a massive and systematic operation against Armenians throughout almost all of the empire was undertaken. The operation was noteworthy for (within designated areas) its simultaneity and for its thoroughness, its pattern, and the scale of its organization. The evidence for it comes in numerous eyewitness accounts from consuls, German and Austrian military personnel, doctors, nurses, and teachers belonging to neutral or pro-German nations, and of course from survivors of the measures themselves. There are also some significant eyewitness accounts from Muslim officers in the Ottoman army, one of whom was present at the measures; these are held in the Public Record Office, London. No trustworthy documents have yet emerged from Turkish archives saying exactly how the operation was organized and carried out. This does not mean that there are no such documents or that the events themselves did not take place; it merely means that either the documents were destroyed at the end of the war (and there is evidence of their destruction), that the censorship up to the present day has been effective, or that the search has not been thorough enough. In assessing the evidence for responsibility for what happened in 1915, the so-called Talaat telegrams are excluded. Controversy still surrounds these documents, which appear to be orders from the Ottoman minister of the interior for the mass killing of Armenians. The documents themselves have disappeared. Publication of them in 1920 was unscholarly, but the analysis of them provided by Professor V. N. Dadrian in the *International Journal of Middle East Studies* (1986) has gone a long way to demonstrating their soundness as well as providing a large amount of circumstantial evidence. However, doubt must remain until and unless the documents or similar ones themselves resurface and are published in a critical edition. In the meantime, the eyewitness evidence of competent observers nevertheless provides the broad outlines of the nature of the events and the official (or otherwise) instigation of them. One other work often cited by Armenians, Mevlanzade Rifaat's *Türk inkilabinin iç yüzü* (The Inner Aspects of the Turkish Revolution), published in Aleppo in 1929, appears to be a fraud and cannot be accepted as sound evidence, at least until a comprehensive bibliographical inquiry is published on the origin of the book and the authenticity or otherwise of its content.

The measures themselves constituted the deportation into the desert or uninhabited wasteland of Armenians from the empire, and hence their extermination. Between April and August 1915 Armenians from almost all major centers of the empire were ordered to leave their homes, then were either killed near their towns or villages or else deported into remote regions, where, denied food and water, they rapidly died. These measures were undertaken against Armenians located both near the international frontier and far from the battle zone; for instance,

Armenians were deported from Kharput in June-July 1915 and from both Angora (Ankara) and Bandirma in August. Therefore claims that the measures were just "wartime relocations" cannot be sustained, especially in the view of the fact that most of the "relocated" people were women and children.

It is indeed virtually impossible to deny—except by those people who have fixed attitudes motivated by present-day political considerations—that the widespread process of assaults on the Armenian community was a policy of extermination: the jailing, beating, and immediate killing of some, and the deportation of the rest to regions where life was insupportable. The similarity of the course of events in the different localities of the empire is too great to be by chance. Much serious work remains to be done by historians on Ottoman policy toward Armenians in 1915-1916, but despite the gaps that exist in our knowledge, enough can be pieced together from what we know to get a picture of what happened and to work out who was responsible for it.

The pattern of the Turks' anti-Armenian measures was observable in very many cases and was too unvarying for chance. It was as follows: All the fit Armenian men from a town or village would be summoned to the government building. They were told that they were going to be moved to another locality and were assured that the government was benevolent. Once the authorities had got hold of them, they were jailed for several days, for no apparent reason. When they were allowed out, they were marched out of town. At the first halting place, they would be shot or bayoneted to death. Shortly afterward the women, children, and old men would be summoned in the same way. They were not jailed, but told that they would have to leave in a few days, for new homes. In actuality, they were made to suffer a terrible fate, much worse than that of the able-bodied men. In the burning summer heat, they were driven on and on, by gendarmes who completely dehumanized them, along designated routes, until they collapsed and died by the wayside. No mercy was shown for pregnant women or nursing mothers. If they would not go on, they were killed. On occasion they were driven the long way round between different localities or backward and forward between different places, until all their strength was gone. Many were told that they were being sent to Mosul; en route they were driven first southwestward in the general direction of Aleppo, which became a main staging post for the deportees; from there they were sent east to locations along the Euphrates River, such as Meskene and Deir ez-Zor, which became vast and pitiless extermination camps, and where death came as a blessing. Only a few ever reached Mosul.

As the Armenians were driven out to die in the wastelands, Muslim refugees (known as *muhajirs*) were resettled in their place. These men and women, numbering some 750,000, were originally from Thrace or Bulgaria, and had left or been driven out during the Balkan War of 1912. From the time of the expulsion of Armenians from Zeitun in April 1915, there are many instances, recorded by eyewitnesses, of *muhajirs* moving in to take over Armenian lands and houses. Although this topic has not yet received systematic analysis, it clearly points to official complicity at a very high level, since *mujahirs* from Thrace could not reach Cilicia or Turkish Armenia without organization and planning.

The first Ottoman town from which Armenians were systematically deported in 1915 was Zeitun, and the deportations began on April 8, almost two weeks before the events in Van that Turkish apologists often cite as justifying the measures. However, the Armenians of Zeitun had by no means been quiet, loyal citizens. They had a tradition of confrontation with the authorities dating back to their revolt in 1862, and their attitudes were shaped by the centuries of semi-independence that preceded that revolt. It has been asserted that in 1915 there had been, since February, secret communication with the Caucasian headquarters of the Russian army. If this was the case, nothing came of it. The Zeitun Armenians, moreover, had failed to enlist at all in the army; this, although legal (on payment of an "exemption" tax), was unwise, and the Turkish general, Fakhri Pasha, who had been in Zeitun with 3,000 soldiers since late March 1915, ordered enrollment of Zeituntsis. Despite the advice of the older generation, the young men refused and fled to the hills, occupying a strategically placed monastery. A battle ensued in which 300 Turkish soldiers were killed before the Turks captured the monastery and burned it.

Thereupon, on April 8, the process began whereby the Armenians of Zeitun were driven out to die of thirst and exposure in the rough byways of Anatolia, Syria, and Mesopotamia. Initially they were sent westward to Sultania; then back to Aleppo, and on to Deir ez-Zor, which became, with the arrival of more and more Armenians, an immense and frightful concentration camp. Into their houses in Zeitun the authorities settled some *muhajirs,* who had been in the vicinity ever since General Fakhri had arrived in March.

After the expulsions from Zeitun, other Cilician towns suffered a similar fate. None of the Armenians knew what was actually happening

to them; many believed the government's affirmations of good faith—
that they were being sent to new homes and would be cared for on their
journey; whereas in fact they were driven continuously until they
dropped.

Two points should be noted about the Zeitun and Cilician deportations of April. (Other deportations from this region followed—for
instance, Hadjin's Armenians were deported over the period June-
September.) In the first place, the blows against Zeitun occurred before
a government edict or law had been passed, giving the actions any sort
of real authority. Second, they occurred before the events in Van, which
the Ottoman government cited as providing the justification for its
anti-Armenian measures.

The condition of Van in April-May 1915 has been described by
Turkish apologists as that of an Armenian uprising, but an examination
of the events reveals that the Armenians did no more than protect
themselves against the brutality of the government. In no manner, as has
been claimed, were their actions coordinated with the movements of the
Russian army.

Since February 1915 the governor *(vali)* of Van had been Jevdet
Bey, brother-in-law of Enver Pasha. He had led the unsuccessful campaign to capture Khoi in Persia, and on failing to take it, he had ordered
the killing of 800 villagers in the Salmast district. Cruelty and a penchant
for violence were indeed two of his distinguishing characteristics.
During the period of the arms searches, he conducted a reign of terror
in the many Armenian villages around Van. (Van was the only Ottoman
province where Armenians were in a majority over the Turkish and
Kurdish populations.)

The attitude of the Armenian community leaders to Jevdet was one
of great caution. They were determined not to give him a pretext for
violence. When he demanded 4,000 Armenian men for the army, they
offered him 400 and the rest in legally permitted exemption tax, an offer
Jevdet deemed unacceptable. Then there was an incident in Shadakh,
south of Van—a demonstration in favor of an imprisoned Armenian—and
Jevdet asked a commission made up of four Turks and four Armenians to
go there and sort things out. En route, on April 16, the Armenian members
of the commission were murdered, almost certainly by government
agents. At the same time government terror was continuing in the countryside. In one incident the Armenians resisted some gendarmes. This
angered the governor. From this point, the testimony of Dr. Clarence
Ussher (1917) is essential in tracing what happened in Van and in

assessing whether the situation was an uprising or self-defense. Ussher, an American missionary, was technically neutral, but undoubtedly favored the Armenians. Nevertheless, the factual data in his account have never been called into question; he was too high-minded a man to lie on such matters. The Armenian leaders turned to him, asking him to try to mediate for them, but he considered that mediation would be pointless.

Violence in the countryside around Van reached a peak on April 19; almost the entire male population (numbering about 2,500) of Akantz, northeast of Van, were killed on that day. Three, feigning death, escaped to tell the tale. Throughout the entire province 55,000 Armenian men, women, and children were killed. Muslims were forbidden, on pain of death, to shelter Armenians.

A small local incident was sufficient to spark off, on April 20, the battle that many sensed had been inevitable. In the city of Van itself, the Armenians, expecting the attack, had been strengthening their quarters for some weeks. Now both the old city, where the houses clustered beneath the rock of Van, and the Aikestan garden suburb were protected. The initial assault was resisted, and the Armenians organized an efficient administration to run the besieged city. They had 1,300 men under somewhat makeshift arms—defending a population of 30,000. With tenacity, shrewdness, and above all bravery, they were able to fend the Turks off for four weeks. The Turks were forced to withdraw on May 16, as the Russian army approached, and a few days later the Russian general Nikolaev confirmed the Armenian administration in power. For six weeks this body ruled Van, until the Russians were in turn forced to retreat, taking with them as many Van Armenians as could get away.

Even at present the claim is made that the events in Van were a revolutionary uprising. However, a study of the chronology of what happened, from Jevdet's reign of terror in the countryside (following naturally from his vindictive behavior in Salmast) to the murder of the four Armenian leaders, shows that each time the government took the initiative for violence and confrontation. None of Jevdet's actions was that of a man defending the established government against a revolutionary attempt to seize power. Only when the government's provocation became too intense did the Armenians take up weapons. They wished at least to spare the city's 30,000 inhabitants from the fate of the 55,000 in the countryside.

Nevertheless, the Ottoman government took the Armenian defense of Van as a pretext for extreme measures. Turkey had been under great pressure from the Allied naval attack on the Dardanelles, but this had been called off on March 18. The Allied landings did not commence until April 25. In the interval the Turks moved against the Armenians. Initially on April 23-24, they arrested 235 community leaders in the capital, writers and educators, holding them at the central police station for three days, before exiling them to the villages of Ayash and Chankiri in central Anatolia.

A second wave of arrests brought the figure to 600, and later 5,000 working class Armenians were taken too. Most were murdered in the vicinity. The really important Armenian public figures were sent on toward Diarbekir; these included parliamentary deputies Vartkes (Hovhannes Serenkiulian) and Krikor Zohrab, arrested on May 21 and later shot just outside Urfa.

These exilings and killings do not feature in Turkish accounts of the period. Stanford and Ezel Kural Shaw in their 1977 history of the Ottoman Empire ignore them completely. Nevertheless, they were obviously central to the government's plans for Armenians; and the natural conclusion to draw from the brutal destruction of the empire's Armenian leadership is that it was the beginning of a wider campaign against Armenians.

The Constantinople arrests were justified by Interior Minister Talaat Pasha to U.S. Ambassador Henry Morgenthau as "self-defense." But it would seem that the definition of self-defense had to be fairly elastic to take in such a deadly response to the mere existence of Armenian community leaders.

Despite the deportations from Zeitun, the slaughter of villagers in Van province before April 20, and the Constantinople deportations and murders, no law had been enacted against Armenians. The minister of the interior and the Ittihadist (Young Turk) group around him had sidestepped constitutional procedures, however shadowy, and were acting simply as a party dictatorship. In order to regulate the situation, a "Temporary Law of Deportation" was approved by the Council of Ministers on May 30, 1915, although it was published officially in the press three days earlier, on the twenty-seventh. This law authorized army commanders and lesser military personnel to suppress armed resistance or attacks from the population (article 1) and to deport the populations of towns and villages "whom they suspect of being guilty of treason or espionage" (article 2). Since the deportations and massacres had already begun, the law would appear to have been passed to provide a facade of legality to the proceedings. As it was in the process of being adopted by the Ottoman Council of Ministers, provisions were added to the law that appeared to mitigate its harshness: these concerned the safeguarding of the deportees; compensation to them for their houses, goods, and lands; and the obligation of officials to abide by the law. Since none of these extra provisions was put into practice, all seem simply to have been a cloak with which to cover the great and terrible violence that the Armenians actually, observably endured.

In the provinces, Erzerum was perhaps the most sensitive town, apart from Van, as far as the Armenians were concerned. It was a significant Armenian intellectual and political center—it was here that the Dashnakist congress had been held the previous year; and it was also the headquarters of the Ottoman Third Army, commanded in 1915 by Mahmud Kiamil Pasha.

Erzerum was also the headquarters of the "Special Organization" (Teshkilat-i Makhsusiye), which played a central and pivotal role in the extermination of the Armenians. The significance of this organization was recognized by historian Arnold Toynbee even during his Turkophile phase, when (in his 1922 book, *The Western Question in Greece and Turkey*) he wrote of

> Turkish "political" chettes [irregulars] . . . reinforced by convicts released for the purpose from the public prisons, [who] carried out the designs of the Union and Progress government against the Armenians in every province of Anatolia except the vilayet [province] of Aidin. The Armenian civil population was "deported" from the villages and towns and marched off for "internment" under the escort of uniformed gendarmes: but at the first point on their road out of range of western observers, the chettes appeared and executed the massacre. (Toynbee, 1922, p. 280)

The status and nature of the Special Organization are complex matters: the organization was secret, and research on it has been patchy. At inception (probably in late 1914) there appear to have been two Special Organizations, one directed by the Ministry of War and the other by the ruling party, the Committee of Union and Progress. The first was responsible for encouraging Caucasian and Iranian Muslims to stage revolts in favor of the Ottoman Empire. However the functions of the two overlapped in the matter of exterminating Armenians: following the failure of Ottoman Turkey's operations against Russian Transcaucasia (January 1915), the military Special Organization personnel were redeployed internally against Armenians. One of the principal leaders of the organization, Eshref Kushjubashi, confirmed that the Special Organization was principally concerned with internal security, and noted that it had "its own cadres, uniforms, treasury and uniforms . . . carrying out the state's internal and external policies [involving] important and dangerous missions." (Dadrian, 1993, p.9) It specifically targeted the empire's non-Muslim populations.

The total strength of the Special Organization has been estimated at 30,000-34,000. Its membership (as Toynbee indicated) was largely made up of criminals released from jail, who were given a week's training. They were known as *chettes* (modern Turkish: *çeteler*]. German undercover agent Colonel Stange described them as "scum . . . [who] in the area of Terdjan killed without exception all the Armenians of the convoy coming from Erzerum. This happened with the assistance of the military escort. This is an incontestable fact." The German consul in Aleppo, Walter Rössler, noted on July 27, 1915, that the Ottoman government had "released convicts from prison, put them in soldiers' uniforms and sent them to areas which the deportees are to pass." In 1918, following an inspection tour arranged by the Ittihad government, journalist Paul Weitz of the *Frankfurter Zeitung* wrote of "the extermination *[Ausrottung]* of Armenians perpetrated by bands organized in Constantinople." The Special Organization, when acting against Armenians, was secretly directed from the center of the political bureau of the Committee of Union and Progress, and apparently masterminded by Talaat himself.

Operationally, the Special Organization was first active against Armenian civilians in Ardahan and Artvin, regions captured from the Russians in November-December 1914. Here local Armenians were dealt with in brutal fashion. Armenians in other areas lost to the Russians in late 1914 suffered massacre when the Turks gained control, especially around Ardanuch, Olti, Alashkert, and Diadin. (Almost all the Armenian villages around Alashkert were destroyed following the December 12, 1914, retreat of the Russians.) Thus violent anti-Armenian activities were observable five to six months before the April-May 1915 confrontation in Van, which is often cited as the prelude to the genocide of Armenians.

In operational charge of the Special Organization, directing the massacres of Armenians in the east, was a Paris-educated doctor, Behaeddin Shakir (1877-1922). He has been described as one of the important members of the CUP, and his opinion carried weight in the Ottoman War Office. He was in Erzerum for some months in 1914, when plans were coalescing for the Armenian genocide, and he returned there in the spring of 1915, when the measures were put into practice. Further evidence of his part in the genocide was given in a series of articles (signed "A. Bil," a pseudonym) which were published in the Turkish newspaper *Vakit* from November 1933 to February 1934. Behaeddin's brutal direction of the mass killing of Armenians in the eastern provinces was the subject of a serious indictment by Vehib Pasha, who was appointed commander of the Ottoman Eastern Front in February 1916. Vehib called him the mastermind of the atrocities, and described in some detail the criminality and savagery of the Special Organization *chettes* which were under his control.

Other important figures in this shadowy but brutal organization were the Geneva-educated Dr. Nazim, described by London *Times* correspondent Philip Graves as a "bleak fanatic" (Graves, 1941, p.163); Cherkez Ahmed, the killer of Vartkes and Zohrab, who also organized with exceptional cruelty the massacres in Trebizond province; Ismail Janbolat, Talaat Pasha's right-hand man; Dr. Reshid, governor of Diarbekir province; and General Mahmud Kiamil Pasha, commander of the Ottoman Third Army until relieved by Vehib Pasha. All these men (who included intellectuals and soldiers, as well as merely hardened criminals) were heavily implicated in the organization and execution of atrocities.

The governor of Erzerum was Hasan Tahsin, an equivocal figure. Formerly governor of Van, until Jevdet's appointment there, he had been in Erzerum since February 1915. Superficially, he showed a measure of concern for Armenians; but nothing that he did in reality benefited any Armenian, and it is possible that he acted unaggressively merely not to upset German liaison officer General Posselt.

On April 18, at a mass meeting just outside the city, held by the Turks, Armenians were denounced as traitors and enemies of the empire. Muslims were ordered not to shield Armenian friends; if they did so, they would suffer the fate of Armenians. However, General Posselt noted on April 26 that "the Armenians will stay calm if they are not pressured or molested by the Turks," and added: "The behavior of the Armenians has been perfect" (Lepsius, 1919, p. 51).

In the following weeks Armenians from the towns and villages of Erzerum province were attacked. In mid-May there was a slaughter of the Armenians of Khnus (Hinis) and its thirty-eight surrounding Armenian villages; 19,000 Armenians killed on the spot, without being deported. From other villages in the province the Armenians were driven to the city of Erzerum. Most died from dehydration, hunger, exhaustion, and the elements. These factors became the authorities' allies in dispatching the Armenians. Those who survived were driven westward, past Erzinjan, to the Kemakh gorge, where they were thrown over a steep escarpment into the fast-flowing river below. Kemakh was the head-quarters of the *chettes,* who were organized to despoil, torture, and murder Armenians.

On the matter of the Armenian villagers from the plains, German consul von Scheubner-Richter wrote thus to his ambassador in Constantinople on June 2:

> The discussion which I have had with the commander in chief on the subject of the expulsion of the Armenians has yielded nothing positive. The Armenian inhabitants of all the plains—doubtless too those of the plain of Erzerum—will be deported to Deir ez-Zor. Such a transfer of population is tantamount to a massacre, since, in the absence of any means of transport, hardly half of them will arrive alive at their destination, and it is possible that this operation will cause the ruin not only of the Armenians, but of the whole country. One cannot justify these measures by military considerations, since it is not a question of a revolt among the Armenians of the region, and the people who are being deported are old men, women, and children. The Armenians who have converted to Islam have not been expelled. Travelling in the abandoned Armenian villages, I have found them pillaged, like the monastery of Kizilvank, whose church has been ransacked. (Lepsius, 1919, p. 80)

Throughout June and July men, women, and children were deported from the city of Erzerum. Most appear to have been driven to the Kemakh gorge to be dispatched; but many were sent vast distances—to Aleppo, Raqqa, or Mosul—where a few managed to survive. Left in Erzerum were only 80 to 100 Armenians, most of whom were needed for essential military services. In this way 65,000 Armenians from the city of Erzerum and its surrounding villages were driven to death or parched exile.

At this time Erzinjan and Baiburt were also in the province of Erzerum. The Armenians from both towns were deported in early June 1915. At Erzinjan they were actually given seven days in which to prepare for the journey; but once they had started, the horrors began, ending for most of them in the mass slaughter at the Kemakh gorge. Baiburt Armenians left in the belief that they were going to safety; but their fate was if anything grimmer than that of those from Erzinjan. Just outside their town, while they were in the process of being sent via Erzinjan to the Kemakh gorge, the process of threatening began. The Turks took levies of money and marketable girls, giving a false promise of safety. Past Erzinjan the attacks from the *chettes* in the hills increased, and the deportees, driven beyond endurance, attempted to flee back to Erzinjan, only to be fired on by gendarmes.

Thus the heartland of northern Turkish Armenia was despoiled of its Armenians. The assaults were virtually simultaneous, and the pattern so similar that official organization is beyond doubt. The Turkish government rationalization for what happened—that deportees were led in a kindly fashion to new homes far from the battle zone, and being given food and water along the way—is contradicted by every eyewitness report, and consuls like Scheubner-Richter knew what really lay behind the deportations. There were no "new homes"; just a string of open-air concentration camps along the Euphrates in northern Syria, or houses and hovels where the few lucky survivors hid themselves from the authorities in the empire's Arab provinces.

While the province of Erzerum was being thus emptied of Armenians, the southern heartland of Turkish Armenia was being cleared in a more summary fashion by the vengeful figure of Jevdet Bey, with his "butcher battalions" (*kesab taburi*): After his failure at Van, he joined forces with Halil, who was in retreat from Urmia, and advanced in a southwesterly direction toward Sairt (or Sghert), whose Armenian and other Christian population he largely destroyed in late May. It is an interesting reflection on Ottoman priorities during the war that the skill, energy, and troops of leading commanders such as Jevdet and Halil were mobilized to such an extent for slaughtering part of the empire's own population. After Sairt, the columns advanced, together with reinforcements sent from Erzerum, toward Bitlis.

In Bitlis the attitude of the Armenians was entirely law-abiding. A number of them were attending the war-wounded in field hospitals. Nevertheless, Jevdet entered the town intent on confrontation. He raised a ransom from the Armenians, then hanged a number of them. The town was surrounded and cut off on June 25, and after a short siege the Armenian quarter capitulated. Almost all the men were shot, the attractive women "distributed" to the local population, and the rest driven south to be drowned in the Tigris. In all about 15,000 are estimated to have died in Bitlis. Turkish and Kurdish *muhajirs* were settled in the houses of the dead Armenians. An attack on the Armenian villages near Bitlis followed. This type of racial killing demanded the deaths of the peasantry as much as the educated townspeople.

From Bitlis, Jevdet Bey struck northwest to Mush. He arrived here after the measures against Armenians had begun. The villages of the

Mush plain and Bulanik district had been attacked in May. Sasun, too, where the population had been augmented by fleeing plainsmen, was under siege from Turks and Kurds; a stalemate ensued, and a truce was arranged. However, with the arrival of Jevdet's forces in late June and of reinforcements from Kharput and Erzerum, the whole region was subjected to fierce attack. Torture of leading Armenians became widespread. The villagers of the Mush plain were rounded up by units of the Special Organization on July 10 and almost all the menfolk were bayoneted. In the town of Mush resistance lasted for four days before the inhabitants were overwhelmed. The men were all summarily dispatched; the rest driven out of the city, where they were observed by a Muslim Arab lieutenant in the Ottoman army:

> In a village of the suburbs of Mush over 500 Armenians, mostly women and children, were herded into a stable and locked in. The gendarmes threw flaming torches through an opening in the ceiling. They were all burnt alive. I did not go near, but I distinctly saw the flames and heard the screams of the poor victims.

This account exactly tallies with a report published in Tiflis in November 1915, and later printed in the Bryce-Toynbee collection of documents published in Britain as a Blue Book (Great Britain, 1916).

After Mush, the forces turned against Sasun, which had been peaceful since the May truce. The Armenian population here had doubled with the influx of refugees from the Mush plain. Fighting flared up in late July, and the defenders were hard-pressed by hunger too. The mixed Turkish and Kurdish forces assaulted the mountainous region from all sides, pressing the Armenians to the upper slopes of Mount Andok. The Armenians defended themselves as well as they could; but with food and ammunition low, and with the skill and ferocity of the Turkish attack, the capture of Andok was only a matter of time, and it occurred on August 5. Thereafter only a handful of Armenians remained to carry on guerrilla attacks.

The outright military assaults on Bitlis, Mush, and Sasun were the less common means by which the authorities attacked the Armenian people. More often the method chosen was that employed at Erzerum—deportation conducted by the gendarmerie. Local variations occurred along the coast of the Black Sea, where Armenians were embarked in boats that were then capsized.

Kharput (Kharpert) lay far from the "border regions" from which, the Turks claimed, the Armenians were being deported as a wartime necessity. Its importance lay in the fact that the Armenian community there was well established and that the American missionaries had set up an institute of learning there in 1876, initially called Armenia College but later renamed Euphrates College. Here Armenians had, within a few decades, gained a modern, practical, and critical outlook on the world; and the institution had forged strong links between the Armenian community and the United States. None of this was any protection against the violence, cruelty, and destructiveness of the Young Turk-led authorities; indeed, it seems to have increased official vindictiveness.

Arrests and arms searches took place here as elsewhere, as did trumped-up Turkish allegations of sedition. Thirteen thousand Ottoman Armenian soldiers who had been stationed there were reliably reported to have been led out of the town under escort and shot.

The Armenian population of Kharput was deported from late June to August 1915. Four professors from Euphrates College were on the first convoy; they died with the others on the desolate road to Diarbekir, after enduring extreme tortures and beatings. The deportations from Kharput were witnessed by the American consul, Leslie A. Davis. He noted that Kharput was first used as a concentration point for deportees from Erzerum and Erzinjan, many of whom camped outside the town. Of these deportees, Davis comments:

> A more pitiable sight cannot be imagined. They are almost without exception ragged, filthy, hungry, and sick. That is not surprising in view of the fact that they have been on the road for nearly two months with no change of clothing, no chance to wash, no shelter, and little to eat. The government has been giving them some scanty rations here. I watched them one time when their food was brought. Wild animals could not be worse. They rushed upon the guards who carried the food and the guards beat them back with clubs hitting hard enough to kill sometimes. To watch them one could hardly believe that these people were human beings. (Davis, quoted in "Document," 1984, p. 95)

There were few men among them, Davis continued, since most had been killed on the road; and those at the encampment represented only a small portion of those who had started. It was clear that this would be the fate of those about to leave from Kharput. "The entire movement seems to me the most thoroughly organized and effective massacre this country has ever seen." Indeed, about 800 men from Kharput and Mezre had already been taken, roped together, to an uninhabited part of the locality, and then been shot or bayoneted to death. Only two or three escaped. "No charge of any kind had ever been made against any of these men. They were simply arrested and killed as part of the general plan to dispose of the Armenian race (ibid., pp. 96-97).

Northwest of Kharput lies Sivas. The fate of this town is linked to the name of a famous Armenian guerrilla fighter, Murad of Sivas. From the Turkish entry into the war until March of the following year, there had been persecution of Armenians in Sivas—general robbery, arms searches accompanied by extreme torture, official violence, murder, and hangings. When Murad was told to appear before the governor in March 1915, he failed to do so, having been tipped off by some Turkish friends. The reign of terror throughout the province increased in severity; Murad escaped with a few comrades, and after a number of encounters with Turkish soldiers escaped from a harbor near Samsun on the Black Sea. The campaign against Armenians throughout the Sivas district intensified after Murad's escape. The decisive measures began occurring in late June, with the deportation of the villagers. Armenians from the town of Sivas began to be deported on July 5.

An account of a deportation from Sivas was published in English in 1978 (*The Urchin;* published in the United States with the title *Some of Us Survived*). The author, Kerop Bedoukian, was a child at the time, and relates with a sharp truthfulness the main features of the deportation. An atmosphere of terror was fostered before the deportations; men were abducted at night; the deportees were systematically despoiled once they were on the road; and most soon accepted that there was no particular destination and that an end would only come with death. They reached Aleppo after about six months, but were ordered on to Birejik because of the spread of typhus. There the survivors remained until the end of the war.

Northwest of Sivas is Marsovan (Mersifon), at the very edge of any possible description of Turkish Armenia, and well beyond it even for some patriotic Armenians. Yet here the deportations were carried out with a rigor and ruthlessness that characterized them elsewhere. For Armenians, perhaps the main significance of Marsovan was Anatolia College, an American educational establishment founded and run by Protestant missionaries. The college itself was initially able to protect a number of Armenians from the measures, when most of the town's 12,000 Armenians were being deported in June and July. The president of the college, Theodore Elmer, sought an assurance for the safety of the Armenians within the college walls from his ambassador in Constantinople; Henry Morgenthau responded that he had received such an assurance from Enver and Talaat. But the district governor of Marsovan alleged that he had received orders that the Armenians in the college were to be deported, and with the precise attention to detail that characterizes an agent of mass murder, he sought out the remaining Armenians in the college and had them expelled into the desert wilderness, where they died.

Even farther west lies Angora (Ankara). Here the larger part of the Armenian population was Catholic (about 15,000-20,000), polished and sophisticated people, speaking Turkish, devoid of any Armenian nationalist aspirations, and not even calling themselves Armenians. But they too were deported, at the end of August, after the deportation of members of the Armenian Apostolic Church. The Austrian ambassador, Count Pallavicini, tried to exert some pressure on their behalf, but nothing effective resulted.

Trebizond, like Angora, lay outside historic Armenia. But here too the Committee of Union and Progress was meticulous in ensuring that Armenians were rounded up and killed. The precise, polished manners of the CUP leaders have been especially noted by Leon Surmelian (1946), whose narrative of his boyhood deportation is outstanding. Another good account of the Trebizond deportation is given by Italian consul Gorrini, who was very sensitive to the horror of the proceedings going on around him, as well as being a careful witness (Great Britain, 1916, pp. 291-92).

These two reports, taken together, create a valuable picture of the Armenian genocide of 1915. They tell of the sophisticated, educated party bosses of the Committee of Union and Progress, with their Western dress and smart shoes, ordering the (sometimes unwilling) local Turkish/Kurdish population to carry out violent and horrific acts against Armenians. They make it clear that the policy was quintessentially a party one, and not a racial or religious one. (The picture that they create is far from the popular European-American image of wild and dirty *mullahs* wielding swords and chanting Muslim curses—a piece of gratuitous orientalism that obscures what really happened.) The main qualities of the CUP's actions against Armenians derived directly from the politbureau politics that had been introduced into the Ottoman

Empire with the revolution of 1908. If the pre-1908 allegiances had been based on an amalgam of religion and community, with a small measure of ethnic awareness, and on respect for the established families or "notables" belonging to any community, the dominant factor in Ittihadist Turkey was the party. Other matters were subordinated to the dictates of the party. The old allegiances were of value only if they could be made to work for the party's decisions. Even the government was an instrument of the party; eyewitnesses reported that provincial governors were forced to work in accordance with the suggestions, and even orders, of the local party functionaries. The party politicization of many levels of the administration of the Ottoman Empire at this period is essential for understanding what was happening to Armenians at this time, and it is underlined by the course of events in Trebizond. According to Consul Gorrini: "We did, in fact, secure numerous exemptions, but these were not subsequently respected, owing to interference by the local branch of the 'Union and Progress Committee' and to fresh orders from Constantinople" (Great Britain, 1916, p. 291).

At Trebizond, too, we see the other aspect of party dictatorship: the manner in which the carrying out of party decisions seems to absolve the participant from any need to regard the objects of his antipathy—in this case the Armenian people—as human beings. Brutal party policy led to an appalling dehumanization of Armenians. Armenian life was never highly valued in the Ottoman Empire, except sometimes in the capital; but at least in the days of Abdul-Hamid, before the emergence of politbureau politics, human beings were not reduced to racial stereotypes to be killed as economically as possible. In the 1890s Armenians had been killed with great violence; but there was the possibility that the massacre would run out of steam "before it reaches our street." The bureaucratic methods of the CUP did not allow for such an eventuality.

Of the 14,000 Armenians Gorrini estimated living in the city of Trebizond before the massacre, barely 100 remained by the date of his departure, July 23, 1915. They had all been driven out, and that included the Catholic Armenians. Many were driven south along the valley of the Deyirmen River, and were murdered at the village of Jevizlik, six hours away. A Macedonian resident of Trebizond reported that every day the river brought naked and mutilated corpses to the sea, the women's bodies with their breasts cut off.

Some of the most vivid and incontrovertible eyewitness testimonies of massacres are those contributed by four Arab Muslim Ottoman officers who defected to the Russians at Kermanshah and were subsequently handed over to the British and interviewed by Sir Mark Sykes. One of these officers, Lieutenant Said Ahmed Mukhtar al-Ba'aj, was stationed at Trebizond in July 1915. In his testimony he mentions that the order to deport the Armenians came from the capital, and, being a member of the court martial (that is, one of the wartime courts established by the government to deal with the security of the empire), he knew that deportation meant massacre. He also records that an imperial *irade* (decree) was issued, ordering that all deserters, when caught, should be shot without trial. Lieutenant Said Ahmed added: "The secret order read 'Armenians' in lieu of 'deserters'" (Great Britain, Public Record Office). The implication of this is important. The authority in Constantinople (whether the government or the Young Turk party cannot be determined) was issuing a double set of orders, one *en clair* and one secret. It is hard to find any other motive for this action other than that the authorities believed their actions were more akin to criminality than to defense of the empire, and that they were, at all costs, determined never to be found out. The mass extermination, or genocide, of the Armenians would certainly fit into the category of a criminal-like policy. The leaders of the empire seem to have understood the nature of their actions and realized the implication for themselves of the Allied declaration of May 23, 1915.

The same lieutenant gave an important firsthand account to Sir Mark Sykes of the procedure of extermination (officially known as "deportation") in the city of Trebizond.

> The children were kept back at first. The government opened up a school for grown-up children, and the American consul at Trebizond instituted an asylum for infants. When the first batches of deported Armenians arrived at Gumush-khana all able-bodied men were sorted out with the excuse that they were going to be given work. The women and children were sent ahead under escort with the assurance by the Turkish authorities that their final destination was Mosul, and that no harm would befall them. The men kept behind were taken out of town in batches of 15 or 20, lined up on the edge of ditches prepared beforehand, shot, and thrown into the ditches. Hundreds of men were shot every day in a similar manner. The women and children were attacked on their way by the *shotas [chettes]*, the armed bands organized by the Turkish government, who attacked them and seized a certain number. After plundering and committing the most dastardly outrages on the women and children they massacred them in cold

blood. These attacks were a daily occurrence until every woman and child had been gotten rid of. The military escorts had strict orders not to interfere with the *shotas*.

The children that the government had taken in charge were also deported and massacred.

The infants in the care of the American consul at Trebizond were taken away with the pretext that they were going to be sent to Sivas, where an asylum had been prepared for them. They were taken out to sea in little boats. At some distance out they were stabbed to death, put in sacks, and thrown into the sea. A few days later some of the little bodies were washed up on the shore at Trebizond.

In July 1915 I was ordered to accompany a convoy of deported Armenians. It was the last batch from Trebizond. There were in the convoy 120 men, 700 children, and about 400 women. From Trebizond I took them to Gumush-Khana. Here the 120 men were taken away, and, as I was informed later, they were all killed. At Gumush-Khana I was ordered to take the women and children to Erzinjan. On the way I saw thousands of bodies of Armenians unburied. Several bands of *shotas* met us on the way and wanted me to hand over to them women and children. But I persistently refused. I did leave on the way about 200 children with Muslim families, who were willing to take care of them and educate them. The *mutessarif* of Erzinjan ordered me to proceed with the convoy to Kemakh. At the latter place the authorities refused to take charge of the women and children. I fell ill and wanted to go back, but I was told that as long as the Armenians in my charge were alive I should be sent from one place to the other. However, I managed to include my batch with the deported Armenians that had come from Erzerum. In charge of the latter was a colleague of mine, Mohammed Effendi, from the gendarmerie. He told me afterwards that after leaving Kemakh they came to a valley where the Euphrates ran. A band of *shotas* sprang out and stopped the convoy. They ordered the escort to keep away, and then shot every one of the Armenians and threw them in the river.

At Trebizond the Muslims were warned that if they sheltered Armenians they would be liable to the death penalty.

Government officials at Trebizond picked up some of the prettiest Armenian women of the best families. After committing the worst outrages on them they had them killed.

Cases of rape of women and girls, even publicly, are very numerous. They were systematically murdered after the outrage.

The Armenians deported from Erzerum started with their cattle
and whatever possessions they could carry. When they reached
Erzinjan they became suspicious, seeing that all the Armenians had
already been deported. The *vali* of Erzerum allayed their fears, and
assured them that the first convoy should leave for Kemakh, the others
remaining at Erzerum until they received word from their friends
informing them of their safe arrival at their destination. And so it
happened. Word came that the first batch had arrived safely at
Kemakh, which was true enough. But the men were kept at Kemakh
and shot, and the women and children were massacred by the *shotas*
after leaving that town.

The Turkish officials in charge of the deportation and extermination were: at Erzerum, Behaeddin Shakir Bey; at Trebizond, Nail
Bey; at Kemakh, the member of parliament for Erzinjan. The *shotas'*
headquarters were also at Kemakh. (Great Britain, Public Record
Office, p. 7)

This is perhaps the clearest and most authentic account yet available by a participant in the mass extermination of Armenians. It is
important to determine what methods the authorities used against the
Armenians and whether there was any ambiguity in their actions.

In the first place, the government made a calculated attempt to
deceive: It opened a school for children, and then deported the children
and massacred them. Men were told they were going to be given work,
but in reality they were taken out of town and shot. Women and small
children were sent off with reassuring words about their final destination, but soon became the prey of the *chettes,* whose actions were
coordinated by the authorities. Lieutenant Said Ahmed was kept in the
dark as to the fate of the convoy of Armenians that he was accompanying. The men were taken from him and killed. For some time he managed
to keep the *chettes* away from the women and children, but they
outwitted his colleague when he had taken charge. Moreover, the
purpose of the journey, as related to the lieutenant in Erzinjan, was
simply to keep walking since "as long as the Armenians in my charge
were alive I should be sent from one place to the other." It is hard to
construe any policy from his account of what happened other than that
of mass extermination—a centrally organized plan of genocide.

By the end of August 1915 a large proportion of the Armenian
population of the empire had been exterminated or was in the process
of being so. Constantinople's Armenian leadership had been

destroyed; Cilicia had been emptied; Armenians from Van, Bitlis, Mush, and Sasun had been slaughtered by Jevdet and his "butcher battalions"; and the rest of Turkey's Armenians had been killed using the deportation procedure.

However carefully the Ottoman government tried to conceal the measures from the outside world, they soon became known. Refugees escaped into Transcaucasia or Europe to tell their stories. On April 27, 1915, the catholicos in Echmiadzin petitioned the neutral United States and Italy to intervene. But these powers recognized the dangers of intervening—that a declaration might make things worse. The Allies themselves issued a declaration on the Armenian massacres on May 23. It began: "For about the last months Kurds and the Turkish population of Armenia have been engaged in massacring Armenians with the help and often the connivance of the Ottoman authorities." After naming the areas where the massacres were known to have taken place, it concluded: "In the face of these fresh crimes committed by Turkey the Allied governments announce publicly that they will hold all members of the Ottoman government as well as such of their agents as are implicated personally responsible for such massacres" (Walker, 1980, p. 231). This declaration obviously did nothing to mitigate the massacres, but it was important in view of the postwar fate of the men responsible for planning, organizing, and executing the killings.

Beyond issuing that declaration, the Allies were powerless during World War I to do anything about the massacres. However, official attitudes in Britain were given substance by the publication in 1916 of the documents collected as a British government Blue Book, with the title *The Treatment of Armenians in the Ottoman Empire* (Great Britain, 1916). An extensive private campaign of private humanitarian concern and charity also was launched in Ententist Europe and the United States. Large sums were raised to feed and clothe the survivors of the Turkish measures, most of whom had fled to Transcaucasia.

However, the authorities continued to deport and massacre the Armenians. From August 1915 those in Central and Western Anatolia were deported, two months after the main deportations elsewhere. A vivid account of one such exile, from Bandirma, on the Sea of Marmora, was published in English in 1981 by Elise Hagopian Taft. Bandirma was a peaceful town, hundreds of miles from the Russian frontier. The author, born Elise (Eliz) Hagopian in 1906, relates a story with a familiar pattern: the hanging of the town's intellectuals for no reason, the coordination of the activities of the authorities and bands of criminal scavengers. Young male Armenians were taken away and shot; the others were sent on a long journey, partly by train and partly on foot, toward Aleppo. They met other convoys, and fell victim to the violence of the *chettes*. Most died of exhaustion and thirst, walking in the burning sun through wild and inhospitable regions.

At Azaz, near Aleppo, the authorities separated those Armenians with skills (real or alleged) from those without. The former were sent to Aleppo, where there was a possibility of meager survival; the others were dispatched to the death camp at Deir ez-Zor. Our author was fortunate to be sent south, where she survived by an oasis in the Hauran, Syria, until the end of the war. The local population was largely friendly, which goes to show that the anti-Armenian attitudes of this time owed nothing to religion.

There occurred, when she was near Aleppo, an epidemic of spotted typhus among the Armenians. "Every day hundreds and hundreds of dead were buried in common graves" (Taft, 1981, p. 61). The conditions among the deportees were ideal for the spread of infection, and since many corpses were left unburied or thrown into rivers, disease could easily have spread to all sections of the population. Turkish apologists today claim that 2 million Turks and Kurds died in the area during World War I. Whatever the figure, the Turkish/Kurdish population died largely as a result of the Ottoman policy of killing Armenians, whose unburied corpses inevitably brought disease and death to non-Armenians.

Although 1915 was a year of disaster for Armenians, one notable success should be recorded—the rescue of the mountain-dwelling community from Musa Dagh, near Antioch. Their order for deportation came in July; but most of the inhabitants defied the government, and escaped to higher ground. For over seven weeks they outwitted the authorities, until they were rescued by a French vessel that had seen their signals of distress. Over 4,000 were shipped to safety in Port Said, Egypt. From there some of the fighting men were enrolled in the *Legion d'Orient,* which saw service in the Allied cause in the later stages of the war, notably in the battle of Arara, Palestine, on September 19, 1918.

A few Turks opposed the violent policies of the Committee of Union and Progress, both at the official and the popular level; how many, it is difficult to ascertain. It is significant that in several localities— notably at Van, Trebizond, and Urfa—decrees were passed making it illegal for Muslims (i.e., Turks and Kurds) to shelter Armenians. Often the penalty was death. This is important in two ways. It shows the authorities had doubts about the popularity of their measures at the local level, and it shows the strength of official determination not to let the Armenians survive. However, many local families violated such orders, and after the war thousands of Armenian children reemerged, who had been kept in Muslim houses for the duration of the conflict (Lepsius, 1919, p. 495).

Of the Ottoman officials (some Turkish, some of other nationalities) who opposed the orders that related to Armenians, one of the best known is Jelal Bey, of Aleppo. He said, "It is the natural right of a human being to live. . . . The Armenians will defend themselves" (Lepsius, 1919, p. 193). He refused to obey the orders for death and deportation, and forbade any such measures to be carried out in the province of Aleppo. As a result he was removed from his post in June 1915.

The Austrian correspondent von Tyszka reported on September 30, 1915: "The governors of Smyrna, Rahmi Bey, and of Adrianople, Hadji Adil Bey, have explained that they do not wish to expel the Armenians. According to a report which has reached the Minister of the Interior, both are abiding by their decisions" (Lepsius, 1919, p. 156).

Ali Suad Bey was subgovernor of Deir ez-Zor, the vast open-air concentration camp to which many deportees were consigned. He was a humane man and did what he could to mitigate their sufferings. Some were allowed to earn a little money by selling wares. But this kindness led to complaints to the authorities in the capital, and he was removed from his post and sent to Baghdad. In his place Zeki Bey was appointed, an official who exercised his authority with maximum cruelty.

These and other examples (for instance, the subgovernor of Midiat) show that some Ottoman officials were prepared to defy the authorities. Even Jemal Pasha, though his attitude remains equivocal, claims in his memoirs, "Just as I had nothing to do with the aforementioned negotiations about the deportation of Armenians, I am equally innocent of ordering any massacres; I have even prevented them and caused all possible help to be given to all emigrants at the time of the deportations." Further documentation is needed to substantiate Jemal Pasha's claims. But his words indicate that he knew that the deportations were more than mere relocations, saying that "The crimes perpetrated during the deportations of 1915 justly roused the deepest horror" (Djemal, 1922, pp. 279-80).

Among the Germans, too, there were those who risked upsetting the alliance between the two powers in order to protest Turkey's extermination policy, undertaken in the name of wartime defensive measures. But such actions must be seen against a more general picture of German moral blindness, since most of the time it passively connived in her ally's anti-Armenian measures. Baron von Wangenheim, German ambassador at Constantinople for most of 1915, restricted his comments and complaints to fairly minor matters; he never seems to have faced up to the reality of the vast, carefully coordinated and deadly measures that the Committee of Union and Progress were undertaking against Armenians, even though his consuls were giving him a good idea of what was happening.

It was not until Germany's third wartime ambassador, Count von Wolff-Metternich, arrived in the Ottoman capital that any real assessment of the Armenian situation took place. His dispatch of June 30, 1916, gives an important picture of the way in which the CUP, through the Special Organization, was acting as a shadow government alongside the actual government and appears to have been making all the important decisions itself. Wolff-Metternich wrote:

> No one has any longer the power to control the many-headed hydra of the Committee, to control the chauvinism and the fanaticism. The Committee demands the annihilation of the last remnants of the Armenians, and the government must bow to its demands. The Committee is not only the organization of the ruling party in the capital; it is spread all over the provinces. At the side of each provincial-governor, and on down to each *kaimakam,* a Committee member stands, with instructions either to support or supervise. The expulsion of the Armenians has begun everywhere anew. But the hungry wolves of the Committee can no longer expect anything from these unhappy people except the satisfaction of their fanatical rage for persecution. Their goods have long since been confiscated, and their capital has been liquidated by a so-called commission, which means that if an Armenian owned a house valued at, say £T100, a Turk—a member or friend of the Committee—could have it for around £T2. (Lepsius, 1919, p. 277)

Dr. Johannes Lepsius, founder of the Deutsche Orient-Mission and the Armenians' strongest supporter inside Germany, was himself allowed to visit Constantinople in 1915, but his pleas to Enver on behalf of the Armenians were fruitless, and on his return to Germany his campaign, among German pastors and representatives of humane societies, had little effect. Although his publication in the summer of 1916 of *Bericht über die Lage des armenischen Volkes in der Türkei* (Report on the Situation of the Armenian People in Turkey) created a stir and caused tension between Berlin and Constantinople, the situation of the Armenians did not improve. When the German consulates themselves assessed matters in early 1917, they found that conditions had not changed much since 1915. Lepsius was not an eyewitness of the measures against Armenians, but a number of Germans were; aside from the various consuls, they include the workers for the Deutscher Hilfsbund, some of whose members contributed testimonies to the Bryce/Toynbee Blue Book. One German who knew a great deal of what was happening was Dr. Armin T. Wegner. He went to Turkey as a volunteer sanitation officer, attached to the Sixth Ottoman Army under Field-Marshal von der Goltz. He took a vast archive of photographs, most of which have not been published or cataloged, and was active after the war in promoting the Armenian cause. He wrote an open letter to President Wilson in 1919 pleading the Armenian cause and giving details of his experiences (Hofmann, 1985, pp. 68-69).

Also noteworthy was Dr. Martin Niepage. He taught at the German *Realschule* (technical school) at Aleppo. His testimony of 1916 (translated into English as *The Horrors of Aleppo* in 1917) raises a serious problem often overlooked by those who are anxious to seek out underlying political motives and to avoid sensationalism. This is the issue of the extreme cruelty of the Turks in killing the Armenians.

Cruelty on the scale of that practiced by the Turks at that time does not fit easily into modern historiography; yet from many eyewitness accounts, it is undoubtedly true that the practice of prolonging death by means of extreme cruelty, not to extract information, but for its own sake, was widespread. Some of the cruelties can perhaps be traced to the underlying policy of race extermination, such as the practice of slitting open the bellies of pregnant women—a demonstration of the intention to destroy Armenians for the present and the future. Other cruelties, such as those witnessed by Herr Spiecker, a German traveler, and related by Dr. Niepage, in which the Turks tied together Armenian men, fired several volleys of small shot into the human mass, and went off laughing while their victims died slowly in convulsions, are more problematic, as is the story related to Niepage by the German consul at Mosul, who informed him that many children's hands had been hacked off and littered the road in a number of places between Aleppo and Mosul. These things appear arbitrary, random, and unrelated to any political process; they bespeak a horror and a human darkness for which straightforward explanations fail. Many other cruelties were committed against defenseless and often dying Armenians. Indeed, the inhuman manner in which the Turks carried out the extirpation of Armenians from Greater Armenia, Cilicia, and Anatolia became one of the main platforms for Armenia's quest for entire separation from Turkey after the war, and for its land to be large and secure enough for there to be no repetition of the cruelties.

Another important German witness was August Bernau, who was the Aleppo representative of an American company. His vivid description of the concentration camps along the Euphrates remains one of the most powerful and shocking documents relating to Armenians, and a rebuttal of the theory that Armenians were being deported to new homes rather than being sent to places of death. All the available eyewitness accounts make it clear that Turkish actions toward the Armenians in 1915-1916 amounted to mass murder, or genocide.

There remains the vexing question of how many Armenians were killed in the Ottoman Empire during the war in the extermination process begun in 1915. These numbers are often revised, usually in accordance with political expediency, since the subject of the Armenian genocide of 1915 has become a central preoccupation of the Turkish government today. Several decades ago, the most commonly accepted figure was 1,500,000 Armenians killed. This was the figure given by Professor Bernard Lewis in his classic study, *The Emergence of Modern Turkey* (1968), which he used in the book's first edition and left unchanged in the work's extensively revised second edition. Since then Turkish area studies (including Lewis) appear to have lost some of their independence and to have become very close to the foreign policy of Ankara, at least as far as Armenians are concerned, and the figure has been revised downward. Armenians themselves have been ill-advised in sometimes revising the figure upward.

Dr. Lepsius took considerable care with the figures he used, although perhaps he should have been more circumspect in accepting the figure of 1,845,450 given by the Armenian patriarchate in Constantinople as the number of Armenians living in the Ottoman Empire. Nevertheless, it is unlikely to be far wrong, if we accept the figures that Enver Pasha gave to Dr. Ernst Jäckh as early as the end of August 1915 for the number of Armenians dead (300,000) and those quoted by the German Embassy on October 4, 1916. Of the approximately 2 million Armenians living in the empire, 1,500,000 had been deported and between 800,000 and 1,000,000 of those had been killed. Lepsius initially estimated the number of Armenians who had died in the empire

at 1,000,000; in the 1919 edition of the *Bericht* he revised that figure to
1,100,000. Lepsius put the number of eastern Armenians killed during
the Ottoman invasion of Transcaucasia in 1918 at between 50,000 and
100,000. Another German closely involved at the time, Ernst Sommer
of the Deutscher Hilfsbund, estimated in 1919 that 1,400,000 Armenians
had been deported, of whom at the time scarcely more than 250,000
were alive (Sommer, 1919).

Lepsius also estimated that the number of Armenians forcibly
converted to Islam was between 250,000 and 300,000. There was no
religious element in the forced conversions to Islam at this time. The
Ittihadist rulers of the empire were unbelievers. By contrast, some
Turkish Muslim leaders, *imams* and *hodjas,* expressed disapproval at
what the Armenians were compelled to endure. The harsh measures
against the Armenians of Kutahia were declared theologically invalid
by the local *mufti.* Forced conversion had instead a political motive: to
destroy the Armenians' identity, to turn Armenians into "Turks" so that
they would appear in the other column of statistics and thus weaken or
nullify any Armenian demands for autonomy or independence. Some
Armenians appear to have returned to their faith after the armistice, but
no figures exist for them.

The evidence from memoirs, published documents, and articles
written by participants and observers, presents an overwhelming case
for affirming that a planned genocide of the Armenian people took place
in the Ottoman Empire in 1915-1916. The strongest evidence comes
from Turkish or German sources and includes the material from German
consular sources, the official Ottoman indictments of the leading CUP
men at their trials in 1919, the condemnation of the killings by Vehib
Pasha, as well as the 1933-1934 articles by "A. Bil." Eyewitness
observation from neutral or pro-Turkish observers is also incontrovertible. Some material also emerged during the Republic of Turkey's 1926
treason trials against the old CUP men. Despite the destruction of
archives, and without using questionable sources, the large amount of
remaining material points to a systematic campaign of mass killing
perpetrated by the Committee of Union and Progress against almost the
entire Armenian people of the Ottoman Empire.

There is also the massive testimony of Armenian survivors, which
makes clear the deliberation and ferocity of the campaign against their
people. All the evidence, together with accounts of the sporadic campaigns against Armenians which stretched on into the postwar period,
is so strong that only those with fixed ideological preconceptions can

deny that what occurred, in its violence, horror, cruelty, and destruction, was indeed a genocide.

FOR FURTHER INFORMATION

For the sources of, or more information on, the material in this chapter, please consult the following (full citations can be found in the Bibliography at the end of this volume).

Ahmad, 1969.

Allen and Muratoff, 1953.

Arlen, 1975.

Armenian Review, 1984.

Bedonkian, 1978.

Dadrian, 1989, 1991, 1992, 1993.

Davis, 1989.

Emin, 1930.

Great Britain, 1916.

Hovannisian, 1967, 1980, 1986, 1992.

Taft, 1981.

Walker, 1980.

9

ARMENIA'S ROAD TO INDEPENDENCE

Richard G. Hovannisian

The upheavals of World War I, from 1914 to 1918, were to have a decisive effect on the course of Armenian history. The Armenian population of the Ottoman Empire was eliminated by the Young Turk dictatorship in its scheme to create a new pan-Turkic empire extending from Constantinople to the Caspian Sea and beyond. These designs also had a profound impact upon the Eastern Armenians living in the Transcaucasus region of the Russian Empire. War and revolution would lead first to the separation of Transcaucasia from Russia and then to its fragmentation into the republics of Georgia, Azerbaijan, and Armenia.

Armenians, Georgians, and Muslims of Transcaucasia

On the eve of World War I, there were some 2 million Armenians in the Russian Empire. All except 300,000 lived to the south of the Caucasus Mountain range in the region known as Transcaucasia. There they were dispersed into every province. The part of the historic Armenian plateau which had come under Russian rule in the nineteenth century was known unofficially as Russian Armenia or Eastern Armenia. It included the provinces of Kars and Erevan, together with the contiguous Armenian-populated sector of Tiflis province (Lori and Akhalkalak) and the eastern sector of Elisavetpol province (Kazakh, Mountainous Karabagh, and Zangezur).

The demographic complexity in Transcaucasia was reflected by statistics showing that the heaviest concentration of Armenians was in Erevan province but that the 670,000 Armenians there made up only 60 percent of the total population. In Kars province the 145,000 Armenians were outnumbered by the other ethnic groups combined. On the other hand, 415,000 Armenians lived in Tiflis province, making up 30 percent of the population. In the city of Tiflis, they were the largest element and dominated the economic, cultural, and political life of this historic capital of eastern Georgia. The 420,000 Armenians in Elisavetpol province constituted a third of the population, but in the highlands contiguous to Erevan province—Mountainous Kazakh, Mountainous Karabagh, and Zangezur—they were an absolute majority. Significant Armenian settlements also existed in eastern Transcaucasia, at Nukhi, Aresh, Geokchai, Shemakha, and especially Baku, where thousands of Armenians were employed in the petroleum industry. Armenians were everywhere—at the major Black Sea port city of Batum, along the Abkhazian coast at Sukhum, on the Caspian Sea at Derbent, and in the many towns and cities of the North Caucasus.

In some ways, the broad dispersal of Armenians in the Caucasus worked in their favor. They prevailed in commerce and the professions and had reliable contacts and associates wherever they went. For as long as Transcaucasia constituted a single unit within the Russian Empire, Armenians were at ease no matter where they lived or traveled in the region. It did not matter so much that the native Russian Armenian provinces were kept rural and agrarian as a part of tsarist economic policies, for Armenian capital found lucrative outlets in Batum, Tiflis, Baku, and elsewhere. Ironically, however, the very advantage that Armenians seemed to enjoy by their dispersal was to cripple them once Transcaucasia had broken up into separate states and Armenians became second-class citizens in their primary economic, cultural, and political centers, which fell within Georgia and Azerbaijan.

The 1,700,000 Georgians of Transcaucasia made up almost 23 percent of the total population. They were no more numerous than the Armenians, but they were concentrated in their historic lands, now the provinces of Tiflis, Kutais, and Batum. There were no significant Georgian colonies or dispersion, in sharp contrast with the Armenian case. Semiautonomous Georgian monarchs had reigned until the nineteenth century, and the traditional social structure was largely intact even after decades of Russian rule. Historically, Georgia had been spared many of the invasions that had devastated Armenia; geographically, Georgia had an extensive seacoast and easy access to the outside world; economically, Georgia was rich in agricultural and mineral wealth. Tiflis, once the seat of Georgian kings, was now the administrative center of the Caucasus and the residence of the Russian viceroy (namestnik).

Although Georgians and Armenians were Christian peoples and shared many traditions, they had in some ways become rivals. The competition stemmed from the increasing influence of the Armenian bourgeoisie and the extension of Armenian capital into Tiflis and other cities and from there into the Georgian countryside. Armenian merchant capital contributed to the ongoing corrosion of the position and economic base of the vitiated Georgian aristocracy. Tiflis itself virtually became an Armenian city, with all classes of people represented. More Armenians lived in Tiflis than in any other city of the Russian Empire. Armenian political parties were born there; Armenian educational institutions, cultural societies, libraries, and printing presses flourished there; and the city duma and administration, including the office of mayor, were almost monopolized by the Armenians.

The rivalry between Armenian bourgeoisie and Georgian aristocracy was ridiculed by many Armenian and Georgian intellectuals who had espoused the tenets of socialism, but the belief that they could unite against the exploiting bourgeoisie of the one people and the parasitic aristocracy of the other proved to be illusive. The mantle of Armenian socialism was apparently much too thin and that of Georgian socialism much too nationalistic. Georgian political thought found its strongest expression in Marxist ideology. A number of Georgian Marxists held important posts in the Russian Social Democratic Workers' Party and gained prominence in the international labor movement. Nearly all, with such notable exceptions as I. V. Jugashvili (Stalin), adhered to the Menshevik faction and branded the Bolshevik program as unorthodox and opportunistic. Subsequent events were to drive most Georgian Mensheviks out of the Russian theater and back to their native land, where they became the leaders of the Georgian republic in 1918. As the Georgian government, they were to invoke socialist slogans and legislation as a means of ending the era of Armenian predominance. Class warfare could serve as a convenient cover for actions really based on nationality and nationalism.

Like the Armenians, the Muslims were scattered into every province of Transcaucasia. Of the 3 million Muslims, almost 1,800,000, or

23.6 percent, of the total population of Transcaucasia belonged to the Shi'a sect and formed an absolute majority in eastern Transcaucasia, except for the city and environs of Baku. They made up a sizable portion of the population of Tiflis and Erevan provinces, and were an actual majority in some counties *(uezds)*. The descendants of Turkic invaders from as early as the eleventh century, they were mostly peasants and herders, but they also had a powerful landed aristocracy made up of khans, beks, and aghas. Referred to inaccurately as "Tatars" by Russians, Armenians, and others, these people had prevailed during the centuries of Turkic and Iranian hegemony in the Caucasus. Only after the region had come under Russian rule in the nineteenth century were the Armenians able to regain numerical superiority in their very heartland, the province of Erevan, and did the Christian peoples combined become a slight majority in Transcaucasia as a whole.

By the turn of the twentieth century, rivalry between Armenians and Muslims had reached a critical level, as Armenian peasants in Elisavetpol province and elsewhere no longer accepted the status of tenant or sharecropper in villages owned or controlled by the Muslim semifeudal landlords and as Armenian capital penetrated into eastern Transcaucasia. Once again class and nationality interacted, as Armenians were proprietors, managers, foremen, engineers, and white-collar workers in the petroleum industry of Baku and the Apsheron peninsula, whereas Muslims overwhelmingly were unskilled, meagerly paid laborers. The intercommunal clashes known as the "Armeno-Tatar" war, from 1905 to 1907, were exacerbated by tsarist bureaucrats, who were accused of stoking the smoldering mutual resentment in pursuance of the policy of divide and rule, especially at a time when the rest of the Russian Empire was in revolt against the tsarist autocracy. Only after the 1905 revolution had subsided two years later did Russian armed forces intervene to prevent further bloodshed in the Caucasus.

By the eve of World War I, the Muslims of the Caucasus had made considerable organic progress. Schools and newspapers had been founded and cultural and political societies formed. The Musavat (Equality) Party, drawing membership from the intellectuals, emerging Muslim bourgeoisie, and enlightened landed notables, became the most pervasive of the various Muslim organizations. Influenced both by pan-Islamic and pan-Turkic ideologies, the party called for the political, economic, and social regeneration of Muslim peoples; the adoption of liberal constitutional reforms; and free association and cooperation among Muslim peoples within and beyond the Russian Empire. Muslim intellectuals were torn between their cultural-religious affinity with Shi'a Iran (Persia) and their racial affinity with Turkey. But following party founder Mehmed-Emin Rasulzade, many bent increasingly toward the Turkish orientation. It was ultimately these "Tatar" intellectuals who would choose the name Azerbaijan for their country and rename themselves as Azerbaijanis or Azeri Turks.

World War I and the Eastern Armenians

The Armenians of the Russian Empire had become alienated by the policies and practices of imperial officials during the Armeno-Tatar conflict and the years of reaction and repression that followed the Russian revolution of 1905. In 1912, however, the government of Tsar Nicholas II took measures to win back Armenian loyalty. War clouds were gathering over Europe, and an alienated Armenian population on the borders of Turkey and Persia might become a potential threat to the security of the empire. Hence, hundreds of Armenians were released from prison or allowed to return from exile, and the Russian government again showed itself to be concerned with the plight of the Western Armenian population of the Ottoman Empire. The viceroy for the Caucasus, Count Illarion I. Vorontsov-Dashkov, encouraged the Armenian supreme patriarch, Catholicos Gevorg V, to appeal to Tsar Nicholas to champion the cause of the Ottoman Armenians. The viceroy also permitted the formation of the Armenian National Bureau in Tiflis to assist the catholicos, to represent Armenian interests, and to serve as a channel of communication and coordination with Armenian communities throughout the Russian Empire and abroad.

Toward the end of 1912, Catholicos Gevorg appointed Boghos Nubar Pasha, son of a former prime minister of Egypt, to lead diplomatic efforts on behalf of the Western Armenians as the powers gathered in London to settle the Balkan War between Turkey and its former subject states. Russian officials in Constantinople also took the lead in negotiating the final Armenian reform measure in the Ottoman Empire. The signing of the compromise program by Russian and Turkish officials in February 1914 was greeted with celebration and anticipation by Armenians worldwide, but in fact added to Turkish suspicions of the Armenians and may have contributed to the Young Turk decision to eliminate the Armenian Question by eliminating the Armenians. The cover of world war was to provide the opportunity to implement that decision.

After Russia and its partners of the Triple Entente—Great Britain and France—had declared war on the Central Powers, headed by Germany and Austro-Hungary, in the summer of 1914, Vorontsov-Dashkov consulted with Tiflis mayor Alexandre Khatisian, the primate of Tiflis, Bishop Mesrop, and prominent civic figure Dr. Hakob Zavriev about the possibility of creating Armenian volunteer detachments to be prepared for action in case Turkey entered the war as a part of the Central Powers. As most Russian Armenian youth had already been drafted into the regular armed forces and sent to the European theater, the volunteer units would be made up of Armenians who were not citizens of the empire or not otherwise obliged to serve. Thousands of Western Armenians now lived in the Caucasus, and many of them were impatient to take arms to liberate their homeland. The volunteers could be of significant assistance as scouts and the avante guard for the regular armed forces. The Armenian National Bureau accepted the offer of arms, matériel, and finances from the Russian army and organized four volunteer detachments, each led by a seasoned revolutionary figure: Andranik (Ozanian), Dro (Drastamat Kanayan), Hamazasp (Srvandztian), and Keri (Arshak Gafavian).

The Ottoman Empire entered the war in October 1914 by bombarding Russian installations along the Black Sea. The attack came two months after the Young Turk dictators, headed by Enver and Talaat, had secretly committed the empire to the Central Powers in return for various concessions, including the right of Turkey to annex parts of the Caucasus. Obsessed with his pan-Turkic objectives, Minister of War Enver Pasha slipped away to Erzerum to surprise the Russians with a massive invasion in deep winter when nearly all military activity on the Armenian plateau was at a standstill. The plan to capture Sarikamish and Kars before the Russian defenders knew what was happening and then to advance upon Tiflis, Erevan, and Baku was put into operation in December 1914 with an army of nearly 100,000 men. But the severity of the Armenian winter and the determined defense of several Russian and Armenian battalions thwarted Enver's designs. Abandoning the ruins of an entire army, he returned to Constantinople in search of a scapegoat to rationalize the setback. The Ottoman Armenians were to fit the role and pay the price.

While the shadow of death spread over the Western (Turkish) Armenians, a spirit of elation uplifted the Eastern (Russian) Armenians. The Russian military authorities showered the Armenian volunteers with commendations and authorized the formation of three additional detachments, to which volunteers from Europe and the United States hastened. The fifth, sixth, and seventh volunteer battalions were led by Vardan, Grigor Avsharian, and Hovsep Arghutian. All now looked toward the impending liberation of Western Armenia.

The onset of the deportations and massacres of the Ottoman Armenians in April 1915 caught the victims by surprise. Resistance was offered in a few localities, usually ending in death of all defenders. The most notable exception was at Van, where the large Armenian population, headed by Aram Manukian and Armenak Erkanian, took arms and for a month withstood the siege of Governor Jevdet Bey, Enver's brother-in-law. The proximity of Van to the frontiers of Persia and the Russian Empire made possible a rescue operation. On May 16 the Armenian battalions led Russian regulars into Van amid a delirious welcome by the Christian population. Once again the Armenian volunteers earned the praise of the Russian command, which confirmed Aram Manukian as temporary governor of the region.

The Armenian volunteers were impatient to advance along the southern shore of Lake Van to liberate the 100,000 Armenians trapped in Bitlis, Sasun, and Mush. But just as Andranik's detachment reached Tatvan on the western edge of the lake in mid-July, the Russian command ordered a general retreat because of a Turkish counteroffensive to the north. Van too was evacuated, as the Armenians who had defied Jevdet Bey for weeks now had to flee to Russian Armenia. The withdrawal spelled years of misery and exile for the natives of Van, but it brought immediate massacre to virtually all men, women, and children of Bitlis, Sasun, and Mush. When the Russian army reoccupied Van in September 1915 and advanced into Mush and Bitlis in early 1916, there was no one left to liberate. The Russian victories now elicited little rejoicing among the Armenians of the Caucasus.

By the end of 1915, a shift in the Russian official attitude toward the Armenians had become evident. The tsar's uncle, Grand Duke Nicholas, replaced Vorontsov-Dashkov as viceroy and quickly revealed impatience and disdain toward the non-Russian nationalities. He imposed strict censorship on the Armenian press and proscribed discussion of the future of Western Armenia and other vital issues. In December the Russian command ordered the liquidation of the Armenian volunteer battalions and the integration of the men into regular army units. The Armenians were shocked and demoralized.

The explanation for these developments could be found in the secret agreements that were being negotiated among the Entente Powers regarding the future partition of the Ottoman Empire. Among the several wartime pacts, the so-called Sykes-Picot agreement carved up the Arab-speaking provinces into French and British zones of direct or indirect control and provided for the expansion of Russia into the eastern Ottoman provinces of Trebizond, Erzerum, Bitlis, and Van. The remainder of Turkish or Western Armenia—that is most of the provinces of Sivas (Sebastia), Mamuret-ul-Aziz (Kharpert), and Diarbekir (Dikranagerd)—were, together with Cilicia, to be included in the French sphere of influence. Hence, rather than an autonomous Western Armenia under Russian auspices, the Entente had planned the division of the region into Russian and French zones. After accepting this arrangement, Russian Foreign Minister S. D. Sazonov wrote Grand Duke Nicholas that Armenians and other local peoples "in certain areas might exercise educational and ecclesiastical freedom, be permitted to use their mother tongue, and be granted municipal and rural self-administration" (Russia, 1924, pp. 208-9). Some within the Russian ruling circles even suggested repopulating the region with Cossacks. Although the terms of the Entente agreements remained secret, the shift in Russian attitude was clearly manifest.

During the military campaigns of 1916, the Russian armies occupied all territories reserved for the Russian Empire by the Sykes-Picot agreement. One after another Bitlis, Mush, Khnus, Kghi, Erzerum, Erzinjan, Baiburt, and Mamakhatun fell to the imperial armed forces, while along the Black Sea they occupied the strategic port city of Trebizond and the coast of Lazistan. The days of the Ottoman Empire seemed numbered, and the Russian command was confident that Constantinople would soon capitulate. In June the Russian government established a temporary administration for areas of the Ottoman Empire "occupied by the right of war." The region was made into a military governorship, with the governor and his assistants all officers of rank. Confiscated goods and lands were to be used solely for the needs of the Russian armed forces. The governor general was to uphold law and order; protect the life, property, and religious liberties of all inhabitants; and consider all nationalities equal, guaranteeing them the possibility of free and tranquil labor on condition they submit fully to Russian rule (Hovhannisian, 1926, pp. 91-93). Nowhere in the decree was there any mention of Armenia or Armenians. In fact, Armenian refugees who had fled to Transcaucasia were not permitted to return to their homes in the occupied zone. It seemed that the longtime goal of Russian chauvinists, the acquisition of "Armenia without Armenians," had been achieved.

The March Revolution

Cracks in the Russian autocracy became increasingly wider as the world war dragged on and the ineptitude of the Russian bureaucracy and governing structure became more pronounced. That structure came crashing down in the spontaneous revolution that toppled Tsar Nicholas and the Romanov dynasty in March 1917. A caretaker administration, known as the Provisional Government, was installed, headed first by Prince G. E. Lvov and then by Alexandr Kerenskii. The "democratic revolution" was hailed throughout the world, as the Provisional Government ended censorship, proclaimed civil liberties, and gave assurances to the other Entente governments that Russia would remain faithful to the alliance.

Embittered by tsarist policies toward the subject nationalities, the Armenians, Georgians, and Muslims of Transcaucasia hailed the revolution that ended the 300-year reign of the Romanov dynasty. The leaders of the peoples of the Caucasus, spurred by the emotions of the moment, united in appeals for regional solidarity and brotherhood within the great Russian federative democracy that surely would rise from the ashes of the Romanov autocracy. In Transcaucasia, as throughout Russia, the political parties of the left organized councils (soviets) of workers, peasants, and soldiers deputies to keep watch on the new official government and to serve as the conscience of the revolution. It was argued that this was the first, "democratic" stage of the revolution. The second, "socialist" stage would follow sometime in the future when conditions were right. The democratic revolution was to usher in the period of preparation for the triumph of socialism.

Shortly after taking power, the Provisional Government replaced Grand Duke Nicholas's administration in the Caucasus with the five-member Special Transcaucasian Committee, known by the acronym Ozakom (Osobyi Zakavkazskii Komitet). The Ozakom, whose membership included Constitutional Democrat Mikayel Papadjanian, was expected to heal the wounds inflicted by the old regime, relieve the critical food shortage, dispel national antagonisms, strengthen the military front, and foster just rule. Actually, the Ozakom had neither the means nor the will to undertake such a comprehensive program. Instead, in pursuance of the Provisional Government's tactic to delay sweeping reforms until the All-Russian Constituent Assembly had been elected and convened to determine the future form of government and basic policies, the Ozakom tried to slow the pace of agrarian and political revolution.

The cautiousness of the Ozakom aside, the Armenians were excited by the Provisional Government's favorable pronouncements about the future status of Western Armenia. In May, Dr. Hakob Zavriev was instrumental in having the government issue a new decree about the administration of the occupied Ottoman territories. This new document identified these territories specifically as "the land of Turkish Armenia" and removed them from the jurisdiction of the military authorities. The region was to have a general commissar and an assistant for civil affairs and was to be subdivided into the districts of Trebizond, Erzerum, Bitlis, and Van, each with its own administration. The decree was a major concession to the Armenians, as Western Armenia was removed from the arena of the Ozakom and local Transcaucasian rivalries and placed under the central government and through it under immediate Armenian jurisdiction. It already had been decided that Dr. Zavriev would serve as the assistant for civil affairs and he in turn would see to it that most civil officials were Armenian. Moreover, the Provisional Government removed the obstacles to repatriation of the Armenian refugees. During the summer months of 1917, some 150,000 Armenians returned to the devastated towns and villages of Erzerum, Bitlis, Mush, and Van, feverishly rebuilding their homes and sowing their fields in time for an autumn harvest. If the front held stable and a favorable peace was concluded between Russia and Turkey, the revival of the Armenian plateau and the formation of an autonomous Armenian state could be at hand.

Armenian confidence was somewhat undermined by the disintegration of the Russian armies on every front. Weary of war and swept along by the slogan "Peace without annexations and indemnities," Russian soldiers mutinied and deserted. Bolshevik defeatist propaganda urged the wretched soldiers to turn their weapons not on the poor workers and peasants in uniform facing them but rather on their own officers and to transform the imperialist war into a class struggle. In view of the unstable conditions along the front, Zavriev, Garegin Pasdermadjian (Armen Garo), and other Armenian spokesmen prevailed upon the Provisional Government to transfer thousands of Armenian soldiers in the regular army from the European theater to the Caucasus front. The reassignment of these troops had just begun, however, when the operation was interrupted by the Bolshevik revolution in Russia.

The fluid situation in 1917 prompted the interparty council of Eastern Armenians to summon a national congress to determine Armenian policies and to select an executive board to act as the collective voice of the Armenian people. The congress, held in Tiflis in October, brought together more than 200 delegates from many parts of the old Russian Empire. Only the Armenian Bolsheviks, still but a handful of men, refused to participate, alleging that the congress would be nothing more than a bourgeois-clerical assembly. By political affiliation the majority of the delegates were Dashnakists (113), followed by the Armenian Populists or Democrats (43), Social Revolutionaries (23), and Social Democrats (9). The Armenian Populist Party (Hai Zhoghovrdakan Kusaktsutiun) had been formed in March 1917 by advocates of liberal, evolutionary reforms, and the free enterprise system. The counterparts of the Western Armenian Constitutional Democrats (Sahmanadir Ramkavars), the Populists drew most of their support from among the professional-commercial classes of Tiflis and Baku. The two cities were also the centers of the small Armenian Social Revolutionary (SR) and Social Democrat (SD) circles, which, like the Populists, found little support in the native Armenian provinces. The Armenian SRs and SDs were internationalists and either had no separate Armenian organization or else operated as component units of the all-Russian parties. Earlier, in feuds with the Dashnaktsutiun, both groups had accused the dominant Armenian party of ultranationalism, excessive involvement in Turkish Armenian affairs, and failure to participate whole-heartedly in the Russian revolutionary movement. In 1917, however, neither Armenian Social Revolutionaries nor Social Democrats could disregard questions related to the future of the Armenian plateau.

The Armenian National Congress, upholding the Provisional Government's strategy of continuing a "defensive war" against the Central Powers and paying lip service to the principle of harmony and collaboration among the peoples of Transcaucasia, also called for the long-overdue administrative reorganization of the region. It recommended that the provincial boundaries be redrawn along ethnic and topographic lines. The Armenian lands would thereby encompass the existing province of Erevan and several contiguous districts in the provinces of Kars, Tiflis, and Elisavetpol. Although similar schemes had been proposed since 1905 at conferences sponsored by tsarist officials, it was felt that the likelihood of adoption was greater now that the forces of democracy had triumphed in Russia. The territories marked for inclusion within the Armenian sector of Transcaucasia were nearly identical with those subsequently claimed by the Republic of Armenia.

In firm control of the National Congress, the Dashnaktsutiun nevertheless sought the collaboration of the other minor parties in the formation of a permanent executive body, to be known as the Armenian

National Council. The Dashnakists therefore accepted a compromise formula that allotted them six of the fifteen seats and assigned two seats each to the Populists, Social Revolutionaries, and Social Democrats and three places to nonpartisans. As the situation in Russia deteriorated during the following months, the responsibilities of the National Council, chaired by noted writer and Dashnakist intellectual Avetis Aharonian, increased. It was this body that ultimately proclaimed the independence of the Republic of Armenia.

That the Dashnaktsutiun, its compromises aside, retained the solid support of the Armenian masses was demonstrated in the elections to the All-Russian Constituent Assembly in November 1917. The Georgian Mensheviks, Muslim Musavatists, and Armenian Dashnakists garnered among themselves more than 75 percent of the total vote in Transcaucasia. This figure would have been even higher had the Russian soldiers stationed in the area not been included in the Transcaucasian electorate, for they augmented considerably the Social Revolutionary and Social Democrat (mainly Bolshevik) vote. Of the fifteen slates on the ballot, the following six posted the highest totals: Social Democrat (Menshevik), 661,934; Musavat, 615, 816; Dashnaktsutiun, 558,440; Muslim Socialist Bloc, 159,770; Social Revolutionary, 117,522; Social Democrat (Bolshevik), 93,581. The parties were awarded one delegate for each 60,000 votes received (Ananun, 1926, p. 672).

Some Transcaucasian delegates were still en route to Petrograd when the All-Russian Constituent Assembly, having convened for a single day on January 18, 1918, was dispersed by order of the new Bolshevik-controlled government of Russia. Nearly all Transcaucasia denounced the Bolshevik tactic, just as it had condemned the November revolution that, two months earlier, had overthrown the Provisional Government of Russia and brought to power the Council of People's Commissars (Sovnarkom). With Baku the only significant exception, all of Transcaucasia firmly denied the Sovnarkom recognition and called instead for the liquidation of the "Bolshevik adventure" and the restoration of the "Russian democracy."

The Bolsheviks and Armenia

Bolshevik strategies perplexed the Armenians. Throughout 1917 V. I. Lenin (Vladimir Ulianov) demanded the withdrawal of the Russian forces from Turkish Armenia and the right of self-determination for the Armenian people. Yet Lenin's words seemed full of cynicism. How was it possible, Armenians asked, to exercise the right to self-determination if the Russian armies abandoned the front and allowed the Turkish armies to reoccupy Western Armenia? Moreover, at the same time that Lenin called for a separate, even independent, Armenian state, he denounced the secret Entente treaties that were "to rob" Turkey and other countries. Even on the eve of the November revolution, Lenin continued to couple Armenian self-determination with Russian withdrawal from the occupied portions of the Ottoman Empire. The maneuver, calculated to win the support of the thousands of war-weary soldiers and to undermine the Provisional Government, seemed sinister to the Armenians.

The Armenian interpretation of self-determination entailed regional autonomy in Transcaucasia and national-territorial autonomy in Western or Turkish Armenia. The Provisional Government's arrangements had made possible Armenian repatriation to much of Western Armenia and implied that this region would enjoy autonomy under Russian supervision. Only with the protection of Russia could the fruits of victory be secured.

The Bolsheviks, submitting to Lenin's insistence that the time for the second stage of the revolution had arrived, seized power in Petrograd and Moscow in November, 1917. In the Russian Civil War of the next four years, the Red Army struggled to withstand and overpower the many domestic and external enemies of Bolshevism. In this campaign the Soviets sought the support of the colonial world, especially the Muslims of Asia. Immediately after the coup the Council of People's Commissars declared "that the treaty on the partition of Turkey and the wresting of Armenia from her is null and void," and the Second Congress of Soviets, repudiating the secret Entente agreements, called for a just peace without annexations or indemnities (Russia, 1957, pp. 34-35).

The contradictions in Bolshevik policy nonetheless continued. In January 1918 the Sovnarkom issued its decree "About Turkish Armenia." Bolshevik activists Vahan Terian, a talented poet, and Sargis Lukashin were instrumental in drafting the decree, but they argued forcefully for the retention of Russian troops in the Western Armenian provinces in order to guarantee the right of Armenian self-determination. Sovnarkom Chairman Lenin and Commissar of Nationalities I. V. Stalin incorporated parts of the draft in the final version but refused to keep Russian troops on the Turkish front. Their decree called for the withdrawal of all armed forces from Turkish Armenia and the formation of an Armenian militia to secure the person and property of the inhabitants; the unhindered return of Armenians forcibly exiled during the war; and the creation of a temporary people's administration in the form of a soviet of Armenian deputies, elected by democratic procedures. In reality the decree only hastened abandonment of the Turkish front, while it lacked any means to implement the other provisions relating to Armenian repatriation and a provisional Armenian administration.

A blow even harsher than the Soviet demand to evacuate Western Armenia was Soviet acquiescence in the Treaty of Brest-Litovsk. The crushing treaty, signed on March 3, 1918, between Soviet Russia and the Central Powers, culminated weeks of negotiations and hostilities, during which the German armies drove deeper into Belorussia and the Ukraine. To save the spark of the Russian revolution in order to make possible the elimination of all national boundaries through a future world revolution, Lenin adopted the policy of peace at any price. That peace took from Russia a million square miles with 60 million people and the country's most productive lands.

As the ally of Germany, the Turkish government, too, demanded concessions. Envoys of Enver and Talaat tried to persuade the Germans to require Russian withdrawal from all occupied Ottoman territories as well as from the districts *(sanjaks)* of Kars, Ardahan, and Batum, which Russia had annexed in 1878. Initially the Germans tried to limit Turkish pretensions to the restoration of the Turkish Armenian provinces, but ultimately they gave in to Enver's insistence that the three districts beyond the prewar frontier also should be awarded to the Ottoman Empire.

Article 4 of the Treaty of Brest-Litovsk read:

> Russia will do all within her power to insure the immediate evacuation of the provinces of Eastern Anatolia and their lawful return to Turkey.
>
> The sanjaks of Ardahan, Kars, and Batum will likewise and without delay be cleared of Russian troops. Russia will not interfere in the reorganization of the national and international relations of these districts, but leave it to the population of these districts to carry out this reorganization in agreement with the neighboring states, especially Turkey. (Wheeler-Bennett, 1938, pp. 405-6)

One of the terms of the secret annex to the treaty read:

The Russian Republic assumes the responsibility to demobilize and dissolve the Armenian bands, composed of Russian and Turkish subjects, which are found in Russia as well as in the occupied Turkish provinces, and will completely disperse these bands. (Russia, 1957, pp. 199-200)

The Armenians, who had tried to man the front in spite of the massive Russian desertions, now accused the Sovnarkom of a nefarious betrayal. Was this the implementation of the decree about Turkish Armenia? Armenian leaders insisted that Soviet Russia was not recognized in Transcaucasia and had no jurisdiction over the region. Hence, the decisions at Brest-Litovsk regarding land beyond the Caucasus Mountains were null and void. The argument did not impress Enver Pasha, who prepared his armies to advance into the territories restored to Turkey by the treaty.

The Transcaucasian Commissariat and the Seim

After the Bolshevik seizure of power in central Russia, a multinational congress of Transcaucasian representatives met in Tiflis in November 1917 to create a provisional regional executive body, the Commissariat, for the purpose of maintaining order until the establishment of a democratic, federative Russian republic. The eleven-member Commissariat was headed by Georgian Menshevik Evgenii Gegechkori and included three Armenians, Khachatur Karjikian and Hamazasp Ohandjanian (Dashnakists) and Ghazar Ter-Ghazarian (Social Democrat), who held the portfolios of finance, public welfare, and provisions. Only the Baku Soviet, chaired by Stepan Shahumian, rejected the legitimacy of the Commissariat and instead pledged loyalty to the Soviet government.

In February 1918, after the Bolsheviks had dispersed the All-Russian Constituent Assembly, the deputies from Transcaucasia organized a regional legislative body, the Seim, with prerogatives in all local matters. Like the Commissariat, the Seim sat in Tiflis and was presided over by a Georgian Menshevik, Nikolai Chkheidze, who had reached a position of prominence in the international socialist movement. The Seim included thirty-three Social Democrat Mensheviks, nearly all Georgian; thirty members of the Musavat-Muslim nonpartisan bloc; twenty-seven Dashnakists; and twenty-two deputies distributed among seven other parties.

The Commissariat and the Seim were heavily encumbered by their pretense that Transcaucasia formed an integral unit of the (nonexistent) Russian democracy, while in fact they were being driven to cope with situations that demanded independent action. The longer Transcaucasia held to the myth of union with Russia, the deeper it sank into contradiction and confusion. The Armenian deputies persistently rejected the slightest suggestion of separation from Russia. Only under the aegis of a powerful Russia, they believed, could Eastern and Western Armenia exist as a progressive autonomous region. The Georgian Menshevik leadership also held to the principle of a united, democratic Russia but gradually tilted in the direction of party veteran Noi Zhordania in his call to organize Transcaucasia into a legal political entity. Most Muslim spokesmen initially advocated a federated Russian republic, yet many were soon drawn by racial and religious bonds toward association with Turkey.

In December 1917 the Commissariat and the (anti-Bolshevik) Russian Army Command of the Caucasus negotiated with the Turkish army a truce that left most of Western Armenia under Transcaucasian control. Because the regular Russian regiments were deserting en masse, the Russian Command authorized the formation of an Armenian Army Corps commanded by General Tovmas Nazarbekian (Foma Nazarbekov), with Dro as civilian commissar. The corps was made up of three substrength divisions commanded by Generals Mikhail Areshian, Movses Silikian, and Andranik Ozanian, a cavalry regiment under Colonel Korganian, several Western Armenian partisan detachments, and various technical and auxiliary units. The Armenians took up positions along the demarcation line from Van to Erzinjan, while a small Georgian force filled in along the Black Sea coast west of Trebizond. Thus, several thousand men now tried to defend a 300-mile perimeter formerly secured by up to a half million Russian regulars.

At the beginning of 1918, the Transcaucasian Commissariat was hurtled into chaos by a well-calculated Turkish maneuver—a proposal to begin bilateral negotiations for a permanent peace. The Commissariat, by its own definition, was an interim body empowered to deal only with local affairs. Moreover, both Georgian and Armenian leaders knew that, alone, Transcaucasia could wield little power at the bargaining table. Nevertheless, unsuccessful in efforts to strike upon a satisfactory alternative and aware that the Soviets were negotiating at Brest-Litovsk, the Commissariat finally accepted the Turkish offer in mid-February 1918. Then on March 1 the Seim announced its "realistic" and "moderate" bases for peace. Transcaucasia would waive its right to the Western

Armenian provinces and would assent to the restoration of the Russo-Turkish frontier of 1914 on condition that certain provisions be made regarding the self-administration of Western Armenia within the framework of the Ottoman Empire. The Armenian deputies, a minority in the Seim, clearly understood that adoption of this program would shatter the cherished vision of a liberated Western Armenia, most of which still remained under the control of the Armenian Army Corps. Yet equally aware that adamance would isolate them and bring even greater misfortune to their people, they sullenly yielded to the plan sponsored by the Georgian and Muslim factions of the Seim.

The Trebizond Conference

Just as the Transcaucasian delegation was about to depart for Trebizond to conduct negotiations with officials of the Turkish government, a wire from Brest-Litovsk announced that Soviet Russia had recognized the right of the Ottoman Empire to regain all of Turkish Armenia and to occupy the districts of Kars, Ardahan, and Batum. The Sovnarkom's action left Transcaucasia in an untenable bargaining position yet with no choice but to begin negotiations. When the Trebizond conference commenced on March 14, 1918, it became apparent that the fears of the Armenians were well founded. Husein Rauf Bey, the chief Turkish delegate, proved intractable in his demand that the Treaty of Brest-Litovsk serve as the basis for all further proceedings. He was not in the least impressed with the arguments that the Sovnarkom had no jurisdiction in Transcaucasia and that Turkey and Transcaucasia had already agreed to negotiate before the Treaty of Brest-Litovsk was concluded.

The large Transcaucasian delegation, headed by Georgian Menshevik A. I. Chkhenkeli, was rendered helpless not only by the overbearing Turkish attitude but also by strident internal discord. The divergent views of the Georgian, Muslim, and Armenian delegates reflected the basic differences among the three peoples. The Muslims, bound by race, religion, language, and ideology to the rulers of Turkey, favored prompt acceptance of all Ottoman demands. They kept Rauf Bey fully informed about the private caucuses of the Transcaucasian delegation. The Georgians recognized the inevitability of making a number of further concessions, but these, they maintained, should focus on Kars, an Armenian district, in order to save Batum, the vital seaport and terminus of the oil pipeline and railway from Baku. The Armenian

delegates angrily retorted that Transcaucasia could never survive without the mighty bastion of Kars and insisted that the conditions for peace
as voted by the Seim should constitute the maximum concession.

Away from Trebizond, the growing disunity among the Transcaucasian peoples racked the Commissariat and the Seim and erupted into
armed conflict between Muslims and Christians in every province of
Transcaucasia. With the land torn by civil strife, the political leverage of
the Turkish representatives in Trebizond was further strengthened. But
Enver Pasha and his fellow military commanders did not intend to await
the outcome of the diplomatic wrangling. Instead they had already issued
the necessary orders for the Turkish army to advance and occupy all
territories awarded to the Ottoman Empire by the Treaty of Brest-Litovsk.
Claiming that Armenian bands had perpetrated atrocities against Muslims
in the occupied eastern provinces, the Third Army, headed by General
Mehmed Vehib Pasha, violated the demarcation line established by the
December truce and advanced toward Erzerum. The sparsely manned
Armenian lines could not resist the powerful Turkish offensive. General
Andranik, who had arrived in Erzerum at the beginning of March to
organize the defense, found it impossible to control the panic or stem the
stream of civilians and soldiers fleeing through deep snowdrifts toward
Kars. On March 12 a Turkish division, commanded by General Kiazim
Karabekir, entered Erzerum and took possession of 400 large fortress
guns, great stockpiles of military matériel, and, most important, the
strategic center of the Armenian plateau. To the south, the thousands of
Armenians who had returned to the provinces of Bitlis and Van had to
take the road to exile once again as the Turkish armies moved forward.
Van fell to the Turkish Fourth Army Corps on April 7, the Armenians fled
toward Erevan, northern Persia, and Mesopotamia. The battle for Turkish
Armenia had ended; the struggle for Russian Armenia was now at hand.

At Trebizond, Chkhenkeli, as head of the Transcaucasian delegation, informed Rauf Bey on April 5 that the Treaty of Brest-Litovsk was
accepted as the basis for negotiations. Chkhenkeli then wired the governing bodies in Tiflis and his Menshevik comrades, urging them to
confirm his unauthorized action as the only possible means of saving
Batum, Transcaucasia's window to the outside world. The mood prevailing in Tiflis, however, contrasted sharply with the cold realism of
Akakii Chkhenkeli. Menshevik orators in the Seim outdid one another
in exclaiming that submission to the terms of Brest-Litovsk would be
tantamount to the self-destruction of the Caucasus. Expressing greater
determination than ever before, the Georgians pledged, to the resound-

ing applause of the Armenian deputies, a resolute defense of the front. But while Georgian sabers rattled in the Seim, Muslim spokesmen made it known that they would not take arms against a kindred people and that they were prepared to support those elements seeking "a just and lasting settlement." Unaffected by this ominous declaration, the now-united Armeno-Georgian bloc ordered Chkhenkeli's delegation to return to Tiflis and acknowledged the existence of a state of war between Transcaucasia and Turkey (Georgia, 1919, pp. 163-87).

The Transcaucasian Federative Republic

The resolve of the Georgians to defend Transcaucasia was short-lived. On April 14, 1918, only hours after the Seim had recalled its delegation from Trebizond, Turkish regiments captured Batum, thus dampening Georgian zeal. The Menshevik faction of the Seim now bowed to the Ottoman conditions for the resumption of negotiations—a declaration of Transcaucasia's total separation from Russia and the recognition of the territorial rights of Turkey. Thus, on April 22, 1918, the Mensheviks, supported by all Muslim factions, proposed the establishment of the independent democratic Transcaucasian Federative Republic. It was Lev Tumanov (Tumanian) of the small Social Revolutionary faction who upbraided those who pretended that Transcaucasia would become independent. The Seim should at least acknowledge that in the existing circumstances "independence" only meant servitude to imperialist Turkey, he said (Georgia, 1919, pp. 200-18). Once again the Armenians were cast upon the horns of a dilemma. Their army corps still held the fortress of Kars and, according to military experts, could stave off the Turkish offensive for at least two months. And yet, if the Armenians should reject the combined Georgian-Muslim tactic in the Seim, they would have to continue the struggle alone. Desperately trying to avoid isolation as the specter of new massacres loomed ever nearer, the dejected Armenian deputies bitterly endorsed the proclamation of Transcaucasian independence. Some of the Armenian deputies left the legislature to spare themselves from hearing Hovhannes Kachaznuni's brief declaration: "Citizens, Members of the Seim, the faction of the party Dashnaktsutiun, clearly cognizant of the great responsibility that it takes upon itself at this historic moment, joins in favor of declaring a separate Transcaucasian government" (Georgia, 1919, pp. 219-20). There was no Armenian pretense, rationalization, or self-deception.

Independence was an act dictated by external military force and regarded as a huge and horrifying stride toward consummation of the pan-Turkic goals of the Young Turk dictatorship.

Akakii Chkhenkeli, the proponent of peace, was entrusted with the formation of the cabinet of the Transcaucasian Federated Republic. While still premier-designate, however, Chkhenkeli ordered General Nazarbekian and the Armenian Army Corps to surrender Kars. The instructions, issued without the knowledge of either the Seim or the Armenians who had agreed to serve in the cabinet, threw the populace of Kars into utter panic. Within a few hours thousands of Armenians were fleeing eastward toward the borders of Erevan province. On April 25, 1918, components of the Ottoman Third Army marched into the fortress and seized its enormous stockpiles of arms and matériel.

The Armenian leaders in Tiflis, learning belatedly of Chkhenkeli's furtive maneuver, rescinded their decision to participate in his cabinet and indignantly demanded the overthrow of the "perfidious" Georgian. Menshevik leaders admitted that Chkhenkeli had acted in bad faith but would agree to topple him only if an Armenian, preferably Kachaznuni, took the reins of government. The Georgians were well aware that the Armenians could not accept such a proposal, for the Turks would regard its adoption as the installation of a war cabinet. With Kars already lost, the possibility of an effective Armenian defense had vanished, and with Kachaznuni as prime minister of Transcaucasia, a renewed Turkish offensive would bring added tragedy to the Armenians. Thoroughly humiliated, the Dashnakists now withdrew their resignations and joined Chkhenkeli's cabinet, which was confirmed by the Seim on April 26, 1918. Once again Georgian Mensheviks took the most important portfolios—foreign affairs, internal affairs, military affairs, and agriculture—in the thirteen-member cabinet. Dashnakists Alexandre Khatisian, Hovhannes Kachaznuni, and Avetik Sahakian and Social Democrat Aramayis Erzinkian accepted the portfolios of finance, welfare, provisions, and labor. The deeply wounded Armenians continued to collaborate with the Georgians. There was no other way to spare the remaining districts of Eastern Armenia from the Turkish onslaught.

The Batum Conference

As premier and foreign minister of the Transcaucasian Federative Republic, Chkhenkeli led a new delegation to Batum to resume negotiations. His government was now prepared to accede to all provisions of the Treaty of Brest-Litovsk. During the first session on May 11, however, the Turkish representative, Halil Bey, announced that this concession no longer sufficed. Since blood had been shed after the Trebizond conference, he explained, the original Turkish terms could no longer be proffered. Then declaring any further discussion unnecessary, Halil presented a draft treaty and demanded its immediate acceptance. The Ottoman Empire now laid claim not only to Turkish Armenia and the districts of Kars, Ardahan, and Batum, but also to the counties of Akhaltsikh and Akhalkalak in Tiflis province and to the western half of Erevan province, including the Araxes River Valley and the railway that connected Kars and Alexandropol with Julfa on the Persian border. Moreover, the truncated Transcaucasian Republic was to be fully subservient to the Ottoman Empire. Chkhenkeli feebly protested that the terms precluded the emergence of a friendly buffer state between Turkey and Russia.

Without troubling to allow time for the Transcaucasian government to accept or reject the new terms for peace, Turkish military authorities ordered the invasion of Erevan province. After a spirited but short Armenian defense, the Turkish army captured Alexandropol (Soviet Leninakan, now Gumri) on May 15 and struck out in two directions: southward along the Erevan-Julfa railway and eastward along the Karakilisa-Tiflis-Baku line. A week later Turkish troops and Muslim irregulars had nearly surrounded Erevan on one front and were pressing on Karakilisa (Soviet Kirovakan, now Vanadzor), the gateway to Tiflis, on the other. Reinforced by these successes in the field, the Turkish delegation in Batum then presented Chkhenkeli an ultimatum that set aside another slice of Erevan province for Turkish annexation and required unconditional acceptance of the amended draft treaty within seventy-two hours. The very existence of the Armenian people seemed at an end.

Germany, the senior ally of the Ottoman Empire, opposed Turkish violations of the Treaty of Brest-Litovsk and repeatedly directed Enver Pasha to shift his attention and military forces to the beleaguered fronts in Mesopotamia and Palestine. Germany had entered into bilateral negotiations with Soviet Russia on the future status of the Caucasus and was nearing a settlement that would place the Baku region in Moscow's sphere of influence while securing for Germany abundant raw materials, especially sorely needed petroleum. Because the Turkish offensive in Transcaucasia strained relations between Moscow and Berlin and

threatened Germany's designs on this strategic crossroad, the Berlin
government admonished Enver to honor the Brest-Litovsk boundaries,
adding that it would make no further excuses for Turkish excesses
against the native Christian population.

When German political and military authorities learned that negotiations between Turkey and Transcaucasia were to resume at Batum,
they dispatched an observer, General Otto von Lossow, to defend
Germany's interests. Von Lossow reported to his government that Enver
and Talaat were bent on annihilating all remaining Armenians and
annexing not only much of the provinces of Erevan and Tiflis but also
Elisavetpol and Baku. Enver had already sent his half-brother, Nuri Bey,
to organize Muslim partisans in the Caucasus as the "Army of Islam" to
capture Baku from the local Soviet, which drew its strength from an
unusual coalition of Bolsheviks and the Dashnakist-dominated Baku
Armenian National Council and military detachments. During the
Batum conference, General von Lossow maneuvered to halt the Turkish
invasion by proposing that he mediate. When his services were spurned,
von Lossow urged his superiors to force the Turkish strategists into
submission through a show of force. Rudely treated by Halil Bey, who
rejected every German attempt to interfere, von Lossow finally informed
the Transcaucasian delegation of his helplessness and departed on the
night of May 25, 1918. Only the Georgian members of the delegation
knew that he was headed for the nearby port of Poti.

By May of 1918 Georgian political leaders had concluded that the
salvation of their people depended on the intervention of Germany,
while the German government, unable to restrain the Turks in Armenia,
a land with no readily accessible raw materials, had resolved to bring at
least Georgia into Berlin's sphere of influence. Therefore, in secret
meetings at Batum, von Lossow and Georgian officials drafted a provisional treaty whereby Germany would extend protection to Georgia in
return for economic concessions. The implementation of this plan
required that the Georgians withdraw from the floundering Transcaucasian Republic and abandon the Armenians. By the time von Lossow set
sail from Batum, all had been arranged. Georgia would declare its
independence and send a delegation to Poti to seal officially the
German-Georgian accord. With these decisions made, Georgian spokesmen in Batum engaged in informal talks with the Muslim members of
the Transcaucasian delegation. A view pervading these discussions was
that one of the three constituent peoples of the Transcaucasian Federative Republic would fall victim to Turkish aggression but it was hoped

that the other two, Georgians and Muslims, could maintain cordial mutual relations. It was anticipated that the Armenians would figure no longer in the politics of Transcaucasia.

Three Independent Republics in Transcaucasia

The Transcaucasian Seim gathered for its final session on the afternoon of May 26, 1918. There Menshevik orator Iraklii G. Tsereteli justified the calculated Georgian tactic. Condemning the disloyalty of the Transcaucasian Muslims and praising the valiant efforts of the Armenians, who, however, had now been defeated, Tsereteli announced that the Georgians had to fend for themselves. Belief in a common Transcaucasian homeland, in a united delegation at Batum, in a community of interests had proved illusory. Thus, the Georgians had no choice but to proclaim independence and form a separate government. Once again it was the Social Revolutionaries who cried that the Armenians, still battling the enemy, were being abandoned and that the Russian revolution was being betrayed by the Georgian Mensheviks (Georgia, 1919, pp. 317-30). Such protests went unheeded as the Seim adopted the Menshevik-sponsored motion: "Because in the questions of war and peace there arose basic differences among the peoples who had created the Transcaucasian Republic, and because it became impossible to establish one authoritative order speaking in the name of all Transcaucasia, the Seim certifies the fact of the dissolution of Transcaucasia and lays down its powers" (Uratadze, 1956, p. 74; Vratzian, 1928, p. 129).

That same evening the Georgian National Council ceremoniously proclaimed the independence of Georgia and named Noi Ramishvili to head a provisional cabinet. The premier's first official act was to hasten to Poti to confirm the treaty between the German Empire and the Republic of Georgia. In Tiflis, the German flag was hoisted alongside the Georgian banner; the Georgians had been saved.

On May 27 the Muslim National Council, meeting in Tiflis, resolved to declare the independence of Azerbaijan, a republic that was to encompass "southern and eastern Transcaucasia." The act was officially proclaimed on the following day, and the governing body of the Transcaucasian Tatars, now Azerbaijanis, selected Ganja (Russian Elisavetpol, Armenian Gandzak, Soviet Kirovabad) as the republic's temporary capital, since Baku still languished under the control of a coalition of Armenian and Bolshevik forces. Ottoman military authorities had already promised to assist in the liberation of Baku, and during the summer of 1918 the Azerbaijani cabinet of Fathali Khan Khoiskii received extensive Turkish support, both in men and matériel. In September, after weeks of battle, the combined Turkish and Azerbaijani armies swept into the city. Much of the Christian population had taken to the ships, but there was neither room nor time for all to flee. An estimated 15,000 Armenians were put to the sword. The Republic of Azerbaijan had at last acquired its natural capital.

The dissolution of the Transcaucasian Federative Republic voided the final effort of the Armenians to forge a united front with their neighbors. On the night of May 26, 1918, the enraged Armenian National Council hurled accusations of treachery at the Mensheviks and denounced the Georgian tactic but failed to reach any positive policy decisions. The Social Revolutionary and nonpartisan members scorned the concept of a separate Armenian state, for without a doubt it would either be obliterated by or made subservient to the Turks. The Armenian Social Democrats, emulating their Georgian Menshevik colleagues, together with most Populists, insisted that there was no alternative but to declare independence. The Dashnakist members of the National Council were sharply split. Only after an emotion-charged emergency party conference did the Dashnaktsutiun recommend that the National Council assume dictatorial powers over the Armenian provinces. On their return to Tiflis, Hovhannes Kachaznuni and Alexandre Khatisian, the Armenian members of Chkhenkeli's delegation in Batum, advised like action, for only a declaration of independence and an immediate peace with Turkey might possibly save the situation so fraught with tragedy. After agonizing hours the National Council finally accepted this view and at noon on May 28, 1918, dispatched Kachaznuni, Khatisian, and Mikayel Papadjanian to Batum with unlimited powers to conclude peace on behalf of the Armenian people or in the name of independent Armenia. In such an inauspicious manner was born the Republic of Armenia.

This decision made, the Armenian National Council still postponed a public proclamation. Only after another extraordinary Dashnakist conference had determined that Armenia should be a republic under a provisional coalition government led by Kachaznuni did the National Council issue the following statement on May 30, 1918:

> In view of the dissolution of the political unity of Transcaucasia and
> the new situation created by the proclamation of the independence of

Georgia and Azerbaijan, the Armenian National Council declares itself to be the supreme and only administration for the Armenian provinces. Because of certain grave circumstances, the National Council, deferring until the near future the formation of an Armenian national government, temporarily assumes all governmental functions, in order to take hold of the political and administrative helm of the Armenian provinces. (Ananun, 1926, p. 683; Vratzian, 1928, pp. 131-32)

The declaration, intentionally vague, made no mention of independence or republic. Only after news of Armenian military successes near Erevan and the conclusion of peace at Batum had been verified did the National Council venture to use those terms publicly.

The Final Battles and Peace

As the Armenian National Council moved toward painful decisions in Tiflis, the Armenian people were making a final desperate stand in the province of Erevan, where Aram Manukian had been proclaimed "popular dictator." Four Turkish divisions, bolstered by irregulars, pressed over Hamamlu (Spitak) toward Karakilisa and upon Bash-Abaran and Sardarabad, the strategic approaches to Erevan, the last remaining Armenian city. It seemed that there would be no deliverance for the thousands of natives and refugees in the province. To the astonishment of friend and foe alike, the unexpected came to pass. The temper of the defenders and populace transformed; resolution replaced panic. On three fronts the peasants and soldiers engaged in battle.

On May 24 General Tovmas Nazarbekian counterattacked from Karakilisa; only after four days of frenzied fighting and the arrival of a second Turkish division did he draw his troops back to Dilijan. To the south Colonel Daniel Bek Pirumian's regulars and partisans at Sardarabad and Dro's men at Bash Abaran stood only a few hours march from Erevan. The Turkish divisions attacked on May 21, but after three days of fierce combat the Armenians remained firm and the Turkish regiments were in retreat for the first time since the offensive had begun. Inspired by the uplifting experience of victory, front commander General Movses Silikian now called his men to a crusade to liberate Alexandropol. And yet, with the troops almost in sight of the fortress city, General Nazarbekian ordered the Armenian Corps to halt. The

National Council in Tiflis had informed him that a cease-fire had been arranged at Batum and that negotiations for peace were in progress. Such an announcement coming a few days earlier would have been greeted with thanksgiving, but it now drew angry jeers from soldiers and peasants alike. The decision of the military and political leaders was dictated, however, by the knowledge that the ammunition depots were almost empty and fresh Turkish reinforcements were nearby. Should the tide of battle again turn in favor of the Turks, the Armenian catastrophe would be unfathomable. Rejection of the cease-fire could not be risked. So it was that the tragedy-laden hostilities between Turks and Armenians abated. General Andranik, denouncing the Russian Armenian leaders and his former Dashnakist comrades for abandoning Western Armenia, refused to acknowledge the Republic of Armenia. With loyal followers and a mass of Western Armenian refugees, he marched toward Persia in the hope of joining up with the British expeditionary force. When he encountered a Turkish division near Julfa, Andranik backtracked and ascended into the highlands of Zangezur, where for the duration of the world war he overran one Muslim village after another.

Negotiations for peace between Armenia and the Ottoman Empire began at Batum on May 29. Halil Bey now pressed for immediate acceptance of the boundaries set forth in his earlier ultimatum to the combined Transcaucasian delegation. The Armenians would be allowed to retain some 4,000 square miles, less than half of the province of Erevan. On June 2, after news of the Armenian victories around Erevan had reached Batum, the Turkish delegation, assenting "for the sake of friendly relations" to a minor territorial rectification, grudgingly allotted Armenia an additional 400 square miles. That was the maximum concession. The Treaty of Peace and Friendship between the Republic of Armenia and the Ottoman Empire, signed on June 4, 1918, left to Armenia the county of Nor-Bayazit and the eastern sectors of the counties of Alexandropol, Echmiadzin, Erevan, and Sharur-Daralagiaz. Other important provisions bound Armenia to grant full religious and cultural liberties to Muslim inhabitants, to reduce drastically the size of the army, to expel all representatives of nations hostile to the Central Powers, and to ensure the unhindered transit of Turkish troops and supplies across the republic. Should Armenia fail to honor these obligations, the Turkish army reserved the right to intervene. The exchange of ratified copies of the treaty was scheduled to take place at Constantinople within a month. Georgia and Azerbaijan also concluded treaties with the Ottoman Empire that day, but the settlement imposed upon Georgia lacked several of the harsh terms of the Armenian treaty, while the Azerbaijani-Turkish document was more in the nature of an alliance.

On June 6 the Armenian peace delegation returned to Tiflis and presented the onerous Treaty of Batum to the National Council. Study of the document revealed that Transcaucasia had been sheared of more than 17,000 square miles, approximately 20 percent of its territory. Almost 75 percent of this loss had been in the provinces of Kars and Erevan. In the surrendered territories the majority of the 1,250,000 prewar inhabitants had been Armenian, with more than 400,000 in the ceded sector of Erevan province alone. During the Turkish invasion most of these people had fled northward into Georgia and beyond the Caucasus Mountains or had crowded into the eastern districts of Erevan province.

In mid-1918 the remnants of the Armenian people were left a mangled bit of land that, for lack of a better term, they called a republic. But as pitiful a state as was the Republic of Armenia in May 1918, its very existence was, nevertheless, an amazing accomplishment. The inglorious birth of the republic followed four years of devastating warfare, the decimation of the Western Armenian population, the illusory hopes prompted by the first Russian revolution of 1917, the disastrous policy of the Sovnarkom at Brest-Litovsk, the relentless Turkish invasion of 1918, the disintegration of Transcaucasia, and, finally, the frantic efforts of the Armenian leaders to save the nation from total annihilation. The decision for independence had been extremely difficult to reach, but the Armenians were soon to find that they faced far greater tribulations in making independence something more than a declaration. The new government turned to the problems of a barren and isolated land, abounding with rocks and mountains, orphans and refugees, heartache and misery.

FOR FURTHER INFORMATION

Ananun, 1926.   Khatisian, 1950.

Beylerian, 1983.   Lepsius, 1919.

Hovannisian, 1967.   Pipes, 1964.

Hovhannisian, 1926.   Sachar, 1969.

Kazemzadeh, 1951.

10

THE REPUBLIC OF ARMENIA

Richard G. Hovannisian

From mid-1918 through the end of 1920, the Armenians strove to emerge from the tragedy of war and revolution, genocide and devastation into a viable, democratic republic. The obstacles to creating the first Armenian sovereign state in centuries were enormous, yet the entire world had made grand manifestations of sympathy and the Entente Powers and their allies were pledged both to the restoration, rehabilitation, and emancipation of the Armenians and to the punishment of the Young Turk perpetrators. It seemed that a new dawn might indeed break for the exhausted Armenian people.

The history of the Republic of Armenia passed through several phases. The first period, from May to November 1918, was the most trying, as the Armenians labored to organize the rudiments of government at a time when all of Western Armenia and most of Eastern Armenia were under Turkish occupation. Even Erevan was within range of Turkish artillery. The end of the world war ushered in the period of a coalition government, November 1918 to June 1919, during which the boundaries of the republic expanded and Armenian spokesmen at the Paris Peace Conference advanced their case for a united Armenia. The year from mid-1919 to mid-1920 was characterized by serious efforts to establish a parliamentary democracy, to define the mutual relations between party and state, and to find a way to settle the territorial disputes with Georgia and Azerbaijan. On the external front, Armenia continued to seek political, military, and economic support from the West, but the Allied Powers had already begun to redefine their obligations toward the Armenians.

A new phase began with an abortive Bolshevik rising in May 1920 in the immediate aftermath of the sovietization of Azerbaijan and continued defiance of the Muslim-populated districts of the republic. Now the highest organ of the party Dashnaktsutiun took the reins of government to crush both Bolshevik and Muslim insurgency. At the same time envoys were sent to Soviet Russia to seek a modus vivendi. But the Dashnakist leaders were never able to abandon their Western orientation, on which the hopes of a united Armenia rested. As it turned out, the West would make a paper award of a moderately sized united Armenian state but would do nothing to implement the decision. The Armenians now had to face a new Turkish invasion and Soviet pressure. In the end there was no Western orientation left to choose, and the hard-pressed Armenian leaders had to pick between Nationalist Turkey and Soviet Russia. It was in fact no choice at all.

The First Months

Having traveled the treacherous road to independence, the Republic of Armenia in mid-1918 was faced with the urgent need to organize a system of administration and to maintain the precarious peace with the Ottoman Empire. Under these circumstances the Dashnaktsutiun sought but failed to organize a coalition cabinet. The Social Revolutionaries and Social Democrats refused to enter a cabinet that included the bourgeois Zhoghovrdakan-Populists, and the Populists insisted that the Dashnaktsutiun, having been discredited by the collapse of Western Armenia and the Turkish occupation of most of Eastern Armenia, should withdraw from the political arena. It was not until the end of June that the Armenian National Council confirmed an abbreviated cabinet slate in which all except the nonpartisan military minister were Dashnakists:

Position	Name
Prime Minister (Minister-President)	Hovhannes Kachaznuni
Foreign Affairs	Alexandre Khatisian
Internal Affairs	Aram Manukian
Financial Affairs	Khachatur Karjikian
Military Affairs	General Hovhannes Hakhverdian

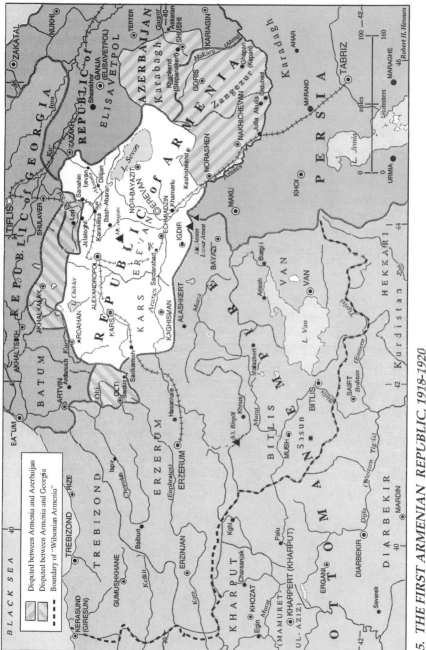

5. *THE FIRST ARMENIAN REPUBLIC, 1918-1920*

With great difficulty the Armenian leaders transferred from Tiflis, with its many conveniences, to Erevan, the unimposing, overgrown town that was to serve as the capital of the republic. Taking over from popular dictator Aram Manukian on July 19, Prime Minister Kachaznuni tried to lay the foundations of government without the benefit of a preexisting national administrative apparatus. The central chancellories, arsenals, printing presses, railway garages, and financial and commercial institutions all lay behind in Tiflis, becoming a part of the rich inheritance of the Republic of Georgia.

Establishment of the parliamentary system of government required the existence of a legislature, but because elections were then out of the question, the Armenian National Council agreed to triple its membership and serve as an interim legislative body, the Khorhurd (Soviet). Thus, when the Khorhurd convened on August 1, it was composed of eighteen Dashnakists, six Social Revolutionaries, six Social Democrats, six Zhoghovrdakan-Populists, two nonpartisans, and, representing the minorities, six Muslims, one Russian, and one Yezidi. In calling the legislature to order, Avetik Sahakian reviewed the tragic events leading to the formation of the republic but, in the presence of German and Turkish envoys, concluded optimistically: "I believe that our borders will expand with the iron force of life, with the defense of our just and indisputable right to the occupied lands."

Two days later, Kachaznuni delivered his inaugural address, in which he described the existing state of affairs as "chaos without bounds." His cabinet would not present grandiose plans but rather labor to employ practical methods to bring the chaos within limits, reopen the avenues of communication and transportation, and assist the refugee population. In foreign affairs, the Armenian government would honor all treaty obligations and seek Turkish withdrawal from at least the occupied parts of Erevan province and the return of the wretched refugees to their native districts (Vratzian, 1928, pp. 164-66).

Although a coalition cabinet had not materialized, Armenia nonetheless was guided along coalitional lines through the multiparty legislative standing committees for finance, administration, education, provisions, refugees, land, labor, local government, and medical-sanitary affairs. Even in these extraordinary conditions, the Khorhurd tried to exercise parliamentary democracy, the debates on the floor often reaching a high pitch and the opposition parties using this legal forum to keep watch on the cabinet. The six-member Social Democrat faction even included one Bolshevik, Arshavir Melikian, whose stinging criticisms were often tempered by his clear understanding of the stark realities facing the Armenian people.

As the government grappled with the chaos caused by the breakdown of law and order, the plight of more than a quarter million refugees, and the complete hostile encirclement of the landlocked state, its envoys in the capitals of the Central Powers attempted to win diplomatic and economic support. For five months, from June until the end of the world war in November 1918, they toiled under trying, often humiliating, conditions, with petitions, statistics, and logic as their only weapons. In Berlin, Dashnakist Hamazasp Ohandjanian and Social Democrat Arshak Zohrabian attempted to persuade the German government to restrain its Turkish allies and force them to honor the boundaries of the Treaty of Brest-Litovsk, thereby returning the Araxes River Valley to Armenia. German encouragement inspired hope, but as the weeks turned into months the sense of optimism faded. Germany would not or could not bring about a Turkish withdrawal or even the repatriation of Armenian refugees.

Another Armenian delegation, composed of Avetis Aharonian, Alexandre Khatisian, and Mikayel Papadjanian, had traveled to Constantinople, the capital of the Ottoman Empire. Initially, based on assurances of German military representatives in the Caucasus, the Armenians were led to believe that a general conference of the Central Powers and Transcaucasian states would redraft the terms of the onerous Treaty of Batum, which Germany found unacceptable. When it became apparent that no such conference would take place, the Armenian delegation sought to deal directly with the Turkish government. The reports of Aharonian and his colleagues lay bare the depth of their emotions as they had to express gratitude to Enver and Talaat for allowing the existence of an Armenian state. During these discussions Talaat cast the blame for Armenian misfortunes on the Kurds, the military authorities, irresponsible local officials, and the Armenians themselves. Enver, the most candid of the Young Turk leaders, offered no sympathy and categorically rejected all entreaties for Turkish withdrawal. The Committee of Union and Progress, he observed, had after considerable deliberation consented to a small Armenian state on former Russian territory provided that it could never have the means to interfere with the interests of the Turkish empire. The borders as laid down in the Treaty of Batum would remain firm.

Only in September, when the Turkish armies were being driven back in the Balkans and in Palestine, did Turkish leaders intimate that the Armenian republic might soon be allowed to expand to the Brest-Litovsk boundary. Then, at the end of the month, Talaat Pasha announced that his government was prepared to make several major concessions to the Armenians. But time had run out for the Young Turk dictatorship. Their cabinet fell in early October, allowing General Ahmed Izzet Pasha to prepare for surrender to the Allied Powers.

The Ottoman Empire capitulated by terms of the Mudros Armistice on October 30, and Germany surrendered on November 11, 1918. World War I was at an end. Armenians everywhere rejoiced. The time of reckoning was at hand. The Allies were pledged to punish the Turks and to reward the Armenians. Yet a careful reading of the terms of the Mudros Armistice indicated that there was good cause for misgivings. While the British negotiators were firm in demands relating to Allied control of the strategic waterways, the disarmament of the Straits, the immediate release of prisoners of war, and Turkish withdrawal from northern Persia and the occupied sector of Transcaucasia, they consented to alter the term requiring evacuation also of the six eastern Ottoman provinces known as Turkish Armenia. Instead, article 24 of the armistice simply reserved the right of the Allied Powers to occupy any part or all of the region "in case of disorder." Turkish military and civil authorities, therefore, would continue to control the area until its fate had been determined by the world peace conference that was to gather in Paris. Even though the Turkish resistance movement against Allied, Greek, and Armenian encroachments was to take form in this very region and a great deal of "disorder" would occur, the Allied Powers were never to implement article 24 of the armistice.

In their evacuation of Erevan province, the Turkish armies stripped everything clean, taking food supplies, livestock, implements, clothing, furniture, and even doors and windows and railway ties. When the Armenian army reoccupied Alexandropol on December 6, 1918, not a single operative locomotive or freight car remained on the entire railway line. Nonetheless, almost 6,000 square miles of fertile territory had been returned to the Armenians, who were further heartened by the landing of British armed forces at Batum and at Baku. The Allies were now present in the Caucasus and would surely help to protect the Armenians while the Allied political leaders found a way to guarantee the Armenians a secure national future.

The Coalition Government

The momentous changes on the international scene had a wholesome effect on the political situation in Armenia. Many who had previously used the terms "independence" and "republic" with skepticism and even disdain now began to feel that perhaps an independent republic could be something more than self-delusive fantasy. The Armenian professionals and businessmen who made up the Populist Party in particular indicated a willingness to participate in the affairs of government. State Controller Minas Berberian and Central Committee Chairman Samson Harutiunian traveled from Tiflis to Erevan to explore the possibility of a coalition cabinet. They found the Dashnakists to be receptive, not only because of the important skills and experience the Populists could bring to Armenia but also because the socialist Dashnaktsutiun wanted to send a clear signal to the Allied Powers that Armenia would be a politically moderate state worthy of Western support and open to foreign investment. In the resulting coalition cabinet, the Dashnakists contented themselves with less than half the portfolios, but they held firmly to the premiership and the strategic ministries of foreign affairs and internal affairs:

Position	Name	Party
Prime Minister	Hovhannes Kachaznuni	Dashnaktsutiun
Foreign Affairs	Sirakan Tigranian	Dashnaktsutiun
Internal Affairs	Aram Manukian	Dashnaktsutiun
Welfare	Khachatur Karjikian	Dashnaktsutiun
Financial Affairs	Artashes Enfiadjian	Populist
Judicial Affairs	Samson Harutiunian	Populist
Education and Culture	Mikayel Atabekian	Populist
Provisions	Levon Ghulian	Populist
Military Affairs	Hovhannes Hakhverdian	Nonpartisan
State Controller (nonvoting)	Minas Berberian	Populist

The coalition cabinet was optimistic that the Allied Powers would soon create a viable, united Armenia and provide for its defense and development. But even in the best of circumstances, the winter of 1918-1919 would have claimed an extremely heavy toll. The homeless refugee masses, lacking food, clothing, and medicine, suffered excruciating months under freezing winds and blizzards. The starving people sometimes rioted for food, but these sporadic outbursts were of no avail; the state granaries were empty. Interior Minister Aram Manukian at times used high-handed methods to requisition food from the districts least impacted by the Turkish occupation, drawing bitter protests from the affected peasantry and critics in the legislature. Aram "Pasha" also took harsh measures against the lawless bands identified by the Mauser revolvers that many carried. Guerrillas and freedom fighters in the years of struggle against Turkish oppression, the Mauserists now robbed and looted in broad daylight, a government unto themselves. It took all the determination and prestige that Aram commanded to deal with freedom fighters turned outlaws.

By the beginning of the winter season, Armenia was already starving. American and Allied officials who came to Erevan brought hope that relief supplies would arrive before long. Until then the nation had to endure. But soon even this hope vanished. An American eyewitness described the misery:

> A terrible population! Unspeakably filthy and tatterdemalion throngs; shelterless, death-stricken throngs milling from place to place; children crying aloud; women sobbing in broken inarticulate lamentation; men utterly hopeless and reduced to staggering weakness. . . . As a picture of the Armenians most in evidence in Armenia I can think of nothing better than this, unless I turn to other kinds of mobs: Large numbers here and there, wide-eyed, eager, hands outstretched in wolfish supplication; teeth bared in a ghastly grin that had long since ceased to be a smile—an emaciated, skin-stretched grin, fixed and uncontrollable. (Egan, 1919, p. 14)

From all over the country reports of famine and epidemic inundated the government:

> The populace is feeding upon the bodies of dead cats and dogs. There have even been cases when a starving mother has eaten the kidneys or liver from the body of her child. . . . The skeleton-like women and children rummage in refuge heaps for moldered shoes and, after cooking them for three days, eat them. (Mikayelian, 1960, p. 108)

The famine was so acute that daily bread rations were steadily reduced until they reached four ounces a day, and this only for those who were fortunate enough to qualify.

The pitiful multitude lay in the snow, in partially destroyed buildings, on doorsteps of churches, eventually too weak to protest or even to beg any longer. They lived in the "land of stalking death," waiting with sunken face and swollen belly for release. And death came, delivering from anguish thousands upon thousands of refugees and native inhabitants alike. Many who withstood the exposure and famine were swept away by ravaging epidemics. Typhus was the main killer, striking in every district and at every age group, taking its largest toll from among the children. During the winter of 1918-1919, nearly 200,000 Armenians—20 percent of the population of the Armenian republic—succumbed to the triple-headed hydra—famine, exposure, pestilence. For each 1,000 persons there were 8.7 births and 204.2 deaths in 1919. The genocide was still in progress.

American Relief

American relief first reached the Armenians through private agencies. As early as 1915 an influential group of missionaries, philanthropists, industrialists, and educators founded the Armenian Relief Committee to assist the refugees. Even after Turkey severed diplomatic relations with the United States in April 1917, some American missionaries remained at their posts and tried to protect as many Armenians as they could. The defeat of the Central Powers at the end of 1918 enabled the American public to renew and intensify relief operations. The Armenian Relief Committee, now operating as the American Committee for Relief in the Near East (ACRNE), raised nearly $20 million in private donations in 1919. In January the president of ACRNE, James L. Barton, led a commission to study firsthand the needs of the region. The field party that visited the Caucasus brought back appalling reports. It was not until March that the first ACRNE medical teams reached Armenia where, by agreement with the government, ACRNE took charge of eleven hospitals and ninety orphanages with 13,000 children. Many others among the 30,000 orphans in the country were eventually taken in by ACRNE, whose president declared:

> The hope of the future of the Armenian nation is wrapped up in large measure with the orphan and women problem which we are attempting to solve. . . . The children who survived the terrible ordeal of the past five years have matured prematurely and reveal unexpected

recuperative capacity. Thousands of the weaker children have perished; we deal with the survivors. (Barton, 1930, p. 119)

By summer's end ACRNE, incorporated in August as the Near East
Relief (NER), had dispatched more than 30,000 metric tons of food and
clothing, with more than half the supplies being distributed to the
destitute in Constantinople and the western provinces of Anatolia. But
even if all private American charity in the Near East had been directed
to the Republic of Armenia, it could not have met the basic needs of the
utterly dependent population. It was the United States government and
its American Relief Administration (ARA) that were to come to the
rescue. In a year when much of the world lay in ruins, gripped by famine,
the United States responded with more than $1 billion in worldwide
relief. In this great American crusade the trickle of supplies that reached
Armenia was enough to shore up the republic for its second, hopefully
brighter, year of existence.

Congress created the ARA in February 1919 to administer a $100
million appropriation to assist nonenemy countries as well as "Armenians, Syrians, Greeks, and other Christian and Jewish populations of
Asia Minor, now or formerly subjects of Turkey." Herbert Hoover
headed the ARA and served simultaneously in Europe as the Allied
director general of relief. The first shipment of supplies destined for
Armenia reached Batum in April, followed by two more steamers in
May and three in June. These deliveries totaled more than 20,000 metric
tons of flour, grain, condensed milk, and other foodstuffs. The final four
shipments of ARA supplies arrived in August, bringing the total to some
50,000 metric tons. For each ARA shipment, the Armenian government
issued promissory notes to be deposited in the United States Treasury,
whereas the ACRNE contributions were the direct gifts of the American
people to the Armenian people. The total deliveries of both ACRNE and
ARA goods was almost 84,000 metric tons in 1919. While this figure
represents only 2 percent of the worldwide distribution, it was sufficient
to give the Armenian people a new grasp on life.

Workings of the Coalition Government

Such were the conditions under which Kachaznuni's coalition cabinet
functioned. Most of the country lay beyond the firm control of the
government and contributed nothing to the state revenue, whereas the

inhabitants of the government-controlled districts did their utmost to evade the onerous obligations imposed on them. Many peasants, reluctant to leave their families amid starvation and insecurity, attempted to avoid military service. A government did exist in Erevan, but it was hardly the embodiment of the self-administration so long coveted by politically aware Armenians. Morcover, the Western Armenian refugees did not consider this their country. The Erevan republic, bearing the strong imprint of Russia, was alien to them, for their national consciousness had developed more rapidly than that of the Eastern Armenian masses.

The burden of several hundred thousand unsheltered and unemployed people was enough in itself to cause economic calamity. Even in normal times the land under the government's jurisdiction could not have supported so needy a population. Industry had never been developed in Eastern Armenia during the century of Russian rule. Erevan province retained its agrarian character, with the Shustov cognac and wine works being the only significant source of industrial income. Home manufacture of furniture, textiles, implements, and handicrafts accounted for nearly all other nonagricultural revenue, but in 1919 this was extremely limited because of the scarcity of raw materials and the widespread devastation of the country. Industrial income had never been high, but in that year it totaled only 8 percent of the prewar level.

The outcome of the dislocation was that, compared with the 748,000 acres of land cultivated in 1914, less than a fourth, 204,000 acres, was sown in 1919. Tremendous losses were registered in grain, fruits and vegetables, and cotton. The overall agricultural decline exceeded 80 percent. The sharp decrease in livestock and farm implements paralleled the ruin in industry and agriculture. Thousands of animals had been slaughtered for food by the Turkish armies of occupation and thousands more were driven toward Kars when those same armies withdrew at the end of 1918. Most of the remaining animals were eaten by refugees or else succumbed to the same diseases that ravaged the population. Thousands of farmers were left without a single draft animal. The slump in livestock when compared with 1914 exceeded 65 percent.

A soaring inflation resulted from these heavy losses. The unsecured paper money became nearly worthless as the price of food and essential items doubled and multiplied time and again. The government was faced with a catastrophe that it had not created but for which it was held accountable.

Compounding its difficulties, the coalition government lost several key figures during the winter of 1918-1919. In November, Welfare

Minister Khachatur Karjikian was assassinated by a deranged political comrade who blamed him for collaborating with the Georgian Mensheviks and contributing to the fall of Kars and the subsequent disaster. The typhus epidemic took two other members of the cabinet in January. First to succumb was State Controller Minas Berberian, a wealthy patriot who had been instrumental in bringing about Populist participation in the coalition government and who had abandoned his position and life of ease in Tiflis to serve Armenia. The heaviest blow fell on January 26, when Aram Manukian lost his battle against the raging epidemic. Aram Pasha, as he was known to friend and foe alike, had been a veritable founder of the Armenian republic. While the Commissariat and Seim harangued in Tiflis, Aram had established a dictatorship in Erevan and took an active role in the successful defense against the Turkish offensive in May of 1918. Following the declaration of Armenian independence, Aram and Dro, as the de facto administration in Armenia, continued in power until Kachaznuni's cabinet finally transferred to Erevan in July. And even after the cabinet had begun to function, there were many who believed that Aram Manukian operated as a virtual dictator. His impatience with the slow pace of parliamentary procedures was evident, and under the existing conditions it was not difficult for the minister of internal affairs to find ample justification for strong, swift, centralized measures. Aram's death deepened the gloom in Erevan. The ministry of interior devolved upon Alexandre Khatisian, but it would never again command the power, prestige, and awe that characterized the critical era of Aram Manukian.

The fundamental, vexing issues notwithstanding, Kachaznuni's cabinet labored assiduously to bring order out of chaos. The Populist ministers, having been given the opportunity to put their ideals into practice, were especially enthusiastic. Samson Harutiunian, an outstanding jurist and civic leader, undertook to reorganize Armenia's judicial system to include branches for civil, criminal, and administrative law, appellate courts, a supreme court, and the jury system. Finance Minister Artashes Enfiadjian laid plans for the introduction of a national currency, a sound budgetary system, and a progressive income tax. Mikayel Atabekian initiated studies for the eventual adoption of a general curriculum based on universal, secular, compulsory elementary education, with emphasis on technical training and the trades. He hoped to transfer the Gevorgian Academy (Jemaran) of Echmiadzin to the capital as the first step toward founding a state university. The idealistic fervor of the Populist ministers eschewed reality, but it inspired hope at a time when pessimism was the prevailing sentiment among many circles in Armenia.

The coalition cabinet also took some immediate practical measures. The Shustov cognac and wine complex, one of the few immediate sources of state revenue, was nationalized. Several textile mills were renovated, providing employment for a few hundred refugee women. Hospitals were opened even though basic equipment and medications were lacking, and thousands of orphans were made wards of the state. In February 1919 teams of civil and mining engineers and technicians from other parts of the Caucasus and from southern Russia were employed to study the soil, survey mineral deposits, assess the industrial potential, and formulate plans for the reconstruction of Armenia. The government also took concrete steps to improve the routes of transportation and communication. When the winter snows thawed, crews of laborers repaired the railways and the depots that had been badly damaged during the Turkish invasion, and they restored and expanded the telegraph network.

The ruling to substitute the Armenian language for Russian in the performance of all official functions was perhaps the most difficult administrative measure to implement. To discard a system developed during a hundred years of Russian dominion was no easy task. Few of the more experienced bureau chiefs could read or write Armenian. They had passed through Russian schools, had entered the Romanov civil and military hierarchy, and had served in various parts of the empire. The Armenian government could conceivably dismiss those who did not know Armenian, or it could teach them to read, to write, and in many cases to speak the language. Either alternative held in store a host of troubles. Still, if Armenia was to rise as an independent republic and gain the loyalty of all its people, the agonizing process of transition had to begin. By April 1919 a few ministries had initiated the awkward and cumbersome move toward Armenianizing the administrative hierarchy.

The structure of the military establishment posed another formidable obstacle. The army command, adept in the tsarist school of traditional warfare, found it extremely difficult to adjust to the needs of a small, emerging state. The military cadre knew little Armenian, used Russian in administrative work and training programs, and even included many Russian officers. The top-heavy structure decreased the combat potential of the army as did the lack of weapons, ammunition, and spare parts. The men under arms were continuously involved with Muslim insurgency and never enjoyed a calm long enough for advanced military training or effective reorganization. In dealing with the problem, the government reshuffled the military hierarchy in March 1919, elevating Colonel Kristapor Araratian to the rank of major general and naming him minister of military affairs. Dro, the experienced partisan leader, was picked as assistant military minister. It was hoped that the pair would be able to create a tight, disciplined, yet flexible army command.

When the various ministerial vacancies were filled and the realignments completed in the spring of 1919, the political balance of the coalition government remained unchanged. The Dashnaktsutiun, in control of the strategic ministries, still held fewer than half the posts:

Position	Name	Party
Prime Minister	Hovhannes Kachaznuni	Dashnaktsutiun
Foreign Affairs	Sirakan Tigranian	Dashnaktsutiun
Internal Affairs	Alexandre Khatisian	Dashnaktsutiun
Welfare	Sahak Torosian	Dashnaktsutiun
Judicial Affairs	Samson Harutiunian	Populist
Financial Affairs	Artashes Enfiadjian	Populist
Education	Gevorg Melik-Karageozian	Populist
Provisions	Kristapor Vermishian	Populist
Military Affairs	Kristapor Araratian	Nonpartisan

Transcaucasian Relations

Foreign affairs during the coalition government focused on attempts to regulate relations with the neighboring states of Transcaucasia and on advancing the Armenian case at the Paris Peace Conference and in Allied countries. The breakup of Transcaucasia into three separate states created enormous problems that would take years to sort out and resolve. Relations were always strained. The Armeno-Georgian territorial dispute focused on the southern districts of Tiflis province. The Armenians staked historic, ethnographic, and geographic claims to Lori and Akhalakalak. These districts along the northern perimeter of Erevan province were a part of the Armenian plateau and were populated overwhelmingly by Armenians. In fact, an Armenian plurality existed right up into the city of Tiflis, now the capital of the Georgian republic. When the Turks evacuated the province of Kars, the dispute was to spill over into its two northern counties, Olti and Ardahan. Georgian kingdoms had extended into all these areas at one time or another, and if the Armenians were now a majority in certain districts, this, said the Georgians, was owing to the hospitality of the Georgian people, who for decades had made room for the Armenians fleeing from the Ottoman Empire.

The dispute led to a brief armed conflict in Lori in December 1918, deeply embarrassing the two peoples who had lived in peace down through the centuries. The British military authorities in Tiflis finally arranged a truce, whereby the southern portion of Lori remained occupied by the Armenians, while the northern sector was made into a neutral zone. Armenian leaders could not forget that the republic's rail lifeline from the port of Batum passed through Georgia and that the half-million Armenians remaining in Georgia were vulnerable. Fortunately, the scope of Armenian-Georgian disagreements could be defined and localized. Both governments realized that the survival of one republic was essential for the well-being of the other. By mid-1919 the two sides were putting forward compromise proposals to settle the remaining disputes. Subsequently, in 1921, the Lori neutral zone became a part of Soviet Armenia. Georgia held on to Akhalkalak. In the long run neither side was to have Ardahan and Olti.

Hostility between Armenians and Azerbaijanis was deep-seated and widespread. Racial, religious, and cultural differences were only the backdrop to the bitter territorial feuds. Azerbaijan claimed all of the provinces of Baku and Elisavetpol, a part of Tiflis province, most of Erevan province, and all of Kars and Batum. According to Azerbaijani maps, the Republic of Azerbaijan would extend from the Caspian to the Black Sea, entirely encircling a small Armenian state at Erevan. Armenia, on the other hand, advanced historic, economic, cultural, and strategic claims to the whole of Erevan province and the western, highland sector of Elisavetpol province, from Kazakh to Mountainous Karabagh and Zangezur.

Armenian-Azerbaijani relations in 1919 were characterized by repeated clashes along the still-undefined borders and even deep within the two republics. The Muslim-populated districts to the south of Erevan refused to acknowledge the authority and officials of the Armenian republic and, with arms and money from Turkey and Azerbaijan, maintained a semiautonomous existence. The Armenians of Karabagh and Zangezur, on the other hand, rejected Azerbaijani claims and declared themselves integral parts of the Armenian republic. When the world war ended, Andranik struck out from Zangezur toward Shushi, the main city of Karabagh, but his force was stopped short of its objective when Allied officers intercepted him and insisted that he return to Zangezur and await the just decision of the Paris Peace Conference. A redoubtable warrior, Andranik could not bring himself to defy the great allies of the West and therefore withdrew his force to Goris in Zangezur. That action was to have a decisive effect on the fate of Karabagh.

The British command at Baku came to accept the Azerbaijani rationale for provisional jurisdiction in Karabagh and Zangezur and assented to the appointment of Dr. Khosrov Bek Sultanov as governor general. The Zangezur Armenians effectively defied this arrangement and threw back every Azerbaijani attempt to seize the district. Karabagh too, through its national assembly and national council, refused to hear of even temporary Azerbaijani jurisdiction. But the acts of Armenian defiance led to the massacre and razing of four Armenian villages in June. Caught up in its desperate struggle for survival, the Erevan government could afford little assistance to the isolated Karabagh Armenians. Finally, in August 1919, the Karabagh National Assembly yielded to provisional and conditional Azerbaijani jurisdiction. The twenty-six conditions strictly limited the Azerbaijani administrative and military presence in the region and underscored the internal autonomy of Mountainous Karabagh.

Violations of those conditions by Azerbaijan culminated in an abortive rebellion in March 1920. In retribution, the Azerbaijani forces burned the beautiful city of Shushi, hanged Bishop Vahan, and massacred much of the population. It was the end of Armenian Shushi. After Armenia was sovietized at the end of 1920, Soviet Azerbaijan ceded Karabagh and the other disputed districts to Armenia, but the decision was soon reversed. Then, in 1923, a part but not all of Mountainous Karabagh was formed into an autonomous region *(oblast')* within Soviet Azerbaijan. Armenian resentment smoldered down through the years until in 1988 it erupted into mass demonstrations for Karabagh's reunification with Armenia.

While Armenians and Azerbaijanis were at loggerheads over the disputed territories, the Turkish armies finally complied with terms of the Mudros Armistice and evacuated the province of Kars in February 1919. Arms, supplies, and demobilized Turkish officers were left behind to assist the local Muslim population organize an autonomous administration and prevent Armenian expansion into the area. The Armenian army, with the support of the British command, nonetheless succeeded in occupying Kars in April, allowing thousands of refugees from the province to return as far as Kaghisman, Sarikamish, and the surrounding villages. Thousands of Western Armenians also pressed into Kars to be closer to their native provinces, now just beyond the prewar frontier.

In May, Dro headed an expeditionary force, again with British cooperation, southward into the Muslim-populated districts of Erevan province. An Armenian administration was installed at Nakhichevan, and Armenian representatives traveled all the way to Julfa, where they relayed greetings to the Persian government. If the railway from Erevan to Nakhichevan and Julfa resumed operations, Armenia could take advantage of trade and communications with and over Persia. By mid-1919 the Republic of Armenia had filled out into most of the region formerly known as Russian Armenia, expanding from its initial 4,500 square miles to nearly 17,000 square miles. This was no mean feat, and if the Paris Peace Conference acted favorably, the new Armenia might be more than double that size.

The Paris Peace Conference

The heads of state of many countries gathered in Paris in January 1919 to conclude peace with the defeated Central Powers and to establish the mechanism of a world organization to maintain peace—the League of Nations. The participants included President Woodrow Wilson and Prime Ministers David Lloyd George of Great Britain, Georges Clemenceau of France, Vittorio Orlando of Italy, and scores of delegations from large and small states and from internationally recognized and nonrecognized governments. It was here that the Armenians were to present their case and to call on the Allied and Associated Powers to fulfill the solemn pledges regarding the future of Armenia and the Armenian people. Lloyd George had captured the essence of public indignation when he condemned the perpetrators of the Armenian genocide and promised that Armenia, "the land soaked with the blood of innocents," would never again be restored to the "blasting tyranny of the Turk" (Great Britain, 1917, col. 2220).

In November 1918, shortly after the end of the world war, the Armenian legislature named Avetis Aharonian to head an Armenian delegation to Paris, along with Hamazasp Ohandjanian (Dashnakist), who was already in Europe, and Mikayel Papadjanian (Populist). After heated debate, the legislature instructed the delegation to advance claims to the six Turkish Armenian provinces and an outlet on the Black Sea. Some deputies proposed unsuccessfully that Cilicia and a Mediterranean outlet should be included in these claims.

It took the Armenian delegation many weeks to travel to Paris, and when it arrived in February, it discovered that Boghos Nubar Pasha and the Armenian National Delegation were already hard at work. A world congress of Western Armenian representatives then taking place in Paris was emphatic that Cilicia must be included in the new united Armenian state. Aharonian's Western Armenian Dashnakist political comrades were no less adamant and persuaded Aharonian, for the sake of presenting a united front, to adopt the claim to Cilicia. Hence, when Boghos Nubar and Aharonian appeared before the Supreme Allied Council on February 26 as the Delegation of Integral Armenia, they made their case for an Armenian state extending from Transcaucasia and the Black Sea to Cilicia and the Mediterranean Sea. Subsequently ridiculed as being unrealistic and perhaps even imperialistic, the Armenian claims nonetheless closely paralleled those already secretly sketched in the British Foreign Office and in the United States Department of State. The French had their own plans for Cilicia and were not pleased with the Armenian claim, but Clemenceau ultimately assented to Cilicia's inclusion in Armenia if the United States would assume a protective mandate for the country.

The Paris Peace Conference, among its first acts, had already declared that "because of the historical misgovernment of the Turks of subject peoples and the terrible massacres of Armenians and others in recent years, the Allied and Associated Powers are agreed that Armenia, Syria, Mesopotamia, Palestine and Arabia must be completely severed from the Turkish Empire." Armenia and the other states could be recognized provisionally as independent nations "subject to the rendering of administrative advice and assistance by a mandatory power" (United States, 1943, vol. 3, pp. 785-86, 795-96).

On the heels of great expectations sometimes follow greater disappointments. Despite the sympathy of the Allied Powers, Armenia was not given a seat at the peace conference, official recognition, or the financial and military support that it sought. Western Armenia stayed under Turkish control, and the refugee population remained homeless. Allied spokesmen advised patience, as many of these issues would be resolved once a peace settlement had been imposed on Turkey and the boundaries of Armenia had been determined. The extent of those boundaries depended on whether a mandatory power was found for Armenia.

President Woodrow Wilson favored an American mandate for Armenia, which was the unanimous choice of the Armenian people as well, yet he decided to hold the issue in abeyance until he could get the Senate to ratify the peace treaty with Germany, which incorporated the Covenant of the League of Nations (including mandate regulations).

In discussions of the mandate question, many Americans with experience in the Near East called for a joint United States mandate over Armenia, Anatolia, and the Constantinople-Straits area. Only in this way could there be uniform progress and could the Armenians be protected. But Armenians and their influential supporters of the American Committee for the Independence of Armenia categorically rejected and denounced that proposal. Armenia should be completely severed from Turkey. Every past reform measure had resulted in bloodshed, and the Armenians demanded absolute and unconditional separation. It would be better to have no mandate at all than a joint mandate, cried Armenian spokesmen. Instead, the United States could recognize the Armenian republic and extend to it financial, administrative, and military aid and advisors.

When the Treaty of Versailles between the Allied Powers and Germany was signed on June 28, 1919, President Wilson still had not put the mandate question to the Senate. And now the Allied heads of state dispersed without having resolved either the Armenian or the larger Near Eastern question. The European powers were not entirely unhappy about the delay, as it gave them time to maneuver for the greatest possible gains in Anatolia and the Arab provinces. But the postponement was a major setback for the Armenians and provided impetus to the emergence of the Turkish resistance movement led by Mustafa Kemal Pasha. Still, nothing was very clear in mid-1919, and the Armenians were encouraged by the sharp rebuke that the Allies gave Turkish Grand Vizier Damad Ferid Pasha when he pled the Turkish case during the closing days of the peace conference.

Damad Ferid, admitting that the Young Turks had committed such crimes as "to make the conscience of mankind shudder with horror forever," asked that the Turkish people not be punished for this aberration and that the territorial integrity of Anatolia be maintained, with the possibility of a border rectification in favor of the new Armenian state (United States, 1943, vol. 4, p. 509). In their reply, the Allied leaders condemned Turkey as the subservient tool of Germany and the perpetrator of massacres "whose calculated atrocity equals or exceeds anything in recorded history." As for leaving alien races under Turkish rule, "the experiment has been tried too long and too often for there to be the least doubt of its results" (United States, 1946, vol. 6, pp. 688-89). A spirit of unbending resolve pervaded the Allied response, giving the Armenians fresh hopes that a favorable settlement was in the wind.

The Act of United Armenia

While Avetis Aharonian and Boghos Nubar tried to put aside their sharp personal differences and the mutual suspicions of Eastern Armenians and Western Armenians to act as the Delegation of Integral Armenia, the coalition government in Erevan became increasingly polarized. The initial enthusiasm of the Populist ministers soon faded into distress and disillusion. The conditions in Erevan made life unbearable. The Armenian bourgeoisie, accustomed to the comforts and luxuries of Tiflis, found adjusting to the situation especially difficult. But the magnetism of Tiflis and the misery of Erevan were not all that disenchanted the Populists. As members of a liberal constitutional party, they were bitterly disappointed that there was little possibility for the early establishment of true parliamentary democracy. They felt intimidated by the brashness of Dashnakist militants and frustrated by the disorganization that still prevailed. More than one Populist minister found occasion to depart for Tiflis on "pressing" business. Their absence from Erevan was sometimes prolonged and for two ministers, Atabekian and Ghulian, it was permanent. Still, as late as April 1919, a show of unity was maintained as Dashnakist Prime Minister Kachaznuni and Populist Finance Minister Enfiadjian embarked on a joint mission to Europe and America to secure financial loans and assistance for the republic.

It was the Declaration of United Armenia, proclaimed during the celebration of the republic's first anniversary on May 28, that provided the immediate cause for the collapse of the coalition cabinet. In preparing for the anniversary, the cabinet, with the concurrence of the Populist ministers, decided to declare the symbolic union of Eastern and Western Armenia, even though no part of Western Armenia was yet under Armenian rule. May 28 was a day of rejoicing, as Armenia had pulled through the terrible winter, American flour had arrived, and the organs of government had begun to function. Townspeople and orphans lined the streets decorated with the Armenian red, blue, and orange tricolor flag and applauded as the military band struck up with the strains of the national anthem, "Mer Hairenik" (Our Fatherland).

Two floats, one depicting the tragedy of Western Armenia and the other, in white, holding forth the promise of a bright future, passed along the parade route to the legislature. There Acting Prime Minister Alexandre Khatisian proclaimed the Act of United Armenia, which read in part:

> To restore the integrality of Armenia and to secure the complete freedom and prosperity of its people, the Government of Armenia, abiding by the solid will and desire of the entire Armenian people, declares that from this day forward the separated parts of Armenia are everlastingly combined as an independent political entity. . . .
>
> Now in promulgating this act of unification and independence of the ancestral Armenian lands located in Transcaucasia and the Ottoman Empire, the Government of Armenia declares that the political system of United Armenia is a democratic republic and that it has become the Government of the United Republic of Armenia.
>
> Thus, the people of Armenia are henceforth the supreme lord and master of their consolidated fatherland, and the Parliament and Government of Armenia stand as the supreme legislative and executive authority conjoining the free people of United Armenia. (Khatisian, 1930, pp. 129-30)

Twelve Western Armenian deputies were then seated in the Khorhurd to give symbolic meaning to the symbolic act.

A few days later, in a startling reversal, the Populist central committee in Tiflis declared that the proclamation had been an act of usurpation. Boghos Nubar and his Armenian National Delegation spoke for the Western Armenians, yet they had not been consulted regarding the act, and the Erevan government had illegally arrogated to itself legislative and executive authority over "United Armenia." The act was therefore null and void, and the Populist ministers, as a sign of protest, were withdrawing from the coalition cabinet. Not mentioning the fact that four Populist ministers had affixed their signatures to the controversial act, the central committee's announcement veiled deeper underlying dissatisfaction with the policies and practices of the Dashnaktsutiun. The Populists hoped that once a united state had actually been formed a coalition with the Western Armenian Constitutional Democrats (Sahmanadir Ramkavars) and other nonsocialist elements aligned with Boghos Nubar might successfully challenge the Dashnaktsutiun for political ascendancy.

Parliamentary Elections

The crisis surrounding the Act of United Armenia evolved amid a brisk campaign for the first popularly elected parliament of Armenia. In keeping with progressive, democratic principles, the election regulations enfranchised all adults regardless of sex, race, religion, and provided that the elections be conducted on the basis of general, direct, equal voting and proportional representation. That the Armenian Revolutionary Federation would gain an absolute majority in a popular election was a foregone conclusion, as the Dashnaktsutiun had struck root throughout the Caucasus and had directed collective Armenian action since the turn of the century. Even if it had been possible to conduct the electoral campaign under ideal conditions, the opposition parties would be overshadowed. The Armenian affiliate of the Social Revolutionary Party, other than emphasizing the need for integral bonds with Russia and interracial harmony, offered little that was not already contained in the platform of the Dashnaktsutiun. The small Marxist Social Democrat groups were split into at least five rival factions, composed mainly of students and intellectuals, and handicapped by the absence of a significant proletariat in the Armenian provinces. The liberal Armenian Populist Party, like the socialist opposition parties, functioned under the anomaly of having more followers in Tiflis and Baku than in Erevan and of directing organizational affairs through a central body situated outside the Armenian republic. But unlike the Social Revolutionaries and Social Democrats, the Populists had shared authority in the coalition cabinet from December 1918 to June 1919, and the rank-and-file members identified increasingly with the concept of national independence. The party had the potential of becoming the catalyst for the various nonsocialist elements. Hence, even though the Populists could not have won many seats in 1919, their decision to withdraw their slate of candidates and declare a boycott on the eve of the elections was a setback for the democratic experiment in Armenia.

Disappointments and shortcomings aside, Armenia's first national election was conducted as scheduled, June 21-23, 1919. The totals posted by the central election bureau showed that the Dashnaktsutiun had received nearly 90 percent of the popular vote, as compared with 5 percent for the second-place Social Revolutionary Party. Some observers believed that the Dashnaktsutiun had used the ruse of a democratic process to tighten its control over the government rather than to place the state on more popular foundations. The Armenian Revolutionary

Federation, on the other hand, was not a monolithic organization, since it had provided a broad umbrella in the emancipatory struggle. The Dashnakist deputies could be expected to stand unanimously on the principle of free, independent, united Armenia, but their divergent social and economic views could easily give rise to internal cleavages and expose the rivalry between the generally conservative and traditionalist Western Armenian leaders and the more radical, internationalist Eastern Armenian intellectuals.

The Parliament (Khorhrdaran) of Armenia convened on August 1, 1919, in an air of excitement enhanced by the arrival from Rostov-on-Don, Baku, Tiflis, and Constantinople of several of the recently elected eighty deputies, three of them women. Alexandre Khatisian was called upon to form the council of ministers, which the Parliament confirmed on August 10. As it was hoped that a coalition government of integral Armenia would result from negotiations with the National Delegation's representatives, then en route from Paris, four of the Dashnakist ministers each temporarily assumed two portfolios:

Position	Name
Prime Minister	Alexandre Khatisian
Foreign Affairs	Alexandre Khatisian
Internal Affairs	Abraham Giulkhandanian
Judicial Affairs	Abraham Giulkhandanian
Provisions	Sargis Araratian
Financial Affairs	Sargis Araratian
Welfare and Labor	Avetik Sahakian
Agriculture and State Properties	Avetik Sahakian
Education and Culture	Nikol Aghbalian
Military Affairs	General Kristapor Araratian

At forty-five years of age, Khatisian was by disposition and experience a man of government. Laying aside a degree in medicine early in his career, he had entered the public arena, rising rapidly to become mayor of Tiflis and president of the Union of Caucasian Cities. Following the Russian revolutions, he served as a member of the Armenian National Council, the several peace missions, and the Transcaucasian federative government, as minister of internal affairs in Kachaznuni's coalition cabinet, and, since April of 1919, as acting prime minister. Although his cabinet was Dashnakist, Khatisian believed that his party should uphold the government without interfering in its day-to-day operations and that the principal criteria for civil service should be training and talent. Hence, every state ministry included nonpartisans, Populists, Social Revolutionaries, and Social Democrats, several of whom were division and bureau chiefs. Khatisian's critics complained that it was unreasonable to stand on cumbersome democratic procedures or expect the peasantry to remain patient amid worldwide social ferment and the apparent reluctance to sweep away the tsarist class structure. Not sterile legalisms, but swift, revolutionary action held the key to Armenian survival. Moreover, the enlistment of so many comrades in governmental work hindered the task of rebuilding the party and raised the specter of tainting it with the inevitable shortcomings of the administration. By and large, however, Khatisian's views prevailed until mid-1920, and under his direction the departments of government gained increasing independence from the party.

The question of party-state relations was debated heatedly during the ninth world congress of the Dashnaktsutiun, which took place in Erevan from late September to early November 1919. Arguing that direct party control of the government was essential in steering the country through great peril, veteran revolutionary Ruben Ter-Minasian stood at the fore of those delegates demanding unqualified submission of the Dashnakist ministers to the supreme party Bureau. At the other extreme, Khatisian's adherents emphasized the party's history of unrelenting opposition to authoritarian regimes and its wholesome tradition of democratic decentralization. If Armenia was to avoid the Bolshevik malady of party-government synonymity and self-perpetuating elitism, the independence of the state machinery had to be maintained and the Bureau's influence channeled through the Dashnakist faction of the legislature. The exchanges gave way to bitter taunts before it was decided that the party faction, in consultation with the Bureau, would select the candidate for prime minister, who in turn would then secure the faction's approval of his proposed ministerial slate before submitting it to the full parliament for confirmation. Comrades in the cabinet were to hold no party post, and members of the Bureau who might enter the government were required to withdraw from active participation in the supreme party organ during that tenure. The Dashnakist faction would discharge its organic legislative duties without undue external interference, although it would admit the Bureau's right to enforce the decisions of the world congresses. While Ter-Minasian criticized the cumbersome features of the scheme and protested that the parliamentary faction had essentially been given the power to neutralize the Bureau in the affairs of state, Khatisian and other champions of the distinction between party and government were gratified by the prospect of mutual cooperation rather than unilateral dictation.

Khatisian's Government

Under Alexandre Khatisian's administration, Armenia remained beset by many serious problems. A disgruntled and impatient refugee population caused an enormous strain on the resources of the state. The bitter territorial disputes with Azerbaijan continued unabated, and, to make matters worse, a Muslim uprising within Armenia drove Armenian administrators and thousands of peasants out of Sharur and Nakhichevan and sealed the route to Persia. Under these circumstances, financial solvency was not possible. Expenditures exceeded income many times over. More than 70 percent of the outlay was allocated to the ministries of welfare, provisions, and military affairs—the agencies involved in sustaining the population rather than rebuilding the country. As unsecured paper money rolled off the press, inflation became rampant, and corruption was commonplace.

Since the peasantry of Armenia made up nearly 90 percent of the population, land reform and agrarian revival were of pressing importance. The Dashnaktsutiun had always advocated the right of the tillers to enjoy the benefit of their toil. Yet the legislation setting maximum limits to individual land ownership and requiring the breakup of the relatively few large estates remained, with few exceptions, unimplemented. The peasantry fell deeper into debt and often prey to shrewd speculators. Khatisian's cabinet tried to deal with this situation by annulling the forced sales and establishing boards of conciliation to compensate the buyers, but significant progress in land reform was never achieved.

A slight revival of industrial output was registered by the end of 1919. Some 5,000 workers were employed in 300 small factories and 400 distilleries. Although the government's labor plank included guarantees against exploitation, harsh working conditions prevailed. The ministry of welfare and labor called attention to the violation of fair employment practices and ordered government inspectors to enforce the eight-hour work day, the prohibition of child labor, the procedures for dismissal, and other laws designed to protect the workers. Owners and managers were to be warned that failure to comply with these regulations would result in fines and prison terms of up to six months. There is no evidence, however, that sentences of that type were ever imposed. Until 1920 labor unrest was limited to economic demands, which were usually couched in expression of patriotism and loyalty. The Dashnaktsutiun tried to keep abreast of the movement by patronizing the professional unions, but it soon became apparent that some of the workers in the railway center at Alexandropol and in the post-telegraph union had been radicalized beyond the control of their union leaders.

The unremitting struggle for survival obscured most of the small, positive achievements in the republic. Yet conditions had improved significantly. A thousand miles of roads were operative, several segments being upgraded for automobile traffic between Erevan and the district towns, and hundreds of miles of telegraph lines were repaired and extended. The first intercity telephone link was opened with service between Erevan and Echmiadzin. The Armenian Railway Administration, which had begun to function in 1918 with 2 locomotives, 20 freight cars, and 5 miles of track, had expanded to more than 400 miles, with 2 complete passenger trains, 32 locomotives, and some 500 freight cars and cisterns. Daily service was introduced on the Alexandropol-Kars and the Erevan-Tiflis runs, and the volume of freight increased tenfold.

Unable to satisfy the land hunger, the agricultural administration was nonetheless one of the best staffed and organized departments of government. Functioning with divisions for agriculture, veterinary medicine, water resources, mountain resources, forestry, and state properties, the administration introduced a number of projects that would bring many long-range benefits if the republic endured. Programs of horticultural instruction were developed; five field research stations and a school of agriculture were opened; a nationwide campaign of animal inoculation was launched and five of sixteen projected ambulatory stations were set up; breeding farms and model dairies were organized in Kars and Lori; workshops to manufacture simple farm implements were equipped; and a comprehensive study was commissioned with the goals of harnessing the Zangu (Hrazdan), Arpa, Kazakh, Garni, and Abaran rivers for hydroelectric energy and bringing an additional half million acres of land under cultivation. A state campaign to plant every field in 1920 resulted in the purchase and distribution of 65,000 tons of seed grain, which was sufficient to produce the largest wheat crop since the early years of the world war.

Small but significant gains were also registered in the other state ministries. Under the direction of the ministry of internal affairs, the municipal charters were liberalized and broad prerogatives were granted the city administrations in public works, enlightenment, local economy, and provisions. Rural self-administration through the medium of local and county assemblies *(zemstvos)* had long been an objective of nearly all liberal and revolutionary societies in the Caucasus, and after months of preparation the first elections for county assemblies were held in January 1920 in Erevan, Echmiadzin, and Alexandropol. In legal affairs, the ministry of justice had to begin the long process of reversing the deep-rooted popular aversion to the courts. Litigation in the Russian language, terrifying preliminary investigations, and the bleak prospect of gaining favorable decisions without influential intermediaries had kept most Armenians away from the courts. It was now necessary to nationalize the legal system and create a judicial hierarchy with courts of cassation and a supreme court. These had been organized by 1920, and in March, after weeks of preparation, Armenia's first trial by jury took place. The case was simple and the jury's verdict was swift in coming, but there was much ado about the event. The newspapers hailed it as a milestone in justice, and Prime Minister Khatisian spoke in the courtroom of its significance in the evolution of a democratic republic. The actual legal proceedings were awkward and even amusing, as the prosecutor, public defender, and judges of the tribunal groped for the proper Armenian legal terminology, but there was above all a sense of exhilaration. After centuries of submission to the courts and discriminatory regulations of alien governments, the Armenians had succeeded in introducing the jury system in their national language.

The ministry of education and culture was headed by Nikol Aghbalian, a man of boundless optimism who planned to replace the old-style parochial school system with compulsory five-year elementary education based on a progressive curriculum. While the existing harsh realities did not permit the enrollment of all school-age children in 1919-1920, the 420 elementary schools had 38,000 pupils, and with the opening of new gymnasia at Erevan, Alexandropol, Dilijan, and Karakilisa the number of secondary schools increased to twenty-two, with more than 5,000 students. Although these figures do not take into account the erratic operation or closure of some schools because of lack of heating fuel or because of requisitions for hospitals and orphanages, they nonetheless stand in sharp contrast with the previous year's statistics of 135 elementary and 10 secondary schools, with a combined enrollment of 14,000. Adult literacy classes and people's universities were opened in several cities, and in January 1920 the State University was inaugurated with much fanfare at Alexandropol, giving cause for new hope and celebration.

During the spring of 1920, Prime Minister Khatisian hoped to advance from the emergency measures needed to sustain a dependent population toward a program of national reconstruction. Negotiations with Boghos Nubar's envoys for a united Armenian government had not succeeded, so the various ministries were reorganized or expanded to prepare for the reconstruction campaign. All except the minister of military affairs and the state controller were Dashnakists:

Position	Name
Prime Minister	Alexandre Khatisian
Foreign Affairs	Alexandre Khatisian
Internal Affairs	Abraham Giulkhandanian
Judicial Affairs	Artashes Chilingarian (Ruben Darbinian)
Communications	Arshak Djamalian
Financial Affairs	Sargis Araratian
Agriculture and State Properties	Simon Vratzian
Labor	Simon Vratzian
Welfare and Reconstruction	Artashes Babalian
Education and Culture	Nikol Aghbalian
Military Affairs	Kristapor Araratian
State Controller	Grigor Djaghetian

Yet whatever the composition of the cabinet, Armenia could not achieve lasting independence without the help of a major power. The Armenian gaze remained fixed on the United States and the European Allied Powers.

Retreat of the West

Armenia's Western orientation was founded on the firm conviction that there was no other way to achieve a viable united state. But by the beginning of 1920, the West was in retreat. Despite its long record of humanitarian and religious involvement with the Armenians, the United

States, after months of vacillation, finally rejected President Wilson's request to assume the Armenian mandate. The president had been tactless in dealing with the Republican majority in the Senate, which refused to ratify the German peace treaty, including the League of Nations Covenant and its regulations regarding the assumption of mandates. Instead, the United States extended diplomatic recognition to the Armenian republic in April 1920 and received Garegin Pasdermadjian (Armen Garo) as minister plenipotentiary.

Because of the Senate's rejection of the Versailles treaty and because the United States had not actually declared war on the Ottoman Empire, the Department of State gave notice to the Allied Powers that the United States would no longer participate in the Turkish peace settlement. Meanwhile, Turkophile sentiment began to resurface among European colonial and mercantile circles, which warned of the dire economic consequence of a drastic partition of the Ottoman Empire and of the unrest that such a measure would arouse in the Muslim-populated colonies of Great Britain and France. Jealous and suspicious of one another, the Allied governments were also individually torn by sharp internal division and dissension. In January 1920, for example, the Supreme Allied Council granted recognition to the three Transcaucasian republics as a reaction to the defeat of the Russian White Armies and the southward thrust of the Red Army. In that context British Foreign Secretary Lord Curzon won a decision to provide the Armenian army with surplus uniforms, equipment, and weapons, but the British War Office, headed by Winston Churchill, delayed delivery for more than six months in the belief that any matériel given the Armenians and Georgians would end up in Bolshevik or Turkish hands. Ironically, the War Office's calculated delays contributed in no small measure to the fulfillment of its own prophecy.

The European Allies worked on the Turkish settlement in London and at San Remo, Italy, from February through April 1920. The beginning of these meetings coincided with the receipt of alarming reports that the Armenians of Cilicia were being massacred. Following the world war, more than 150,000 Armenians had returned to the cities and villages of Cilicia, which was placed under French supervision. By the beginning of 1920, however, the Turkish Nationalist resistance movement had chosen this region for its first test of strength. The battle for the city of Marash culminated on February 10 with the withdrawal of the French garrison, the crazed Armenian flight into a raging blizzard that claimed thousands of lives, and the massacre or captivity of those

Armenians who were unable to escape. The struggle for Cilicia would continue until 1922, when the Armenians were forced to abandon the Taurus and Amanus mountains and the great alluvial plain of Adana and pass into permanent exile.

The problems in Cilicia reinforced the view of the Allied leaders that the new Armenian state should, in the interest of the Armenians themselves, be awarded territories that could be readily defended and where the Armenians could attain a majority within a few years. Hence, Armenian pretensions to Cilicia and the western half of Turkish Armenia could not be accepted. Rather, the new united Armenian state should extend only into the three easternmost Ottoman provinces of Van, Bitlis, and Erzerum, with an outlet on the Black Sea. The Allies took no action on the many petitions by Armenians and their supporters to include at least the region of Kharpert and even expressed grave misgivings about awarding the city and fortress of Erzerum to Armenia.

In their halfhearted attempts to draw an Armenian boundary without having to commit armed forces to implement their decision, the Allied leaders struck upon a clever way out of the dilemma. At Lloyd George's suggestion they invited President Wilson to draw the final boundaries within the limits of the provinces of Van, Bitlis, Erzerum, and Trebizond. The strategy was intended to coax the United States back into the perplexing Armenian settlement and to shift some of the responsibility for future developments on to the shoulders of the American president. Wilson took the bait and agreed to appoint a commission to draw Armenia's boundaries within the specified limits. Thus, the European Allies were able to announce to the world that they had fulfilled their solemn pledges to the Armenian people.

When the Treaty of Peace with the Ottoman Empire was finally signed at Sèvres on August 10, 1920, the Turkish government committed itself to accept the boundary that President Wilson would lay down within the four provinces. Turkey also recognized Armenia as an independent, sovereign state and accepted the obligation to assist in the repatriation and restoration of the Armenian survivors, in the rescue of Armenian women and children still held in Muslim households, and in the prosecution of the perpetrators of the Armenian genocide. Avetis Aharonian, as the delegate of the Republic of Armenia, was a signatory to the treaty, and both he and Boghos Nubar signed an additional protocol guaranteeing religious, cultural, and other freedoms to Armenia's minorities.

As a signatory to the Treaty of Sèvres, Armenia received formal diplomatic recognition of all other signatory states. Moreover, in the

Western Hemisphere, Argentina, Brazil, and Chile joined the United States in granting recognition. Armenian legations or diplomatic personnel operated in London, Paris, Rome, Brussels, Berlin, Belgrade, Bucharest, Sofia, Athens, and Constantinople; in Tehran, Tabriz, Baghdad, Djibouti, and Addis Ababa; in Tiflis, Baku, Batum, Sukhum, Vladikavkaz, Rostov-on-Don, and other parts of the former Russian Empire; and in Harbin and Yokohama. The assimilated communities of Central and Eastern Europe stirred with renewed consciousness and sent representatives to Erevan to explore the possibility of returning to the homeland after centuries in the dispersion. If Armenia could endure as an independent state, a reversal of the unceasing tides of exodus could bring back hundreds of thousands of partially assimilated Armenians living on five continents.

It was not until November 1920 that President Wilson submitted his decision on the Armenian boundaries. "Wilsonian Armenia" encompassed most of Van, Bitlis, and Erzerum, with exclusion of the southernmost and westernmost sectors for ethnographic, economic, and geographic reasons. The city and port of Trebizond were added to Armenia along with much of the coast of Lazistan to give the republic a broad outlet to the sea. A viable, united Armenian state had been created—on paper. For the Armenians it was both sad and ironic that Wilson's decision was relayed to the Allied governments in Europe at the very time that the Republic of Armenia was waging a losing struggle to preserve its existence.

Soviet-Turkish Relations and Armenia

While the Allied Powers proceeded with plans to partition the Ottoman Empire without facing up to the fact that military enforcement of the terms would be required, Mustafa Kemal (Ataturk) and other Turkish resistance leaders sought Soviet support in the struggle against the common adversaries. Soviet leaders, in their turn, recognized the potential role that Turkish influence could play in stirring the Muslim colonial world against the Western powers and thereby saving the Bolshevik revolution and Soviet state. Preliminary contact had already been made through the deposed Young Turk fugitives who had found haven in Germany, Russia, and the Caucasus. Although Mustafa Kemal regarded the Young Turk clique headed by Enver and Talaat to be his political rivals, he did not hesitate to use their good offices in efforts to draw

Soviet Russia into the Turkish struggle for political survival. Mustafa Kemal and General Kiazim Karabekir, the commander of the 15th Army Corps at Erzerum, also dispatched their own agents to contact the Bolshevik underground in Baku with the goal of forming a land bridge between Russia and Turkey. This was to be achieved by placing Azerbaijan in the Soviet sphere, neutralizing Georgia, and crushing Armenia. In Azerbaijan, the dominant Musavat Party aspired to national independence but was not immune to Turkish pressure and prestige. Several thousand Turkish officers and civilians served in that republic as military cadre, administrators, and police officials. Moreover, Young Turk fugitives such as Halil Pasha and Nuri Pasha were treated as honored guests. They were to play a significant role in the sovietization of Azerbaijan.

In April 1920, immediately after the Turkish Nationalists had organized in Ankara (Angora) a countergovernment to that of the sultan in Constantinople, Mustafa Kemal acknowledged Soviet Russia as the champion of colonial peoples and gave assurances of Turkish support against the imperialist powers. He wrote Foreign Affairs Commissar Grigorii Chicherin that once Russia had gained sway over Georgia and brought about the expulsion of the last remaining British garrison at Batum, the Turkish Nationalists would begin military operations against "the imperialist Armenian government" and exert pressure on Azerbaijan to enter the Soviet state union. To hasten effective collaboration, Soviet Russia should supply arms, food, technical assistance, and financial aid, including an initial shipment of 5 million gold liras (Türk Devrim Tarihi Enstitüsü, 1964, pp. 304-5).

Events were already unfolding swiftly in Transcaucasia. Soviet Russia, having overpowered General A. I. Denikin and his Volunteer Army in the Russian civil war, had reached the flanks of the Caucasus Mountains and now gave orders to capture the rich oil fields of Baku and to sovietize Azerbaijan. The Red Army advanced across the frontier on the night of April 27, and by dawn the first echelons had entered Baku in a near-bloodless coup. Armenian reaction to Azerbaijan's sovietization was not all unfavorable. In fact, many Armenians welcomed the change, reasoning that the Christian minority in eastern Transcaucasia would be safer under any form of Russian rule than under the Musavat regime. Some Armenian officials even believed that the Soviet leaders could be persuaded that a united, independent Armenia would be in the best interest of Russia itself. An Armenian mission departed for Moscow on April 30 to propose a treaty of friendship based on Soviet recognition of the independence of the Armenian republic, inclusive of Karabagh, Zangezur, and Nakhichevan; acceptance in principle of the goal of a united Armenian state; and permission for Armenian refugees in Russia to emigrate with all their movable belongings to the Caucasus.

The three-man delegation of Levon Shant, Hambardzum Terterian, and Levon Zarafian arrived in Moscow on May 20 and soon began discussions with Foreign Affairs Commissar Chicherin and Assistant Commissar Lev Karakhan. The two officials gave assurances that Soviet Russia had no desire to subvert the Armenian government and would assent to the transfer of the refugees to Armenia. The Armenian republic, they agreed, should include the disputed territories of Zangezur and Nakhichevan, while the fate of Karabagh could be decided through arbitration or plebiscite. Armenia, on the other hand, should recognize the need of Soviet Russia and Nationalist Turkey to collaborate against the Western imperialists and should desist from any measure that might hinder communication and cooperation between the two revolutionary movements. Chicherin implied that at least a part of Western Armenia should be included in the Armenian republic and offered Soviet mediation in bringing about an equitable settlement with the Turkish Nationalists. Encouraged by the cordial reception and swift pace of the discussions, the Shant delegation wired the Erevan government on June 10 that agreement in principle had been reached on the major issues and all that remained was the need to work out the details and give substance to the treaty.

The anticipated treaty, however, did not materialize. The delay of a positive response from Erevan may have been attributable to difficulties in communication but possibly also to the Armenian government's concern that the premature announcement of a friendship treaty with Soviet Russia might adversely affect the disposition of the Allied Powers, which had recently determined that the Armenian republic should be awarded much of the Ottoman eastern provinces. But there was more to the Soviet decision to interrupt the negotiations and insist upon their continuation in Erevan. A Turkish Nationalist delegation was en route from Ankara with proposals for a Soviet-Turkish alliance, the new Soviet Azerbaijani government bitterly opposed any modus vivendi that would give Nakhichevan, Zangezur, and possibly even Mountainous Karabagh to Armenia, and Armenian Bolsheviks such as Anastas Mikoyan and Avis Nurijanian had intensified their denunciations of the Erevan government before the party leaders in Moscow. A bloody Dashnakist reign of terror, the Caucasian comrades claimed, had been unleashed against Bolsheviks and their sympathizers who had supported an abortive coup d'état known as the May rebellion. The subject of extensive literature, intense controversy, and significant historical re-evaluation, the May uprising turned the Armenian government toward dictatorial power.

The May Uprising and Bureau Government

The splintering of Transcaucasia into three independent states weakened and undermined the Bolshevik organizations in the region. The nationality question added to the dissension within the ranks, but finally the Baku comrades took the lead in concluding that the best way to break the grip of the dominant anti-Bolshevik parties was to accommodate national sentiment by calling for the creation of Soviet republics federated with Russia. Most veteran Bolsheviks in Georgia and Armenia, having denounced Musavat, Menshevik, and Dashnakist separatism, rejected the proposal as an unorthodox ideological deviation. But in the end even Lenin concurred that revolutionary work in the de facto border states would be facilitated through advocacy of separate Soviet republics and even separate national party organizations joined at the regional level as affiliates of the Russian Communist Party.

In contrast with Azerbaijan, Armenia had no significant proletariat or any of the objective conditions considered necessary for a Marxist revolution. The country was overwhelmingly agrarian and had been so terribly devastated that even veteran Bolsheviks such as Arshavir Melikian argued that, instead of militant revolutionary activity, there should be a long period of peaceful agitation and education of the masses. While the younger Communists repudiated their teachers and demanded the immediate overthrow of the Dashnakist "lackeys of imperialism," Bolshevism did not gain a significant following in Armenia before 1920. In fact, when the Georgian Mensheviks cracked down on their Marxist competitors, the Armenian government granted haven to many Armenian Communists and provided them employment as teachers and civil servants. This influx in 1919, together with the efforts of professional cadre sent by the party's regional committee, produced a loose organizational network, with the auto and rail garages in Alexandropol becoming the most active link. Still, at the end of the year, there were according to Soviet statistics fewer than 500 Bolsheviks in all Armenia. During the first party conference at Erevan in January 1920, the twenty-two participants restructured the Armenia Committee (Armenkom) of the Russian Communist Party and charged it with the responsibility of coordinating preparatory measures for the eventual seizure of power. Resolutions and exhortations aside, most local Bolsheviks continued to believe that success could be achieved only with the supportive intervention of the Red Army. The Armenkom's own behavior between January and May reflected this attitude, in deed if not in word.

The sovietization of Azerbaijan in late April and the approach of the Red Army toward the Armenian frontiers excited and emboldened the Bolsheviks. By that time some elements of the army and citizenry had been radicalized because of the Allied failure to extend measurable political and military support, the inability of the government to meet the basic needs of the populace, the repressive actions of partisan bands, and the general fatigue of many Eastern Armenians and their yearning for a return to normalcy under the accustomed wing of Russia. During the May Day celebrations in Erevan, the Dashnakist-organized meetings were countered by Bolshevik orators and marchers, while in Alexandropol a public rally turned into an angry manifestation of anti-Dashnakist and anti-government sentiment. Securing the neutrality or tacit sympathy of the local army garrison, the Alexandropol Bolsheviks seized the railway station on May 2 and organized the Revolutionary Committee of Armenia (Revkom) there five days later. Then, on May 10, the Revkom declared Armenia a Soviet republic and the "Dashnak government of mauserist and imperialist speculators" liquidated.

Disturbances of lesser proportions and shorter durations also occurred at Sarikamish, Kars, Dilijan, Nor-Bayazit, and several other towns and villages. Yet the conspirators did not act with the requisite resolve and aggressiveness. The Armenkom in Erevan was caught off guard by the Alexandropol rising and failed to respond decisively to the unexpected situation. Even the more militant Revkom assumed a basically defensive stance, not venturing out of its armored-train headquarters or taking advantage of the friendly disposition of the Russian Molokan and Muslim villages around Alexandropol. The inability of either the Armenkom or the Revkom to provide clear direction and to capitalize on the temporary confusion of the government made suppression of the movement inevitable. On the night of May 13/14, loyal troops and Western Armenian partisan units moved into Alexandropol, dispersing the Revkom. Several rebel leaders were executed, and many more fled to Baku. But the Armenian Bolsheviks had received the baptism of fire and offered up a small pantheon of martyrs, memorialized in Soviet literature and monuments.

The May revolt resulted in widespread demoralization within the country and the loss of trust and prestige abroad. The gradualistic, evolutionary policies of Alexandre Khatisian were discredited, and on May 5 his cabinet was replaced by the entire Bureau of the Dashnaktsutiun:

Position	Name
Prime Minister	Hamazasp Ohandjanian
Foreign Affairs	Hamazasp Ohandjanian
Internal Affairs	Ruben Ter-Minasian
Military Affairs	Ruben Ter-Minasian
Financial Affairs	Abraham Giulkhandanian
Judicial Affairs	Abraham Giulkhandanian
Communications	Arshak Djamalian
Agriculture and State Properties	Simon Vratzian
Labor	Simon Vratzian
Education and Culture	Gevorg Ghazarian
Welfare and Reconstruction	Sargis Araratian

The Bureau justified its violation of the restrictions imposed upon it by the party's world congress on grounds that the very existence of the republic was in jeopardy. The loyalty of all non-Bolshevik parties during the uprising and the spirit of unity in the celebrations marking the republic's second anniversary strengthened the Bureau's position. During the summer of 1920, Ohandjanian's Bureau-government drove the Bolsheviks underground or out of the country and turned the regular army and Western Armenian detachments against the constantly defiant Muslim-populated districts from Zangibasar and Vedibasar in the vicinity of Erevan to Sharur and the lower Araxes River Valley. The triumphant sweep to the south, after two years of a policy of containment, vindicated Ruben Ter-Minasian's position in the eyes of many previous skeptics. But if patriotic dictatorship was the answer to Armenia's crises, there was not to be enough time to prove the point.

The strain in Armenian-Soviet relations after the May rebellion contributed to the interruption of the negotiations in Moscow. At the beginning of July, Chicherin informed Shant that Boris V. Legran, an official of the foreign affairs commissariat, was assigned to resume the parleys in Erevan and to do whatever possible to resolve the disputes between Armenia and its neighbors. Legran soon entrained for Baku, accompanied by Halil Pasha, who had been pleading the Turkish Nationalist cause in Moscow and was returning with a large Soviet consignment of gold to be delivered in Anatolia. It was not until early August that Shant's delegation was able to procure transportation to the south and not until mid-September that the Armenian envoys returned tardily to Erevan. Meanwhile, Soviet-Turkish negotiations were being conducted in Moscow.

A Draft Soviet-Turkish Treaty

Mustafa Kemal and other Nationalist leaders were gratified by the Soviet disposition to extend military and financial assistance but were wary of the political ramifications. While Chicherin's messages praised the heroic Turkish struggle for independence and welcomed cooperation against the imperialist powers, they also implied that the fate of areas of mixed Armenian, Kurdish, Laz, and Turkish habitation in the eastern Ottoman provinces should be regulated on the basis of the prewar population and the principle of self-determination, taking into account all those people who had been forced to flee. The Soviet government was prepared to serve as a mediator in attaining a just and equitable boundary settlement between Turkey, Armenia, and Persia. In May a Turkish Nationalist delegation headed by Foreign Affairs Commissar Bekir Sami Bey departed for Moscow to deal with such complications and, more important, to formalize relations and hasten the shipment of desperately needed arms and currency.

During the negotiations, which began shortly after Bekir Sami's arrival on July 19, Chicherin and Karakhan readily offered Soviet military and financial aid and concurred that a land bridge between Russia and Turkey should be created quickly. Karakhan revealed that the Eleventh Red Army was already under orders to occupy the Karabagh-Nakhichevan corridor. The Soviet officials nonetheless urged the Ankara government to resolve the Armenian question, which had roused worldwide concern, by assenting to a frontier rectification that would give the Armenians the districts of Van, Bitlis, and Mush and allow Turkey to occupy the strategic mountain passes near Sarikamish. A mixed commission could determine the exact boundaries and facilitate the work of repatriation and any exchanges of population. Adamantly refusing to make territorial concessions for promises of material assistance, Bekir Sami agreed only to apprize his government of Chicherin's suggestions. He maintained that Soviet aid should be dispatched immediately as a sign of good faith and that a preliminary treaty on nonterritorial issues should be concluded. This position was supported by Stalin, who was unsympathetic toward the Armenian case, and by Lenin, whose main concerns at that time were the difficulties on the Crimean and Polish fronts and the broader question of relations with the West.

Hence, on August 24, two weeks after the sultan's plenipotentiaries in Paris had signed the Treaty of Sèvres, which required Turkey to recognize the independence of Armenia and to cede to it the eastern border provinces, a draft Soviet-Turkish Nationalist accord was initialed in Moscow. All previous treaties between Russia and Turkey were declared null and void, Russia would decline to recognize any international act not ratified by the Ankara government, and both sides were to make every effort to open an unobstructed avenue between the two countries for the flow of men and matériel. Other provisions related to trade and transit, the status of nationals of one country living in the other, and future diplomatic relations. Separate protocols on Soviet military and economic aid were also prepared. Yusuf Kemal (Tengirshenk), a member of the Turkish delegation, carried the treaty, together with the first of a promised 5 million gold rubles, to Trebizond. From that Black Sea port, he wired the terms to Ankara on September 18. In their reports to Mustafa Kemal, Bekir Sami and Yusuf Kemal drew attention to the reserved attitude of Chicherin and Karakhan but added that Lenin was sympathetic and had given the impression that Russia would soon assume a more aggressive role in the Caucasus (Çebesoy, 1955, pp. 61-82). Two days after receiving the terms of the draft treaty, Mustafa Kemal authorized General Karabekir to begin the offensive against Armenia. This was the theater chosen by the Nationalist leaders to impress upon the world their rejection of the Treaty of Sèvres.

The Armeno-Turkish War

The Turkish armies captured the strategic border posts and Sarikamish by the end of September and then advanced in the direction of Kars. According to military specialists, the mighty fortress city could withstand a lengthy siege, but in one of the worst military fiascos in Armenian history, Kars fell amid uncontrollable panic and desertion on October 30, 1920.

The Armenian will to resist had been broken, and by November 6 the Turks had advanced into Alexandropol, forcing Ohandjanian's government to accept a truce based on the Brest-Litovsk boundaries and permitting temporary Turkish occupation of Alexandropol and its environs. Additional Turkish demands on November 8 for the surrender of large quantities of arms and matériel and for control of the entire railway from Alexandropol to Julfa elicited a final desperate defense effort, but within a week Armenia was compelled to submit. Alexandre Khatisian departed for Alexandropol on November 23 to begin negotiations with Karabekir Pasha for an Armeno-Turkish treaty of peace.

Despite the need for a Russo-Turkish alliance, the Soviet government viewed the Turkish offensive with apprehension and tried unsuccessfully to halt the fighting through its good offices. The resulting friction did not obscure the desirability for cooperation with Turkey, however, and preparations to dispatch additional arms and money to Anatolia were not interrupted. Meanwhile, on October 11, Boris Legran and his Soviet mission finally arrived in Erevan to resume negotiations with the Shant delegation. Previously, Legran had been denied entry into Armenia pending Shant's return from Moscow. This had not, however, prevented communication between the two sides, and on August 10 Armenian envoys Arshak Djamalian and Artashes Babalian concluded an accord with Legran in Tiflis. Armenia accepted the provisional Red Army occupation of Zangezur and Nakhichevan, whereas Soviet Russia acknowledged the independence and sovereignty of the Armenian republic and assented to its administration of the railway running from Erevan through Nakhichevan to Julfa. The guidelines for resolving the Armeno-Azerbaijani territorial disputes would be included in the forthcoming treaty to be negotiated in Erevan between Legran and Shant. Ironically, Armenia's acquiescence in the encroachment of the Red Army came on the same day that Avetis Aharonian affixed his signature to the Treaty of Sèvres, creating united, independent Armenia.

Even though Shant returned to Erevan on September 14, Legran did not arrive there until October 11, two weeks after the Turkish offensive had begun. Conditions had changed so drastically that he now called upon the Armenian government to renounce the Sèvres treaty, permit the free movement of men and supplies between Turkey and Soviet Russia and Azerbaijan, and seek Russian mediation in the conflict with Turkey. The Red Army, Legran urged, should be invited to protect the country. Unwilling to turn away from the long-sought European solution to the Armenian question or to condone foreign military occupation, Ohandjanian's cabinet nonetheless did accept the offer of friendly intercession. Moreover, according to terms of a draft treaty concluded by Legran and Shant on October 28, Soviet Russia was to relinquish all sovereign rights over the former Russian Armenian provinces and influence Turkey to bring about the union of a part of Western Armenia with the Armenian republic. The status of Mountainous Karabagh, Zangezur, and Nakhichevan was to be settled by mutual concessions or plebiscite. Russia was to have free transit privileges through Armenia and, if Zangezur and Nakhichevan were awarded to Armenia, was to be granted telegraph, radio, and other facilities to maintain communication with friendly or allied governments. When Legran put the draft treaty before the Communist Party's Caucasian Bureau (Kavburo) in Baku, serious objections and reservations were expressed. Since Kars had now fallen and there was no time for consultations in Moscow, Legran returned to Erevan to demand Armenia's sovietization. Comrade Budu Mdivani accompanied him to serve as the Soviet mediator in the Armenian-Turkish conflict, but General Karabekir summarily rejected the attempted intercession.

Sovietization and Peace

Defeated and discredited, Armenia's Bureau-government gave way on November 23 to a cabinet headed by Simon Vratzian. To that last cabinet fell the heavy obligation to conclude peace and preserve the physical existence of the Armenian people at almost any price. Only the Social Revolutionary Party agreed to enter a coalition government at that grave moment:

Position	Name	Party
Prime Minister, Foreign Affairs, and interim Internal Affairs	Simon Vratzian	Dashnaktsutiun
Military Affairs	Dro (Drastamat Kanayan)	Dashnaktsutiun
Agriculture and State Properties	Arshak Hovhannisian	Dashnaktsutiun
Financial Affairs and interim Welfare	Hambardzum Terterian	Dashnaktsutiun
Judicial Affairs and interim Commercial Affairs	Arsham Khondkarian	Social Revolutionary

Position	Name	Party
Education and Culture	Vahan Minakhorian	Social Revolutionary

For a few days, Vratzian tried to persuade Legran that sovietization would invite greater tragedy, since Armenia would be blockaded by Georgia and deprived of external economic aid at a time when Russia itself was gripped by famine. Renunciation of the Sèvres treaty, moreover, would be tantamount to a sentence of death on the Armenian question, bringing to naught the untold sacrifices in the national movement for emancipation. On November 30 Legran announced that the decision to sovietize Armenia was irreversible. He demanded that Armenia break all bonds with the Western imperialists and unite with the Russian workers and peasants. A few Armenian Bolsheviks had already crossed the frontier on November 29 from Azerbaijan into Karvansarai (Ijevan), where they proclaimed Armenia a Soviet republic and appealed for the intervention of the Red Army.

In these circumstances, Vratzian's government bowed to the inevitable and appointed Dro and Hambardzum Terterian to arrange for the transfer of power. The treaty signed by Legran and the Armenian representatives on December 2 gave some ground for hope. Armenia became an independent Soviet Socialist Republic, and Soviet Russia acknowledged as indisputable parts of that state all lands that had been under the jurisdiction of the Armenian government prior to the Turkish invasion, Zangezur included. Russia was to take immediate steps to furnish the requisite military force to consolidate and defend the republic. Neither the army command nor members of the Dashnaktsutiun and other socialist parties were to be persecuted for their previous activities. Power would pass temporarily to a military revolutionary committee composed of five members appointed by the Communist Party and two left-wing Dashnakist members, selected with the approval of the Communist Party. Until that body was organized, the government would be entrusted to Dro, the military commander, and to Otto A. Silin, the plenipotentiary of Soviet Russia. For the government of independent Armenia, all that remained was to issue its final decree: "In view of the general situation in the land created by external circumstances, the Government of the Republic of Armenia, in its session of December 2, 1920, decided to resign from office and to relinquish all military and political authority to Dro, the commander in chief, now appointed as minister of war" (Baldwin, 1926, p. 32).

The announcement of Armenia's sovietization did not remove the Turkish menace, since Karabekir threatened to resume the offensive unless his government's peace terms were accepted forthwith. Those terms obliged Armenia to renounce the Treaty of Sèvres and all claims to Turkish Armenia and the province of Kars, to accept temporary Turkish jurisdiction in Sharur-Nakhichevan, to recall all representatives from Europe until the Ankara government had settled its differences with those adversary states, and to reduce the size of the Armenian army to 1,500 men. In case of need, Turkey would extend military assistance to the remaining small Armenian state. Only after all these terms had been fulfilled would the Turkish army withdraw from the Alexandropol region and establish the Arpachai River as the new international frontier. Even though his government had officially relinquished power, Khatisian signed the Treaty of Alexandropol (Gümrü) shortly after midnight on December 3. Denounced and branded a traitor by Soviet and other non-Dashnakist authors, Khatisian justified his action as an exigency measure taken with the knowledge of the new Erevan government and intended to give time for the Red Army to enter Armenia in sufficient numbers to block a further Turkish advance. Realizing that he had no legal jurisdiction, Khatisian hoped that the new Soviet government, with the support of Russia, would repudiate his action and force the Turks to withdraw at least to the prewar boundaries. As it turned out, these calculations proved ill-founded. The efforts of the Soviet Armenian government to recover a part of the lost territories were supported only with mild diplomatic notes by Soviet Russia, which proceeded toward normalization of relations with the Ankara government.

The Aftermath

The Military Revolutionary Committee of Armenia arrived in Erevan on December 4, followed two days later by the first echelons of the Red Army. The Revkom, dominated by young, vindictive Bolsheviks, immediately repudiated the treaty negotiated between Legran and the former Armenian government on December 2 and initiated an aggressive course of War Communism. Hundreds of former government officials and non-Bolshevik political leaders were imprisoned, the army officer corps was exiled, and a harsh regime of retribution and requisition was imposed. These oppressive policies, coupled with the trenchant anti-Russian and anti-Bolshevik sentiment of the Western Armenian refugee population and the collusion of some Dashnakist partisan leaders, produced a surge of rebellion in February 1921. The Revkom was driven out of Erevan and a Salvation Committee was swiftly organized under Simon Vratzian's presidency to coordinate the movement sweeping the countryside.

Not until Georgia had been sovietized in March were sufficient Red Army reinforcements brought in to suppress the revolt. In April the Salvation Committee and thousands of insurgents and civilians withdrew into Zangezur, where the battle was continued under the command of Garegin Nzhdeh until a reorganized Soviet Armenian government issued an amnesty and gave assurances that Zangezur would become a part of Soviet Armenia. Lenin had already chided his Caucasian comrades for their overzealousness and advised that conditions in the local republics necessitated a "slower, more careful, and more systematic transition to socialism" (Eudin and North, 1957, p. 55). Alexandr Miasnikian, a trusted veteran party professional, was transferred from the European theater to head the Armenian government. In July 1921, as Miasnikian began to implement the more cautious measures of the New Economic Policy, thousands of anti-Bolshevik rebels and bewildered civilians crossed the Araxes River into Persia to begin the bitter life reserved for expatriates and exiles.

On the international front, Soviet Russia sacrificed the Armenian question to cement the Turkish alliance. Having rejected all attempts at mediation, Mustafa Kemal even made a ploy to occupy Batum and the border districts of Akhaltsikh and Akhalkalak in Georgia. The maneuver, apparently intended to win additional concessions regarding Armenia, bore results. By the Treaty of Moscow (March 1921), which established normal relations and friendship between Soviet Russia and the Ankara government, Turkey dropped its claims to Batum and the other districts in return for Russian abandonment of efforts to redeem for Soviet Armenia the Surmalu district of Erevan. In that sector, the new Turkish boundary was extended to the Araxes River, thus incorporating the fertile Igdir plain and Mount Ararat. What was more, the treaty provided that Sharur-Nakhichevan would not be attached to Soviet Armenia but would instead be constituted as an autonomous region under Soviet Azerbaijan, even though it was separated from eastern Transcaucasia by intervening Armenian territory. Whatever qualms Chicherin and Karakhan might still have had were sublimated to the decisive support the Turkish delegation received from Stalin. As stipulated by the Treaty of Moscow, almost identical terms were included in the Treaty of Kars (October 1921) between Turkey and the three Transcaucasian Soviet republics. Described by a Soviet historian later purged by Stalin as one of the most oppressive and ignominious treaties in the annals of history, that document clamped the lid on the Armenian question and locked Soviet Armenia within its limited, landlocked territory (Borian, 1929, pp. 163, 300). The European Powers put their own seal on the Armenian question two years later by renegotiating the Treaty of Sèvres. The Turkish victory in the resultant Lausanne treaties was so thorough that neither the word "Armenia" nor "Armenian" was allowed to appear anywhere in the texts. It was bitterly ironic for the Armenians that, of the several defeated Central Powers in the World War, Turkey alone expanded beyond its prewar boundaries and this, only on the Armenian front.

The interlude of Armenian independence had ended. Born of desperation and hopelessness, the Armenian republic lacked the resources to solve its awesome domestic and international problems. Yet within a few months it had become the fulcrum of national aspirations for revival, unification, and perpetuity. Limitations and shortcomings aside, the rudiments of government were created and organic development did occur. The failure to achieve permanent independence left a worldwide Armenian dispersion with unrequited grief, frustration, and resentment. Nonetheless, the legacy of the Armenian republic was not lost. Armenian government and statehood had been recovered for the first time in centuries. The staggering Armenian sacrifices had not been entirely in vain, for the core of the Republic of Armenia continued as the Armenian Soviet Socialist Republic, where a part of the nation would strive to etch a place in the sun.

FOR FURTHER INFORMATION

For the sources of, or more information on, the material in this chapter, please consult the following (full citations can be found in the Bibliography at the end of this volume).

Aftandilian, 1981.   Kazemzadeh, 1951.
Barton, 1930.   Kerr, 1973.
Bedoukian, 1978.   Khatisian, 1930.
Egan, 1919.   Nassibian, 1984.
Elliot, 1924.   Pipes, 1964.
Gidney, 1967.   Swietochowski, 1985.
Hovannisian, 1971-1996.

11

SOVIET ARMENIA

Ronald Grigor Suny

The short-lived experiment in Armenian independence collapsed late in 1920 as the isolated republic came between the dual threats of advancing Soviet power and the Turkish Nationalists in Anatolia. With Western Armenia in the hands of the triumphant Kemalists, only Eastern Armenia, that small portion of historic Armenia that had been under Persian rule until 1828 and then part of the Russian Empire until 1917, remained under the control of Armenians at the end of the Russian civil war (1918-1921). When General Dro (Drastamat Kanayan), the plenipotentiary of the Dashnakist government of Armenia, and Silin, the representative of Soviet Russia, proclaimed Armenia an "independent socialist republic" on December 2, 1920, the country was at the nadir of its modern history. Armenians had been driven out of the Turkish-held parts of the Armenian plateau in the genocidal massacres and deportations of 1915. The population of Russian Armenia had also fallen precipitously since the outbreak of World War I because of warfare, migration, and disease. By 1920 only 720,000 lived in Eastern Armenia, a decline of 30 percent. Moreover, almost half of that population was made up of refugees. Many of the social and political institutions that Armenians in the Caucasus and in Turkey had built up over centuries had been destroyed. The Armenian middle class, the once-privileged elite of Tiflis and Baku, was now suspect in the eyes of the new Soviet governments in Georgia and Azerbaijan. Their unenviable choice was either to accommodate themselves to the alien socialist order or to emigrate to the West. In the seven years of war, genocide, revolution, and civil war (1914-1921), Armenian society had in many ways been "demodernized," thrown back to its precapitalist agrarian economy and more traditional peasant-based society.

The first tasks of the new Soviet government in Erevan were to rebuild the economy, feed the "starving Armenians," and establish their new political order. The Dashnakists and Communists had agreed that all power was to be handed over to a Revolutionary Committee (Heghkom) made up of five Communists and two Dashnakists, the latter to be approved by the former. No repressive measures were to be carried out against the Dashnaks or other non-Communists. It was generally understood that the Dashnaktsutiun remained the most popular party among the Armenians and that the Communists had very little support in the country, except for a few hundred radical intellectuals and workers. The population was weary of war, hungry, sick, and politically apathetic. There was no resistance to the entry of the Red Army into Erevan. Rather than protest, silence greeted the new government. The "revolution" that brought the Communists to power had been allowed to happen in order to prevent Eastern Armenia from being overrun by the Turks, and Armenians hoped that the Red Army would drive the Turks from Alexandropol and other parts of occupied Armenia.

The first Soviet government, headed by Sarkis Kasian (1876-1937), was made up of very young and militant Communists, such as Askanaz Mravian, Avis Nurijanian, Ashot Hovhannisian, and Alexandr Bekzadian. Marked by years of underground work, these young Communists were deeply hostile to the Dashnaks, who, after all, had suppressed the revolts by Armenian Bolsheviks and executed some of their comrades. Completely inexperienced as administrators, insensitive to the weariness and desperation of the people they now governed, the Heghkom moved quickly to impose its authority. A secret police organization modeled on the Russian Cheka was set up within days, and all governmental institutions of the old republic were abolished. Disregarding the agreement creating a coalition government, the Communists arrested many Dashnaks. The old Russian imperial law code, which had been used in the independent republic, was replaced by the legal statutes of the Soviet Russian republic. And most onerous of all, the economic policy, later known as War Communism—nationalization of banks and industries, confiscation of foodstuffs, severe restrictions on the market—was imposed on Armenia.

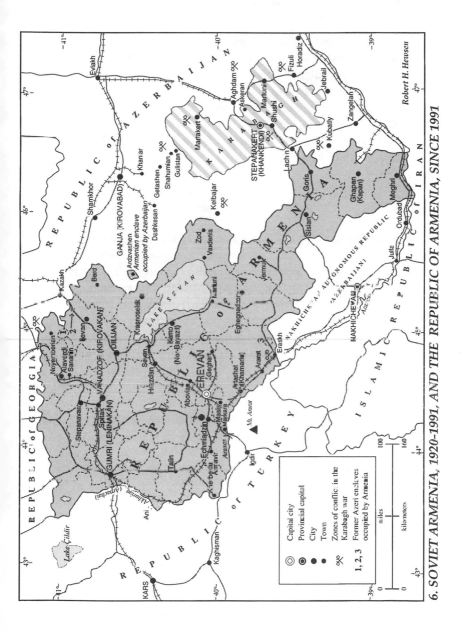

6. *SOVIET ARMENIA, 1920-1991, AND THE REPUBLIC OF ARMENIA, SINCE 1991*

The harshness of the Communists' initial policies created great dissatisfaction with the Soviet government. Red Army men moved into villages and seized grain from the peasants to feed soldiers and townspeople, but the new government proved unable to alleviate the shortages of food and fuel, caused in part by the Menshevik Georgian blockade of Armenia. The hope that the Red Army would drive out the Turks proved illusory. Bolshevik Russia viewed the Turkish Nationalists as allies against Western imperialism and was reluctant to challenge them in Armenia.

An early Soviet historian, Bagrat Borian, wrote candidly about the economic terror of the first Soviet Armenian government:

> The Revolutionary Committee started a series of indiscriminate seizures and confiscations, without regard to class, and without taking into account the general economic and psychological state of the peasantry. Devoid of revolutionary planning, and executed with needless brutality, these confiscations were unorganized and promiscuous. Unattended by disciplinary machinery, without preliminary propaganda or enlightenment, and with utter disregard of the country's unusually distressing condition, the Revolutionary Committee issued its orders nationalizing food supply of the cities and the peasantry. With amazing recklessness and unconcern, they seized and nationalized everything—military uniforms, artisans tools, rice mills, water mills, barbers' implements, beehives, linen, household furniture, and livestock. (Borian, 1929)

In January 1921, the Communists rounded up and exiled 560 Armenian army officers, including General Tovmas Nazarbekian (Foma Nazarbekov) and General Movses Silikian. General Dro was "invited" to go to Moscow. The next month Hovhannes Kachaznuni, the former prime minister of independent Armenia who had stayed behind in Erevan, was arrested and placed in a Cheka prison. But he remained there only eight days. When the Red Army marched out of Armenia to overthrow the Mensheviks in Georgia in February 1921, Dashnak leaders saw their opportunity to rid themselves of the hated Communist regime. The initial Dashnakist resistance to Soviet rule was outside the capital, in Zangezur, and in the contested mountainous region of Karabagh, led by the Bulgarian Armenian colonel Garegin Nzhdeh. On the morning of February 18, Dashnak insurgents entered Erevan, driving the Communists before them. The Bolsheviks made their last stand at the railroad station, and at noon an armored train carried them from the city toward Nakhichean in defeat. The Red Army, busy sovietizing Georgia, was unable to come to their rescue. The new government was headed by Simon Vratzian, who appealed to the West to aid the new Armenia. Armenians fought Armenians for the next few months, with Russian troops shelling Erevan. When the Cheka prisons were opened, a scene of horror greeted the liberators. Seventy-five bodies were discovered, hacked by axes. Among the dead were the Dashnakist heroes, Hamazasp (Srvandztian) and Colonel Dmitrii Korganov, shot February 1, 1921. The Dashnaks responded by arresting Bolsheviks, some of whom were subsequently killed. Having subdued Georgia, the Red Army returned to Armenia, overcoming the resistance of the Dashnakist forces. The Soviet troops entered Erevan on April 2. The Dashnaks and thousands of civilians fled into the mountains of Zangezur where they held out until July.

The rebellion had a sobering effect on the Communists. Moscow replaced the militant Heghkom with a new government headed by Alexandr Miasnikian (1886-1925), a man trained in the law but with a long period of service fighting on the Western front during the Russian civil war. He was commissioned by Lenin, the chairman of the Soviet government in Moscow, to carry out a more moderate policy toward the Caucasus. In an often-reproduced letter to his Caucasian comrades, Lenin pointed out that the Soviet republics in Transcaucasia were more backward, "more peasant than Russia," and that socialist policies had to be implemented very slowly. He called on the party to exercise "greater gentleness, caution, concessions in dealing with the petty bourgeoisie, the intelligentsia, and especially the peasantry." Lenin was suspicious that many Communists were not sensitive to local and ethnic peculiarities, that their "internationalism" and calls for unity with Soviet Russia were really disguised forms of Russian nationalism. "Scratch a Communist," he once said, "and you will find a Great Russian chauvinist!" A degree of autonomy for the smaller nationalities was necessary, he believed, in order to win them over to the Soviet cause.

The second Soviet Armenian government came to Erevan far more willing to compromise the more extreme goals that had marked the period of the civil war. By now Russia had adopted the moderate economic policy known as the New Economic Policy (NEP), which denationalized much of the economy and gave the peasants the right to control their own grain surpluses. Lenin called this new policy a tactical retreat to "state capitalism." Rather than fully nationalizing the economy and eliminating the market, NEP decreed that only the "commanding heights" of the economy, large-scale enterprises, railroads, and banks, were to be nationalized. Much smaller scale production was to remain in private hands. Most important, the grain requisitioning by the state was ended, and peasants were left free to run their own farms after paying a set tax to the government. The years of NEP, roughly 1921 to 1928, were a period of relative economic "liberalism," and the Armenian republic gradually recovered from the war and the revolution under the limited market system of NEP. In early 1920 about 90 percent of Armenians lived on the land, and the government's first priority was to restore agriculture. Canals, such as that in Shirak, were built; desert areas, notably the Sardarabad desert, were irrigated; and hydroelectric plants were constructed to bring electricity to the farms. Peasant life improved steadily. By 1926 agricultural production had reached 71.5 percent of its prewar level. And as a result of improving conditions and economic outlook, a certain degree of reconciliation was achieved between the state and the peasant population.

In the towns and cities of Armenia, progress was slow but steady. Even at the end of the 1920s, only about 20 percent of Armenians in Armenia lived in towns. Erevan, which had had a population of about 30,000 in 1913, reached nearly 65,000 in 1926. But many were refugees from Turkey and other parts of the Middle East, and nearly one-half of urban workers were out of work. Industry barely recovered its prewar level by 1928, and it remained basically small scale, little mechanized, and based on artisanal labor. Less than 13 percent of Armenia's population could be considered "proletarian," even by the most generous definition of that term. In 1928 there were only 6,000 factory workers and 8,000 artisans in Armenia. The Communist Party, which in its own self-image was the vanguard of the urban working class, was in fact an isolated elite governing an overwhelmingly peasant population. Instead of building a socialism based on a preexisting capitalist industrial system, as had been envisioned by their founding theorist, Karl Marx, the Soviet Communists were faced with the daunting prospect of creating an industrial economy from the limited resources of an impoverished agrarian society.

Given the weakness of Soviet Armenia—the dismal economic situation, the fragility of popular backing for the regime, and the fact that more Armenians lived outside Armenia, in Georgia and Azerbaijan, than in Armenia itself—the Communists of Armenia were desperately interested in closer ties with the Georgian, Azerbaijani, and Russian Soviet republics. On September 30, 1921, Armenia signed a treaty of alliance with the Russian Soviet Federated Socialist Republic (RSFSR) that established financial cooperation. A few months later Armenian delegates attended the All-Russian Congress of Soviets in Moscow, demonstrating their close links with the RSFSR. While the Georgians, who were economically better off than the Armenians, hesitated to create economic ties with other republics, Armenia pushed for the establishment of a Transcaucasian economic union. Miasnikian supported the efforts of Sergo Ordjonikidze, the leading Communist in Transcaucasia, and his mentor, Joseph Stalin, to integrate the three republics in Transcaucasia into a single republic. On April 14, 1921, all railroads in Transcaucasia were put under one authority. Two weeks later foreign trade was placed under a single agency, the Obvneshtorg. In May and June custom barriers and border guards were removed between the republics and between Transcaucasia and the RSFSR. Work began on the touchy matter of delineating the frontiers of the republics and determining the fate of areas such as Akhalkalak, Lori, Karabagh, and Nakhichevan, which were desired by several republics. The negotiations continued into 1923, and though Armenia received Lori, it lost two areas that historically had been part of the Armenian states—Karabagh and Nakhichevan. Both were awarded to the Azerbaijani republic, which was economically stronger than Armenia. Nakhichevan had a largely Muslim population, but Karabagh was overwhelmingly Armenian. Armenian Communists protested the decision of July 5, 1921, that placed Karabagh in Azerbaijan, but at the time they were more concerned about unity with the other Transcaucasian peoples and economic recovery than state sovereignty over historically Armenian territories.

Through 1921 and 1922 the progressive whittling away of the prerogatives of the individual republics and the consolidation of Transcaucasia into a single unit continued. In November 1921 the party organizations in Armenia and Azerbaijan approved a proposal calling for the political unification of Transcaucasia. Ordjonikidze was able to get the Georgia party congress to approve the measure, against the advice of the Georgian Central Committee. On March 12, 1922, representatives from Armenia, Azerbaijan, and Georgia signed the treaty forming the Federal Union of Soviet Socialist Republics of Transcaucasia (FSSSRZ). This rather loose arrangement was a compromise between the centralizers who wanted closer ties between the republics and the RSFSR, and the Georgians, who favored greater autonomy for the republics. But the centralizers were not satisfied with this arrangement, and in September 1922 Stalin introduced a plan to bring all the national republics—Armenia, Azerbaijan, Belorussia, Georgia, and Ukraine—into the RSFSR as autonomous republics. This would have effectively ended their independence and made them completely subordinate to the leadership in Moscow. Lenin opposed this centralizing effort, and though he was mortally ill, he was able to stop Stalin's design. Instead of merging into the RSFSR, the five national republics and the RSFSR entered a new political federation— the Union of Soviet Socialist Republics, which came into existence formally in December 1922. At the same time the FSSSRZ was dissolved, and a slightly more centralized federation, the Transcaucasian Federated Soviet Socialist Republic (ZSFSR), was created. On December 30, the ZSFSR entered the USSR. The Soviet republic of Armenia, thus, was a member of the Transcaucasian Federation, which in turn was part of the Union of Soviet Socialist Republics.

Essentially Soviet Armenia existed within a pseudofederal system in which the final decision-making power lay outside the republic. The all-important matter of who should decide the budget was resolved in favor of the center, and Armenia's budget became part of the budget of the ZSFSR, which was part of the budget of the whole USSR. The ruling party of Armenia was not a separate and independent Communist party but a constituent part of the All-Russian Communist Party (RKP[b]), a local branch of a highly centralized political organization directed by a small group of men in Moscow.

Through the early 1920s, Armenia's political structure came to resemble that of the RSFSR. In January 1922 the First Congress of Soviets of Armenia adopted a constitution modeled on that of the RSFSR. Everywhere the emphasis was on standardization and uniformity in the interest of building a strong, unified country. The leaders of Soviet Armenia did not resist centralization, as did the Georgians up to 1923, but worked together with Stalin and the centralizers, who ultimately had their way. Lenin, too ill to fight any longer, died in January 1924. His brainchild, the Soviet Union, survived, but his conception of it as a union of relatively autonomous republics was buried along with him.

Within Armenia a monopoly of power was assured the Communist Party. All other political organizations were eventually eliminated. Under pressure from the dominant political movement, the Dashnaktsutiun in Erevan formally abolished its local organization in November

1923. Within a few years of the establishment of Soviet power, Armenia had ceased in any real sense to be a sovereign state, though officially in Soviet law it was so designated. Within the republic, as throughout the Soviet Union, representative government had ceased to have any reality. A one-party state ruled by men with loyalty to the central Communist leadership in Moscow had been established in Armenia. As the Russian Politburo fell year by year under the influence of one man, Joseph Stalin, so in Armenia those Communists who could prove their loyalty to Stalin came to power and those who could not were removed. The Communist Party of Armenia—headed by Ashot Hovhannisian from 1922 to 1927, Haik Hovsepian in 1927, and Haikaz Kostanian from 1928 to 1930—refused to tolerate non-Communist intellectuals in positions of influence. In 1927 the independent Marxist ("Spetsifist"), Davit Ananun, a brilliant social critic and political analyst, was thrown out of his job as part of a campaign against "counterrevolutionary nationalists." Other former Dashnaks and Mensheviks were also purged from institutes and party cells. One hundred twenty members of the Trotskyist opposition were arrested in April 1927, and in the turmoil of these purges, First Secretary Hovhannisian was dismissed for underestimating the dangers of deviant Marxists. These purges, part of the Stalinist consolidation of power, ended the period of relative intellectual tolerance in Armenian and Soviet political circles.

Making Armenia Armenian

While politically Soviet Armenia was a dictatorship of one party, in the 1920s it was mixed economically, with state enterprises coexisting with private businesses and independent peasant agriculture. Socially and culturally the country was also relatively pluralistic, with Marxist artists and scholars coexisting with the old prerevolutionary intelligentsia in an uneasy arrangement. The Communists made an effort to realize certain national aspirations of the Armenians, particularly in the cultural sphere. The policy of *korenizatsiia* (rooting) or "nativization," first outlined in a resolution of the Tenth Party Congress (March 1921), was directed at encouraging members of local nationalities to run their own republics. Local administration, economic organs, scholars, theaters, newspapers, and other institutions were to operate in the native language of the region. Cadres of the local nationality were to administer each republic, and the national language and national culture were to be nourished by state support. Communists were warned to avoid all colonial aspects of imperial Russian rule, to work to eliminate social and ethnic inequalities between the center and the peripheries. These lofty intentions were proclaimed by the Communist Party, and though in practice such ideals were seldom completely realized, the aims of the leadership attracted many members of the minority nationalities.

As a result of *korenizatsiia,* Armenia became more Armenian in the 1920s. A social and cultural "renationalization" took place in the tiny republic. Thousands of displaced Armenians migrated to Armenia. Refugees from the genocide, victims of war and the upheavals of the Russian revolution, moved into Erevan and the surrounding areas. Armenians who had lost their privileged position in Georgia and Azerbaijan because of the nativization of those republics traveled to Armenia to find new opportunities. Armenians from Greece, the Middle East, and France joined in Armenia the migrant intellectuals and dispossessed bourgeois from Tiflis, Baku, and Moscow. Poor peasants came in from the countryside and settled in the towns, looking for work. A new urban population made up of very disparate elements was formed. Speaking different dialects, bringing in varied customs, foods, and experiences, these migrants melded together to make up the first generation of the new Soviet Armenian nation.

While integrating the new immigrants into Armenian society, the republic also engaged in a program of "cultural revolution," making Armenian the language of state administration, education, art, and science. In September 1921 the Council of People's Commissars of Armenia issued a decree that required all illiterate and semiliterate citizens from sixteen to fifty to study the Armenian language. Circles were set up throughout the republic to teach reading and writing. By 1940 the Armenian government could announce that full literacy of the adult population had been achieved. At the same time a new school system was set up to teach children. In 1924-1925 a network of seven-year village schools was created for the peasant population. Workers could attend special schools established for those active in production. Teachers' colleges were opened, and in 1926 Erevan State University graduated its first thirty-seven students. Almost all instruction was in Armenian.

For the first time since the Middle Ages, Armenian became a language of science. In 1921 an institute for cultural and historical studies was opened in Echmiadzin, and four years later the Institute of Science and Art (later the Academy of Sciences) was formed in Erevan. Historians such as Leo (Arakel Babakhanian) and Hakob Manandian, scholars of language such as Hrachia Ajarian and Manuk Abeghian published their work under state sponsorship—with all the advantages and disadvantages such an arrangement implies. A new literary language, based on the Erevan dialect was developed, along with a new orthography. Established artists such as Martiros Saryan, writers Alexandr Shirvanzade, Avetik Isahakian, and Eghishe Charents, and musicians such as Alexandr Spendiarov, pursued their art under the auspices of official support from an Armenian government. A state dramatic theater was founded in Erevan in January 1922. The following year the government established a conservatory of music. So poor was the country that Armenian supporters of the Soviet republic living abroad sent money and musical instruments to keep the conservatory operating. In 1925 the actor-director Hamo Bek-Nazarov directed the first fiction film from the Armenian film studio, *Armenkino*. Based on the novel *Namus* (Honor) by Shirvanzade, the film portrayed pre-revolutionary provincial life with its barbarous traditions that destroy two young lovers. In 1935 Bek-Nazarov made the first sound film from Armenia, *Pepo,* adapted from the nineteenth-century play by Gabriel Sundukian. From the point of view of Armenian artists, the 1920s was a period of rebirth, experimentation, and new creativity.

At the same time, however, the Soviet state had its own agenda. Though it tolerated artists and intellectuals who were not fully committed to the building of a socialist society, it also imposed strict restrictions on their expression. Nationalism was officially condemned, though much of what intellectuals produced could have been construed as nationalistic. No overtly antisocialist or anti-Soviet writing or painting or teaching was permitted. Religion was allowed, but antireligious propaganda was encouraged and supported by the state.

As the Soviet government attempted to reshape Armenia, making it both more Armenian and socialist, it met considerable resistance from the most ancient of Armenian institutions, the national church. The Catholicos of All Armenians, Gevorg V (1911-1930), refused to recognize the atheist regime at first. Antireligious zealots closed churches and insulted clergymen. Sevana Vank, the medieval monastery on Lake Sevan, was turned into a rest area for artists. Education was taken out of the hands of priests, and religious instruction was restricted to the homes. In 1922 the government set up a Free Church made up of Soviet sympathizers to rival the Armenian Apostolic Church. Since the mass of the peasants was still religious, the antireligious campaign struck at the heart of the worldview of the majority of Armenians.

Only in the mid-1920s was an uneasy reconciliation achieved between church and state. By order of Deputy Foreign Affairs Commissar Lev Karakhan, an Armenian, the medieval manuscripts that had been taken from Echmiadzin to Moscow earlier in the decade were returned to Armenia and placed in a new repository, the Matenadaran. In 1927 the catholicos acknowledged the Soviet government as the lawful authority in Armenia. But periodic anticlerical campaigns by the party continued to plague church-state relations. At the very end of the decade, militant atheists again closed churches in certain villages, despite the admonitions of moderate Communists such as Sahak Ter-Gabrielian, who warned that emancipation from the influences of religion could not be forced but would come only through education. By this time, however, the NEP was coming to an end, and the state was about to engage in a concerted assault on the whole peasant way of life.

Stalin's Revolution

As impressive as the successes of the New Economic Policy had been up to the last years of the 1920s, party leaders could not avoid the conclusion that the Soviet Union was not growing fast enough economically. While peasant agriculture was thriving, investment in new industry was simply inadequate to produce the quantities of industrial goods needed to trade with the peasants for their surplus grain. By the end of 1927 the amount of grain collected from the peasantry was steadily declining. Low agricultural prices and the shortage of industrial goods convinced peasants to hold on to their produce until the terms of trade with the towns improved for them. When food shortages were felt in the cities, the party leaders decided to take "extraordinary measures," forcing the peasants to give up their grain. Stalin, who by 1928 was the most powerful party leader in the Soviet Union, became convinced that only a tough line toward the peasantry could save the regime. His opponents gathered around his former ally, Nikolai Bukharin, and argued in favor of a continuation of the moderate NEP. They were defeated, however, in the fall of 1928 and systematically excluded from key decision-making positions. The road was now clear for the launching of an ambitious assault on the countryside and an all-out effort to industrialize the country. On Stalin's urging the Sixteenth Party Conference (April 1929) adopted the most radical version of the First Five-Year Plan.

Communists throughout the Soviet Union were dedicated to the idea that their country would someday have to overcome its peasant backwardness and become an industrial giant able to defend itself from external enemies. But within the party many Old Bolsheviks considered Stalin's "general line" of very rapid industrialization and collectivization of agriculture to be destructive of the peasant-worker "alliance" that had been painstakingly built up in the 1920s. Many leaders in Transcaucasia tried to convince Moscow to exempt their region from the harsh policy toward the peasantry. After all, Transcaucasia had always been an importer of foodstuffs, not self-sufficient, and was certainly unable to produce agricultural surpluses in grain for export. But the central leaders rejected such an argument, and in November 1929 Moscow dismissed the Georgian First Secretary of the Transcaucasian Party Committee, Mamia Orakhelashvili, and replaced him with an outsider, Alexandr Krinitskii, a man who did not know the local scene. The radical policies of Stalin were then systematically applied to Armenia, Azerbaijan, and Georgia. Not only were peasants forced to join collective farms and give up their grain to state collection agencies, but they were subjected to another antireligious campaign. Churches were closed; icons broken; and the heavy veils torn off devout Muslim women.

In late 1929 and early 1930 workers and students were sent from the cities into villages to force peasants to form collective farms (kolmtesutiunner in Armenian, kolkhozy in Russian). Where the workers failed or were resisted, police and soldiers intervened. Those better-off peasants, considered kulaki ("fists" in Russian), were thrown off their land and exiled either to inferior lands or to Siberia. Peasants resisted by killing off their livestock rather than surrendering them to the collectives. From 1928 to 1933 Armenia lost 300,000 head of cattle and over 500,000 sheep and goats. In some places armed bands were formed to fight off the intruders, but resistance proved futile. On paper at least it seemed as if peasant households were being collectivized. Whereas in December 1929 only 3.9 percent of Armenian peasant households were in the collective farms, by early February 1930 that figure had risen to 65.6 percent. Obviously this process has not been voluntary. Rather, physical threats and actual violence had compelled peasants to join the collective farms.

Suddenly, on March 2, 1930, just as peasant resistance throughout the Soviet Union was spreading, Stalin himself intervened in the rural revolution. He published an article, "Dizziness from Success," in which he condemned local authorities for forcing peasants into the collectives. By this move he brought the pell-mell collectivization to a temporary halt and shifted the blame for the excesses in the countryside from the top leaders onto local officials. Immediately peasants began leaving the unpopular collectives. By April 1, 1930, only 25 percent of peasant households were still in the collectives in Armenia, and by August the number had dropped to under 10 percent. The Armenian Communist Party was forced to admit that it had acted too precipitously in pushing peasants toward socialist agriculture and in the process had allowed "*kulak* and Dashnak elements" to turn the anticollectivization movement into an anti-Soviet campaign. Only gradually, in the fall of 1930, was the collectivization drive renewed, this time at a more moderate pace. Nevertheless, resistance flared up in several districts. In Daralagiaz the party organization itself came out against collectivization and sided with the peasants. Such rebellion was not tolerated, and in 1932 Russian troops were brought in to crush the resistance. By the end of that year about 38 percent of peasant households in Armenia were collectivized. By the end of the decade almost all Armenian peasants were working in either collective or state farms.

Collectivization was a profoundly revolutionary change for the majority of the Armenian population. Once and for all, it ended independent private farming. Peasants lost control over their own household economy and became producers for the state procurement agencies. The Communist Party increased its political hold over the peasants and created the instruments with which it could extract by force and heavy taxation the grain needed for cities and workers. Village headmen *(tanuter),* who had been the traditional leaders of rural society, were now treated as *kulaki* and exiled from their homes. Peasants became a second-class social group in Soviet society—not included in the social security system, underpaid for their produce and labor, and regarded as a backward element. After 1932 when internal passports were issued for urban dwellers in the USSR, peasants were not given the precious documents and therefore could not freely leave the collectives. Yet they thwarted the law, and thousands of villagers left the countryside and migrated to the towns where they made up the greater part of the expanding industrial labor force. Those who remained in the villages suffered enormously, though eventually the state allowed them the right to cultivate small household plots and to sell some of their output on collective farm markets.

Collectivization can be seen as a war by the state against the peasantry, and its effects reached far beyond agriculture. As a result of the mass migrations from the countryside, collectivization aided in the creation of a new working class. But more ominously, the vast increase of party power and the expanded use of violence against the most numerous class in the population created an atmosphere in which police rule became the norm in Soviet life. What had been used against the peasantry would soon be turned against the better-off people in society, particularly members of the Communist Party.

The 1930s was also a time of enthusiasm for the project of building socialism in one country, and Soviet propaganda effectively portrayed the USSR as the alternative to a worldwide capitalism suffering in the Great Depression and as the major bulwark against a growing fascist threat. As a result of the "Stalin Revolution" of the 1930s, Armenia became more industrial, more "proletarian." The number of workers in Armenia grew by 2.5 times in the 1930s, until they made up 31.2 percent of Armenia's population in 1939. By 1935 industry accounted for 62 percent of economic production. The years of industrialization were a time of upward social mobility. Peasants became workers; many workers became foremen or managers; managers became party and state officials. But this new industrial society, in which quantities of output were emphasized at the expense of quality of product or safety of workers, did not empower workers. Rather, Soviet-style "socialism" created a society in which the workers were politically powerless, trade unions were agencies of the state, and factory managers acting as "little Stalins" dominated the process of production.

The "Stalin Revolution" of the 1930s ended market relations in the Soviet Union—except for the collective farmers' markets and the illegal, underground "black markets." Along with the end of commercial transactions and the collapse of "state capitalism," the old merchant middle class was eliminated. The entire economy was put under state control; everything was nationalized; and this "command economy" was declared to be "socialism" in 1936. The original Marxist concept that under socialism the producers themselves would run the economy and society was buried under a mountain of rhetoric about capitalist encirclement, dangers from Fascist aggressors in central Europe, and "enemies of the people" at home. Stalin's ideologists argued that the closer the Soviet Union moved toward the classless society, the stronger the state would have to become in order to beat back the enemies of communism.

Anyone who questioned these innovations in Marxist theory was considered disloyal, and all questioning of the official party line was punishable by imprisonment, exile, or even death. Under the Stalinist regime established in the 1930s the police became all-powerful, subjecting even loyal party members to torture and execution. Purges periodically cleansed the party and state apparatus of anyone who might be considered skeptical about the new order or its self-ordained leader.

The leadership of the Armenian Communist Party in the early 1930s was made up of loyal Stalinists. At the head of the party was Aghasi Khanjian (1901-1936), a young Communist born in Van. A Marxist from his teenage years, Khanjian had worked in Leningrad in the 1920s, where he was involved in purging the local organization of the anti-Stalinists. In 1928 he had been transferred to Erevan and rose rapidly in the party ranks. One by one he removed the old Armenian Bolsheviks who had governed Armenia since the early 1920s. Khanjian benefited enormously from the patronage of Stalin, and in May 1930, at the age of twenty-nine, he was named first secretary of the Armenian Communist Party. Though he presided over collectivization (in its second phase), Khanjian achieved a degree of popularity and was seen by many as a defender of the aspirations of the Armenians. But by the mid-1930s Khanjian had come into conflict with the most powerful party leader in Transcaucasia, Lavrenti Beria, a Georgian close to Stalin. Early in July 1936 Khanjian was called to Tiflis. Suddenly and unexpectedly it was announced that the Armenian party chief had committed suicide. Though the circumstances of his death are murky, it is believed that Beria had ordered Khanjian's death to remove a threat to his own monopoly of power.

With Khanjian out of the way, Beria's appointee to head the Armenian party, Haik Amatuni, began a purge to rid the party of a newly discovered heresy, Khanjianism. Throughout the Soviet Union deviant and even mildly critical Communists were being removed from office. By 1937 they were being arrested, tried, and either shot or exiled to prison camps. Apparently the pace and ferocity of the purges in Armenia were not satisfactory to Stalin, and the Armenian leaders. Amatuni and his deputy, Stepan Agopov, were chided for leniency. Despite this criticism from Moscow, the Armenian Communists did not remove their leaders but reelected them to their high posts. From Moscow the Politburo decided to intervene directly and end this insubordination. On September 8, 1937, Stalin wrote to the Bureau of the Armenian Central Committee, accusing it of covering up enemies of the Armenian people. A week later two of Stalin's closest associates, Georgii Malenkov and Anastas Mikoyan, arrived in Erevan with Beria. The year-old leadership of the Armenian party was arrested, and Beria's protégé, Grigor Harutiunian (Arutiunov), former head of the Tbilisi party committee, was named first secretary in Armenia. Immediately the systematic decimation of Armenian Communist ranks began. One after another the men who had ruled Armenia in the first fifteen years of Soviet power were arrested and shot: Aramayis Erzinkian (1879-1937), commissar of agriculture (1921-1930); Sargis Kasian (1876-1937), head of the first Soviet government in Armenia; Avis Nurijanian (1896-1937), a member of that first government; Sahak Ter-Gabrielian (1886-1938), Armenian representative in Moscow (1921-1928) and chairman of the Council of People's Commissars in Armenia (1928-1935); Haik Hovsepian (d. 1937), once head of the Armenian Communist Party; and Haik Amatuni, who had been appointed to lead the party by Beria after Khanjian's death.

The purges hit not only the top party leaders but the lower ranks and non-Communist intellectuals as well. The writer Aksel Bakunts perished for the crime of "bourgeois nationalism." The leading Soviet Armenian poet, Eghishe Charents, who earlier had been one of the most ardent supporters of Soviet power in Armenia, was accused of "right deviationism" and nationalism for his poem "Message." On the surface the poem appeared to be standard verses in praise of Stalin, but when one read the second letter in each line vertically a secret message read: "O Armenian people, your only salvation lies in your united strength!" Charents died in prison, as did Vahan Totovents, a brilliant short-story writer from Western Armenia. Few writers were as fortunate as Gurgen Mahari to emerge after decades in Stalin's prisons to a brief period of freedom in the twilight of their lives.

Historians are still divided as to the motivations of the Great Purges of 1936 to 1938. Perhaps the results give some clues to the causes for the massive bloodletting. Once the purges were called off in early 1939, Stalin was secure in his autocratic powers. No longer did any factions or prominent personalities pose an alternative to his absolute rule. The party ranks and leaders had been tamed by the political police, the NKVD, and Stalin remained unchallenged until his death in 1953. A second major result of the purges was the removal of the older generation of Bolsheviks from positions of authority. The men and women who had made the revolution, led the country through the periods of civil war, NEP, and the early Stalin Revolution were viciously eliminated, and in their place a younger generation of Soviet-educated technicians and managers was thrust into power. That "Stalin generation" would remain in commanding positions well into the early 1980s. One ruling elite, more cosmopolitan and steeped in the prerevolutionary Marxist movement, had been physically destroyed; another, largely recruited from the working class and technical intelligentsia, and presumably more loyal to the new order, was rapidly elevated to administrative positions and rewarded with power, prestige, and privileges. And, finally, the purges ended any pretension by regional or republic leaders to autonomy from the center. Stalinism created a hypercentralized political system in which all important decisions were made in Moscow and communicated downward to loyal and unquestioning subordinates.

The Stalin Revolution was not only a brutal transformation of the economy and the political hierarchy; it also had an effect on state policy toward the nationalities. After an initial promotion of the nativization policy in the years of the First Five-Year Plan (1928-1932), official enthusiasm for *korenizatsiia* began to fade. The learning of Russian was encouraged, and in 1938, it was made compulsory for all Soviet students. Most Armenians in school were still receiving instruction only in Armenian (77.7 percent at the end of the 1930s), and only a small minority (2.8 percent) were studying in Russian. But in the years after 1938 the percentage of those studying in Russian steadily rose. Stalin's policy was to make Russian the lingua franca of the whole country, while permitting the continuation of the national languages within the individual republics. Russian was recognized as "the language of the socialist revolution," the most "progressive" language in the USSR. Many Russian word forms were introduced into Armenian. The word *hanrapetutiun* (republic) was replaced by *respublika, kusaktsutiun* (party) by *partiia, khorhrdayin* (Soviet) by *sovetakan*.

At the same time that local nationalism was denounced, Soviet patriotism, which was often a disguised form of Russian nationalism, was promoted. Lenin had always emphasized the greater danger posed to the socialist cause by Great Russian chauvinism, but in 1934 Stalin told the Seventeenth Party Congress that local nationalism was as great a danger to socialist unity as Great Russian chauvinism. Gradually, nearly imperceptibly, Russians were elevated to the level of a superior people and the nationalities lowered to a second-class category. While nineteenth-century writers, such as Raffi and Rafayel Patkanian, and even certain Soviet Armenian writers were condemned as "nationalists," films depicting Peter the Great, General Suvorov, Ivan the Terrible, and

Alexandr Nevskii—all Russian historical figures—were praised. All artists had to conform to the norms set down by the state-run writers' union, and these included Stalin's famous dictum that Soviet culture must be "national in form, socialist in content." What this meant in practice was that official Soviet views were to be expressed in national languages and idioms. The canons of Socialist Realism, an aesthetic theory created in the 1930s, were to be applied to all writers, artists, filmmakers, and musicians. Negative aspects of Soviet life had to be played down or eliminated altogether. Writers and artists were required to create positive heroes who could serve as models for young readers. Fiction was to be realistic in style but highly romanticized in content. A beautiful, bright picture of the future was to be drawn.

By the outlook of the World War II in 1939, the essential features of the Stalinist order had been established. The Soviet Union had become a new kind of political and social system in which an all-encompassing state had eliminated all centers of autonomy and resistance to its monopoly of power. Civil society and the economy had been swallowed by the state. Political decision making was tightly held in the hands of Stalin himself and his closest associates—Beria, Molotov, Malenkov, Zhdanov, and Mikoyan. The secret police dominated all sections of the party, eliminating the remnants of the autonomous prerogatives of the national republics or local administrations. State-directed terror guaranteed political conformity and passivity. Armenians were free to celebrate the economic and cultural achievements of the Soviet system and the benefits it brought to the Armenian people, but they were not free to criticize the system or to suggest that Armenia might be better off independent. Any hint of separatism was condemned as Dashnakism, and nationalist expression, even of the most innocent variety, could lead to ruined careers or loss of life.

World War II and the Cold War

On June 22, 1941, Hitler's armies crossed the Soviet border and initiated the most colossal military confrontation between two nations in human history. By the time the Soviet army had driven the Nazis back into Germany, the Soviet people had lost 7,000,000 soldiers and 20,000,000 civilians. The enormous costs of the war were borne by all peoples in the USSR, among them the Armenians. Though precise figures are not available, it is known that the population of Soviet

Armenia dropped 12 percent (by 174,000 people) between 1941 and 1945. Not until 1952 would Armenia's population again reach the prewar level of approximately 1,360,000. Though the Wehrmacht was stopped north of the Great Caucasus and Armenia proper was spared German occupation, the loss of life and the severe material privations of the war years left the country in dire straits by 1945. Early in the war Armenian military units were thrown into some of the heaviest fighting at the front and suffered great casualties. In the republic there was fear that the Turks would use the opportunity of Russia's weakness to launch an attack on Armenia. All able-bodied men were at the front, and there were few police, let alone soldiers, to keep law and order at home or to guard the frontier.

The Soviet government mobilized all its resources for the mortal struggle with the Fascists. Both in Russia and in Armenia a reconciliation was arranged with the church. State-church relations in Armenia had been strained since the mysterious death of Catholicos Khoren I Muratbekian (1933-1938). It was widely believed that he had been murdered by Beria's secret police. The government refused the Armenian Apostolic Church permission to elect a successor to the catholicos, and Archbishop Gevorg Chorekjian directed the church as acting head. With the outbreak of war, however, the government softened its policy. Several churches were reopened in Armenia; some exiled clergymen returned from Siberia. In April 1943 a Council of Ecclesiastical Affairs was created in Soviet Armenia. And most astonishing of all, Stalin himself received Archbishop Chorekjian in the Kremlin on April 19, 1944. The Armenian Church was permitted to open a seminary and to reestablish its printing press. For its part, the church supported the fight against the Nazi invaders in every way—blessing the troops, raising money for Armenian military units, and rallying the people behind the war effort. The alliance between the church and the Soviet state repaired some of the damage done in the 1930s to popular support for the government. While such radical social transformations as collectivization, industrialization, and the purges had alienated many Armenians from the Soviet order, the war provided the Soviet government with a new legitimacy as the defender of the country. Patriotism was combined with appeals for a brighter future and brought many Armenians back into the Soviet fold.

At the same time, however, other Armenians broke decisively with the Soviet regime and went over to the Germans. Certain Berlin-based Dashnakists, though repudiated by the official party organs, made an agreement with the Nazis in 1942 to support the Germans against the Soviet Union in the hope of liberating Armenia. General Dro Kanayan, a one-time leader of the independent Armenian government, helped to form an Armenian legion on the Eastern front. As the Red Army drove the Germans back in 1944-1945, many Armenians living in the North Caucasus and Ukraine retreated with the Germans, ending up in refugee camps in Germany. Eventually most of them would be allowed to emigrate to the United States. Thus, Armenians fought on both sides of the Soviet-Germany front, though the great majority—including almost 500,000 Soviet Armenian soldiers—backed the anti-Nazi campaign. Sixty Armenian generals fought in the Soviet Army, including the future Marshal of the Soviet Union, Ivan (Hovhannes) Baghramian.

Just after the war in Europe ended in May 1945, Armenian clergymen and laity gathered in Echmiadzin for the election of a new Catholicos. Archbishop Chorekjian was chosen as Gevorg VI (1945-1954) and, unlike his predecessor, was allowed to live in Echmiadzin. The new catholicos had proven his ability to work with the Soviet authorities, and the Soviet government approved his election. A new era seemed to be opening in state-church relations and in closer ties between Soviet Armenia and the diaspora *(spiurk)*. With the support of the conclave that had elected him, Gevorg VI sent a series of messages to Stalin urging repatriation of diaspora Armenians to Soviet Armenia and the return of Armenian lands in Turkey to Armenia. "The Armenian people," he wrote, "are firmly convinced that the Great Russian people will aid them in realizing their patriotic and humane aspirations of recovering their national patrimony" (Lazian, 1957, p. 353; Mouradian, 1979, p. 80).

The repatriation campaign *(nergaght)* and the Soviet claims to Kars and Ardahan, areas held by Russia from 1878 to 1921, were supported by the Armenian Church throughout the world, as well as by the liberal Ramkavar Party, with its financial resources from middle-class and wealthy Armenians, and the socialist Hnchak Party. Even the anti-Soviet Dashnaktsutiun joined the campaign for repatriation. Most of the refugees, about 80 to 85 percent, were in the Middle East and Greece, and in the years 1945 to 1948, more than 100,000 "returned" to the "homeland." These *hairenatartsner* (repatriates) made up less than 10 percent of the Armenian diaspora and were primarily Armenians who lived at some time in their lives in historic Armenia or Cilicia. Survivors of the genocide or children of survivors, their emigration to Soviet Armenia had more to do with Armenian nationalist sentiments than with commitment to Soviet-style "social-ism." With great joy and enthusiasm the repatriates embarked for Armenia, only to find on their arrival that the country was ill-prepared to receive them. The war had left great poverty and destruction in the Soviet Union, and local Armenians were often reluctant to share the little they had with the *aghberner* (pejorative for "brothers"), as these Western Armenians were derisively called. And as the Cold War began to chill, the government itself turned against the refugees, suspecting them of being too Western. Many repatriates ended up in prison camps, where they remained until Stalin's death. When the opportunity arose in the late 1950s and 1960s to leave Armenia, thousands emigrated once again, this time to Europe and the United States.

At the same time as it agitated for repatriation, the Soviet gov-ernment raised the "Armenian Question" for the first time since the sovietization of Armenia. On June 7, 1945, Foreign Minister Viacheslav Molotov told the Turkish ambassador in Moscow that the Kars and Ardahan districts, which had been formally ceded to Turkey by Soviet Russia in 1921, would now have to be returned to the Soviet Union. Although the Turks wanted peaceful relations with the USSR, they were unwilling to make territorial concessions. Soviet pressure pushed Turkey toward an alliance with the West. Through 1945 and 1946 the Soviet Union made repeated claims against Turkey, both in the name of the Armenian and Georgian republics. On October 27, 1947, Ambassador Andrei Vyshinskii spoke at the United Nations in favor of the return of Kars and Ardahan to Georgia, compromising the moral and political claims of the Armenians. Meanwhile Armenians in Europe and America tried to influence their governments in favor of the annexations. A delegation of prominent Armenians visited Secretary of State Dean Acheson to plead their case, but the United States and Britain decided to back Turkey against what they perceived to be Soviet aggression. Once the Cold War broke up the Grand Alliance of the Soviet Union, Great Britain, and the United States, agreement on Armenian irredenta became impossible. The issue died shortly after Stalin's death in 1953, when Molotov publicly announced that the governments of Armenia and Georgia had waived their terri-torial claims against Turkey. The "Armenian Question" was once again buried by the diplomats, though Armenian organizations and publicists periodically raised the issue. Historic Armenia remained divided, not only between the USSR and Turkey, but also between two hostile camps—the Soviet Bloc and the NATO alliance.

The Cold War ended the period of direct relations between the diaspora and Soviet Armenia. For nearly a decade travel became nearly impossible. The years of late Stalinism were marked by a fierce anti-Western propaganda. A policy of tighter control over the population was instituted in the late 1940s, and a new campaign was launched against nationalism. The all-too-brief flowering of wartime cultural life came to an end. In November 1948 the Armenian Communist Party's congress condemned scholars and other writers for "idealizing the historical past of Armenia," for "ignoring the class struggle" in the history of Armenia, and for being too attracted by the "reactionary culture of the bourgeois West." Historians were attacked for their failure to recognize the "progressive" significance of the annexation of Armenia by Russia. The nineteenth-century nationalist writer Raffi, who had been republished as late as 1947, was once again castigated. Even the internationally famous composer Aram Khachaturian had to submit an apology for having written "bourgeois" music. In this culturally cramped atmosphere real creativity became impossible, and any slight expression of Armenian pride was once again condemned as nationalism. In 1949 it was announced that a Dashnak underground existed in the republic. Thousands of Armenian families were exiled to the Altai region of Central Asia.

Stalin died on March 5, 1953, and with his passing an entire era in Soviet history came to an end. Stalinism had radically changed Armenia. From a basically agrarian country with a small-holding peasantry, Armenia had become increasingly industrial and urban. But even as it entered modernity, Armenia was severely restricted in its cultural and national formation. Education and social mobility made Armenians more eager to explore the world and experience what modern life offered. Stalin's revolution had created rising expectations, a hunger for a richer material and cultural life, but at the same time Stalinism prevented people from fully achieving their potential. The contradiction between the achievements and the new aspirations created great frustration, but discontent could not be expressed openly in the police state ruled by the Georgian dictator. At the same time Armenians were pulled in two directions; on the one hand, their country had become more Armenian, more homogeneously Armenian, more conscious of its heritage; on the other, strict limits shut off avenues of national expression. The material and spiritual tensions built up under Stalin manifested themselves in a new nationalism in the decades after the dictator's death.

The Years of Reform: Khrushchev (1953-1964)

At the time of Stalin's death, the Soviet Union was economically stagnant, its agriculture displaying the signs of permanent structural weakness. Though the country had largely recovered from the devastation of the World War II, industrial growth had slowed down and disproportionately high investments in heavy industry had left consumers with little to buy. Internationally the USSR was isolated from the other Great Powers, who were organized into the anti-Soviet North Atlantic Treaty Alliance (NATO), and at that moment were fighting the Chinese and North Korean Communists on the Korean peninsula. Anticommunism dominated the political discourse both in the United States and Western Europe, and the Cold War hostility toward Stalinism made negotiations with the Soviet Union nearly impossible. Within the country a repressive political system stifled innovation, initiative, and cultural expression.

The leadership that inherited Stalin's empire had the difficult political choice either to continue the policies of their dead chief, complete with domestic terror, or to embark on internal reforms and a more conciliatory foreign policy. A general consensus was shared in the Kremlin that consumer needs had to be met to a greater degree, that the harsh exploitation of the peasantry had to be alleviated, and that a less confrontational posture had to be adopted toward the rest of the world. The new leader of the party, Nikita Sergeevich Khrushchev, convinced other members of the ruling Presidium that the first step was to eliminate the threat of the secret police. Beria was arrested and executed, and the police were once again subordinated to the party. Within months Beria's lieutenants, both in the center and in Transcaucasia, were removed from their positions.

Although there were significant shifts in Transcaucasia after Beria's fall, the Armenian Communist leadership proved somewhat resistant to purging itself. A cohesive group of Armenian Communists, schooled and promoted during the long period of Arutiunov's rule (1937-1953), made no move to demote their chief. Only Second Secretary Zaven Grigorian was dismissed. Mir Jafar Baghirov, head of the Azerbaijani party, was arrested, and in September 1953 the Georgian party was given a new leadership; but not until November 1953, and only after the Moscow Central Committee pressured the Armenians, was Arutiunov replaced by Suren Tovmasian. The new first secretary had come up through the Arutiunov machine and had been a member of the Central Committee since 1938. Moreover, the chairman of the Council of Ministers, Anton Kochinian, another Arutiunov protégé, retained his position as head of the government. This renewed elite, with deep roots in the Stalinist party, remained in charge of the Armenian republic with relatively little change for the next two decades. Though Tovmasian was replaced by a relative outsider, Iakov Zarobian, in 1960, Kochinian held onto his post until he stepped into Zarobian's place in 1966. Notoriously corrupt, Kochinian remained the dominant Armenian politician until his political disgrace in November 1974. Thus, for two decades after Stalin's death and the end of Beria's satrapy in Transcaucasia, the Armenian party continued to be dominated by the generation of men who had come to power in the late 1930 at the time when the Great Purges carried away the Old Bolsheviks of the revolutionary generation.

Much more significant change in Armenia occurred at the social and cultural level. The Khrushchev period (1953-1964) was the most intensive time of reform that the Soviet Union had experienced since the 1930s. Even before Khrushchev's so-called secret speech to the Twentieth Party Congress in February 1956, a period of "thaw" began in culture. Anastas Mikoyan, now a close colleague of Khrushchev, went to Erevan in March 1954 to reverse the antinational policy of the local Communist Party. The Armenian writers who had been condemned as nationalists were to be published. In 1954 the works of Armenian writers who had survived the prison camps, such as Gurgen Mahari, Vagharshak Norents, and Vahram Alazan, appeared, alongside those of pre-revolutionary writers such as Raffi and Patkanian. And several of the writers of the 1920s and 1930s who had not survived the purges, most notably Eghishe Charents and Aksel Bakunts, were now praised as good Communists. At the same time political figures, such as Sahak Ter-Gabrielian and Aghasi Khanjian, who had been killed by Beria's police, were rehabilitated. Thousands of political prisoners returned to Erevan and told of their years of torture and deprivation in the Gulag (prison camp system). Everywhere the "cult of personality," a euphemism for Stalinist dictatorship and terror, was condemned. Young people particularly began to question more seriously the system that had given rise to Stalin, and the seamless fabric of ideological conformity that had marked the 1930s and 1940s began to shred, never to be sewn together again. The campaign against Stalin, launched by Khrushchev and Mikoyan at the Twentieth Party Congress, culminated in the early 1960s with the removal of the largest statue of Stalin in Erevan. Years later a huge monument to "Mother Armenia" was placed on the empty pedestal on which the "Father of All Peoples" had stood.

Khrushchev's rule in the Soviet Union was marked by continual experiments in government and economy. The overly centralized Stalinist "command economy" had worked to industrialize the USSR rapidly on the eve of World War II and to restore the devastated economy after the Nazi invasion and occupation. But the investment in heavy industry and the creation of large, inefficient collective farms did not allow for the provision of abundant goods and food supplies or adequate housing for the working population. The elite lived a privileged life, with special shops in which to buy what they needed, but workers and peasants lived poorly and lost much incentive to produce. A series of economic reforms—the permitting of greater initiative for peasants in agriculture, the "Virgin Lands" program in Kazakhstan to open up new farms, the creation of regional economic councils *(sovnarkhozy)* in 1957—was launched to revitalize the economy without giving up party control over the levers of economic power. For Armenia the experiments meant more local initiative, though ultimate planning and budgetary control remained with Moscow. Industrial enterprises in the republic were placed under the local Ministry of Industry and local farming under the local Ministry of Agriculture. The huge collective farms of the late Stalin period were broken up into smaller farms, still collectivized but more manageable. The poorly educated farm chairmen were now to be better trained. Whereas in May 1950 Armenia had been ordered to supply its own grain, the new policy allowed the republic to specialize in crops that better suited its terrain. Besides grain, which still made up 40 percent of sown acreage, Armenians planted wine grapes, fruits, vegetables, and tobacco in greater amounts. Livestock production expanded, and agricultural productivity per unit of cultivated land rose. Between 1950 and 1978 agricultural output increased by 218 percent. Though farm incomes improved in Armenia, the republic remained close to the bottom of any union republic in per capita farm income.

The shift from farm to factory, village to town, continued through the 1950s, 1960s, and 1970s. In the Soviet Union as a whole, the percentage of the labor force working in agriculture and forestry dropped from 46 percent in 1950 to 39 percent in 1960 and 22 percent in 1975. The Armenians started below the Soviet average in 1950. Fifty percent of Armenian labor worked in agriculture and forestry in the last years of Stalin, but that figure rapidly dropped to 35 percent in 1960 and to 20 percent in 1975. As for industry, Armenian workers made up only

24 percent of the labor force in 1950 and grew to 32 percent in 1960 and to 38 percent in 1975, thus reaching the all-USSR level and surpassing the levels of Azerbaijan (28 percent) and Georgia (27 percent). Armenian peasants, who had made up over 80 percent of the republic's population in 1920, were only 20 percent by the end of the 1970s. Only a third of Armenians continued to live in the countryside in the early 1980s, while two-thirds lived in towns and cities. After sixty years of Soviet-style modernization, Armenia had become a predominantly urban and industrial society.

The post-Stalin decades were marked by rapid industrial growth in Armenia. From 1950 to 1978 Armenian industrial output rose at an average annual rate of 9.9 percent, exceeding the rates of Georgia (8.2 percent) and Azerbaijan (7.4 percent) as well as that of the USSR as a whole. However, on a per capita basis Armenia (and Georgia and Azerbaijan as well) grew slower industrially than the USSR average. Nevertheless, from a minuscule industry based almost entirely on copper mining and cognac distilling, Armenia has developed an advanced machinery industry with a highly skilled labor force. Forty percent of industrial workers in Armenia were in the machine industries, building electrical equipment, motors, and machine tools. By 1978 Armenian industrial production was 335 times greater than it had been in 1913. Though poorer by most indices than the Soviet Union in general, Armenia was significantly better off materially than its Muslim neighbors, Turkey and Persia, and had obviously benefited economically from its association with the rest of the Soviet Union.

The welcome changes from Stalinist centralization gave the Armenian party-state leadership greater power over the local economy and at the same time greater opportunity to misuse the resources of the state economy. A continual tension existed between local Armenian managers and bureaucrats and the authorities in Moscow over increasing production and productivity. Local officials in Transcaucasia allowed the creation and development of a widespread underground, illegal "second economy." Favors were done in return for services and goods. Money and material were stolen from state enterprises. Workers worked on special jobs for private reimbursement outside their regular jobs. And buying and selling of coveted but otherwise unavailable goods was carried on relatively openly, though prohibited by law. Corruption, "speculation," black-marketeering, and simply "doing favors" *(papakh)* became the normal way of doing business in Armenia. Everything depended on whom one knew; what was needed was "pull," or in the Armenian variant, "kh-ts-b" *(khnaminer, tsanotner, barekam-ner*—in-laws, acquaintances, and relatives).

The "second economy" reached its height in the early 1970s under Kochinian's rule. Central Soviet authorities tried to bring it to an end by appointing an unknown young man from outside the Stalinist political establishment to head the Armenian party. Karen Demirchian (born 1932) was an engineer who had graduated from the Higher Party School in Moscow, worked in Leningrad, and had held party positions in Armenia only from the mid-1960s. His task was to cleanse the party and state of careerists and profiteers and to rebuild the morale of the political elite. But the "second economy" proved impossible to uproot. Family circles and friendship networks worked against the government's attempts to penetrate the illegal operations. As long as the state sector proved unable to supply Armenians with the necessities and luxuries they demanded, the population resorted to illegal and semilegal methods to obtain their goods and services. Demirchian managed to improve the economic situation, and for his relative success he was rewarded with support from Moscow, which kept him in power for over a decade. But like his predecessors, Demirchian eventually accommodated himself to the corrupt political system he inherited. By the mid-1980s he headed a political machine in Erevan that enriched itself with little regard for the Armenian population at large.

The Rise of the New Nationalism

Both Western social scientists and Soviet analysts had long predicted that, over time, the national differences among the peoples of the USSR would diminish, ultimately leading to assimilation of the smaller ethnic groups into the Russian mass. But the experience of the Armenians and other nationalities belied this expectation. Not only did the federal structure of the USSR permit a legal existence for an Armenian political formation, but the policy of *korenizatsiia* encouraged ethnic distinction and local control. Though its long-range goals were to create a single "Soviet people," the Soviet state, rather than pushing a consistent policy of forced Russification, settled for political loyalty to the Communist Party and tolerated cultural diversity. In Transcaucasia at least, educators and politicians pushed for bilingualism, not the suppression of local languages. A compromise was reached between the maximal goals of the central party leaders (*sblizhenie* [rapproachment of various nation-

alities] and *sliianie* [their eventual melding into a single nationality])
and the aspirations of ethnic communities and local Communists.

Within Armenia, the process of national development created the
most homogeneous republic in the USSR. Of Armenia's population,
89.7 percent was Armenian in 1979. The rate of increase among Armenians (23.4 percent) was higher than that of non-Armenians (9.9 percent). Even after sixty-five years of Soviet rule, most Armenians in
Armenia preferred to communicate in the Armenian language. Among
Armenians in Armenia 99.4 percent considered Armenian to be their
native language. Even many members of ethnic minorities in the republic, such as the 50,000 Kurds and the 160,000 Azeris, used Armenian as
a lingua franca. In the late Soviet period, however, many better-educated
urban Armenians preferred sending their children to Russian-language
schools in order to enhance their career horizons. Despite the attractive-
ness of Russian among young Armenians and the widespread bilingualism, Armenians did not face any danger of Russification or assimilation
in Armenia—in contrast to the evident threats to western Slavs and the
Baltic peoples. When in 1978 the Soviet authorities considered remov-
ing the clause in the Georgian and Armenian constitutions that established the local languages as the official state languages, protests in
Tbilisi compelled the government to back down, and the Armenians
were spared the need to defend their language rights.

At the same time, however, Armenians were the most dispersed
people in the USSR, except for the Jews. Only 65.5 percent of Soviet
Armenians (2,725,000 out of 4,151,000) lived in the Armenian republic in 1979. Educated Armenians, anxious to better their prospects for
interesting careers and for their children's future, often left Armenia
for Russia or other parts of the Soviet Union. These emigrant Armenians faced a real possibility of losing their language, of intermarrying
with non-Armenians, and over time of assimilating with Russians.
This trend of assimilation moved in a direction opposite of what was
happening in Soviet Armenia itself. On the positive side, it should be
noted that in 1959, Armenians in Soviet Armenia represented only
55.7 percent of all Armenians in the USSR; by the late 1970s, they
represented two-thirds. Immigration, a fairly strong birth rate, and a
sense of pride in being Armenian worked to strengthen the ethnic
cohesion of Armenians in Armenia.

The conflict in the Soviet Union between ethnic consolidation, on
the one hand, and potential acculturation and assimilation, on the other,
created fears among small nationalities that their national distinctiveness

might be lost in the near future. Such fears, as well as more positive aspirations to improvements in the status of the nationalities, created a renewed sense of nationalism in various parts of the Soviet Union. Unlike the nationalisms of Georgia, Ukraine, and Estonia, Armenian nationalism was distinct in that it was directed not so much against the dominant Russians as against the traditional enemy, the Turks. The Communist government of Armenia not only made concessions to nationalism but often subtly encouraged it. Since Armenian nationalism was no threat to the unity of the USSR, except in certain militant forms, the Soviet government could afford to be tolerant of its manifestation—within limits. Thus, one can speak of an orthodox or official nationalism, which the party accepted, and an unorthodox or dissident nationalism, which it condemned and punished.

The line between orthodox and dissident nationalism was not always easy to determine, and as the party's tolerance of national expression increased or diminished, certain poets or politicians found themselves on the wrong side of the line. The Armenian intelligentsia continually raised issues of language policy, repatriation of Armenians abroad, and territorial adjustments in favor of Armenia. The government made moderate concessions, such as the establishment of an Association for the Preservation of Armenian Historical Monuments in 1965 or the erection of monuments to Armenian national heroes such as Vardan Mamikonian, General Andranik (Ozanian), and the Western Armenian poet and victim of the genocide Daniel Varuzhan. A complex of statues and buildings was built in 1968 at Sardarabad in a neo-Urartian style to commemorate the battle in May 1918 that prevented the Turkish army from overrunning Erevan. Local lore recounted how the fierce-eyed eagles that line the approach to the ensemble were first set up to face Turkey, but later, when this was seen as too provocative, were turned with their backs to the border. In the late 1960s the original Armenian word for "republic" *(hanrapetutiun)* was restored in the official designation of the Armenian SSR.

The first major outbreak of dissident nationalism within Soviet Armenia occurred on April 24, 1965, when thousands of Armenians in Erevan demonstrated on the fiftieth anniversary of the 1915 deportations and massacres. Crowds gathered at the Spendiarian Opera House as a quiet official commemoration was being held inside. Soon the observers became angry; rocks were thrown, and the protesters demanded that the Turks return the Armenian lands to Armenia. Armenians called upon the Russians to aid them in retrieving their irredenta. Government officials were unable to calm the crowd, and even the Catholicos Vazgen I, a man regarded by many as the true head of the nation, had difficulty in restoring some semblance of order. The demonstration was an extraordinary event in the Soviet Union, and its consequences were impressive. Order was restored without recourse to armed suppression and bloodshed, in contrast to what had occurred nine years earlier when Georgians in Tbilisi (Tiflis) had demonstrated their national concern about the criticisms of Stalin. But the Armenian party leader, Iakov Zarobian, was dismissed, and his successor, Anton Kochinian, denounced him for permitting "local nationalism" and tolerating "the poor situation in ideological work in Armenia." At the same time the party leadership made it clear that a monument would be built in Erevan to commemorate the victims of the genocide. In November 1967 Kochinian inaugurated the Dzidzernakaberd monument to the genocide, fifty-two years after the events and forty-seven years after the sovietization of Armenia.

By the 1970s national expression in Armenia could not be contained without official bounds. On January 20, 1974, a young man of twenty-five, Razmik Zohrabian, set fire to a portrait of Lenin in Erevan's central square. He announced that he was protesting "the anti-Armenian internal and foreign policy" of the Soviet government and the repression of Armenian patriots and dissidents. Investigations revealed that the young protester was a member of a secret underground Armenian nationalist party, the National Unity Party, a small group of young Armenians who demanded the return of Nakhichevan, Karabagh (Artsakh), and Western Armenia to the Armenians and the formation of a united independent state. This separatist movement had been formed in 1967 by Stepan Zatikian and others, who managed to put out one issue of an illegal journal, *Paros,* before they were rounded up, tried, and imprisoned in 1974. Some eighty Armenians had been tried and imprisoned for nationalist activity in the decade up to 1974. Soviet authorities later reported that Zatikian broke with the more moderate members of his party while in prison and began to advocate terrorism. On January 8, 1977, a bomb exploded in the Moscow subway killing seven and injuring thirty-seven. Two years later TASS announced that Zatikian, along with Hakob Stepanian and Zaven Baghdasarian, had been secretly tried, found guilty of the bombing, and summarily executed.

The separatists of the National Unity Party were the most extreme and violent of the dissidents who emerged in Armenia in the late 1960s and 1970s. A Human Rights Group, much more moderate and concerned with broader civil rights issues, was set up in Erevan in April 1977 to monitor Soviet compliance with the Helsinki Agreement of 1975. The five members of this small group made contact with similar groups in Russia, Ukraine, and Georgia, but by December of that year they had all been arrested. In its first declaration the Armenian "Helsinki Group" combined issues of human rights with specific Armenian national aspirations, namely the repatriation of Armenians to Armenia, Armenian membership in the United Nations, and the rejoining with the Armenian republic of Mountainous Karabagh and Nakhichevan, which were then included in the territory of Azerbaijan. This last issue, the question of Karabagh, remained the single most volatile political demand of Soviet Armenians through the 1980s.

The renewed nationalism among Soviet Armenians was less the product of resistance to forced Russification than it was the result of social, economic, and political developments both under Stalinism and in the years of gradual reform since 1953. Armenia had developed economically into a more urban and industrial country under successive Soviet governments. At the same time its territory and people had become more ethnically homogeneous. Armenians were better educated, knew their history, language, and culture more completely, and had maintained their national culture even during the repressive years of Stalinism. Once the terror of the 1930s and 1940s was replaced by the greater tolerance of the 1950s and 1960s, the pent-up demand for greater national and personal expression exploded in the form of a new nationalism. Armenians were both more Armenian in consciousness and more eager to express their ethnic distinctiveness and protect it against incursions from the central power.

Rather than groaning under a government that in no way satisfied their aspirations, Armenians were involved through the years of Leonid Ilyich Brezhnev's rule (1964-1982) in a complex and constant series of negotiations, both with the local Soviet Armenian administration and with the central Soviet government. Their discontents were multiple, particularly concerning the low level of material life compared with more developed Western countries. Armenians continually pushed the limits of national expression, while the government tried both to keep that expression within acceptable bounds and satisfy those popular desires that did not threaten the Communist Party's monopoly of power.

From Renewed Reform to National Revolution

Brezhnev died in November 1982 and was succeeded by the former head of the KGB Yuri Andropov (1982-1984). Beginning cautiously with calls for greater labor discipline and a concerted struggle against corruption, Andropov initiated moderate reforms that began a long process of social and political change in the USSR. After a brief interregnum under Konstantin Chernenko (1984-1985), Andropov's protégé Mikhail Gorbachev came to power in March 1985, and within a few years he shook the conservative party regime to its foundations. Gorbachev boldly began a program of restructuring the Soviet economic and political system *(perestroika),* expanding enormously the bounds of free expression *(glasnost),* and decentralizing political control and increasing democratic participation *(demokratizatsiia).* For the non-Russian peoples he promised greater autonomy and more respect for national cultures and languages, but opposed any moves toward separation from the Soviet Union.

In Armenia three concerns combined to stimulate a broad-based national movement by 1988. The transformation of Armenia into an industrial-urban country had brought in its wake severe ecological problems, most important of which was the threat from a nuclear plant at Metsamor. Second, many Armenians were angered by the pervasive corruption and arrogance of the Demirchian regime. Third and most immediate, they were concerned about the fate of Karabagh, where more than 100,000 Armenians lived under Azerbaijani rule and had been cut off from Armenian culture. Petitions and protests over Karabagh had had no effect either on the Azerbaijani party or on the central Soviet leadership.

Suddenly, unexpectedly, on February 13, 1988, Karabagh Armenians began demonstrating in their capital, Stepanakert, in favor of unification with the Armenian republic. Six days later they were joined by mass marches in Erevan. On February 20 the Soviet of People's Deputies in Karabagh voted 110 to 17 to request the transfer of the region to Armenia. This unprecedented action by a regional soviet brought out tens of thousands of demonstrators both in Stepanakert and Erevan, but Moscow rejected the Armenians' demands. In response to the demands, Azerbaijanis in Sumgait, an industrial town on the Caspian, went on a rampage for two days, and at least thirty-one people died before Soviet troops ended the pogrom.

After the events at Sumgait, the peaceful transfer of Karabagh to Armenia became impossible. Through the next year, while Moscow hesitated to take decisive action, Armenians increasingly grew disillusioned with Gorbachev and the program of *perestroika,* and Azerbaijanis organized into a powerful anti-Armenian nationalist movement. In May 1988 Demirchian was replaced as Armenian party chief by Suren Harutiunian, but the Communist Party's authority continued to decline rapidly. The popular movement, led by the Karabagh Committee in Erevan and the *Krunk* (Crane) Committee in Stepanakert, continued to grow until its leaders were effectively the most popular and influential political forces among the Armenians. In July demonstrators attempted to take over Erebuni airport outside of Erevan, and one young man was killed. Sporadic fighting broke out in and around Karabagh, and in the fall hundreds of thousands of Armenian and Azerbaijani refugees fled (or were forced to move) to their native republics. A special commission set up by Moscow to govern Karabagh proved unable to contain the continuing crisis.

On December 7, 1988, a massive earthquake devastated northern Armenia, killing at least 25,000 people and rendering hundreds of thousand homeless. World attention focused here for several weeks, and aid poured in from many countries. Gorbachev flew to Armenia to survey the damage, but he was received hostilely because of his Karabagh policies. Even as the country lay crippled by the earthquake, the party decided to arrest the Karabagh Committee members and place the region under the direct administration of Moscow.

Through 1989 relations between the peoples of Transcaucasia grew worse. The arrests of the Karabagh leaders and the January decision to set up a special administration for Karabagh not only engendered Azerbaijani resistance but made governance of Armenia by the local party nearly impossible. Shootings were a daily occurrence in Karabagh. Soviet troops were ineffective in enforcing peace, though they stood between the hostile nationalities to prevent further bloodletting.

In Armenia the attempt by the Communist Party to rule without the popular representatives of the national movement only worsened the political crisis. In March 1989 many voters boycotted the general elections. Massive demonstrations started up again in early May, demanding the release of the members of the Karabagh Committee, and in the elections to the Congress of People's Deputies in May, Armenians chose people identified with the Karabagh cause. Finally, on the last day of May, the Karabagh Committee members were released to the cheers of demonstrators who greeted their arrival in Erevan.

For the next six months the Armenian Communist leadership and the national movement worked as uncomfortable allies. Already emerging as the most important of the movement's leaders, the philologist Levon Ter-Petrosian made it clear that the Committee had a broader vision than merely the solution of the Karabagh question. Ultimately determined to bring full democracy and independence to Armenia, the trajectory of the movement would bring it into head-on collision with the party. In June the mushrooming unofficial organizations joined together to form the Pan-Armenian National Movement (Hayots Hamazgayin Sharzhum, HHSh), and the government gave them official recognition.

The Azerbaijani-Armenian conflict escalated steadily in the summer and fall of 1989. Both the HHSh and the newly formed Azerbaijani Popular Front (APF) called for abolition of the special administration, headed by Gorbachev's deputy Arkadii Volskii. The Armenians held to their position that Karabagh must become part of the Armenian republic, and radical Azerbaijanis called for the abolition of Karabagh autonomy altogether. As hundreds of thousands of Azerbaijanis demonstrated in Baku, the blockade of Karabagh and Armenia tightened. Karabagh Armenians responded by electing their own National Council, which on August 23 declared the secession of Karabagh from Azerbaijan and its merger with Armenia. The Armenian Supreme Soviet then declared the Karabagh National Council as the sole legitimate representative of the Karabagh people. The Azerbaijani Supreme Soviet responded by abrogating the autonomy of Karabagh and Nakhichevan. On November 28, in frustration at its inability to bring the parties together, the USSR Supreme Soviet voted to replace the Special Administration Committee in Karabagh with an administration subject largely to Azerbaijan. A republic organizing committee on a parity basis was to be created, and the Nagorno-Karabagh provincial soviet and its executive committee (suspended by the January 12, 1989 decree) were to be restored. A Union Monitoring and Observation Commission, subordinate to the Supreme Soviet of the USSR, would supervise the sociopolitical situation, and special troops from the USSR Ministry of Internal Affairs would remain under conditions normalized. A new law was to be worked out within two months to guarantee the full development of Karabagh. No changes in the demographic situation were to be permitted.

Neither side was satisfied. Demonstrations were held both in Erevan and Baku against the decision. In Stepanakert people burned copies of the resolution. The Armenian Supreme Soviet rejected Moscow's decision and on December 1 declared Karabagh a part of Armenia. Forty thousand demonstrators were mobilized on December 5 to surround the Supreme Soviet building and demand the end of colonialist practices; the abolition of article 6 of the Soviet Constitution, which gave the Communist Party a leading political role; and the renaming of the republic as "Republic of Armenia." By the late fall of 1989, the cooperative relationship between the Armenian Communist authorities and the HHSh had come to an end, and the open contest for power between the nationalists and the Communists accelerated.

By 1990 Gorbachev's strategy to reform the political structure while preserving a renewed Communist Party had led to a deep polarization of Soviet politics. His policies had failed to revive the stagnating Soviet economy and instead threatened the unity of the Soviet Union. His extraordinary foreign policy successes were generally acknowledged, but inside the USSR he was faced by ever more frequent and ever more threatening crises. In Transcaucasia, as in the rest of the disintegrating Soviet Union, the cycle of economic decline and radicalized politics fed on each other. Both the incomplete political reform, in part democratic, in part preserving the old structures, and the national revolts had negative effects on the economy. In January, under HHSh pressure, the Armenian Supreme Soviet revised the republic's constitution and gave itself the power to validate USSR laws. Central state authority withered, and the writ of the Kremlin could be enforced by police and soldiers.

After more than two years of the Karabagh conflict, Armenians had moved from being one of the most loyal Soviet nations to completely losing confidence in Moscow. They perceived a pro-Azerbaijani slant to official media coverage that treated both sides as equally just in their claims and equally culpable for the cascading violence. Gorbachev's unwillingness to grant Karabagh to Armenia and his failure to end the blockade convinced people that the Kremlin calculated political advantage in backing the Muslims. In Armenia the Communist Party, under Suren Harutiunian, was torn between the Kremlin's refusal to allow the merger of Karabagh with Armenia and the growing popular movement that would be satisfied with nothing less.

Suddenly, on January 13, 1990, as a quarter of a million Azerbaijanis listened to speeches in the central square in Baku, groups of young people broke away and began running through the city beating and killing Armenians. Two days later the central Soviet government declared a state of emergency in Azerbaijan and launched a series of maneuvers, first in Karabagh and other areas and then toward Baku. On January 20, as the Popular Front organized a haphazard defense of the city, the Soviet Army stormed Baku, killing hundreds. Most Armenians were evacuated, and the military restored the power of the Communist Party of Azerbaijan and repressed the Popular Front. What had begun as a peaceful constitutional movement for Armenian rights in Karabagh had, by the spring of 1990, degenerated into vicious pogroms in Azerbaijan, the evacuation of the Armenian community of Baku, and a guerilla war between two nations in the southern Soviet Union.

With the Communist Party in rapid decline and the popular nationalist forces far from united, a vacuum of power could be felt in Armenia. Allied intellectually and politically with the democratic opposition that had formed in Russia around Boris Yeltsin, the Armenian National Movement was committed to dismantling the Communist system, preparing for eventual political independence, and marketizing the economy. With the resignation of Harutiunian as first secretary of the Armenian Communist Party (April 6, 1990) and the elections of the spring and summer of 1990, the old political elite gradually made way for a new political class that had matured in the two years of the Karabagh movement. At first Communists and their opponents appeared equally strong at the polls, and Ter-Petrosian spoke of a possible coalition government. But by late July it became clear that the non-Communists would win a parliamentary majority. After several rounds of voting, the newly elected Armenian parliament chose as its chairman Levon Ter-Petrosian instead of the new Communist chief, Vladimir Movsesian.

With the HHSh in power and the Communists in opposition, Armenia began a rapid transition from Soviet-style government to an independent democratic state. The Armenian national movement leaders argued that Armenians must abandon their reliance on a "third force," rethink their traditional hostility toward and fear of the Turks, and be prepared to create their own independent state by themselves now that the opportunity had arisen. The HHSh was prepared to deal more directly and forthrightly with the Turks and believed that the question of Armenian lands in Turkey had to be deferred until the issue of full sovereignty and independence was resolved.

The new government faced a nearly complete collapse of order in the republic. Buildings had been seized by armed men in Erevan, and several independent militias operated there as well as on the Azerbaijani frontier. Frustrated by the Azerbaijani blockade and determined to defend their republic and Karabagh, Armenian *fedayis* (a term that recalls the revolutionaries of the turn of the century) raided arsenals and police stations to arm themselves for the coming battles. In April 1990 a crowd attempted to storm the KGB building in the capital, and a month later a clash between Soviet troops and Armenian irregulars at the Erevan railroad station left twenty-four dead. When Gorbachev threatened military intervention if the independent militias of Armenia were not disarmed within fifteen days, Ter-Petrosian's government set out to restore order in Erevan.

As Armenians faced Armenians and the new national leadership tried to establish its authority, Armenia formally declared its intention to become a sovereign and independent state (August 23, 1990) with Karabagh an integral part of the new Republic of Armenia. The Armenian nation was defined broadly to include not only those on the territory of the republic but the worldwide diaspora as well. And the government set out to redefine Armenian national interests, recognizing but laying aside for the moment the painful question of the Armenian genocide and seeking improved relations with Turkey and Iran.

Gorbachev's revolution from above was spinning out of control by the fall of 1990, and former supporters of the Soviet president feared that democracy would soon fall victim to social chaos and political conservatism. Ter-Petrosian was wary about Gorbachev's efforts to renew the Soviet federation through the signing of a new union treaty. While visiting the United States in September, he made it clear that he favored a confederation of equal, sovereign states (Zoryan Institute, 1990, p. 7).

While Gorbachev struggled to stave off the collapse of his state, the Armenian parliament, led by the HHSh, refused to participate in the referendum on the union treaty. At the beginning of March, the Armenian Supreme Soviet announced that the republic would hold its own referendum on September 21 to comply with the Soviet law on secession. Through the spring Armenia paid a high price for its moves toward independence. In May, Soviet paratroopers landed, without notifying the Armenian government, at Erevan airport to protect Soviet defense installations in Armenia. Fighting broke out on the border of Armenia and Azerbaijan, and Armenians accused Soviet troops once again of deporting Armenians from Getashen (Chaikend) and Martunashen in Azerbaijan. The Azerbaijanis claimed that only documents were being checked and that armed militants were in the area, but eyewitnesses told of beatings and people being forced to sign documents that they were willing to leave their villages. Ter-Petrosian issued a statement on May 6: "To all intents and purposes, the Soviet Union has declared war on Armenia" (*Current Digest of the Soviet Press*, 1991, p. 9). Voskepar, a village inside Armenia in the Novemberyan district, was destroyed by invading MVD (Ministry of Internal Affairs) troops under Azerbaijani control. Combat continued in the Goris district, where hostile soldiers entered six villages. In retaliation, Armenians in Dilijan disarmed sixty Soviet soldiers and held them hostage.

On the morning of August 19, the world awoke to hear the stunning news that a self-proclaimed Emergency Committee had overthrown Gorbachev and taken control of the Soviet government. For three tense days the forces loyal to Russian president Boris Yeltsin and the democratic movement withstood the threats from the conservative leaders of the army, KGB, and the party. In his Crimean isolation Gorbachev refused to give in to the coup organizers, and after a strained stalemate the army and police refused to obey the plotters. The coup collapsed, but with it so did the last hopes of a union treaty.

While Azerbaijan's Communist boss Ayaz Mutalibov had welcomed the coup, and Georgia's president Zviad Gamsakhurdia vacillated, Ter-Petrosian resolutely opposed the plotters. He believed that Gorbachev's personnel blunders, indecisiveness, and concessions to the conservatives were to blame for the coup. Armenian leaders hoped that a more powerful Russia under Yeltsin would provide the economic and political support that the central government under Gorbachev had denied them. At the same time there was an awareness that some kind of relationship, particularly in the realm of economics, was essential between Armenia and whatever remained of the Soviet Union.

Within the first two months of the failed coup, Armenians went to the polls twice: the first time on September 21, to reaffirm the commitment to independence; the second on October 16, to elect Levon Ter-Petrosian president of the republic. Receiving 83 percent of the votes cast, Ter-Petrosian now had a popular mandate to carry out his vision of Armenian independence and self-sufficiency.

As the power of the central state rapidly withered away through the fall of 1991, almost all the Soviet republics established themselves as independent states. At the same time a series of attempts were made to resurrect some form of central authority or at least linkages between republics. Gorbachev tried in vain to resurrect the union treaty, but interrepublic cooperation could be achieved only on the economic level. In early October ten republics, including Armenia, agreed to an economic treaty, though only eight (including Armenia) actually signed it on October 18. Armenia did not join in Gorbachev's efforts in November to form a new confederation, the Union of Sovereign States.

On December 8 the leaders of the three Slavic republics—Russia, Ukraine, and Belarus—announced that the USSR had ceased to exist and that the three republics had set up a commonwealth, to which other republics were invited to join. An economic declaration linked the three republics in a common currency system and a joint economic program. In Erevan Ter-Petrosian offered "full support" for the initiative and signaled Armenia's intention to join the new commonwealth. On December 25, 1991, the Soviet Union ceased to exist.

Ethnically the most homogeneous of Soviet republics, Armenia was perhaps the most unfortunate economically—nearly a quarter of its population was homeless, the victims of both political and natural earthquakes. Armenia had a population of about 3,283,000. Neighboring Azerbaijan had a population of 7,029,000, and Georgia, 5,449,000. With less than 16 million people, Transcaucasia represented just under 6 percent of the whole Soviet population. Armenia made up only 1.1 percent of the Soviet population, produced only 0.9 percent of the USSR's national material product (NMP) (1.2 percent in industry, 0.7 percent in agriculture), retained 1.4 percent of the state budget revenue, delivered 63.7 percent of its NMP to other republics, and exported 1.4 percent abroad. It was highly integrated into the Soviet economy. Its exports flowed almost entirely to other parts of the Union, and its imports came from its sister republics. Along with Estonia and Tajikistan, Armenia had the highest level of imports of any Soviet republic. Forty percent of all enterprises in Armenia were devoted during Soviet times to defense and were now in particular trouble.

For all its faults, Soviet-style communism and imperialism had managed a rough peace throughout the Soviet empire, both within the USSR and along its borders, that precluded interethnic warfare and interstate hostilities. With the end of Pax Sovietica, each republic was confronted with internal ethnic problems and external security threats that it would have to deal with on its own. Armenia entered its second period of independence in the twentieth century with war raging on its frontiers. The Ter-Petrosian government tried to distance itself from the

Karabagh problem by portraying it as an internal Azerbaijani matter, but at the same time it was aware that Armenia had a moral and political commitment to support its compatriots in Karabagh. The Armenian voters of Karabagh responded to the collapse of the Soviet Union by declaring themselves an independent republic. Both Armenia and Karabagh seized the opportunity presented by the collapse of the Soviet empire to shape their own futures. The post-Communist governments of the Republic of Armenia and of Karabagh combined a cautious pragmatism with a bold faith that they could construct stability and prosperity in the troubled and treacherous world in which they were forced to live.

FOR FURTHER INFORMATION

Baldwin, 1926.   Matossian, 1962.
Borian, 1929.   Pipes, 1964.
Elliot, 1924.   Suny, 1983, 1993.
Mathieson, 1975.   Walker, 1991.

12

THE ARMENIANS IN AMERICA

Robert Mirak

The Armenian communities in North and South America are products of the cataclysmic events that uprooted the Armenian populations of the Middle East: first, in the turbulent period from the Russo-Turkish War of 1877-1878 to the 1920s; and then, in the upheavals in Egypt, Syria, Lebanon, Iran, and Soviet Armenia in the twenty-five years after 1965. Adjusting with alacrity to a variety of social and political systems, Armenian communities nevertheless have attempted to maintain their separate cultural and social identities.

Most important is the community in the United States. Approaching 1 million in number, it is the largest Armenian community outside of Armenia, and it continues to attract the homeless, the dispossessed, and ambitious among the Armenian people. It is also the wealthiest and best educated. Growing in prominence through recent arrivals from Lebanon and Iran is the Canadian Armenian community. Other noteworthy communities exist in Uruguay, Argentina, and Brazil.

The Formation of the Communities

The single largest number of Armenians came to the New World from the Ottoman Empire in the late nineteenth and early twentieth centuries.

Set in motion by the Hamidian pogroms of 1894 to 1896, this wave brought over 100,000 men, women, and children to the Americas before immigration to the United States was restricted in the 1920s. Prior to this exodus, smaller numbers of Armenians had settled in the Americas. A few adventurers and planters arrived in the British colony of Virginia and in Spanish South America as early as the seventeenth century, but systematic migration did not begin until the early 1800s, when American missionaries arrived in Turkey. Seeking to convert the Armenians to Congregationalist Protestantism, they established schools, missions, hospitals, printing presses, and eventually secondary schools (called "colleges") to educate Armenians. Missionaries also encouraged young Armenian males to further their education in the United States so that they would return to Turkey to assist in the education and conversion of fellow Armenians. By the early 1880s word about America—"promising everything" to the poorer provincial laboring and peasant classes, especially on the Kharpert (Kharput) plain, a focus of missionary activity—stirred others to leave for the "Promised Land." But passage was expensive, traveling was dangerous, and a 5,000-mile trip was not easily undertaken by young men who had never traveled beyond their small villages.

A powerful explosive force was required to stir an exodus, and this was provided by the Hamidian massacres of the mid-1890s. The slaughter of 100,000 men, women, and children and the devastation of Armenian communities from Constantinople to Van sent countless thousands fleeing for their lives to Russia, Eastern Europe, France, England, and the New World. By the century's close, 15,000 Armenians had succeeded in making the arduous journey to the Americas, while many more sought shelter in countries closer to home.

Once begun, the movement grew annually from 1900 to World War I. Some Armenians left because of continuing political persecution—the massacres of 1904 and 1909, the lawlessness of Turks and Kurds engendered by the sultan's misrule, and the Muslim-Christian hatreds and fears stirred by the Balkan Wars of 1912-1913. Others fled because Turkey was poor, because the Turks exploited instead of encouraged ambitious minorities, and because the government, on the verge of bankruptcy, broke its subjects' will with onerous taxes. The Young Turk regime, which overthrew the hated Sultan Abdul-Hamid in 1908, made emigration easier for Ottoman subjects; and beginning in 1909 some young Armenians fled the threat of being drafted into Turkish armies. By the outbreak of World War I, when international hostilities cut off the escape, 67,000 Armenians had migrated to the United States and Canada and another 45,000 had settled in South America. Of the immigrants landing in the United States, 77 percent were males, 87 percent were between the ages of fourteen and forty-five, and 40 percent were from nonagricultural backgrounds. In addition, three out of four immigrants were literate in Armenian, a high ratio in comparison with the other Southern and Eastern European and Middle Eastern immigrants streaming to America. It was a movement of the young, able-bodied, skilled, and literate.

Immigration resumed with the war's end and continued until the imposition of the quota system by the U.S. Immigration Act of 1924, which virtually ended immigration from Southern and Eastern Europe and the Middle East. In these few years 23,000 more Armenians settled in North America and perhaps 8,000 in South America, including many women who had been orphaned or widowed by the genocide of World War I. In many instances these survivors were brought to the Americas by the heroic efforts of their relatives, often aunts or older sisters, who searched through Syria and Turkey to find them in orphanages and refugee camps or with Turkish families that had befriended them. International assistance through the so-called Nansen passports (named after the Norwegian humanitarian Fridtjof Nansen) rescued many other needy survivors.

These were the last of the founding generation—the over 100,000 Armenians drawn almost entirely from Turkey (only three in every hundred came from Russia or elsewhere) who established the Armenian community in the New World. This was the pioneering generation.

Twenty-five years later a second wave of immigrants began to flow to the New World, again chiefly from the Middle East. The movement began just after World War II, with the arrival of a few thousand Armenians admitted under the Displaced Persons Act of 1948 (an exception to the quota system). It was followed in the 1950s by the migration of about 8,500 Armenians displaced by the Arab-Israeli conflict in Palestine. But the largest numbers migrated after the mid-1960s, when the U.S. Immigration Act of 1965 ended the discriminatory quota system and when the successive crises in Egypt, Turkey, Lebanon, and Iran undermined the once large, prosperous, and stable communities in those countries. After 1975 several hundred Armenians annually left Soviet Armenia for the New World. Many of these newcomers originally had repatriated to Armenia after World War II from Europe, the Middle East, and the United States and had found it impossible to adjust to the socialist regime. Soon other Soviet Armenians, benefiting from American refugee legislation and Soviet easing of immigration restrictions and left destitute by political crises and the catastrophic 1988 earthquake, swelled the total to nearly 11,000 in 1988 alone, after which new American refugee policy sharply reduced the flow.

By and large, the arrivals from the Middle East after 1965 were even more educated, skilled, youthful, and ambitious than their predecessors. Indeed, many political and community leaders regarded their departure from Istanbul, Beirut, and Tehran as an ominous threat to Armenian national survival, since these once-powerful communities close to the historic homeland were bastions of Armenian identity in the diaspora. The flight of thousands annually from Soviet Armenia in the late 1980s also caused severe recriminations. Once the Azerbaijani blockade of Armenia is lifted and American immigration restrictions ease, many more will probably seek to leave for the United States.

Patterns of Settlement

Of the over 100,000 Armenians who arrived in North and South America in the late nineteenth and early twentieth centuries, the vast majority landed in the United States, chiefly at the port of New York. Because of proximity to transportation and jobs, they settled first in the metropolitan areas of the Northeast and Middle Atlantic states: 60 percent settled in Massachusetts, New York, Rhode Island, Connecticut, New Jersey, and Pennsylvania. In 1910 New York City claimed the largest number of foreign-born Armenians (2,616), with Providence (1,970), Worcester (1,584), and Boston (1,189) following close behind. Significantly smaller Armenian settlements in the Midwest were in Cleveland and Akron, Ohio; Detroit and Grand Rapids, Michigan; Racine, Wisconsin; Chicago, Waukegan, and East St. Louis, Illinois. Others pushed farther north through the enclaves in upper New York State and Detroit into Canada's province of Ontario, where they established tiny communities in Brantford, Gault, and St. Catharines. Immigrants shunned rural areas—the single important exception being the large agricultural colony in Fresno County, California—and rarely ventured into the Rocky Mountain states or the deep South. They remained an overwhelmingly urban population.

Settlement followed a regular pattern. First, the bachelors or married men who had left their families behind moved into communal boardinghouses and tenements. There they endured severe overcrowding, poor sanitation, and abysmal diets. The living quarters of the 120 Armenian textile workers in Lawrence, Massachusetts, in 1913 were located in two of the most densely populated blocks in the entire state. In time women and children began to arrive from the Old Country, alleviating the worst of these urban living conditions by providing some domestic amenities and eliminating the necessity of sending money home. As the neighborhoods filled up with families, the unmarried men moved on to the Midwest, where there was less competition for jobs, and reestablished the boardinghouse system.

In Fresno, California, the proportion of immigrants coming in family units was high from the beginning. Many of the Fresno Armenians had first labored for years in eastern mills or factories to save money. They then moved on to Fresno to invest in vineyards, raise their families (for children were needed to help in the vineyards), and build their homes.

Beginning in 1920 the immigrant families who had remained in the East also began to move out of the central cities; economic success, the availability of interurban transportation, and the arrival in their neighborhoods of new and unwelcome immigrant groups prompted their departure. A few were too poor or too attached to the "little Armenias" to abandon them, however, so the Armenian neighborhoods, although considerably diminished, did remain.

Jobs beckoned many to the Midwest, especially to Detroit, chiefly as the result of Henry Ford's guarantee in 1914 of a $5 workday; by 1930 Detroit's Armenian population (3,508) ranked second only to New York City's (6,919).

California, especially Fresno County, had the most rapid growth until the 1930s, expanding from about 10,000 in 1919 to 18,000 a decade later. Despite, or perhaps because of, their increasing numbers, Fresno Armenians were kept from spreading out of their original neighborhoods by antipathy from German Russian immigrants and by restrictive covenants against Armenians, Japanese, Chinese, Negroes, and Mexicans. Meanwhile, the small, sleepy towns surrounding Fresno—Parlier, Fowler, Dinuba, and Yettem ("Eden" in Armenian—the only town exclusively settled by Armenians in the United States) were rapidly populated with Armenian farmers. This expansion phase ended temporarily with the Great Depression (1929-1939), which was ruinous to California's agriculture. Many young Armenians were forced off the land in Fresno and joined the unemployed in San Francisco or Los Angeles.

After World War II new highway systems, suburban housing developments, and greater affluence encouraged Armenians to leave the old settlements for new ones farther outside the city, but communal roots persisted. Some of the easterners again looked to Fresno and Los Angeles as the new paradise; in Fresno, the outlawing of restrictive codes in 1948 finally permitted Armenians to move into middle-class neighborhoods.

The approximately 5,000 to 10,000 immigrants who came annually after 1965 from Soviet Armenia and the Middle East also bypassed the older settlements for suburban ethnic neighborhoods. Haverhill, Massachusetts, closed its Protestant Armenian Church in 1977 for lack of parishioners. Watertown, Massachusetts, remains an active center of Armenian community life, and New York City attracts some newcomers, but more are going to California, especially to the San Francisco Bay Area and Los Angeles County, which now has 250,000 Armenians and is the largest Armenian community in the diaspora.

The growth of Armenian communities in Canada has been substantial since World War II. Canadian immigration restrictions were less severe than in the United States before 1965, and a booming economy in the provinces of Ontario and Quebec attracted newcomers chiefly to the metropolitan centers of Toronto and Montreal. The Canadian Armenian community has reached about 100,000; the newcomers, unlike those in the United States, far outnumber the original settlers who came between 1890 and 1924.

Estimates in 1992 placed the number of Armenians in South America as high as 150,000. The largest communities are in Argentina (80,000), Brazil (25,000), and Uruguay (15,000). As in North America, settlement is highly urbanized: 65,000 Argentinean Armenians live in Buenos Aires alone, and virtually all of the Brazilian community dwells in São Paulo or in Rio de Janeiro.

Economic Life

When the immigrants arrived in the New World in the late nineteenth century, the industrial revolution was in full sway. The vast majority of the newcomers—who were poverty-stricken, without usable New World economic skills, and unable to speak English—entered the economy at its lowest levels, as unskilled and semiskilled factory and mill workers. In the United States, they were the wirepullers, rubber workers, and laborers in the foundries and textile and shoe factories of New England, the operatives in the foundries and shirt and collar factories of upper New York State, and the furniture workers in Racine, Wisconsin. Across the border in Canada, they found jobs tending the furnaces in the mills of St. Catharines and Gault.

Without the protection of labor unions and exploited by entrepreneurs, Armenians endured the classic abuses of the new industrial order: minimal wages; dangerous, heavy work; monotony; and exhaustion at sixty-hour-a-week jobs. Probably the most grueling jobs were those of Russian Armenian laborers in the Riverside, California cement works, who lugged ninety-four-pound sacks of cement all day while breathing the poisonous, dust-laden air of the cement grinders overhead. But factory jobs everywhere in nineteenth-century industrial America were taxing, underpaid, and hazardous. Indeed, as an example of the wretched safety conditions in which the immigrants worked, the *Worcester* (Massachusetts) *Daily Telegram* carried many stories of how inexperienced wire mill recruits caught their hands or feet in the whirring machines. One factory was called the "Amputator." The introduction to industrial America was a brutalizing experience.

But immigrants adapted to the "dark, Satanic mills" for two major reasons: to save enough money to return to their families in Turkey, hence their stay in the mills was temporary; or because they dreamed of one day leaving the factories to open a small store or buy a farm in far-off California. Very few joined the nascent American labor movement; more often they were exploited as strikebreakers.

By the end of the migration (1924), many had left factory life, often for small businesses. One of the favorite occupations was shopkeeping—as barbers, shoemakers, grocers, tailors, and butchers in Boston, New York, and Philadelphia. Some became prominent in photoengraving and photography. Shopkeeping entailed financial risks and hours as long as those in the factories, but it paid better, represented freedom from industrial serfdom, and presented the opportunity to be their "own bosses," a highly valued cultural and economic trait of the immigrants from Turkey with small-trades backgrounds.

The rich agricultural prospects and healthy climate of Fresno, California, lured many others. Investing funds carefully saved from labor in the East, Armenian settlers worked alongside their children in the fields and packing houses; and by good business management, saving, and risk taking, they enjoyed substantial success. In fact, by World War I they had outstripped in wealth the neighboring German Russian, Danish, and even Japanese raisin growers of the San Joaquin Valley.

At the same time, in the major metropolitan centers of the East and Midwest, Armenians virtually monopolized the Oriental rug business. Exploiting the late Victorian craze in Oriental goods and using their connections with markets in Constantinople, London, and Persia, these able businessmen, many of whom were the sons of Old World rug merchants, established flourishing wholesale and retail outlets; one family, the Karagheusians of New York and Connecticut, pioneered the large-scale manufacture of the "domestic Oriental" rug.

The immigrant generation succeeded because of their Old World business and skilled-trades backgrounds, their high literacy rate, their experience as a minority in their native land, and the fact that after the devastation of the homeland in the 1890s and especially after World War I, most knew they were in the United States to stay and hence had to sink roots.

Although a few Armenians pursued education through special citizenship classes, the vast majority could not afford the time to study as they worked to establish themselves in the new land. But the immigrants considered education for their children of paramount importance. *"Tbrots kna vor mart ellas"* (Go to school to be a man) was an immigrant injunction, and older children took jobs to make sure that their younger brothers and sisters would receive the prized high school or college diploma. Indeed, their efforts led to college degrees and white-collar occupations for the second generation. As early as 1921 one study noted that Armenians had the highest percentage of children in higher education of all the newer immigrant groups in America (Gilbert and Bridgeman, 1921, pp. 156-57). Oral history interviews of Armenian survivors of the 1915 genocide revealed that although they most often worked at unskilled or semiskilled jobs, their children were frequently doctors, engineers, or teachers (Harold Takooshian, communication to the author, June 1977). Their upward mobility was further accelerated in the third generation. A 1976 study of Armenians in academic life in the United States noted that they were significantly overrepresented in academic endeavors, especially in science, academic medicine, and engineering (Armenian Assembly, 1975, pp. 1-2).

Yet the attraction of business remained strong. The sons and grandsons of the original California farmers in time established flourishing agricultural communities in Fresno as well as in the Coachella

Valley of Southern California. Kirk Kerkorian, a Las Vegas entrepreneur and the major stockholder in Metro-Goldwyn-Mayer, is a folk hero in the ethnic press. Moreover, Armenians, breaking with entrepreneurial traditions, have moved into the higher echelons of corporate America. One second-generation Armenian was the chief executive officer of the Bank of Boston, one of the country's oldest financial institutions and the sixteenth largest. And among professionals, property ownership and business investments are common.

The recent immigrants from the Middle East are also making their mark in the economy. Most of those from Armenia and the Arab countries arrived with limited skills and took jobs as unskilled and semiskilled workers. But through savings and assistance from family and Armenian philanthropies, they are graduating to the traditional Armenian small stores, filling stations, and auto body shops, especially in the East. Real estate and the jewelry business also attract many: 30 percent of all Los Angeles jewelers are Armenians and in one sixteen-story building, 70 of the 240 jewelers are Armenian. Others from Iran, Iraq, and Lebanon who arrived with resources and experience in the capitalistic economies of those nations succeeded rapidly; for example, the Hovnanian brothers, sons of Iraq's largest road builder, are prominent in real estate from New Hampshire to Florida. For most Armenians, the transition to American capitalism was easy. However, some Armenians from Erevan, many of whom were poor but well-educated professionals and artists who had experienced a cradle-to-grave socialist economic life, at first found life in a capitalistic economy difficult.

Family and Society

The earliest social entities of the immigrant generation were the male-oriented boardinghouses and restaurants, which appeared as early as the 1880s and 1890s in the major settlements. In these three-story tenements, immigrants shared their food and living space to cope with loneliness and to save funds for their return to Turkey. The boardinghouses and restaurants became critical sources of friendship, job information, and assistance during hard times; there, gambling and Old Country songs provided relief from the factory routine. After the 1890s family life began to be established as women migrated to the small Armenian enclaves. However, because males outnumbered females four to one until about World War I, a number of immigrant males traveled to the Old Country or to Marseilles and Beirut after 1920 to find brides; others sent photographs of themselves to prospective mates abroad.

Armenian writers have perhaps idealized Armenian immigrant family life as unified, warmly sharing, and good humored. The family exercised strict control over its younger members through hard work and often harsh discipline; perhaps as a result, juvenile delinquency was virtually unknown. Desertion and divorce were also rare in immigrant life. Pitched battles occurred over the prospect of intermarriage with *odars* (non-Armenians), as parents insisted that their children marry within the group to preserve family ways and culture, while the young people, exposed in public schools and through Hollywood to the concept of romantic love, struggled for social independence. Because of family strife, some either fled their homes or never married. However, the family was an important vehicle of adjustment to the new environment. Families in the New World were magnets for relatives still in the Old Country; newcomers obtained jobs through family members already employed in mills and farms; and husbands, wives, and children often worked together in the home or on the farm. Moreover, the family was the hub of social activity. This meant visiting, often weekly, among relatives and friends from Old Country villages; gatherings of compatriotic societies based on Old World hometown affiliations (these societies raised funds for the villages in Turkey); and the immigrant theater, which by the 1920s flourished in all the sizable Armenian communities. The men were drawn to the social life of the political clubs and the women to that of the Armenian Relief Society, an important charity; both sexes participated in the Armenian General Benevolent Union, the largest charitable organization of Armenians in the United States.

After World War II greater affluence, mass culture, and almost universal education up to the college years transformed this family ethos. The next generations adopted middle- and upper-middle-class American values. Intermarriage increased among the children of the immigrants, and more than 70 percent of all third- and fourth-generation Armenian Americans married non-Armenians, raising troubling prospects for the perpetuation of the culture and ethnic identity. Furthermore, few were learning the language. In college-educated offspring the traditional respect for those older than themselves was replaced by concepts of egalitarianism and meritocracy. Socially, debutante balls, church-sponsored sports, bingo, men's and women's organizations, and the country clubs supplanted the earlier communal forms. Other signs of a new ethos are a higher incidence of divorce in Armenian marriages, though still below the American norm, and the appearance of juvenile delinquency. Brushes with the law among children of immigrants from Armenia and the Middle East indicate the possible presence of severe generational problems among the newest arrivals.

In common with other late nineteenth and early twentieth century immigrants from the Middle East who were derided by racist Americans as the "scum of the Levant," Armenians faced harsh discrimination, not only in places like Lynn, Massachusetts, where they were involved in strikebreaking, but especially in Fresno, where their darker complexions, clannishness, and aggressive business ways in a racially troubled community led to overt discrimination in landowning, employment, and membership in social groups. Armenians were ousted from a Protestant church they helped establish (1894). Attempts to abridge their rights to land and even to citizenship were made before and after World War I, only to be finally settled in 1924 in the Tateos Cartozian case, which affirmed Armenians' Caucasian ancestry and hence their right to be American citizens. For years, however, natives referred to them as "Fresno Indians" and "lower-class Jews." In the East they battled local Irish groups, which referred to them as "Turks."

The major social division facing Armenians after 1965 came from within the community itself, from discord between the older generation of Armenians and the newer immigrants from the Middle East. The newcomers, many of whom are skilled and ambitious, rely on the assistance of the older generation to make their way in the New World; once established, however, they are accused of forgetting those who first welcomed and aided them. The newer immigrants also have assumed from the older immigrants the leadership of Armenian American organizations and headed those organizations with inflexible, Old World, hierarchical methods unfamiliar to the older generation. Furthermore, in California many Soviet Armenian immigrants were charged with living off the welfare system—an anathema to the self-reliant older generation.

The newer immigrants, however, accused the older Armenians of failing to retain their ethnic identity, since these older Armenians, or at least their children, do not speak fluent Armenian. The newcomers think of themselves as more loyal to the historic culture, and they feel patronized by those longer in the land. The newcomers' aggressive attitudes have alienated not only the older generation but also the second, third, and fourth generations, many of whom yearn to contribute but feel neglected and are in danger of being lost to the community. In time, however, and with intermarriage between the offspring of the older immigrants and the newcomers, the differences between these communities, like those that troubled Eastern and Western European Jews in the United States in the late nineteenth century, may ease.

Religion and Education

Armenian religious institutions grew rapidly in the New World. The first Armenian Apostolic Church was consecrated in Worcester, Massachusetts, in 1891; the first Armenian Protestant Church, also in Worcester, dates from 1901. By World War I both groups had established churches in the major communities of the East Coast, Midwest, and California (although Boston lacked an Apostolic church until the mid-1920s). Today the churches, coupled with community centers, are fixtures throughout the United States, Canada, and South America.

The building of the churches in the New World was not without its severe problems, some of which remain to this day. First, the seats of power and authority of the Armenian Apostolic Church (in Constantinople and Echmiadzin) were at great distances from the New World. Troubled by the turbulent events of the mid-1890s, the holocaust of 1915, and the Soviet takeover of Armenia in 1920, the church could not adequately care for its far-flung parishes in North and South America. Furthermore, because of its long decay, its political problems, and the rise of secularism, it lacked a highly qualified clergy worldwide. The clergy in the United States were particularly ill-fitted by training (many had very poor clerical educations) to cope with the problems of an immigrant group in a modern, secular, industrial society. Finally, there were the political problems.

Like the Polish Catholic Church and other Eastern churches, the Armenian Church has always been identified with the nation and has been involved in political issues. In the United States the church has generally taken a conservative stance. In the early 1890s it staunchly opposed the preaching of revolutionary doctrines on its premises, and its clergy battled the anticlerical, Marxist Hnchak and Dashnak parties in that period. But the church did not become crippled by political issues until the 1930s. Then a grievous political battle that culminated in the assassination of an Armenian archbishop on Christmas Sunday, 1933, while he was celebrating the divine liturgy in an Armenian church in New York City, split the church into two rival factions, a schism that exists to this day. As a result many communities now support two

Apostolic churches—one that espouses loyalty to Echmiadzin and the other that is tied to the Cilician hierarchy in Antelias, Lebanon.

Because of these problems and the difficulties in promoting religious life in a secular society, the church has experienced major changes. Most obvious is the diminution of the religious life as it was known in the Old Country—the 160 fast days, the daily matins and vespers, the frequent resort to prayer. At the same time the church has adopted many American ways, such as the increased use of English in the service, the promotion of men's and women's clubs, athletics, and even bingo in the church halls and community centers.

Powerful conservative forces appear, however, to be keeping the church alive. The fear of assimilation has strengthened the church and its social and educational activities as a national focus; a strong effort is being made to promote an American-educated clergy, especially through the establishment of St. Nersess Seminary in New York State; second- and third-generation Armenian Americans participate in a beehive of church-related activities; and despite assimilation and intermarriage, the church is still relied upon for the central rites of marriage, baptism, and death. Meanwhile, powerful efforts are being made by the laity and clergy on both sides of the schism to bring about a reconciliation of the two churches, now recognized as critical in light of crises overseas—the 1988 earthquake, political independence, and the struggle with Azerbaijan over the issue of Karabagh. As in the past, Old World turmoil has invigorated Armenian consciousness and moves toward unity in the New World.

The Armenian Protestant Church, which ministers to perhaps 10 percent of the community, has suffered less in transplanting. The product of the American missionary movement in Turkey and the United States, and often relying on American-educated clergy, the Protestant churches have successfully maintained and extended their role in community affairs. Once regarded as outside the pale of the nation ("There are no Armenians outside of the Apostolic Church," the old saying went), the Protestants are often relied on as neutral arbiters in political and communal issues. Gathered into the Armenian Evangelical Union of North America, and with an active charitable arm—the Armenian Missionary Association of America—the Armenian Protestant community recently has adopted more ceremonial practices in the service and has participated in national rites such as the annual commemorations of the 1915 genocide, all attesting to its full membership in the diaspora community.

A third community is formed by the Armeno-Catholics. With a handful of churches and perhaps 10,000 communicants, the Armenian Catholics, who follow the Eastern rite, are under the jurisdiction of the Armenian Mekhitarist Order of Vienna or the Armenian Catholic patriarch in Beirut.

Politics and the Press

Born of the frustration of the decade after the Treaty of Berlin (1878) and inspired by the example of Greek and Balkan nationalist movements, Armenian paramilitary organizations led the immigrant generation in their quest for political rights for their brethren in Turkey and Russia. By far the most important formal institutions in the immigrant world, these parties (the Armenian Revolutionary Federation or Dashnaks, Social Democratic Hnchak Party, Reformed Hnchak Party, and the Ramkavar Party) organized immigrant colonies into party cells, raised large sums of money for weapons and political work in Turkey, established the immigrant press, and lobbied for American support for Armenian rights. The parties also established a host of ancillary institutions such as libraries, reading rooms, clubs, and marching and dramatic societies, all to preserve and enhance the Armenian community in the diaspora until the time for repatriation arrived.

Although the parties all supported Armenian rights, their positions differed dramatically in the period before and after World War I. Divisions were based on sharp ideological and personal animosities and on different approaches to the use of violence, all of which often alienated potential followers, especially younger Armenian Americans.

In the 1890s conservatives battled the revolutionary Hnchaks and Dashnaks over the dangers involved in mounting armed opposition to the Ottoman regime. In the conservatives' view, help could come only from reliance on the European concert of nations and enforcement of the Treaty of Berlin. After the 1894 to 1896 massacres, the Hnchak and Dashnak committees were suspected not only of having precipitated the massacres but even of having deliberately provoked the Turks into massacres as a way of forcing European intervention, a charge that embittered the debate about how Armenians could obtain justice. The allegation of Armenian complicity in the massacres had some historical backing but has recently been thrown out by Armenian and non-Armenian scholars (Walker, 1980, pp. 171-72; Suny, 1994, pp. 257-58).

Since the Armenian republic's absorption by Soviet Russia in 1920 until the end of the Cold War, the major political lines were drawn on the basis of attitude toward the Soviet situation. For the Dashnaks, who espoused a nationalist and irredentist cause, the destiny of the Armenians lay only in a free and independent Armenia; under the pre-glasnost regimes, the quest for political and religious liberty was only weakened and perverted; the head of the Armenian Apostolic Church in Echmiadzin was merely a tool of the Marxist government; Soviet rule was the antithesis of statehood.

By contrast, the conservative Ramkavars accepted Soviet rule in 1920 as an inevitable and beneficial step toward ensuring eventual independence by providing a great-power mandate over the beleaguered Armenians. In their view Soviet rule was infinitely preferable to an independence threatened with annihilation by numerically and militarily superior Turkish forces. The pro-Communist Armenian Progressive Party, established in the 1930s, followed the international Communist Party line with respect to Soviet Armenia and had no interest in liberation.

Notwithstanding their earlier differences, between 1985 and 1991—the period of glasnost and perestroika—all diaspora parties more closely identified with the social, political, and economic aspirations of the Soviet Armenian citizenry. Beginning with environmental concerns and expanding to demands for Karabagh and self-defense against Azerbaijani nationalist repression, the positions had the full support of the Dashnaks and Ramkavars. The tragedy of the 1988 earthquake also deepened cooperation among the political parties.

Independence in 1991 raised new hopes and ambitions. However, the diaspora parties—the Ramkavars and especially the Dashnaks, which had labored as a quasi-government in exile for over half a century—were crushed in parliamentary and presidential elections by the Armenian National Movement and its leader, Levon Ter-Petrosian. Seeking political talent and ties with the diaspora, the new government enlisted Armenian Americans at the highest levels: Raffi Hovannisian became foreign minister of the republic, Matthew Der Manuelian headed the North American diplomatic desk, Jirair Libaridian later served as deputy foreign minister, and Sebu Tashjian as minister of energy. Quickly, the Ramkavars closed ranks behind the ANM (Armenian National Movement), albeit with some reservations, while the Dashnaks formed a vocal opposition. The issue of Karabagh and especially territorial acquisitions sharply divided the more conservative government from the Dashnaks, who espoused full independence for Karabagh. Although both diaspora parties in time clashed with the ruling ANM, Armenia differed markedly from other states of the former Soviet Union in that democratic, parliamentary institutions and methods—not force and insurrection—were the hallmarks in politics.

An important product of the political formation was the immigrant press. The first Armenian-language papers in the United States actually predated the parties but they were all short-lived, unable to attract outside support. The first long-lasting political journal was *Hairenik* (Fatherland), established by the Dashnaks in New York City in 1899 but afterward moved to Boston. A daily since the pre-World War I period, *Hairenik* (now a weekly) remains an important Armenian-language newspaper. *Baikar* (Struggle), also a daily until 1984 and published in Watertown, Massachusetts, dates from 1923 as an organ of the Ramkavar Party but is no longer published in the United States. Their counterparts in California are the *Asbarez* (Arena) daily (founded 1908) and the *Nor Or* (New Day) semiweekly (founded 1922). Both major parties publish an English-language weekly: the *Armenian Weekly* (Dashnak) (founded 1934 in Boston) and the *Armenian Mirror-Spectator* (Ramakar) (founded 1932 in Watertown). Other Armenian-language newspapers include the Armenian Progressive *Lraber* (Messenger) (founded 1937 in New York and suspended in 1991), the Hnchak *Eritasard Hayastan* (Young Armenia) (founded 1903 in Boston) and more recently the *Masis* (founded 1981 in California). The success of the weekly English-language *California Courier* (founded 1958 in Fresno), the *Armenian Observer* (founded 1971 in Los Angeles), the *Armenian Reporter* (founded 1967 in New York), the bilingual *New Life* (founded 1978), and the monthly *AIM (Armenian International Magazine)* (founded 1990), all three in Los Angeles (founded in 1985), suggests that independent, nonpolitical journals are able to survive.

Armenian politics entered the American political arena in the late nineteenth century. In the aftermath of the Hamidian slaughter of 100,000 Armenians and the threat to American missionaries and property in Turkey, Americans at all levels urged President Grover Cleveland to take strong action, including a declaration of war against the Turks. However, Cleveland's conservatism, the fact that the United States was not a signatory to the Treaty of Berlin, and the brewing Spanish-American War limited American involvement. Nonetheless, American charities, nurtured by seventy years of missionary work with the Armenians in Turkey, were instrumental in relieving widespread hunger and disease.

World War I summoned forth the greatest humanitarian crusade in America's history. Organized through Near East Relief, the sole agency incorporated by Congress to aid refugees "in Biblical lands," Americans contributed to Armenian relief by building refugee camps and hospitals and by distributing food and clothing to hundreds of thousands of the destitute and orphaned. Many first-generation Armenian Americans owe their survival to Near East Relief.

However, American involvement peaked with the war. In 1919 President Woodrow Wilson, aware of the great sufferings of the Armenians and the bankruptcy of Ottoman rule, called for an American mandate over the embattled Armenian republic; and the geographical boundaries of "Wilson's Armenia" became the basis for Armenian territorial aspirations. Although the United States recognized the republic in 1920, conservative opposition to the League of Nations and the rejection of Wilsonian internationalism soon doomed the mandate and the cause.

The impetus for American involvement in Armenian issues in the years since World War II has come from an American-born generation that is entering the American political arena. The first Armenian American to gain prominence in American politics was Steven Derounian, a congressman from New York from 1952 to 1964. Since then substantial numbers have held local, state, and national office, especially in California, where Charles Pashayan (b. 1941) was elected to the House of Representatives and George Deukmejian was elected governor for a second term in 1987. At the same time the Armenian Assembly, founded in 1972, has encouraged Armenian representation in politics by sponsoring summer internships in the nation's capital, lobbying for Armenian causes, and educating the community in political responsibilities.

Meanwhile, the Armenian political parties, after decades of internecine warfare and now stirred by the immense challenges of a nascent but struggling Armenia, are acting in concert on specific issues affecting Armenians worldwide. In the 1980s the political parties, elected officials, and interested citizens urged American support for the recognition, in opposition to well-financed Turkish propaganda, of the enormity of the Armenian genocide. Since the earthquake in 1988 the focus has shifted to appeals for humanitarian, economic, and especially political support for Armenia. United States governmental grants in the millions of dollars, coordinated relief efforts for hospitals, housing and energy supplies, and pro-Armenian positions in Washington on the Karabagh issue are the fruits of the collaborative efforts.

On non-Armenian issues the majority of the community leans toward the Republican Party, upholds conservative, middle-class attitudes toward crime and government (Governor Deukmejian, for example, championed limited government and capital punishment), taxes, education, and a forceful American foreign policy. Despite the conservatism of the Armenians, however, presidents Woodrow Wilson, Franklin Delano Roosevelt, and John F. Kennedy remain heroes to the immigrants and still stand among the community's most revered political figures.

Culture and Group Maintenance

As soon as the immigrants had built up sufficient numbers in the New World, they established a strong cultural life, based on Old World traditions; by the eve of World War I communities from Boston to Fresno boasted Armenian food stores, Turkish Armenian music and cuisine, Armenian dance, theater, and newspapers. By the 1920s, however, changes were already apparent. The language succumbed to American pressures most rapidly. Editors wrote columns lambasting the laborers' use of American slang and swear words, and the second generation, educated in the American public school system, learned kitchen Armenian while speaking English on the streets. Equally powerful was the influence of American mores, the media, and virulent American nationalism, which regarded foreign habits and languages as dangerous and subversive to the United States. Children of immigrants taunted by Anglo-Saxons and others longer in the land than themselves felt embarrassed by their parents "foreign" clothes, "funny foods," and Old World language. They faced the classic conflict of adolescents caught between the demands of their homes and the pressures of their environment.

Americanization most directly affected the written language. Armenian newspapers continued to exist, as they do to this day, but by the 1930s both major political parties, the Dashnaks and Ramkavars, brought out English-language weeklies to perpetuate the Armenian heritage among the second generation which was unable to read in Armenian. Men of letters fared less well. On the one hand, first-generation intellectuals eked out livings as party functionaries and editors, but because of poverty and because the Turks historically stifled free expression, the culture supported little intellectual life on its own—

outside of politics or the political press. By the 1940s and 1950s only a few Armenian-language magazines existed and they soon expired.

On the other hand, Armenians moved into American literature. Most noteworthy was William Saroyan. A proud and enormously gifted second-generation Armenian whose writings gave evidence of the harsh anti-Armenian feelings of his native Fresno, Saroyan dazzled the literary world with his debut, *A Daring Young Man on the Flying Trapeze* (1934), won the Pulitzer Prize in 1939 for his play *The Time of Your Life,* and poured out volumes of plays, short stories, and memoirs, many of which were based on his Armenian background. Michael Arlen, Jr., is known for *Exiles* (1970) and *Passage to Ararat* (National Book Award, 1975); and Diana Der Hovanessian is a noted poet. An important spokesman for the arts both Armenian and non-Armenian, is Vartan Gregorian, former president of the New York Public Library and then president of Brown University. The appearance in 1960 of *Ararat,* an English-language literary quarterly sponsored by the Armenian General Benevolent Union, has created an important forum for young Armenian American writers, but its press run (currently 1,200) testifies to the fact that the community, now entering is fourth generation, has not fostered a large literary subculture.

The cultural aspirations of the community lend themselves more readily to music and dance, forms that were unfettered in Turkey. Folk and liturgical music, compiled in part by the modern composer Gomidas Vartabed (1869-1935), expressed the religious, national, and cultural yearnings of the nation. Armenian operas were produced by popular touring companies in the 1920s. The most celebrated singer was Armen Shah Muradian (1878-1939), whose recordings had a place in every Armenian home. Since the 1950s professionally led choral groups have enjoyed widespread success. Armand Tokatyan (1899-1960), Lucine Amara (b. 1927), Paolo Ananian and Lily Chookasian (b. 1925) have had careers in opera. Composers whose works often draw on Armenian sources for inspiration are Richard Yardumian (1917-1988) and Alan Hovhaness (b. 1911). Dance also remains extremely popular, both in small informal groups and in professionally led troupes. Visiting dance, choral, and orchestral troupes from Armenia draw capacity crowds everywhere. Church groups often provide scholarships for promising musicians and composers. The newest popular music derives its inspiration from the modernized, Western idiom of Lebanon in contrast to the more traditional style of immigrant generation music. Conversely, a new movement toward ethnic purism has led to criticism of the inclusion of Turkish dances and songs in Armenian repertories.

Since the 1960s powerful efforts have been made to revive the Armenian American community's cultural and political awareness. These efforts have emphasized maintenance of the language and heritage, active pursuit of Old World claims against the strident Turkish campaign to expunge the historical reality of the Armenian genocide, and, most recently, aid to rebuild and assist independent Armenia. As external pressures—cultural penetration, intermarriage, and other evidences of acculturation—increase, vigorous conservative forces and Old World demands seek to preserve the threatened heritage and historical past.

The origins of the communal awakening lie in the Armenian Studies movement. In 1959 the Armenian American community, through the National Association for Armenian Studies and Research, established a chair of Armenian studies at Harvard University. The $300,000 donation indicated both a deep commitment to learning and a fear that, unsupported by a political state, Armenian culture would eventually disappear. This and subsequent endowments at Columbia University, the University of California, Los Angeles (UCLA), and Berkeley, the University of Michigan, Tufts University, and California State University, Fresno, underscored the quest for cultural continuity. Programs at Wayne State University in Detroit, the University of Chicago, Glendale City College in California, and elsewhere now attract students to the Armenian past.

The rapid development in the 1970s and 1980s of the Armenian primary and secondary parochial school system reveals the new stress on language and cultural maintenance. In the past, afternoon and Saturday schools had operated vigorously but on limited resources; meager funding, old-fashioned materials, and competition with sports limited their success. In the late 1960s and 1970s, a more prosperous community, expanded by newcomers from the Middle East and buoyed by the national revival of ethnic studies, established full-day professionally staffed and well-financed schools with Armenian and non-Armenian curricula. To some, ethnic survival was and is inextricably tied to the survival of the language itself. To others, it is obvious that the flourishing community is already led by many non-Armenian-speaking sons and daughters and that a renaissance of the language would in any case not revive Armenian letters. Nonetheless, in addition to the currently bolstered Saturday language-school system with more than sixty schools and 4,500 students, there are twenty-one full-time schools with an enrollment of about 5,000 and every prospect of expanding.

The growth of parochial schools, as part of well-endowed community centers, is even greater in the Canadian Armenian community, where the Canadian government, prompted by the French-speaking minority in Quebec Province, has especially since 1971 encouraged multiculturalism and given financial support to ethnic minorities.

In South America academic groups also led a renaissance. In Brazil university-educated youths founded the Brazil-Armenian society in 1954, and others established a chair in Armenian Studies at the State University of São Paulo in 1962. As in Canada and the United States, a community center begun in São Paulo in 1980 capped the efforts of the rejuvenated Brazilian Armenians.

The quest for survival and political recognition of past injustices has been intensified by the ominous developments of the past quarter century. The deterioration of Armenian communities in the Middle East—especially in Lebanon and Iran—brought thousands of immigrants to the United States; and they, with fierce political and cultural commitments to their heritage, swiftly assumed control of much of Armenian American organizational life. Injecting new blood, they also disrupted traditional leadership and methods, leaving a residue of strife and bitterness. In the 1970s especially, the Armenian terrorist movement, fed on the unbridled frustration of the young men of the turbulent and destabilized Armenian communities of the Middle East, and erupting in bombings and assassinations in Europe and the United States, heightened the political debate. At the same time, in the intellectual arena, Armenian academicians led by Professor Richard Hovannisian of UCLA, redoubled efforts to inform Armenian and non-Armenian audiences about the historical reality of 1915 and to repel the attempts, perpetrated by pro-Turkish scholars, to whitewash the genocide. The Armenian National Institute was established in Washington, D.C. in 1997 to gain international reaffirmation of the genocide and to combat denial. However, the intense concentration on the genocide, replete with documentaries, workshops, tape-recordings of survivors, an Armenian Research Center at the University of Michigan–Dearborn, and above all the drive to recognize April 24 by the American Congress as "A Day of Remembrance" has to some a negative side effect. For, like the Jewish absorption with the Holocaust, the Armenian fixation on 1915 tends to create a "garrison mentality" in which a self-critical attitude toward Armenian issues is often avoided.

A final potent and burgeoning source of heightened group consciousness has come from Armenia. The modern opening of contacts
between Armenian Americans and Soviet Armenia dates from 1959,
when at the end of the Stalinist period, Armenian Americans traveled
on tours to the homeland. By the early 1980s about 1,200 Armenian
Americans annually were spending two to three weeks in Erevan,
Echmiadzin, and the countryside while, in the same period, from Soviet
Armenia, dance and music groups and monthly English- and Armenian-
language journals were enthusiastically received in the United States.
Interest in and interchange with Soviet Armenia expanded after 1985
with the opening of trade, borders, communication, and travel. All this,
however, was a prelude to a new chapter in diaspora-Armenia relations
beginning in 1988. For, with the Erevan demonstrations over Karabagh,
the earthquake of 1988, the nationalist movement culminating in independence in September 1991, and the ensuing blockade and war with
Azerbaijan, Armenia became the vital center of Armenian diaspora
consciousness.

In this period, in addition to political efforts to aid the republic,
Armenian Americans, in conjunction with worldwide support, took
extraordinary humanitarian steps to rebuild the earthquake-stricken
towns and villages. As the crises grew, a Children's Milk Fund, the
Women's Reproductive Health Care Center in Erevan, a Medical Out-
reach Program, the ABGU's (Armenian General Benevolent Union's)
Plastic and Reconstructive Surgery Unit at the Mikayelian Institute, and
a host of ad hoc medical groups aimed to aid health in Armenia. The
founding of the American University of Armenia, affiliated with the
University of California, and the establishment of the Haigazian University College School of Management in Erevan, sponsored by the
Armenian Missionary Association of America, supported educational
demands. Operation Winter Rescue (1992 and 1993) brought food,
medicine, and warm blankets, while Project Winter (1994) promised
$21 million in home heating fuel. Clearly, the wounds of Armenia—a
nation living without heat, hot or cold water, or electricity for two
winters—and its aspirations—for health, education, and liberty—have
evoked powerful responses in the diaspora.

As it moves into its second century, the Armenian American
community is caught in the dilemma common to a diaspora community.
On the one hand, it has been pulled by forces and institutions inherited
from the Old World, and its Armenian consciousness will continue to
be heightened by the destabilization of the Middle East, the quest for

political recognition of the genocide, and the fear of cultural extinction. Most important, the independence of Armenia and the perils to its existence stir Armenian Americans. On the other hand, the Armenian American community has integrated itself successfully into the economic, social, and political fabric of the host nation. And in a Westernized society with its public education system, mass media, mobility, and its very congeniality and tolerance toward different cultures, the community's trend toward integration and acculturation will continue. The situation of the Armenians in Canada and in South America is quite similar. Thus, it is likely that the Armenian American community—the largest of its kind outside of Armenia—and its brethren to the north and south will enjoy continued cultural and social strength amid growing acculturative pressures.

FOR FURTHER INFORMATION

For the sources of, or more information on, the material in this chapter, please consult the following (full citations can be found in the Bibliography at the end of this volume).

Arlen, 1975.   Hekimian, 1990.
Avakian, 1977.   Kaprielian, 1987.
Bakalian, 1993.   Mirak, 1980, 1983.
Harney, McCarthy,   Waldstreicher, 1989.
    and Kaprielian, 1982.

13

THE ARMENIAN DIASPORA

R. Hrair Dekmejian

Armenian Diasporas: A Conceptual Framework

The creation of diasporas throughout Armenian history has been the consequence of destabilizing forces that have affected the homeland since early times. These forces have ranged from economic crises and deprivation, to political instability, conquest, religious persecution, massacre, and deportation. Secondary catalysts of emigration from the homeland included the pursuit of foreign trade, educational opportunities, and military careers as mercenaries. Between the fourth century A.D. and the massacres of 1915 to 1922, successive waves of Armenian immigrants and refugees established hundreds of expatriate communities in over thirty different lands throughout the world. Despite the ravages of history, much has survived about the life of these diaspora communities, many of which were to suffer extinction.

The life cycle of diasporas—their genesis, development, and extinction—is determined by a plethora of events and dynamic social forces operating in global, regional, and local environments. Once diasporas are established, their life and destiny become intimately shaped by their immediate national milieu—by the host country's dominant ideology, political system, socioeconomic structure, cultural traditions, and domestic and foreign policies. As a particular diaspora community develops within the political, socioeconomic, and cultural parameters of the host country, it creates its indigenous institutions and structures—religious, political, and socioeconomic—which shape the individual and collective behavior of diaspora members, who also are influenced by ties to the homeland, interaction with other diasporas, and the larger world environment.

With the passage of time diaspora communities tend to adjust themselves to the changing conditions of the host countries. This process of adjustment can be a difficult process. Indeed, the degree to which a community accommodates itself to the host country's prevailing conditions may well determine its long-term integrity and survival.

The Contemporary Diaspora: Formative Events (1894–1990)

The formation of the contemporary dispersion of the Armenian people can be traced to the great massacres of 1894 to 1896 perpetrated under the rule of Sultan Abdul-Hamid II. These massacres, and the subsequent repressive rule of the "Red Sultan," triggered the first major wave of Armenian emigration from the Ottoman Empire.

The Young Turk revolution of 1908 brought a hiatus in the persecution of the Ottoman Armenians. However, the promises of the ruling Ittihad Party to institute reforms proved illusory when, in 1909, 30,000 Armenians were massacred in Adana and other places in Cilicia. Because of its localized character, the Adana massacre did not induce a large population outflow. Indeed, the available evidence suggests that the Armenian leadership in Constantinople and large segments of the population deluded themselves by believing in the capacity of the European powers to press the Young Turk regime to introduce reforms and safeguard basic human rights. These hopes and expectations were cruelly extinguished when the Turkish government began to implement its secret policy of mass deportations and genocide in the spring of 1915.

The defeat of Ottoman Turkey in October 1918 and the promises of the Allied Powers to establish an Armenian state prompted the return home of many survivors of the 1915 massacres. Soon, however, the failure of the Allies to occupy the interior provinces of the empire prevented the demobilization of a substantial portion of paramilitary and regular military units, some of which continued to victimize the remnants of the Armenian population, prompting new waves of refugees from the subsequent Turkish Republic. Meanwhile, the establishment of the independent Republic of Armenia in May 1918 provided the impetus for immigration to the nascent state, which itself was under threat from the advancing Turkish forces. In December 1920 Armenia became a Soviet republic as the leadership of the independent state and its supporters left the country.

The Diaspora in Crisis (1920–1939)

The sovietization of Armenia formalized the duality in the life of the Armenian people between those living under semi-indigenous authority and those in dispersion. Indeed, the establishment of Soviet power over a legally designated territorial entity called Armenia introduced important elements of stability and instability into Armenian life. The main element of stability was the promise of physical security and cultural autonomy for the Armenians living in the republic and those throughout other parts of the Soviet Union. The destabilizing factors concerned the politically and culturally repressive policies under Stalin as well as the ideological dichotomy between the Communist order of the homeland and the pluralism of the diaspora. The upshot was the polarization of the diaspora marked by intense ideological conflicts between the various Armenian parties and groups. Virtually every Armenian diaspora community was split along partisan cleavages, which affected families, cultural societies, educational institutions, and ultimately the Armenian Church.

The Armenian Soviet regime and the political parties of the diaspora played leading roles in the bifurcation of the community. In keeping with its revolutionary creed, the Armenian Communist government sought to maximize its following among diaspora Armenians through propaganda and the neutralization of the Armenian Revolutionary Federation (ARF). As the dominant party in the government of the independent republic, the ARF sought to consolidate its hold on the diaspora communities after its displacement by the Soviets in 1920. The ARF's efforts were opposed by the Social Democrats Hunchak Party (Hunchakian), the Armenian Progressive League (Harachdimakan), and the Armenian Democratic Liberal Party (Ramkavar Azatakan).

The interparty confrontation climaxed in the assassination of Archbishop Levon Tourian in New York City on December 24, 1933, for which several ARF members were inculpated. This tragic episode marked the deepening of the cleavage in the American Armenian community that has persisted until the present time. While the ARF was legally exonerated from any direct complicity in the assassination, the organization and its members were ostracized by the opposition parties. Two consequences of the Tourian episode were the split in the Armenian Church in the United States and a concomitant weakening of the ARF, although the party was able to reinvigorate itself after World War II, by its forthright opposition to Communist rule.

World War II and Repatriation (1939–1948)

During World War II the Armenians fought on all fronts against the Axis powers. In view of the tacit alignment of Turkey with Nazi Germany in the early war years, the Armenians feared the consequences of an Axis victory. On the Soviet side they fought with uncommon valor and sustained the highest battle casualties among the Soviet nationalities. Four Armenians rose to the rank of Marshal of the Soviet Union—a distinction granted only to a dozen top Soviet commanders. Armenians also fought in the American and French armies as well as in the French resistance against the German occupation.

The immediate postwar period was one of misplaced optimism for the Armenian diaspora. Two important events caused a temporary heightening of Armenian hopes after the war's ravages. The first was the call to return to the homeland. To the diaspora, the call from the homeland was embodied in the magic word *Nergaght* (Repatriation)— which spoke to the deepest yearnings of the Armenian people. The decision to permit the repatriation of the Armenians had been made at the highest councils of the Soviet Communist Party and by Stalin himself. In response, 150,000 Armenians from Syria, Lebanon, Iran, France, Greece, Egypt, the United States, and other countries immigrated to the Armenian Soviet Republic.

The second development that heightened the political consciousness of the Armenian diaspora was the reopening of the territorial question between Turkey and the USSR in the wake of Germany's defeat. At the war's end the USSR requested the return of the Kars, Ardahan, and Artvin provinces that had been ceded to Turkey in 1921 at a time of Soviet weakness. These claims were made in the name of the Armenian and Georgian republics that occupied contiguous areas to the provinces in dispute. For Armenians the world over, the return of these areas meant the reconstruction of their homeland along the territorial expanse of the independent Armenian republic of 1918 that had been supported by the Allied Powers. However, the Soviet Union's principal Western allies—Great Britain and the United States—were not prepared to permit Soviet territorial expansion to the detriment of Turkey. The Soviet territorial claims were shelved during the mid-1950s in the context of the Cold War and the bipolar struggle between the Soviet Union and the Western powers. Soon after Stalin's death, the Soviet Union formally renounced its claims on Turkey and inaugurated a policy of rapprochement with the Ankara government which had become a member of the North Atlantic Treaty Organization (NATO) in 1950.

The shelving of the Soviet territorial claims had a disheartening impact on the Armenians who considered the provinces a part of historic Armenia and as a partial reparation by Turkey for the massacres of 1915. Significantly, all shades of Armenian political opinion, including the anti-Soviet ARF, supported the Soviet territorial claims. More disappointing was the mass repatriation to the homeland. By the late 1940s, Soviet authorities halted the repatriation of the Armenians. Due to the ravages of war, no more newcomers could be absorbed by a country suffering serious economic deprivation. Indeed, it soon became apparent that the new immigrants had become a major socioeconomic burden for the Armenian government. In the heady milieu of repatriation, many immigrants had forsaken their economically comfortable and politically tolerant existence in the diaspora, in exchange for the economic hardships of the homeland ruled by Stalinist totalitarianism. Indeed, the expatriates had performed *nergaght* despite the appeals of many host governments, particularly in the Arab world, who had urged the Armenians to remain. Moreover, the repatriations were a hardship for the indigenous Armenian population, which had to share with the newcomers the country's meager resources.

The Diaspora in the Cold War (1948–1958)

The breakup of the wartime alliance against the Axis powers triggered the Cold War between the Soviet bloc and the Western countries led by the United States. The ensuing ideological and military confrontation seriously affected the Armenian diaspora. It would not be an exaggeration to state that the Cold War was fought in every Armenian community regardless of its size or location.

Emboldened by the West's challenge to Soviet hegemony over Eastern Europe, the ARF emerged from its wartime status of defensiveness to take the lead against the opposition parties. In the pro-Western countries of the diaspora, the ARF sought to maximize its influence as a counterweight to the Armenian Soviet authorities. While these efforts were not always successful, the ARF was able to force the opposition Hnchak, Ramkavar, and Progressive parties into the defensive, in view of their vocal support of Soviet Armenia. The interparty struggle was characterized by ideological coloration, along with certain inconsistencies between ideology and policy. As Marxist parties, the Hnchakists and the Progressives were consistent in their support of the Communist regime of the homeland. In contrast, the Ramkavar ideological position manifested inconsistencies when compared with the party's class base and orientation toward Soviet Armenia. Traditionally, the Ramkavars were the party of the Armenian bourgeoisie, which had opposed the ARF's socialist and populist orientation. Consequently, Ramkavar support for Soviet Armenia, at least in part, flowed from its opposition to the ARF. Moreover, the Ramkavars were at pains to emphasize that their support for the Armenian Soviet regime was based on patriotism rather than ideological sympathy. As to the ARF, clearly its socialist ideology had to be diluted in view of the party's alliance with the Western powers.

The death of Stalin in March 1953 and Nikita Khruschev's de-Stalinization campaign contributed to the gradual relaxation of Soviet-American relations. In the Armenian diaspora, however, the Cold War was reaching its zenith. In their internecine struggle, the political parties succeeded in writing some of the darker pages of Armenian history.

Once again the struggle centered on the church and its administrative apparatus. The passing of Catholicos Garegin of the Cilician See in Antelias, Lebanon, in 1952 prompted a struggle for succession. Bishop Zareh of Aleppo, Syria, was elected catholicos by the National Ecclesiastical Assembly, over which the ARF had considerable influence. The bishop's election was opposed by a coalition of anti-ARF parties that had the tacit backing of the Armenian Soviet authorities. Consequently, the Catholicos of All Armenians based at Echmiadzin in Soviet Armenia refused to recognize the legitimacy of Bishop Zareh's election. Despite the negative stance of the Echmiadzin Holy See, Bishop Zareh was consecrated Catholicos of Cilicia on February 20, 1956, and proceeded to extend his administrative authority over the dioceses of Greece, Iran, Venezuela, Kuwait, and American dissident parishes, thereby deepening the political bifurcation of the diaspora. This controversy acutely polarized the large community of Lebanon, leading to internecine warfare in the context of the Lebanese civil strife of 1958. Armenian militants fought on both sides of the conflict, with the ARF supporting President Camille Chamoun, while the Hnchak-Ramkavar-Progressive coalition joined the Arab nationalists led by Prime Minister Rashid Karami and Kamal Junblat.

Beginnings of Détente (1958–1965)

While the communal Cold War raged in the diaspora, the homeland was beginning to enjoy the benefits of de-Stalinization. Significantly, First Secretary Nikita Khruschev's momentous initiative of de-Stalinization had found a vocal supporter in Anastas Mikoyan, the Politburo's sole Armenian member. One consequence of the Soviet liberalization drive was the establishment of close cultural relations between the homeland and the diaspora. Beginning with the late 1950s, increasing numbers of expatriate Armenians visited the republic. Simultaneously, many Soviet-Armenian writers, musicians, composers, scientists, and dance ensembles toured the diaspora centers. These contacts had a powerful effect on the ethnic life and regeneration of the cultural ethos of diaspora Armenians. Equally important was the growing spiritual impact of the Holy See of Echmiadzin, which had been accorded considerable latitude by the Soviet authorities to minister to the religious needs of the diaspora. The relaxation of official controls on the Holy See was also instrumental in strengthening the administrative ties between the clerical hierarchies of the homeland and the expatriate communities. For the first time in modern history, the supreme catholicos was able to pay visits to his flock in dispersion. The successive pastoral visits of His Holiness Vazgen I to France, Egypt, Italy, England, and the United States evoked mass enthusiasm and adulation.

Another consequence of de-Stalinization was the progressive remission of the Cold War amid efforts by the superpowers to forge a *modus vivendi*. After a half decade's lag, the Armenian diaspora began to experience the atrophy of its own cold war. Thus, the mid-1960s saw a decrease in intracommunal political conflict and a pervasive quest for communal harmony. Meanwhile, unforeseen political developments in both the homeland and abroad came to influence Armenian life in the diaspora.

Alienation and the New Nationalism (1965–1985)

Concurrent with the decline of ideological fervor and interparty cleavages was a general increase in the economic well-being of Armenian communities throughout the world. Having suffered the ravages of massacre and deportation during World War I, the Armenians had achieved a significant degree of economic prosperity in virtually every host country. This was accomplished through a combination of hard work, self-reliance, and entrepreneurial ingenuity—attributes that had served them well in their long history of struggle against difficult odds. However, economic well-being was not accompanied by a sense of contentment and happiness. Several factors were discernible after the mid-1960s as being responsible for feelings of discontent:

1. The gradual realization of the permanence of diasporic existence, in view of the prevailing sociopolitical conditions of the homeland.
2. The persistent concern with the threat of assimilation and loss of identity.
3. The pervasive feeling of political impotence in the world community of nation-states because of the lack of national independence.
4. The deep sense of loss and moral outrage against Turkey for the massacres perpetrated during and after World War I, which had gone unacknowledged by the world community and denied by the Turkish government.

In combination, these factors worked in a mutually reinforcing manner to magnify communal discontent and frustration. Behind the veneer of socioeconomic well-being lurked the tormented soul of the Armenian that bore the scars of suffering and genocide.

The feelings of subdued rage and political impotence were to produce a peculiar personality type in diaspora settings: the confident, extroverted, and good-natured member of Western society bent on conformity and success, and the perpetual rebel and persistent alien, scarred by the burdens of the tragic past, who viewed the world with deep cynicism, despair, and metaphysical anguish. Significantly, this psychospiritual dichotomy, which was also shared by the Armenians of the homeland, finally surfaced during the 1960s and 1970s in an upsurge of militancy in every community from the Armenian republic to the Middle East, Europe, and the United States. The first manifestation of this nationalist fervor occurred in April 1965, on the fiftieth anniversary of the 1915 massacres, when mass demonstrations broke out in the streets of Erevan. These demonstrations, unprecedented in the history of the USSR, were directed against Soviet policies of rapprochement with Turkey and the concomitant efforts to suppress anti-Turkish gatherings to commemorate the massacres and to protest Turkish control over former Armenian territories. The predictable Soviet response included a party purge and arrests of "bourgeois nationalists." However, the authorities made some concessions sanctioning the public commemoration of the massacres and building a lofty memorial outside Erevan for the victims of the genocide.

The events of April 1965 were to have important repercussions in the homeland and the diaspora. A new spirit of national consciousness appeared in the Soviet Armenian literature that found its echo in the cultural life of the diaspora. The example set by the Armenians of the republic in challenging the Soviet authorities was a source of pride and inspiration for the dispersion. In retrospect, this challenge provided the impetus for the emergence of a new wave of national consciousness that turned into militancy under the impact of incipient crises besetting the diaspora. The immediate catalysts included the displacement and deprivations suffered by the large Armenian communities of Lebanon, Iran, and Turkey. The emigration from Armenia itself added to the widespread demoralization. The Lebanese civil war exposed that country's Armenians to the radicalizing influences of their revolutionary milieu. Hence the beginning of armed militancy against the Turkish government, which had persisted in its denial of the genocide and instituted a massive campaign to distort history and to denigrate the Armenian people in worldwide propaganda.

Profiles of Diaspora Communities

Iran

Sizable Armenian communities have lived in Iran for over 1,700 years. There have been significant historical and cultural affinities between the Armenians and Persians rooted in their common Zoroastrian-Aryan past, despite the subsequent religious separation brought on by Armenia's Christianization and Persia's Islamization.

The rise of Persian nationalism in the 1890s against the dual imperialism of Britain and Russia was supported by Armenian leaders such as Malcom Khan, who emerged as a major exponent of Persian constitutionalism and nationalism. As a consequence of the 1915 massacres in Turkey, the arrival of numerous refugees swelled the ranks of the Armenian communities of Iran. With the establishment of the Pahlavi dynasty by Reza Shah, the Armenians flourished in such urban centers as Tehran, Tabriz, Abadan, Isfahan, and Rasht. Indeed, the Armenians constituted Iran's largest non-Muslim community, numbering over 200,000. Being mostly apolitical, the Iranian Armenians were not greatly affected by the authoritarian nature of the regime; indeed, given their entrepreneurial predilections, the Armenians fitted well into Iran's free-wheeling oil economy. In addition, they were given substantial autonomy in all aspects of communal life. For those Iranians seeking to rediscover their pre-Islamic identity, the Armenians provided an unbroken cultural bond to their Aryan past.

The onset of the Iranian revolution of 1979 and the establishment of the Islamic Republic triggered a wave of emigration that included many Armenians. However, the remaining Armenians still constitute the largest non-Muslim presence in Iran, despite the periodic imposition of social and educational constraints by Islamic militants. As one of Iran's oldest communities, the Armenians have been spared the persecutions of Iran's Jewish and Bahai minorities. Under the Islamic regime's Shari'a law, the authority of the Armenian Church has been expanded and two Armenian deputies represent the community in the *majles*—the country's parliament.

Turkey

The 1915 genocide perpetrated by the Ittihadist leaders of the Ottoman Empire found its culmination under the Turkish nationalist regime of Mustafa Kemal (Ataturk). Between 1922 and 1930 the survivors of the 1915 massacres from the regions of Cilicia, Kharpert, Diarbekir, and the Sanjak of Alexandretta experienced death, persecution, and deportation. All that remained was a community of 80,000 in Istanbul and small groups in the interior provinces, many of whom were forcibly Turkified. Some of these provincial Armenians have been brought to Istanbul by the patriarchate in recent years and reintegrated into the Armenian community. During World War II, the Armenians of Turkey along with Greeks and Jews were subjected to the payment of a wealth tax, *varlik vergisi*, which was arbitrarily imposed on non-Muslims to bring about their pauperization. Those unable to pay these heavy taxes were deported to eastern Turkey and condemned to hard labor. The postwar period witnessed some improvement in the community's situation. However, in 1955 the Armenians and Greeks of Istanbul were terrorized by the desecration of their churches and cemeteries by Turkish mobs enraged over the Cyprus issue and incited by government officials. Meanwhile, the patriarchate and its parochial schools were placed under arbitrary restrictions. As a result, significant numbers of Armenians have immigrated to Europe, Canada, the United States, and South America. In addition, the community has had to cope with the Turkish government's displeasure at the manifestations of Armenian activism in various diaspora centers during the last two decades. Despite their difficult circumstances, the Armenians of Turkey, numbering about 50,000, managed to endure under the perspicacious leadership of Patriarch Shnork Kalustian. After the passing of the patriarch in February 1990, the community experienced the flagrant intervention of the Turkish authorities in the election of a new patriarch.

Egypt

Armenians have been living in Egypt since the sixth and seventh centuries. During Arab rule a number of Islamized Armenians assumed key military and administrative positions as viziers, governors, and generals. With the onset of the Muhammad Ali dynasty, the Armenians were granted unprecedented opportunities to contribute to the socioeconomic development of Egypt. Of the many high officials, Nubar Pasha was the most prominent as prime minister. By the late nineteenth century, there were 10,000 Armenians in Egypt—a number that progressively increased to 40,000 because of the massacres and deportations from Turkey. They were mostly engaged in commerce, industry, the service professions, and skilled crafts. In subsequent years, the size of the community decreased because of immigration to the Armenian SSR, Australia, and North America. During the first decade of the 1952 revolution, the Armenians were commended for their loyalty and were not compelled to emigrate as were the Jews, Italians, and Greeks. However, the regime's socioeconomic reforms, particularly after the socialist laws of 1961, had an enervating effect on the Armenians, some of whom incurred economic losses. At present about 6,000 Armenians are concentrated in Cairo and Alexandria, where they maintain community schools, newspapers, churches, and cultural and athletic associations.

Ethiopia and the Sudan

Small Armenian communities existed in Ethiopia as early as the seventh century, perhaps as a reflection of the religious ties between the Ethiopian and Armenian churches, which share a common theology. By late nine-teenth century, the Armenians were centered in Addis Ababa, Harar, and Diradawa, where they had gained prominence in business, government, and diplomacy. The Armenians participated in the Ethiopian armed resistance to the Italians; after the Italian conquest of 1936, the community decreased because of persecution and emigration. Under Emperor Haile Salassie close religious ties were maintained as Bishop Terenik Poladian of Lebanon was appointed dean of the Ethiopian Theological Seminary. Since the emperor's overthrow in 1974, the community has shrunk in size to several hundred persons, although it still maintains a church and a school.

The Armenian community in the Sudan was established in the early nineteenth century only to dwindle during the Mahdist revolution of the 1870s. After General Kitchener's reconquest (1896-1899), the number of Armenians increased until the 1960s. The growing instability of the country in the 1980s resulted in considerable emigration, although about 300 remain in Khartum, where they maintain a church, a primary school, and cultural organizations.

Syria, Lebanon, and Iraq

Armenian settlements have existed in the Fertile Crescent area since the time of King Tigran (95-55 B.C.). In recent times, the Hamidian massa-cres (1895) marked the beginning of successive waves of new im-migrants settling in Aleppo, Beirut, and other cities of Syria and Lebanon. During World War I the Arabs were reluctant to carry out the Ottoman government's order of *jihad* and instead gave the fleeing Armenians aid and protection. In this sense the Arabs became one of the few benefactors of a people marked for destruction. Over 200,000 Armenians took refuge in the eastern Arab lands, mainly in Syria, Lebanon, Egypt, Iraq, and Palestine. Initially, few of them envisaged a long-term settlement; they expected to return to the land of Armenia. Soon, however, reality forced them to plan for a more permanent stay in the Arab lands; hence the need for the rapid mobilization of the community and the establishment of religious and cultural institutions, an elaborate school system, and the means for economic well-being. It was a familiar pattern of group behavior that had repeated itself through-out Armenian history. Having just "returned from the dead," the Arme-nians were determined to survive and to compensate for their losses and deprivations of the past by a drive to excel in a brief time span.

This peculiar dynamism was in sharp contrast to the Middle East's traditional socioeconomic environment. In the Ottoman context, because of their ties to the West, the Armenians had Westernized earlier than the other inhabitants of the empire. While their higher developmental level accorded the Armenians confidence and even feelings of superiority vis-à-vis the host society, it also produced intercommunal tensions, especially after the rise of Arab nationalism. The Armenians became visible, particularly in the economic life of Syria and Lebanon, since there were important technical and entreprencurial roles to be filled in these developing countries. Also the Armenians' familiarity with Western languages and cultures made them the key "brokers" in foreign commerce and "mediators" between the European mandatory authorities and the indigenous population. In general, the Armenians shied away from involvement in political affairs; they remained urbanites with petit bourgeois outlooks, lacking sufficient concern with the political and social currents influencing Arab society. The radicalization of Arab nationalism after the rise of Israel and the consequent establishment of leftist Arab military regimes had a detrimental effect on Armenian life.

After World War I, Syria became home to over 100,000 Armenian refugees, emerging as the fourth largest center of the Armenian dispersion after the Soviet Union, the United States, and Iran. Over half the Armenians lived in Aleppo, where they constituted one fourth of the city's inhabitants. Others lived in Damascus, Hama, Homs, and Lataqiyyah and the oasis towns of Jarablus, Dayr al-Zur (Deir ez-Zor), al-Hasaka, and al-Qamishli. In short order, a network of over sixty schools was established in addition to political societies, newspapers, and cultural and athletic associations. During Syria's struggle for independence, the Armenians rebuffed French efforts to turn them against the Arab nationalist movement, a stance that the newly established Syrian government lauded. Consequently, the Armenians of Syria enjoyed a large measure of communal autonomy until the formation of the Syrian-Egyptian union in February 1958. In a milieu of radical nationalism and anti-Western sentiment, the authorities suppressed the Armenian Revolutionary Federation for its allegedly pro-Western activities and sharply circumscribed the Armenian press and political groups. Meanwhile, community schools and their curricula were brought under direct state control. These restrictive policies induced a precipitous rise of emigration from Syria. The progressive radicalization of the Ba'thi regime in the mid-1960s was reversed after the takeover by General Hafiz al-Asad in November 1970. Under the Asad government the situation of the Armenian community has substantially improved. The secular stance of President Asad's Ba'thi regime and its success in defeating the fundamentalist insurrection of the late 1970s have provided once again a propitious environment for the Syrian Armenian community of some 120,000.

Armenians who took refuge in Mount Lebanon during the nineteenth century were partially assimilated into the Maronite and Protestant communities. In the mid-eighteenth century, Armenian Catholic monks established the monastery of Bzummar, while two Armenian Catholics, Dawud Pasha and Ohannes Pasha Kuyumjian, served as the Ottoman governors of Mount Lebanon from 1861 to 1868 and from 1912 to 1915, respectively. The successive massacres in Turkey and emigration from Syria contributed to the establishment of a large community, mostly centered in Beirut. Prior to the outbreak of the Lebanese civil war in 1975, the Lebanese Armenian population numbered over 200,000, which supported about 80 schools and numerous newspapers and political and cultural associations. In addition, the town of Antelias near Beirut has been since 1930 the seat of the Catholicosate of Cilicia in the patriarchal reigns of Sahag II (Khabayan) and Coadjutor Catholicos Papken I (Giulesserian), Bedros I (Saradjian), Garegin I (Hovsepian), Zarch I (Payaslian), Khoren I (Paroyan), Karekin (Garegin) II (Sarkissian; subsequently Garegin I of the Holy see of Echmindzin) and Aram I (Keshishian). Until the civil war, Lebanon provided a most ideal setting for the Armenians. There existed a perfect fit between the Armenians' propensity for business and Lebanon's capitalistic system. More important, Lebanon's sectarian sociopolitical milieu gave the Armenians complete communal autonomy and substantial political participation both in parliament and the cabinet. Indeed, Lebanon became a second homeland for the Armenians, and the civil war of 1975 was a special tragedy. The internecine bloodletting of the 1958 conflict was not repeated, as the Armenian political societies united to assume a neutral stance between the warring factions. The community's militia fought only when Armenian-populated areas were threatened. The Armenian reluctance to fight the leftist-Muslim-Palestinian coalition brought armed retaliation from some Maronite factions. Meanwhile, a large number of Armenians along with many other Lebanese sought refuge in Syria, Canada, the United States, France, and other European countries, many on a temporary basis, waiting to return after the establishment of peace. As to Lebanon's future, the Armenians remain ardent exponents of independence and a rejuvenated consociational system.

The roots of the present community in Iraq can be traced to Shah Abbas's forced relocation of the Armenians to Iran, some of whom subsequently moved on to Mesopotamia. The ranks of Iraq's Armenians swelled with the arrival of 25,000 survivors who had fled from the Turkish Armenian provinces during World War I. These Armenians, along with Chaldean and Nestorian refugees, were housed at a camp in Baquba by the British military authorities. In due course, the Armenians left Baquba and other camps in Mosul and Basrah to work in the cities as technicians, craftsmen, minor government functionaries, and petroleum workers. After the revolution of 1958, the government of Brigadier General 'Abd al-Karim Qasim proscribed the activities of some Armenian societies for their alleged pro-Western tendencies and placed the Armenian Church under close surveillance. These unsalutary developments coupled with political instability resulted in substantial emigration from Iraq. The Ba'thi takeover in mid-1968 brought a measure of stability to the Armenian community, which now numbers about 10,000. During the 1980s, the Armenians benefited from President Saddam Hussein's modernization efforts as the community rebuilt its cultural institutions and even consecrated an imposing cathedral in Baghdad. Along with other Iraqis, the Armenians suffered during the Iran-Iraq War (1980-1988) and the Gulf War of 1991.

Jerusalem, Israel, and Jordan

Armenians settled in the Holy Land as early as the fourth and fifth centuries, as Jerusalem became an important center of learning and pilgrimage. The patriarchate of Jerusalem was established during the seventh century to guard the rights and sanctuaries of the Armenian Church. Since early times communal life was centered in the Armenian Quarter of the Old City, dominated by the patriarchal monastery of St. James, which was generously endowed throughout the centuries by Armenian royal and princely families and wealthy benefactors. Despite periodic persecutions under Muslim rule, the patriarchate survived as protector of Armenian rights in the Holy Land and as a center of scholarship.

Several thousand Armenian refugees settled in Palestine after World War I, but the community was shaken by the 1948 Arab-Israeli war and the partition of the country. During the war, most Armenians living in the coastal towns and the New City took refuge in the walled monastery, but after the armistice were prevented from returning home by the Israelis. During the 1950s some Palestinian-Armenian refugees were admitted to the United States as stateless persons. The Israeli occupation in 1967 reunited the Armenians of the Old City and the West Bank with the small congregations that had remained in Haifa and Jaffa.

Armenian community life in Jerusalem experienced considerable internal turmoil arising from internecine conflicts within the St. James Order, which oversees the affairs of the holy sites in Jerusalem. The election of Archbishop Tiran Nersoyan as patriarch in 1957 was overturned by the Jordanian government, and Archbishop Eghishe Derderian became patriarch, causing substantial dissension within the order and the diaspora at large. The accession of Archbishop Torkom Manoogian upon Patriarch Derderian's death in January 1990 may have opened a new era of reconstruction and renewal in this age-old center of Armenian religious life although dissension still exists.

A small community of 1,000 lives in Amman, Jordan, in a hospitable environment under the Hashemite monarchy. As a consequence of the oil boom, large numbers of Armenians from Syria, Lebanon, Jordan, and Iraq settled in the Arab sheikhdoms of the Gulf. 20,000 Armenians are working in Kuwait, Saudi Arabia, Bahrain, Qatar, and the UAE. A community of 10,000 has prospered in the liberal Kuwaiti environment, where it maintains a church, school, and a vibrant cultural life.

Cyprus, Greece, and Bulgaria

Armenians appeared in Cyprus as early as the fourth century. After World War I, several thousand Armenians took refuge in Cyprus, where they flourished until the Turkish conquest and occupation (1974) of the northern part of the island. At present a community of 2,500 is mostly centered in Nicosia and Larnaca. The Melkonian College established in 1926 in Nicosia has provided a well-rounded education to generations of needy Armenian students mostly recruited from Middle Eastern countries.

Between 1916 and 1923 a total of 45,000 Armenian refugees moved to Greece from Turkey. Despite the efforts of the Greek authorities, these refugees faced severe deprivations in a country saddled with the absorption of 1,200,000 Greeks expelled from Turkey. Eventually many of the Armenian newcomers found their way to France, the Arab countries, and the United States, while some remained to establish roots in Greece, mostly in Athens and Thessaloniki. During World War II the Greek-Armenians joined the indigenous guerrilla movement and fought the Nazi occupation army. In recent decades the community numbering 15,000 has continued to prosper in a hospitable environment.

The earliest Armenian migrations to Bulgaria date back to the eleventh century. These apparently included Armenian Paulicians from Thrace who, around A.D. 1000, joined the Bulgarians in revolt against the Byzantines. In the early nineteenth century there were over 10,000 Armenians in Bulgaria—a number that more than tripled after the Balkan War of 1912-1913 and the massacres of 1915. In the early 1900s Bulgaria became a haven for Dashnakist revolutionaries, such as Kristapor Mikayelian. At present the Armenian community numbers around 15,000, mostly centered in Varna, Plovdiv, and Sofia.

Romania, Hungary, and Poland

Sizable Armenian communities lived in Romania beginning with the fourteenth century. These communities declined under Ottoman rule, although by the mid-nineteenth century there were 20,000 Armenians still living in Romania. Beginning with 1895, there were substantial influxes from the Ottoman Empire. After World War II, large numbers of Romanian-Armenians migrated to the Armenian SSR and to the United States. The present size of the community is estimated at several thousand centered in Bucharest and Constanta. The most distinguished Romanian-Armenian is Catholicos Vazgen I (1955-1994).

In contrast to the more tolerant Orthodox milieu of Romania, the sizable Armenian communities in neighboring Hungary and Poland did not survive. Numbering 15,000 in the early nineteenth century, the Hungarian community was mostly assimilated because of the pressures by the Hapsburgs to accept Catholicism. A similar fate awaited the Armenians of Poland. By the eighteenth century these large communities had become mostly assimilated under the protracted campaigns of the Roman Church.

The Asian Diasporan Communities

Despite their historical significance, little remains today of the Armenian communities of India, Burma, Indonesia, Singapore, and China. In the eighteenth century Armenian life flourished in Madras, Bombay, and Calcutta. A century later India's prosperous Armenian communities had declined; a small community now survives in Calcutta. Similarly, the Burmese-Armenian community, which had produced traders, generals, and palace functionaries in the seventeenth century, had dwindled in the nineteenth century. The Armenian church still stands in Rangoon, but there are no Armenians left. Meanwhile, the Indonesian island of Java had become a center of Armenian settlement. In 1831 a church was built in Batavia (Jakarta) and then another in Surabaya to accommodate immigrants from Persia and India; by the latter part of the twentieth century this community had become extinct.

Until the onset of Chinese Communist power in 1949, a small Armenian community endured in Shanghai and Harbin, Manchuria. During the war years, the parish priest of the Harbin community, the Very Reverend Asoghik Ghazarian, was interned by the Japanese authorities and subsequently incarcerated by the Chinese Communist regime until his expatriation in 1951. Today there are no Armenians in China, although about a thousand Armenians are spread throughout Japan, Hong Kong, and the Philippines, without any organized community life.

While the Asian diasporas have become virtually extinct, Australia and New Zealand have emerged as new centers of Armenian settlement. The bulk of the immigrants arrived after World War II, mostly from the Middle East. The present community numbers about 20,000, mostly living in Sydney and Melbourne. The growing population has prompted the establishment of a church diocese, schools, and many social and cultural organizations, political societies, radio programs and newsletters. A community of 400 Armenians has grown up in nearby New Zealand.

Russia

In recent centuries Russia emerged as a haven for Armenians escaping persecutions, resulting in the establishment of Armenian communities in dozens of urban centers. New waves of immigrants arrived in the nineteenth century, including students, political activists, and intellectuals because of instability in the Ottoman and Persian realms. Russian Armenians became prominent as generals in the tsar's armies and as leading revolutionaries at the top echelons of Lenin's Bolsheviks. After the establishment of Soviet power, there was substantial emigration from the Armenian SSR to the European and Asiatic parts of the Soviet Union, mainly for reasons of employment. Until the late 1980s, 1,300,000 Armenians lived outside the Armenian SSR, with large concentrations in Georgia, Azerbaijan, Central Asia, Kharkon and other cities of the Ukraine, and major urban centers of European Russia such as Moscow, Leningrad, Krasnodar, and Rostov. The Soviet Union's demise in 1991 triggered a reverse flow of Armenians from the Islamic republics into European Russia and Armenia itself.

Georgia and Azerbaijan

Armenians have lived in Georgia since early times. In the nineteenth century Tiflis rivaled Constantinople as a major center of Armenian intellectual and political life. Until the civil strife preceding the collapse of the Soviet Union, about 400,000 Armenians lived under culturally favorable circumstances in mainly Tbilisi, Akhalkalaki, and Sukhumi. The Abkhasian separatist conflict uprooted the Armenians of Sukhumi, and the civil war and economic crisis have created an uncertain future for Georgia and its large Armenian communities.

In contrast to Georgia, Azerbaijan has been less hospitable to its large Armenian minority. The emergence of Baku as an oil-producing center in the early 1900s provided employment and business opportunities for large numbers of Armenians, some of whom joined the ranks of the nascent Bolshevik movement. After the withdrawal of Russian armies in 1917, the Armenians of Baku were subjected to pogroms and persecutions under a Turkish-sponsored regime. Although the sovietization of Azerbaijan in 1920 halted these persecutions, Stalin's incorporation of Nagorno-Karabagh and Nakhichevan into Azerbaijan created a long-term destabilizing element in Armenian-Azerbaijani relations. Soviet president Gorbachev's policies of openness set the stage for Armenian demands to reunite Nagorno-Karabagh with the Armenian Republic. In 1988 these demands triggered pogroms and massacres by Azerbaijanis against the Armenians of Sumgait, Baku, and Kirovabad (Ganja), prompting the hasty exodus of 400,000 Armenians who took refuge in Armenia, Russia, and other parts of the Soviet Union.

Western Europe

The growing economic and political influence of the West European countries since the 1600s became a magnet for Armenian merchants, students, and expatriate intellectuals and political activists. In view of its historical ties to the Cilician kingdom and its tradition of liberty, France became the largest center of Armenian settlement. Around the turn of the century, Paris became a haven for Armenian expatriate revolutionaries and intellectuals as a prelude to the onrush of over 50,000 immigrants between 1921 and 1925, which swelled to 70,000 in the late 1930s. A significant number of French-Armenians distinguished themselves in the French resistance against the Nazi occupation. The growing instability of the Middle East in the 1970s brought new waves of immigration to France particularly from Iran and Lebanon. In the early 1980s the community was estimated at 200,000, mainly living in Paris, Marseilles, Lyon, Vienne, and Valence. The Armenian community has become an integral part of French society while maintaining a vibrant ethnocultural life centered around the Armenian Church and numerous political and educational institutions. French Armenians have been at the forefront of political activism in the pursuit of Armenian interests in European councils and in helping the nascent Republic of Armenia.

Armenian settlers first arrived in Great Britain in the thirteenth century, escaping from the Mongol invasion. During the eighteenth century, Armenian merchants went to Britain from India, and by mid-nineteenth century Armenian traders had settled in Manchester. In the 1910s a small community had grown around London, which now exceeds 10,000 with recent arrivals from the Middle East. Churches are maintained in Manchester and in London, which now boasts a score of Armenian cultural, social, athletic, and political societies.

Commercial ties with Germany were established during the Crusades and renewed after the seventeenth century. In the mid-1800s Armenian students entered German universities, including such renowned figures as Gomidas (Komitas) and the Catholicos Garegin Hovsepiants. Since the 1950s several thousand Armenians have settled mostly in German urban centers, particularly in Cologne and Frankfurt.

Prior to the establishment in Vienna of the Roman Catholic Mekhitarist Order in 1811, the Armenian presence in Austria consisted of merchants who had arrived in the seventeenth century. The community grew in the early 1900s with new arrivals from the Middle East. Aside from the educational work of the Mekhitarist fathers, the Vienna Armenian Apostolic community, now numbering over 1,000, maintains a church and cultural organizations.

Before its decline during the Napoleonic conquests, the Armenian community of Holland had distinguished itself in the economic and cultural spheres. The first Armenian church in Europe was opened in Amsterdam in the seventeenth century. In the 1600s Armenian merchants played a dominant role in the Dutch silk trade with Persia. In 1660 a monk from Echmiadzin established a printing press and published the first printed book in the Armenian language. Currently small communities exist in Amsterdam and Amalu.

The first center of Armenian settlement in Belgium was Antwerp, where a printing press was established in 1695—another milestone in

Armenian cultural history. Beginning in late nineteenth century, Belgium attracted Armenian students and merchants. The interwar years saw the expansion of the community, which was further augmented by recent immigrants from the Middle East. At present about 2,000 Armenians reside in Belgium, mostly in Brussels, where they have a church and other community organizations.

In the late nineteenth century a small community took root in Geneva as Swiss universities began to attract Armenian students from the Russian and Ottoman empires. The prevailing democratic order provided a propitious environment for the establishment of Armenian revolutionary societies at the turn of the century in Geneva and Lausanne. In recent decades the ranks of the community have swelled with Middle Eastern immigrants. The present community of about 2,000 is centered in Geneva, which serves as the religio-cultural center of Swiss-Armenians.

Despite the presence of Armenian traders, no significant Armenian community took root on the Iberian peninsula except for a small settlement in Cadiz in the eighteenth century. In recent years small Armenian communities have taken shape in both Portugal and Spain. Lisbon serves as headquarters of the Calouste Gulbenkian Foundation and the site of the renowned Gulbenkian Museum of Art.

Sizable Armenian communities sprang up in the large Italian cities during and after the Renaissance period, only to become assimilated under the religious constraints imposed by the papacy. In 1717 the Mekhitarist order of expatriate Armenian Catholic monks founded one of the foremost centers of Armenian learning on the island of San Lazzaro near Venice. Apart from their literary and cultural contributions, the Mekhitarists established a network of schools throughout the diaspora, many of which have remained active until the present. Today several thousand Armenians live in Rome, Milan, and other Italian cities. The largest concentration is in Milan, which is the site of the only Armenian Apostolic Church in Roman Catholic Italy.

Latin America

Armenians began to settle the Latin American countries mainly after World War I. Since the 1950s additional immigrants have arrived, mostly from the Middle East. The largest Armenian community, of about 80,000 resides in Argentina, where it maintains a variety of religious, cultural, and educational institutions in Buenos Aires and

Cordoba. Much smaller is the Armenian community of Brazil, numbering 20,000, mostly in São Paulo. Also, there is a community of about
15,000 in Montevideo, Uruguay, and about 2,000 Armenians residing
in Caracas, Venezuela. Small communities of several hundred reside in
Chile, Mexico, and the Central American republics.

Canada

Armenians first migrated to Canada in large numbers after World War
I as refugees from Turkey. There has been a continuous flow of new
immigrants since the early 1950s because of the progressive destabliza-
tion of the Middle East. The current Armenian presence is about 45,000,
mostly centered in Montreal and Toronto, with smaller communities in
Vancouver, Hamilton, St. Catharines, and other urban centers. Cana-
dian-Armenians enjoy a vibrant community life clustered around both
Apostolic and Protestant churches, cultural societies, schools, and political associations. As a response to the rapid growth of the Armenian
population, the Echmiadzin and Cilician sees have established independent dioceses to minister to the religio-cultural needs of their flocks.

United States

The first large influx of immigrants came after the Hamidian massacres
of 1895-1896. A second but smaller wave of immigration occurred in
the aftermath of the Adana massacres of 1909 as a prelude to a massive
third wave of refugees escaping the massacres and deportations of 1915
to 1922. Armenians tended to cluster in the industrial urban centers of
the Northeast, the Midwest, and the West Coast, with the notable
exception of the farmers who settled in California's San Joaquin Valley.
As in the case of other newcomers, the early Armenian immigrants
formed their communal ghettos where they built their churches and
clubs. Major centers included Boston, New York, Philadelphia, Detroit,
Chicago, and Los Angeles along with some medium-size cities—
Worcester, Providence, Hartford, Troy, Binghamton, Syracuse, Niagara
Falls, Cleveland, Racine, Granite City, and Fresno. Armenians did not
settle in the Southern states in large numbers, although in recent decades
communities have sprung up in Georgia, Florida, Louisiana, Tennessee,
Texas, New Mexico, and Arizona.

    Initially, most of the immigrants were employed as factory work-
ers and small shopkeepers. However, this pattern of employment has

virtually disappeared since World War II with the emergence of small and large entrepreneurs and professionals. This evolution in occupational patterns reflects the overall betterment in the socioeconomic status of the community as well as the class composition and aspirational orientation of the immigrants arriving since World War II. In contrast to the immigrants of the 1890s and 1909 to 1923, who included large numbers of farmers and artisans, the newcomers were mostly from the Middle East's urban centers, with typically middle-class backgrounds and aspirations. While the early immigrants possessed generally modest levels of education, the new arrivals were usually well educated and proficient in English and other languages. These generational, cultural, and socioeconomic differences were destined to create significant social tensions within the American-Armenian community particularly during the 1970s, when a new influx of immigrants began to arrive from Lebanon, Turkey, Iran, and Soviet Armenia. Another important characteristic distinguishing the recent immigrants from their older compatriots was a sense of political worldliness and self-confidence, which predisposed some of them toward greater involvement in the American political process. The newcomers also include an intelligentsia that has faced the difficult task of establishing roots in the American setting.

As a consequence of the new immigration, the American-Armenian community is estimated as approaching 1 million, of which nearly half live in California. The election of George Deukmejian as governor in 1982 represented an indication of the political vigor of the Armenian community of California.

The growth of the community has led to an unprecedented church-building effort along with the establishment of many full-time community schools and the multiplication of newspapers, journals, and cultural and athletic organizations. The two sees of the Apostolic Church have 130 parishes. An additional thirty churches are maintained by the Armenian Protestant and Armenian Catholic communities. Because of its growing size and wealth, the American-Armenian community has assumed a leading role in the development of the homeland and the diaspora.

Diasporas in Evolution: Dominant Patterns

The evolution of Armenian communities in dispersion throughout history suggests certain characteristics and patterns that seem to repeat themselves with great regularity. The identification of these patterns enables the social scientist to analyze the life cycle of diaspora communities of the past and the causal factors shaping their evolution. The discernment of these general patterns of historical experience should prove useful to scholars and those seeking to guide the development of present-day diasporas. At the most general level, ten patterns can be identified.

1. Primacy of Coercion as Causal Factor

The primary trigger of large-scale Armenian emigration from the homeland virtually always involved some form of coercion—deportation, religious persecution, political oppression, forced relocation, or escape from physical annihilation. Historically, the Armenians tended not to abandon their homeland en masse in quest of better economic opportunities. The recent emigration from Armenia represents an exception to the historical pattern.

2. Transience of Diaspora Existence

Since historical times, Armenians have perceived the diaspora as a temporary phenomenon—a transient place of existence that would culminate in the inevitable return to the homeland. This psycho-spiritual predisposition has been a pervasive and persistent feature of Armenian life until the present, although with the passage of time many diaspora communities have had to establish roots and a sense of permanence.

3. Patterns of Survival and Assimilation

The natural response to life in dispersion was to make intensive and protracted efforts to maintain ethnic identity through communal insularity against overwhelming odds, until ties to the homeland were severed because of distance, passage of time, or crisis conditions that made communication impossible. The inevitable consequence was acculturation and assimilation. In general, there was an inverse relationship between the rate of assimilation and the incompatibility of the religio-cultural environment. For example, the rate and likelihood of Armenian assimilation was much lower in the Muslim lands than in the Christian countries. Moreover, there existed an inverse relationship between hostile diaspora milieux and the rate and likelihood of assimilation. In other words, the more inhospitable the host country, the greater the probability of Armenian survival.

4. Deprivation—Compensation—Elitism

The persecutions suffered in the homeland, the denial of the opportunity to develop their own country, and their minority status in dispersion have combined to propel the Armenians to excel whenever conditions were reasonably propitious. Thus, the persistent quest for economic well-being and cultural achievement in diaspora settings was a form of compensation for the Armenians' inability to develop their homeland as well as a mechanism to achieve a sense of security in foreign environments. Yet this quest for excellence and sociocultural and economic elitism has often proven detrimental to many Armenian communities, since the achievement of prominence inevitably brings visibility, which in turn triggers negative reactions from the dominant majority, ranging from socioeconomic pressures, to persecution, deportation, and ultimately liquidation. Despite the Armenians' pride in serving their hosts, they have harbored deep feelings of anguish and frustration for their inability to serve the independent Armenia of their dreams. Indeed, throughout two millennia Armenian generals led the armies of Byzantium, Egypt, Russia, and Persia but seldom their own, and despite their renowned wealth, Armenian merchants and entrepreneurs could not ameliorate the plight of their poor kinsmen at home. The pervasive feeling has been: "We serve others well, but not ourselves."

5. Bourgeois Lifestyles

Despite the prominence achieved by many Armenians in the political and military affairs of some countries, the rank and file of diaspora communities usually have tended to shun political activism or even involvement in host country politics, even in hospitable democratic contexts. This tendency may be attributable to the centuries of subservience to foreign rule and the deep conviction that political involvement is ultimately dangerous; hence the redirection of efforts toward economic well-being and intellectual, cultural, and religious endeavors. As a consequence, diaspora Armenians have sought to adopt bourgeois lifestyles marked by an innate conservatism and eschewal of politics.

6. Heightened Intracommunal Politics

While Armenians generally abstain from deep involvement in host country political affairs, the internal life of diaspora communities is often marked by vigorous competition between the various political societies and groups. Historically, intracommunal politics has involved struggles among leaders, ideologies, and political groups seeking to dominate the church and the community. These political conflicts are often exacerbated by generational differences, class conflicts, and cultural cleavages between the newcomers and natives, and among groups of immigrants from different countries.

7. Religio-Cultural Nationhood

As founders of the first Christian state in around A.D. 301, Armenians have always felt a sense of mission as the privileged bearers of the divine grace. The early years of Armenian Christianity were marked by extensive missionary work among the peoples of the Caucasus until the onset of the Zoroastrian persecutions and the spread of Islam. In these circumstances of adversity, the Armenians viewed themselves as the "flock of New Israel" *(uz-hod nor Israeli)* committed to the Christian faith, which eventually became the ideological foundation of a peculiar religio-cultural nationhood centered in the Armenian Apostolic Church.

Thus, the fifth-century fusion of revivalist Christianity and resurgent ethnocultural identity produced a religio-cultural symbiosis that served as the ideological bedrock of Armenian nationhood for 1,500 years both in the homeland and the diaspora. It was significant that Armenians through the ages have regarded themselves not simply as a "people"—*zhoghovurd*—but as a "nation"—*azg*—even after the loss of independent statehood. This sense of ancient nationhood has also persisted in diverse diaspora settings throughout the centuries.

8. Social Insularity and Cultural Parochialism

As in the case of other ethnic groups, Armenian communities tend toward social insularity in diaspora settings. While economic ties are quickly established with the larger society, Armenians tend to view excessive social and cultural relations with non-Armenians as being inimical to their survival as a close-knit community. Centuries of persecution have deepened the sense of paranoia toward "outsiders"—

odars—who, even in democratic settings, are sometimes regarded with apprehension lest they marry Armenians, thereby hastening the community's assimilation. On the other hand, *odars* are welcomed into the community should they show readiness to integrate themselves into the Armenian cultural milieu. In recent decades there has been a decline in communal insularity in the Western countries such as France, Britain, and the United States.

However, the propensity for self-encapsulation often transcends social relations to affect the intellectual life of contemporary Armenian communities, particularly in America and Europe. Complaisant within the boundaries of their "cultural ghetto," many Armenians remain impervious to the powerful sociopolitical and intellectual currents swirling in their larger environment. In their self-criticism, some Armenians have correctly diagnosed this parochialist syndrome and termed it *ailamerzhutiun*—which implies a reluctance to accept outside influences that could prove detrimental or at best are unworthy of emulation. The combined effect of this parochialist worldview and the Armenians' petit bourgeois outlook has produced certain salient behavioral patterns among the new generation of the diaspora—a causal relationship that requires further empirical investigation. In the choice of educational specializations and career goals, for example, Armenian college students appear to favor the applied professions rather than abstract theoretical subjects, music, the arts, literature, and advanced fields of research in the social and behavioral sciences. While the traditional Armenian emphasis on education has persisted, the quest for knowledge for its own sake has given way to pragmatic goal-oriented education. These factors may have blunted the potential for creativity and hindered the emergence of a "world-class" Armenian intelligentsia of writers, scientists, musicians, and scholars.

9. Postgenocide Syndrome

The genocide of 1915 to 1922 has had both a long- and a short-term social-psychological impact on recent generations. There has been little empirical research on the dimensions of this impact, although certain of its attributes can be tentatively identified, particularly in child-rearing practices. It has been observed that children of the first and second generations after the genocide of 1915 to 1922 were raised in overprotective homes where parents displayed persistent concern about their safety. As a consequence, the postgenocide generations grew up with a pervasive sense of insecurity and dependency, which left psychological scars on some and impeded their normal development. On the other hand, those who were not deeply affected by the genocide syndrome responded to the tragic past with determination to establish successful lives and flourishing communities.

10. The Armenian Church as National Bastion

The patterns of migration, settlement, survival, and extinction over the last fifteen centuries of dispersion point to the epicentric role of the Armenian Apostolic Church as preserver of ethnocultural identity. The church followed the immigrants wherever they went, and church buildings functioned as the centers of Armenian cultural life. Consequently, the Armenian Church was called upon to transcend its spiritual mission to become the cultural stewart of the diaspora. Indeed, during the centuries since the loss of political independence, the church had become the sole repository of the Armenian heritage in the homeland. Yet it was infinitely more difficult for the church to pursue its socializational goals in the diaspora where its ethnocultural role sometimes overshadowed its spiritual mission. Despite the contradiction between these dual roles, the church had no real choice—since without securing the cultural identity of its faithful it would be left without a flock to spread Christ's message. The church's cultural stewardship was particularly crucial in communities lacking well-developed educational and political organizations. Axiomatically, the church's strong institutional presence and vigorous cultural activism combined to forestall the assimilation process in many communities. With an unbroken institutional life of seventeen centuries, the Armenian Church remains potentially a powerful spiritual and organizational force in both the homeland and the dispersion. The poet Vahan Tekeyan called it "a shining shield," while to Patriarch Malachia Ormanian, the church was "the visible soul of the absent fatherland."

The Diaspora in Transition

The unfolding of momentous events and developments in the Soviet Union since 1985 have had a powerful impact on the Armenian diaspora in terms of its structure, institutional makeup, ideological orientation, morale, and sense of priorities. These changes primarily were triggered by the cataclysmic earthquake that devastated northern Armenia in December 1988, the subsequent demise of Soviet power, the proclamation of Armenia's independence, the Karabagh crisis and the ensuing Azerbaijani-Armenian confrontation.

The impact of these successive crises galvanized the diaspora communities outside the Soviet Union. As the full dimensions of the troubles besetting Armenia began to unfold, it became apparent that the external diaspora would be called upon to play a crucial role in sustaining the homeland. Indeed, the survival of Karabagh and the newly independent republic required a mobilized diaspora that could provide not only economic assistance, but also political support and even military aid. These were awesome burdens for the geographically disparate Armenian communities still beset by their ideological and sectarian divisions and the ravages of the Lebanese civil war and instability in the Middle East.

Diaspora's Economic Role

Soon after the earthquake, Armenians throughout the world initiated successive campaigns to dispatch funds, medicine, equipment, and basic essentials to provide short-term aid to the thousands left destitute. The imposition of an Azerbaijani-Turkish blockade and the Soviet government's failure to implement reconstruction programs further underlined the imperative of systematic planning in the diaspora in order to provide comprehensive assistance to the republic's economy on a long-term basis. An important manifestation of such a strategy was the establishment of the United Armenian Fund (UAF)—composed of seven major diaspora church and relief organizations, backed by Kirk Kerkorian's Lincy Foundation—which dispatched planeloads of supplies to the homeland on a regular basis. Simultaneously, Armenian political groups successfully lobbied their home governments to extend economic assistance to the beleaguered republic.

These protracted efforts brought a gradual realization that the resources of the diaspora were insufficient to sustain the homeland's faltering economy. In fact, a conflict of priorities soon beset the diaspora communities, which were forced to postpone or reduce support for their own needs for the benefit of the homeland. This conflict in priorities became exacerbated by the needs of a growing number of immigrants from Armenia and other parts of the former Soviet Union.

Diaspora's Political Restructuring

The demise of the Soviet Union and the consequent rise of nationalist groupings in the Armenian republic brought about significant ideological and institutional changes in the diaspora communities. Specifically, the discrediting and subsequent collapse of Soviet political institutions in Armenia undermined the ideological legitimacy of the pro-Soviet political parties in the diaspora. Faced with these hard realities, the political stance of some of these parties became anachronistic. In contrast, the traditional nationalist ideology of the Armenian Revolutionary Federation (ARF) and its call for independence assumed maximal legitimacy, as the tricolor of the pre-Soviet Armenian republic gained general acceptance in the homeland and throughout the dispersion.

At first this ideological transformation did not induce a heightening of interparty conflict, as each affected political group reoriented its respective ideological stance to conform with the new realities of the homeland. Indeed, a general quest for interparty cooperation was necessitated by the deteriorating economic and political conditions in the homeland. These cooperative efforts also involved the two sees of the Armenian Church and other cultural and professional organizations.

However, this short interregnum of relative ideological quiescence came to an end soon after the proclamation of independence and the onset of interfactional politicking in the new republic. The transformation of the Karabagh Committee into the Armenian Pan-National Movement (APM) and its rise to political dominance in the homeland set the stage for renewed interparty competition in the diaspora. Prompted by the nascent democratic milieu, the three parties of the diaspora established their presence in the republic in order to participate in the evolving political process. Having engaged in seventy years of often-bitter politicking, now these parties had the opportunity to engage in electoral contests and to assume the responsibilities of governing and parliamentary opposition—tasks in which neither the APM nor the diaspora parties had much experience. The election of Levon Ter-Petrosian as president by a lopsided majority and his decision to govern through the APM placed the ARF and the other groups into the opposition. Consequently, the political struggles of the homeland were exported to the diaspora, where the APM sought to build its own constituency. To be sure, these manifestations of heightened interparty politics could be regarded as a normal part of democratic political life, as patterned after the Western democracies. The problem was that conditions in the homeland were not normal; nor were democratic norms and practices firmly rooted in the republic and the diaspora. Yet despite the emergency conditions brought on by the Azerbaijani blockade and the Karabagh fighting, there were no serious attempts to suspend the divisive inter-party struggle through the formation of a national unity government that would unite the parties and factions within Armenia and the diaspora at a time of national peril.

In the foreseeable future, developments in the Republic of Armenia and Karabagh can be expected to exert a strong influence on diaspora life. Relations between the homeland and the diaspora will remain a delicate problem given the different priorities, agendas, and interests that the two sides are destined to pursue, as determined by their different milieux. The stabilization of Armenia's political life under a constitutional order remains the best guarantee for the development of mutually beneficial ties between the homeland and diaspora communities. The creation of such an effective symbiotic relationship is a challenge that requires enlightened leadership in both the diaspora and the homeland itself.

FOR FURTHER INFORMATION

For the sources of, or more information on, the material in this chapter, please consult the following (full citations can be found in the Bibliography at the end of this volume).

Abrahamian, 1964.

Alboyadjian, 1941, 1955, 1961.

Armstrong, 1976

Dédéyan, 1982.

Dekmejian, 1975, 1976.

Hourani, 1947.

Hovannisian, 1962, 1974, 1993.

Hudson, 1968.

Kardashian, 1943.

Kevorkian, 1954–67/68.

Mserlian, 1947.

Sanjian, 1965.

Suleiman, 1967.

Suny, 1983.

Walker, 1980.

Wyszomirski, 1975.

BIBLIOGRAPHY FOR VOLUMES I AND II

Abovian, Khachatur. 1858. *Verk Hayastani* (Wounds of Armenia). Tiflis.

Abrahamian, A. G. 1964. *Hamarot urvagids hai gaghtavaireri patmutian* (Concise Outline of the History of Armenian Expatriate Communities). Erevan.

Abu, Salih. 1865. *The Churches and Monasteries of Egypt and Some Neighbouring Countries.* Trans. B. T. A. Evetts. Oxford.

Acoghic. See Stepanos Asoghik (Taronetsi).

Adontz, Nicholas. 1970. *Armenia in the Period of Justinian.* Trans. and Comm. by Nina Garsoïan. Lisbon.

Aftandilian, Gregory. 1981. *Armenia: Vision of a Republic: The Independence Lobby in America.* Boston.

(Agathangelos). 1970. *The Teaching of Saint Gregory: An Early Armenian Catechism.* Trans. and comm. R. W. Thomson. Cambridge, MA.

Agathangelos. 1976. *Agathangelos, History of the Armenians.* Trans. and Comm. R.W. Thomson. Albany, NY.

Ahmad, Feroz. 1969. *The Young Turks.* Oxford.

Ahmed Emin (Yalman). See Emin (Yalman), Ahmed.

Ajarian, Hrachia. 1942-1962. *Hayots andznanunneri bararan* (Dictionary of Armenian Personal Names). 5 vols. Erevan.

Akinian, Nerses. 1958. "Zruits bghndze kaghaki" (The Tale of the City of Bronze). *Handes Amsorya.*

al-Baladhuri. 1968. *The Origins of the Islamic State.* Trans. Ph. K. Hitti. 2 vols. New York. Originally published in 1916.

Alboyadjian, Arshak. 1941, 1955, 1961. *Patmutiun hay gaghtakanutian* (History of Armenian Emigrations). 3 vols. Cairo.

Alishan, Ghevond (Leonce M.). 1888. *Léon le Magnifique.* Translated from Armenian. Venice.

Alishan, Ghevond. 1893. *Sisakan.* Venice.

Allen, W.E.D., and Paul Muratoff. 1953. *Caucasian Battlefields.* Cambridge, UK.

Amasiatsi, Amirdovlat. See Amirdovlat Amasiatsi.

Amirdovlat Amasiatsi. 1459. *Akhrapatin.* Preserved in Matenadaran Institute of Manuscripts, no. 8871.

Amirdovlat Amasiatsi. 1926. *Angitats anpet*. Ed. K. V. Basmajian. Vienna.

Amirdovlat Amasiatsi. 1940. *Ogut bzhshkutian* (Utility of Medicine). Ed. St. Malkhasian. Erevan.

Ammiani Marcellini res gestae libri qui supersunt. Ed. and trans. R.C. Rolfe. 3 vols. Loeb Classical Library.

(Anania Shirakatsi) (Anania of Shirak) Anania Širakac'i. 1964. "Autobiographie d'Anania Sirakac'i." Trans. H. Berbérian. *Revue des études arméniennes*, n.s. 1.

(Anania Shirakatsi) (Anania of Shirak) Ananias of Širak. 1992. *The Geography of Ananias of Širak (Ašxarhac'oyc'): The Long and the Short Recensions*. Trans. R. H. Hewsen. Beihefte zum Tübinger Atlas des Vorderen Orients, Reihe B, 77. Wiesbaden.

Ananian, Paolo. 1961. "La data e le circonstanze della consecrazione di S. Gregorio Illuminatore." *Le Muséon* 74. Original Armenian version published in *Pazmavep* (1959-1960).

Ananias of Širak. See Anania Shirakatsi.

Ananun, Davit. 1926. *Rusahayeri hasarakakan zargatsume* (The Social Development of the Russian Armenians). Vol. 3, *1901-1918*. Venice.

Anasian, Hakob. 1957. *Haykakan aghbiurnere Biuzantiayi ankman masin* (Armenian Sources on the Fall of Byzantium). Erevan. English trans. in A. K. Sanjian (Cambridge, MA, 1969), and with commentary in *Viator* 1 (1970).

Anasian, Hakob. 1961. *XVII dari azatagrakan sharzhumnern arevmtian Hayastanum* (The Seventeenth Century Freedom Movements in Western Armenia). Erevan.

Anderson, M. S. 1966. *The Eastern Question, 1774-1923*. London.

Andreasyan, H. D. 1964. *Polonyali Simeon'un seyahatnâmesi, 1608-1619*. Istanbul.

Aparantsi, Simeon. See Simeon Aparantsi.

Appian. "The Mithridatic Wars." *Appian's Roman History*. Ed. and trans. Horace White. Vol 2. pp. 240/1-476/7. Loeb Classical Library.

Appian. "The Syrian Wars." *Appian's Roman History*. Ed. and trans. Horace White. Vol 2. pp. 104/5-236/7. Loeb Classical Library.

Arakel Tavrizhetsi (Arakel of Tabriz). 1896. *Patmutiun* (History). Vagharshapat.

Arakelian, A. 1964. *Hay zhoghovrdi mtavor mshakuiti zargatsman patmutiun* (The History of the Development of the Intellectual Culture of the Armenian People). Vol. 2, *XIV-XIX Centuries*. Erevan.

Areveltsi, Vardan. See Vardan Areveltsi.

Aristakēs Lastivertc'i. See Aristakes Lastiverttsi.

(Aristakes Lastiverttsi) (Aristakes of Lastivert) Aristakes de Lastivert. 1973. *Aristakes de Lastivert. Récit des malheurs de la nation arménienne*. Trans. M. Canard and H. Berbérian. Brussels.

(Aristakes Lastiverttsi) Aristakēs Lastivertc'i. 1985. *History.* Trans. R. Bedrosian. New York.

Arkomed, S. T. 1929. *Pervaia gruppa revoliutsionerov armian na Kavkaze.* Tiflis.

Arlen, Michael J. 1975. *Passage to Ararat.* New York.

Armenian Academy of Sciences. 1971-1984. *Hay zhoghovrdi patmutiun* (History of the Armenian People). Vols. 1-4. Erevan.

Armenian Assembly. 1975. *Directory of Armenian Scholars.* Washington, D.C.

"An Armenian Catholic Bishop of Nakhichevan." 1837. *Journal Asiatique* (March).

Armenian Delegation. 1919. *Réponse au mémoire de la Sublime-Porte en date du 12 février 1919.* Constantinople.

Armstrong, John A. 1976. "Mobilized and Proletarian Diasporas." *American Political Science Review* 70, no. 2 (June).

Arrian. *Anabasis Alexandri.* Ed. and trans. E. I. Robson. 2 vols. Loeb Classical Library.

Arutjunova-Fidanjan, A. 1986-1987. "Some Aspects of the Military-Administrative Districts and of Byzantine Administration in Armenia during the 11th Century." *Revue des études arméniennes,* n.s. 20.

Arutyunian, N. V. 1970. *Biainili (Urartu): Voenno-politicheskaia istoriia i voprosy toponimiki* (Biainili [Urartu]: Military-Political History and Questions of Place-Names). Erevan.

Asar Sebastatsi (Asar of Sebastia). 1993. *Girk bzhshkakan arhesti* (Book on the Medical Art). Ed. D. M. Karapetian. Erevan.

Asdourian, P. 1911. *Die politischen Beziehungen zwischen Armenien und Rom vom 190 v. Chr. bis 428 n. Chr.* Venice. Armenian edition (1910).

Asoghik, Stepanos. See Stepanos Asoghik.

Avakian, Arra. 1977. "Armenians in America: How Many and Where." *Ararat* 18, no. 1 (Winter).

Avdall, Johannes. 1841. "On the Laws and Lawbooks of the Armenians." *Journal of the Royal Asiatic Society of Bengal* 111.

Aydenian, Arsen. 1866. *Critical Grammar of Ashkharhabar or the Modern Armenian Language* (in Armenian).

Azarpay, Guitty. 1968. *Urartian Art and Artifacts: A Chronological Study.* Berkeley.

Baberdatsi, Ghazar. See Ghazar Baberdatsi.

Bakalian, Anny. 1993. *Armenian-Americans: From Being to Feeling Armenian.* New Brunswick, NJ.

Balcer, J. M. 1984. *Sparda by the Bitter Sea.* Chico, CA.

Baldwin, Oliver. 1926. *Six Prisons and Two Revolutions.* London.

Baltrusaitis, Jurgis, and Dickran Kouymjian. 1986. "Julfa on the Arax and Its Funerary Monuments." In *Armenian Studies/Etudes Arméniennes: In Memoriam Haïg Berbérian,* ed. Dickran Kouymjian. Lisbon.

Barkan, O. L. 1958. "Essai sur les données statistiques des registres de recensement dans l'Empire ottoman aux XVe et XVIe siècle." *Journal of the Economic and Social History of the Orient.* Vol. 1.

Barsoumian, Hagop. 1982. "The Dual Role of the Armenian Amira Class with the Ottoman Government and the Armenian *Millet* (1750-1850)." In vol. 1 of *Christians and Jews in the Ottoman Empire,* eds. B. Braude and B. Lewis. New York.

Barton, James L. 1930. *Story of Near East Relief, 1915-1930.* New York.

Basmadjian, Garig. 1971. "Armenian Poetry: Past and Present." *Ararat* (Spring).

Bauer-Manndorff, Elizabeth. 1984. *Das Frühe Armenien.* Vienna.

Bedoukian, Kerop. 1978. *The Urchin: An Armenian's Escape.* London. Published in the U.S. under the title *Some of Us Survived* (New York, 1979).

Bedoukian, P. 1978. *Coinage of the Artaxiads of Armenia.* London.

Bedoukian, P. Z. 1962. *Coinage of Cilician Armenia.* New York.

Bedrosian, Margaret. 1991. *The Magical Pine Ring: Armenian-American Literature.* Detroit.

Berbérian (Perperean), Haïg. 1965. *Niuter K. Polsoy hay patmutian hamar* (Material for the History of the Armenians in Constantinople). Vienna. Originally published as a series of four articles in *Handes Amsorya.*

Beylerian, Arthur. 1983. *Les grandes puissances: L'Empire Ottoman et les Arméniens dans les archives françaises, 1914-1918.* Paris.

Boase, T. S. R. 1978. *The Cilician Kingdom of Armenia.* Edinburgh, New York.

Boase, T. S. R. 1979. *The Cilician Kingdom of Armenia.* 2nd ed. Danbury, CT.

Borian, B. A. 1929. *Armeniia, mezhdunarodnaia diplomatiia i SSSR.* Vol. 2. Leningrad.

Borisov, A. A. 1965. *Climates of the U.S.S.R.* Trans. R. A. Ledward. Chicago.

Bournoutian, George A. 1983. "The Ethnic Composition and the Socio-Economic Conditions of Eastern Armenia in the First Half of the Nineteenth Century." In *Transcaucasia: Nationalism and Social Change,* ed. R. Suny. Ann Arbor.

Bournoutian, George A. 1992. *The Khanate of Erevan under Qajar Rule, 1795-1828.* Costa Mesa, CA.

Bournoutian, George A., trans. 1994. *A History of Qarabagh.* Costa Mesa, CA.

Brosset, M. F. 1874. *Collection d'historiens arméniens.* Vol. 1. St. Petersburg.

Buniat Sebastatsi (Buniat of Sebastia). 1644. *Girk bzhshkutian tomari* (Book of Medicine). Preserved in Matenadaran Institute of Manuscripts no. 1023.

Busse, H., ed. and trans. 1972. *History of Persia under Qajar Rule.* New York.

Buxton, Noel and Harold. 1914. *Travels and Politics in Armenia.* London.

Cahen, Claude. 1968. *Pre-Ottoman Turkey.* London.

Cambridge History of Iran. 1983, 1985, 1991. Vol. 2, *The Median and Archaemenian Periods,* ed. Ilya Gershevitch. Vol. 3, *The Seleucid, Parthian, and Sasanid Periods,* ed. Ehsan Yarshater. Vol. 7, *From Nadir Shah to the Islamic Republic,* ed. Peter Avery et al. Cambridge, UK.

Campbell, George Douglas (Duke of Argyll, 8th Duke). 1896. *Our Responsibilities for Turkey.* London.

Carswell, John. 1968. *New Julfa, The Armenian Churches and Other Buildings.* Oxford.

Cartwright, John. 1611. *The Preacher's Travels . . . through Syria, Mesopotamia, Armenia, Media, Hircania, and Parthia. . . .* London.

Çebesoy, Ali Fuat. 1955. *Moskova hâtıraları* (21/11/1920-2/6/1922) (Moscow Memoirs [November 21, 1920–June 2, 1922]). Istanbul.

Chamchian, Mikayel. 1784-1786. *Hayots patmutiun* (Armenian History). 3 vols. Venice.

Charny, Israel W. 1983. *International Conference on the Holocaust and Genocide.* Book I, *The Conference Program and Crisis.* Tel Aviv.

Chaumont, M. L. 1982. "Tigranocerte: Données du problème et état des recherches." *Revue des études arméniennes,* n.s. 16.

Chelebi, Evliya. See Evliya Chelebi.

Chronicles of the Chaldean Kings (626-556 B.C.). 1961. Trans. D.J. Wiseman. London.

La Chronique attribuée au Connétable Smbat. Trans. G. Dédéyan. 1980. Paris.

Chronique de Matthieu d'Edesse: Bibliothèque historique arménienne. 1858. Trans. E. Dulaurier. Paris.

Clavijo. 1928. *Embassy to Tamerlane, 1403-1406.* Trans. G. Le Strange. London.

Commission of the Churches on International Affairs. 1984. *Armenia: The Continuing Tragedy.* Geneva.

Cook, M. A. 1972. *Population Pressures in Rural Anatolia, 1450-1600.* London.

Cowe, S. P. 1989. "An Allegorical Poem by Mkrtich Naghash and Its Models." *Journal of the Society for Armenian Studies* 4.

Current Digest of the Soviet Press. 1991. 43, no. 18. (5 June).

Dadrian, Vahakn N. 1975. "The Common Features of the Armenian and Jewish Cases of Genocide: A Comparative Victimological Perspective." *Victimology* 4.

Dadrian, Vahakn N. 1986. "The Naim-Andonian Documents on the World War I Destruction of the Ottoman Armenians." *International Journal of Middle East Studies* 8, no. 3 (August).

Dadrian, Vahakn N. 1986a. "The Role of Turkish Physicians in the World War I Genocide of Ottoman Armenians." *Holocaust and Genocide Studies* 1, no. 2.

Dadrian, Vahakn N. 1989. "Genocide as a Problem of National and International Law· The World War I Armenian Case and Its Contemporary Legal Ramifications." *Yale Journal of International Law* 14, no. 2 (Summer).

Dadrian, Vahakn N. 1991. "The Documentation of the World War I Armenian Massacres in the Proceedings of the Turkish Military Tribunal." *International Journal of Middle East Studies* 23, no. 4 (November).

Dadrian, Vahakn N. 1992. "The Role of the Turkish Military in the Destruction of the Ottoman Armenians." *Journal of Political and Military Sociology* 20, no. 2 (Winter).

Dadrian, Vahakn N. 1993. "The Role of the Special Organisation in the Armenian Genocide during the First World War." In *Minorities in Wartime,* ed. Panikos Panayi. Oxford, UK, Providence, RI.

Dandamaev, M. A. 1990. *Political History of the Achaemenid Empire.* Leiden.

Dandamaev, M. A., and V. Lukonin. 1988. *Culture and Social Institutions of Ancient Iran.* Cambridge.

Daranaghtsi, Grigor. See Grigor Daranaghtsi.

Darbinjan, M. O. 1965. *Simeon Lekhatzi, Putevye zametki.* Moscow.

Dashian, Hagovpos, and Kerope Sbenian. 1898. *Study of the Classical Armenian* (in Armenian).

Dasxuranc'i, Movsēs. See Movses Daskhurantsi.

David. 1983. *Definitions and Divisions of Philosophy.* Trans. Bridget Kendall and Robert W. Thomson. Atlanta.

Davis, Leslie A. 1989. *The Slaughterhouse Province.* New Rochelle, NY.

de Lusignan, Levon V. *Chronique d'Arménie.* 1906. In *Recueil des Historiens des Croisades: Documents arméniens,* vol. 2. Paris.

Dédéyan, Gérard. 1996. "Les princes arméniens de l'Euphratès et l'Empire byzantin (fin XIe-milieu XIIIe s.)." *L'Arménie et Byzance.* Paris.

Dédéyan, Gérard, ed. 1982. *Histoire des Arméniens.* Toulouse.

Dekmejian, R. Hrair. 1975. *Patterns of Political Leadership: Egypt, Israel, Lebanon.* Albany, NY.

Dekmejian, R. Hrair. 1976. "The Armenians: Historical Memory, Consciousness and the Middle East Dispersion." *Middle East Review* (April).

Der Nersessian, Sirarpie. 1945. *Armenia and the Byzantine Empire.* Cambridge, MA.

Der Nersessian, Sirarpie. 1959. "The Armenian Chronicle of the Constable Smpad'." *Dumbarton Oaks Papers.* No. 13.

Der Nersessian, Sirarpie. 1962. "The Kingdom of Cilician Armenia." In Vol. 2, *A History of the Crusades,* ed. K. M. Setton. Philadelphia.

Der Nersessian, Sirarpie. 1969. *The Armenians.* London.

Der Nersessian, Sirarpie. 1978. *Armenian Art.* London.

Diakonoff, I. M. 1985. *Prehistory of the Armenian People.* Delmar, NY.

Diakonoff, I. M., and V.P. Neroznak. 1985. *Phrygian.* Delmar, NY.

Dio's Roman History. Ed. and trans. E. Cary. 9 vols. Loeb Classical Library.

Djemal Pasha (Jemal Pasha). 1922. *Memories of a Turkish Statesman, 1913-1919.* London.

"Documents: The State Department File." 1984. *Armenian Review* 37/1 (Spring).

Dostourian, A. E. 1993. *Armenia and the Crusades: The Chronicle of Mathew of Edessa.* Boston.

Drasxanakertc'i, Yovhannēs. See Hovhannes Draskhanakerttsi (Yovhannēs Drasxanakertc'i).

Earle, E. M. 1935. *Turkey, the Great Powers and the Bagdad Railway.* New York.

Edwards, R. W. 1987. *The Fortifications of Armenian Cilicia.* Washington, D.C.

Egan, Eleanor Franklin. 1919. "This To Be Said for the Turk." *Saturday Evening Post* 192, 20 December.

Ełišē. See Eghishe.

(Eghishe) Ełishe. 1982. *History of Vardan and the Armenian War.* Trans. R.W. Thomson. Harvard Armenian Texts and Studies, 5. Cambridge, MA.

Elliott, Mabel E. 1924. *Beginning Again at Ararat.* New York.

Emin, Joseph. 1792. *The Life and Adventures of Joseph Emin, an Armenian.* London.

Emin, Joseph. 1918. *Life and Adventures of Joseph Emin, 1726-1809.* 2 vols. Calcutta.

Emin (Yalman), Ahmed. 1930. *Turkey in the World War.* New Haven.

Encyclopaedia of Islam. 1960. 2nd ed. Leiden. See especially, "Armīniya," "Kara-Koyunlu," and "Enwer Pasha."

Erznkatsi, Kostandin. See Kostandin Erznkatsi.

Etmekjian, James. 1964. *The French Influence on the Western Armenian Renaissance, 1843-1915.* New York.

Eudin, Xenia Joukoff, and Robert C. North. 1957. *Soviet Russia and the East, 1920-1927: A Documentary Survey.* Stanford.

Evliya Chelebi. 1896-1928. *Seyahatname* (Travel Account). 10 vols. Istanbul. Partial English trans. Joseph von Hammer-Purgstall, under the title *Travels of Evliya Chelebi,* 2 vols. (London, 1834-1846). Partial Armenian trans. in Safrastian, vol. 3 (Erevan, 1967).

Eznik. 1959. *Eznik, De Deo.* Trans. L. Mariès and C. Mercier. (Patrologia Orientalis. XXVIII 3-4), Paris.

Faroghi, S. 1984. *Towns and Townsmen of Ottoman Anatolia.* Cambridge.

Fontenrose, Joseph. 1959. *Python: A Study of Delphic Myth and Its Origins.* Berkeley.

Forbes, Thomas B. 1983. *Urartian Architecture.* BAR International Series, 170. Oxford.

Frik. 1952. *Frik Divan.* Ed. Archbishop Tirair. New York.

Galanus, Clemens. 1650, 1690. *Conciliationis Ecclesiae Armenae cum Romana.* 2 vols. Rome.

Gandzaketsi, Kirakos. See Kirakos Gandzaketsi.

Garitte, G. 1952. *La Narratio de Rebus Armeniae.* Louvain.

Garsoïan, Nina. 1967. *The Paulician Heresy.* The Hague and Paris.

Garsoïan, Nina. 1984-1985. "The Early Medieval Armenian City: An Alien Element?" *The Journal of Ancient Near Eastern Studies* 16-17.

Garsoïan, Nina. 1985. *Armenia Between Byzantium and the Sasanians.* London.

Garsoïan, Nina. 1994. "Reality and Myth in Armenian History." In *The East and the Meaning of History.* Rome.

Garsoïan, Nina. 1997. "The Armenian Church between Byzantium and the East." *Morgan Library Symposium* (1994). New York.

Garsoïan, Nina G., T. F. Mathews, and R. W. Thomson, eds. 1982. *East of Byzantium: Syria and Armenia in the Formative Period.* Washington, D.C.

Genocide: Crime against Humanity. 1984. Special issue of *Armenian Review* 37, no. 1 (Spring).

Georgia. 1919. *Dokumenty i materialy po vneshnei politike Zakavkaz'ia i Gruzii.* Tiflis.

Ghazar Baberdatsi (Ghazar [Lazar] of Baberd). n.d. Bible. Preserved in Matenadaran Institute of Manuscripts, no. 351. Erevan.

(Ghazar Parpetsi) Ghazar P'arpec'i. 1985. *History of the Armenians.* Trans. R. Bedrosian. New York.

(Ghazar Parpetsi) Łazar P'arpec'i. 1991. *The History of Łazar P'arpec'i.* Trans. and Comm. R. W. Thomson. Atlanta.

(Ghevond) Lewond. 1982. *The History of Lewond.* Trans. Z. Arzoumanian. Philadelphia.

Ghukas Vanandetsi. 1699. *Gandz chapoy, kshroy, tvoy, ev dramits bolor ashkharhi* (Treasury of Measures, Weights, Numeration, and Currency from All Over the World). Amsterdam.

Gidney, James B. 1967. *A Mandate for Armenia.* Kent, OH.

Gilbert, Charles K., and Charles T. Bridgeman. 1921. *Foreigners or Friends.* New York.

Girk Tghtots (The Book of Letters). 1994. Jerusalem.

Graves, Philip. 1941. *Briton and Turk.* London.

Great Britain. Foreign Office. 1916. *The Treatment of Armenians in the Ottoman Empire. See* Toynbee, Arnold J., ed. 1916.

Great Britain. Foreign Office. 1928. *British Documents on the Origins of the War, 1898-1914.* Eds. G. P. Gooch and Harold Temperley. Vol. 5. London.

Great Britain. Parliament. 1878. *Sessional Papers*. Vol. 83, c. 1973, Turkey no. 22.

Great Britain. Parliament. 1878a. *Sessional Papers*. Vol. 83, c. 2083, Turkey no. 39.

Great Britain. Parliament. 1895. *Sessional Papers*. Vol. 109, c. 7894, Turkey no. 1.

Great Britain. Parliament. 1896. *Sessional Papers*. Vol. 95, c. 7923, Turkey no. 1.

Great Britain. Parliament. House of Commons. 1917. *The Parliamentary Debates*. 5th series. London.

Great Britain. Public Record Office. Classes 371 and 424.

Grégoire de Narek. See Grigor Narekatsi.

Gregorian, V. 1972. "The Impact of Russia on the Armenians and Armenia." In *Russia and Asia*, ed. W. S. Vucinich. Palo Alto.

Gregory, J. S. 1968. *Russian Land, Soviet People: A Geographical Approach to the U.S.S.R.* New York.

Griboedov, A. S. 1953. "Proekt uchrezhdeniia Rossiiskoi Zakavkazskoi kompanii." In *Sochineniia*, ed. V. Orlov. Moscow.

Grigor Daranaghtsi (Grigor of Daranagh). 1915. *Zhamanakagrutiun* (Chronology). Jerusalem. French trans. M. F. Brosset in vol. 1 of *Collection d'historiens arméniens* (St. Petersburg, 1874).

Grigor Magistros (Gregory the Magister) Pahlavuni. 1910. *Grigor Magistrosi Tghtere* (The Letters of Grigor Magistros). Ed. K. Kostaniants. Alexandropol.

Grigor Narekatsi (Gregory of Narek) (Grégoire de Narek). 1961. *Grégoire de Narek: Le Livre de Prières*. T. Kéchichian. Paris.

Grigor Tatevatsi (Grigor of Tatev). 1729. *Girk hartsmants* (Book of Questions). Constantinople.

Hachakhapatum. 1927. "Ausgewählte Reden aus dem Hatschachapatum vom hl. Mesrop." Trans. S. Weber and E. Sommer. In *Ausgewählte Schriften der armenischen Kirchenväter*, ed. S. Weber, vol. 1. Munich.

Hairapetian, S. 1995. *A History of Ancient and Medieval Armenian Literature*. Delmar, NY.

Hakobian, H. 1932. *Ughegrutiunner* (Travel Accounts). Vol. 1, *1253-1582*. Erevan.

Hakobian, V. A. 1951, 1956. *Manr zhamanakagrutiunner XIII-XVIII dd.* (Minor Chronicles, XIII-XVIII Centuries). 2 vols. Erevan.

Hakobian, V., and A. Hovhannisian. 1974. *Colophons of Seventeenth Century Armenian Manuscripts*. Vol. 1, *1601-1620*. Erevan.

Halasi-Kun, T. 1963. "The Caucasus: An Ethno-Historical Survey." *Studia Caucasica* 1. The Hague.

Hammer-Purgstall, Joseph von. 1827-1835. *Geschichte des Osmanischen Reiches.* 2nd ed. 10 vols. Pesht. French trans. J. J. Hellert under the title *Histoire de l'Empire ottoman,* 18 vols. (Paris, 1835-1841).

Hammer-Purgstall, Joseph von, trans. 1834-1846. *Travels of Evliya Chelebi.* 2 vols. London.

Harney, Robert F., Anne McCarthy, and Isabel Kaprielian, eds. 1982. "Armenians in Ontario." *Polyphony* 4, no. 2 (Fall/Winter).

Harvard Encyclopedia of American Ethnic Groups. 1980. Stephan Thernstrom, Ann Orlov, and Oscar Handlin, eds. Cambridge, MA.

Haykakan Sovetakan Hanragitaran (Armenian Soviet Encyclopedia). 1974-1986. 12 vols. Erevan.

Hekimian, Kim. 1990. "Armenian Immigration to Argentina: 1909-1939." *Armenian Review* 43, no. 1/169 (Spring).

Heratsi, Mkhitar. See Mkhitar Heratsi.

Herodotus. 1954. *The Histories.* Trans. Aubrey De Selincourt. London.

Herodotus. Trans. A. D. Godley. 4 vols. Loeb Classical Library

Hertslet, Edward. 1891. *The Map of Europe by Treaty.* Vol. 4. London.

Hetoum. 1988. *A Lytell Cronycle.* Toronto.

Hetum of Korikos. 1529. *La Flor des Estoires de la Terre d'Orient.* Paris.

Hewsen, Robert H. 1978-1979. "Introduction to Armenian Historical Geography: The Nature of the Problem." *Revue des études arméniennes,* n.s. 13.

Hewsen, Robert H. 1983. "Introduction to Armenian Historical Geography: II. The Boundaries of Achaemenid Armenia." *Revue des études arméniennes,* n.s. 17.

Hewsen, Robert H. 1984. "Introduction to Armenian Historical Geography: III. The Boundaries of Orontid Armenia." *Revue des études arméniennes,* n.s. 18.

Hewsen, Robert H. 1992. *The Geography of Ananias of Shirak: Introduction, Translation and Commentary.* Wiesbaden.

Hofmann, Tessa. 1985. "German Eyewitness Reports of the Genocide of the Armenians 1915-16." In *A Crime of Silence: The Armenian Genocide,* Permanent People's Tribunal. London.

Hourani, Albert H. 1947. *Minorities in the Arab World.* London.

Housepian, Marjorie. 1972. *Smyrna 1922: The Destruction of a City.* London.

Hovannisian, Richard G. 1962. "The Armenian Communities of Southern and Eastern Asia." *Armenian Review* 15 (Autumn).

Hovannisian, Richard G. 1967. *Armenia on the Road to Independence, 1918.* Berkeley, Los Angeles.

Hovannisian, Richard G. 1971-1996. *The Republic of Armenia.* 4 vols. Berkeley, Los Angeles, London.

Hovannisian, Richard G. 1974. "The Ebb and Flow of the Armenian Minority in the Arab Middle East." *Middle East Journal* 28, no. 1 (Winter).

Hovannisian, Richard G. 1991. "Altruism in the Armenian Genocide of 1915." In *Embracing One Another*, eds. Samuel and Pearl Oliner. New York.

Hovannisian, Richard G. 1993. "The Armenian Diaspora and the Narrative of Power." In *Diasporas in World Politics*, eds. Dimitri C. Constas and Athanassios G. Platias. London.

Hovannisian, Richard G. 1994. "The Etiology and Sequelae of the Armenian Genocide." In *The Conceptual and Historical Dimensions of Genocide*, ed. George J. Andreopoulos. Philadelphia.

Hovannisian, Richard G. 1994a. "Historical Memory and Foreign Relations: The Armenian Perspective." In *The Legacy of History in Russia and the New States of Eurasia*, ed. S. Frederick Starr. Armonk, NY, and London.

Hovannisian, Richard G., ed. 1980. *The Armenian Holocaust: A Bibliography Relating to the Deportations, Massacres, and Dispersion of the Armenian People, 1915-1923.* Cambridge, MA.

Hovannisian, Richard G., ed. 1986. *The Armenian Genocide in Perspective.* New Brunswick, NJ.

Hovannisian, Richard G., ed. 1992. *The Armenian Genocide: History, Politics, Ethics.* London, New York.

(Hovhannes Draskhanakerttsi) Yovhannēs Drasxanakertc'i. 1987. *Yovhannēs Drasxanakertc'i, History of Armenia.* Trans. K. H. Maksoudian. Atlanta.

Hovhannes Makuetsi (Yovhannes Makuec'i) (Hovhannes of Maku). 1969. "Oghb Hayastanay Ashkharhi Erevanay ev Jughayu" (Lament on the Land of Armenia, Erevan, and Julfa). In *Hay mijnadarian patmakan oghber* (Medieval Armenian Historical Laments), ed. P. M. Khachatrian. Erevan.

(Hovhannes Mamikonian) Yovhannēs Mamikonean. 1993. *Pseudo-Yovhannēs Mamikonean, The History of Tarōn (Patmutiwn Tarōnoy): Historical Investigation, Critical Translation and Historical and Textual Commentaries.* Trans. Levon Avdoyan. Atlanta.

(Hovhannes Mandakuni) Johannes Mandakuni. 1927. "Reden des armenischen Kirchenvaters Johannes Mandakuni." Trans. J. Blatz and S. Weber. In *Ausgewählte Schriften der armenischen Kirchenväter*, ed. S. Weber, vol. 2. Munich.

(Hovhannes Odznetsi) Johannis Ozniensis. 1834. *Johannis Ozniensis Opera.* Trans. J. Aucher. 2 Vols. Venice.

Hovhannes Tlkurantsi (Hovhannes of Tlkuran). 1958. *(Khev) Hovhannes Tlkurantsi Taghagirk* (Book of Tagh Poems by [Crazy] Hovhannes of Tlkuran). Ed. N. Bogharian. Jerusalem.

Hovhannisian, Ashot, comp. 1926. *Hayastani avtonomian ev Antantan: Vaveragrer imperialistakan paterazmi shrdjanits* (Armenia's Autonomy and the Entente: Documents from the Period of the Imperialistic War). Erevan.

Hovnatan, Naghash. 1983. *Tagher* (Tagh Poems). Ed. A. Mnatsakanian. Erevan.

Hudson, Michael C. 1968. *The Precarious Republic: Political Modernization in Lebanon.* New York.

Hughes, Byron O. 1939. "The Physical Anthropology of Native Born Armenians." PhD. diss., Harvard University. Published as "Occasional Paper no. 6 of the Society for Armenian Studies." Photocopy (1986).

Ibn Ḥawḳal. 1964. *Configuration de la terre.* Trans. J. H. Kramers and G. Wiet. 2 vols. Paris.

Inglisian, V. 1963. "Die armenische Literatur." In *Armenisch und kaukasische Sprachen,* ed. G. Deeters (Handbuch der Orientalistik, 1, 7).

İslam Ansiklopedisi. 1945-88. 1st ed. See especially "Ak-Koyunlu" and "Kara-Koyunlu," Vladimir Minorsky. Istanbul.

Jahukian, G. B. 1987. *Hayots lezvi patmutiun: Nakhagrayin zhamanakashrjan* (The History of the Armenian Language: The Pre-Literate Period). Erevan.

Jennings, R. 1976. "Urban Population in Anatolia in the Sixteenth Century: A Study of Kayseri, Karaman, Amasya, Trabzon and Erzurum." *International Journal for Middle Eastern Studies* 7.

Johannes Mandakuni. See Hovhannes Mandakuni.

Johannis Ozniensis. See Hovhannes Odznetsi.

Kapoïan-Kouymjian, Angèle. 1988. *L'Egypte vue par les Arméniens.* Paris.

Kaprielian, Isabel. 1987. "Migratory Caravans: Armenian Sojourners in Canada." *Journal of American Ethnic History* 6, no. 2 (Spring).

Karakashian, Madatia. 1895. *Critical History of the Armenians* (in Armenian).

Kardashian, Ardashes. 1943. *Niuter Egiptosi Hayots patmutian hamar.* (Materials for the History of the Armenians of Egypt). Cairo.

Karst, J., ed. 1905. *Armenisches Rechtsbuch.* 2 vols. Strassburg.

Katerdjian, Hovsep. 1849, 1852. *Tiezerakan Patmutiun* (Universal History). 2 vols. Venice.

Kayaloff, Jacques. 1973. *The Battle of Sardarabad.* The Hague.

Kazemzadeh, Firuz. 1951. *The Struggle for Transcaucasia, 1917-1921.* New York, Oxford.

Kazemzadeh, Firuz. 1974. "Russian Penetration of the Caucasus." In *Russian Imperialism from Ivan the Great to the Revolution,* ed. Taras Hunczak. New Brunswick, NJ.

Kazhdan, A.P. 1975. *Armiane v sostave gospodstvuiushchego klassa Vizantiiskoi Imperii v XI-XII vv.* Erevan.

Kecharetsi, Khachatur. See Khachatur Kecharetsi.

Kerr, Stanley E. 1973. *The Lions of Marash: Personal Experience with American Near East Relief, 1919-1922.* Albany, NY.

Kevorkian, Garo. 1954-67/68. *Amenun taregirke* (Everyone's Almanac). Beirut.

Khachatur Kecharetsi (Khachatur of Kecharis). 1958. *Khachatur Kecharetsi xiii-xiv dd.* Ed. T. Avdalbegian. Erevan.

Khachikian, Levon. 1950. *Colophons of Fourteenth Century Armenian Manuscripts* (in Armenian). Erevan.

Khachikian, Levon. 1955, 1958, 1967. *Fifteenth Century Armenian Manuscript Colophons* (in Armenian). 3 vols. Erevan. Partial English trans. A. K. Sanjian. Cambridge, MA, 1969.

Khachikian, Levon. 1972. In *Hay zhoghovrdi patmutiun* (History of the Armenian People), Armenian Academy of Sciences, vol. 4. Erevan.

Khatisian, Alexandre. 1930. *Hayastani Hanrapetutian dsagumn u zargatsume* (The Creation and Development of the Republic of Armenia). Athens.

(Khatisian, Alexandre) Khatissian, Alexander. 1950. "The Memoirs of a Mayor, Part IV." *The Armenian Review* 3, no. 2 (Summer).

Khorenatsi, Movses. See Movses Khorenats'i.

Kirakos Gandzaketsi (Kirakos of Gandzak). 1961. *Patmutiun hayots* (History of the Armenians). Ed. K. A. Melik-Ohanjanian. Erevan.

Kirakos Gandzaketsi. 1986. *History of the Armenians.* Trans. R. Bedrosian. New York.

Kiuleserian, Babgen. 1939. *Patmutiun katoghikosats Kilikioy (1441-en minchev mer orere)* (History of the Catholicosate of Cilicia [from 1441 to Our Days]). Antelias.

Kiumurjian, Eremia Chelebi. 1913, 1932, 1939. *Stampoloy patmutiun* (History of Istanbul). 3 vols. Vienna.

Kloian, Richard D., comp. 1985. *The Armenian Genocide: News Accounts from the American Press, 1915-1922.* 3rd ed. Berkeley.

Knapp, Grace H. 1915. *The Mission at Van.* New York.

Knik Havatoy (The Seal of Faith) 1974 Louvain

Koriun. 1964. *The Life of Mashtots.* Trans. B. Norehad. New York. Reprinted 1985 in the *Delmar Classical Armenian Text Series.* New York.

Kostandin Erznkatsi (Constantine of Erzinka). 1962. *Tagher* (Tagh Poems). Ed. A. Srapian. Erevan.

Kouymjian, Dickran. 1975. "The Canons Dated 1280 A.D. of the Armenian Akhî-Type Brotherhood of Erzinjan." In part I, vol. 2 of *Actes du XXIXe congrès international des orientalistes, Paris, 1973.* Paris.

Kouymjian, Dickran. 1982. "L'Arménie sous les dominations des Turcomans et des Ottomans (X^e-XVIe siècles)." In *Histoire des Arméniens,* ed. Gérard Dédéyan. Toulouse.

Kouymjian, Dickran. 1983. "Dated Armenian Manuscripts as a Statistical Tool for Armenian History." In *Medieval Armenian Culture,* T. Samuelian and

M. Stone, eds. University of Pennsylvania Armenian Texts and Studies, vol. 6. Chico, CA.

Kouymjian, Dickran. 1988. "A Critical Bibliography for the History of Armenia from 1375 to 1605." *Armenian Review* 41/1 (Spring).

Kouymjian, Dickran. 1994. "From Disintegration to Reintegration: Armenians at the Start of the Modern Era, XVIth-XVIIth Centuries." *Revue du monde arménien* 1.

Krikorian, Mesrob K. 1978. *Armenians in the Service of the Ottoman Empire, 1860-1908.* London.

Kuper, Leo. 1982. *Genocide: Its Political Use in the Twentieth Century.* New Haven, London.

Kurat, Y. T. 1967. "How Turkey Drifted into World War." In *Studies in International History,* K. Bourne and D. C. Watt, eds. London.

Kurkjian, Vahan M. 1958. *A History of Armenia.* New York.

Landau, Jacob M. 1981. *Pan-Turkism in Turkey: A Study of Irridentism.* London.

Lang, David Marshall. 1981. *The Armenians: A People in Exile.* London.

Lang, David Marshall, and Christopher J. Walker. *The Armenians.* Minority Rights Group, no. 32 (revised). London.

Lastivertc'i, Aristakēs. See Aristakes Lastiverttsi.

Laurent, J. 1919. *L'Arménie entre Byzance et l'Islam.* Paris. Revised and enlarged edition by M. Canard (Lisbon, 1980).

Łazar P'arpec'i. See Ghazar Parpetsi.

Lazian, Gabriel. 1957. *Hayastan ev hai date* (Armenia and the Armenian Question). Cairo.

Le Strange, Guy. 1939. *Lands of the Eastern Caliphate.* Cambridge, UK.

Le Strange, Guy, ed. and trans. 1926. *Don Juan of Persia, A Shi'ah Catholic, 1560-1604.* New York, London.

Lebon, J. 1929. "Les citations patristiques du Sceau de la foi." *Revue d'histoire ecclésiastique* 5.

Lehatsi, Simeon. See Simeon Lehatsi.

Lepsius, Johannes. 1897. *Armenia and Europe: An Indictment.* London.

Lepsius, Johannes. 1916, 1919a. *Der Todesgang des armenischen Volkes.* Potsdam.

Lepsius, Johannes, ed. 1919. *Deutschland und Armenien, 1914-1918.* Potsdam.

Lewis, Bernard. 1968. *The Emergence of Modern Turkey.* 2nd ed. London, New York.

Lockhart, L. 1938. *Nadir Shah.* London.

Lockhart, L. 1958. *The Fall of the Safavid Dynasty and the Afghan Occupation of Persia.* Cambridge, UK.

Luckenbill, Daniel David. 1989. *Ancient Records of Assyria and Babylonia.* 2 vols. Reprint, London.

Lydolph, P. E. 1970. *Geography of the U.S.S.R.* 2nd ed. New York.

Lynch, H. F. B. 1901. *Armenia: Travels and Studies.* 2 vols. London.

Lynch, H. F. B. 1990. *Armenia: Travels and Studies.* 2 vols. London, 1901. Reprint, New York.

Maalouf, A. 1984. *The Crusades Through Arab Eyes.* New York.

Magistros, Grigor. See Grigor Magistros (Grigor the Magister) Pahlavuni.

Mahé, J.-P. 1993. "L'Eglise arménienne de 611 à 1066." In *Histoire du christianisme,* vol. 4, ed. J.-M. Mayeur et al. Paris.

Maksoudian, Krikor. 1988-1989. "The Chalcedonian Issue and the Early Bagratids: The Council of Širakawan." *Revue des études arméniennes* 21.

Makuetsi, Hovhannes. See Hovhannes Makuetsi.

Mallory, J. P. 1989. *In Search of the Indo-Europeans: Language, Archaeology and Myth.* London.

Mamikonean, Yovhannēs. See (Hovhannes Mamikonian) Yovhannēs Mamikonean.

Manandian, Hakob. 1963. *Tigrane II et Rome.* Lisbon. Original Armenian edition, Erevan, 1940.

(Manandian) Manandyan, Hakob. 1965. *The Trade and Cities of Armenia in Relation to Ancient World Trade.* Trans. and ed. Nina Garsoïan. Lisbon.

Mandakuni, John (Johannes). See Hovhannes Mandakuni.

Mandelstam, André. 1917. *Le sort de l'empire Ottoman.* Paris, Lausanne.

"Manifest II. II. Dashnaktsutian" (Manifesto of the Armenian Revolutionary Federation). 1958. In *Droshak: Hai Heghapokhakan Dashnaktsutian Organ, 1890-1897* (n.p.)

Mariès, L. 1924. "Le De Deo d'Eznik de Kolb. Etude de critique littéraire et textuelle." *Revue des études arméniennes* 4.

Mathews, T. F., and A. K. Sanjian. 1991. *Armenian Gospel Iconography: The Tradition of the Glajor Gospel.* Dumbarton Oaks Studies, 29. Washington, D.C.

Mathieson, R. S. 1975. *The Soviet Union: An Economic Geography.* New York.

Matossian, Mary Kilbourne. 1962. *The Impact of Soviet Policies in Armenia.* Leiden.

Meillet, Antoine. 1936. *Esquisse d'une grammaire comparée de l'arménien classique.* 2nd ed. Vienna.

Mekhitar, Abbot. 1749. *Dictionary of the Armenian Language* (in Armenian).

Mekhitar, Abbot. 1985. *Grammar in Armeno-Turkish* (in Armenian).

Melson, Robert F. 1992. *Revolution and Genocide: On the Origins of the Armenian Genocide and the Holocaust.* Chicago, London.

Metzopetsi, Tovma. See Tovma Metzopetsi.

Mikayelian, V. A. 1960. *Hayastani giughatsiutiune Sovetakan ishkhanutian hamar mghvads paikari zhamanakashrdjanum (1917-20)* (The Peasantry of Armenia during the Period of Struggle for Soviet Power, [1917-1920]). Erevan.

Minorsky, Vladimir. 1953. *Studies in Caucasian History.* London.

Minorsky, Vladimir. 1953a. "Thomas of Metsop on the Timurid-Turkman Wars." In *To Professor M. Shafi.* Lahore.

Minorsky, Vladimir. 1958. *A History of Sharvān and Darband.* Cambridge and London.

Mirak, Robert. 1980. "Armenians." In *Harvard Encyclopedia of American Ethnic Groups,* Stephan Thernstrom, Ann Orlov, and Oscar Handlin, eds. Cambridge, MA.

Mirak, Robert. 1983. *Torn Between Two Lands: Armenians in America, 1890 to World War I.* Cambridge, MA.

Mkhitar, Gosh. 1975. *Girk datastani* (Judicial Manual). Ed. Kh. Torosian. Erevan.

Mkhitar Heratsi. 1832. *The Consolation of Fevers* (in Armenian). Venice.

Mkhitar Heratsi (Mekhitar of Her). 1971. In *Hay groghner* (Armenian Writers). Jerusalem.

(Mkhitar Sasnetsi) Mxit'ar Sasnec'i (Mekhitar of Sasun). 1993. *Theological Discourses.* Trans. S. P. Cowe. Vol. 21 (in Armenian), and vol. 22 (in English) of *Corpus Scriptorum Christianorum Orientalium.* Louvain.

Mkrtich Naghash. 1965. *Mkrtich Naghash.* Ed. E. D. Khondkarian. Erevan.

Morgenthau, Henry. 1918. *Ambassador Morgenthau's Story.* Garden City, NY.

Mouradian, Claire. 1979. "L'immigration des Arméniens de la diaspora vers la RSS d'Arménie, 1946-1962." *Cahiers du Monde russe et sovietique* 20, no. 1 (January-March).

Mouradian, Claire. 1990. *De Staline à Gorbachev: Histoire d'une République sovietique. l'Arménie.* Paris.

(Movses Daskhurantsi) Movsēs Dasxuranc'i. 1961. *The History of the Caucasian Albanians.* Trans. C.J.F. Dowsett. London.

(Movses Khorenatsi) Moses Khorenats'i (Moses of Khoren). 1978. *History of the Armenians.* Trans. and Comm. Robert W. Thomson. Cambridge, MA.

Mserlian, Kevork. 1947. *Akanavor hayer Ekibtosi medj* (Distinguished Armenians in Egypt). Cairo.

Mutafian, Claude. 1993. *Le royaume arménien de Cilicie, XIIe-XIVe siècle.* Paris.

Naghash, Mkrtich. See Mkrtich Naghash.

Nalbandian, Louise. 1963. *The Armenian Revolutionary Movement.* Berkeley, Los Angeles.

Nalbandian, Mikayel. 1940-1948. *Erkeri liakatar zhoghovatsu* (Complete Collection of Works). 4 vols. Erevan.

Nassibian, Akaby. 1984. *Britain and the Armenian Question, 1915-1923.* London.

Nerses Shnorhali (Nerses the Gracious). 1973. *Oghb Edesioy* (Lament on Edessa). Ed. M. Mkrtchian. Erevan.

Nersissian, V. 1984. "Medieval Armenian Poetry and Its Relation to Other Literatures." In *Armenia: Annual Volume Review of National Literatures,* ed. Vahé Oshagan, vol. 13. New York.

Nève, F. 1861. "Exposé des guerres de Tamerlane et de Schah-Rokh dans l'Asie occidentale, d'après la chronique arménienne inédite de Thomas de Medzoph." In *Académie royale des sciences, des lettres et des beaux-arts de Belgique: Mémoires, couronnés,* vol. 11/4. Brussels.

Niepage, Martin. 1975. *The Horrors of Aleppo.* London, 1917. Reprint, New York.

Olmstead, A. T. 1948. *History of the Persian Empire.* Chicago.

Orbelian, Stepanos. 1859. *History of the Region of Sisakan by Stepanos Orbelian, Archbishop of Siunik‘* (in Armenian). Ed. K. Shahnazariants. Paris.

Orbelian, Stepanos. 1864. *Histoire de la Siounie par Stépannos Orbelian.* Trans. M.-F. Brosset. St. Petersburg.

Ormanian, Malachia. 1912, 1914, 1927. *Azgapatum* (National History). Vols. 1-2, Constantinople. Vol. 3, Jerusalem.

Ormanian, Malachia. 1955. *The Church of Armenia.* Trans. Marcar Gregory. 2nd ed. London.

Oshagan, Vahé. 1982. *The English Influence on West Armenian Literature in the Nineteenth Century.* Cleveland.

Oshagan, Vahé. 1986. "Literature of the Armenian Diaspora." *World Literature Today,* 60.2.

Oshagan, Vahé, ed. 1984. *Armenia: Annual Volume Review of National Literatures.* Vol. 13. New York.

Pahlavuni, Grigor. See Grigor Magistros (Gregory the Magister).

P‘arpec‘i, Łazar. See Ghazar Parpetsi.

Papazian, H. 1972. In *Hay zhoghovrdi patmutiun* (History of the Armenian People), Armenian Academy of Sciences. Vol. 4. Erevan.

Papikian, Hakob. 1909. *Adanayi egherne* (The Adana Calamity). Constantinople.

Pavstos Buzand P‘awstos Buzand. 1989. *The Epic Histories: Attributed to P‘awstos Buzand (Buzandaran Patmut‘iwnk‘).* Trans. and comm. N. G. Garsoïan. Harvard Armenian Texts and Studies, 8. Cambridge, MA.

Pechevi. 1961. *Ta’rikh* (History). In *Contemporary Turkish Sources on Armenia and the Armenian* (in Armenian), ed. A. Safrastian, vol. 1. Erevan.

Perikhanian, A. 1967. "Une inscription araméenne du roi Artašēs trouvée à Zanguézour (Siwnik‘)." *Revue des études arméniennes,* n.s. 3.

Permanent People's Tribunal. 1985. *A Crime of Silence: The Armenian Genocide.* London.

Piotrovsky, B. B. 1967. *Urartu: The Kingdom of Van and Its Art.* Trans. P. Gelling. London. Originally Published as *Vanskoe tsarstvo (Urartu)* (Moscow, 1959).

Pipes, Richard. 1964. *The Formation of the Soviet Union.* Cambridge, MA.

Pitcher, D. E. 1972. *An Historical Atlas of the Ottoman Empire.* Leiden.

Pliny. *Natural History.* Trans. H. Rackham. 10 vols. Loeb Classical Library.

Plutarch. "Crassus." *Lives.* Trans. B. Perrin. Vol. 3. pp. 314/5-422/3. Loeb Classical Library.

Plutarch. "Lucullus." *Lives.* Trans. B. Perrin. Vol. 2. pp. 470/1-610/1. Loeb Classical Library.

Plutarch. "Pompey." *Lives.* Trans. B. Perrin. Vol. 5. pp. 116/7-324/5. Loeb Classical Library.

Polybius. *The Histories.* Trans. W. R. Patron. 6 vols. Loeb Classical Library.

Procopius. "Buildings." *Works.* Trans. H.B. Dewing. Vol. 7. Loeb Classical Library.

Procopius. "The Gothic War." *Works.* Trans. H.B. Dewing Vols. 3-5. Loeb Classical Library.

Procopius. "The Persian War." *Works.* Trans. H.B. Dewing Vol. 1. Loeb Classical Library.

Pseudo-Sebeos. See Sebeos.

Qazvini. 1919. *The Geographical Part of the Nuzhat-al-Qulub of Hamd-Allah Mustawfi of Qazvin.* Trans. G. Le Strange. London.

Recueil des Historiens des Croisades: Documents arméniens. 1906. Vol. 2. Paris.

Renfrew, Colin. 1987. *Archaeology and Language: The Puzzle of Indo-European Origins.* New York.

Renoux, C. 1993. "Langue et littérature arméniennes." In *Christianismes Orientaux,* ed. M. Albert et al. Paris.

Res Gestae Divi Augusti. Ed. and trans. F. W. Shipley. Loeb Classical Library.

Rudt-Collenberg, W. H. 1963. *The Rupenides, the Hethumides, and Lusignans.* Paris.

Russell, James R. 1982. "Zoroastrian Problems in Armenia: Mihr and Vahagn." In *Classical Armenian Culture,* ed. T. J. Samuelian. University of Pennsylvania Armenian Texts and Studies, vol. 4.

Russell, James R. 1984. "Pre-Christian Armenian Religion." In *Aufsteig und Niedergang der Römischen Welt,* II.18.4, ed. W. Haase and H. Temporini.

Russell, James R. 1987. "A Mystic's Christmas in Armenia." *Armenian Review* 40, no. 2-158 (Summer).

Russell, James R. 1987a. *Yovhannēs T'lkuranc'i and the Medieval Armenian Lyric Tradition.* Atlanta.

Russell, James R. 1987b. *Zoroastrianism in Armenia.* Harvard Iranian Series, 5. Cambridge, MA.

Russell, James R. 1989. "The Craft and Mithraism Reconsidered." *Proceedings of the American Lodge of Research* (Masonic), New York.

Russell, James R. 1993. "Tork' and Tarkhu." *Proceedings,* Second International Conference on the Armenian Language, Erevan, September 1987.

Russia, Ministerstvo Inostrannykh Del SSSR. 1924. *Razdel Aziatskoi Turtsii po sekretnym dokumentam b. ministerstva inostrannykh del.* Ed. E. A. Adamov. Moscow.

Russia, Ministerstvo Inostrannykh Del SSSR. 1957. *Dokumenty vneshnei politiki SSSR.* Vol. 1. Moscow.

Sachar, Howard M. 1969. *The Emergence of the Middle East, 1914-1924.* London.

Safrastian, A. 1961, 1964, 1967, 1972. *Contemporary Turkish Sources on Armenia and the Armenians* (in Armenian). 4 vols. Erevan.

Sanjian, Avedis K. 1965. *The Armenian Communities in Syria under Ottoman Dominion.* Cambridge, MA.

Sanjian, Avedis K. 1969. *Colophons of Armenian Manuscripts, 1301-1480: A Source for Middle Eastern History.* Cambridge, MA.

Sarkissian, A. O. 1938. *History of the Armenian Question to 1885.* Urbana, IL.

Sarkissian, Karekin. 1965. *The Council of Chalcedon and the Armenian Church.* London.

Sasnec'i, Mkhitar. See Mkhitar Sasnetsi.

The Scriptores Historiae Augustae. Ed. and trans. D. Magie. 3 vols. Loeb Classical Library.

Sebastatsi, Asar. See Asar Sebastatsi.

Sebastatsi, Buniat. See Buniat Sebastatsi.

Sebeos. 1904. *Histoire d'Heraclius.* Trans. F. Macler. Paris

Setton, K. M., ed. 1969-1990. *A History of the Crusades.* 6 vols. Madison, WI.

Shalian, A. 1964. *David of Sassoun.* Athens, OH.

Shiragian, Arshavir. 1976. *The Legacy.* Boston.

Shirakatsi, Anania. See Anania Shirakatsi.

Shirinian, Lorne. 1990. *Armenian-North American Literature: A Critical Introduction.* New York.

Shnorhali, Nerses. See Nerses Shnorhali.

Simeon Aparantsi (Simeon of Aparan). 1969. "I veray arman Tavrizoy" (On the Capture of Tabriz). In *Hay mijnadarian patmakan oghber* (Medieval Armenian Historical Laments), ed. P. Khachatrian. Erevan.

Simeon Lehatsi (Simeon of Poland). 1936. *Ughegrutiun* (Travel Journal). Ed. Nerses Akinian. Vienna. Russian trans. M. Darbinjan (Moscow, 1965). Partial Turkish trans. H. Andreasyan (Istanbul, 1964). Partial French trans. Angèle Kapoïan-Kouymjian, *L'Egypte vue par les Arméniens* (Paris, 1988). Partial Polish trans. Zbigniew Kosciow (Warsaw, 1991).

Siurmeian, A. 1935. *Tsutsak hayeren dzeragrats Halepi* (Catalogue of Armenian Manuscripts of Aleppo). Jerusalem.

Sommer, Ernst. 1919. *Die Wahrheit über die Leiden des armenischen Volkes in der Türkei während des Weltkrieges.* Frankfurt.

Soviet Armenia. 1972. Moscow.

Sprengling, M. 1953. *Third Century Iran: Sapor and Kartir.* Chicago.

(Stepanos Asoghik) Acoghic. 1883. *Etienne Acoghic de Daron, Histoire Universelle.* Trans. E. Dulaurier. Books 1 and 2. Paris.

(Stepanos Asoghik) Asołik. 1917. *Etienne Asołik de Taron, Histoire Universelle.* Trans. F. Macler. Book 3. Paris.

Strabo [of Amasia]. 1961. *The Geography.* Ed. and trans. H. L. Jones. Loeb Classical Library.

Strom, Margot Stern, and William S. Parsons. 1982. *Facing History and Ourselves: Holocaust and Human Behavior.* Watertown, MA.

Sue, Eugene. 1991. *The Wandering Jew.* Dedalus European Fiction Classics Series. New York.

Suleiman, Michael W. 1967. *The Political Parties in Lebanon: The Challenge of a Fragmented Culture.* Ithaca, NY.

Suny, Ronald Grigor. 1972. *The Baku Commune, 1917-1918.* Princeton.

Suny, Ronald Grigor. 1983. *Armenia in the Twentieth Century.* Chico, CA.

Suny, Ronald Grigor. 1993. *Looking Toward Ararat: Armenia in Modern History.* Bloomington, IN.

Surmelian, Leon Z. 1946. *I Ask You, Ladies and Gentlemen.* London.

Swietochowski, Tadeusz. 1985. *Russian Azerbaijan, 1905-1920: The Shaping of National Identity in a Muslim Community.* Cambridge, MA.

Synodicon Orientale, ou Receueil des synods nestoriens. 1902. J. B. Chabot. Paris.

Tacitus. *Annales.* Ed. and trans. J. Jackson. 3 vols. Loeb Classical Library.

Taft, Elise Hagopian. 1981. *Rebirth.* Plandome, NY.

Tallon, M., trans. 1955 "Livre des Lettres. Ier Groupe: Documents concernant les relations avec les Grecs" (Book of Letters). *Mélanges de l'Université de S. Joseph.* 32, fasc. 1. Beirut.

Tatevatsi, Grigor. See Grigor Tatevatsi.

Tavrizhetsi, Arakel. See Arakel Tavrizhetsi.

Ter Ghewondian, A. 1976. *The Arab Emirates in Bagratid Armenia.* Trans. Nina Garsoïan. Lisbon.

Ter Minassian, Anahide. 1973. "Le mouvement révolutionnaire arménien, 1890-1903." *Cahiers du monde russe et sovietique* 14, no. 4 (October-December).

Thierry, J. M., and P. Donabedian. 1989. *The Art of the Armenians.* Paris.

Thomas Artsruni. See Tovma Artsruni.

Thomson, R. W. 1988-1989. "The Anonymous Story-Teller (also known as Pseudo-Šapuh)." *Revue des études arméniennes,* n.s. 21.

Thomson, R. W. 1994. *Studies in Armenian Literature and Christianity*. Variorum. Aldershot, UK.

Thomson, R. W. 1995. *A Bibliography of Classical Armenian Literature to 1500 AD*. Turnhout.

Tlkurantsi, Hovhannes. See Hovhannes Tlkurantsi.

Toumanoff, Cyril. 1963. *Studies in Christian Caucasian History*. Washington, D.C.

Toumanoff, Cyril. 1966. "Armenia and Georgia." In *Cambridge Medieval History*, vol. 4, 2nd ed.

Toumanoff, Cyril. 1969. "The Third-Century Arsacids: A Chronological and Genealogical Commentary." *Revue des études arméniennes*, n.s. 6.

Toumanoff, Cyril. 1976. *Manuel de généalogie et de chronologie pour l'histoire de la Caucasie chrétienne*. Rome.

Tournebize, François. 1910. "Léon V de Lusignan dernier roi de l'Arméno-Cilicie." *Etudes publiées par des pères de la Compagnie de Jésus* 122 (Paris).

Tournebize, François. 1910a. *Histoire politique et religieuse de l'Arménie*. Paris.

(Tovma Artsruni) Thomas Artsruni. *History of the House of the Artsrunik'*. Trans. and Comm. R. W. Thomson. Detroit 1985.

Tovma Metzopetsi (Thomas of Metzop). 1860. *Patmutiun Lank Tamuray ev hadjordats iurots* (History of Timur Lang and His Successors). Paris. Partial French trans. F. Nève (Brussels, 1861).

Tovma Metzopetsi (Thomas of Metzop). 1892. *Colophon*. Tiflis.

(Tovma Metzopetsi) T'ovma Metsobets'i. 1987. *History of Tamerlane and His Successors*. Trans. R. Bedrosian. New York.

Toynbee, Arnold J. 1915. *Armenian Atrocities: The Murder of a Nation*. London.

Toynbee, Arnold J. 1917. *Turkey: A Past and a Future*. London.

Toynbee, Arnold J. 1922. *The Western Question in Greece and Turkey*. London.

Toynbee, Arnold J., ed. 1916. *The Treatment of Armenians in the Ottoman Empire 1915-16: Documents Presented to Viscount Grey of Fallodon, Secretary for Foreign Affairs*. London.

Türk Devrim Tarihi Enstitüsü. 1964. *Atatürk'ün tamim, telgraf ve beyannameleri* (Ataturk's Circulars, Telegrams, and Declarations). Vol. 4, *1917-1938*. Ankara.

Turkey. 1919. *Memorandum of the Sublime Porte Communicated to the American, British, French and Italian, High Commissioners on the 12th February 1919*. Constantinople.

Ukhtanes. 1985, 1988. *Bishop Ukhtanes of Sebastia: History of Armenia*. Trans. Z. Arzoumanian. 2 Parts. Fort Lauderdale, FL.

United States vs. Cartozian. 1925. 6 Federal Reporter, 2nd Series, 919 (District Court of Oregon).

United States. Department of State. 1943, 1946. *Papers Relating to the Foreign Relations of the United States 1919: The Paris Peace Conference.* Vols. 3-4, 6. Washington, D.C.

United States. National Archives. Record Group 59.

Uratadze, G. I. 1956. *Obrazovanie i konsolidatsiia Gruzinskoi Demokraticheskoi Respubliki.* Munich.

Ussher, Clarence D. 1917. *An American Physician in Turkey.* Boston.

Vanandetsi, Ghukas. See Ghukas Vanandetsi.

Vardan Areveltsi. 1981. In *Hay grakan knnadatutian krestomatia* (Chrestomathy of Armenian Literary Criticism), ed. Zh. A. Kalantarian. Erevan.

(Vardan Areveltsi) Vardan Arewelc'i. 1989. "The Historical Compilation of Vardan Arewelc'i." Trans. R. W. Thomson, in *Dumbarton Oaks Papers.* 43, pp. 125-226.

Velleius Paterculus. *Compendium of Roman History.* Ed. and trans. F. W. Shipley. Loeb Classical Library.

Vratzian, Simon. 1928. *Hayastani Hanrapetutiun* (The Republic of Armenia). Paris.

Vryonis, Speros. 1971. *The Decline of Medieval Hellenism in Asia Minor and the Process of Islamization from the Eleventh through the Fifteenth Century.* Berkeley, Los Angeles, London.

Waldstreicher, David. 1989. *The Armenian Americans.* New York.

Walker, Christopher J. 1980. *Armenia: The Survival of a Nation.* London, New York.

Walker, Christopher J., ed. 1991. *Armenia and Karabagh: The Struggle for Unity.* London.

Wheeler-Bennett, John W. 1938. *Brest Litovsk: The Forgotten Peace, March 1918.* London.

Winkler, G. 1994. *Koriwns Biographie des Mesrop Mastoc'* (Orientalia Christiana Analecta, 245), Rome.

Woods, John. 1976. *The Aq-Quyunlu: Clan, Confederation, Empire, A Study in 15th/9th Century Turko-Iranian Politics.* Minneapolis.

Wyszomirski, M. J. 1975. "Communal Violence: The Armenians and Copts as Case Studies." *World Politics* 27, no. 3 (April).

Xenophon. *Anabasis.* Ed. and trans. C. L. Brownson. 2 vols. Loeb Classical Library.

Xenophon. *Cyropaedia.* Ed. and trans. W. Miller. 2 vols. Loeb Classical Library.

Yovhannēs Drasxanakertc'i. See Hovhannes Draskhanakerttsi.

Yovhannēs Mamikonean. See Hovhannes Mamikonian.

Yuzbashian, K. 1975-1976. "L'administration byzantine en Arménie aux Xe et XIe siècles." *Revue des études arméniennes,* n.s. 10.

Yuzbashian, K. 1988. *Armianskie gosudarstva epokhi Bagratidov i Vizantiia IX-XI vv.* Moscow.

Zarbhanalian, Garegin. 1905. *Patmutiun hayeren dprutian* (History of Armenian Literature). Vol 2. 2nd ed. Venice.

Zulalian, M. K. 1959. "*'Devshirme'-n* (mankahavake) osmanian kaysrutian medj est turkakan ev haikakan aghbiurneri [The *'Devshirme'* (Child-Gathering) in the Ottoman Empire According to Turkish and Armenian Sources]." *Patma-Banasirakan Handes* (Historical-Philological Journal), nos. 2-3. Erevan.

Zulalian, M. K. 1966. *Jalalineri sharzhume* (The Jelali Movement). Erevan.

NOTES ON THE CONTRIBUTORS

HAGOP BARSOUMIAN has concentrated on studies of the Armenian community in the Ottoman Empire in the nineteenth century. He has published articles on the Armenian *amira* class and the constitutional movement. He prepared a draft of the chapter included in this volume while he was teaching at the Haigazian College in Beirut. Unfortunately, Dr. Barsoumian was abducted and disappeared in 1996 during the Lebanese civil war. The editor of this volume has completed the writing of his chapter.

GEORGE BOURNOUTIAN is Professor of History at Iona College in New York. He is the author of five books on Armenian history, including his popular two-volume *A History of the Armenian People* (1993-1994), and has contributed to the *Armenian Review, Journal of the Society for Armenian Studies, Encyclopaedia Iranica,* and the *Journal of Iranian Studies.*

R. HRAIR DEKMEJIAN is Professor of Political Science at the University of Southern California. He has authored numerous books and articles on the Islamic world, ethnic politics, political elites, and international affairs. He has served as a specialist consultant to governmental agencies and to the media.

RICHARD G. HOVANNISIAN is the Holder of the Armenian Educational Foundation Chair in Modern Armenian History at the University of California, Los Angeles. He is the author of *Armenia on the Road to Independence* (1967) and *The Republic of Armenia,* 4 vols. (1971-1996), and he has edited three volumes on the Armenian genocide. A Guggenheim Fellow, he was elected to the National Academy of Sciences of Armenia in 1991 and awarded an honorary doctorate from Erevan State University in 1994.

DICKRAN KOUYMJIAN is the Holder of the Haig and Isabel Berberian Chair in Armenian Studies and Director of the Armenian Studies Program at California State University, Fresno. He held the position in Armenian at the Institute for Oriental Languages of the University of Paris from 1988 to 1991. His most recent publications are on Armenian art, the artistic organization of early Armenian Gospels, and inscribed Armenian manuscript bindings.

FATHER KRIKOR MAKSOUDIAN is the director of the Krikor and Clara Zohrab Information Center of the Eastern Diocese of the Armenian Church of America in New York City. He is a member of the brotherhood of St. James in Jerusalem and taught Armenian language and literature at Columbia University for several years. Among his publications is a translation, with introduction and commentary, of the history of Hovhannes Draskhanakerttsi.

ROBERT MIRAK has taught at Harvard University and Boston University and is the author of *Torn Between Two Lands: Armenians in America, 1890 to World War I* (1983) and has contributed to the *Harvard Encyclopedia of American Ethnic Groups.*

VAHÉ OSHAGAN teaches the history of Armenian culture at Macquarie University in Sydney, Australia. He is the author of several books of Armenian poetry and fiction, including *Inknutiun* and *Hampuyr* (both 1996), as well as scholarly monographs on Armenian literature.

RONALD GRIGOR SUNY is Professor of Political Science at the University of Chicago. He was the first holder of the Alex Manoogian Chair in Modern Armenian History at the University of Michigan and has also taught at Oberlin College, Stanford University, and the University of California, Irvine. Among his published works are *The Baku Commune* (1972), *The Making of the Georgian Nation* (1988), *Looking Toward Ararat* (1993), and *The Revenge of the Past: Nationalism, Revolution, and the Collapse of the Soviet Union* (1993).

CHRISTOPHER J. WALKER is a researcher and journalist residing in London. He is the author of *Armenia: Survival of a Nation* (1980), *Armenia and Karabagh* (1991), and *Visions of Ararat* (1997). He has edited and contributed to publications dedicated to minority rights and human rights.

INDEX

Russia, 18, 23, 42, 54, 58, 59, 64, 68, 69, 74, 79,
82-137 *passim,* 149, 175-76, 177, 178,
179, 180, 190, 200, 207, 208, 209, 211,
221, 233, 234, 236, 239, 242, 275, 280,
282, 283, 284, 285, 286, 287, 288, 289,
290, 293, 295, 313, 315, 333, 334, 335,
336, 337, 340, 343, 366, 369, 375, 378,
383, 385, 386, 390, 391, 402, 421, 430,
431, 437
Russian Armenia, 106, 121, 122, 125, 131, 150,
214, 275, 281, 292, 319, 347. *See also*
Eastern Armenia.
Russian Armenians, 135, 212, 233, 430
Russian Army Command of the Caucasus, 290
Russian Communist Party, 336 37. *See also*
Communist Party.
Russian Empire, 106, 110, 113, 115, 124, 126,
127, 130, 133, 137, 149, 207, 215, 216,
275, 276, 277, 278, 279, 281, 282, 285,
333, 347
Russian General Oil Company, 125
Russian Orthodox Church, 115
Russian Revolution, 137
Russian Social Democratic Workers' Party
(RSDRP), 134, 277
Russian Social Revolutionaries, 216
Russian Soviet Federated Socialist Republic
(RSFSR), 353
Russian State Duma, 135
Russians, 125, 126, 131, 136, 207, 208, 251, 254,
262, 278, 376
Russification, 128-29, 137
Russo-Japanese War, 124
Russo-Ottoman War, 102
Russo-Persian War, 100, 104, 105, 110, 112
Russo-Swedish War, 87
Russo-Turkish War, 74, 105, 112, 126, 127, 207,
239, 389
Rustam, 29, 36
Rustum, 5, 6
Rustum, Karakoyunlu, 8

Sabaheddin, Prince, 228, 229, 232
Safavid Empire, 87, 93, 97
Safavid Iran, 1
Safavid (language), 2
Safavids, 8-9, 14, 15, 17, 21, 22, 31, 55, 81, 82,
85-86, 94
Safyan sheikhs, 8
Saghatelian, Hovhannes, 135
Sahag II (Khabayan; Sahak Khapayan), Catholi-
cos of Cilicia, 426
Sahakian, Avetik, 294, 306, 325
Sahmandir Ramkavars, 227
Said Halim, 237
Saint Catharines Ontario, 392, 395, 434
Saint Gregory, 38, 44
Saint Hermoni Vank, 36
Saint Hripsime, 44, 66
Saint James, 25
Saint James Order, 428

Saint Karapet, 26, 42
Saint Nersess Seminary, 401
Saint Petersburg, 87, 91, 92, 99, 106, 110, 113,
118, 134, 142, 148, 149, 163, 165
Saint Pierre, Bernardin, de, 156
Saint Sargis, 57
Saint Theodorus, 42
Sairt (Sghert), 257
Salisbury, Lord Robert, 209, 210, 221, 239
Salmast, 18, 25, 213, 251
Salonika, 229, 230
Salvation Committee, 345
Samsun, 260
Samuel of Ani. *See* Samvel Anetsi.
Samvel Anetsi, 70
San Francisco Bay Area, 394
San Joaquin Valley, California, 396, 434
San Lazzaro, 143, 433
San Stefano, 208, 210
Sanahin, 5, 24, 35, 42
Sanjak of Alexandretta, 422
São Paulo, 394, 409, 434
Sarafov, Movses of Atrakhan, 91
Sarajev, D.S., 124
Sardarabad, 96, 104, 299, 376
Sargis, Bishop, 39
Sargis, Khizan/artist, 44
Sarikamish, 245, 319, 337, 339, 340
Saroyan, William, 407; *A Daring Young Man on
the Flying Trapeze,* 407, *The Time of
Your Life,* 407
Saryan, Martiros, 357
Sasun, 26, 199, 219, 221, 223, 227, 258, 266, 281
Sasunites, 219, 220
Saudi Arabia, 428
Savior Officers, 232
Sayat Nova, 93, 148
Sazonov, Sergei D., 136, 282
Sbenian, Father Kerope, 157; *Study of the Classi-
cal Armenian,* 157
Scheubner-Richter, von, German Consul, 256,
257
Schiller, Johann, 150
Schleiermacher, 176
Scott, Sir Walter, 147, 156, 168
Sea of Azov, 55
Sea of Marmora, 266
Sebastia, 2, 6, 192, 282. *See also* Sivas.
Sebeos, 70
Second Congress of Soviets, 287
Second Socialist International, 217
Selim the Grim, Sultan, 1, 26, 30, 39, 43
Selim II, Sultan, 13, 14-15, 154
Selim III, Sultan, 178
Seljuk invasion, 24
Seljuk (language), 2
Seljuks, 1, 7, 52
Semal, 219
Serbia, 178, 208, 210, 232
Serbs/Serbians, 177-78, 179, 180, 183, 206
Serenkiulian, Hovhannes. *See* Vartkes.